The Anticorruption Manual

A Guide for State Prosecutors

The Anticorruption Manual

A Guide for State Prosecutors

Amie N. Ely
Marissa G. Walker

EDITORS

NATIONAL ASSOCIATION OF ATTORNEYS GENERAL

Published by
National Association of Attorneys General
1850 M Street, NW, 12th Floor
Washington, DC 20036
(202) 326-6000

The Anticorruption Manual: A Guide for State Prosecutors
First Edition

Library of Congress Control Number: 2021908858
ISBN 978-1-946357-03-8

Dedication

This book is dedicated to the innumerable men and women who faithfully and honestly serve the public in the states and territories of the United States. These government employees work day after day and year after year without using their positions to seek personal recognition, fame, or unearned wealth. Together, they quietly maintain the integrity of our great system simply by carrying out each of their professional duties with earnest dedication. For those who never run afoul of the laws and rules discussed in this book, we are grateful.

Table of Contents

Chapter 1.2

Chapter 1.3

Section Two

Chapter 2.1

CHAPTER 2.4

CHAPTER 2.5

Chapter 2.8

Section Three

Chapter 3.1

Section Six

Civil & Administrative Enforcement, Asset Forfeiture, & Collateral Consequences of Corruption

Chapter 6.1

Administrative Remedies: How Ethics Boards Deter & Punish Corrupt Behavior

Chapter 6.3

Chapter 6.4

Indices

Acknowledgements & Disclaimers

The editors would like to acknowledge the many individuals who contributed to the preparation of this Manual. Each chapter was researched and written by different authors with expertise in each substantive area. Although the authors are noted on each chapter along with their biographical information, we would like to thank them again here for their effort and dedication:

> Stacy Aronowitz, Brenda Bauges, Wes Cheng, Michael Chu, Carrie Cohen, Dan Cort, Alice Dery, Katie Duhig, Robert Falin, Steve Grimes, Peter Henning, Michelle Henry, Johnjerica Hodge, Christine Hoffman, Brian Kane, Peter Lee, Beverly Ma, Ann Ratnayake Macy, Howard Master, Thomas McGoldrick, Glen McGorty, Dave Navarro, Victor Olds, Jeff Perconte, Anthony Picione, Daniel Pietragallo, Rebecca Ricigliano, Jessica Roth, Rob Shapiro, Darrin Sobin, Steve Solow, Kevin Steele, and Tim VanderGeisen.

We are particularly grateful to Peter Henning. In addition to contributing an essential chapter to this Manual, he has devoted significant efforts to studying and understanding public corruption and how to prosecute it. His treatise, *The Prosecution and Defense of Public Corruption: The Law and Legal Strategies*, cited throughout this Manual, is a trusted and formidable work in the field of anticorruption law. For his scholarship and his dedication to the cause of preventing and prosecuting public corruption, we are grateful.

We would also like to acknowledge the contributions of individual professionals and students who helped with the editing process. From Columbia Law School's Center for the Advancement of Public Integrity, we thank Executive Director Berit Berger, former Executive Director Jennifer Rodgers, Kori Cooper, Benjamin Costanza, Kelsey Dennison, Frank (Haojun) Feng, Tara Hofbauer, Amelie Hopkins, Jenn Katz, Martin McSherry, Anisha Mohin, Mai-Lee Picard, and Olivia Smith. We also thank Darrell E. White II, Charlotte Janovyak, Alexandra Santana, E. Davis Martin, and Carol Ottolenghi for their help with research and review, and Rory Callison for his assistance with preparing other related instructional materials. We thank our invaluable team members, Emily Myers, Allison Gilmore, Lisa Jeter, Ashley Wynstra, and Zayn Hasan, for their tremendous work in seeing this book through to production.

Please note that in some chapters, the authors refer to specific vendors of services or resources available to investigators and attorneys. That information is provided for informational purposes only. The National Association of Attorneys General (NAAG) and the National Attorneys General Training & Research Institute (NAGTRI) do not endorse or approve of any of the products, services, or opinions of any other corporation, organization, or individual.

Throughout the Manual, we intend the language and guidance to be gender neutral. Depending on the context, in some instances, we refer to the third-person singular when no gender-neutral noun is appropriate. In those instances, use of the masculine pronoun is not intended to exclude the feminine—nor is the use of the feminine pronoun intended to exclude the masculine.

The information provided in this Manual does not constitute legal advice. All content and references are for informational purposes only. We urge the reader to consult this Manual as a starting point only and the reader should not act on any particular legal matter solely on the basis of this Manual without seeking legal advice in the relevant jurisdiction or, if the reader is an attorney, without performing independent legal and factual research. Use of this Manual does not create an attorney-client relationship between any reader and any contributor, author, or editor of this Manual.

The views expressed in this Manual are those of the individual authors writing in their individual capacities only. The authors do not necessarily express the views of their respective employers, of NAAG, or of NAGTRI.

The Anticorruption Manual

A Guide for State Prosecutors

FOREWORD

The Importance of Confronting & Prosecuting Corruption

Chris Toth

Chris Toth is the executive director of the National Association of Attorneys General.

By virtue of the fact that you are reading this it is clear that you have an interest in confronting corruption. Perhaps you are already a seasoned corruption prosecutor. Or perhaps you are just now embarking on your first corruption case. If the former, hopefully what follows provides affirmation, and adds to what you have already experienced and learned. If the latter, hopefully what follows will steel you for the coming challenges you will face.

If you are an academic, we hope this book provides a reminder that successful corruption enforcement also occurs outside of federal courts: as you'll learn, in one state, an attorney general's office successfully prosecuted the corrupt powerful speaker of the house;[1] in another, a local prosecutor successfully prosecuted the corrupt attorney general.[2] Given the limits the United States Supreme Court has imposed on the reach of federal statutes to prosecute local and state officials,[3] local and state prosecutors are increasingly the only sheriffs in town with the authority to investigate and prosecute certain corrupt officials. If you are a citizen who is interested in reducing corruption, we expect you will

---

1 *See* Chapter 1.3, Part III(C).

2 *See* Chapter 1.2.

3 *See, e.g.*, Kelly v. United States, 140 S. Ct. 1565, 1571 (2020); McDonnell v. United States, 136 S. Ct. 2355, 2373 (2016).

find this Manual to be an interesting view of how people on the front lines are fighting this battle.

Enforcing corruption laws is a uniquely important and noble endeavor. The very success of democracy depends on the rigorous and robust enforcement of anticorruption laws. It is no coincidence that the higher a nation scores on Transparency International's Corruption Perception Index (CPI), the more likely the nation is a healthy democracy; the lower the score, the more likely the nation is an oppressive dictatorship that violates basic human rights.[4] Healthy democracies are not immune to corruption. But what makes a democracy healthy is that it has institutions dedicated to the rooting out of corruption before it can take hold and completely poison the entire system. Institutions, of course, are simply made up of individuals and ideas. For our system to succeed, it takes tireless and ever-vigilant people armed with an unwavering commitment to the rule of law.

What makes corruption different than other crimes is that a corrupt act victimizes not just one person or a group of people, but everyone in the jurisdiction where it is committed. Corruption is insidious. Left unchecked, it undermines trust in government and creates a cynical citizenry. A cynical citizen is less likely to be civically involved. Corruption creates business and economic inefficiencies that unnecessarily drive prices up, such as when laws regarding bidding are flouted, which in turn lead to reduced standards of living.[5] Corruption can make day-to-day life less safe if someone is paid off to ignore building or environmental codes. Corruption destroys the morale of honest public servants, leading them to give up or get out, which in turn leads to less dedicated and less ethical people in positions of public trust.

Understanding corruption—and thus being better able to confront it—begins with knowing that corruption is almost always a process. Most corrupt officials do not start off with one grand act of corruption. Corruption is very often a learned habit that starts small and grows over time. It usually starts not with major legal lines being broken, but with small forays over ethical lines that are easily rationalized: "it's a stupid rule, anyway," "I'm only helping a friend," or "I can't survive on this salary and I'm not hurting anyone." Then the lines

---

4 *See Corruption Perceptions Index 2020*, Transparency Int'l, https://www.transparency.org/en/cpi/2020/index/nzl (last visited June 12, 2021).

5 *See* Chapter 1.4.

shift a bit and then shift some more. A typical fact pattern provides an example of this: an official is treated to monetarily insignificant gifts, that turn into paid lunches, that turn into paid expensive dinners, which finally turn in to out-and-out bribes. Corrupt officials don't often think of themselves as bad people. More likely, they think of themselves as *good* people. Good because they have put themselves in a pot of water that didn't reach boiling all at once, but by one degree at a time and every so often, and they don't know it's time to scream because of the gradual nature of their line crossing. Good because in their minds they are doing what they need to do for their family or their friends. Good because they don't feel fairly compensated and because they have an exaggerated sense of their own worth to an organization. Good because "you should see what the other guys are doing."

It takes courage to prosecute corruption. Everyone (except for the defendant's friends and family) loves a prosecutor who prosecutes a murderer. The importance of such a case is universally understood and supported. But corruption cases are more complicated in the eyes of many of the public. Yes, in the abstract everyone will say they are angry about the existence of corrupt officials, but not everyone is necessarily angry about the acts of *their own corrupt official.* Successful government officials, whether appointed or elected, are more often than not charming, very likable people. Public officials who are corrupt often make it a point to trade in favors and thus develop very loyal constituencies. That is in large part how they get and stay where they are. Individuals who are largely disliked usually don't get very far in politics. And disliked officials who are committing corrupt acts often don't last for long, because they usually have long lists of people eager to turn them in. When you prosecute a public official it is very likely that official is admired and has a great deal of personal support. He or she will have constituencies invested in his or her continued tenure. History, ancient and recent, is full of corrupt officials who were revered by large segments of the population—even when their corruption is openly acknowledged by their constituents.[6] Bad behavior—even rising to the level of open

---

6 Indeed, some corrupt politicians have been reelected after corruption charges have been filed—or even after their conviction. *See, e.g.*, Emily Opilo, *Allentown Mayor Ed Pawlowski has been Re-Elected. What if He's Convicted?*, Morning Call (Nov. 17, 2017), https://www.mcall.com/news/local/allentown/mc-nws-allentown-whats-next-post-election-20171115-story.html (discussing the reelection of Ed Pawlowski as mayor of Allentown, Pennsylvania after being charged with corruption-related offenses); *Mayor Convicted of Corruption Elected Again in Connecticut*, CBS News (Nov. 5, 2015), https://www.cbsnews.com/news/mayor-convicted-of-corruption-elected-again-in-connecticut/ (discussing the reelection of Joseph Gamin as

corruption—by an official who "delivers" to constituents may be acceptable to many. Accordingly, when you prosecute corruption be prepared that some people may vilify you. The first refuge of any indicted corrupt scoundrel may be to question the motives—political, personal, or otherwise—of the prosecutor.

Also be prepared that some otherwise fundamentally honest people will not cooperate with your efforts. Whether it is because they are afraid of getting involved or of potential adverse personal or political consequences, or because they do not want to help "ruin" the life of someone they otherwise like, otherwise upstanding citizens may balk at providing information in a corruption case. Prosecute even a few corruption cases and you will face this phenomenon.

That's the bad news. Corruption undermines the rule of law, erodes trust in government, makes people less safe, and leads to inefficiencies that hurt people. Fighting corruption can be a lonely affair that can have real, personal consequences to those fighting it.

Here is the good news: confronting corruption protects the rule of law, reinforces trust in government, makes people safer and improves the lives of people in very tangible ways. And no matter the temporary popularity of any corrupt actor and no matter how lonely the fight, history remembers and smiles favorably on those who have the courage to do the right thing.

There are very few pursuits as important to the continued health of our democracy as investigating and prosecuting corruption. We hope this Manual will be of just some assistance in this noble effort. Always remember justice wears a blindfold for a reason. Investigate your cases thoroughly, honor the facts, stay true in your resolve and courage, and remember what you do impacts not only this generation, but also those to come.

As this Manual was being finalized, the world was facing an unprecedented challenge: a pandemic that transcended borders, causing healthcare systems across the globe to stretch to, and sometimes beyond, capacity and economies to crash. We are predicted to face a long, slow recovery involving trillions of economic stimulus dollars from the federal government. These funds will no doubt help many who need and deserve assistance. But they will

mayor of Bridgeport, Connecticut five years after being released from seven-year federal prison sentence for accepting bribes and extortion).

also draw bad actors. While a close treatment of all of the expected issues is outside the scope of this Manual, we expect many of the general lessons will be instructive. We expect that the guidance in these pages about investigating[7] and trying[8] complex crimes, in particular, will be useful for the prosecutors and investigators who are tasked with rooting out COVID-19-related fraud.

Many heartfelt thanks to all our contributors. They offered their efforts not in the pursuit of fame or fortune, but in the spirit of true public service. My particular thanks go to Amie Ely, the director of the NAGTRI Center for Ethics and Public Integrity and editor of this Manual. Amie embodies the very best in passionate and ethical service to the rule of law.

Finally, I am thankful that these few pages have brought us together for a few moments, and I am thankful for all you do.

---

7 *See* Section 2.
8 *See* Section 4.

Section One

Species of Corruption Cases

This section covers some of the patterns of corruption you might find in:

- The three branches of the government—judicial, executive, or legislative;
- Certain governmental systems—such as the process to bid for contracts and elections;
- Local government—an area perhaps particularly germane to state and local prosecutors;
- Police corruption—which includes information about methods used by federal prosecutors (including cooperation agreements, non-prosecution agreements, and immunity orders) to secure witnesses' testimony; and
- Union leadership—which includes a discussion of the use of monitors, an oversight mechanism more commonly employed by federal prosecutors, but one that state and local prosecutors may want to consider in cases involving entities that have been corrupted.

Our authors explore these species of corruption using a combination of case studies, often from their own practice as prosecutors who investigated and charged the cases they discuss, and from general principles. Some chapters, like the Executive Corruption chapter recounting the prosecution of former Pennsylvania Attorney General Kathleen Kane by Kevin Steele and his team, dive deeply into just one case. Others, like the scholarly approach to Legislative Corruption by Howard Master, highlight some of the unique legal issues that may arise when prosecuting one particular type of case. The case studies illustrate how corruption manifests in various factual and legal contexts.

Chapters throughout the Manual intentionally intersect. The Manual's primary audience is a busy prosecutor seeking guidance on a specific issue. Many chapters focusing on one issue refer to other sections or chapters for a fuller discussion of related issues. As an example, several chapters in this section briefly discuss the use of wiretaps. Those chapters also refer to a chapter in Section Two that focuses in more detail on that powerful investigative technique. This structure means that the reader who consumes the Manual from beginning to end should have a good understanding of both technique and application across a wide area of issues of interest to the corruption prosecutor, with repetition reinforcing concepts.

CHAPTER 1.1

Judicial Corruption: A Threat to Justice

Daniel G. Cort

Daniel G. Cort serves as First Deputy Commissioner of the New York City Department of Investigation, which is New York City's Inspector General, with independent oversight of city government. From March 2014 to December 2018, Mr. Cort served as chief of the Public Integrity Bureau of the New York Attorney General's Office. Prior to that, he was an assistant district attorney at the New York County District Attorney's Office for nineteen years, most recently serving as chief of that office's Public Integrity Unit. He has investigated, prosecuted, and supervised the investigation and prosecution of several judges.

> Take all the robes off all the good judges that have ever lived on the face of the earth, and they would not be large enough to cover the iniquity of one corrupt judge.
>
> —Henry Ward Beecher[1]

INTRODUCTION

Perhaps no type of corruption is more corrosive to the rule of law than judicial corruption. Our legal system relies on the honesty, fairness, and impartiality of the judiciary. Corrupt actors within the judiciary who violate the

1 WILLIAM DRYSDALE, PROVERBS FROM PLYMOUTH PULPIT: SELECTED FROM THE WRITINGS & SAYINGS OF HENRY WARD BEECHER 63 (1887).

public trust shake the foundations of that system. Judges wield tremendous power. Judicial rulings can have significant effects on both the societal and economic standing of the individuals who appear before them. Those decisions can even limit or completely take away their liberty. Corrupt judges deny litigants the right to equal access to the courts. Judicial corruption victimizes the non-corrupt party, future litigants, and the integrity of the judicial system. Trial court decisions are frequently final and not appealable, either because of the nature of the ruling or because appeals are too costly.[2] If a corrupt appellate court judge issues a precedent-setting decision for corrupt reasons, future cases—even those handled by honest judges—might apply an erroneous legal standard and potentially undermine the legitimacy of the decisions relying on the corrupt ruling. When corruption is discovered and rulings are overturned, both crime victims and litigants suffer when cases they thought were settled are reopened. In a system that relies on the honesty and impartiality of judges, corruption erodes citizens' faith in government.

I. Judicial Corruption Defined

The anticorruption organization Transparency International (TI) defines corruption as the "abuse of entrusted power for private gain."[3] TI defines judicial corruption as "any inappropriate influence on the impartiality of the judicial process by any actor within the court system."[4] While TI's definition includes everyone in the court system, this chapter focuses primarily on corrupt judges, with some reference to the judges' coconspirators in bribery cases.

---

2 For example, a trial court's finding that a witness is not credible may be all but impossible to overturn on appeal. *See, e.g.*, Fed. R. Civ. P. 52(a)(6) ("Findings of fact, whether based on oral or other evidence, must not be set aside unless clearly erroneous, and the reviewing court must give due regard to the trial court's opportunity to judge the witnesses' credibility.").

3 *What Is Corruption?*, Transparency Int'l, https://www.transparency.org/en/what-is-corruption (last visited Apr. 14, 2021).

4 Transparency Int'l, Global Corruption Report 2007: Corruption in Judicial Systems xxi (2007), https://issuu.com/transparencyinternational/docs/global_corruption_report_2007_english.

A. *Types of Judicial Corruption*

Every decision, ruling, and discretionary action by a judge is a potential point of corruption. Reported acts of judicial corruption have come in many forms: bribery, extortion, tampering with records, dismissing charges, reducing sentences, manipulating the case assignment system, increasing bail in exchange for kickbacks from a bail bond agency, granting litigants favorable money judgments, improperly making fiduciary appointments, and abusing court proceedings for personal gain and for the benefit of friends and family.[5]

B. *Corruption Distinguished from Unethical Conduct*

While corrupt judges are unethical, not all unethical conduct is criminal. For example, a judge who knowingly presides over a case involving a company in which the judge has an "economic interest,"[6] personally solicits or accepts campaign contributions,[7] acts intemperately,[8] or even renders judicial decisions for the wrong reasons[9] might violate a code of judicial ethics relating to bias, impartiality, or judicial decorum, but those acts would not necessarily be prosecutable as crimes of corruption. There can be overlap, however, between conduct that is unethical and conduct that is criminal. While an ex parte communication between a judge and a litigant or his lawyer may not itself violate a criminal statute, a corrupt judge may engage in ex parte conversations, for example, to solicit a bribe.[10] Directly soliciting campaign contributions may

---

5 A discussion of every type of judicial corruption is beyond the scope of this chapter, but for a comprehensive discussion of its myriad forms, see Stratos Pahis, Note, *Corruption in Our Courts: What It Looks Like and Where It Is Hidden*, 118 Yale L.J. 1900, 1906 (2009) (addressing judicial bribery, which the author defines as "the selling and purchasing of legal decisions") and Geoffrey P. Miller, *Bad Judges,* 83 Tex. L. Rev. 431, 431 (2004) (addressing the problem of "judges and magistrates who are incompetent, self-indulgent, abusive, or corrupt").

6 Model Code of Judicial Conduct r. 2.11(A)(3) (Am. Bar Ass'n 2020).

7 *See id.* r. 4.1(A)(8); Williams-Yulee v. Fl. Bar, 575 U.S. 433, 440 (2015) ("[M]ost . . . [s]tates prohibit judicial candidates from soliciting campaign funds personally, but allow them to raise money through committees.").

8 Model Code of Judicial Conduct r. 2.8(B).

9 *Id.* r. 2.2.

10 Rule 2.9 of the Model Code of Judicial Conduct prohibits ex parte communications in most instances. *Id.* r. 2.9(A). For examples of how ex parte communications furthered corruption, see Robert J. McCarthy & Dan Herbeck, *Judge Michalek Says He Took Bribes as Corruption Probe Moves to Pigeon*, Buffalo News (June 29, 2016), http://buffalonews.com/2016/06/29/judge-michalek-will-plead-guilty-taking-bribe-pigeon-faces-charges-thursday/ and discussion of Gerald Garson in Part VI(C).

not only be unethical but may be criminal if there is a quid pro quo agreement between the contributor and the judge.[11]

C. *How Common is Judicial Corruption?*

There are fewer than 1,500 federal judges in the United States.[12] As of 2010, there were over 31,000 judges in state courts.[13] Because there are far more state judges, it is perhaps not surprising that most reports of corruption involve state judges.[14] A 2006 survey conducted by TI reported that two percent of North Americans surveyed who had contact with the judiciary had paid a bribe.[15] But regardless of whether corruption is common or rare, the tremendous influence that judges and courts have on peoples' lives makes any judicial corruption a threat to the rule of law that must be investigated and prosecuted.

D. *Who Prosecutes Judicial Corruption?*

The Public Integrity Section of the United States Department of Justice "has sole responsibility for the investigation and prosecution of federal judges due to the potential appearance issues that might arise" if local United States Attorney's Offices investigated allegations of wrongdoing by federal judges

---

11 *See* McCormick v. United States, 500 U.S. 257, 273-74 (1991).

12 Approximately 890 federal judges require Senate confirmation. *Judicial Vacancies*, United States Courts, http://www.uscourts.gov/judges-judgeships/judicial-vacancies (last visited Apr. 14, 2021). This number includes 179 federal circuit court judges, 28 U.S.C. § 44(a) (2018), 663 federal district judges, *id.* § 133(a), and 316 bankruptcy judges, *id.* § 152(a)(2). In addition to those positions requiring confirmation, about 570 federal magistrate judges serve eight-year terms. Peter G. McCabe, A Guide to the Federal Magistrate Judges System 2 n.7 (Oct. 2016), https://www.fedbar.org/wp-content/uploads/2019/10/FBA-White-Paper-2016-pdf-2.pdf (536 full-time and 34 part-time magistrate judges as of September 2015); *Status of Magistrate Judge Positions & Appointments—Judicial Business 2018*, United States Courts, https://www.uscourts.gov/statistics-reports/status-magistrate-judge-positions-and-appointments-judicial-business-2020 (last visited Apr. 14, 2021) (555 full time, 27 part time, and 3 combined in 2020).

13 Nat'l Ctr. for State Courts, Number of Authorized Justices/Judges in State Courts, 2010 (2012), http://www.courtstatistics.org/~/media/Microsites/Files/CSP/SCCS/2010/Number_of_Authorized_Justices_and_Judges_in_State_Courts.ashx.

14 *See* Pahis, *supra* note 5, at 1922.

15 The survey defined "North America" as Canada and the United States. Transparency Int'l, *supra* note 4, at 11 n.3. As one commentator reasoned, it is unlikely that judicial bribery is more pernicious in Canada than the United States, which suggests that aggregate data accurately reflects the experiences in both countries. *See* Pahis, *supra* note 5, at 1905 n.7. The TI survey included bribes of others involved in the justice system, including clerks, lawyers, prosecutors, and court employees. Transparency Int'l, *supra* note 4, at xx, 12; Pahis, *supra* note 5, at 1905.

before whom they regularly appeared.[16] Attorneys general,[17] district attorneys,[18] and federal prosecutors have also investigated and prosecuted corrupt state judges.[19]

II. Judicial Corruption Commonalities

One study concluded that all the judges who were removed from the bench after bribery scandals or convicted of bribery charges between 1967 and 2000 served at the trial court level.[20] That is certainly due, in part, to the fact there are far fewer appellate judges.[21] Appellate courts are also structurally less able to be corrupted as the judges generally sit in panels of three or more. It is more difficult to corrupt a multi-judge panel than it is a single judge.

The structure of both federal and state court systems may also help explain the increased vulnerability to corruption of courts at the trial court level. Trial courts are factfinders, which gives them a greater ability to sway the outcome of a case by making credibility findings in favor of a briber's witnesses—a power that may be difficult to uncover as corrupt, as it involves the exercise of discretion, and also difficult to reverse on appeal. Appellate judges are generally confined to determining whether the law was correctly applied to a case, making it harder for them to tip a case in favor of a briber and more likely that a patently incorrect application of the law would be discovered.

---

16 Pub. Integrity Section, U.S. Dep't of Justice, Report to Congress on the Activities & Operations of the Public Integrity Section for 2017 11 (2017), https://www.justice.gov/criminal/file/1096306/download.

17 The New York State Attorney General's Office prosecuted former Judge John Michalek. *See* McCarthy & Herbeck, *supra* note 10.

18 The New York County District Attorney's Office prosecuted Surrogate's Court Judge Nora Anderson for campaign finance violations in a case that resulted in an acquittal, but a later public censure of the judge. *See* John Eligon, *Manhattan Surrogate's Court Judge Is Acquitted*, N.Y. Times (Apr. 1, 2010), http://www.nytimes.com/2010/04/02/nyregion/02judge.html. The Kings County District Attorney's Office prosecuted former Judge Gerald Garson. See discussion in Part VI(C) of Gerald Garson.

19 Federal prosecutors brought a case against Mississippi trial lawyer Richard "Dickie" Scruggs for attempting to bribe a state judge. Nelson D. Schwartz, *The Legal Trail in a Delta Drama*, N.Y. Times (Jan. 20, 2008), http://www.nytimes.com/2008/01/20/business/20blake.html.

20 *See* Pahis, *supra* note 5, at 1922.

21 *See id.* (trial court judges comprise approximately 98% of the state and 89% of the federal judiciary).

Finally, as with federal judges, the lack of reported corruption among appellate judges may also be explained by a more rigorous selection process, the relatively higher salaries for federal and appellate judges, and the greater prestige associated with the appellate position, suggesting appellate judges are more qualified and less likely to face the economic pressures that can incentivize corruption.[22] To the extent that trial-level judges are more likely to be elected than appellate-level judges, they may be under more pressure to raise money for campaigns in both legal and illegal ways.[23]

Certain types of courts also appear more prone to corrupt judges. Courts of limited or specialized jurisdiction—such as traffic court, juvenile court, surrogate's (trusts and estate) court, and matrimonial court—are insular, may be less likely to issue written decisions that can be easily obtained and reviewed, and require specialized knowledge. All these factors can create fertile environments for corruption.[24] First, the same lawyers appear each day in front of the same judges. Such familiarity can foster a culture where formalities can break down, shortcuts can be taken, and corruption may be tolerated or accepted. Second, in courts that rarely issue written decisions explaining their rulings, it is easier for judges to conceal corrupt dealings. It is more difficult and expensive to obtain transcripts of oral rulings—assuming that the proceedings were even recorded—than copies of written orders. Finally, if a specialized court does issue a decision, whether written or oral, that contains an analysis that has been infected by corruption, it is less likely that the decision will raise red flags if it involves the application of laws that are not well-understood by "outsiders."[25]

Courts where judges are involved in the case assignment system can also be vulnerable to corruption. It becomes easier for dishonest court employees and judges to, for example, ensure a case involving an attorney willing to pay a bribe is assigned to a judge willing to be induced to rule in that attorney's favor, and to solicit their own kickbacks for this corrupt service.

---

22 *See id.* at 1923-24.

23 *See id.* at 1922-23, 1924 (noting that elected judges at trial and appellate levels were caught accepting a larger number of bribes relative to the number of cases that they handle).

24 *See* discussion *infra* of Kids for Cash judges (Part VI(B)) and Gerald Garson (Part VI(C)).

25 For example, in the "Kids for Cash" case discussed in Part VI(B), one of the judges adopted procedures that avoided the appointment of counsel for juveniles and the creation of a normal court record. INTERBRANCH REPORT, *infra* note 78, at 19.

Judges who are authorized to appoint fiduciaries may likewise be subject to more temptation.[26] Fiduciary appointments can be lucrative.[27] Appointees may seek to illegally curry favor with a judge to seek a valuable appointment and judges may be all too eager to leverage their appointment power to obtain money or favors.[28]

III. Identifying and Detecting Judicial Corruption

Judicial corruption is difficult to detect and to investigate. Judicial corruption is generally a complex and hidden consensual crime involving, at a minimum, a judge and a litigant. Since individuals who are not parties to the corruption often do not know it is occurring, they are not able to report the crime. Additionally, judicial conduct organizations are generally designed to handle ethical complaints rather than criminal wrongdoing and are often overburdened. According to one source, more than ninety percent of the complaints made to judicial conduct organizations each year are dismissed.[29]

Although difficult, it is obviously not impossible to uncover judicial corruption. Judicial corruption, like most other types of public corruption, may be discovered as a result of an investigation into another crime. Individuals who engage in one type of criminal activity may be aware of other types of illegality. Other sources of investigative leads are complaints from the public and dissatisfied litigants. Newspaper articles and other types of investigative journalism can be fruitful sources of information. Civil court filings for lawsuits involving judges in their personal capacities may be a source of improper financial dealings. In such a case, the court file could be a source of further investigative

---

26 *See* Miller, *supra* note 5, at 436-37.

27 Although in many cases the fees are relatively small or even non-existent, in some cases they can be quite lucrative. N.Y. Unified Ct. System, Report of the Commission on Fiduciary Appointments § II.A. (Dec. 2001), https://www.nycourts.gov/ip/gfs/fidcommreport.html; *see also* Dan Herbeck, *Michalek, as Judge, Approved Receiver Fees for Ex-Boss and Political Booster Sorrentino*, Buffalo News (Jul. 10, 2016), http://buffalonews.com/2016/07/10/michalek-as-judge-approved-receiver-fees-for-ex-boss-and-political-booster-sorrentino/ (involving more than $89,000 in fees).

28 *See, e.g.*, McCarthy & Herbeck, *supra* note 10.

29 Cynthia Gray, *The Line Between Legal Error & Judicial Misconduct: Balancing Judicial Independence & Accountability*, 32 Hofstra L. Rev. 1245, 1245 (2004).

leads, including the names of potential witnesses and details about assets that could be evidence of unexplained wealth.

Because of the corruption risks associated with fiduciary appointments, court rules or state law may require disclosure of these appointments, the amount of money involved, and the frequency that a judge appoints a certain fiduciary.[30] Analyzing this information can help detect corruption.[31] For example, in the prosecution by the New York Attorney General's Office of former Buffalo judge John Michalek, a review of court filings required of a judge when appointing a receiver not on the usual list (along with emails obtained by search warrant) showed that Judge Michalek had appointed an unqualified fiduciary for corrupt reasons.[32]

A judge's disciplinary record may reveal a judge who is not only willing to engage in unethical conduct, but perhaps worse. A lawyer with a disciplinary record who becomes a judge may merit close scrutiny. For example, Gerald Garson, whose judicial corruption case is discussed *infra*, was disciplined as an attorney, prior to becoming a judge, for improperly providing gifts to a judge.[33] A confidential informant or cooperator who has information about a corrupt judge can help to uncover this type of corruption, but these are rare.[34]

IV. Investigating Judicial Corruption

Every corruption investigation is unique, but some investigative tools and approaches may be consistently useful when investigating judicial corruption.

Investigating a judge's lifestyle to determine if he is living above his means can lead to evidence of corruption. Obtaining ethics filings or financial

---

30 *See, e.g.*, 1 Tex. Admin. Code § 171.9 (2020); Tex. Gov't Code Ann. § 71.035(b) (2020); N.Y. Ct. Rules Part 36 (2017).

31 *See, e.g.*, Miller, *supra* note 5, at 437 n.54 (citing N.Y. Unified Ct. System, *supra* note 27).

32 Christine Streich, *Political Operative Admits to Bribing Judge*, WKBW Buffalo (Sept. 28, 2018), https://www.wkbw.com/news/political-operative-admits-to-bribing-judge.

33 *In re Garson*, 471 N.Y.S.2d 331, 331 (N.Y. App. Div. 1984) (Garson censured for "conferring gifts, gratuities and benefits upon a Civil Court Judge, by paying for a weekend stay at a resort hotel for the Judge and his wife").

34 *See* discussion *infra* of Gerald Garson.

disclosure forms, some of which can be found online, may yield information about the judge's lifestyle.[35] Asset searches, FinCEN reports,[36] and credit bureau reports can also help the investigator understand a judge's finances. These searches generally require access to specialized databases that may only be available to law enforcement agencies and, as to credit bureau reports, require state prosecutors to obtain a court order.[37] Credit bureaus may notify targets that their records have been requested by law enforcement, but including a non-disclosure requirement in the court order may help protect a covert investigation.

The first round of subpoenas and court orders can reveal lines of credit and relationships with previously unknown entities. Records obtained from banks, car dealerships, credit card companies and other financial institutions may reveal unusual or suspect transactions. They may also provide the names of potential witnesses, subjects, or targets. If, for example, the target judge has a co-signer on an account, investigating the relationship with the co-signer may yield evidence of a crime. Once again, a non-disclosure order in a subpoena may prevent disclosure of the investigation. In some cases, delaying a request for documents from an entity with a close relationship with the target may also prevent disclosure.

---

35 Financial disclosure forms for federal judges are available online through organizations such as Judicial Watch, Inc. *See Financial Disclosure Documents*, Judicial Watch, http://www.judicialwatch.org/judicial-financial-disclosure/ (last visited Apr. 14, 2021). For state court judges, disclosure forms may be available through the state government website. *See, e.g.*, *Financial Disclosure Forms*, N.Y. State Unified Court System, https://ww2.nycourts.gov/IP/ethics/FDform.shtml (last visited Apr. 14, 2021) (disclosure forms of New York judges); *Search for Financial Disclosures*, S. Ct. of Nev. Admin. Off. of the Cts., https://nvcourts.gov/AOC/FinancialDisclosures/FDSearch.aspx (last visited Apr. 14, 2021) (providing a search function for financial disclosures of Nevada judges); *2018 Judicial Financial Disclosure Statements*, Haw. State Judiciary, https://www.courts.state.hi.us/2018-judicial-financial-disclosure-statements (last visited Apr. 14, 2021) (providing links to the disclosure statements of Hawaiian judges).

36 FinCEN is the Financial Crimes Enforcement Network. Law enforcement officers and prosecutors can obtain access to its databases through FinCEN's Office of Law Enforcement Support. *See Support of Law Enforcement*, Financial Crimes Enforcement Network, https://www.fincen.gov/resources/law-enforcement/support-law-enforcement (last visited Apr. 14, 2021).

37 The Fair Credit Reporting Act permits the issuance of a credit report "[i]n response to the order of a court having jurisdiction to issue such an order, or a subpoena issued in connection with proceedings before a Federal grand jury." 15 U.S.C. § 1681b(a)(1) (2018).

Surveillance may be helpful to learn with whom the target judge is meeting and it can also be useful to understand the judge's lifestyle and financial means. So-called "sneak and peek" or "delayed notice" search warrants, which enable law enforcement to search a location without providing immediate notification of the search, could be used to surreptitiously enter a judge's chambers during the covert stage of an investigation.[38] A wiretap of a judge's phone or a listening device placed in her chambers or a robing room are other potential investigative tools, subject to any applicable judicial privilege.[39]

Undercover officers or confidential informants can be incredibly useful tools to investigate corrupt judges. Sham cases have been used occasionally in undercover operations to catch a corrupt judge misusing his authority without imperiling an actual prosecution or civil case.[40] This investigative technique may be subject to legal and ethical requirements.

While judges sometimes act alone in engaging in corruption, such crimes often involve lawyers and court employees, including clerks, court officers, secretaries, or clerical staff, and even law enforcement officers[41] It can be difficult for litigants and judges to have direct contact with each other, as such contact

---

38 *See* 18 U.S.C. § 3103a(b) (2018) (setting forth requirements for delayed notice warrants in federal courts). For a discussion of federal law considering the permissibility of the practice before the statute was enacted, *see generally* Kevin Corr, *Sneaky but Lawful: The Use of Sneak & Peek Search Warrants*, 43 U. Kan. L. Rev. 1103 (1995). Delayed notice search warrants may also be subject to state law.

39 *See* discussion *infra* of judicial privilege. For a discussion of wiretap requirements, see Chapter 2.3.

40 For more on this tool, see Chapter 2.5. A federal case against a municipal court judge in Philadelphia used confidential informants and a sham prosecution to build a case against the judge and his coconspirators. *See* Rhodi Lee, *FBI Snares Allegedly Corrupt Judge with Invented Defendant & Pretend Arrest & Court Appearances*, Tech Times (Sept. 30, 2014), http://www.techtimes.com/articles/16711/20140930/fbi-snares-allegedly-corrupt-judge-with-invented-defendant-and-pretend-arrest-and-court-appearances.htm; Jeremy Roebuck, *Former Phila. Judge Gets Two Years for Trying to Fix Cases*, Phila. Inquirer (Jan. 22, 2015), http://www.philly.com/philly/news/20150123_Former_Phila_judge_gets_two_years_for_fixing_cases.html. Note that some courts may not be hospitable to the use of sham processes or cases. *See* United States v. Hammad, 858 F.2d 834, 839-40 (2d Cir. 1988) (disapproving of use of sham grand jury subpoena in undercover operation).

41 *See, e.g.*, Special Comm'n on the Admin. of Justice in Cook Cty., Final Rep. (1988), https://jenner.com/system/assets/assets/SpecialCommissionAdminJusticeSolovyReport1988.pdf (discussing Operation Greylord). Over seventy individuals, including judges, lawyers, clerks, police officers, and deputy sheriffs, and court personnel were convicted of federal crimes relating to case fixing, bribes, extortion, and other crimes. *Id.* at 13.

may raise suspicion. An intermediary, therefore, is often used to carry out the corruption. Those intermediaries, because they have contact with both the judge and the litigant, may be more susceptible to detection than the primary participants and may be helpful in covert investigations.[42] Finding a cooperative low-level court employee can be useful in uncovering corruption involving judges, particularly if the cooperator can implicate superiors up to and including the judge.

V. How to Deal with the Challenges of Investigating Judicial Corruption

Investigation of judicial corruption not only poses the same problems inherent in any white collar crime investigation, but it also presents unique challenges. Some of the challenges are logistical and practical, while others are legal—like the shield of judicial privilege.

A. *Logistical Challenges*

The most obvious issue is the problem of obtaining court process from a judge who may be a colleague of the target judge. When investigating a judge, it is often necessary to involve a supervising or administrative judge outside of the target judge's courthouse to obtain court process, such as subpoenas, search warrants, and eavesdropping warrants. Seeking court process from a non-supervising judge may put the investigation at risk. A judge on the same level as the judge who is being investigated may inadvertently—or even purposely—compromise the investigation. Asking a judge in the same court as a target judge to issue court process against a target judge puts that judge in, at best, an awkward position. It is generally a good idea, if the jurisdiction allows it, to go to the highest-level supervisor or administrative judge possible to obtain court process in any judicial investigation. The prosecutor should, of course, exercise caution in choosing which supervising judge to approach.

Not only might judges who work with the target judge reveal the investigation, it is possible that courthouse staff may do the same. Even if the prosecutor need not involve a judge to get a subpoena or a wiretap, it is often

---

42 *See* discussion of Gerald Garson in Part VI(C).

necessary to request assistance from others in the courthouse.[43] For example, it may be necessary to ask court employees to retrieve a court file, court records, emails, or other documents located on the court system's computer server. Courthouse employees who are friendly with or answer to the corrupt judge may be tempted to warn the target judge about requests for documents related to that judge.

B. *Judicial Deliberative Privilege*

Proving judicial corruption can be complicated by the judicial deliberative privilege, which is the privilege against compelled disclosure of a judge's deliberative thought process. This relatively obscure privilege protects "confidential communications among judges and their staffs in the performance of their judicial duties."[44] In the first reported case to recognize and discuss the privilege, the court stated that "a judge should not be compelled to state the reason of his decision."[45] The judicial deliberative privilege has been explicitly recognized in a number of jurisdictions including Connecticut,[46] Illinois,[47] Iowa,[48] Massachusetts,[49] New York,[50] New Hampshire,[51] Pennsylvania,[52] West Virginia,[53] the Third Circuit,[54] and the Eleventh Circuit.[55] This privilege can

---

43 While the case did not involve a judge, charges filed in November 2017 against a county courthouse deputy clerk serve as a reminder of the potential damage a corrupt courthouse employee can do. Local prosecutors allege that the clerk warned drug dealers when she saw search warrants that targeted locations they controlled, providing them with time to remove contraband before the warrants were executed. *See* Angenette Levy, *Prosecutor: Clerk Tipped Drug Dealers to Search Warrants*, Local12.com (Nov. 16, 2017), http://local12.com/news/local/former-court-clerk-employee-alleged-accomplice-accused-of-tipping-off-crooks.

44 *In re* Certain Compls. Under Investigation by an Investigating Comm., 783 F.2d 1488, 1520 (11th Cir. 1986).

45 *In re* Estate of Cohen, 174 N.Y.S. 427, 428 (N.Y. Surr. Ct. 1919).

46 Statewide Grievance Comm. v. Burton, 10 A.3d 507, 514 (Conn. 2011).

47 Thomas v. Page, 837 N.E.2d 483, 490-91 (Ill. App. Ct. 2005).

48 Office of Citizens' Aide/Ombudsman v. Edwards, 825 N.W.2d 8, 19 (Iowa 2012).

49 *In re* Enforcement of a Subpoena, 972 N.E.2d 1022, 1027-28 (Mass. 2012).

50 *Estate of Cohen*, 174 N.Y.S. at 428.

51 Phelan v. Thompson, 161 F.R.D. 7, 8 (D.N.H. 1994); New Hampshire *ex rel.* Childs v. Hayward, 248 A.2d 88, 90 (N.H. 1968).

52 Leber v. Stretton, 928 A.2d 262, 270 & n.12 (Pa. Super. Ct. 2007).

53 West Virginia *ex rel.* Kaufman v. Zakaib, 535 S.E.2d 727, 735 (W. Va. 2000).

54 Grant v. Shalala, 989 F.2d 1332, 1344 (3d Cir. 1993) (discussing administrative law judges).

55 *In re* Certain Complaints Under Investigation by an Investigating Comm., 783 F.2d 1488, 1520-21 (11th Cir. 1986).

sometimes pose challenges to proving bribery or other crimes. If faced with the potential assertion of this privilege, the prosecutor should set up a taint team or other method to ensure that the investigation team does not review privileged material. The privilege does not apply to non-deliberative events such as "whether a judge was subjected to 'extraneous influences' or ex parte communications during the deliberative process."[56] Some jurisdictions may also recognize a crime-fraud exception to the privilege.[57]

VI. Examples of Judicial Corruption

An analysis of three cases of judicial corruption shows the commonalities, successful investigative methods, and potential preventative measures in these types of cases.

A. *Martin Thomas Manton*

1. Fact Summary

In 1916, President Woodrow Wilson appointed Martin Thomas Manton to the Southern District of New York.[58] Manton was connected to New York's Tammany Hall Political Machine and was, at age thirty-six, the youngest federal judge in the country at the time he was appointed.[59] He was elevated to the Second Circuit in 1918 and was even considered in 1923 for an appointment to the Supreme Court.[60] He eventually became the presiding judge of the Second

---

56 *In re* Enforcement of a Subpoena, 972 N.E.2d 1022, 1033 (Mass. 2012) ("By definition, such influences and communications lie outside the protected sphere of the judge's internal deliberations.").

57 *See In re* Estate of Cohen, 174 N.Y.S. 427, 428-29 (N.Y. Surr. Ct. 1919) ("It seems a judge could well be questioned regarding acts which were directed against the proper administration of the law, as for example, his advice to destroy public records in his office, or direction to commit forgery or perjury.").

58 Allan D. Vestal, *A Study in Perfidy*, 35 Ind. L.J. 17, 17 (1959) (providing a detailed discussion of the Martin Thomas Manton bribery case).

59 *Ex-Judge Manton of U.S. Bench Here; Head of the Appeals Court Who Served Time for Accepting $186,000 Dies Up-State*, N.Y. Times (Nov. 18, 1946), https://timesmachine.nytimes.com/timesmachine/1946/11/18/93181150.pdf (Manton obituary); *see also* Gerald Gunther, Learned Hand: The Man and the Judge 431 (2d ed. 2011).

60 David J. Krajicek, *Powerful Judge with Humble Brooklyn Roots Sent to Jail in 1939 for*

Circuit. In his time on the federal bench, he wrote over 650 decisions.[61] He was also the first federal judge to be convicted of a bribery-related charge.[62]

Manton suffered severe financial losses as a result of the Great Depression and took loans from individuals and companies with cases pending before his court.[63] An investigation revealed that he took bribes to fix civil cases and, in at least one instance, a criminal case.[64] Manton had repeatedly overridden case assignment rules, designating himself as a district court judge to hear certain cases, particularly so he could reward those who provided him with loans by giving them lucrative receiverships.[65] Even while he was accepting bribes and subverting justice, Manton held himself out as a pillar of ethics, giving rousing speeches at national and state bar associations about honorable lawyers who typically needed "[n]o regulations of conduct,"[66] and writing the foreword to the first edition of a federal practice treatise.[67]

The USDOJ and the Manhattan District Attorney, Thomas Dewey, investigated the corruption allegations.[68] This investigation included obtaining statements Manton made about his assets and liabilities in connection with financial transactions and proceedings before regulators, along with a careful examination of various corporations that were associated with the judge.[69] This evidence revealed both that Manton was willing to lie about his assets and that his net worth went from negative $500,000 to positive $750,000 during an eleven-month period in the mid-1930s—a $1.25 million increase then, which would

---

Bribe Scandal, N.Y. Daily News (Jan. 30, 2016), http://www.nydailynews.com/new-york/judge-brooklyn-jail-bribe-scandal-1939-article-1.2514804; Max Minzner, *Saving Stare Decisis: Preclusion, Precedent, and Procedural Due Process*, 2010 BYU L. Rev. 597, 626 (2010).

61 *See* Vestal, *supra* note 58, at 18.

62 Peter J. Henning, The Prosecution and Defense of Public Corruption: The Law and Legal Strategies § 1.02[5] (Matthew Bender, 2020 ed.).

63 *See* Vestal, *supra* note 58, at 20-21.

64 *Id.* at 35-36. A lawyer who had bribed Manton was himself charged with taking a bribe. After the charges were filed, Manton took money from this lawyer, which he promised would be used to bribe the district judge who had the lawyer's case. That judge dismissed the case; when the lawyer was arrested again, he eventually appealed. Manton presided over that appeal, and—unsurprisingly—ruled in the lawyer's favor. *Id.*

65 *Id.* at 22-23, 24-26 (describing Manton's flouting of court rules to sit as a district court judge so he could appoint receivers).

66 *Id.* at 29-30 (speeches in Michigan (to the American Bar Association) and Vermont).

67 *Id.* at 39.

68 *Id.* at 40.

69 *Id.* at 25, 30-31.

be worth approximately $24 million in 2021.[70] Dewey proved that Manton took approximately $435,000 in bribes[71]—nearly $8.5 million today.[72] Manton resigned, and was later indicted, convicted after a jury trial, and sentenced to two years in federal prison.[73] The Second Circuit granted re-hearings in the cases in which Manton took bribes, but not for later cases that relied upon legal principles enunciated in Manton's tainted decisions, raising interesting *stare decisis* issues.[74]

2. Lessons Learned

The Manton case shows that not all corruption involves state court trial level judges. Although most reported cases of corruption do, in Manton's case, a federal appellate judge was corrupted.

Had Manton been subject to financial reporting requirements at the time he committed his crimes, some of his unusual financial dealings may have been revealed sooner. This shows the need to scrutinize a suspect judge's financial disclosure forms. Manton facilitated his corruption using his control over the assignment of cases. This demonstrates the importance for any investigator looking at potential judicial corruption to determine who has control over case assignments. Manton also carried out some of his schemes by choosing to sit as a district court judge, demonstrating that trial court judges have more discretion as individuals—including over matters like potentially lucrative appointments—than do appellate court judges. Finally, the Manton case reminds us that even powerful judges who preach about ethics may still be susceptible to corruption—and of the importance of careful, fearless investigation to uncover corruption in even very high places.

One corrupt judge can cause serious damage to the judicial system. Manton's corruption affected not only the rulings for which he was bribed,

---

70 *See* Krajicek, *supra* note 60. *See CPI Inflation Calculator*, Bureau of Labor Statistics, https://www.bls.gov/data/inflation_calculator.htm (last visited Apr.14, 2021) (January 1935 to March 2021).

71 Vestal, *supra* note 58, at 40.

72 *See CPI Inflation Calculator*, *supra* note 70 (January 1935 to March 2021).

73 *Ex-Judge Manton of U.S. Bench Here*, *supra* note 59 (noting Manton served 19 months of his sentence).

74 Minzner, *supra* note 60, at 627-29.

but later decisions that cited those tainted decisions.[75] It was reported that one district court judge, even in recent years, had instructed his clerks never to cite a decision written by Manton[76] and the Second Circuit was said to have had an "informal rule to avoid relying on decisions where Manton's vote made the difference."[77]

B. *Kids for Cash Judges: Mark Ciavarella and Michael Conahan*

1. Fact Summary

A more recent example of judicial corruption involved former judges Mark Ciavarella and Michael Conahan in Luzerne County, Pennsylvania.[78] Ciavarella and Conahan were involved in the "Kids for Cash" scandal. Conahan was, at one time, both president judge of the Luzerne County Common Pleas Court and a juvenile court judge and Ciavarella was a juvenile court judge in the same county.[79] As president judge, Conahan was the chief administrator of the court.

The investigation began with allegations that Ciavarella was denying juveniles the right to counsel.[80] A public interest law firm filed a petition with the Pennsylvania Supreme Court detailing these allegations, and the Pennsylvania AGO filed an amicus brief urging the state supreme court to review the case.[81] While that petition was initially denied, Ciavarella was eventually found to have wrongfully denied over 1,800 juveniles the right to counsel between 2003 and May 2008.[82]

The investigation expanded beyond those allegations, revealing that both judges entered into kickback agreements with the owner and developer of

---

75 *Id.*

76 Benjamin Weiser, *Hang Him Up? A Bad Judge and His Image*, N.Y. Times (Jan. 27, 2009), http://www.nytimes.com/2009/01/28/nyregion/28portrait.html.

77 Minzner, *supra* note 60, at 629.

78 For an in-depth analysis of this case, *see* Interbranch Commission on Juvenile Justice, Report (May 2010), http://www.pacourts.us/assets/files/setting-2032/file-730.pdf?cb=4beb87 [hereinafter Interbranch Report].

79 *Id.* at 5-6, 13.

80 *Id.* at 8.

81 *Id.*

82 *Id.* at 8 (denying petition), 9 (vacating order denying petition after the two charged in federal court).

private juvenile detention facilities. Conahan used his powers as president judge to strip funding from the county's existing juvenile detention facility, causing it to close, and then helped two related private facilities obtain county contracts to house juveniles.[83] Ciavarella then detained a large proportion of the young offenders who appeared before him, and they served their time in those private facilities.[84] Between 2000 and 2009, when they were indicted by a federal grand jury, both men received continuing payments from the owner of the two detention facilities based on the number of juveniles placed there, thus earning the "Kids for Cash" moniker.[85]

Conahan pleaded guilty to racketeering conspiracy and was sentenced to more than seventeen years in federal prison.[86] Ciavarella was found guilty after trial of racketeering, honest services mail fraud, tax evasion, and money laundering. He was sentenced to twenty-eight years in prison and ordered to pay $1.17 million in restitution.[87]

The corruption caused significant disruption in the Luzerne County justice system. The Pennsylvania Supreme Court expunged approximately 4,000 convictions in juvenile cases that Ciavarella handled from 2003 to 2008.[88]

After the indictments, other evidence emerged that suggested Ciavarella and Conahan routinely abused their power on the bench. In one instance, for example, Ciavarella heard a friend's speeding case. The police officer testified that the judge's friend had been driving at a speed of eighty miles per hour,

---

83 *Id.* at 9.

84 *Id.*

85 Michael Rubinkam, *Former Pa. Judges Indicted in Kids-For-Cash Scheme*, NEWSDAY (Sept. 10, 2009), http://www.newsday.com/news/nation/former-pa-judges-indicted-in-kids-for-cash-scheme-1.1436586.

86 *Judge Gets 17 1/2 Years in Kickbacks Case,* BOS. GLOBE (Sept. 24, 2011), https://www.bostonglobe.com/news/nation/2011/09/23/judge-gets-years-kickbacks-case/wVXIVKfKGD50GRirHG7oRP/story.html.

87 Warren Richey, *'Kids for Cash' Judge Sentenced to 28 Years for Racketeering Scheme*, CHRISTIAN SCI. MONITOR (Aug. 11, 2011), http://www.csmonitor.com/USA/Justice/2011/0811/Kids-for-cash-judge-sentenced-to-28-years-for-racketeering-scheme. Some of Ciavarella's convictions have been reversed on statute of limitations grounds. United States v. Ciavarella, No. 09-Cr-272, 2018 U.S. Dist. LEXIS 2785, *39 (M.D. Pa. Jan. 8, 2018); James Halpin, *Judge Rules in Ciavarella's Favor in Kids-for-Cash Appeal*, CITIZEN'S VOICE (Jan. 9, 2018), http://citizensvoice.com/news/judge-rules-in-ciavarella-s-favor-in-kids-for-cash-appeal-1.2288319.

88 *In re* Expungement of Juvenile Records & Vacatur of Luzerne County Juvenile Court Consent Decrees or Adjudications from 2003-2008, No. 81 M.M. 2008, 2009 Pa. LEXIS 2286, *9 (Pa. Oct. 29, 2009); INTERBRANCH REPORT, *supra* note 78, at 12.

well over the fifty-five miles per hour speed limit. After the officer testified, Ciavarella said "No, I think he was just going 60. Matter closed."[89] In another, Conahan assigned the case of one of his cronies—an associate of an organized crime figure who was suing a local paper for defamation when it reported he was the target of a federal investigation—to Ciavarella, who, after a bench trial, issued a $3.5 million verdict in favor of Conahan's associate.[90]

The two judges engaged in other problematic conduct that should have raised red flags for investigators and auditors. They bought an expensive Florida condominium together, apparently using bribe money to fund the purchase.[91] In one strange instance, one of their associates sued the owner of a Florida yacht club where a yacht all three men used was docked. Instead of suing in Florida, the associate sued the yacht club in Luzerne County. A colleague of the judges ruled in favor of the judges' associate.[92] In 2006, a courthouse whistleblower sent an anonymous letter to the Pennsylvania Judicial Conduct Board.[93] The letter laid out in painstaking detail—including names, dates, and docket numbers—allegations that Conahan and Ciavarella were abusing their authority by, among other things, fixing cases and presiding over cases in which they had a conflict of interest.[94] But despite the Judicial Conduct Board's practice of referring complaints of criminal wrongdoing to law enforcement, no referral was made.[95]

There were also signs that suggested Ciavarella was handling juvenile cases differently than other judges and Conahan was impeding any efforts to question how juvenile justice was meted out. In 2002, over half of all juveniles in Ciavarella's court waived their right to an attorney; the average waiver in the state was only 7.4 percent.[96] In 2003, the year after the juvenile facility was first opened, Ciavarella placed juveniles in secure facilities at twice the state average.[97] In 2005, Conahan used his powers as president judge to transfer one judge

89 Ian Urbina, *Despite Red Flags About Judges, a Kickback Scheme Flourished*, N.Y. Times (Mar. 27, 2009), http://www.nytimes.com/2009/03/28/us/28judges.html.

90 Interbranch Report, *supra* note 78, at 14-16.

91 Urbina, *supra* note 89.

92 *Id.*

93 Interbranch Report, *supra* note 78, at 27-28.

94 *Id.*

95 *Id.* at 29.

96 *Id.* at 40 (54.8 percent waived in Ciavarella's court).

97 *Id.* at 39 ("In 2003, Ciavarella ordered 330 juveniles from Luzerne County into placement. That was twice the statewide average. More significant, in a county that represented less than

who raised questions about funding of the juvenile facilities.[98] Around the same time, auditors found that the juvenile facilities were overbilling the county, but efforts to subpoena additional information from the facilities resulted in litigation; the case ended up before Conahan, and he ruled—unsurprisingly—for the juvenile facilities that had been bribing him, which caused the audit to grind to a halt.[99] While in isolation, these indicators may not have been sufficient to warrant opening a formal investigation, together they were troubling and suggested something might be awry.

2. Lessons Learned

Many lessons can be learned from the Kids for Cash case. The first is that small corruption may lead to larger corruption, and that patterns of misconduct may well include the violation of criminal laws that are designed to punish corruption. When Judge Ciavarella did not recuse himself from hearing the speeding case involving his high school friend and then found him not guilty in the face of overwhelming evidence, alarm bells should have rung. Conahan's transfer of the judge who raised questions about his conduct was yet another warning sign of corruption. When a person is willing to break the rules for something small, it is quite possible he is willing to commit much more egregious crimes. While none of these incidents may have themselves violated criminal statutes, collectively they provided grounds to look more closely at the judges. A closer examination might well have revealed some of the instances in which they violated criminal statutes, in addition to ignoring the Pennsylvania Code of Judicial Conduct.

This case involved a specialized or insular court. As the only juvenile judge in Luzerne County, Ciavarella was able to wield absolute power. That allowed him to avoid following usual procedures and explaining his decisions—one factor an investigative commission later singled out for reform when it recommended that juvenile judges be required to state the reasons for dispositions on the record.[100] Similarly, the strange statistical anomalies, such as the large number of juveniles being sent to detention facilities from Luzerne County and the large number of pleas that were taken without lawyers, were

---

3 percent of Pennsylvania's population, this single judge was responsible for 22 percent of the juvenile placements throughout all of Pennsylvania.").

98 *Id.* at 25.

99 *Id.* at 25-26.

100 *Id.* at 53.

investigative predicates that could have warranted opening an investigation earlier. Additionally, both Ciavarella's and Conahan's unusual spending, such as the purchase of expensive Florida condominiums, should have been warning signs for auditors and investigators.

While federal authorities eventually brought charges against the judges, it was only after years of their use of the courthouse to line their own pockets, resulting in loss of liberty for juveniles who should not have been incarcerated, cost to taxpayers who had to subsidize the corrupt contracts with the owner of the private juvenile detention facilities that bribed the judges, and substantial harm to the rule of law in the county in which they served. Had these warning signs been recognized and investigated, these two judges could have been stopped much sooner.

C. *Gerald Garson*

1. Fact Summary

Former judge Gerald Garson was a Brooklyn (Kings County), New York trial judge who heard matrimonial cases and was convicted of taking bribes from a lawyer named Paul Siminovsky.[101] Garson's corruption was uncovered when a woman who was seeking a divorce contacted Nissim Elmann, a person in her Brooklyn neighborhood who was known to be able to influence the outcome of divorce cases.[102] When the woman approached Elmann, he told her that she was too late because her husband had already paid him to influence the case.[103]

Upon hearing that, the woman went to the Kings County District Attorney's Office to report the corruption.[104] With the woman's consent, the District

---

101 People v. Garson, 848 N.E.2d 1264, 1265 (N.Y. 2006); Michael Brick, *Former Judge is Convicted of Bribery in Divorce Court*, N.Y. Times (Apr. 20, 2007), http://www.nytimes.com/2007/04/20/nyregion/20judge.html.

102 People v. Garson, 775 N.Y.S.2d 827, 839-40 (N.Y. Sup. Ct. 2004); Andy Newman, *Court Officer Convicted in Brooklyn Bribery Case*, N.Y. Times (Sept. 21, 2004), http://www.nytimes.com/2004/09/21/nyregion/court-officer-convicted-in-brooklyn-bribery-case.html.

103 Jennifer Medina, *On Tape, Assurances That a Judge Would Help*, N.Y. Times (Aug. 31, 2004), http://www.nytimes.com/2004/08/31/nyregion/on-tape-assurances-that-a-judge-would-help.html?_r=0.

104 *Garson*, 775 N.Y.S.2d at 839.

Attorney's office surreptitiously recorded a conversation between the woman and Elmann.[105] The investigators then obtained an eavesdropping warrant and recorded conversations between Elmann and Siminovsky, the dishonest lawyer who had direct contact with Garson.[106] Elmann would take money from litigants and would refer the bribe-paying litigant to Siminovsky.[107] Investigators approached and flipped Siminovsky, who agreed to record his conversations with Garson.[108] In addition, without informing Siminovsky, investigators obtained authorization from the administrative judge of the court to place a video and audio recording device in the judge's robing room.[109] The recording devices captured the judge giving advice to Siminovsky about how to try his cases, promising to rule for one of Siminovsky's clients, and accepting cash and gifts from Siminovsky.[110]

During Garson's trial, Siminovsky testified that the recording devices reflected just one instance of his ongoing bribery of Garson. He said he had given Garson drinks, meals, cigars, and cash to give him advice and to get favorable treatment for his clients during other cases,[111] and that Garson repeatedly coached Siminovsky about what arguments to make and then ruled in favor of his clients.[112]

Two bribe payers, a court officer, Elmann, Siminovsky, and Garson were all convicted for their roles in the scheme, although the judge's courtroom clerk was acquitted.[113] Garson received a sentence of three to ten years in prison and eventually served two and a half years.[114]

---

105 *Id.*

106 *Id.* at 840.

107 Michael Vecchione & Jerry Schmetterer, *Crook is Disrobed: New Book Details How Brooklyn D.A. Nabbed Corrupt Judge*, N.Y. Daily News (Nov. 8, 2015), http://www.nydailynews.com/new-york/new-book-details-brooklyn-nabbed-corrupt-judge-article-1.2427076.

108 *Garson*, 775 N.Y.S.2d at 841-42.

109 *Id.* at 840-41.

110 People v. Garson, 848 N.E.2d 1264, 1265-66 (N.Y. 2006).

111 *Id.*

112 *Id.*

113 Newman, *supra* note 102; *Garson*, 848 N.E.2d at 1265; Brick, *supra* note 101.

114 Scott Shifrel & Larry McShane, *Crooked Judge Gerald Garson Leaves Halfway House; Served 6 Months Less Than Minimum Sentence*, N.Y. Daily News (Dec. 23, 2009), http://www.nydailynews.com/news/crime/crooked-judge-gerald-garson-leaves-halfway-house-served-6-months-minimum-sentence-article-1.437114.

Before Garson became a judge, he had been disciplined as an attorney for giving gifts to a sitting judge.[115] The judge had been suspended from the bench for six months for accepting those gifts and for other ethical breaches.[116] Perhaps because of the local "political machine" in which Garson and his family members were important and familiar cogs,[117] this episode did not prevent him from becoming a judge.

2. Lessons Learned

Garson, like the Kids for Cash judges, had been willing to cut ethical corners in the past. While one ethical misstep does not necessarily tar a judge as corrupt, that Garson had been censured as an attorney for providing gifts to a judge made him an appropriate target when there were credible allegations he was accepting bribes. Given that he and the judge to whom he had given gifts were both punished, he was certainly aware that accepting gifts from the attorneys who appeared before him was, at minimum, a breach of the ethical rules.

The Garson case also shows how, as in the Kids for Cash case, specialized or insular courts may be especially vulnerable to corruption. Because the corrupt lawyer appeared before Garson frequently, it fostered an environment that made the corrupt dealings possible. Judges and lawyers can abuse opaque assignment systems in matrimonial court and other specialized courts in an effort to influence cases. Finally, Garson's willingness to engage in unethical ex parte communications facilitated his bribery scheme.

---

115 *In re* Garson, 471 N.Y.S.2d 331, 331-32 (N.Y. App. Div. 1984).

116 *In re* Vaccaro, 1977 N.Y. LEXIS 2603, *3-4 (N.Y. Jud. Ct. Sept. 26, 1977).

117 Andy Newman, *Politics Laid Bare: Success and Scandal in Family of Judges*, N.Y. Times (July 5, 2003), http://www.nytimes.com/2003/07/05/nyregion/politics-laid-bare-success-and-scandal-in-family-of-judges.html.

Conclusion

Corruption within the judicial system damages one of the pillars of our democracy: a free and fair judiciary. Despite the unique challenges presented by these crimes, it is essential for investigators and prosecutors to thoroughly and aggressively pursue judicial corruption of all kinds. While certain types of courts—like specialized trial courts—may be, for structural reasons, more fertile grounds for corruption, any type of judge may be corrupted. These cases remind us that careful, thorough, and fearless investigations are necessary to probe and prosecute judicial corruption.

Chapter 1.2

Executive Corruption: The Trial of the Pennsylvania Attorney General

Kevin R. Steele, Michelle A. Henry, Thomas W. McGoldrick, Robert M. Falin

Kevin R. Steele serves as District Attorney for Montgomery County, Pennsylvania.

Michelle A. Henry serves as First Deputy Attorney General for the Pennsylvania Office of Attorney General.

Thomas W. McGoldrick serves as Deputy District Attorney for Montgomery County, Pennsylvania.

Robert M. Falin serves as Deputy District Attorney for Montgomery County, Pennsylvania.

Introduction

The public expects law enforcement agencies, including prosecutor's offices, to do the right thing for the right reason. A corrupt prosecutor can undermine the public's trust in her office and even poison other law enforcement agencies. In those situations, it is incumbent upon those other agencies to seek justice and help restore the public trust.

The 2016 case of *Commonwealth of Pennsylvania* v. *Kathleen G. Kane* presented this very scenario. Kane, then the Attorney General of Pennsylvania, was charged with leaking secret grand jury material and then illegally trying to cover up the leak.[1] After a week-long trial in state court, she was convicted. This successful prosecution made it clear to the public that no one—not even the chief law officer of the Commonwealth[2]—is above the law. It also showed that, despite Kane's abuse of authority, her office still retained dedicated civil servants, including some who testified against her at her trial.

This chapter, written by some of the prosecutors who investigated and prosecuted Kane, first provides a factual and procedural background of the case. Then, it discusses several unique challenges that law enforcement personnel faced during the prosecution: inheriting an investigation begun by another entity; effectively investigating the elected head official of a state law enforcement agency; and corroborating the testimony of several key witnesses at trial, including by obtaining and using federal wiretap evidence. It closes by discussing some lessons learned from the case.

I. Factual and Procedural History

Kathleen Kane was elected Attorney General for the Commonwealth of Pennsylvania on November 6, 2012.[3] When she was administered the Oath of Office on January 15, 2013, Kane swore to "support, obey and defend the Constitution of the United States and the Constitution of this Commonwealth" as well as "discharge the duties of [her] office with fidelity."[4] Kane then began what was supposed to be a four-year term as Attorney General.

Shortly after Kane became Attorney General, one of her Deputy Attorneys General, Frank Fina, resigned from the Attorney General's Office to join the Philadelphia District Attorney's Office (DAO).[5] While he was with the

---

1 Richard Pérez-Peña, *Pennsylvania Attorney General, Kathleen Kane, Charged in Leak Case*, N.Y. Times (Aug. 6, 2015), https://www.nytimes.com/2015/08/07/us/pennsylvania-attorney-general-kathleen-kane-charged-in-leak-case.html.

2 Pa. Const. art. IV, § 4.1.

3 *Kathleen Kane Elected Pennsylvania Attorney General, First Woman to Hold the Office*, Lehigh Valley Live (Nov. 7, 2012), http://www.lehighvalleylive.com/elections/index.ssf/2012/11/kathleen_kane_elected_pennsylv.html.

4 Pa. Const. art. VI, § 3.

5 Years after Fina left the AGO, the public learned that his tenure there had been tainted

AGO, Fina managed an undercover sting operation involving a confidential informant named Tyron Ali; that operation, sometimes called the "Ali investigation," uncovered evidence that six public officials had taken bribes. After Kane declined to pursue criminal charges, the Ali investigation was adopted by the Philadelphia DAO, which subsequently charged six defendants, five of whom pleaded guilty or no contest, and one of whom has been convicted after trial.[6]

On March 16, 2014, *The Philadelphia Inquirer* published an article highly critical of Kane.[7] The *Inquirer* article reported that Kane had decided not to prosecute the six public officials targeted in the Ali investigation.[8] As her trial later revealed, Kane was incensed by the *Inquirer* article, and she believed Fina provided information to the reporters who wrote it. Publicly, however, Kane denied being angry with Fina. In March 2014, Kane issued a press release which stated: "I do not have any animosity toward the lead prosecutor of this case. I do not know the former prosecutor any more than I know the individuals targeted in this investigation."[9]

Also in March 2014, Kane held a press conference to address the *Inquirer* article. During it, Kane claimed that the investigation was racially motivated

---

by misconduct. As a result of actions Fina took in investigating Jerry Sandusky and Penn State, the Supreme Court of Pennsylvania suspended Fina's license for a year and a day. Office of Disciplinary Counsel v. Frank G. Fina, No. 166 DB 2017, Att'y Reg. No. 71711, Order (Feb. 19, 2020), http://www.pacourts.us/assets/opinions/DisciplinaryBoard/out/166DB2017-Fina.pdf. Fina also was involved in a scandal, related to the Kane case, in which many employees of the AGO received and forwarded racially and sexually offensive emails, violating ethical rules. *See* Charles Thompson, *Sandusky Prosecutor's Actions Called 'Reprehensible' in Disciplinary Board Report*, Penn Live (June 6, 2019), https://www.pennlive.com/news/2019/06/sandusky-prosecutors-actions-called-reprehensible-in-disciplinary-board-report-license-suspension-recommended.html.

6 *See* Mark Scolforo, *State Lawmaker from Philly Convicted of Bribery Resigns 'Under Protest'*, Pittsburgh Post-Gazette (Dec. 12, 2018, 9:03 AM), https://www.post-gazette.com/news/politics-state/2018/12/12/State-lawmaker-philadelphia-vanessa-brown-convicted-of-bribery-resigns-under-protest/stories/201812120118.

7 Angela Couloumbis & Craig R. McCoy, *Kane Shut Down Sting that Snared Phila. Officials*, Phil. Inquirer (Mar. 16, 2014), http://www.philly.com/philly/news/20140316_Kane_shut_down_sting_that_snared_Phila__officials.html.

8 *Id.*

9 Affidavit of Probable Cause at 4, Commonwealth v. Kane, Nos. 6239-2015, 8423-2015 (Pa. Ct. of Common Pleas Aug. 6, 2015), https://www.montcopa.org/ArchiveCenter/ViewFile/Item/2504.

and "so poorly handled by her predecessors that it could not be prosecuted."[10] In the weeks following this press conference, the *Inquirer* published additional articles about the Ali investigation critical of Kane.

Evidence admitted at her trial showed that Kane believed Fina was mainly responsible for the critical newspaper articles and sought to use the power of her office to retaliate against him. Kane instructed certain AGO employees to review a 2009 grand jury investigation into the possible misuse of grant funding that Fina oversaw.[11] The 2009 investigation led to the conviction of two individuals; another individual, J. Whyatt Mondesire, had also been investigated but never charged.[12]

Seeking revenge, Kane decided to launch a personal attack intended to harm Fina's reputation. She believed that Fina's reputation would suffer if the press reported that he somehow prevented Mondesire from being prosecuted. Kane thus directed the Special Agent in Charge of the Bureau of Special Investigations to interview an agent who worked on the 2009 investigation so she could learn more about that investigation.[13] That interview, which revealed information about grand jury proceedings, was recorded and transcribed; then, one copy of that transcription was printed and given to Kane.[14]

After she reviewed the transcript, Kane directed her First Assistant Attorney General, Adrian King, to deliver the transcript, along with emails and an internal AGO memorandum written about the case (which also referred to grand jury materials) to her political consultant.[15]

---

10 *Id.* Subsequently, a Philadelphia Grand Jury investigating some individuals involved in the Ali case issued a report stating, among other things, "[a]s the grand jurors represent a cross-section of Philadelphia citizens, we were particularly sensitive to the explosive charge that the defendants were racially targeted . . . . We found, however, that the claims of racism in this instance were simply false." Hans von Spakovsky, *Two Pennsylvania Legislators Indicted for Accepting Bribes*, CNBNews (Dec. 19, 2014), https://www.gloucestercitynews.net/clearysnotebook/2014/12/two-pennsylvania-legislators-indicted-for-accepting-bribes.html (quoting and linking to grand jury presentment).

11 Commonwealth v. Kane, Nos. 6239-2015, 8423-2015, 2017 Pa. Dist. & Cnty. Dec. LEXIS 3228 at *5-6, *13 (Mar. 2, 2017).

12 *Id.* at *9-12.

13 *Id.* at *15-16.

14 *Id.* at *16-17.

15 *Id.* at *17, *21.

Kane called her political consultant after he received the materials from King to ask him to leak those materials to the press. The consultant agreed, and—after redacting the documents, at Kane's suggestion, to remove most of the names except Fina's—delivered the materials to a reporter for the *Philadelphia Daily News*.[16] As he later testified, her consultant understood the purpose of the leak to be "to show that Frank Fina shut down [the Mondesire] investigation, the same way Kathleen [Kane] shut down the investigation with the [Ali] sting."[17]

Before publishing an article about the 2009 investigation, the *Philadelphia Daily News* reporter contacted several people whose names appeared in the leaked documents, including Fina. Fina told the reporter that the materials he had contained grand jury information, which was illegal to disseminate. Fina later notified the Honorable William R. Carpenter, the supervising judge of the statewide investigating grand jury, that it appeared there had been a leak of confidential information. Judge Carpenter then appointed a special prosecutor, Tom Carluccio, and permitted Carluccio to use the grand jury to investigate the apparent breach.[18]

On June 6, 2014, an article appeared in the *Philadelphia Daily News* written by the reporter to whom Kane's political consultant leaked documents.[19] The article contained detailed information about the 2009 investigation; it also cited the leaked documents and the transcript.[20] Mondesire's photograph was featured prominently in the print edition.

Carluccio's grand jury investigation was already underway when the *Daily News* article was published. It lasted about seven months, during which time dozens of witnesses were called to testify. Kane herself testified, under

---

16 *Id.* at *22-23.

17 *Id.* at *22.

18 While outside the scope of this chapter, Kane—represented by private counsel—unsuccessfully tried to have the appointment of the special prosecutor quashed. *In re* Thirty-Fifth Statewide Investigating Jury, 112 A.3d 624, 629-30 (Pa. 2015) (finding inherent authority for a grand jury's supervising judge to appoint a special prosecutor to investigate potential criminal conduct by a prosecutor).

19 Chris Brennan, *State A.G. Probed Philly NAACP Leader Mondesire's Finances 5 Years Ago*, Phila. Daily News (June 6, 2014), https://www.inquirer.com/philly/news/20140606_State_A_G__probed_Philly_NAACP_leader_Mondesire_s_finances_5_years_ago.html.

20 *Id.*

subpoena, before the grand jury on November 17, 2014.[21] On December 18, 2014, the grand jury returned a presentment recommending that criminal charges be filed against Kane for unlawfully leaking confidential information.[22] The next day, Judge Carpenter referred the matter to the Montgomery County DAO for criminal investigation.[23]

Pursuant to the referral, the Montgomery County DAO began an independent investigation into the matter. Personnel executed numerous search warrants and interviewed dozens of witnesses. As a result of this investigation, a criminal complaint was filed against Kane on August 6, 2015.[24] It charged her with perjury,[25] false swearing,[26] obstructing the administration of law or other governmental function,[27] and abuse of office/official oppression,[28] and with conspiring to violate several of the substantive statutes with which she was charged.[29]

Shortly after Kane's arrest, a longtime AGO executive assistant and notary, Wanda Scheib, read the criminal complaint against Kane.[30] Scheib saw that Kane had testified that she had no obligation to keep confidential information from the Twenty-Ninth Statewide Investigating Grand Jury, which conducted the investigation involving Mondesire, because she had not signed a secrecy oath for that grand jury. But Scheib had notarized a "historical oath"

---

21 Brad Bumsted, *AG Kane Believed Leaked Documents Not Grand Jury Material, Lawyer Says*, Trib Live (Nov. 17, 2014, 1:52 PM), http://triblive.com/news/adminpage/7173944-74/grand-jury-kane. Kane had unsuccessfully sought to quash the subpoena; when that failed, she chose not to exercise her Fifth Amendment right to remain silent. *Id.*; *see also In re* Thirty-Fifth Statewide Investigating Jury, No. 175 MM 2014, 2015 Pa. LEXIS 1894, at *11-12, *68 (Aug. 26, 2015).

22 *In re* Thirty-Fifth Statewide Investigating Grand Jury, No. 18 MM 2015, 2015 Pa. LEXIS 1890, at *8-9 (Aug. 26, 2015).

23 *Id.*

24 Police Criminal Complaint, Commonwealth v. Kane, Nos. 6239-2015, 8423-2015 (Pa. Ct. of Common Pleas Aug. 6, 2015), https://www.montcopa.org/ArchiveCenter/ViewFile/Item/2504.

25 18 Pa. Cons. Stat. § 4902 (2019).

26 *Id.* § 4903.

27 *Id.* § 5101.

28 *Id.* § 5301.

29 *Id.* § 903.

30 Anna Orso, *A Secretary Blew the Whistle on Kathleen Kane—Now She's Not a Notary Anymore*, BillyPenn (Aug. 11, 2016, 10:55 AM), https://billypenn.com/2016/08/11/a-secretary-blew-the-whistle-on-kathleen-kane-now-shes-not-a-notary-anymore/.

that Kane signed, which bound her to secrecy regarding the Twenty-Ninth Statewide Investigating Grand Jury.[31] Scheib realized that Kane had lied in her testimony before the grand jury that indicted her and informed then-First Deputy Attorney General Bruce Beemer that she had notarized Kane's historical oath.[32] Beemer subsequently relayed this information to the Montgomery County DAO.

As a result of Beemer's information, Montgomery County detectives executed a sealed search warrant at AGO. Seized items included Scheib's notary logbook and several signed secrecy oaths, including Kane's signed secrecy oath for the Twenty-Ninth Statewide Investigating Grand Jury. On October 1, 2015, a second criminal complaint was filed against Kathleen Kane charging her with perjury, false swearing, and related offenses as a result of her false testimony before the grand jury about her signed secrecy oath.[33]

The two criminal cases were subsequently consolidated for trial,[34] which began August 8, 2016 before the Honorable Wendy Demchick-Alloy.[35] Seven days later, the jury convicted Kane on all charges.[36] Two days after her conviction, Kane resigned as the Attorney General of Pennsylvania.[37]

About two and a half months later, Kane was sentenced. During that sentencing, Judge Demchick-Alloy said that Kane's decisions to abuse her power reflected her inability to transition from being a politician to public servant once she was elected, and that citizens' trust and confidence in the court system

---

31 Commonwealth v. Kane, Nos. 6239-2015, 8423-2015, 2017 Pa. Dist. & Cnty. Dec. LEXIS 3228 at *33 (Mar. 2, 2017), https://www.montcopa.org/ArchiveCenter/ViewFile/Item/3644.

32 Orso, *supra* note 30.

33 Police Criminal Complaint, Commonwealth v. Kane, Nos. 6239-2015, 8423-2015 (Pa. Ct. of Common Pleas Oct. 1, 2015), https://www.montcopa.org/ArchiveCenter/ViewFile/Item/2632.

34 Craig R. McCoy & Laura McCrystal, *AG Kane Held for Trial on New Perjury Charge*, Pittsburgh Post-Gazette (Nov. 10, 2015, 10:57 PM), http://www.post-gazette.com/news/politics-state/2015/11/10/Kane-held-for-trial-on-new-perjury-charge/stories/201511100172.

35 *Timeline: The Rise & Fall of Kathleen Kane*, Morning Call (Nov. 30, 2018), https://www.apnews.com/fa4f6543e0054e4c94b67b2e1ace0a57.

36 Maryclaire Dale, *Pennsylvania Attorney General Kathleen Kane Found Guilty on All Charges in Perjury Trial*, NBC Phila. (Aug. 15, 2016, 7:28 AM), https://www.nbcphiladelphia.com/news/local/Kathleen-Kane-Trial-Perjury-Closing-Arguments-Jury-390168381.html.

37 Amy B. Wang, *Pennsylvania Attorney General Kathleen Kane Resigns After Criminal Conviction*, Wash. Post (Aug. 16, 2016, 4:29 PM), https://www.washingtonpost.com/news/post-nation/wp/2016/08/16/pennsylvanias-top-prosecutor-kathleen-kane-found-guilty-on-nine-criminal-charges/?utm_term=.8cfa21a059e8.

had been "completely eroded and undermined" by Kane's crimes.[38] Judge Demchick-Alloy sentenced Kane to ten to twenty-three months of incarceration to be served at the Montgomery County Correctional Facility, followed by eight years of consecutive probation.[39] The judge granted Kane's request to remain out on bail pending her appeal.[40] On May 25, 2018, the intermediate appellate court affirmed all convictions and wrote that "[t]his matter implicates constitutional issues, the rule of law, and a fundamental tenet underlying our legal system—the truth and sanctity of testimony under oath."[41] The defendant then petitioned for an allowance of appeal to the Supreme Court of Pennsylvania. On November 26, 2018, the Supreme Court denied the petition.[42] Kane reported to prison on November 29, 2018.[43] On March 22, 2019, the Disciplinary Board of the Supreme Court of Pennsylvania issued a disbarment order, ending Kane's career as a lawyer.[44] On July 31, 2019, Kane was released after serving about eight months in prison.[45]

II. Challenges

Our office faced many challenges in the case, including: its unique posture; the position held by the target; and our need to rely on the testimony of several key witnesses, which we addressed by, among other things, obtaining access to evidence from a federal wiretap.

---

38 Peter Hall, *Kathleen Kane Gets 10 to 23 Months in Jail, Judge Chides Her for Political 'Ego'*, Morning Call (Oct. 24, 2016, 10:55 PM), https://www.mcall.com/news/pennsylvania/mc-pennsylvania-former-attorney-general-kathleen-kane-sentencing-20161024-story.html.

39 *Id.*

40 Angela Couloumbis & Craig R. McCoy, *Ex-Attorney General Kathleen Kane Headed to Jail After Appeal Fails*, Pittsburgh Post-Gazette (Nov. 26, 2018, 7:04 PM), https://www.post-gazette.com/news/politics-state/2018/11/26/Attorney-General-Kathleen-Kane-appeal-fails-jail-pennsylvania-perjury/stories/201811260153.

41 Commonwealth v. Kane, 188 A.3d 1217, 1221 (Pa. Super. Ct. 2018).

42 Commonwealth v. Kane, 197 A.3d 1180, 1180 (Pa. 2018).

43 Joe Hermitt, *Ex-Attorney General Kathleen Kane Arrives at Pa. Prison*, Penn Live (Nov. 29, 2018), https://www.pennlive.com/news/2018/11/kathleen-kane-has-arrived-at-prison-heres-what-shell-face.html.

44 Office of Disciplinary Counsel v. Kane, 2019 Pa. LEXIS 1711, *1 (Mar. 22, 2019).

45 Craig R. McCoy, *Former AG Kathleen Kane Released from Jail; 'Grateful,' She Says*, Phila. Inquirer (July 31, 2019), https://www.inquirer.com/news/kathleen-kane-released-jail-attorney-general-pennsylvania-grand-jury-leak-20190730.html.

A. *Inheriting an Investigation from Another Entity*

One of the greatest challenges we faced was inheriting an extensive investigation performed by another entity that was not a law enforcement agency. The effects of inheriting an investigation included lost opportunities to engage in any covert investigation,[46] to fully investigate key witnesses before they spoke to law enforcement or to the grand jury, and to control the number of statements witnesses provided to authorities.

Special prosecutor Tom Carluccio investigated the case from May 2014 through the grand jury's presentment and the referral to our office in December 2014. Although Carluccio was a veteran criminal defense attorney and former prosecutor, he was handling a complicated investigation essentially solo. His seven-month investigation included testimony before the grand jury by dozens of witnesses, some of whom testified several times.

Following Judge Carpenter's December 19, 2014, referral, then-District Attorney Risa Vetri Ferman assigned a team of Montgomery County detectives and prosecutors to conduct an independent investigation. The team obtained transcripts and evidence from Carluccio's investigation and executed sealed search warrants upon the AGO to obtain additional documents. In addition, detectives interviewed many potential witnesses, some of whom had already testified during the special prosecutor's grand jury investigation, to follow up on or to clarify their earlier testimony. These interviews also addressed new evidence uncovered by our independent investigation. We had to work backwards to ensure that witness statements and testimony were complete.

Working backwards is not an ideal way to conduct an investigation. Had we been able to handle the investigation from the beginning, we would have gathered evidence and obtained witness testimony in a logical and strategic fashion. As one example, before approaching key, and possibly uncooperative witnesses, we would have become as knowledgeable as possible about their roles, and been prepared to impeach them with other evidence, if necessary.

One clear example of a missed opportunity was Kane's testimony before the grand jury. When Carluccio called Kane to testify on November 17, 2014, he did not have the benefit of evidence that we later uncovered, including Kane's

46 For more on covert investigations, see Chapter 2.2.

signed secrecy oath regarding the Twenty-Ninth Statewide Investigative Grand Jury. As a result, Carluccio could not thoroughly question Kane about several areas, including that she had sworn not to divulge information about that grand jury. We are not second-guessing the special prosecutor, who was doing a solid job alone under trying circumstances, but use this example to show the limitations of a one-man investigation of a high public official, and the challenges posed by an inherited investigation.

The multiple witness statements also complicated the case. Because many witnesses had already testified before the grand jury and were re-interviewed during our investigation, defense counsel had ample opportunity to cross-examine them about any inconsistencies across their grand jury testimony, interview statements, and trial testimony. Having more control over the investigation may have allowed us to control the number of statements witnesses provided, potentially reducing defense counsel's ability to cross-examine them on their multiple statements to authorities.

B. *Investigating the Elected Head Official of a State Law Enforcement Agency*

Another significant challenge we faced was the fact that our county law enforcement agency was investigating the elected head official of a statewide law enforcement agency. Kathleen Kane remained Attorney General of Pennsylvania—the state's largest law enforcement agency with more than 800 employees—throughout the entire investigation and during her trial. In that role, she had the power to fire AGO employees if they cooperated with the investigation. She also had a much greater ability to access information about the investigation, particularly when Carluccio was using the grand jury.

Kane's unlawful plans to retaliate against Frank Fina by finding a case that embarrassed him, generating documents about that case, and then leaking those documents to a reporter were largely hatched within the walls of the AGO. As she chose to use AGO personnel to carry out several of these tasks, most of the witnesses to these crimes were necessarily current or former employees of the AGO. Seeking the cooperation of witnesses who are employed by the target of the criminal investigation is problematic, at best. When the target has the power to terminate any employee at any time—and is the chief law enforcement officer of the Commonwealth—those employees are placed under tremendous pressure not to cooperate with the investigation.

The prospect of having to cooperate and testify against their boss, and the specter of having their careers destroyed if she chose to retaliate against them, most certainly had a chilling effect on AGO employees who possessed information of Kane's guilt.[47] Fortunately, several courageous AGO employees, including the former First Deputy Attorney General and the executive assistant who notarized Kane's grand jury secrecy oath, testified truthfully during Kane's trial. Without the cooperation of these brave people, the Kane prosecution surely would not have succeeded.

Other logistical challenges arose in investigating the top law enforcement officer of our state. The grand jury that the special prosecutor used for his work had been originally empaneled at the request of the AGO to investigate unrelated criminal activity the AGO was investigating. The AGO had thus been entrusted with handling the administrative functions associated with its grand jury, like keeping of notes of testimony, subpoenas, and evidence. When the special prosecutor used the AGO's grand jury to, in effect, investigate the AGO's actions over the leak, the AGO's usual role in assisting the grand jury's administrative functions posed challenges, including a heightened risk of leaks between grand jury personnel and AGO personnel. To ameliorate this risk, the court issued a protective order—but not every person complied with that order.[48]

C. *Corroborating Key Trial Witnesses*

Three witnesses provided critical testimony during *Commonwealth* v. *Kane*: Wanda Scheib, the AGO executive assistant who notarized Kane's secrecy oath and transcribed the interview leaked to the press; former First Deputy Attorney General Bruce Beemer; and political consultant Joshua Morrow. We expected that defense counsel would seek to undermine these witnesses' credibility, given the importance of their expected testimony. As a result, we

---

47 One long-time employee of the AGO was, in fact, terminated after he testified before the special prosecutor's grand jury. Through her spokesperson, Kane stated that the employee's termination had nothing to do with his testimony before the grand jury. This employee was reinstated to his position once Kane was convicted and resigned her post. Teresa Bonner, *Deputy Attorney General Fired by Kathleen Kane Gets His Job Back*, PennLive (Oct. 27, 2016), https://www.pennlive.com/news/2016/10/deputy_attorney_general_fired.html.

48 A member of Kane's protective detail was later convicted of contempt after he violated the protective order by accessing emails to learn about the grand jury's probe of the leak. Commonwealth v. Reese, 156 A.3d 1250, 1254 (Pa. Super. Ct. 2017).

obtained evidence to corroborate their testimony—including phone records, text messages, and other written records—and highlighted it during Kane's trial.

1. Lay Witness Wanda Scheib

Wanda Scheib testified about notarizing Kane's grand jury secrecy oaths, including historical oaths in which Kane swore to keep confidential information from the Twenty-Ninth Statewide Investigating Grand Jury that heard evidence about the 2009 investigation.[49] Kane had testified before the grand jury that she signed no such oaths—and that it would be "improper" to sign a historical oath.[50] Scheib's testimony was thus crucial to prove (1) that Kane was not permitted to leak information about the Twenty-Ninth Statewide Investigating Grand Jury; and (2) that Kane lied to the Thirty-Fifth Statewide Investigating Grand Jury when she testified that she was not required to keep confidential information from the earlier grand jury. To corroborate her, we introduced as evidence Kane's signed oath and Scheib's notary logs that reflected a contemporaneous record of her notarizing Kane's oath.[51]

Scheib also testified about transcribing, at the request of the Special Agent in Charge of the Bureau of Special Investigations, the recorded interview with an agent involved in the 2009 investigation subsequently leaked to the press.[52] Scheib testified that she had printed out only one copy of that transcript and provided it to the Special Agent in Charge.[53] To corroborate Scheib on this point, we introduced electronic records that showed that she had printed the

---

49 Transcript of Record at 56-70, Commonwealth v. Kane, Nos. 6239-2015, 8423-2015 (Pa. Ct. of Common Pleas Aug. 11, 2016, A.M. Session), https://www.montcopa.org/ArchiveCenter/ViewFile/Item/3284.

50 Affidavit of Probable Cause, Commonwealth v. Kane, Nos. 6239-2015, 8423-2015 (Pa. Ct. of Common Pleas Oct. 1, 2015), https://www.montcopa.org/ArchiveCenter/ViewFile/Item/2632; Affidavit of Probable Cause at 34, Commonwealth v. Kane, Nos. 6239-2015, 8423-2015 (Pa. Ct. of Common Pleas Aug. 6, 2015), https://www.montcopa.org/ArchiveCenter/ViewFile/Item/2504.

51 Transcript of Record at 56-70, Commonwealth v. Kane, Nos. 6239-2015, 8423-2015 (Pa. Ct. of Common Pleas Aug. 11, 2016, A.M. Session), https://www.montcopa.org/ArchiveCenter/ViewFile/Item/3284.

52 *Id.* at 50-53.

53 *Id.* The Special Agent in Charge, in turn, testified that he provided that one copy to Kane. Transcript of Record at 49-52, Commonwealth v. Kane, Nos. 6239-2015, 8423-2015 (Pa. Ct. of Common Pleas Aug. 10, 2016 P.M. Session), https://www.montcopa.org/ArchiveCenter/ViewFile/Item/3297.

transcript only once, just as she told the jury.[54] Thanks to this corroboration, Scheib's demeanor and personality, and the fact that she came forward despite her obvious fears Kane would retaliate against her, the defense did little to diminish Scheib's credibility during her cross-examination.

2. Lay Witness Bruce Beemer

We called Bruce Beemer to establish several non-controversial facts, including the structure of the AGO, how AGO operated grand juries and conducted grand jury investigations, and the need for grand jury secrecy.[55] He also identified the materials that were the subject of the grand jury leak and explained the background of the 2009 investigation.[56] One way we corroborated him was through a notebook he used to jot down reminders and contemporaneous notes in 2014.[57] That notebook allowed us to introduce information about dates on which certain events happened as past recollections recorded and prior consistent statements.[58]

Based on statements Kane had made to the press, we expected that the defense would argue that Beemer wanted Kane removed from office so that he could become attorney general.[59] We also expected that the defense would highlight the conflicts between the two when Beemer was Kane's first deputy, and suggest that Beemer had animus toward Kane that infected his testimony. However, defense attempts to challenge Beemer's credibility were muted by the contemporaneous recordings of incidents in his notebook, and Kane's lawyers

---

54 Transcript of Record at 52-53, Commonwealth v. Kane, Nos. 6239-2015, 8423-2015 (Pa. Ct. of Common Pleas Aug. 11, 2016, A.M. Session), https://www.montcopa.org/ArchiveCenter/ViewFile/Item/3284.

55 Transcript of Record at 93-102, Commonwealth v. Kane, Nos. 6239-2015, 8423-2015 (Pa. Ct. of Common Pleas Aug. 9, 2016, P.M. Session), https://www.montcopa.org/ArchiveCenter/ViewFile/Item/3281.

56 *Id.* at 107-17.

57 Transcript of Record at 22-25, Commonwealth v. Kane, Nos. 6239-2015, 8423-2015 (Pa. Ct. of Common Pleas Aug. 10, 2016, A.M. Session), https://www.montcopa.org/ArchiveCenter/ViewFile/Item/3283.

58 *See, e.g.*, Fed. R. Evid. 803(5) (past recollections recorded); *id.* 801(d)(1)(B) (prior consistent statements).

59 Beemer had left the AGO by the time the trial started and had accepted a governor-appointed position as inspector general, which reduced somewhat the power of this defense argument.

focused their cross-examination on eliciting testimony they hoped would be favorable to their client.[60]

3. Immunized Witness Joshua Morrow

Kane's former political consultant, Joshua Morrow, testified pursuant to an immunity order.[61] Immunized witnesses are typically subjected to greater scrutiny by jurors than are lay witnesses, making it important to fully debrief and corroborate Morrow, and to handle his direct testimony carefully.[62]

Morrow testified at trial about his agreement with Kane to leak materials about the 2009 investigation to the *Daily News* reporter, and then their attempt to cover up that crime by testifying falsely before the grand jury.[63] He told the jury about their efforts to craft a story that was consistent with the evidence and would wrongly place the blame for the unlawful disclosure of grand jury material on Adrian King, who served as Kane's First Deputy and had delivered the sealed box to Morrow with the grand jury materials.[64]

When Morrow agreed to cooperate with the prosecution of Kane, he admitted his role in the original leak and the cover up that followed. Earlier in the investigation, however, Morrow, like Kane, had lied to the grand jury and to investigators from our office.[65] We expected that he would be confronted by the

---

60 Transcript of Record at 51-78, 95-101, Commonwealth v. Kane, Nos. 6239-2015, 8423-2015 (Pa. Ct. of Common Pleas Aug. 10, 2016, A.M. Session), https://www.montcopa.org/ArchiveCenter/ViewFile/Item/3283.

61 Order of Immunity, Commonwealth v. Kane, Nos. 6239-2015, 8423-2015 (Pa. Ct. of Common Pleas Aug. 10, 2016), https://www.montcopa.org/ArchiveCenter/ViewFile/Item/3270. For more on immunized witnesses, see Chapter 1.8, Part II(A)(iii).

62 For example, a federal pattern instruction directs jurors to examine the testimony of an immunized witness "with greater care than the testimony of an ordinary witness . . . to determine whether or not it is colored in such a way as to place guilt upon the defendant in order to further the witness' own interests . . . ." 1-7 Modern Federal Jury Instructions-Criminal ¶ 7.01 (2018).

63 Transcript of Record at 134-35, Commonwealth v. Kane, Nos. 6239-2015, 8423-2015 (Pa. Ct. of Common Pleas Aug. 11, 2016, A.M. Session), https://www.montcopa.org/ArchiveCenter/ViewFile/Item/3284.

64 Transcript of Record at 50-52, Commonwealth v. Kane, Nos. 6239-2015, 8423-2015 (Pa. Ct. of Common Pleas Aug. 11, 2016, P.M. Session), https://www.montcopa.org/ArchiveCenter/ViewFile/Item/3285.

65 Transcript of Record at 113-18, Commonwealth v. Kane, Nos. 6239-2015, 8423-2015 (Pa. Ct. of Common Pleas Aug. 11, 2016, A.M. Session), https://www.montcopa.org/ArchiveCenter/

defense about these false statements. Before being willing to rely on Morrow, or to ask the jury to believe him, we looked at his emails, memoranda, phone records, and other documents to see if they were consistent with his expected testimony. We later obtained evidence from a federal wiretap investigation that included calls intercepted between Morrow and one of his associates, who was the target of the wiretap order.[66]

Morrow provided us with his tablet device, which contained text messages that he had exchanged with Kane that corroborated his description of their scheme.[67] They reflected that, just as Morrow said, Kane and Morrow conspired to illegally disclose confidential material to a news reporter as an act of revenge directed toward Fina. The text messages also demonstrated that Kane and Morrow then conspired to cover up their illegal actions. These text messages were perhaps the most important evidence in the trial: they reflected Kane, in her own words, plotting to abuse the powers of her office and then cover up her crimes by using her knowledge about a legal system she swore to support and obey. They also corroborated Morrow on key points, making it more likely that the jury would also credit his recollections of conversations that were not recorded.

One particular exchange of text messages provided our theme for the trial. In an effort to suggest she had no motive to leak the grand jury materials about the 2009 investigation, Kane claimed she had no animus toward Fina and, in fact, would not even recognize him. Morrow, however, testified that Kane was angry with Fina after the article about her failure to prosecute the Ali investigation appeared in the *Inquirer*, and leaked the 2009 investigation materials to retaliate against Fina by generating similarly negative press about him.

Text messages between Morrow and Kane reflected that Morrow was telling the truth, and that Kane was gleefully seeking revenge against Fina. The *Daily News* reporter who received the leaked material told Morrow that Fina said it was illegal to disclose grand jury information. Morrow relayed that conversation to Kane in a text message, commenting: "Oh, man, Frank's

---

ViewFile/Item/3284.

66 *Id.* at 139-50. For more on obtaining authorization to use wiretaps in an investigation, see Chapter 2.3.

67 Trial Exhibits C-51, C-52, C-53, Commonwealth v. Kane, Nos. 6239-2015, 8423-2015 (Pa. Ct. of Common Pleas Aug. 11, 2016, A.M. Session), https://www.montcopa.org/ArchiveCenter/ViewFile/Item/3284.

reaction was priceless." Later, Morrow texted Kane again, "What's the saying about revenge?" Kane responded, "Best served cold. Are we eating out soon?" The theme of Kane seeking to "serve" revenge was repeated by prosecutors throughout the trial.[68]

Telephone records also corroborated Morrow's testimony. For instance, Morrow testified that his grand jury appearance was on November 14, 2014, via telephone,[69] and that he told Kane about his grand jury testimony during two calls very late that same night.[70] Telephone records established a six-minute call between Morrow and Kane starting at 12:23 a.m. on November 15, 2014 and another twenty-three-minute call starting at 1:01 a.m., less than half an hour later.[71] Corroboration about the existence and timing of those calls made Morrow's description of their contents more credible, which included that Kane somehow knew even before they spoke that Morrow had testified before the grand jury and not appeared in person, despite the confidential nature of the grand jury proceedings.[72] These facts helped us show that Kane was obtaining access to the grand jury proceedings.

We were also able to corroborate Morrow by using calls intercepted during an unrelated 2014 federal wiretap investigation. We learned about those calls after a federal prosecutor contacted our office in May 2015 to tell us that the Middle District of Pennsylvania's U.S. Attorney's Office had recorded conversations that could be relevant to the Kane case. We sought and received an order from a federal judge to obtain access to these calls so we could review them. After reviewing the calls, we found calls with Morrow that provided key insights into his role in the scheme to leak grand jury material. Once we determined that we wished to introduce those calls at Kane's trial, we had to seek another order from the federal judge who supervised the wiretap investigation so that we could use those calls in our case, as a state court subpoena for

---

68 *Id.*

69 Transcript of Record at 112-13, Commonwealth v. Kane, Nos. 6239-2015, 8423-2015 (Pa. Ct. of Common Pleas Aug. 11, 2016, A.M. Session), https://www.montcopa.org/ArchiveCenter/ViewFile/Item/3284.

70 Transcript of Record at 68-72, Commonwealth v. Kane, Nos. 6239-2015, 8423-2015 (Pa. Ct. of Common Pleas Aug. 11, 2016, P.M. Session), https://www.montcopa.org/ArchiveCenter/ViewFile/Item/3285.

71 *Id.* at 69-72 (including Trial Exhibits C-70, C-71).

72 Kane believed that Morrow had appeared via video-teleconference rather than a telephone call—a detail that, if anything, helped reveal that Morrow was a careful, credible witness, as he would have likely just reported that she knew he appeared via phone if he made up the details of the call.

materials maintained by the federal government would be unenforceable due to sovereign immunity.[73] With assistance from the U.S. Attorney's Office, we obtained the necessary approval from the supervising judge to use the wire-tapped calls at our trial.

Obtaining that order allowed us to introduce a call intercepted on April 22, 2014, that proved critical.[74] As other trial evidence revealed, Kane asked then-First Assistant Attorney General Adrian King to deliver a sealed package to Morrow on that day.[75] That package—apparently unbeknownst to King—contained the 2009 investigation materials Kane wished to have leaked to the press. That same day, as Morrow testified, Kane called Morrow to tell him about the package and request that he leak the materials to the press.[76]

Later that day, the wiretap intercepted a phone call between Morrow's friend, who was the subject of the wiretap, and Morrow. During that call, Morrow discussed his reservations about leaking the materials and sought guidance about what he should do. Morrow said "so Kathleen called me today and I want to get your advice on this, Kathleen called me today and she's like Adrian has documents for you to leak out . . . . You know and it's all bullshit about like Frank Fina killing a Jerry Mondesire investigation." Morrow's friend presciently responded, "there's not going to be anything good that comes of that."[77]

While Morrow clearly did not abide by his friend's good advice, the call provided unimpeachable corroboration of Kane and Morrow's scheme: it had been recorded as the plan unfolded, without Morrow's knowledge, and long before Morrow had any incentive to curry favor with the prosecution by suggesting that Kane played some particular role in the leak scheme.

---

73 "A state subpoena commanding a federal agency to produce its records or have its employees testify about information obtained in their official capacities violates federal sovereign immunity." *In re* Collins, 524 F.3d 249, 251 (D.C. Cir. 2008). *See also, e.g.*, Commonwealth of Puerto Rico v. United States, 490 F.3d 50, 61 n.6 (1st Cir. 2007); Mir Aimal Kasi v. Angelone, 300 F.3d 487, 503 (4th Cir. 2002); *In re* Elko Cty. Grand Jury, 109 F.3d 554, 556 (9th Cir. 1997); Civiletti v. Municipal Court, 116 Cal. App. 3d 105, 109-10 (Cal. Ct. App. 1981).

74 Transcript of Record at 139-50, Commonwealth v. Kane, Nos. 6239-2015, 8423-2015 (Pa. Ct. of Common Pleas Aug. 11, 2016, A.M. Session), https://www.montcopa.org/ArchiveCenter/ViewFile/Item/3284.

75 *Id.* at 133-35.

76 *Id.*

77 *Id.* at 139-50 (including Trial Exhibit C-57).

Along with corroborating Morrow, we were careful to pull the sting about his perjury before the grand jury and his lies to investigators during his direct examination. By fronting those issues during his testimony as our witness, we reduced the power of the expected cross-examination about Morrow's previous lies and showed the jury that we had nothing to hide.

Thanks to the text messages, phone records, and the wiretapped call, Morrow's testimony was well corroborated. Kane's team of skillful defense attorneys cross-examined Morrow about how he had previously lied about Kane's role in the scheme and argued that there were innocent explanations for the text messages between Morrow and Kane. We had fronted the lies, which reduced the strength of that cross, and were able to remind the jury of the context for the text messages on redirect and in our jury addresses. For example, the defense suggested when Morrow told Kane in a text message that he expected she would "enjoy the read" in a few days, he was referring to an article about a campaign for Congress by Morrow's fiancé. We pointed out that this text was one in a series of messages about the leaked grand jury documents, which made it clear that it referred to the upcoming *Daily News* article—not to an unrelated article about our witness's fiancé.[78]

As we built our case and prepared for trial, we thought carefully about which witnesses provided essential evidence and gathered evidence to corroborate them. For our lay witnesses, this included their own contemporaneous notes—whether in a notary log or a notebook—that reflected that the things about which they testified had indeed occurred. Recognizing that an immunized witness is, rightfully, subject to additional scrutiny, we obtained as much corroborating evidence as possible to ensure and show that Morrow was telling the truth. That evidence allowed the jury to see the scheme as it unfolded: they read Kane's own texts, and they heard Morrow's candid, contemporaneous description of Kane's request that he leak grand jury materials to the press. Of course, not every case will include the fortunate accident of having a key witness intercepted in an unrelated wiretap investigation.

---

78 Transcript of Record at 23-25, Commonwealth v. Kane, Nos. 6239-2015, 8423-2015 (Pa. Ct. of Common Pleas Aug. 11, 2016, P.M. Session), https://www.montcopa.org/ArchiveCenter/ViewFile/Item/3285 (including Trial Exhibit C-64).

The case against Kane was strong; the messages, documents, and wiretaps that corroborated the testimony of our primary witnesses made the case even stronger.

III. Lessons Learned

A. *The Investigation Never Stops*

When we inherited the case from the special prosecutor, our office re-interviewed witnesses and used additional investigative tools to ensure that we were confident in the credibility of key witnesses and obtained sufficient evidence to successfully prosecute Kane. We did not simply rely on the good work that the special prosecutor had already done but used our own investigation and prosecutorial discretion to assess the case and decide whether, and which, charges were appropriate. Our additional work and independence helped insulate the case from legal challenges[79] and ensure the best result at trial.

After the initial charges were filed, as noted above, witnesses came forward with information that suggested Kane lied in the grand jury. The prosecution team investigated these new allegations, including obtaining a search warrant for AGO files, which led to additional charges against Kane. Even after initial charges are filed, prosecutors should be willing to—particularly in cases involving the abuse of the legal process—pursue additional charges such as obstruction of justice or perjury when warranted.

Finally, when we learned about a federal wiretap that could provide important corroboration of a key witness, we used appropriate legal mechanisms to obtain it.

---

79 Our independent investigation and exercise of discretion was, in the view of one Pennsylvania Supreme Court judge, necessary to deny Kane's later motion for quo warranto relief on the grounds that Judge Carpenter lacked authority to appoint the special prosecutor. *In re* Thirty-Fifth Statewide Investigating Jury, 112 A.3d 624, 636 (Pa. 2015) (Baer, J., concurring).

B. *Providing Information Can Help Restore Trust in the Rule of Law*

Our office provided access on our official website to public documents in the case, including the two complaints filed against Kane, motions filed by the defense and by the prosecution, the entire trial transcript, and decisions by the judge.[80] Providing this information helped ensure that the media accurately reflected what was happening in the case and that interested citizens had access to information that could be made public. Given that the charges in the case involved the abuse of the grand jury process—one that is, by necessity, secret and one that prosecutors are entrusted to use properly—increased transparency was an important step to recover citizens' trust in prosecutors in our state.

We believe that this prosecution helped the community regain trust in our legal system and provided some measure of comfort for victims. One sad footnote to our case is that J. Whyatt Mondesire's reputation was unfairly, and permanently, tarnished by Kane. After the *Daily News* published the article suggesting he had been a target of the grand jury, Mondesire was ostracized from institutions he helped build and his health declined; he died a broken man less than a year later.[81]

Conclusion

Hopefully, cases like this will be rare. When they do arise, however, they pose "important issues of constitutional law and, more fundamentally, the rule of law itself."[82] The public must be able to trust that law enforcement agencies

---

80 The complete archive of court documents related to the proceedings against Kane is available on the Montgomery County website. *See Archive Center: Commonwealth v. Kathleen Granahan Kane*, Montgomery County, PA, https://www.montcopa.org/Archive.aspx?AMID=158&Type=&ADID= (last visited Apr.14, 2021). For more on what information can and cannot ethically be provided by prosecutors to the public, see Chapter 5.3.

81 Wallace McKelvey, *"It Just Took a Toll," Says Partner of Alleged Kane Leak Subject J. Whyatt Mondesire*, Penn Live (Aug. 12, 2016), http://www.pennlive.com/news/2016/08/kathleen_kane_mondesire.html.

82 Commonwealth v. Kane, Nos. 6239-2015, 8423-2015, 2017 Pa. Dist. & Cnty. Dec. LEXIS 3228 at *1 (Mar. 2, 2017), https://www.montcopa.org/ArchiveCenter/ViewFile/Item/3644.

will faithfully abide by the law. As difficult as these cases may be to prosecute, we are duty-bound to use the resources necessary to seek justice.

To successfully prosecute a member of another law enforcement agency for public corruption requires a thorough investigation. In our case, that meant conducting a long investigation even after there was a grand jury presentment and public attention was on the case. It also helps if other members of the law enforcement agency under investigation cooperate. Thankfully, in our case, there were brave men and women willing to come forward and put their livelihoods at risk.

The successful prosecution of these cases may also require the involvement of other state and federal agencies. Without that involvement in this case, we would not have obtained the Morrow wiretap. Through investigation, cooperation, and shared involvement of other agencies, we could build a case that was strong, convincing, and corroborated on many levels. Fully restoring the public trust may take more time, but this successful prosecution of the sitting Pennsylvania Attorney General for her crimes was a necessary step toward that goal.

Chapter 1.3

Legislative Corruption

Howard S. Master

Howard S. Master has served as Special Counsel to the Suffolk County District Attorney since 2018, where he supervises prosecution of public corruption offenses, among other responsibilities. Prior to that, he served as Senior Enforcement Counsel to the New York State Attorney General, Deputy Chief of the Criminal Division of the United States Attorney's Office for the Southern District of New York (SDNY), and a member of SDNY's Public Corruption Unit. Over the course of his career, Mr. Master has investigated, prosecuted, and supervised the investigation and prosecution of several legislators. Mr. Master also serves as Adjunct Professor at the University of Pennsylvania School of Law, where he co-teaches a class titled Public Corruption and the Law.

Introduction

Legislative bodies possess enormous power to make the laws that other officials enforce, as well as control the funding necessary for other officials to carry out enforcement priorities. Legislators also often have significant influence over a host of governmental activities in their capacity as representatives of constituents with matters pending before the government. Legislatures' status as a locus of power makes them subject to overt and lawful efforts to curry favor and exert influence such as lobbying and campaign contributions. But that same power makes legislatures vulnerable to unlawful forms of influence peddling, potential conflicts of interest, and other official misconduct. In addition, corrupt conduct by an elected representative of the people may serve as a source of greater public outrage and injury to public confidence in government than corruption by an unelected bureaucrat.

For these and other reasons, corruption units should be prepared to aggressively investigate and to prosecute legislative corruption where it exists.

Before doing so, however, prosecutors should be aware of the significant challenges, both legal and practical, that will confront them. They also should take advantage of some of the unique sources of evidence that may be available to help jumpstart or advance legislative corruption investigations. A summary of some of these unique challenges and resources is set forth below.

I. Unique Challenges Associated with Prosecuting Legislative Corruption

A. *Legislative (Speech or Debate) Privilege*

The United States Congress and many state legislatures possess unique constitutional protections from investigation and prosecution. The source of these protections is referred to as the Speech or Debate privilege, or sometimes more generally as legislative privilege.[1]

Members of the United States Congress obtain protection from the Speech or Debate Clause of the United States Constitution, which reads as follows:

> The Senators and Representatives shall . . . in all Cases, except Treason, Felony and Breach of the Peace, be privileged from Arrest during their Attendance at the Session of their respective Houses, and in going to and returning from the same; and for any Speech or Debate in either House, they shall not be questioned in any other Place.[2]

An academic survey revealed that forty-three state constitutions have an analogous provision, sometimes identically- or similarly-worded, that protects members of their legislatures in connection with their legislative work.[3] While

---

1 This concept is also discussed in Chapter 4.3, Part VIII.

2 U.S. Const. art. I, § 6, cl. 1.

3 *See* Steven F. Huefner, *The Neglected Value of the Legislative Privilege in State Legislatures*, 45 Wm. & Mary L. Rev. 221, 224 (2003); *see also, e.g.*, N.Y. Const. art. III, § 11 ("For any speech or debate in either house of the legislature, the members shall not be questioned in any other place."); Wis. Const. art. IV, § 16 ("No member of the legislature shall be liable in any civil action, or criminal prosecution whatever, for words spoken in debate.").

many state constitutions' Speech or Debate clauses have not been construed definitively by their respective states' highest courts,[4] the scope of the federal Speech or Debate clause has been heavily litigated in recent decades, and recent state jurisprudence has drawn on federal decisions concerning the United States Constitution to guide interpretation of state Speech or Debate clauses.[5] Accordingly, while different states' Speech or Debate jurisprudence may vary significantly from the federal example, the discussion below summarizes the scope of the federal Speech or Debate protection as a guide to the potential application of Speech or Debate privilege in the states.

Speech or Debate clauses arose out of the English experience of legislative oppression by the executive, particularly arrest and intimidation by members of law enforcement answerable to the King. The U.S. Constitution's Speech or Debate Clause can be traced to the English Bill of Rights of 1689, which was the "culmination of a long struggle for parliamentary supremacy."[6] The Clause "was designed to assure a co-equal branch of the government wide freedom of speech, debate, and deliberation without intimidation or threats from" another branch of government, specifically the executive branch.[7] As the United States Supreme Court stated in *United States* v. *Johnson*:

> There is little doubt that the instigation of criminal charges against critical or disfavored legislators by the executive in a judicial forum was the chief fear prompting the long struggle for parliamentary privilege in England and, in the context of the American system of separation of powers, is the predominate thrust of the Speech or Debate Clause. In scrutinizing this criminal prosecution, then, we look particularly to the prophylactic purposes of the clause.[8]

Because state prosecutors and other state law enforcement agents are agents of executive power, they are co-equal to state legislatures and thus are bound by the restrictions of state Speech or Debate clauses. Note, however,

---

4 Huefner, *supra* note 3, at 225.

5 *See, e.g.*, Edwards v. Vesilind, 790 S.E.2d 469, 476 (Va. 2016); Hamilton v. Hennessey, 783 A.2d 852, 860 (Pa. Commw. Ct. 2001) ("when interpreting the Speech or Debate Clause of the Pennsylvania Constitution, it is appropriate to look to decisions interpreting the federal Speech and Debate Clause"), *aff'd*, 800 A.2d 927 (Pa. 2002).

6 United States v. Johnson, 383 U.S. 169, 178 (1966).

7 *Edwards*, 790 S.E.2d at 477 (quoting Gravel v. United States, 408 U.S. 606, 616 (1972)).

8 *Johnson*, 383 U.S. at 182.

that federal authorities are, under the United States Constitution's Supremacy Clause, not co-equal with state legislatures.[9] Thus, for example, the Supreme Court has held that federal prosecutors are able to investigate and prosecute state legislative corruption even where state legislative immunity rules may have prevented a state prosecutor from doing so.[10]

1. What Is Covered

All "legislative activity" is covered by the Clause—i.e., all activity that is "an integral part of the deliberative and communicative processes by which Members participate in committee and House proceedings with respect to the consideration and passage or rejection of proposed legislation or with respect to other matters which the Constitution places within the jurisdiction of either House."[11] This includes, most clearly, speeches on the floor of the legislature,[12] votes on any matter, and other matters related to the business of considering and passing legislation, e.g., committee work.

Any discussion of what *is* covered by the Clause, however, must include an assessment of what is *not* covered. Caselaw has not developed a definitive rule, but the following conduct has been found not to be protected by the Clause and thus subject to prosecution:

- Criminal agreements themselves, including agreements to exchange official action for bribes, are not privileged. A criminal quid pro quo is not protected even where the official action to be exchanged for the bribe is legislative and thus is itself covered by the Clause. As stated in *United States* v. *Brewster*, "Taking a bribe is, obviously, no part of the legislative process or function; it is not a legislative act."[13] This is because the public official's agreement to take a bribe in exchange for legislative action is the crime, regardless of whether the legislator in fact performs a legislative act pursuant to the agreement.

---

9 *See* United States v. Gillock, 445 U.S. 360, 370 (1980).

10 *See id.* at 373-74 (state legislative immunity does not bar federal prosecution of state legislators; Supremacy Clause overrides state speech or debate/legislative immunity).

11 *Gravel*, 408 U.S. at 625.

12 *Johnson*, 383 U.S. at 173-74.

13 United States v. Brewster, 408 U.S. 501, 526 (1972).

- Political activities of a legislator that are not related to the consideration of legislation or other work on legislative committees or bodies are not privileged. As summarized by *Brewster*, political activity includes:

> [A] wide range of legitimate 'errands' performed for constituents, the making of appointments with Government agencies, assistance in securing Government contracts, preparing so-called 'news letters' to constituents, news releases, and speeches delivered outside the Congress. The range of these related activities has grown over the years. They are performed in part because they have come to be expected by constituents, and because they are a means of developing continuing support for future elections. Although these are entirely legitimate activities, they are political in nature, rather than legislative, in the sense that term has been used by the Court in prior cases. But it has never been seriously contended that these political matters, however appropriate, have the protection afforded by the Speech or Debate Clause.[14]

- Publication of information to third parties, or remarks made outside of the confines of the legislature, are unprotected by the Clause, thus subjecting legislators to potential prosecution for disclosing classified information or to use of their extra-legislative statements against them in prosecutions or litigation.[15]

- Personnel management decisions, including acts that may constitute discrimination in violation of law, are not privileged.[16]

- Campaign finance and other campaign activities are not privileged. Thus, legislators may be prosecuted for campaign finance violations or other crimes related to their political campaigns.[17]

---

14 *Id.* at 512.

15 Hutchinson v. Proxmire, 443 U.S. 111, 130 (1979); *Gravel*, 408 U.S. at 622-24.

16 Bastien v. Office of Campbell, 390 F.3d 1301, 1318 (10th Cir. 2004).

17 *See, e.g.*, United States v. Hunter, No. 18 Cr. 3677 (S.D. Cal. Jul. 9, 2019) (denying Congressman Duncan Hunter's motion to dismiss campaign finance indictment under Speech and Debate Clause); Ken Stone, *FBI Raid on Duncan Hunter's El Cajon Office Violated Rights, Appeals Court Told*, Times of San Diego (Sept. 6, 2019), https://timesofsandiego.com/

2. Who Is Covered

All legislators, staff, and committees are protected for conduct covered by the Clause. "[T]he Speech or Debate Clause applies not only to a Member but also to his aides insofar as the conduct of the latter would be a protected legislative act if performed by the Member himself."[18] In addition, some state court decisions have deemed legislatures' interactions with consultants retained for legislative purposes also to be covered by state Speech or Debate clauses.[19]

3. Effect of Coverage

The Clause exerts a powerful effect on prosecutions that involve acts that fall in whole or in part within its scope. First, it creates an evidentiary privilege protecting members of Congress "against inquiry into acts that occur in the regular course of the legislative process and into the motivation for those acts,"[20] and it "precludes any showing of how [a member of Congress] acted, voted, or decided."[21] This evidentiary privilege prohibits evidence of legislative acts from being introduced against a legislator at trial, even if the acts that the prosecution would otherwise seek to introduce are public (e.g., votes, speeches on the floor of Congress).[22]

Second, while the United States Supreme Court has not yet ruled on the matter, lower federal courts have found that material covered by the Clause cannot be obtained by compulsory process, at least from legislative bodies or facilities.[23] In *United States* v. *Rayburn House Office Building, Room 2113,*

---

politics/2019/09/06/fbi-raid-on-duncan-hunters-el-cajon-office-violated-rights-appeals-court-told/. Hunter pled guilty to misusing campaign funds and was sentenced to eleven months in prison; however, he was pardoned in December 2020. *Former GOP Rep. Duncan Hunter Gets Full Pardon from Trump*, CBS L.A. (Dec. 22, 2020), https://losangeles.cbslocal.com/2020/12/22/trump-pardons-former-gop-rep-duncan-hunter/.

18 *Bastien*, 390 F.3d at 1310 (quoting *Gravel*, 408 U.S. at 618).

19 Edwards v. Vesilind, 790 S.E.2d 469, 481-82 (Va. 2016); Arizona Indep. Redistricting Comm'n v. Fields, 75 P.3d 1088, 1098 (Ariz. Ct. App. 2003).

20 United States v. Brewster, 408 U.S. 501, 525 (1972).

21 *Id.* at 527.

22 United States v. Johnson, 383 U.S. 169, 184-85 (1966) (holding that evidence of a speech given on the floor of Congress is inadmissible in criminal prosecution of Congressman due to Speech or Debate Clause protection).

23 The United States Constitution's Secrecy Clause, which states that "Each House shall keep a Journal of its Proceedings, and from time to time publish the same, *excepting such Parts as may in their judgment require Secrecy*," U.S. Const. art. I, § 5, cl. 3 (emphasis added), also supports

Washington, D.C. 20515,[24] for example, the D.C. Circuit considered whether a search warrant concerning an investigation into a Member of Congress's corruption in office could be executed lawfully in a Congressional office building by federal law enforcement agents.[25] The Circuit found that "a search that allows agents of the Executive to review privileged materials without the Member's consent violates the Clause."[26] Similarly, subpoenas to Members of Congress or legislative bodies seeking legislative materials have been quashed.[27] Other courts, however, have limited the reach of this non-disclosure privilege where material outside the scope of the Clause is sought.[28]

A. McDonnell *Challenges*

In 2016, the United States Supreme Court decided *McDonnell* v. *United States*,[29] a closely-watched ruling that changed the landscape of federal corruption prosecutions. The case involved former Virginia Governor Robert F. McDonnell, who was convicted of bribery-related offenses for accepting hundreds of thousands of dollars in exchange for alleged efforts to assist his bribe-payer with obtaining a variety of benefits from Virginia state government for his purported nutritional supplement business.[30]

The benefits sought by the bribe-payer included coverage for the supplement by the state's health benefits system and state-funded research into the health benefits of the supplement.[31] Governor McDonnell met on multiple occasions with the payer and publicly promoted the product at an event.[32] He also contacted state officials under him who had responsibility for health benefits

---

Congressional claims that it is not required to disclose items sought by the Executive Branch unless it chooses to do so.

24 497 F.3d 654 (D.C. Cir. 2007).

25 *Id.* at 655-56.

26 *Id.* at 663.

27 *See* Brown & Williamson Tobacco Corp. v. Williams, 62 F.3d 408, 423 (D.C. Cir. 1995); SEC v. Comm. on Ways & Means of the U.S. House of Representatives, 161 F. Supp. 3d 199, 239-45 (S.D.N.Y. 2015).

28 *In re* Fattah, 802 F.3d 516, 531 (3d Cir. 2015) (declining to quash search warrant for emails of Congressman investigated for corruption offenses); United States v. Renzi, 651 F.3d 1012, 1039 (9th Cir. 2011).

29 136 S. Ct. 2355 (2016). For more on *McDonnell* defenses, see Chapter 4.3, Part II.

30 *Id.* at 2361.

31 *Id.* at 2362.

32 *Id.* at 2363.

coverage and medical research to request that those individuals grant access to the bribe-payer and consider his requests for state support.[33] The bribe-payer did not, however, secure either health benefits coverage or state-supported research before the scheme was uncovered and McDonnell was charged.[34] After McDonnell was convicted at trial and his conviction was affirmed by an intermediate appellate court, McDonnell's case was heard by the United States Supreme Court.[35]

McDonnell argued to the Supreme Court that he had not engaged in criminal bribery because the relevant federal bribery statute required an agreement to perform an official act in exchange for the payments, and he claimed that the actions he took, which he asserted consisted of promoting the product; providing access to himself and others in state government; and making calls and arranging meetings, were insufficient to satisfy the "official act" threshold.[36]

The Supreme Court agreed, holding that the text of the applicable federal statute defining "official act," as well as Supreme Court precedent and constitutional concerns, required a narrow definition of "official act" that specifically excluded from its reach access, meetings, calls, and events, standing alone.[37] In particular, the Supreme Court expressed concern that if campaign contributions or minimal payments could supply the quid, and meetings, contacts, and other non-decisional actions could supply the quo in a criminal quid pro quo, as the federal government argued to the Supreme Court, it "could cast a pall of potential prosecution" over routine relationships between constituents and elected representatives, adversely affecting representative government: "Officials might wonder whether they could respond to even the most commonplace requests for assistance, and citizens with legitimate concerns might shrink from participating in democratic discourse."[38]

Legislators' daily activities are filled with acts that, standing alone, may no longer meet the "official act" threshold of *McDonnell*. These activities include meetings with constituents, donors, and advocates; attendance at events; and contact with executive branch agencies on behalf of constituents.[39] While

---

33 *Id.* at 2364.
34 *Id.* at 2364-65.
35 *Id.* at 2367.
36 *Id.*
37 *Id.* at 2371-72.
38 *Id.* at 2372.
39 *See* United States v. Silver, 948 F.3d 538, 564 (2d Cir. 2020) (Speaker of the New York State

legislators also are involved in actions that clearly would meet the threshold for "official action" even after *McDonnell*, including drafting and voting on legislation, much of this material may be entitled to Speech or Debate Clause protection, presenting unique potential challenges in post-*McDonnell* bribery prosecutions of legislators.[40]

State and local prosecutors can adopt several different approaches to avoiding these issues, however. First, they can seek to distinguish state statutory definitions related to official action from the definition at issue in *McDonnell*. Efforts to make such a distinction thus far have been mixed.[41] Second, they can rely on state statutes with a different or lower evidentiary burden than the bribery charges at issue in *McDonnell*, including gift bans and prohibitions on official misconduct that do not require demonstrating a quid pro quo agreement to exchange cash for official acts.[42] Third, they can focus investigations and prosecutions on conduct that unambiguously constitutes official action and that falls outside of Speech or Debate Clause protections. Each of these strategies should be considered when evaluating a potential investigation or prosecution of legislative corruption in the post-*McDonnell* environment.

Assembly's effort to assist bribe-payer with navigating a local permitting process "is not an official act" after *McDonnell*, even while several other actions taken by Sheldon Silver on behalf of the bribe-payer and others did meet the official act threshold). Note: The author served as co-lead counsel in the investigation and prosecution of Silver.

40 These challenges were lessened in *Silver* because as a state legislator, Silver's legislative acts were not shielded from scrutiny or admissibility at a federal criminal trial. *See* United States v. Gillock, 445 U.S. 360, 374 (1980).

41 *See* United States v. Ferriero, 866 F.3d 107, 125 (3d Cir. 2017) (New Jersey bribery statute unaffected by *McDonnell*); United States v. Tavares, 844 F.3d 46, 56-57 (1st Cir. 2016) (interpreting Massachusetts state statutory definition of "official act" in light of *McDonnell* to exclude meetings and contacts); Commonwealth v. Veon, 150 A.3d 435, 447-48 (Pa. 2016) (interpreting Pennsylvania's conflict of interest statute as prohibiting only private financial gain, rather than a benefit political in nature); Commonwealth v. Degnan, 73 N.E.3d 823, 828 (App. Ct. Mass. 2017) (interpreting the Massachusetts state bribery statute in light of federal case law including *McDonnell*).

42 *See, e.g.*, N.Y. Penal Law § 195.00 (2020) (defining misdemeanor crime of Official Misconduct as occurring when, e.g., a public servant, "with intent to obtain a benefit or deprive another person of a benefit . . . commits an act relating to his office but constituting an unauthorized exercise of his official functions, knowing that such act is unauthorized," without requiring "act relating to [the public servant's] office" to be official or requiring the act to occur in exchange for any benefit from a third party).

B. *Practical Challenges*

Prosecuting legislative corruption is challenging not only because of constitutional provisions and doctrine, but also because of practical considerations associated with pursuing legislative misconduct. Legislators draft and approve the legislation that governs their own conduct as well as that of other public servants. Legislators who are both powerful and corrupt may thus be able to use their power to craft or use existing gaps in the law to shield their conduct from prosecution or public scrutiny.

For example, the New York State Legislature had long resisted exposing to public scrutiny details of their members' sources of outside income.[43] It was only after several prosecutions of legislators on corruption charges, and a push by the state's governor to adopt greater transparency, that the legislature agreed to greater disclosure.[44] Other states may have similar stories of legislation that has the effect (if not the purpose) of imposing challenges to prosecution of legislators for misconduct.[45]

In addition, state legislators adopt the budgets that fund, directly or indirectly, all or substantial portions of government operations, including funds dedicated to prosecutorial and other law enforcement resources, and they have the ability to call for legislative hearings or adopt legislation to cabin the authority of prosecutors if they choose to do so.[46] Elected legislators also may be of different political parties from elected prosecutors or have taken policy positions on certain issues that are adverse to those of elected prosecutors, allowing

---

43 *See Governor Cuomo, Majority Leader Skelos & Speaker Silver Announce Agreement on Historic Ethics Reform*, N.Y. State (June 3, 2011), https://www.governor.ny.gov/news/governor-cuomo-majority-leader-skelos-speaker-silver-announce-agreement-historic-ethics-reform (quoting comments characterizing the legislation as "long-awaited changes . . . unraveling what has for decades been the Gordian knot of ethics reform").

44 *See Governor Cuomo Signs Ethics Reform Legislation*, N.Y. State (Aug. 15, 2011), https://www.governor.ny.gov/news/governor-cuomo-signs-ethics-reform-legislation.

45 *See, e.g.*, Ga. Code Ann. § 45-15-17(d) (2020) ("Nothing contained in this Code section shall authorize the Attorney General to commence or carry on any investigation or to issue any subpoenas to anyone for the purpose of investigating any member of the General Assembly while the General Assembly is in any regular or called session.").

46 *See, e.g.*, Luther Strange, *Sen. Luther Strange: The Importance of Taking on Corruption*, AL.com (Mar. 7, 2019), https://www.al.com/opinion/2017/12/sen_luther_strange_the_importa.html (describing how, after his office charged a powerful state legislator, other legislators threatened to reduce corruption prosecutor's budget to zero).

some legislators to argue (whether or not the argument is well founded) that a particular investigation or prosecution is politically motivated.[47] In addition, individuals may be wary of informing on legislators because of their power. Using these levers of power, a corrupt legislator may try to deter or undermine efforts to expose his or her misdeeds, or to create legal ambiguity in a potential prosecution of those misdeeds.

Prosecutors must be prepared to address each of these practical challenges through deep knowledge of the law under which they are investigating or prosecuting any legislator, and through use of measures to protect the integrity of any investigation or prosecution in the event it is challenged.

II. Unique Assets Available to Prosecutions of Legislative Corruption

While prosecuting legislative corruption presents unique challenges, unique resources are available to prosecutors investigating a member of the legislature. Investigators have access to a wealth of public information concerning legislators and their conduct in and out of office, including the following:

- Campaign finance records, including the identities of contributors and the amounts of their contributions, expenditures and the recipients of those expenditures, and the staff employed by the campaign;
- Campaign-related material, including fliers, websites, speeches, and debates,
- Records of legislation introduced, sponsored, or voted on;
- Statements at public hearings;
- Financial disclosure forms, which vary by jurisdiction, but which typically require disclosure of potential conflicts of interest;

---

47 It is, as an ethical matter, inappropriate for prosecutors to allow political considerations to guide their decision-making. *See* Chapter 5.1, Part I.

- Lobbying disclosure forms, which may identify the lobbyist, the entities hiring the lobbyist, the legislators lobbied, and the issues or legislation on which they were lobbied; and

- Records of organizations funded through any legislative earmarks or member items (also known colloquially as "pork barrel" funding), and tax returns of any tax-exempt organization funded through these earmarks.[48]

Different jurisdictions may have more information on the legislative process or individual legislators that can be tapped in support of investigations.

By accessing these public resources and comparing them with each other and with the allegation of misconduct that is being investigated, it may be possible to determine if the allegation has some merit even before taking any overt step in the investigation. For example, mining legislative documents, financial disclosures, and nonprofit tax returns enabled federal prosecutors to uncover use of a member item "slush fund" by members and aides of the New York City Council to route public funds to sham nonprofits that in turn, kicked money back to the public officials.[49] Many other schemes involving legislative misconduct were uncovered by members of the media or the public who similarly were scrutinizing public statements and records and whose findings were pursued by prosecutors.

III. Case Studies

A. *Sheldon Silver*

Sheldon Silver's case illustrates many of the challenges associated with prosecuting powerful legislators, as well as the value of public information in holding legislators accountable for misconduct. Silver was the powerful

48 For example, the website Guidestar provides searchable access to publicly-filed Form 990s (federal tax-exempt organization tax returns). *See Guidestar Products*, GuideStar, https://learn.guidestar.org/products/ (last visited Apr. 14, 2021).

49 *See* Alice McQuillan, *Former Councilman Gets 5 Years for Slush Fund Fraud*, NBCNewYork.com (Dec. 15, 2009), https://www.nbcnewyork.com/news/local/councilman-martinez-sentenced/2117736/.

Speaker of the New York State Assembly (one of the chambers of New York's State Legislature) for over twenty-five years. Over time, New York State government aggregated power over budgets and the most significant legislation in the hands of three individuals: the assembly speaker (Silver's position), the senate majority leader, and the governor. Negotiations among those three figures (until recently all men, leading the practice to be known colloquially as "Three Men in a Room") historically have occurred in secret, and the product of those negotiations is presented to the Legislature for a vote as a *fait accompli*, with no public hearings, minimal debate, and low risk of rejection.[50]

As established by evidence presented at Silver's trials, Silver took full advantage of the traditionally secretive practices of New York State government to enrich himself to an extent that the public did not know for years, using means that also were concealed for years.[51] Among other things, Silver used his control over the legislative process to gain power not only over legislation, but over substantial funding streams that were not subject to public disclosure. Silver also approved legislation that gave him power to veto any significant state financing done by public authorities through an entity called the Public Authorities Control Board (PACB). Silver used his power over secret funding streams to induce a doctor to send referrals for lucrative cases to a law firm in exchange for hundreds of thousands of dollars in state research funding and other forms of assistance to the doctor. The law firm, in turn, paid Silver millions of dollars in salary and referral fees. Silver used his power over the PACB, and legislation of importance to real estate developers more generally, to induce real estate developers who were especially reliant on Silver to send him business that generated hundreds of thousands more dollars in referral fees in exchange for Silver's favorable consideration of their requests for PACB funding and their legislative priorities. These corrupt practices were undiscovered for years,

---

50 *See generally* SEYMOUR P. LACHMAN WITH ROBERT POLNER, THREE MEN IN A ROOM: THE INSIDE STORY OF POWER AND BETRAYAL IN AN AMERICAN STATEHOUSE (2006).

51 The case has been heavily litigated at the trial and appellate level. A detailed accounting of the facts of the case and its procedural history may be found in the following opinions: United States v. Silver, 184 F. Supp. 3d 33 (S.D.N.Y. 2016) (denying motion for judgment of acquittal and new trial after conviction in first trial); United States v. Silver, 864 F.3d 102 (2d Cir. 2017) (vacating and remanding for new trial in view of intervening decision in *McDonnell*), *cert. denied*, 138 S. Ct. 738 (2018); United States v. Silver, No. 15 Cr. 93 (VEC), 2018 U.S. Dist. LEXIS 158216 (S.D.N.Y. Sept. 17, 2018) (denying motion for judgment of acquittal and new trial after conviction in second trial); United States v. Silver, 948 F.3d 538 (2d Cir. 2020) (vacating three counts of conviction but affirming remaining counts); United States v. Silver, No. 18-2380, 2020 U.S. App. LEXIS 10183 (2d Cir. Apr. 1, 2020) (denying petition for stay pending writ of certiorari).

in part because Silver ensured that legislation mandating greater disclosure of outside income was stymied.

It was only after a series of scandals involving leaders of New York State government, including several sitting state legislators, and the election of a new governor who ran on an ethics platfom, that Silver was pressured into agreeing to greater (though still limited) public disclosure of outside income. Those greater disclosures revealed, however, that Silver's outside income far outstripped that of any other member of the Assembly, exceeding $750,000 per year. Moreover, Silver's disclosure form reflected that this income was being generated for purported legal work, primarily on personal injury cases, yet publicly-available court filings and docket entries reflected that Silver had not filed a notice of appearance or submitted papers for any paid clients in either state or federal court.

These substantial red flags, as well as source information suggesting that Silver was willing to trade on his power as Assembly Speaker to enrich himself through his law practice, led federal prosecutors and agents, including this author, to initiate an investigation of Silver and to discover the truth about the reason why Silver had earned millions of dollars while serving as Speaker. Silver was indicted in January 2015 and convicted after trial in November 2015 of several federal bribery and extortion offenses, as well as engaging in certain prohibited financial transactions involving the proceeds of his crimes.

Because Silver was investigated and ultimately prosecuted federally, he was not protected by New York State's Speech or Debate Clause.[52] Silver did, however, benefit greatly from the ruling in *McDonnell*, which was decided by the Supreme Court in 2016, after Silver's initial conviction in 2015. The Supreme Court's decision led the Second Circuit to conclude that the jury instructions in the initial trial concerning "official action" needed to be changed to reflect *McDonnell*'s holding, and it sent the case back for retrial. After the jury instructions were changed to address *McDonnell*, Silver was retried, and again was convicted of all counts. Even then, however, the Second Circuit found fault with one aspect of the trial court's interpretation of *McDonnell*'s requirements. Although the Second Circuit confirmed that the Government had proven Silver had participated in two bribery schemes and a money laundering scheme, and it affirmed Silver's conviction on four counts, three counts were dismissed,

---

52 *See* United States v. Gillock, 445 U.S. 360, 370 (1980).

and because federal criminal law does not contain an analogue to New York's official misconduct statute that could have avoided *McDonnell* issues, no alternative charges could be brought on those counts. Silver was sentenced to seventy-eight months in prison.[53]

B. *Robert Menendez*

The recent prosecution of United States Senator Robert Menendez, which resulted in a hung jury and a later dismissal of all charges, reflected the challenges of overcoming Speech or Debate Clause and *McDonnell* challenges in addition to those typically attendant to prosecution of a bribery scheme involving political contributions and parties with connections extending beyond the political sphere.

Robert Menendez is one of two United States Senators for the State of New Jersey. He has served in powerful positions on various Senate committees. As set forth in the Third Circuit's opinion denying Senator Menendez's pre-trial motion to dismiss the indictment that had been filed against him in 2015 on Speech or Debate Clause grounds:

> A 22-count indictment . . . charges that from 2006 to 2013 United States Senator Robert Menendez of New Jersey solicited and accepted numerous gifts from his friend Dr. Salomon Melgen, a Florida-based ophthalmologist. In exchange, Senator Menendez allegedly used the power of his office to influence, among other things, an enforcement action against Dr. Melgen by the Centers for Medicare and Medicaid Services . . . and to encourage the State Department and the U.S. Customs and Border Patrol . . . to intervene on Dr. Melgen's behalf in a multi-million dollar contract dispute with the Dominican Republic.[54]

Because the prosecution was brought by a federal prosecutor against a federal legislator, the Speech or Debate Clause of the United States Constitution applied. While Senator Menendez's pre-trial Speech or Debate Clause challenge

---

53 Benjamin Weiser & Jesse McKinley, *Sheldon Silver, Former N.Y. Assembly Speaker, Will Finally Go to Prison*, N.Y. Times (July 20, 2020), https://www.nytimes.com/2020/07/20/nyregion/sheldon-silver-sentencing-prison.html.

54 United States v. Menendez, 831 F.3d 155, 159 (3d Cir. 2016).

was unsuccessful, the Third Circuit's opinion illustrates the challenges faced by prosecutors who were bound by its limitations: prosecutors were required to litigate whether legislative employees could be compelled to testify before a federal grand jury about matters allegedly outside the scope of the Clause,[55] and then to litigate and defend on appeal a pre-trial motion to dismiss the indictment as a whole, as well as individual charges, on Speech or Debate Clause grounds.

Senator Menendez's pre-trial Speech or Debate Clause motion ultimately was unsuccessful, and the case proceeded to trial. At trial, the defendants asserted that the benefits provided to Senator Menendez by Dr. Melgen were gifts to a friend, and Senator Menendez's acts benefiting Dr. Melgen were done on the merits and to help a friend—in other words, for reasons unrelated to the gifts Dr. Melgen had provided to him. At trial, the jury could not reach a unanimous verdict on the charges.[56] On motions to dismiss prior to retrial, the trial court resolved challenges to the sufficiency of the evidence of official actions satisfying the *McDonnell* standard, as well as challenges based on caselaw requiring a quid pro quo to be "explicit" where the alleged quid is a political contribution otherwise protected by the First Amendment.[57] While the trial court denied the *McDonnell* challenge, it granted the defendants' motion to dismiss the counts premised on a political contribution quid, finding insufficient evidence of an explicit quid pro quo to exchange those contributions for official acts.[58] Considering this adverse ruling, limits imposed by Speech or Debate Clause and *McDonnell* issues, and proof that was insufficient to persuade all members of the jury at the first trial, the government declined to re-prosecute the case.[59]

---

55 *Id.* at 163.

56 *See* Nick Corasaniti & Nate Schweber, *Corruption Case Against Senator Menendez Ends in Mistrial*, N.Y. Times (Nov. 16, 2017), https://www.nytimes.com/2017/11/16/nyregion/senator-robert-menendez-corruption.html.

57 *See* United States v. Menendez, 291 F. Supp. 3d 606, 612-13 (D.N.J. 2018) (trial court ruling on pre-verdict motion to dismiss and quoting McCormick v. United States, 500 U.S. 257, 273 (1991) ("The receipt of such contributions is also vulnerable under the [Hobbs] Act [which prohibits extortion by public officials] . . . , but only if the payments are made in return for an explicit promise or undertaking . . . .")).

58 *See Menendez*, 291 F. Supp. 3d at 634-35.

59 *See* Nick Corasaniti & Kate Zernike, *After Years of Investigation, a Sudden Folding of the Case Against Menendez*, N.Y. Times (Feb. 4, 2018), https://www.nytimes.com/2018/02/04/nyregion/menendez-corruption-trial-new-jersey.html. Melgen was convicted in a separate healthcare fraud-related case; however, his sentence was commuted to time served in January

C. *Mike Hubbard*

The case against Mike Hubbard, former Speaker of the Alabama House of Representatives, illustrates how a committed attorney general's office can overcome challenges posed by the corruption of a powerful state legislator. As described by an opinion of the Alabama Supreme Court, Hubbard led the effort to revise the state's Ethics Code to add provisions that he would later be convicted of violating after he ran into financial difficulties and turned to those seeking official action from him for income:

> [S]hortly after the 2010 election, the Governor called a special session of the new Republican-majority legislature to reform the Ethics Code. At the beginning of the session, Hubbard was elected Speaker of the House. Under Hubbard's leadership, the legislature revised the Ethics Code to, among other things, tighten restrictions on gifts to public officials and employees from lobbyists and their employers.
>
> Soon thereafter, Hubbard began experiencing personal financial difficulties. In January 2011, [International Sports Properties, Inc., a broadcasting company that paid Hubbard a salary,] was purchased by International Management Group, which laid off Hubbard two months later. Hubbard began looking for ways to replace his lost income. In particular, he began seeking clients with which he could contract as a consultant. To that end, he enlisted the aid of Will Brooke, an executive of an asset-management firm and the then chairman of the Business Council of Alabama . . . . Brooke was ultimately unable to find any clients for Hubbard, but Hubbard eventually obtained several clients through other means.
>
> In 2012, Hubbard experienced further difficulties when Craftmaster Printers, Inc. . . . , a printing company in which he held a 25 percent interest, was teetering on the edge of financial

---

2021. Dustin Racioppi, *Dr. Salomon Melgen, Who Stood Trial with Sen. Bob Menendez, Gets Clemency from Trump*, NORTHJERSEY.COM (Jan. 20, 2021), https://www.northjersey.com/story/news/new-jersey/2021/01/20/salomon-melgen-friend-bob-menendez-pardoned-president-trump/210560001/.

> collapse. Hubbard again reached out to Brooke, who crafted a turnaround plan for the company. To implement the plan, Hubbard located eight investors who each contributed $150,000 in exchange for Craftmaster stock.[60]

As reflected in the Supreme Court's opinion, many of the clients whom Hubbard obtained to meet his financial needs also sought Hubbard's use of his power and influence as the Speaker of the House, and Hubbard in fact used that power and influence to benefit several of the people and entities who hired him.[61]

The elected Attorney General of Alabama, Luther Strange, recused himself from the case, having used Craftmaster to print election mailings in the 2010 election.[62] After indictment, Hubbard aggressively fought the charges against him, accusing recused Attorney General Strange of targeting him politically. He also accused prosecutors handling the case of leaking grand jury material and engaging in misconduct.[63] Hubbard also alleged that the ethics legislation he had helped sponsor was unconstitutionally vague and overbroad.[64]

Ultimately, the case proceeded to trial and Hubbard was convicted of twelve of the counts that had been filed against him. He was sentenced to four years' imprisonment but the sentence was stayed while he filed numerous appeals. On April 10, 2020, the Alabama Supreme Court affirmed Hubbard's conviction on six of the counts of conviction and vacated his conviction on the remaining counts.[65] Because the charges of conviction were premised on alleged violations of state-specific ethics rules governing Alabama public officials' conduct, which the Alabama State Legislature had decided would apply to its own

---

60 *Ex parte* Hubbard, No. 1180047, 2020 Ala. LEXIS 54, *2-3 (Ala. Apr. 10, 2020).

61 *See, e.g., id.* at *28-29.

62 Brian Lyman, *AG Luther Strange Explains Recusal in Hubbard Case*, MONTGOMERY ADVERTISER (June 11, 2015), https://www.montgomeryadvertiser.com/story/news/local/alabama/2015/06/11/attorney-general-luther-strange-explains-recusal-in-hubbard-case/71071446/. For more on recusals and conflict walls, see Chapter 5.1, Part I(B).

63 *See* Strange, *supra* note 46.

64 Brian Lyman, *The Mike Hubbard Case: A Timeline*, MONTGOMERY ADVERTISER (May 19, 2016), https://www.montgomeryadvertiser.com/story/news/politics/southunionstreet/2016/05/19/mike-hubbard-case-timeline/84542986/.

65 *See Hubbard*, 2020 Ala. LEXIS 54, at *56.

legislators, neither *McDonnell* nor Alabama's Speech or Debate Clause limited the Attorney General Office's ability to prosecute and prevail on those counts.

Conclusion

The work that legislators do is extremely important and has an impact on every citizen. Legislators also are elected specifically to represent the people. Thus, it is vital that the people's representatives provide that service honestly and with integrity. Legislative corruption can be challenging to investigate and prosecute. But public resources, media, and citizens can help identify and corroborate corruption where it exists. While voters always serve as a primary check on their representatives' corruption, prosecutors play a vital role in holding to account those who violate their oaths of office to enrich themselves or harm others, and in deterring others, both inside and outside the legislature, who may be tempted to corrupt the legislative process. Prosecutors who use available resources effectively and who know the relevant legal doctrine will be prepared to root out corruption where it exists and help secure the people's right to honest government.

Chapter 1.4

Bid Rigging on Public Contracts

Emily Myers

Emily Myers is Antitrust Counsel for the National Association of Attorneys General and Chief Editor for the National Attorneys General Training and Research Institute. She is also the editor of the book State Attorneys General Powers and Responsibilities, *which explores the responsibilities and authority of the office of state attorneys general.*

Introduction

State and local governments enter into thousands of contracts every year for a variety of services and goods, from pharmaceuticals to computers to road paving to construction of arenas. The public contracting process is complex and differs from state to state, but as a rule, the governmental unit seeks bids from competing providers. This competitive process is designed to achieve better value for money, allowing more efficient and effective use of state resources. These benefits of competitive bidding can be lost when bidding companies manipulate the bidding process through bid rigging, bribery, or kickbacks. Interference with the public contracting process can contribute to economic uncertainty and undermine the public's confidence in government. Detecting and prosecuting these crimes fulfills one of the attorney general's duties: to protect the public's interest in the wise use of taxpayer dollars.

This chapter describes several types of corrupt practices associated with public contracting and provides a roadmap for detecting and prosecuting those cases.

I. Types of Anti-Competitive Practices

The public contracting process can be manipulated in a number of ways, including through bid rigging, bribery, and kickbacks. It can involve competitors only, or competitors and public employees. It can occur once or over an extended period of time and a series of contracts.

In general terms, bid rigging occurs when competitors alone or competitors and government purchasing officials collude to interfere with the competitive bidding process. Bid rigging can occur in ways that do not involve corrupt public officials. For example, when all bidders collude to submit very high bids, or collude to ensure that each bidder wins on one project in a group of projects, or when a bidder fabricates bids from other competitors that are higher than his or her own bid. In cases involving the purchasing officer, there are several ways that the bidding process can be manipulated. The government employee may provide bid specifications in advance to the favored bidder or may tailor the bid specifications in a way that favors one bidder. The government employee may pick a bid that is not in fact the lowest bid, or pick a bid from an unqualified bidder, or tell the favored bidder what other competitors have bid. The government employee may form his or her own company to bid on a contract, and award the contract to that company, or may receive bribes or kickbacks to induce him or her to pick the briber's company.

Bribery of public contracting officials also interferes with the competitive bidding process. In this context, bribery is generally defined as the giving or receiving of a thing of value to corruptly influence the actions of a public official in awarding or executing a government contract.[1] Kickbacks are a type of bribe through which, instead of being paid up front, the public officials are typically paid a negotiated percentage of the contract income, incrementally.[2] As a very general rule of thumb, kickbacks are typically solicited by the public official, while bribes are offered by the potential contractors.

---

1 *See Bribery*, Black's Law Dictionary 236 (11th ed. 2019).

2 *See Kickback*, Black's Law Dictionary 1040 (11th ed. 2019).

II. Applicable Federal and State Laws

Bid rigging is often covered by statutes that criminalize antitrust, bribery, or kickback schemes, or that prohibit the making of false statements. While Chapter 3.1 describes and analyzes state bribery and kickback statutes at length, they are discussed in summary fashion here to provide necessary context for this chapter.

A. *Antitrust Laws*

The federal antitrust statute is the Sherman Act (15 U.S.C. § 1), which prohibits "Every contract, combination . . . or conspiracy, in restraint of trade or commerce . . . ."[3] The Sherman Act makes such actions felonies, punishable by fines of $100 million for corporations or $1 million for individuals, as well as imprisonment of up to ten years.[4]

Almost every state has a similar antitrust statute, most of which also have criminal penalties. State antitrust laws tend to follow federal antitrust law, and many state criminal antitrust statutes track the language of § 1 of the Sherman Act, prohibiting combinations, contracts, or conspiracies in restraint of trade.[5] Penalties for criminal violations of state antitrust statutes can be severe. The highest penalties are in Alaska, in which courts may impose a fine of up to $1 million for individuals and $50 million for corporations.[6] In New Jersey, fines are up to $300,000 for individuals and $1 million for corporations, but jail time can be up to ten years.[7]

---

3 15 U.S.C. § 1.

4 *Id.*

5 *See* Alaska Stat. § 45.50.562; Ariz. Rev. Stat. Ann. § 44-1402; Colo. Rev. Stat. § 6-4-104; Del. Code. Ann. tit. 6, § 2103; D.C. Code § 28-4502; Fla. Stat. § 542.18; Haw. Rev. Stat. § 480-4; La. Rev. Stat. Ann. § 51:122; Me. Rev. Stat. Ann. tit. 10, § 1101; Mass. Gen. Laws ch. 93, § 4; Mo. Rev. Stat. § 416.031; Neb. Rev. Stat. § 59-801; N.H. Rev. Stat. Ann. § 356:2; N.J. Stat. Ann. § 56:9-3; N.M. Stat. § 57-1-1; N.C. Gen. Stat. § 75-1; N.D. Cent. Code § 51-08.1-02; Or. Rev. Stat. § 646.725; R.I. Gen. Laws § 6-36-4; S.D. Codified Laws § 37-1-3.1; Tex. Bus. & Com. Code § 15.05; Utah Code Ann. § 76-10-3104; Va. Code Ann. § 59.1-9.5; Wash. Rev. Code § 19.86.030; W. Va. Code § 47-18-3; Wis. Stat. § 133.03. Unless otherwise indicated, all citations to statutes in this chapter refer to the version current at the time of publishing.

6 Alaska Stat. § 45.50.578.

7 N.J. Stat. Ann. §§ 56:9-11(c), 2C:43-6.

A conviction under state criminal antitrust law can also lead to mandatory or optional debarment, which typically prevents the criminal actor from bidding for state and local contracts for a term of years.[8] If the company does a great deal of government contracting business, debarment is a heavy sanction. A criminal antitrust conviction can also result in revocation of licenses held by the criminal actor, whether that is the company itself or individuals.[9] In some states, a criminal conviction can result in dissolution of a corporate charter.[10] Similar license revocation proceedings may follow in other states, based solely on the revocation in the first state.

As described below, bid rigging is a combination within the meaning of these statutes. Many state antitrust laws require that courts interpret them consistently with federal antitrust law.[11] In addition, a number of states also have statutes specifically prohibiting bid rigging.[12] For example, the Colorado statute provides "It is illegal for any person to contract, combine, or conspire with any person to rig any bid, or any aspect of the bidding process, in any way related to the provision of any commodity or service."[13] Iowa's statute states, "A person having substantial control over an enterprise who knowingly and willfully engages in bid rigging or price fixing involving a contract with the state or a governmental agency is guilty of a class 'D' felony."[14]

---

8 *See, e.g.*, HAW. REV. STAT. § 103D-702(b) (three years); MD. CODE ANN. STATE FIN. & PROC. § 16–203(a)(2).

9 *See, e.g.*, N.C. GEN. STAT. § 133-25.

10 *See, e.g.*, S.C. CODE § 39-3-160; TENN. CODE ANN. § 47-25-104(a).

11 *See, e.g.*, DEL. CODE. ANN. tit. 6, § 2113; IOWA CODE § 553.2; MD. CODE ANN., COM. LAW § 11-202(a)(2); MICH. COMP. LAWS § 445.784(2); NEV. REV. STAT. § 598A.050. Note, however, that some state courts have explicitly declined to follow federal precedent. *See, e.g.*, Hyde v. Abbott Labs., Inc., 473 S.E.2d 680, 686 (N.C. App. 1996), *rev. denied*, 478 S.E.2d 5 (N.C. 1996) (North Carolina courts "are not required to construe [North Carolina's] antitrust statute in harmony with the federal antitrust laws").

12 *See, e.g.*, ARIZ. REV. STAT. § 34-252; COLO. REV. STAT. § 6-4-106; CONN. GEN. STAT. § 53a-161a; FLA. STAT. ANN. § 838.22; GA. CODE ANN. § 16-10-22; 720 ILL. COMP. STAT. 5/33E-3; IOWA CODE § 553.14; KY. REV. STAT. ANN. § 45A.325; MD. CODE ANN. COM. LAW § 11-203(b); MINN. STAT. § 325D.53; MONT. CODE ANN. § 30-14-205; NEV. REV. STAT. § 598A.060; N.Y. GEN. MUN. LAW § 103-e; OHIO REV. CODE. ANN. § 4707.151; 62 PA. CONS. STAT. § 4503; UTAH CODE ANN. § 76-10-3112; VA. CODE ANN. § 59.1-68.7; WASH. REV. CODE §§ 9.18.120, 9.18.130; W. VA. CODE ANN. § 17-4-22.

13 COLO. REV. STAT. § 6-4-106.

14 IOWA CODE § 553.14.

B. *Bribery Statutes*

Bribery is discussed in detail in Chapter 3.1. With respect to government purchasing, state bribery statutes generally prohibit conferring or offering to confer a benefit upon a public servant with the intent to influence the public servant's actions[15] or for a public servant to request or receive any such benefit with the understanding that it will have such an influence.[16] Sometimes the actions of the public servant are classified as "[d]emanding or receiving a bribe"[17] or "bribe receiving."[18] Bribery and receiving a bribe are always classified as felonies, with penalties ranging from one year to fifteen years in prison and fines from $500 to $50,000.[19] Those convicted of receiving a bribe are typically required to forfeit their office[20] and are frequently barred from public office forever.[21]

C. *False Statements*

Many states require that contractors submitting bids include, under penalty of perjury, a statement that their bids are not the product of collusion.[22] For example, New York requires the following statement on all public contract bids:

> The prices in this bid have been arrived at independently without collusion, consultation, communication, or agreement, for the purpose of restricting competition, as to any matter relating to such prices with any other bidder or with any competitor;
>
> Unless otherwise required by law, the prices which have been quoted in this bid have not been knowingly disclosed by the bidder and will not knowingly be disclosed by the bidder prior to opening, directly or indirectly, to any other bidder or to any competitor; and

---

15 *See, e.g.*, ALA. CODE § 13A-10-61; COLO. REV. STAT. § 18-8-302; KY. REV. STAT. ANN. § 521.020.

16 *See, e.g.*, NEB. REV. STAT. § 28-917; N.J. STAT. ANN. § 2C:27-10.

17 *See, e.g.*, N.M. STAT. ANN. § 30-24-2.

18 *See, e.g.*, OR. REV. STAT. § 162.025.

19 *See, e.g.*, MINN. STAT. § 609.42.

20 *See, e.g.*, *id.* For more on removal and disqualification from holding office, see Chapter 6.3.

21 *See, e.g.*, KAN. STAT. ANN. § 21-6001(b); MD. CODE ANN., CRIM. LAW § 9-201(d).

22 *See, e.g.*, CAL. PUB. CONT. CODE § 7106; TEXAS GOV'T CODE ANN. § 2155.005.

> No attempt has been made or will be made by the bidder to induce any other person, partnership or corporation to submit or not to submit a bid for the purpose of restricting competition.[23]

Thus, a bidder who is submitting a bid that is part of a bid-rigging scheme or is the subject of bribery or kickbacks may be liable under state statutes prohibiting making false statements, offering a false instrument for filing, falsifying business records, or other similar criminal provisions.

D. *Other Statutes*

In addition to the statutes described above, bidders and public employees charged in connection with bid rigging and other market manipulation may also be charged with violations of the following types of statutes:

- Kickback statutes prohibiting improper compensation to a public employee for past actions[24] ("gratuities," "commissions,"[25] or "rebates"[26]);
- Racketeering-type statutes ("engaging in a pattern of corrupt activity," "corrupt organizations");
- Conflicts of interest ("restricted activities," "official misconduct");[27] and
- General theft statutes ("grand larceny," "theft by deception").

III. Types of Bid Rigging

There are many possible forms of bid rigging. As noted above, bid rigging can be undertaken by colluding competitors without the cooperation of a public employee. Generally, bid-rigging arrangements involving multiple competitors can be divided into several categories.

---

23 N.Y. State Fin. Law § 139-d(1)(a)(1)-(3).

24 *See, e.g.*, Idaho Code § 18-1354; Me. Rev. Stat. Ann. tit. 17-A, § 604.

25 Mich. Comp. Laws § 750.125.

26 S.C. Code Ann. § 16-9-230.

27 For a discussion of state conflict of interest laws, see Chapter 3.4.

- *Complementary bidding*—The colluding bidders agree that all or most of them will submit bids that are either very high or include conditions that are not acceptable to the purchaser. This type of bid rigging gives the appearance of competition and is also known as courtesy bidding. Because these bids are not competitive, the winning bidder selected by the group will be awarded the contract. This is the most common type of bid rigging.[28]

- *Bid suppression*—In this type of bid rigging, several competing bidders agree not to bid on a project, or to withdraw already-submitted bids. This allows the group's selected winning bidder to be awarded the contract.[29]

- *Bid rotation*—Colluding bidders may agree to take turns being the low bidder on a series of contracts. They may distribute the contracts to the different winners based on amount of the contract, or volume of purchases, in order to ensure that all colluding bidders are awarded appropriately. In some cases, the non-participating bidders are then used as subcontractors to the winning bidder, allowing them to share in the profits from the non-competitive prices.[30]

Other bid-rigging arrangements involve only one or a few competitors and a public employee. Schemes in which a public employee is involved are likely to last longer, since a non-corrupt public employee reviewing contract bids may well notice and report the suspicious patterns of bidding outlined above. Several additional types of bid rigging are possible when a government employee colludes with bidders.

- *Repeated awards to favored bidder*—A bidder may offer bribes or kickbacks to a public employee to ensure it is always the favored bidder.

- *Bid tailoring*—A corrupt public employee may work with a favored bidder on bid specifications before those specifications are revealed to the public, allowing the bidder to suggest changes that would favor that bidder and reduce bid competition.

---

28 U.S. Dep't of Justice Antitrust Div., Price Fixing, Bid Rigging, and Market Allocation Schemes: What They Are and What to Look For 2 (2007), https://www.justice.gov/sites/default/files/atr/legacy/2007/10/24/211578.pdf.

29 *Id.*

30 *Id.* at 3.

- *Repeated awards to bidders who do not submit lowest bids*—Certain contract procedures may allow the public employee to award contracts to higher priced bidders in certain circumstances (e.g., the bidder is better established financially and/or can do the job more quickly).

- *Changes in the scope of the contract after it is awarded*—A corrupt public employee may issue bid specifications that are incomplete, award the contract to the favored bidder, and then increase the scope of work to allow the bidder to make more money from the contract.

IV. Finding and Evaluating Public Contracting Crimes

Schemes to manipulate the bidding process for public contracts can be detected by monitoring the bidding process for red flags and by using bid pattern analysis to catch suspicious activity. Documentary evidence and expert analysis can be used in the prosecution of bid-rigging. Factors that may indicate bid rigging include:

1. *Repeated awards to the same bidder*—Repeated awards may frequently be justified, but contract documentation should be reviewed to ensure that other bids were in fact obtained and were higher than the winning bid.

2. *Bidder complaints and protests*—When bidders complain about the bid process or file protests about the award, a third party (from a different state agency or another part of the same agency) should review those complaints to ensure they are not the result of a bid-rigging scheme involving an agency employee.

3. *Bidder behavior and statements*—Possible red flags include competitors regularly socializing or holding meetings shortly before bid deadlines, or meeting as a group with procurement officers to discuss bid terms. Bidder statements such as "our competitors charge about the same" or "that's the way we all do it" may indicate price collusion. Statements such as "we don't sell in that area" or "only company *A* deals with that business" may indicate allocation of contracts among vendors.

4. *Procurement officer behavior*—Possible red flags in purchasing employee behavior include promoting a vendor who is unqualified or provides poor quality goods or services or misses delivery dates; appearing to be overly friendly with a particular vendor; or accepting favors or gifts from a vendor.

5. *Many contracts under a price threshold*—Sometimes contracts above a certain amount will be subject to added scrutiny that might reveal signs of collusion. If there are different procedures for contracts under a certain price threshold, repeated contracts just under that level, especially if several contracts have been issued for a single project, may be an indicator of bid-rigging.

6. *Use of subcontractors*—Repeated use of losing bidders as subcontractors on the contract may be an indicator of collusive bidding.

7. *Analysis of bid documents*—Bid documents may be analyzed for the following indicators of potential collusive activity:

    - Common addresses or telephone numbers on bids by different bidders;

    - Identical errors in bids submitted by different bidders;

    - Identical prices from several bidders on several line items within the contract;

    - Physical alterations to bid documents that indicate last-minute price changes;

    - Bids made as joint ventures by bidders who usually bid alone;

    - A company that is incapable of actually performing the contract submits a bid anyway (this may indicate complementary bidding);

    - Unusual bid patterns, such as a number of bids at one level with one bid much lower, all bids submitted in round numbers, or bids containing prices that are much higher than published prices or estimates by outside experts; and

- If the original bids are rejected and the project is rebid, the rebidding results in the same bidders being ranked in the same order as on the original bidding.

V. Elements of the Crimes

A. *Bid Rigging Under the Sherman Act*

In order to prove a bid-rigging scheme, the prosecutor must show:

1. an agreement or conspiracy,
2. which the defendant entered into voluntarily and intentionally,
3. to interfere with competition for a transaction conducted by bid.[31]

Under the federal Sherman Act and state analogues, the government need only prove the existence of the conspiracy and the defendant's agreement to participate in it. The government need not prove any overt acts in furtherance of the conspirators' agreement. The conspiracy does not need to be formal or written; it requires only a meeting of the minds or mutual understanding that the parties are going to seek to restrain trade. The conspiracy need not be successful to be prosecuted, and a failed attempt to rig bids is no defense to a criminal prosecution. The offense can be proven by direct evidence (e.g., testimony of participating bidders), circumstantial evidence (bid award or pricing patterns), or both direct and circumstantial evidence. Because bid rigging is *per se* illegal, it is no defense that the prices that were fixed were reasonable or that the bid rigging stimulated competition.[32]

B. *Bribery in Connection with Bid Rigging*

The elements of bribery are described in more detail in Chapter 3.1. For purposes of bid manipulation schemes, the elements of bribery are, generally:

---

31 United States v. Guthrie, 814 F. Supp. 942, 949-50 (E.D. Wash. 1993).

32 Jury Instructions, United States v. Glazier Foods Co., Crim. No. H-94-58 (S.D. Tex. Apr. 26, 1994), https://www.justice.gov/atr/case-document/governments-proposed-jury-instructions.

1. a person gives a public officer, or a public officer asks for, receives, or agrees to receive

2. something of value

3. with a corrupt intent to influence an official matter.[33]

In the context of bribery in connection with bid-rigging of government contracts, there is typically no question that a public official is involved. To be guilty of bid-rigging—or to support the conviction of the person who bribed him or her—a public official needs only apparent, not actual, authority over the act for which the bribe has been paid.[34]

An illegal kickback (also known as a commission or rebate) is, like a bribe, a thing of value, given to a public employee. The difference is that the kickback may be paid after the action is taken, rather than before. A bribe is paid to influence an official act. A kickback is paid because of an official act.[35] The elements of a kickback are:

1. a person gives a public officer, or a public officer asks for, receives, or agrees to receive

2. something of value

3. for having engaged in official conduct where the employee was not entitled to any special compensation.[36]

---

33 *See, e.g.*, Colo. Rev. Stat. §18-8-302; Haw. Rev. Stat. § 710-1040; N.D. Cent. Code § 12.1-12-01.

34 *See, e.g.*, Thomas v. State, 992 A.2d 423, 431 (Md. Ct. App. 2010); *see also* R.I. Gen. Laws § 11-7-4(b); Tenn. Code Ann. § 39-16-102(b).

35 *See* Manual of Model Criminal Jury Instructions for the District Courts of the Eighth Circuit § 6.18.201F (Judicial Comm. on Model Jury Instructions for the Eighth Circuit 2011).

36 *See* N.Y. Courts Criminal Jury Instructions, Giving Unlawful Gratuities, http://www.nycourts.gov/judges/cji/2-PenalLaw/200/200-30.pdf.

VI. Double Jeopardy

Bid-rigging schemes may come to the attention of both federal and state authorities. Subject to the limits explained in this part, multiple sovereigns may investigate and prosecute—civilly or criminally—individuals and companies involved in bid rigging. The Double Jeopardy Clause of the Fifth Amendment to the U.S. Constitution provides that no person shall be "subject for the same offense to be twice put in jeopardy of life or limb."[37] In *Bartkus* v. *Illinois*,[38] however, the Supreme Court held that the Double Jeopardy Clause does not bar a state prosecutor from bringing state criminal charges against the same criminal act previously prosecuted under federal law. Similarly, in *Abbate* v. *United States*,[39] the Court held that the Double Jeopardy Clause does not bar a federal prosecutor from bringing federal criminal charges against the same act previously prosecuted under state law. The Court reasoned that such prosecutions represent separate violations punished by separate sovereigns.[40] In 2019, the Court reaffirmed this principle in *Gamble* v. *United States*.[41]

While the federal Constitution imposes no limitation on prosecutions by multiple sovereigns, federal policy and state statutes may prevent the criminal prosecution of a bid rigger on both federal and state charges. United States Department of Justice policy dictates that no federal prosecution may be initiated or continued following a state prosecution based on substantially the same act or acts, absent a compelling federal interest.[42] Some states, including

---

37 U.S. Const. amend. V. The Fifth Amendment's protections extend to persons prosecuted under state law by operation of the Fourteenth Amendment to the U.S. Constitution. *See* Ashe v. Swenson, 397 U.S. 436, 437 (1970) (citing Benton v. Maryland, 395 U.S. 784 (1969)).

38 359 U.S. 121 (1959).

39 359 U.S. 187 (1959).

40 *See Bartkus*, 359 U.S. at 131 ("Every citizen of the United States is also a citizen of a State ... [and] may be said to owe allegiance to two sovereigns, and may be liable to punishment for an infraction of the laws of either ... [even for] the same act.") (quoting Moore v. Illinois, 55 U.S. 13, 20 (1852)). *Bartkus* suggests, however, that double jeopardy might bar a suit by a state following a federal prosecution if the state was acting as "merely a tool of the federal authorities." 359 U.S. at 123-24.

41 139 S. Ct. 1960, 1980 (2019).

42 Federal prosecutors must obtain permission from the appropriate Assistant Attorney General before charging a person who has faced state charges for the same conduct. Justice Manual § 9-2.031 (U.S. Dep't of Justice 2020), https://www.justice.gov/jm/jm-9-2000-authority-us-attorney-criminal-division-mattersprior-approvals#9-2.031.

Florida,[43] Illinois,[44] Maryland,[45] Michigan,[46] and Missouri,[47] have adopted similar policies through legislation prohibiting their attorneys general from commencing a criminal action against an individual or corporation that is a defendant in a federal criminal antitrust action involving substantially the same subject matter. States still may pursue civil damage actions in either federal or state court arising out of the same conduct subject to federal criminal prosecution.[48]

Conclusion

Prosecution of bid rigging plays an important role in protecting public funds and providing the public with the best and most innovative products and services in an open and competitive market. Careful attention to bid documents and bidding procedures and careful development of cases will increase confidence in government and ensure that taxpayer dollars are well spent.

43 Fla. Stat. § 542.21(4).

44 740 Ill. Comp. Stat. 10/6(3).

45 Md. Code Ann., Com. Law § 11-207(e).

46 Mich. Comp. Laws § 445.779.

47 Mo. Rev. Stat. § 416.051(1).

48 *See, e.g.*, California v. Infineon Techs. AG, 531 F. Supp. 2d 1124, 1129-30 (N.D. Cal. 2007) (civil suits brought by states after federal criminal investigation); Press Release, U.S. Dep't of Justice, Samsung Agrees to Plead Guilty and to Pay $300 Million Criminal Fine for Role in Price Fixing Conspiracy (Oct. 13, 2005), http://www.justice.gov/archive/atr/public/press_releases/2005/212002.pdf. *But see* Iowa Code § 553.15 ("The bringing of a criminal prosecution against a person by filing an information or returning an indictment shall be an election of remedies to not bring suit to assess a civil penalty against this person.").

Chapter 1.5

Local Corruption Investigations: The Quintessence of Official Misconduct Prosecutions

David Navarro, Kathleen Farrell Duhig

David Navarro is a Cook County circuit court judge, serving as the supervising judge in the Pretrial Division. He sits on the board of the Hispanic Lawyers Association of Illinois as well as the Illinois Latino Judges Association. He is an adjunct professor at Loyola University School of Law where he teaches Trial Practice. Prior to taking the bench, he was chief of the Public Integrity Bureau at the Illinois Attorney General's Office and was a supervisor at the Cook County State's Attorney's Office.

Kathleen Farrell Duhig is an attorney with the law offices of Farrell & Farrell, Ltd., where she focuses primarily on probate, estate planning, and litigation. Prior to joining the firm, she served as assistant attorney general in the Illinois Attorney General's Office for much of her career. In that role, she prosecuted an array of complex white collar and corruption cases, as well as violent crimes, in both state and federal court. She is president of the Southwest Bar Association, a fellow of the American Bar Association, and a former international fellow of the National Attorneys General Training and Research Institute.

Introduction

We are all familiar with the headlines about elected officials or high-ranking agency heads being charged with misconduct. Certainly, such nefarious activities generate headlines and create distrust among members of the general public, as they should. However, less publicized criminal activities of lower-level government employees make up a significant amount of fraud and corruption in the public sector.[1] While the individual cases may not involve the theft of a large amount of funds, the aggregate effects of this conduct may amount to an appreciable loss of taxpayer money and trust. This chapter highlights some common features of local corruption, including circumstances conducive to employee corruption, measures that local governments can take to prevent corruption, and approaches in investigating and prosecuting low-level corruption. These common features arose in four cases, discussed below, which were prosecuted by the Illinois Attorney General's Office.[2]

I. Conditions Potentially Conducive to Local Corruption

A. *Access to Funds*

Agencies that are responsible for issuing government funds in the form of grants and benefits, as well as those that are responsible for receiving payments, are ripe for abuse.[3] Cash transactions[4] are particularly susceptible to abuse, as are transactions carried out by one individual with little or no oversight.[5] Lack of systematic controls may allow one individual to have unfettered access to funds.[6]

---

1 Adriana S. Cordis & Jeffrey Milyo, *Measuring Public Corruption in the United States: Evidence from Administrative Records of Federal Prosecutions*, 18 Pub. Integrity 127, 130, 137 (2016).

2 Facts relating to those four cases that are not otherwise supported by citations to published authorities are derived from the authors' experience.

3 *See* discussion of the Williamson County Circuit Clerks in Part IV(A) below [hereinafter WCCC].

4 *See* discussion of the Crainville Water Department in Part IV(C) [hereinafter Crainville] and of the Grundy County Health Department in Part IV(D) [hereinafter Grundy] below.

5 Crainville; Grundy.

6 Crainville.

B. *Lack of Oversight*

Because of budget constraints, the checks and balances that should be in place to prevent fraud may be eliminated as a cost-saving measure. For example, the work previously done by two or three employees may be shifted onto one employee. As a result, the same person may be receiving the payments, recording the payments, depositing the payments and, ultimately, reconciling the books to document the deposits.[7] While that structure may allow a government to save money on wages, it provides opportunity for corrupt workers to embezzle money and conceal their theft. Sometimes, a scheme is uncovered when the target goes on vacation or has an unplanned illness, and the replacement notices irregularities in the books.[8]

C. *Et tu, Brute?*

In smaller agencies or small local governments, witnesses may be reluctant to point the finger at the target. Potential witnesses may have worked side by side with the target, possibly for years, and may be slow to believe that the target committed fraud. But just as the target may have friends who do not want to implicate her, she may have enemies who want to do just that. Anonymous whistle-blowers, if properly vetted, may be critical to detecting municipal fraud.[9] Similarly, a municipality's police department may have difficulty investigating a target who is well-known in the community, or the police department

---

7 *See* Crainville (involving one person performing many functions); Grundy. *See also* Antonio Olivo, *Millions of Dollars Are Missing. The Sheriff Is Dead. A Small Virginia Town Wants Answers.*, Wash. Post (Sept. 24, 2019), https://www.washingtonpost.com/local/virginia-news/millions-of-dollars-are-missing-the-sheriff-is-dead-a-small-virginia-town-wants-answers/2019/09/24/1a0be2fe-c061-11e9-b873-63ace636af08_story.html ("The lessons here are that there's a need for better financial accountability . . . People beyond one person who is managing a project where the temptation may be too great."); Henry C. Smith, III et al., *The Horses Take A Nasty Fall*, Fraud Mag. (Nov./Dec. 2012), https://www.fraud-magazine.com/article.aspx?id=4294975467 (discussing a local comptroller who used her position managing "all financial aspects of the city funds" to misappropriate $53 million) [hereinafter Nasty Fall].

8 Crainville (fraud detected while employee was on medical leave). *See also* Henry C. Smith, III et al., *Comptroller, Horse Lady, and Crook*, Fraud Mag. (Sept./Oct. 2012), https://www.fraud-magazine.com/article.aspx?id=4294974482 (city council discovered the fraud when local comptroller went on an extended vacation) [hereinafter Crook].

9 *See* WCCC; Nick Mariano, *Former Clerks Plead Guilty to Theft, Official Misconduct*, The S. Illinoisan (May 15, 2015), https://thesouthern.com/news/local/communities/marion/former-clerks-plead-guilty-to-theft-official-misconduct/article_cfe987eb-610e-5512-ade9-60a3599ac373.html.

itself may be involved in the fraud.[10] In some cases, investigators on a county or state level may want to avoid working with the local police department to avoid potential conflicts.

II. Measures to Prevent Employee Corruption

A prophylactic measure used by at least thirty-three states is an inspector general.[11] An inspector general can have broad oversight,[12] or have authority over just one agency.[13] Inspectors general identify and investigate fraud, waste, and abuse by those they oversee—including lower-level government employees. In many states, an inspector general can refer cases to the AGO for additional investigation and, potentially, prosecution. An inspector general can also often provide more support throughout the course of an investigation. Some AGOs have created bureaus or units dedicated to combating public corruption.[14]

---

10 *See* Olivo, *supra* note 7. *Accord* Chapter 1.8, Part III(B) (discussing challenges of prosecutors investigating police officers with whom they work).

11 *Directory of State & Local Inspector General Agencies*, Assoc. of Inspec. Gen., http://inspectorsgeneral.org/useful-links/directory-of-state-and-local-government-oversight-agencies/ (last visited Apr. 14, 2021).

12 For example, the State of Georgia Office of the Inspector General has oversight over all public officials in the executive branch. *Office of the Inspector General*, State of Ga., https://oig.georgia.gov (last visited Apr. 14, 2021).

13 For example, Maryland's Department of Human Services has its own Office of the Inspector General. *Office of the Inspector General*, Md. Dep't of Hum. Servs., http://dhr.maryland.gov/office-of-the-inspector-general/ (last visited Apr. 14, 2021).

14 For example, the New York AGO has a Public Integrity Bureau. *Public Integrity Bureau*, N.Y. Att'y Gen., https://ag.ny.gov/bureau/public-integrity-bureau (last visited Apr. 14, 2021). In New Jersey, an Office of Public Integrity and Accountability prosecutes corruption and large-scale fraud from state programs, among other crimes, and handles internal affairs investigations of high-level officials. *Combating Public Corruption and Strengthening Public Confidence in Government and the Criminal Justice System in New Jersey*, N.J. Dep't of Law & Public Safety, https://www.njoag.gov/about/divisions-and-offices/office-of-public-integrity-and-accountability-home/ (last visited Apr. 14, 2021). Other states, such as Georgia, designate a unit to handle public corruption enforcement as well as other types of complex fraud. *Organization of the Office*, Ga. Office of the Att'y Gen., https://law.georgia.gov/about-us/organization-office (last visited Apr. 14, 2021) (explaining that the Prosecution Division prosecutes fraud and corruption involving the state's departments and agencies).

Accounting measures and systemic checks may prevent instances of theft.[15] Segregating duties to ensure that one person does not have authority over every aspect of the finances is critical to preventing fraud.[16] Keeping accounting systems updated and performing regular audits may also prevent fraud.[17]

III. Approaches to Investigating Missing Money and Where It Has Gone

An audit is a basic starting point for any investigation.[18] Prosecutors may require the victim agency or municipality to conduct an audit before making any charging decisions.[19] The cost of an audit can be substantial, and many prosecuting agencies and police departments may not have the expertise or resources to undertake such reviews. Importantly, the agency has an interest in knowing the loss it suffered and often is in the best position to determine how deep it wants to dig. The scope of an audit may depend on how long the target has been employed. If the target has been working at the same place for many years, for example, a basic starting point for a forensic audit may be to begin with three years prior to the current date.

It may seem unsophisticated, but stolen money, including cash, often will be deposited in the target's own bank account.[20] This is why it is important to identify all bank accounts held by the target. Since most payrolls are direct deposit, the target's employer will have the bank routing and account information. Regular cash deposits are unusual for most salaried employees, unless the

---

15 *See* discussion of the Illinois Department of Human Services Caseworker in Part IV(B) [hereinafter DHS] (functioning systemic checks detected the fraud).

16 *See* Crainville; Nasty Fall, *supra* note 7.

17 *See* WCCC (arcane accounting system hindered audits).

18 *See* Crainville; Grundy.

19 Upon the discovery of missing funds, the victim agency or municipality may commence an independent audit by an accountant to identify the controls in place as well as any preexisting accounting deficiencies or weaknesses. Further investigation may inform whether the entity made the necessary corrections or ignored the previous finding of deficiency. Of significance is identifying any responsible individuals for correcting negative prior findings and determining whether they made the necessary corrections. If not, the audit should shed light on whether the conduct was nefarious or simply due to a lack of funding or resources.

20 *See* WCCC; DHS; Crainville; Grundy.

government employee operates a cash business (laundromat, car wash, restaurant) on the side.

Understanding the motive of the government employee can guide the investigative theory, and finding where the money is flowing can help establish motive. While the occasional modern day "Robin Hood" may use access to funds to help friends in need, it is more common that the pilfering employee is a standard "Greedy McGee" with a gambling problem,[21] a penchant for expensive horses,[22] or credit card debts to pay.[23]

Careful analysis of the primary bank account may yield a plethora of investigative leads. That account may show checks being written to or from other accounts, payments being made to a credit card issuer, or debit card purchases. If you see withdrawals being made at a local casino, for example, obtain the casino gambling records.[24] While casinos do not keep records on all gamblers, all casinos have player loyalty cards that keep track of how much is gambled and, in turn, the player receives gifts. The target's desire for a free shrimp cocktail can lead to how much money the target spent at the local casino. Spending habits and a lifestyle inconsistent with the target's legitimate salary may be a red flag for investigators.[25] In addition to bank records, posts to social media may document spending and lifestyle habits. In extreme cases, a lavish lifestyle may be well known within a small community.[26]

As well as the personal financial records of the target of the investigation, the agency files may yield important evidence. What types of documents are relevant will depend largely on the kind of agency and the role of the target within that agency. The agency files may contain undocumented receipts, fraudulent billing statements, or evidence of phony shell entities or transactions.[27] If the investigation is covert and the target is still employed at the agency, accessing

---

21 Jennifer Barrios, *Fake Invoices & Gambling Debts: How a County Bureaucrat Stole $6.7 Million*, WASH. POST (Feb. 21, 2019), https://www.washingtonpost.com/local/md-politics/montgomery-official-embezzled-67-million-from-county-federal-prosecutors-say/2018/11/16/5378861c-e85a-11e8-bbdb-72fdbf9d4fed_story.html.

22 Crook, *supra* note 8.

23 Olivo, *supra* note 7.

24 In some extreme cases, the casino itself may raise the initial concern about suspicious activity. *See* Barrios, *supra* note 21.

25 Nasty Fall, *supra* note 7.

26 Crook, *supra* note 8.

27 *See* Barrios, *supra* note 21.

the files without alerting the target may be difficult.[28] If the target is capable of altering or destroying records, investigators may consider whether the risk of exposing the investigation outweighs the risk of allowing the target time to tamper with the files. If the target has been put on leave during the investigation, that reduces the possibility that the target will tamper with files.

Agency records outside of the target's control, including historical records, may yield evidence even if the target has tampered with other files. Such records may reveal individuals close to the target who are involved in or benefitting from the scheme. When the individual is responsible for the distribution of benefits and grants, investigators should also scrutinize the receiving parties.[29]

IV. Case Studies

Cases involving corrupt low-level agency officials often involve the same type of charges: theft, wire fraud, and/or bribery. In Illinois, any one of these crimes coupled with the official discharge of duties can support an official misconduct charge.[30] In some states, a conviction for official misconduct can require the defendant to relinquish his or her pension.[31] For example, in Illinois any member of the General Assembly convicted of a felony relating to or arising out of or in connection with his or her service as a member forfeits pension benefits.[32] Localities may have similar ordinances.[33] In one of the case studies

---

28 For more on covert investigations, see Chapter 2.2, Part I.

29 For example, in Illinois, if an entity receives state grants and is a not-for-profit tax-exempt organization, it must file a Form AG990-IL and disclose that form and other financial information on a public, searchable database. *See* Building Better Charities, Il. Att'y Gen., https://illinoisattorneygeneral.gov/charities/ (last visited Apr. 14, 2021). The Form AG990-IL identifies the three highest paid individuals in the organization. Il. Charitable Org. Annual Report, Form AG990-IL (revised Jan. 2019), http://www.illinoisattorneygeneral.gov/charities/ag990-annualreport.pdf.

30 *See* 720 Ill. Comp. Stat. 5/33-3 (2020).

31 For more on requiring the relinquishment of pensions, see Chapter 6.3, Part I(A)(2).

32 40 Ill. Comp. Stat. 5/2-156 (2020).

33 *See* Jeremy Kohler, *No Pension for Stenger, After St. Louis County Council Changes Ordinance*, St. Louis Post-Dispatch (Aug. 7, 2019), https://www.stltoday.com/news/local/govt-and-politics/no-pension-for-stenger-after-st-louis-county-council-changes/article_9246558b-b01c-5b50-9dea-728b28d871bb.html.

below, the use of that penalty provided funds to compensate the agency that was victimized.[34]

The case studies below provide some examples of how a tenacious investigation can reveal abuses of trust by agency employees, and how prosecutors can play a role in seeking restitution for the agency and deterring other would-be wrongdoers.

A. *Williamson County Circuit Clerks*

The targets of the investigation in this case were deputy clerks for the county circuit court clerk's office who processed fines, fees, and bond money in traffic and criminal cases.[35] Among their duties were to receive bond payments for traffic and criminal cases and conduct a count of the cash drawers at the end of each day.[36]

In August 2013, the elected circuit clerk received an anonymous letter alleging that the deputy clerks had been stealing money from the office. The letter also directed investigators to look under one of the target's desks. When investigators looked under that desk, they found bond receipts totaling over $84,000.[37] The investigation revealed that the funds reflected in those bond receipts had not been deposited in the clerk's office. Because of the arcane system of recordkeeping, an audit could not be performed. Instead, investigators focused on the amount of cash deposited into each individual target's bank accounts. Since the targets had no other employment or legitimate source for large cash deposits, all the cash deposits were believed to have come from the clerk's office.

Personal bank records of each deputy clerk were subpoenaed to detail deposits and expenses in those accounts for each year under investigation. Every one of the employees was getting paid by the county through direct deposit. Their bank records indicated cash deposits between pay periods. Cash deposits typically coincided with issuance of a non-sufficient fund check or

---

34 *See* Crainville. The defendant in that case forfeited her pension contribution and used that to pay restitution. As part of her sentence, she forfeited any future payments she was entitled to receive. For more on pension forfeiture, see Chapter 6.3, Part I(A)(2); for more on restitution and asset forfeiture, see Chapter 6.4.

35 *See* Mariano, *supra* note 9.

36 *Id.*

37 *Id.*

debit item return. Additionally, several cash deposits were made right after a direct deposit had occurred where the account was already overdrawn. Based on that, the targets each pleaded guilty and were convicted of felony theft. They were each ordered to pay restitution to the county and sentenced to probation.[38] Analysis of bank records can be time consuming, but it may be critical to a financial investigation.[39] As a result of this case, the county instituted security changes and a new debt-collection system.[40]

B. *Illinois Department of Human Services Caseworker*

In October 2015, the Local Office Administrator of the Madison County Family Office of the Illinois Department of Human Services (DHS) was alerted that one client had two accounts in the system.[41]

The investigation revealed that the main account was for the actual client. The second account located was for a temporary relief cash account using the same name, date of birth, and social security number as the first account, but with a different mailing address. That relief account address belonged to a DHS caseworker, who created the second account from her computer terminal at the DHS office.[42] Further investigation revealed that the same caseworker manipulated two other accounts using a similar scheme. The total amount of DHS funds misappropriated by this caseworker totaled over $150,000 in just over three years.[43]

---

38 *Id.*

39 Software programs, such as BankScan.com, may facilitate the conversion of bank and credit card statements into standard electronic formats. *See, e.g.*, BankScan.com, https://www.bank-scan.com (last visited Apr. 14, 2021).

40 Nick Mariano, *Plea Deal for Former Circuit Clerk Employee Accused of Theft*, The Southern Illinoisan (Mar. 16, 2015), https://thesouthern.com/news/local/communities/marion/plea-deal-for-former-circuit-clerk-employee-accused-of-theft/article_f202a270-fb69-5866-b751-32f2900a8517.html ("The charges have served as an impetus for instituting security changes in the office and helped spark a new debt collection system for the county that is administered by the state comptroller's office.").

41 *See* Press Release, Il. Att'y Gen., Madigan: DHS Worker Charged with Theft, Official Misconduct (Nov. 19, 2015), http://www.illinoisattorneygeneral.gov/pressroom/2015_11/20151119.html; Sanford J. Schmidt, *Highland Woman Accused of Stealing $160,000 from IDHS*, Telegraph (Nov. 19, 2015), https://www.thetelegraph.com/news/article/Highland-woman-accused-of-stealing-160-000-from-12601249.php.

42 Schmidt, *supra* note 41.

43 Press Release, *supra* note 41.

The caseworker pleaded guilty to theft and was sentenced to four years in prison and ordered to pay restitution.[44]

C. *Crainville Water Department*

Because they receive many cash payments, water departments are particularly vulnerable to internal theft. In one case, during a water department clerk's medical leave, her coworkers discovered that cash reflected in deposit slips had not been deposited into the water department's bank account. That clerk controlled the deposit slips, made bank deposits, and compiled monthly financial reports. After the clerk's coworkers reported what they found, the mayor contacted the Illinois AGO, which directed the mayor to order an audit.[45] Initially, it appeared that the thefts had just been occurring for only a few months before the clerk took her medical leave in June 2012. But the audit revealed that the clerk began stealing from the water department in January 2010 and misappropriated over $70,000. While she started by taking small amounts of cash, by 2012, she was stealing thousands of dollars a month.[46]

This investigation also included a search of the clerk's bank records, which revealed that cash was often deposited in her account around the dates of the missing cash reflected in the water department's deposit slips. Her bank records showed that she was being paid by direct deposit. They also revealed that she was issuing non-sufficient fund checks and debit item returns and was making cash deposits to cover these items.

The clerk had worked for the village for over twenty years and was a trusted member of the community, which may have been one of the reasons her theft went undiscovered for so long. After the investigation, the clerk pleaded

---

44 Press Release, Il. Att'y Gen., Madigan: Former DHS Worker Pleads Guilty, Sentenced to Prison (Jun. 27, 2016), http://www.illinoisattorneygeneral.gov/pressroom/2016_06/20160627.html.

45 The AGO requested that the mayor order an audit to determine the total loss. The findings revealed the total loss was more than they originally thought.

46 Brad Palmer, *Former Crainville Official Pleads Guilty to Stealing from the Village*, WSIU (Sept. 14, 2015), https://news.wsiu.org/post/former-crainville-official-pleads-guilty-stealing-village#stream/0. *See also* Press Release, Il. Att'y Gen., Madigan: Former Water Dep't Official Indicted on Charges of Stealing Nearly $71,000 in Village Funds (Oct. 7, 2013), http://www.illinoisattorneygeneral.gov/pressroom/2013_10/20131007.html (discussing clerk's responsibilities at the Water Department and her indictment for stealing village funds).

guilty to felony theft and official misconduct. She forfeited her pension and was sentenced to felony probation with restitution.

D. *Grundy County Health Department*

In some cases, a corrupt employee may divert all the cash that comes her way. For a six-month period, the bookkeeper for the Grundy Health Department stole all the money received by the health department, rather than sending it to the county treasurer's office. During that time, she was the only individual in control of both recording the income or receipts and making the deposit items to the bank—a red flag.[47]

After an internal audit confirmed that none of the cash received by the health department during the corrupt bookkeeper's term had been deposited in the treasurer's office, the local Sheriff's Department's investigation concluded that the bookkeeper stole the cash.[48] As seen in other cases, it was her job to record the cash received, make the deposits with the treasurer's office, and keep a spreadsheet of the health department's finances. Because she had control over the entire process by which cash came into, was recorded by, and left the health department, she was able to steal tens of thousands of dollars before she was detected.[49]

Once again, investigators obtained the target's bank records, which revealed cash deposits into her account that totaled over $44,000.[50] As she had no source of income other than her bookkeeping job, the cash deposits approximated the funds stolen from the health department, and she was the only person with easy access to the cash and the records, we were confident the bookkeeper was responsible for the theft.

The bookkeeper was convicted of felony theft and ordered to pay restitution to the county.

---

47 *See* Press Release, Il. Att'y Gen., Madigan Charges Former Grundy County Official with Theft, Official Misconduct (June 5, 2014), https://illinoisattorneygeneral.gov/pressroom/2014_06/20140605.html.

48 Jessica Bourque, *Former Grundy County Health Department Bookkeeper Turns Herself in On Theft Charge*, Herald News (May 8, 2014), https://www.theherald-news.com/2014/05/08/former-grundy-county-health-department-bookkeeper-turns-herself-in-on-theft-charge/ai7ioh5/.

49 *See* Press Release, *supra* note 47.

50 *Id.*

Conclusion

As the case studies show, agencies where employees have access to cash, wide discretion, and little oversight can provide opportunities for corruption. Government employees' thefts may be revealed by another employee, an audit, or reports by another agency. It is important to follow the money trail when conducting these investigations: obtain bank records and other evidence to build your case. In the aggregate, corrupt government employees steal large sums of money from the taxpayers and violate the public's trust. Holding them accountable can provide restitution to the government they defrauded, just punishment of the offender, deterrence to others, and may prompt changes in procedures that reduce the opportunity for future fraud. By prosecuting local corruption, prosecutors can also help restore the public's trust in government.

Chapter 1.6

Prosecuting Union Corruption

Glen McGorty, Rebecca Monck Ricigliano

Glen McGorty is managing partner of Crowell & Moring's New York office, a member of the firm's Management Board, and a partner in the firm's White Collar and Regulatory Enforcement Group and Financial Services and Investigations practices. Before joining Crowell, Mr. McGorty served almost fifteen years as a federal prosecutor in the U.S. Attorney's Office for the Southern District of New York and the U.S. Department of Justice in Washington, DC.

Rebecca Monck Ricigliano, a former federal prosecutor, is a partner in Crowell & Moring's White Collar and Regulatory Enforcement Group and a member of its Steering Committee; she is also a member of the firm's Financial Services and Investigations practices. Before joining Crowell, Ms. Ricigliano served as a federal prosecutor in the U.S. Attorney's Office for the Southern District of New York and as the First Assistant Attorney General of New Jersey.

The authors thank Danielle Rowan for her assistance in researching and writing this chapter.

Introduction

Prosecutors have a number of options when charging union officials. The types of corruption and the applicable statutes can have significant overlap and require prosecutors to use discretion when determining the appropriate charges for various factual scenarios. Careful thought should be given to determine which tools to use during the investigation, and which statute or statutes to charge when the investigation is complete. This is especially true when charging corruption in organized labor unions.

I. Anticorruption Laws

A. *Federal Laws*

Under 18 U.S.C. § 201, federal prosecutors can charge individuals with the crime of bribery when there is proof that (1) an individual or public official corruptly gives, offers or promises anything of value[1] (2) with the intent to influence[2] an official act, commit or aid in committing any fraud, or induce to do or omit any act in violation of his or her official duties.[3] It is important to distinguish whether the act is bribery or accepting a gratuity, as the latter requires a looser connection (i.e., the thing of value is given after the fact as thanks, or given with the intent to merely seek favor with a public official) and has a significantly smaller sentencing maximum.[4] Extortion is yet a third way to prosecute the unlawful exchange of money for power, with different elements. Specifically, extortion by a public official involves obtaining of property from another, with his consent, under color of official right.[5]

Congress's first attempt to address union corruption specifically came in the form of the 1935 National Labor Relations Act (NLRA).[6] Congress designed

---

1 A "thing of value" may be defined as "intangibles as well as tangibles." *See* United States v. Girard, 601 F.2d 69, 71 (2d Cir. 1979). Courts typically focus on the value of the bribe to the defendant, rather than the bribe's commercial value. United States v. Williams, 705 F.2d 603, 622-23 (2d Cir. 1983). *See also* Criminal Resource Manual § 2044 (U.S. Dep't of Justice 2020), https://www.justice.gov/archives/jm/criminal-resource-manual. Note that the U.S. Department of Justice appears to be treating the *Criminal Resource Manual* as an archived document.

2 Bribery requires intent to act corruptly, meaning "with a bad or evil purpose" or willfully with "specific intent." Criminal Resource Manual § 2044.

3 18 U.S.C. § 201(b) (2018). Similar statutes exist in all the states. *See* Chapter 3.1.

4 18 U.S.C. § 201(b), (c); Criminal Resource Manual § 2044 (explaining that the intent requirement for section 201(c) is simply that the defendant acted knowingly and purposefully and not by mistake or inadvertence). *See also* United States v. Evans, 572 F.2d 455, 480-81 (5th Cir. 1978).

5 *See* 18 U.S.C. §§ 872, 1951; Criminal Resource Manual § 2404.

6 29 U.S.C. §§ 151-169 (2018).

the law to protect the rights of employees and employers, to encourage collective bargaining, and to curtail certain private sector labor and management practices, which can harm the general welfare of workers, businesses, and the U.S. economy.[7] Under the NLRA's § 7, employees have the right to organize or join a union, and to collectively bargain.[8] The NLRA also prohibits unfair labor practices such as "restrain[ing] or coerce[ing] employees in the exercise of the rights guaranteed them in [§] 7" of the Act, while still allowing a union to "prescribe its own rules with respect to the acquisition or retention of membership therein."[9] Additionally, § 8(b)(1)(B) of the Act makes it unlawful for unions or their members "to restrain or coerce . . . an employer in the selection of his representatives for the purposes of collective bargaining or the adjustment of grievances."[10]

Federal prosecutors have successfully used the Hobbs Act, 18 U.S.C. § 1951, in union bribery and extortion cases. The Hobbs Act states:

> Whoever in any way or degree obstructs, delays, or affects commerce or the movement of any article or commodity in commerce, by robbery or extortion or attempts or conspires so to do, or commits or threatens physical violence to any person or property in furtherance of a plan or purpose to do anything in violation of this section shall be fined under this title or imprisoned not more than twenty years, or both.[11]

To demonstrate a violation of the Hobbs Act, the prosecutor must show that: (1) the defendant induced or attempted to induce the victim to give up property or property rights; (2) the defendant used or attempted to use the victim's reasonable fear of physical or economic harm to induce the victim to give up the property; (3) the defendant's conduct actually or potentially obstructed, delayed, or affected interstate or foreign commerce in any way; and (4) the defendant's actual or threatened use of force was wrongful.[12] In *United States* v.

---

7 *Nat'l Labor Relations Act*, Nat'l Labor Relations Board, https://www.nlrb.gov/guidance/key-reference-materials/national-labor-relations-act (last visited Apr. 17, 2021).

8 29 U.S.C. § 157.

9 *Id.* § 158(a)(1), (b)(1)(A).

10 *Id.* § 158(b)(1)(B).

11 18 U.S.C. § 1951(a) (2018).

12 *See* Criminal Resource Manual § 2403 (U.S. Dep't of Justice 2020), https://www.justice.gov/archives/jm/criminal-resource-manual.

Green, union officials were convicted of extortion under the Hobbs Act when they attempted to compel an employer to pay wages for superfluous, unwanted, and fictitious services.[13] The union was convicted of using and threatening force to obstruct, delay, or affect commerce by extortion. The Supreme Court's decision affirming the conviction was the catalyst for a number of union extortion prosecutions. However, in a 1973 decision, *United States* v. *Enmons*,[14] the Supreme Court reversed the convictions of union members who had used rifles and explosives against an employer's property to "achieve legitimate union objectives"—specifically, higher wages for legitimate work—and gave rise to legislative hearings and acts to address union action.[15] The Court's decision, which was based on the literal language of the Hobbs Act, held that the statute does not prohibit other behaviors beyond extortion, and therefore cannot be used to prosecute violent union members who seek to exact higher wages in return for genuine services.[16]

The 1947 Labor-Management Relations Act (Taft-Hartley Act) gives employees the right to refrain from joining unions and made it a federal crime for employers and unions to give or accept any "thing of value."[17] Like the Hobbs Act, prosecutors can use the Taft-Hartley Act as a basis for charging union officials for bribery and extortion. In *United States* v. *Iozzi*, a union president was convicted under the Taft-Hartley Act for extorting money from contractors by threatening to withhold labor from members of twenty-five local trade unions to the contractors.[18] The Fourth Circuit Court of Appeals held that by accepting $3,000 directly from one of the owners of the employer organization, Iozzi, acting as a union official, violated the Taft-Hartley Act by accepting payment from that employer.[19] International Longshoreman's Association President

---

13 350 U.S. 415, 420-21 (1956) (holding that Hobbs Act criminalized the use of threats or violence by union officials in an effort to obtain a benefit from a company, even if those officials did not directly benefit from those extortionate acts).

14 410 U.S. 396, 398, 411-12 (1973).

15 *See Labor Violence and the Hobbs Act Before the S. Comm. on the Judiciary*, 98th Cong. 1, S. Hrg. 98-1009 (Oct. 25, 1983; Apr. 30, 1984; May 1, 1984).

16 *Enmons*, 410 U.S. at 408-09.

17 Section 302 of the Taft-Hartley Act, 29 U.S.C. § 186, prohibits employers or agents of employers from providing any money or "thing of value" to its employees, a labor organization, its officers, or a representative of employees. 29 U.S.C. § 186(a) (2018). The statute also prohibits "any representative of any employees" from demanding, requesting, or receiving such payments from the employer. *Id.* §186(b).

18 420 F.2d 512, 514-15 (4th Cir. 1970).

19 *Id.*

Joseph Ryan was also convicted for violating the Taft-Hartley Act when he accepted payments from employers of union members.[20] Ryan accepted $1,000 each December from two employers while serving as the president of the International Longshoremen's Association and acting as its representative in collective bargaining negotiations with the employers.[21] The Supreme Court held that § 302 of the Taft-Hartley Act should be broadly read, and "prohibits payments by employers to individuals who represent employees in their relations with the employers."[22] As a result, the payments to Ryan were unlawful.

The most recent update to corruption statutes relevant to labor unions came in 1970. The Racketeer Influenced and Corrupt Organizations Act (RICO)[23] created three new federal crimes for those involved in corrupt union activities: (1) to invest the proceeds of racketeering activity or collection of an unlawful debt in any legal enterprise; (2) to obtain an interest in any enterprise through a pattern of racketeering activity or collection of an unlawful debt that affects interstate commerce; and (3) to conduct or participate in the affairs of an enterprise[24] through a pattern of racketeering activity or collection of an unlawful debt.[25] It is also a crime, under section 1962(d), to conspire to commit any of the three substantive RICO offenses.[26]

Prosecutors have used the RICO statute to convict union officials for extortion and bribery offenses. In 1989, the Eleventh Circuit Court of Appeals upheld a conviction of union members for racketeering activity consisting of taking bribes in the form of unlawful payments from the union's employee welfare benefit plans. The court held that based on the ample evidence that the union members were aware of each other's participation in the bribery scheme, that "government need only prove that [the] defendant conspired to commit the substantive RICO offense and was aware that others had done likewise" in order to support a RICO conspiracy charge.[27] In addition, the court found that based on Congressional intent, any construction work is likely to have an

---

20 United States v. Ryan, 350 U.S. 299, 301 (1956).

21 *Id.* at 300.

22 *Id.* at 307.

23 18 U.S.C. §§ 1961-1968 (2018). For an exploration of the use of RICO by state prosecutors in corruption cases, see Chapter 6.2.

24 An enterprise "includes any individual, partnership, corporation, association, or other legal entity, and any union or group of individuals associated in fact although not a legal entity." 18 U.S.C. § 1961(4).

25 *Id.* § 1962.

26 *Id.* For more on RICO, see Chapter 6.2.

27 United States v. Norton, 867 F.2d 1354, 1359 (11th Cir. 1989).

effect on interstate commerce, particularly when the project includes employee benefit plans.[28] As such, the defendant's actions had satisfied 18 U.S.C. § 1962(b) because the officials and representatives of the benefit funds traveled between Florida and Illinois to discuss the payoffs.[29]

Prosecutors can also use the crimes of theft, embezzlement, and fraud. Theft (conversion) is typically defined as the act of control or dominion over property that seriously interferes with the owner's rights. Embezzlement requires conversion of property, but requires two additional elements: (1) that the property was in the lawful possession of the defendant at the time of its appropriation, and (2) there was the requisite knowledge that appropriation of the property is contrary to the wishes of its owner.[30]

The Labor-Management Reporting & Disclosure Act of 1959 (LMRDA)[31] was the first broadly-written federal statute that dealt with the internal workings of labor unions. Generally, LMRDA regulates union internal affairs and their relationships with their members' employers. Congress intended it to eliminate improper and unlawful actions by those in labor organizations. In addition to granting a bill of rights for union members, it creates reporting requirements for unions, standards for the elections of officers, and bans persons with criminal records from holding office. In *United States* v. *Stockton*, the president of Local 239 UAW was convicted of embezzlement using the LMRDA for misappropriating funds and converting them for his own use.[32] Stockton's bank records showed that all of the checks charged in the indictment were deposited into his accounts and spent on his own personal debts.[33]

More recently, United States Department of Justice prosecutors successfully negotiated a guilty plea from the president of the Council on New York Labor and New York Assemblyman, Brian McLaughlin.[34] Prosecutors used the

---

28 *Id.* at 1359 n.3 (stating "any construction work, regardless of the size or duration of the project, is likely to have an effect on interstate commerce"). *See also* 29 U.S.C. §1001(a) (2018).

29 *Norton*, 867 F.2d at 1359.

30 *See* 29 U.S.C. § 501(c); Chapter 3.2.

31 29 U.S.C. §§ 401-531.

32 788 F.2d 210, 212-13 (4th Cir. 1986).

33 *Id.* at 213-14.

34 Press Release, Dep't of Justice, U.S. Attorney's Office, S. Dist. of N.Y., Former New York State Assemblyman and Labor Leader Brian McLaughlin Sentenced to Ten Years in Prison for Racketeering and False Statement Crimes (May 20, 2009), https://www.justice.gov/archive/usao/nys/pressreleases/May09/mclaughlinbriansentencingpr.pdf.

LMRDA to indict McLaughlin for embezzling more than two million dollars from the State of New York and the unions he represented.[35] Prosecutors were also able to convict Santo Petrocelli, an electrical contractor, for his illegal payments to McLaughlin. Petrocelli paid McLaughlin in return for McLaughlin directing business to Petrocelli.[36] Prosecutors used the reporting requirements of the LMRDA to indict McLaughlin on his inaccurate reporting of union finances, timesheets, and campaign disclosures.[37] These LMRDA violations, paired with McLaughlin's racketeering charges, led to McLaughlin's 120-month sentence.[38]

Prosecutors have also been successful in using certain provisions from the Employee Retirement Income Security Act of 1974 (ERISA) to prosecute union corruption. Under 18 U.S.C. § 664, any individual who embezzles, steals, or converts the funds or assets of an employee welfare benefit plan or employee pension benefit plan may be fined and/or imprisoned up to five years.[39] Further, 18 U.S.C. § 1954 prohibits offering, soliciting, or receiving anything of value because of or with the intent to be influenced with respect to any actions or decisions relating to an employee benefit.[40] Finally, under 18 U.S.C. § 1027, a person who knowingly makes a false statement, or conceals or fails to disclose required information in an employee benefit plan document, commits a felony.[41]

Since ERISA's inception, several union leaders have been charged and convicted using the ERISA statute. A 2010 conviction of the president of the Waterfront Guard Association Local 1852 using § 664 of the ERISA Act resulted in his thirty-month sentence for embezzling funds from the union employee pension plans.[42] In 2012, federal prosecutors used § 664 to convict

---

35 Sealed Indictment, United States v. McLaughlin, No. 1:06-cr-965-RJS (S.D.N.Y. Oct. 16, 2006), ECF No. 1.

36 Press Release, FBI, Former Owner of Petrocelli Electric Company Sentenced in Manhattan Federal Court to Three Months in Prison for Making Illegal Payments to Union Official (Nov. 30, 2009), https://archives.fbi.gov/archives/newyork/press-releases/2009/nyfo113009a.htm.

37 Sealed Indictment, *supra* note 35, at 6-9.

38 Benjamin Weiser, *Ex-Labor Leader Is Sentenced to 10 Years for Racketeering*, N.Y. Times (May 20, 2009), https://nyti.ms/2J5dCsg.

39 18 U.S.C. § 664 (2018).

40 *Id.* § 1954.

41 *Id.* § 1027.

42 *See* James B. Jacobs, *Is Labor Union Corruption Special?*, 80 Social Research 1057, 1073-74 (2013).

the president of the National Association of Special Police and Security Officers for embezzling more than $100,000 from the union's pension fund.[43] These cases are significant, as they demonstrate the types of ERISA violations that are actionable under the statute and are just two examples of the dozens of union-related ERISA violations that have been prosecuted since its passage.[44]

B. *State Laws*

Generally, state laws prohibiting fraud, bribery, embezzlement, and extortion can apply to union corruption. These laws are described elsewhere in this Manual.[45] New York's legislature also enacted an "enterprise corruption" statute designed to specifically curtail labor racketeering.[46] This law makes it a felony to bribe a labor official or for a labor official to receive a bribe. It likewise prohibits union officials from receiving anything of value from an employer whose employees are union members and prohibits employers giving anything of value to a union official. New Jersey's Casino Control Act also has provisions relevant to union corruption.[47]

II. Source Development

Several source development tactics can help compel targeted individuals to cooperate in corruption inquiries. Prosecutors may wish to take advantage of the Witness Security Program, written cooperation agreements, undercover roles, and anonymous witnesses.[48] Each of these tools is discussed below.

---

43 *Id.*

44 *See* Am. Inst. of Cert. Pub. Acct., Employee Benefit Plans DOL Criminal Enforcement Cases January 2006-September 2013 9-13, https://www.kellerowens.com/wp-content/uploads/2014/08/2013-DOL-Criminal-Enforcement-Cases.pdf.

45 *See* Chapter 3.1, Chapter 3.2.

46 N.Y. Penal Law §§ 460.00-460.80 (2020).

47 N.J. Stat. Ann. §§ 5:12-93, 5:12-125 to 5:12-130 (2020).

48 For guidance on using cooperating witnesses, see Chapter 2.5. For more information about cooperation agreements, see Chapter 1.8, Part II(A)(i). Prosecutors investigating union corruption may seek wiretap and stored communication electronic evidence. These investigative techniques and their legal requirements are discussed in detail in Chapters 2.3 and 2.4.

A. *The Witness Security Program*

Since 1970, the Witness Security Program has provided protection for more than 8,600 witnesses and their family members.[49] It should be used in rare circumstances and only when testimony is essential to the success of the prosecution and outweighs the potential danger of relocating the witness into a community. For example, investigators should consider the witness's criminal record, alternatives to providing protection under the witness security program, results of psychological examinations, and the witness's potential to harm innocent victims in the future. For a witness to be considered for the program, investigators and government trial attorneys must also make a timely showing that "there is clear evidence that the life of the witness or a family member is in immediate jeopardy."[50] Prisoners in state or federal prisons are not precluded from participating in the program and are put in the Bureau of Prisons' custody.[51]

As soon as an incarcerated witness starts cooperating, investigators should notify the applicable prison officials to ensure that the witness can be secured and separated from any potential individuals or groups that may harm the witness. This request for separation does not require the witness to formally enter the Witness Security Program and, in at least some federal districts, is routinely made to protect cooperating witnesses.

The USDOJ Office of Enforcement Operations authorizes all agreements to enter the Witness Security Program and documents them in a "memorandum of understanding."[52] This memorandum must include the witness's commitment to testify and the witness's responsibility to avoid criminal activity and any other legal obligations. Notably, this memorandum does not provide legally enforceable rights against the U.S. Attorney General and "[t]he United

---

49 *See* U.S. Marshals Service, *Witness Security Program*, https://www.usmarshals.gov/witsec/ (last visited Apr. 18, 2021). Local or state authorities seeking protection for a witness can work with the U.S. Attorney's Office in their district to submit an application for the Witness Security Program; however, the state will be required to reimburse the United States for costs. Justice Manual § 9-21.140 (U.S. Dep't of Justice 2020), https://www.justice.gov/jm/jm-9-21000-witness-security#9-21.140.

50 *See* Piechowicz v. United States, 885 F.2d 1207, 1212-13 (4th Cir. 1989) (citation omitted).

51 Justice Manual § 9-21.140. For more on proffer and cooperation agreements, see Chapter 1.8, Part II(A)(i).

52 18 U.S.C. § 3521(d) (2018).

States and its officers and employees shall not be subject to any civil liability on account of any decision to provide or not to provide protection."[53] If the agreement is approved, the program will provide suitable documents to enable the witness to establish a new identity, provide housing and other basic needs, and provide the witness with services that are necessary to assist the person in becoming self-sustaining.[54]

B. *Cooperation Agreements*

Frequently, to provide incentives for witnesses to cooperate, prosecutors must enter into written cooperation agreements.[55] These agreements offer investigators leverage in negotiations with witnesses who would not otherwise be willing to testify. The USDOJ has tried to impose uniformity in the format and use of these agreements; however, in practice, the format and use of agreements can vary widely by jurisdiction. Proffer agreements, plea agreements, and cooperation agreements should all be used only when necessary to the public interest.[56]

When determining whether the witness's cooperation is necessary to the public interest, USDOJ has instructed federal prosecutors to weigh all relevant factors, including:

1. The importance of the investigation or prosecution to an effective program of law enforcement, or consideration of other national security or governmental interests;

2. The value of the person's cooperation to the investigation or prosecution;

3. The person's relative culpability in connection with the offense or offenses being investigated or prosecuted and criminal history; and

4. The interests of any victims.[57]

---

53 *Id.* § 3521(a)(3).

54 *Id.* § 3521(b)(1).

55 For more on cooperation agreements and related agreements and orders, see Chapter 1.8. Part II(A)(i).

56 Justice Manual § 9-27.600.

57 *Id.* § 9-27.620.

In addition, the scope of the government's commitment should be limited to "(1) Non-prosecution based directly or indirectly on the testimony or other information or cooperation that has been or will be provided; or (2) Non-prosecution within his/her district with respect to a pending charge, or to a specific offense then known to have been committed by the person."[58] The agreements should not bind other prosecutors or agencies without their consent, and any effects from the agreements should be communicated to the relevant agencies.

C. *Undercover Agents, Informants, and Anonymous Witnesses*

In addition to written cooperation agreements, investigators may also use undercover officers,[59] confidential informants,[60] and anonymous witnesses[61] to collect evidence of corruption. Investigators should determine the barriers to entry for the group in question (i.e., is it possible to use an undercover officer, or would the group exclude new members or outsiders from participating in their activities), and determine which type of informant can provide the evidence that the investigator is seeking. While credibility may be an issue for confidential informants and anonymous witnesses, the use of undercover officers is not always possible. When using undercover officers, investigators should determine whether the officer can use video or audio evidence if the subject of the investigation is not aware they are being recorded, and whether the use of undercover officers infringes on the subjects' Fourth Amendment rights.[62] The U.S. Attorney General's guidelines for use of confidential informants and anonymous witnesses require agents to balance a number of factors including witness reliability, history of substance abuse, criminal history, and whether the witness is believed to be a danger to the public.[63] In addition, an investigator

---

58 *Id.* § 9-27.630.

59 "Undercover officers" refers to police officers or law enforcement agents posing as civilians for the purpose of gathering evidence. For more information about this investigative technique, see Chapter 2.5.

60 "Informant" refers to an individual who provides information to investigators regarding activities that may amount to criminal conduct, typically in exchange for a benefit of some kind (e.g., reduction of a criminal sentence). For more information about this investigative technique, see Chapter 2.5.

61 "Anonymous witness" refers to a witness allowed to "testify under pseudonyms and without revealing their dates and places of birth and home and work addresses." United States v. Ramos-Cruz, 667 F.3d 487, 492 (4th Cir. 2012).

62 *See* United States v. Jacobsen, 466 U.S. 109, 117 (1984); United States v. White, 401 U.S. 745, 752 (1971). *See also* Chapter 2.5, Part V(B)(1).

63 U.S. Gov't Accountability Off., GAO-15-807, Confidential Informants:

should note the treatment of anonymous witnesses in a particular jurisdiction, as courts have not unanimously determined standards for using anonymous witnesses.[64]

III. Teamsters Union Case Study

The year 2015 marked a major shift in the history of the International Brotherhood of Teamsters (IBT). After twenty-five years of supervision by USDOJ, the IBT and Preet Bharara, the U.S. Attorney for the Southern District of New York, entered into a Final Agreement and Order that would phase out the terms of the IBT's 1989 consent decree over a five-year period.

A. *Civil RICO Suit*

After decades of alleged corruption at the local and international level, the IBT was named in a civil RICO suit on June 28, 1988.[65] The claim, brought by then-U.S. Attorney Rudy Giuliani, sought injunctive relief to restrain the IBT's ongoing racketeering activity and to prevent future violations.[66] The suit named the IBT as one of five sets of defendants:

1. The International Brotherhood of Teamsters;
2. Twenty-six La Cosa Nostra (LCN) members;

Updates to Policy and Additional Guidance Would Improve Oversight by DOJ and DHS Agencies 31-35 (2015), https://www.gao.gov/assets/680/672514.pdf (providing a list of provisions from *Attorney General's Guidelines Regarding the Use of Confidential Informants* and *Attorney General's Guidelines Regarding the Use of FBI Confidential Human Sources*).

64 For example, the Fourth Circuit held in United States v. Ramos-Cruz, 667 F.3d 487, 500-01 (4th Cir. 2012) that using pseudonyms for two witnesses without disclosing identifying information did not violate the Confrontation Clause, particularly where the witness testimony was limited in scope. However, in the D.C. Circuit, witnesses using pseudonyms have been required to disclose their names to defense counsel. *See* United States v. Celis, 608 F.3d 818, 829-33 (D.C. Cir. 2010). *See also* United States v. Palermo, 410 F.2d 468, 472 (7th Cir. 1969) ("[W]here there is a threat to the life of the witness, the right of the defendant to have the witness' true name, address and place of employment is not absolute.").

65 James B. Jacobs & Kerry T. Cooperman, Breaking the Devil's Pact: The Battle to Free the Teamsters from the Mob 22 (2011).

66 *Id.* at 33.

3. The Cosa Nostra commission (the organization that the LCN crime families used to resolve disputes);

4. The IBT's general executive board (GEB); and

5. Eighteen former or current members of the IBT's GEB.[67]

The complaint asserted that the IBT was involved in numerous criminal activities involving the LCN crime family, which culminated in a "pattern of racketeering activity that included wire fraud, blackmail, embezzlement, extortion, and murder."[68] In addition to RICO violations, the government asserted that under the LMRDA, discussed above, the IBT defendants "pervert[ed] . . . the democratic principles of trade unionism" by depriving IBT members of economic benefits, including pensions and welfare funds, jobs, and wages.[69] After months of impasse between the USDOJ and IBT, a settlement was entered into on March 13, 1989.[70] The agreement was documented in a consent decree that provided that all IBT members and officers be enjoined from committing racketeering acts and from knowingly associating with any LCN members or associates. It also required that the IBT amend its constitution to include new election rules and strengthened disciplinary violation procedures. The consent decree required oversight by three court-appointed officers: an independent administrator, an investigations officer, and an election officer.[71]

After more than twenty-five years of oversight, the IBT entered into an agreement with the USDOJ to reduce the government's role in its electoral and disciplinary systems and replace government-monitoring with self-monitoring.[72] The January 2015 agreement acknowledged the IBT's success in rooting out corruption in the union and ends the government's role in the union over a five-year phase-out period.[73] The agreement also includes permanent

---

67 *Id.* at 25.
68 *Id.* at 29.
69 *Id.* at 31-32.
70 *Id.* at 40.
71 *Id.* at 41.
72 Press Release, U.S. Dep't of Justice, U.S. Attorney's Office, S. Dist. of N.Y., Manhattan U.S. Attorney Announces Proposed Settlement Agreement in Landmark Civil RICO Action (Jan. 14, 2015), https://www.justice.gov/usao-sdny/pr/manhattan-us-attorney-announces-proposed-settlement-agreement-landmark-civil-rico.
73 *Id.*

injunctions that prohibit IBT members from knowingly associating with organized crime groups or engaging in racketeering activity; and requires the IBT to retain independent review officers and produce election reports for government review.[74] The agreement frees the IBT from the financial burden of the original 1989 agreement, which was estimated by the IBT to cost approximately $170 million, while still retaining many of the reforms that the consent decree mandated.[75]

B. *The Aftermath—Independent Monitors and NLRB*

The USDOJ has prioritized deterring corporate and union-related crime and directs federal prosecutors to consider deferred prosecution and non-prosecution agreements such as consent decrees.[76] These agreements typically include an independent monitor, whose primary role is to analyze and monitor the organizations' compliance with the terms of the agreement.[77] In addition, the independent monitor evaluates and proposes internal controls and compliance mechanisms for the organization and makes recommendations for implementing a well-designed compliance program to address any recurrence of the organization's misconduct.[78] The use of independent monitors in deferred prosecution and non-prosecution agreements is critical, particularly when the alleged crimes are related to a culture of corruption. An effective independent monitor can "reduce[] recidivism of corporate crime and . . . protect[] the integrity of the marketplace."[79]

---

74 *Id.*

75 Marianne Levine & Brian Mahoney, *With End of Teamsters Supervision, An Era Passes*, POLITICO (Jan. 14, 2015), https://www.politico.com/story/2015/01/justice-department-teamsters-union-supervision-ends-114281.

76 *See* JUSTICE MANUAL §§ 9-28.010, 9-28.200, 9-28.1100 (U.S. DEP'T OF JUSTICE 2020), https://www.justice.gov/jm/justice-manual. For an example of a consent decree entered into by a state AGO, see Chapter 1.8, Part IV(B).

77 *See* CRIMINAL RESOURCE MANUAL §§ 163, 166 (U.S. DEP'T OF JUSTICE 2020), https://www.justice.gov/archives/jm/criminal-resource-manual.

78 When deciding whether to charge a business organization, or in negotiating a plea agreement or other agreement, prosecutors may consider the adequacy and effectiveness of the corporation's compliance programs that were in place at the time of the offense. *See* JUSTICE MANUAL § 9-28.300; EVALUATION OF CORPORATE COMPLIANCE PROGRAMS (U.S. DEP'T OF JUSTICE, CRIM. DIV. 2020), https://www.justice.gov/criminal-fraud/page/file/937501/download.

79 CRIMINAL RESOURCE MANUAL § 163.

The United Brotherhood of Carpenters and Joiners is a national labor union overseeing more than 20,000 members in the New York City area.[80] The District Council of New York City and Vicinity (District Council) is responsible for overseeing local unions and coordinating collective bargaining agreements with its members' employers.[81] In 1990, the U.S. government sued the officers of the District Council under the civil RICO statute, and alleged that the District Council had a history of corruption and involvement with organized crime, specifically the Genovese Crime Family.[82] In 1994, the federal government and the District Council settled the case through a consent decree.[83] The consent decree prohibited District Council officers from: (1) committing any act of racketeering activity as defined by the RICO statute; (2) knowingly associating with any member or associate of any LCN members (which includes the Genovese Crime Family) or any other criminal group, or with any person prohibited from participating in union affairs; and (3) obstructing or otherwise improperly interfering with the court-appointed officer's efforts to enforce the consent decree.[84] In addition, the agreement required that an Investigations and Review Officer (IRO) and Independent Hearing Committee implement the consent decree. The IRO had the power to: investigate District Council operations and individuals; bring disciplinary charges; exercise veto authority over officer decisions; recommend organizational reforms; formulate and implement new job referral rules; and organize and supervise the District Council's elections.[85]

The court-appointed review officers oversaw the District Council's actions until December 31, 2014, when the court appointed an independent monitor. While previously the focus had been on eradicating the culture of corruption in the organization and implementing "institutional reforms and compliance-oriented mechanisms" with the approval of an independent monitor, the focus evolved to maintaining and improving existing compliance structures.[86] Since January 1, 2015, the role of the Independent Monitor has

---

80 James B. Jacobs & Kristin Stohner, *Ten Years of Court-Supervised Reform: A Chronicle & Assessment*, 6 Cal. Crim. L. Rev. 3, *3 (2004).

81 *Id.*

82 Complaint, United States v. Dist. Council, No. 90-cv-05722 (S.D.N.Y. Sept. 6, 1990), ECF No. 1.

83 Consent Decree, United States v. Dist. Council, No. 90-cv-05722 (S.D.N.Y. March 4, 1994), ECF No. 410.

84 *Id.* at 3.

85 *Id.* at 7-8.

86 First Interim Report of the Independent Monitor 2, United States v. Dist. Council, No. 90-cv-05722 (S.D.N.Y. July 1, 2015), ECF No. 1628.

been to establish goals and guidelines for the District Council in order to transition its leadership to self-monitoring. This has included: (1) continuing to oversee the transfer of union members to an Out-of-Work List (OWL) system that ensures that journeymen are dispatched to jobsites in accordance with the consent decree; (2) making improvements to the District Council's information technology infrastructure to integrate new compliance controls; (3) investing in leadership practices training for District Council members; (4) working with the District Council to revise its bylaws, its OWL rules, and pilot programs to address various issues; and (5) establishing operational goals for the executive leadership team and developing internal governance and compliance initiatives.[87] In addition, the Independent Monitor has worked with outside auditors and the executive leadership to review the performance of the Taft-Hartley Benefit Funds associated with the Union, leading to the release of those funds from direct monitorship in early 2017.[88] It is the goal of the Independent Monitor and the District Council's executive leadership to transition to a system of limited supervision, while still adhering to the anticorruption principles laid out in the consent decree.

Conclusion

The use of independent monitors, particularly in union corruption cases, can resolve cases without a criminal conviction, eradicate existing corruption, and benefit the organization's membership by reducing recidivism. It gives prosecutors and defendants flexibility in determining what system of oversight is best for them and allows them to tailor the independent monitor's role to the facts of the case. Agreements can establish the independent monitor's duties to evaluate intended reforms and can identify the remedial measures needed to satisfy the independent monitor's mandate. Prosecutors typically will also have flexibility in the duration of the agreement, and therefore can terminate or extend the monitorship based on the results of the reforms. Overall, the use of independent monitors can be an effective way to keep open communication between the government and union defendants and instill public confidence in both parties. Prosecutors should weigh the potential benefits of employing a monitor in their deferred prosecution and non-prosecution agreements and determine what impact a monitor can have on a union's governance.

---

87 Fourth Interim Report of the Independent Monitor 2-7, United States v. Dist. Council, No. 90-cv-05722 (S.D.N.Y. Apr. 7, 2017), ECF No. 1755.

88 *Id.* at 13-18.

CHAPTER 1.7

Election Crimes

Tim VanderGiesen

Tim VanderGiesen serves as Assistant State Attorney and Division Chief of the Public Corruption Unit at Miami-Dade State Attorney's Office. Any opinions or conclusions set forth in this Chapter are solely his and are not attributable to the Miami-Dade State Attorney's Office.

INTRODUCTION

The United States Constitution guarantees that every adult citizen of the United States has an equal right to vote.[1] The Voting Rights Act, which further codifies those constitutional rights, was signed into law in 1965 by President Lyndon Johnson.[2] Citizens hold sacred the right to vote. It is one of the most powerful ways that an individual can affect the functioning of our government.

The modern election process affords citizens ever-expanding choices for when, where, and how they register to vote and cast their ballot. With the expansion of voter choice, opportunities for bad actors to corrupt the process have also expanded. Some state legislatures and courts are providing new ways for citizens to vote while others are imposing new rules that restrict means of voting.[3] Enforcers should research the relevant statutes carefully and should be

1 U.S. CONST. amends. XIV, XV, XIX, XXVI.

2 Voting Rights Act, 52 U.S.C. §§ 10101, 10301-10314, 10501-10508, 10701-10702 (2018).

3 *2021 Election Enactments*, NAT'L CONF. OF STATE LEGISLATURES (Apr. 22, 2021), https://

aware of ways that advancements in technology can create new opportunities for fraud and corruption.[4]

Election-related crimes, like other crimes against public integrity, often result in a diffuse harm. An affected voter often perceives no obvious injury or loss, but the damage is to the integrity of the process and the outcome of the election. The ultimate result is that voters may lose confidence in the electoral process and in the validity of the election results.

This chapter will discuss various issues that investigators and prosecutors face in election-related criminal cases, as well as effective strategies for addressing the complexities surrounding such cases. This chapter will also identify differences and similarities between state and federal enforcement of election laws and specific legal concepts that are often at issue such as criminal intent and residency. Finally, this chapter identifies areas of the elections process that may warrant additional attention from prosecutors.

I. Preparation and Resources

The type of criminal conduct prosecutors and investigators find will vary from state to state because each state uses unique voting equipment and procedures for recording votes.[5] Many states still use the traditional punch card, some states use computers that record the vote directly into the system, and

---

www.ncsl.org/research/elections-and-campaigns/2021-election-enactments.aspx (noting that all fifty states introduced election-related bills in 2021). For an example of expansion, see Kan. Const. art. 4, § 1; Kan. Stat. Ann. §§ 25-431 to 25-440 (2020); Sawyer v. Chapman, 729 P.2d 1220, 1224 (Kan. 1986) (potential for voter fraud and loss of secrecy resulting from voting by mail are outweighed by compelling state interest in increased participation in election process, and thus Mail Ballot Election Act is constitutional). For an example of restrictions, see S.B. 90, 2021 Leg. (Fla. 2021).

4 Use of the term "fraud" in this chapter refers to conduct that violates criminal statutes. In public discourse, "fraud" may be used loosely to refer to actions taken without a criminal intent, or that do not violate the law. It is the author's opinion that prosecutors and investigators should use caution when broadly characterizing all improper or illegal conduct relating to elections as fraud, as we share in the responsibility to protect and ensure the integrity of the voting process, not draw attention to our work through inflammatory rhetoric.

5 *See Voting Methods & Equipment by State*, Ballotpedia, https://ballotpedia.org/Voting_methods_and_equipment_by_state (last visited Apr. 15, 2021).

some states use optical scan ballots in which the voter completes the ballot and then it is scanned into a machine.[6] To investigate and prosecute crimes relating to elections and voting, prosecutors and investigators need to understand the procedures employed in their jurisdiction.

Preparation and anticipation are key to successfully investigating and prosecuting elections-related crimes, so that sufficient resources are in place. Because election-related crimes are sporadic, prosecutors and investigators may not have considerable experience analyzing and applying election laws. To prepare for the challenges that come with elections, prosecutors may wish to consider the following practices:

- Dedicate experienced white collar criminal prosecutors to reviewing complaints, working with investigators, and prosecuting crimes relating to elections. Prosecutors with such experience usually have demonstrated proficiency for protracted, complex, or document-intensive prosecutions, like those involving elections offenses.

- Partner with local police agencies that can assign seasoned white collar investigators to review and respond to complaints, gather evidence, and interview witnesses. As with prosecutors, investigators with a demonstrated proficiency in protracted, complex, or document-intensive investigations will likely transition more easily to elections offenses.

- Team with prosecutors and investigators who are knowledgeable in cybercrimes, search warrants for computers and other technological devices, and the field of cybersecurity. With the increase in cyber- or hacking-related incidents, prosecutors and investigators who are experts in the field are essential.

- Require prosecutors and investigators to work together throughout both the investigation and prosecution. Much like other white collar corruption investigations, if an investigator does not consult with the prosecutor during the investigation, he or she may conduct an entire investigation only to find out that the conduct was not a crime. If consulted, a prosecutor can advise the investigator at the beginning of the investigation if the target's alleged conduct would violate the law.

---

6 *Id.*

- Train investigators and prosecutors in election laws just prior to election season, so they understand the distinction between irregularities that may incur only civil penalties and criminal misconduct.

- Consider combining various agency resources to form a task force to be better equipped to handle a high volume of complaints and produce larger, more intensive investigations. Formation of a task force also creates a presence within the community. This community presence can deter crime and may allow concerned citizens to contact law enforcement easily.

- Require all prosecutors and investigators to familiarize themselves with the races and candidates for each election, as well as campaign consultants and vendors, and public records pertaining to campaign finance.

- Establish a dedicated hotline or similar contact number for election-related tips and complaints. The hotline will invariably field calls that are not criminal in nature that can be directed to the appropriate agency. A hotline will give the community confidence that complaints are being addressed and it ensures that voters get the appropriate response.

- Alert the community to available resources through press conferences, press releases, social media, or other outreach efforts.

- In multilingual communities, ensure that prosecutors and investigators have people working with them who are proficient in relevant languages.

- Train and educate prosecutors, investigators, and other team members to be sensitive to cultural differences and concerns the community may have when cooperating with law enforcement. The more trust that law enforcement builds with the community, the more likely the community will alert authorities to misconduct.

- Respond to all credible complaints of criminal conduct. Even if it appears unlikely that a complaint will result in a viable criminal case, be diligent in investigating all leads.

Because of the political context of election-related crimes, the public may scrutinize how law enforcement reacts and responds to a complaint.

Prosecutors and investigators often have a very small amount of time in which to begin investigating an election complaint before news of the complaint becomes public. If the public becomes aware of a complaint, the investigation can be jeopardized or become subject to an allegation of political motivation. While enduring a certain amount of public scrutiny is inherent in the role of the prosecutor, in the election context the public criticism could undermine the community's confidence in the process. It is essential for prosecutors and investigators to be prepared and responsive.

II. Relationship with Elections Departments

The goal of elections departments[7] is to conduct successful elections in compliance with the law.[8] Elections departments may not consider it their responsibility to investigate or uncover allegations of election crimes. A good working relationship between law enforcement and those running the elections department may help prevent election-related crime and may facilitate investigation and prosecution if a crime occurs. Elections department officials are experts in a very specialized field of administering elections, but may not be focused on ways bad actors may try to corrupt the system they administer. By working with prosecutors and investigators, elections professionals learn what practices they can implement to deter criminal conduct, as well as what suspicious activities may require alerting law enforcement about potential crimes. A good working relationship with the elections department is also important if a crime does occur because it may allow access to most of the relevant records so that investigators and prosecutors can react to disrupt the criminal activity as quickly as possible.

Some of the specific knowledge and practices that will benefit an investigation and prosecution will include:

---

7 For this chapter, "elections department" refers to an agency responsible for administering the voting process. States may refer to such departments as, for example, a Department of Elections, Office of Elections, or Board of Elections.

8 *See, e.g., Mission Statement,* Supervisor of Elections, Nassau County, Fla., https://www.votenassau.com/m/Home/Resources/Mission-Statement (last visited Apr. 18, 2021); *Mission Statement,* Kansas City Board of Election Comm'rs, https://www.kceb.org/board/missionstatement/ (last visited Apr. 18, 2021); *Mission Statement,* Bd. of Elections in the City of New York, https://vote.nyc/page/mission-statement (last visited Apr. 18, 2021).

- Which processes can be completed electronically by the voter and which processes require completion of a hard-copy form.
- Where and how the elections department physically stores hard copies of voter information that has been submitted/received.
- Where and how the elections department maintains voter information submitted/received electronically.
- Whether any outside vendors/contractors are used in the process and what information might be retained by the vendor/contractor.
- What information can be obtained by a request from law enforcement to the elections department and what information will only be provided via a subpoena or warrant.

Since elections officials do not create procedures and processes with bad actors in mind and they are not likely experts in the relevant criminal statutes, investigators and prosecutors must fully understand elections department practices to determine whether or not a crime may have occurred.

III. Initiating an Election-Related Investigation

Prior to any investigation or prosecution into election crimes, two threshold considerations arise: (1) the credibility and nature of the origin of the tip, lead, or complaint; and (2) timing and the stage of the election.

Assessing the quality of the tip, lead, or complaint can help shape any future investigation or prosecution. Some possible factors to consider include:

- Is the origin of the lead political in nature? Some common sources of investigative leads include the elections department, members of the community, media reports, and people associated with political campaigns.
- Is the allegation relating to illegal conduct that is completed, ongoing, or yet to occur?

- Who is the target? Is the complaint against a candidate, political party, employee or volunteer, unaffiliated individual, or employee of the elections department?
- If proven, would the allegation lead to a civil penalty, misdemeanor, or felony?

Timing of the investigation is an important consideration because investigations and prosecutions may undermine the integrity of the election or voting process. The general federal policy for election crimes has traditionally been "not to conduct overt investigations, including interviews with individual voters, until after the outcome of the election allegedly affected by the fraud is certified."[9] Four factors to consider with respect to timing are whether the criminal conduct is ongoing, the identity of the target, the level of criminal conduct, and whether an investigation can occur covertly. Just the initiation of an investigation can have significant repercussions for the outcome of the election.

IV. State or Federal Jurisdiction

State or local prosecutors have jurisdiction over state or local criminal offenses that occur within the boundaries of their jurisdiction irrespective of what office the candidates are seeking.[10] State jurisdiction over investigating and prosecuting election-related crimes belongs to the local prosecutor or

---

9 Richard C. Pilger, Federal Prosecution of Election Offenses 9 (8th ed. 2017), https://www.justice.gov/criminal/file/1029066/download. *See also* U.S. Dep't of Justice, Gov't Ethics Outline, III.F.1.d. (Jul. 5, 2017), https://www.justice.gov/jmd/government-ethics-outline ("No employee may use his official authority or influence to interfere with or affect the result of an election."). In 2020, then-U.S. Attorney General William Barr issued a memorandum that authorized federal prosecutors "to pursue substantial allegations of voting and vote tabulation irregularities prior to the certification of elections in your jurisdictions" if such "clear and apparently-credible allegations of irregularities . . . could potentially impact the outcome of a federal election. . . ." Memorandum from U.S. Att'y Gen. William Barr to U.S. Att'ys, et al. (Nov. 9, 2020), *available at* https://int.nyt.com/data/documenttools/barr-memo-elections-fraud/9bf5cac375012c4c/full.pdf (last visited Apr. 15, 2021).

10 *Accord* Pilger, *supra* note 9, at 8 ("It is the states that have primary authority to ensure that only qualified individuals register and vote, that the polling process is conducted fairly, and that the candidate who received the most valid votes is certified as the winner.").

the attorney general for the area in which the election occurs.[11] So, if conduct violating a state criminal statute occurs in relation to an election for a federal office, the state official with jurisdiction where the crime occurred will have authority to prosecute the offense.

For example, consider a hypothetical situation where ten voters received money to vote for a candidate in a United States Congressional race. The voters were paid the money and voted when they were all physically located in Miami-Dade County, Florida. Florida Statute § 104.045, Vote Selling, states "Any person who . . . [a]ccepts a pecuniary or other benefit in exchange for a promise to vote for or against, or to refrain from voting for or against, any candidate in any election, is guilty of a felony of the third degree."[12] The Miami-Dade State Attorney's Office has jurisdiction to prosecute the offense for violations of the state statute because the conduct occurred in Miami-Dade County, even though it is a federal race.

At the same time, federal authorities have jurisdiction to prosecute elections offenses as long as at least one candidate for a federal race is on the ballot.[13] "[T]he federal election fraud statutes were implemented to protect two aspects of a federal election: the actual results of the election and the integrity of the process of electing federal officials."[14] Once a federal race is on the ballot, federal agents and prosecutors have jurisdiction over all races on the ballot because of a federal interest in the integrity of the election.[15] Therefore, if there is a federal candidate on a ballot, state and federal authorities almost always have concurrent jurisdiction.[16] Under the previous hypothetical, federal authorities have

---

11 For example, the Florida Election Code imposes specific duties upon the supervisor of elections and other public officials, but enforcement of the election laws for which criminal sanctions are imposed lies with the appropriate prosecuting attorneys of the several counties and the determination of guilt in such cases rests with the judiciary. Responsibility for Enforcement of Election Code, Fla. Op. Att'y Gen. 072-331, 1972 Fla. AG LEXIS 108, *1 (Fla. 1972).

12 Fla. Stat. § 104.045 (2020).

13 *See* 52 U.S.C. § 10307(c) (2018); Pilger, *supra* note 9, at 5-7; United States v. McCranie, 169 F.3d 723, 726-27 (11th Cir. 1999) (federal jurisdiction exists even if the federal candidate is running unopposed).

14 *McCranie*, 169 F.3d at 727 (quoting United States v. Cole, 41 F.3d 303, 307 (7th Cir. 1994)).

15 United States v. Olinger, 759 F.2d 1293, 1298 (7th Cir. 1985) (citing Anderson v. United States, 417 U.S. 211, 225-28 (1974)).

16 *See Ex parte* Siebold, 100 U.S. 371, 383 (1880) (finding that Congress assuming control over an area does not necessarily result in exclusive federal control); United States v. Simms, 508 F. Supp. 1179, 1186 (W.D. La. 1979) (explaining that the federal vote-buying statute contemplates cooperation between the federal and state governments).

concurrent jurisdiction over the vote-buying scheme because both federal and state candidates are involved in the election.

V. State or Federal Crimes

State and federal laws allow for prosecution of election-related offenses. Federal elections offenses are prosecuted under:

- 18 U.S.C. § 241, which criminalizes conspiracies of two or more individuals who violate rights or privileges given to an individual by the Constitution or laws of the United States,[17]
- 18 U.S.C. § 242, which criminalizes the deprivation of rights under color of law,[18]

---

17 18 U.S.C. § 241 states in relevant part:

> If two or more persons conspire to injure, oppress, threaten, or intimidate any person in any State, Territory, Commonwealth, Possession, or District in the free exercise or enjoyment of any right or privilege secured to him by the Constitution or laws of the United States, or because of his having so exercised the same . . . [t]hey shall be fined under this title or imprisoned not more than ten years, or both . . . .

18 U.S.C. § 241 (2018).

18 18 U.S.C. § 242 states in relevant part:

> Whoever, under color of any law, statute, ordinance, regulation, or custom, willfully subjects any person in any State, Territory, Commonwealth, Possession, or District to the deprivation of any rights, privileges, or immunities secured or protected by the Constitution or laws of the United States, or to different punishments, pains, or penalties, on account of such person being an alien, or by reason of his color, or race, than are prescribed for the punishment of citizens, shall be fined under this title or imprisoned not more than one year, or both; and if bodily injury results from the acts committed in violation of this section or if such acts include the use, attempted use, or threatened use of a dangerous weapon, explosives, or fire, shall be fined under this title or imprisoned not more than ten years, or both; and if death results from the acts committed in violation of this section or if such acts include kidnapping or an attempt to kidnap, aggravated sexual abuse, or an attempt to commit aggravated sexual abuse, or an attempt to kill, shall be fined under this title, or imprisoned for any term of years or for life, or both, or may be sentenced to death.

18 U.S.C. § 242 (2018).

- 52 U.S.C. § 10307, which sets forth specific criminal voting violations,[19]

---

19 52 U.S.C. § 10307 states in relevant part:

(a) *Failure or refusal to permit casting or tabulation of vote*

No person acting under color of law shall fail or refuse to permit any person to vote who is entitled to vote . . . , or willfully fail or refuse to tabulate, count, and report such person's vote.

(b) *Intimidation, threats, or coercion*

No person, whether acting under color of law or otherwise, shall intimidate, threaten, or coerce, or attempt to intimidate, threaten, or coerce any person for voting or attempting to vote, or intimidate, threaten, or coerce, or attempt to intimidate, threaten, or coerce any person for urging or aiding any person to vote or attempt to vote . . . .

(c) *False information in registering or voting; penalties*

Whoever knowingly or willfully gives false information as to his name, address or period of residence in the voting district for the purpose of establishing his eligibility to register or vote, or conspires with another individual for the purpose of encouraging his false registration to vote or illegal voting, or pays or offers to pay or accepts payment either for registration to vote or for voting shall be fined not more than $10,000 or imprisoned not more than five years, or both: *Provided, however,* That this provision shall be applicable only to general, special, or primary elections held solely or in part for the purpose of selecting or electing any candidate for the office of President, Vice President, presidential elector, Member of the United States Senate, Member of the United States House of Representatives, Delegate from the District of Columbia, Guam, or the Virgin Islands, or Resident Commissioner of the Commonwealth of Puerto Rico.

(d) *Falsification or concealment of material facts or giving of false statements in matters within jurisdiction of examiners or hearing officers; penalties*

Whoever, in any matter within the jurisdiction of an examiner or hearing officer knowingly and willfully falsifies or conceals a material fact, or makes any false, fictitious, or fraudulent statements or representations, or makes or uses any false writing or document knowing the same to contain any false, fictitious, or fraudulent statement or entry, shall be fined not more than $10,000 or imprisoned not more than five years, or both.

(e) *Voting more than once*

(1) Whoever votes more than once in an election referred to in paragraph (2) shall be fined not more than $10,000 or imprisoned not more than five years, or both.

(2) The prohibition of this subsection applies with respect to any general, special, or primary election held solely or in part for the purpose of selecting or electing any candidate for the office of President, Vice President, presidential elector, Member of the United States Senate, Member of the United States House of Representatives, Delegate from the District of Columbia, Guam, or the Virgin Islands, or Resident Commissioner of the Commonwealth of Puerto Rico.

(3) As used in this subsection, the term "votes more than once" does not include the casting of an additional ballot if all prior ballots of that voter were invalidated, nor does it include the voting in two jurisdictions under section

and

- 52 U.S.C. § 20511, which addresses voter intimidation and the procurement or submission of false voter registration applications or ballots.[20]

Many states also have statutes that enable them to prosecute elections offenses relating to the following:

- Submitting false information or false swearing[21]
- Voting when not a United States citizen;[22]
- Tampering with another individual's vote-by-mail ballot;[23]

[10502 of this title], to the extent two ballots are not cast for an election to the same candidacy or office.

52 U.S.C. § 10307 (a)-(e) (2018).

20 52 U.S.C. § 20511 states:

A person, including an election official, who in any election for Federal office—

(1) knowingly and willfully intimidates, threatens, or coerces, or attempts to intimidate, threaten, or coerce, any person for—

(A) registering to vote, or voting, or attempting to register or vote;

(B) urging or aiding any person to register to vote, to vote, or to attempt to register or vote; or

(C) exercising any right under this chapter; or

(2) knowingly and willfully deprives, defrauds, or attempts to deprive or defraud the residents of a State of a fair and impartially conducted election process, by—

(A) the procurement or submission of voter registration applications that are known by the person to be materially false, fictitious, or fraudulent under the laws of the State in which the election is held; or

(B) the procurement, casting, or tabulation of ballots that are known by the person to be materially false, fictitious, or fraudulent under the laws of the State in which the election is held,

shall be fined in accordance with title 18 (which fines shall be paid into the general fund of the Treasury, miscellaneous receipts (pursuant to section 3302 of title 31), notwithstanding any other law), or imprisoned not more than 5 years, or both.

52 U.S.C. § 20511 (2018).

21 *E.g.*, Fla. Stat. § 104.011 (2020) (false swearing); S.C. Code Ann. § 7-25-10 (2020) (false swearing in applying for registration).

22 *E.g.*, Ohio Rev. Code Ann. § 3599.12(A)(1) (2020); State v. Hull, 728 N.E.2d 414, 418 (Ohio Ct. App. 1999) ("The Ohio Constitution and Ohio Revised Code unequivocally establish that a 'legally qualified voter' must be a United States citizen.").

23 *E.g.*, Miss. Code Ann. § 23-15-753 (2020); Sewell v. State, 721 So.2d 129, 131 (Miss. 1998).

- Voting more than once (ballot stuffing);[24]
- Voting using the name of another person;[25]
- Intimidating or threatening a person to prevent them from registering to vote or to influence them to vote a certain way or not to vote;[26]
- Paying a person to vote;[27]
- Providing false address on voter registration;[28]
- Paying or receiving compensation based on the number of voters registered;[29]
- Crimes by elections department employees;[30]

---

24 *E.g.*, OHIO REV. CODE ANN. § 3599.12(A)(2) (2020); State v. Arent, 981 N.E.2d 307, 311 (Ohio Ct. App. 2012).

25 *E.g.*, S.C. CODE ANN. § 7-25-120 (2020) (impersonating a voter).

26 *E.g.*, FLA. STAT. § 104.061(1) (2020); KAN. STAT. ANN. § 25-2415 (2020).

27 OHIO REV. CODE ANN. §§ 3599.01, 3599.02; Op. Att'y Gen. 96-033, 1996 Ohio AG LEXIS 29, *6 (Ohio 1996) (explaining that awarding extra credit violates law prohibiting payment in exchange for voting). Federal courts' interpretation of "payment" in § 10307(c) may be useful for states with statutes that have similar language. 52 U.S.C. § 10307(c) (2018); United States v. Campbell, 845 F.2d 782, 787 (8th Cir. 1988) (explaining that paying a voter and then filling out absentee ballot for voter was the same as paying voter to vote); United States v. Garcia, 719 F.2d 99, 101-102 (5th Cir. 1983) (finding that "payment" in exchange for vote need not be money but can include welfare food voucher); United States v. Lewin, 467 F.2d 1132, 1136 (7th Cir. 1972) (explaining that vote-buying statute does not proscribe efforts by civic groups to encourage people to register).

28 *E.g.*, Jenkins v. State, 468 S.W.3d 656, 672 (Tex. App. 2015). *See also, e.g.*, FLA. STAT. § 104.011 (2020). Once again, federal caselaw may be useful for states with similarly worded statutes. United States v. Collins, 685 F.3d 651, 657-59 (7th Cir. 2012) (finding sufficient evidence to convict of voter fraud where voter used former address for voting while establishing a new permanent residence in a different home); United States v. Boards, 10 F.3d 587, 589 (8th Cir. 1993) (finding that submitting fraudulent information to obtain an absentee ballot violates law prohibiting providing false information in voting); United States v. Howard, 774 F.2d 838, 842-43 (7th Cir. 1985) (finding that using a false address violated federal law even if the voter was entitled to vote using true address).

29 MICH. COMP. LAWS § 168.932c (2020) (prohibiting compensation based on number of voters registered); NEV. REV. STAT. § 293.805 (2020) (same); Busefink v. State, 286 P.3d 599, 607 (Nev. 2012) (finding that the Nevada statute does not violate the first amendment and is not unconstitutionally vague).

30 *E.g.*, KAN. STAT. ANN. § 25-2420 (2020) (election fraud by an election officer is a felony).

- Gambling, betting, or wagering on the outcome of an election;[31]
- Intimidating or interfering with elections workers;[32] and
- Crimes related to petitions.[33]

When there is concurrent state and federal jurisdiction, the illicit conduct that is the basis for federal criminal charges often also satisfies the elements for one or more state or local offenses. In some instances, the state and federal laws are almost identical. For example, Florida Statute § 104.18 and federal 52 U.S.C. § 10307(e) use similar language to prohibit voting more than once in any election.[34]

In other instances, federal and state laws will criminalize the same illicit conduct even though the laws are different in structure or language. States often have criminal statutes that are tailored to a specific course of conduct, whereas federal statutes are often written more broadly to encompass the same conduct as the more narrowly-tailored state statute. Applying current Florida statutes to the facts of *United States* v. *Boards*[35] illustrates the point. In *Boards*, the defendants completed absentee ballot applications in the names of other registered voters, forged the voters' signatures on some applications, and marked some applications with Xs even though the voters were able to sign their own names.[36] They were charged under a predecessor statute to 52 U.S.C. § 10307(c), which prohibited "knowingly or willfully giving false information as to [a person's] name . . . for the purpose of establishing [the person's] eligibility to register or vote."[37] The district court concluded submission of fraudulent absentee ballot applications using the names of other registered voters did not violate

---

31 *E.g.*, N.C. Gen. Stat. § 163-274 (a)(6) (2020).

32 *E.g.*, N.C. Gen. Stat. § 163-275 (11) (2020).

33 Mich. Comp. Laws § 168.544c(8)(a) (2020) (making it a misdemeanor to sign a petition with a name other than one's own); People v. Hall, 884 N.W.2d 561, 570-71 (Mich. 2016) (explaining that a person may be prosecuted for felony perjury as well as misdemeanor elections offense of signing a different name to a petition).

34 *Compare* Fla. Stat. § 104.18 (2020) ("[W]hoever willfully votes more than one ballot at any election commits a felony of the third degree.") *with* 52 U.S.C. § 10307(e)(1) (2018) ("Whoever votes more than once in an election . . . shall be fined not more than $10,000 or imprisoned not more than five years, or both.").

35 10 F.3d 587 (8th Cir. 1993).

36 *Id.* at 588.

37 *Id.*

the statute.[38] In the district court's view, those statutory prohibitions applied only to registering and voting, not to applying for an absentee ballot.[39] The Eighth Circuit Court of Appeals ruled that defendants were properly charged because an absentee ballot application is a "vote" under the federal law's broad definition.[40]

If the facts of *Boards* were to occur today in a Florida election, the applicable Florida statutes would include both § 104.047(1) ("any person who requests a vote-by-mail ballot on behalf of an elector is guilty of a felony") and § 104.011("[a] person who willfully swears or affirms falsely to any oath or affirmation, or willfully procures another person to swear or affirm falsely to an oath or affirmation, in connection with or arising out of voting or elections commits a felony").[41] These two Florida statutes criminalize the same conduct that the federal election statute criminalizes, even though the relevant state and federal laws are not identical.

VI. Criminal Intent

Federal election-related statutes and most state election-related statutes require prosecutors to prove the specific intent of the person committing the offense.[42] Because voters may be confused about practices, procedures, and formalities associated with registering to vote and voting, criminal investigations and prosecutions of election law violations may ensnare those who did not intend to violate the law, but did not educate themselves on the law, failed to seek the proper advice, or were careless in their actions.

A person acting inadvertently—accidentally or by good faith mistake—does not violate a statute that requires knowing or willful conduct.[43] But a

---

38 *Id.* at 589.

39 *Id.*

40 *Id.*

41 Fla. Stat. Ann. §§ 104.011, 104.047 (2020).

42 *See* 52 U.S.C. § 10307 (2018) (prohibiting knowing and willful conduct specified in the statute). One exception is seen in Ohio where certain criminal elections violations are strict liability offenses. State v. Arent, 981 N.E.2d 307, 310 (Ohio Ct. App. 2012) (comparing Ohio Rev. Code § 3599.11 with Ohio Rev. Code § 3599.12).

43 United States v. Cianciulli, 482 F. Supp. 585, 620-21 (E.D. Pa. 1979).

person cannot escape criminal liability by deliberately ignoring obvious facts.[44] A person who falsely swears or affirms that he is legally qualified to register or vote does not have to know the exact law, but needs only to be aware that his actions are in some way illegal to have knowingly or willfully violated the applicable statute.[45]

VII. Legal Residence

An issue that often arises during elections is whether a voter or candidate is a legal resident at the address with which he or she registers to vote. It is not illegal or uncommon for people to move residences for the purpose of running for office in a specific district. A voter's or candidate's residence is determined by state law, but to establish residence, a voter or candidate often must show physical presence and an intent to remain in that location.[46] Once residency is established, it is not illegal for an individual to spend nights at a location that is not his or her claimed residence.[47] To the contrary, courts have found that people can go to another city for work for an extended period of time and maintain their residence in the city they left if their intention is to return once the work is done.[48]

Although residency issues arise with respect to candidates for office, they also arise when people claim residency for the purpose of voting in a specific race. This issue arises in local or state races for powerful positions because the difference between the winning and losing candidate may be only a handful of votes.[49] For example, in *Jenkins* v. *State*,[50] a small group of voters falsified their residency in order to vote in a local election.[51] For almost twenty years leading

---

44 *Id.*

45 *Id.*

46 Maksym v. Bd. of Election Comm'rs, 950 N.E.2d 1051, 1060 (Ill. 2011).

47 *Id.* at 1059.

48 *Id.* at 1059-60.

49 *See* McDuffee v. Miller, 327 S.W.3d 808, 811 (Tex. App. 2010) (ten votes cast, of twelve total votes, for directors of a local utility district were ruled invalid because voters did not establish residency when using local hotel during election with no intention of staying).

50 468 S.W.3d 656 (Tex. App. 2015).

51 *Id.* at 662.

up to the election at issue, defendant Jenkins lived with his family and had been registered to vote at an address outside the boundary of the locality.[52]

One month prior to the election, Jenkins and several others signed a Texas Voter Registration application changing their residence addresses to the address of a Marriott Residence Inn located within the election boundary.[53] On the form, Jenkins listed his twenty-year family home address as his mailing address; he also maintained a homestead exemption on the property.[54] The day before the election, Jenkins and others checked into the hotel.[55] They voted the next day and the challenger candidates, whom they supported, won ten votes to two votes.[56] After the election, the losing incumbent candidates challenged the election results.[57] Jenkins was convicted of illegal voting.[58] The *Jenkins* case is a glaring example of the efforts some people will go to in order to falsify their residency to vote or to become a candidate, even in local elections.

If a complaint arises regarding residency of a candidate or voter, a prosecutor may look to various factors to indicate an intent to remain.[59] Assuming that the person continues to claim the address as his or her residence and does not admit to a mistake or falsification of the paperwork, the issue for investigators and prosecutors to determine is whether there is any evidence tying the individual to the claimed address to support the claim and demonstrate the person's intent.

Although the following list is not exhaustive, evidence that would tend to support or disprove a claim of residence can include whether the individual:

- Leases or owns the property;[60]

---

52 *Id.* at 659-60.
53 *Id.* at 660.
54 *Id.* at 660-61.
55 *Id.* at 661-62.
56 *Id.* at 662.
57 *Id.*
58 *Id.* at 670. Jenkins's conviction was reversed on the grounds that the trial court erred by not giving a proper jury instruction. *Id.* at 682. The conviction of one of his co-defendants was affirmed as the proper instructions were given. Doyle v. State, No. 09-14-00458-CR, 2016 Tex. App. LEXIS 2461, at *2 (Tex. App. Mar. 9, 2016).
59 Bloomfield v. St. Petersburg Beach, 82 So. 2d 364, 368-69 (Fla. 1955).
60 *Id.* at 367-69.

- Has active utilities on the property in the name of the voter or candidate;[61]
- Has a driver's license using the same address;[62]
- Is seen at the property;[63]
- Files taxes at the property;[64]
- Lacks connection to an alternative address;[65]
- Receives mail at the property.[66]

VIII. Vote-By-Mail or Absentee Ballots

A few states today have laws and procedures allowing voting to be done completely through the mail.[67] For the remainder of the states, vote-by-mail is offered as an option either to every voter or to those who assert a reason the state has concluded warrants excusing them from in-person voting; the second category is sometimes referred to as "absentee voting," but is included in the general vote-by-mail discussion here.[68] States have generally increased voting by mail: in 1992, the percentage of ballots cast by mail was less than ten percent, and in 2017, it was approximately twenty-five percent.[69] In 2020, a number of states elected to provide increased access to voting by mail as a result of the COVID-19 pandemic, with at least some allowing all voters who wished to

---

61 Walker v. Harris, 398 So. 2d 955, 958-59 (Fla. Dist. Ct. App. 1981).

62 *Id. But see Bloomfield*, 82 So. 2d at 368.

63 *Walker*, 398 So. 2d at 958.

64 *Bloomfield*, 82 So. 2d at 368.

65 *Id.*

66 Perez v. Marti, 770 So. 2d 284, 290 (Fla. Dist. Ct. App. 2000).

67 *See States with All-Mail Elections*, Nat'l Conf. of State Legislatures (Apr. 21, 2020), https://www.ncsl.org/research/elections-and-campaigns/vopp-table-18-states-with-all-mail-elections.aspx.

68 *See Voting Outside the Polling Place: Absentee, All-Mail and Other Voting at Home Options*, Nat'l Conf. of State Legislatures (Sept. 24, 2020), https://www.ncsl.org/research/elections-and-campaigns/absentee-and-early-voting.aspx.

69 *Voting by Mail & Absentee Voting*, MIT Election Data & Science Lab, https://electionlab.mit.edu/research/voting-mail-and-absentee-voting (last visited Apr. 15, 2021).

do so to submit an absentee ballot.[70] In the future, elections departments may continue increasing access to voting by mail because its convenience results in more voter participation, it avoids bringing together crowds of people, and it may be less costly than operating precincts or polling sites.[71]

Voting by mail creates different issues for prosecutors and investigators than does traditional voting at precincts. Precincts are governed by local, state, or federal laws that regulate access by those associated with candidates and campaigns. For example, the state statute in Florida requires such individuals to remain 150 feet away from a polling location or drop box.[72] That law prohibits others from contacting a voter while the voter is in possession of and voting his or her ballot. The purpose of the law is to prevent harassment, tampering, and influence during the voting process.[73] And poll workers operating the precincts and drop boxes serve as a deterrent for those who would consider violating such laws.

However, coercion or tampering could occur with absentee ballots returned by mail because no access restrictions apply.[74] Candidates and campaigns can obtain lists of voters who vote by absentee ballots and can learn from public information when the absentee ballots are mailed. A campaign can then send someone to the home of the voter to try to influence the vote, mark the ballot of the voter, take possession of the ballot and deliver it or destroy it.[75] Whether it is legal to try to influence a mail-in ballot voter to vote for a candidate or issue is a question of state law.[76] It is generally illegal to possess

---

70 *See, e.g.*, New York City Campaign Finance Board, Voting and Coronavirus (COVID-19): Information for NYC Voters (Sept. 8, 2020), https://www.nyccfb.info/nyc-votes/coronavirus/ ("This fall, all New York voters can vote by mail due to the risk of contracting the coronavirus."); *Pennsylvania Boosting Efforts to Promote Voting by Mail Amid COVID-19 Pandemic*, 6 ABC (Apr. 22, 2020), https://6abc.com/health/pennsylvania-boosting-efforts-to-promote-voting-by-mail/6122146/.

71 *See Voting Outside the Polling Place*, *supra* note 68.

72 Fla. Stat. § 102.031 (2021).

73 Miami-Dade County Grand Jury, Cir. Ct. of the 11th Judicial Cir., Absentee Ballot Voting: Convenience & Its Consequences 3-4 (2012), http://www.miamisao.com/publications/grand_jury/2000s/gj2012s.pdf [hereinafter Absentee Ballot Grand Jury Report].

74 *Voting Outside the Polling Place*, *supra* note 68.

75 Absentee Ballot Grand Jury Report, *supra* note 73, at 1-2 (summarizing both rumored and corroborated problems with absentee ballot voting).

76 *See, e.g.*, Tex. Elec. Code §§ 64.036(a)(3), 276.013(a)(1) (2019) (prohibiting suggesting how a voter should vote, while assisting that voter, and making any effort "to influence the

someone else's ballot, vote or mark someone else's ballot, or destroy someone else's ballot—although that, too, is a question of state law.[77]

Some scholars believe that vote-by-mail fraud is likely more common than fraud with in-person voting.[78] The facts of *United States* v. *McCranie* provide a brazen example of voter fraud relating to absentee ballots.[79] In the elections for county sheriff and county commissioner in Dodge County, Georgia, the incumbent sheriff of thirty years and a county commission candidate were found guilty of two separate conspiracies to buy votes.[80] Evidence at trial included multiple witnesses who testified that they paid twenty to forty dollars to voters after the voter cast his or her absentee ballot.[81] Another witness testified that his "primary role was to physically mark the voters' absentee ballots for McCranie and Jones, no matter what the voters' preferences were."[82] In its opinion, the Eleventh Circuit Court of Appeals noted, "Incredibly, each of the two camps . . . actually set up tables inside the courthouse at opposite ends of the hall, where supporters on both sides openly bid against each other to buy absentee votes."[83] The atmosphere was described as a "flea market" or "auction."[84]

IX. Internet Election Crimes

The risk of bad actors tampering with the voting process through internet hacking is significant.[85] While our diverse and locally-run election process

---

independent exercise of the vote of another in the presence of the ballot or during the voting process").

77 *See, e.g.*, Miss. Code Ann. § 23-15-753 (2020); Sewell v. State, 721 So. 2d 129, 131 (Miss. 1998).

78 *Voting by Mail & Absentee Voting*, *supra* note 69.

79 169 F.3d 723, 725-26 (11th Cir. 1999).

80 *Id.*

81 *Id.*

82 *Id.*

83 *Id.* at 726.

84 *Id.*

85 Elaine Kamark, *States and Localities Are on the Front Lines of Fighting Cyber-Crimes in Elections*, Brookings (Aug. 15, 2019), https://www.brookings.edu/blog/fixgov/2019/08/15/states-and-localities-are-on-the-front-lines-of-election-security/; Sue Halpern, *America Continues to Ignore the Risks of Election Hacking*, New Yorker (Apr. 18, 2018), https://www.newyorker.com/news/news-desk/america-continues-to-ignore-the-risks-of-election-hacking.

mitigates the risk of large-scale cyberattacks,[86] some threat exists in every municipality, county, and state in which a voter registration and a request for a vote-by-mail ballot can be completed on the internet.

As an example, in Miami-Dade County, Florida, during the 2012 elections, vote-by-mail ballots presented several opportunities for criminal interference with the election process.[87] A registered voter could go online and complete a form to request a ballot to be mailed to the person's house. To initiate the process, a person only needed minimal information about a voter such as the last name, date of birth, and house number of the voter, all of which is potentially public information.[88]

Investigators became aware that hundreds of absentee ballots were being requested from the same IP addresses in very short time periods, usually one request every minute or two.[89] The ballots were being requested for individual voters who had no apparent relationship to each other or to the physical addresses that were associated with the IP addresses. An investigation revealed that the requests were made through overseas anonymizers that hid the identity and location of the culprits, but it was clear that the requests were not made by the legitimate voters.[90] Under Florida law, requesting an absentee ballot on behalf of another person and submitting a false affirmation in connection with voting or elections are each a felony offense.[91]

Further investigation revealed that a campaign manager of one of the congressional candidates orchestrated the vote-by-mail request scheme with the intention of persuading those voters to vote for his candidate in a hotly-contested race.[92] The campaign manager, who subsequently became chief of staff

---

86 Nat'l Ass'n of Secretaries of State, *BRIEFING: Key Facts & Findings on Cybersecurity & Foreign Targeting of the 2016 U.S. Elections* 2 (Mar. 20, 2017), https://www.nass.org/sites/default/files/briefing-nass-cybersecurity-election-2016-facts-and-findings-mar17%20(2).pdf.

87 Absentee Ballot Grand Jury Report, *supra* note 73, at 2.

88 *Id.* at 11-12.

89 *Id.* at 14.

90 *Id.*

91 Fla. Stat. §§ 104.047, 104.011 (2020).

92 Patricia Mazzei, *Ex-Aide to Miami Rep. Joe Garcia to Head to Jail in Absentee-Ballot Case*, Miami Herald (Oct. 20, 2013), https://www.miamiherald.com/news/local/community/miami-dade/article1956526.html.

for the winning congressional candidate, was sentenced to ninety days' incarceration for his role in the scheme.[93]

X. Punishment and Precedent

Once an investigation is complete and sufficient evidence supports initiating prosecution, a prosecutor may consider the likely sentence when making a charging decision. While sentencing guidelines may dictate punishment in some jurisdictions, prosecutors may have discretion in recommending punishment even within applicable guidelines. Especially because defendants who commit election-related offenses vary from the confused and unsophisticated to the ill-intentioned and politically motivated, every prosecutor should be mindful of the precedent being set when charging, prosecuting, and resolving an election-related case.

Conclusion

The right to vote is a fundamental feature of our democracy. The ways in which citizens exercise that right and the ways in which the process can become corrupted are continually changing. Investigators and prosecutors who combat election crimes play an important role in maintaining the integrity of the electoral process. Although election-related criminal conduct will vary across jurisdictions and across election cycles, prosecutors and investigators can prepare to meet new challenges by understanding recurrent legal issues and being prepared to investigate and charge those who violate the laws designed to protect our democratic process.

---

93 *Id.*

Chapter 1.8

Police Corruption

Amie N. Ely

Amie N. Ely is the Director of the Center for Ethics & Public Integrity, National Attorneys General Training & Research Institute, National Association of Attorneys General.

Introduction

Police corruption, like several of the other areas of corruption discussed in this section, undercuts citizens' trust in government. Perhaps even worse, it increases the risk of other crimes going uninvestigated and unpunished, as it may reduce the likelihood that citizens will contact the police if they are victimized.

This chapter introduces some types of "traditional" police corruption; discusses some of the investigative steps and tools that may be useful to investigate it; and summarizes some legal issues that may be likely to arise in cases involving police corruption. Finally, the chapter discusses two non-criminal means of addressing police corruption: commissions and consent decrees. Some of the concepts discussed in this chapter may also be relevant in other types of criminal cases involving police officers as witnesses, subjects, targets, or charged defendants.

I. Types of Police Corruption

The traditional scope of police corruption includes: (1) nonenforcement or selective enforcement of the law, which can range from overlooking parking violations outside certain businesses to ignoring serious crimes; (2) mishandling of evidence, including intentionally destroying or stealing money, property, or contraband; and (3) influencing the outcome of a case by causing the judge or prosecutor to dismiss or reduce charges, all done deliberately and often in exchange for a bribe.[1] One commentator who prosecuted corrupt police officers in the Chicago area in the 1970s also described what he called "internal corruption," which included officers paying money to join the police force, for better shifts, promotions, or vacation time, or for assignments that would "yield lucrative kick-backs."[2] Finally, as detailed in the Mollen Commission Report discussed below, police corruption can include officers themselves committing crimes that are aided by the power of their badges.[3]

II. Selected Investigation Challenges

While investigating corruption is always difficult because participants typically conceal their actions, police corruption can be especially difficult to investigate.[4] The "blue wall of silence" is the phenomenon of police obstructing any outside evaluation of officer conduct based on the belief that outsiders lack understanding of the danger and difficulty of police work.[5] Breaking that wall often requires building cases by starting with the civilians who are paying the officers to look the other way, tamper with evidence, or fix cases. In a 1988 manual, the United States Department of Justice recommended that prosecutors first identify citizens who were paying bribes to police officers, induce

---

1 Edward S.G. Dennis, Jr. & Dennis O. Wilson, *Investigation and Prosecution of Police Corruption Cases, in* Prosecution of Public Corruption Cases 65, 68 (U.S. Dep't of Justice 1988), https://www.ncjrs.gov/pdffiles1/Digitization/110010-110033NCJRS.pdf.

2 Herbert Beigel, *The Investigation and Prosecution of Police Corruption*, 65 J. Crim. L. & Criminology 135, 136 (1974), https://scholarlycommons.law.northwestern.edu/cgi/viewcontent.cgi?article=5891&context=jclc.

3 *See* discussion *infra* Part IV(A)(2).

4 Dennis & Wilson, *supra* note 1, at 67.

5 *See* Gabriel J. Chin & Scott C. Wells, *The "Blue Wall of Silence" As Evidence of Bias and Motive to Lie: A New Approach to Police Perjury*, 59 U. Pitt. L. Rev. 233, 237-40 & nn.15-22 (1998).

the payers' cooperation, and develop the investigation from there.[6] As police officers "are the public officials paid to enforce the law," they "have violated the public trust and are the more serious offenders."[7] That manual thus generally recommends that the testimony of bribe payers be secured with immunity or non-prosecution agreements, which are described below, to build a case against bribe-accepting officers.[8]

Two tools have proven effective to investigate police corruption cases: first, the use of cooperation agreements, immunity orders, and non-prosecution agreements to secure the testimony of officers' coconspirators—both the bribers and other officers; and second, the grand jury, which can provide a powerful method to require testimony, impress upon witnesses the seriousness of telling the truth, and obtain truthful testimony from witnesses who might waver when looking at a defendant in open court. Because of the diversity of state law and practice, we primarily describe federal law and practice, with an emphasis on the manner in which these tools are used in the Southern District of New York.

As is true with other types of sensitive corruption investigations, prosecutors and investigators should carefully consider when to transition from covert to overt investigations in cases involving the police, and be familiar with requirements for filing charging instruments and other process under seal.[9] Other potential investigative tools—including using confidential informants and undercover officers,[10] and obtaining wiretaps[11]—may provide powerful evidence to charge corrupt police officers. As these concepts and techniques are addressed elsewhere in this Manual, this chapter does not discuss them at length. However, those embarking on investigations of police corruption should read those chapters and think carefully about the likely impact of an investigation into police corruption becoming known by its targets. Chapter 1.2, which describes the prosecution of a sitting state attorney general, may also be instructive.

Some commentators and federal prosecutors have also suggested that local authorities are rarely able to investigate pervasive corruption in police

---

6 Dennis & Wilson, *supra* note 1, at 69-70.
7 *Id.* at 69.
8 *Id.* at 70.
9 *See* Chapters 2.2 (covert and overt investigations) & 5.2 (timing of charges).
10 *See* Chapter 2.5.
11 *See* Chapter 2.3.

departments with which they work closely.[12] This potential conflict of interest is addressed in Part III(B), below.

A. *Cooperation Agreements, Immunity Orders, and Non-Prosecution Agreements*

While securing the testimony of people who have criminal exposure is not unique to police corruption cases, it is important to understand and be prepared to weigh three standard options, at least in the federal system, to securing testimony of individuals with criminal exposure: (1) cooperation agreements, (2) immunity orders, and (3) non-prosecution agreements.[13] This part also discusses proffers and proffer agreements, which are often used while debriefing witnesses with criminal exposure or defendants who wish to cooperate with the government. State prosecutors should, as always, consult their statutes and case law to determine if these mechanisms exist and are used in the same fashion in their own jurisdiction.

1. Cooperation Agreements

Cooperation agreements require a defendant to enter a guilty plea and to waive Fifth Amendment rights. The cooperation agreement typically requires the defendant to be fully forthcoming with the government, including by truthfully disclosing information about his own and others' crimes; not to commit any additional crimes; to cooperate with the investigation; and, if the government requests, to testify. If the defendant fulfills his end of that bargain, that fulfillment results in "substantial assistance" to the government, and the government files the necessary motion, he will be sentenced pursuant to Section 5K1.1 of the U.S. Sentencing Guidelines and 18 U.S.C. § 3553(e). The filing of this "5K Motion" gives the court the freedom to sentence the defendant in light of the factors set forth in the statute and the guidelines section, and allows for a sentence even below an otherwise-applicable mandatory minimum.[14]

---

12 Dennis & Wilson, *supra* note 1, at 67; Beigel, *supra* note 2, at 135-36 & n.2; Kate Levine, *Who Shouldn't Prosecute the Police*, 101 Iowa L. Rev. 1447, 1447 (2016) (arguing that "a structural conflict of interest arises when local prosecutors are given the discretion and responsibility to investigate and lead cases against the police").

13 *See also* Chapter 1.6, Part II(B).

14 18 U.S.C. § 3553(e) (2018) ("Upon motion of the Government, the court shall have the authority to impose a sentence below a level established by statute as a minimum sentence so as to reflect a defendant's substantial assistance in the investigation or prosecution of another

Cooperation agreements provide perhaps the best set of incentives for truthful testimony. Under such an agreement, if the cooperator has entered a guilty plea and yet refuses to testify or testifies falsely, the government has the unilateral power to withdraw the cooperation agreement or refuse to file a 5K Motion.[15] If that happens, the defendant will still be convicted, but will not be afforded the benefit of being sentenced as a cooperator.[16]

Cooperation agreements ensure that the witness is also held to account for his crimes. This is important both as a matter of policy and practice. As a matter of policy, culpable actors should be held accountable. More practically, there is a risk that a jury will discount the testimony of someone who appears to have escaped justice, or be unhappy that the government appears to be unprincipled in choosing its targets.

That said, a cooperation agreement may not be appropriate for a potential witness who committed a low-level crime that would not otherwise be prosecuted. Proof issues may also prevent a coconspirator from being charged in the first instance, which may make a cooperation agreement impossible, impractical, or even unethical. For such a witness, a non-prosecution agreement or immunity order, discussed below, may be appropriate.

2. Proffer Agreements

In the federal system, before a defendant and the government enter into a formal cooperation agreement, he engages in proffer sessions with the government during which he provides information about the crimes he and his coconspirators committed. Those meetings are typically governed by a proffer agreement. A proffer agreement allows a defendant the opportunity to give investigators candid and truthful statements without fear of those statements being directly used against him. A proffer agreement may also be used to provide protection to a witness with potential criminal exposure even if no cooperation agreement is contemplated. Proffer agreements thus may also be

person who has committed an offense."); U.S. Sentencing Guidelines Manual § 5K1.1 (U.S. Sentencing Comm'n 2018).

15 Wade v. United States, 504 U.S. 181, 186-87 (1992).

16 A district court has the power to consider even ineffective cooperation as part of a defendant's "history and characteristics" when imposing sentence. 18 U.S.C. § 3553(a)(1); United States v. Fernandez, 443 F.3d 19, 34 (2d Cir. 2006). However, the court's discretion would be cabined by any otherwise applicable mandatory minimum sentence.

used in situations that result in non-prosecution agreements, immunity orders, or even no formal agreement or order.

Proffer sessions typically include the prosecutor, law enforcement, the witness/defendant, and defense counsel, and follow the terms of a proffer agreement that is signed by the witness/defendant and the attorneys. That proffer agreement describes the limited ways the government can use the information that the witness/defendant is providing. The proffer agreement tries to incentivize truth-telling by strictly limiting how a speaker's statements can be used against him, unless he lies. It also typically waives the provisions of Federal Rule of Evidence 410, which would otherwise restrict the admissibility of statements made during plea discussions.[17] It typically gives the witness/defendant protection against having his statements used against him in the government's case in chief unless he testifies and makes claims that are inconsistent with what he said during the proffer or his attorney makes an argument that is inconsistent with his proffer admissions. Proffer agreements typically allow the government to use the information obtained during the proffer to develop leads.[18]

An example helps illustrate how a proffer agreement like the one described above will limit the use of information provided during a proffer session. Assume a police officer admitted during a proffer session governed by such an agreement that he:

1. Accepted cash from a business owner;
2. Deposited that money in a bank account in his sister's name; and
3. Corresponded over email with the business owner about the payment using his personal email account.

---

17 *See, e.g.*, United States v. Rosemond, 841 F.3d 95, 107 (2d Cir. 2016) (describing waiver of Rule 410 protections in proffer agreements); United States v. Barrow, 400 F.3d 109, 116-17 (2d Cir. 2005).

18 If the agreement does not explicitly permit this derivative use, however, courts are likely to conclude that information a witness provides during a proffer session cannot be used to develop leads. United States v. Plummer, 941 F.2d 799, 802-03 (9th Cir. 1991); *see also* Criminal Resource Manual § 719 (U.S. Dep't of Justice 2018), https://www.justice.gov/archives/usam/criminal-resource-manual-719-informal-immunity-distinguished-formal-immunity. Note that the U.S. Department of Justice appears to be treating the *Criminal Resource Manual* as an archived document.

Under the terms of the typical federal proffer agreement, the government can use the information the police officer provided to (1) obtain a subpoena for records for his sister's bank account and (2) request a search warrant for his personal email account. If the officer is charged and elects to go to trial, the proffer agreement provides no barrier for the evidence from the bank account and email search warrant to be introduced against him at trial.

The government will generally not be able to call an agent who was present for that proffer to introduce the defendant's statement that he accepted cash from that business owner. However, if the defendant testifies that he did not accept money from the business owner, or if the defense attorney affirmatively argues that his client did not accept that money, the government will be able to introduce the defendant's admissions during the proffer session to rebut those statements.[19] Then, prosecutors may typically (1) cross-examine the defendant about those proffer statements, if he chooses to testify, and (2) during a rebuttal case, call an agent present for the proffer to testify that the defendant admitted doing those things.

3. Immunity Orders

There are two types of immunity: transactional and use. Transactional immunity shields a witness from ever being prosecuted for any offense about which he testifies.[20] Use immunity is narrower, and permits prosecution of the witness if a case can be proved independently from the witness's testimony.[21] If a witness granted use immunity is later prosecuted, the prosecution has "the affirmative duty to prove that the evidence it proposes to use is derived from a

---

19 In *Rosemond*, the Second Circuit summarized some of the arguments and factual assertions that do and do not trigger the provision in the proffer agreement that permits the government to introduce the defendant's proffer statements. 841 F.3d at 109-10.

20 Adam H. Kurland, *The Guarantee Clause as a Basis for Federal Prosecutions of State and Local Officials*, 62 S. Cal. L. Rev. 367, 380 n.35 (1989) (citations omitted). New York provides for transactional immunity for witnesses who are compelled to testify before the grand jury. N.Y. Crim. Proc. L. § 190.40 (Consol. 2020). *See also* Murphy v. Waterfront Comm'n, 378 U.S. 52, 79 n.18 (1964) ("Once a defendant demonstrates that he has testified, under a state grant of immunity, to matters related to the federal prosecution, the federal authorities have the burden of showing that their evidence is not tainted by establishing that they had an independent, legitimate source for the disputed evidence."); United States v. Helmsley, 941 F.2d 71, 79 (2d Cir. 1991) (concluding that state transactional immunity does not prevent future federal prosecution).

21 Kurland, *supra* note 20, at 380 n.35.

legitimate source wholly independent of the compelled testimony."[22] One sovereign cannot use immunized testimony compelled by another.[23]

To illustrate the limitations on using information obtained from an immunized witness, assume that a police officer testified pursuant to an immunity order that—as above—he:

1. Accepted cash from a business owner;

2. Deposited that money in a bank account in his sister's name; and

3. Corresponded over email with the business owner about the payment using his personal email account.

Unlike information obtained pursuant to a standard proffer agreement, information obtained during compelled testimony could not be used to obtain evidence against the officer. If prosecutors learned of the business owner's name from the officer's compelled testimony and seek to have the business owner testify, they will have to prove that the "taint ordinarily attributable to the alleged derivation of the challenged testimony from the defendant's coerced statements is absent because the relationship between the defendant's statements and the challenged testimony [of the business owner] is too remote."[24] They cannot use the officer's immunized testimony as a basis to obtain, for use against that officer, a subpoena for the bank account or a search warrant for the email account. If they are able to obtain from a non-tainted source the leads necessary to reveal the bank or email accounts and use that non-tainted source to obtain that information, they will need to be prepared to show that the evidence came from a source other than the compelled testimony.

Provision of "use immunity" in federal courts and other federal fora—including before Congress—is governed by statute.[25] Section 6002 provides that

---

22 Kastigar v. United States, 406 U.S. 441, 460 (1972).

23 *See Murphy*, 378 U.S. at 79 n.18.

24 United States v. Ghailani, 743 F. Supp. 2d 261, 278 (S.D.N.Y. 2010). Factors include (1) the stated willingness of the witness to testify, (2) the role played by the compelled testimony in gaining his cooperation, (3) the proximity of the compelled testimony to the decision to cooperate and the actual testimony at trial, and (4) the police motivation in engaging in illegal activity. *See id.* at 275 (quoting United States v. Leonardi, 623 F.2d 746, 752 (2d Cir. 1980)).

25 18 U.S.C. §§ 6001-6005 (2018).

if a witness refuses to testify or provide other information on the basis of his privilege against self-incrimination and is nonetheless ordered to do so, "no testimony or other information compelled under the order (or any information directly or indirectly derived from such testimony or other information) may be used against the witness in any criminal case, except a prosecution for perjury, giving a false statement, or otherwise failing to comply with the order."[26] An immunized witness who refuses to testify or provide information may be "confine[d] at a suitable place" until he complies, for as long as the duration of the court proceeding or the term of the grand jury, with a cap of eighteen months.[27]

There are strict limits on federal prosecutors who wish to obtain an immunity order.[28] The district's U.S. Attorney must obtain the approval of the U.S. Attorney General or one of the U.S. Attorney General's designated staff members, and may only seek such approval when the testimony or information the order seeks "may be necessary to the public interest" and the individual who would provide that testimony or information "has refused or is likely to refuse to testify or provide other information on the basis of his privilege against self-incrimination."[29] The Justice Manual recommends that, when possible, an immunity order be sought after the person being compelled to testify has been convicted and requires that any efforts to prosecute someone whose testimony was previously compelled be approved by the U.S. Attorney General.[30]

Every federal circuit court has concluded that only prosecutors have the power to seek an immunity order to compel a witness to testify, as whether to immunize a witness is a "core prosecutorial function . . . [that] necessarily involves weighing the public's need for testimony against the risk that immunity will inhibit later prosecution of criminal wrongdoing."[31]

The safest practice is to wall off or screen prosecutors who wish to charge a person who has use immunity for testimony or information.[32] Because the

---

26 *Id.* § 6002.

27 28 U.S.C. § 1826(a) (2018).

28 *See* Justice Manual §§ 9-23.000 to 9-23.400 (U.S. Dep't of Justice 2020), https://www.justice.gov/jm/justice-manual.

29 18 U.S.C. § 6003(b)(1), (b)(2).

30 Justice Manual §§ 9-23.212, 9-23.400.

31 United States v. Quinn, 728 F.3d 243, 247 (3d Cir. 2013).

32 In the federal tax prosecution of Leona Helmsley, an assistant attorney general who

government will have the burden to prove that compelled information was not used directly or indirectly to investigate or prosecute a defendant,[33] it is important to keep careful records to demonstrate that the prosecutors and investigators who charged a defendant did not have access to information obtained from him through an immunity order.[34] Even that may not be enough, however. In the Oliver North case, the D.C. Circuit Court of Appeals, sitting en banc, concluded that the government must also be able to show that the testimony of witnesses was not shaped by exposure to compelled testimony.[35] The prosecution followed North's compelled testimony before Congress—which was publicized heavily.[36] The exposure of witnesses to a defendants' compelled testimony is less likely to occur in a typical prosecution, but the lessons of *North* are nonetheless important for a prosecutor considering whether to charge a target who was provided with use immunity.[37]

As a practical matter, it may be imprudent to rely upon the trial testimony of a hostile witness, even if that witness is compelled to testify. When possible, prosecutors should require a potentially hostile immunized witness to first testify before the grand jury. This will provide a preview of the testimony and a transcript of the witness's statements to use to impeach him or potentially introduce into evidence as a prior inconsistent statement.[38]

---

attended Helmsley's state grand jury testimony was permitted to be a part of the federal prosecution team only after a federal prosecutor, who acted as a "taint" reviewer, determined that the contents of that state grand jury testimony were "unrelated to the matters the [federal g]overnment was investigating." United States v. Helmsley, 726 F. Supp. 929, 936 (S.D.N.Y. 1989). For more on walls, see Chapter 2.8, Parts II(B)(i), III(C), & Chapter 5.1, Part I(B).

33 Kastigar v. United States, 406 U.S. 441, 442 (1972).

34 The D.C. Circuit referred to one method of showing this as "canning" the testimony of witnesses—that is, making sure witness testimony was obtained and recorded in some fashion before requiring an immunized target to testify. United States v. North, 920 F.2d 940, 942 (D.C. Cir. 1990) (en banc).

35 *Id.* at 941-42.

36 *Id.*; *see also Flashback: Blockbuster Congressional Testimony . . . in 1987*, CBSnews.com (June 7, 2017), https://www.cbsnews.com/news/flashback-blockbuster-congressional-testimony-in-1987-oliver-north/ (comparing North's testimony to the then-upcoming testimony of James Comey, and characterizing North as "a star of congressional testimony who held the country transfixed and deepened the country's partisan divisions").

37 *North* has been described as "the most expansive reading of the Fifth Amendment to date regarding the evidentiary use of immunized testimony." United States v. Helmsley, 941 F.2d 71, 82 (2d Cir. 1991). Prosecutors should, as always, research the caselaw in their own jurisdiction.

38 *See, e.g.*, FED. R. EVID. 613(b). For an example of a state case that used testimony from an immunized witness, see Chapter 1.2, Part II(C)(3).

4. Non-Prosecution Agreements

Voluntary agreements between the prosecutor and a witness that the witness will not be prosecuted in exchange for cooperating with the government do not implicate the witness's Fifth Amendment rights, as the witness is choosing to waive the right to remain silent.[39] Nor do these voluntary agreements bind another prosecutor—state or federal—in the way an immunity order would.[40]

While non-prosecution agreements are often a non-public matter between the prosecutor and the witness, a 2018 agreement not to prosecute a media outlet for an illegal campaign contribution was made public and sheds light on the process.[41] That agreement contained typical non-prosecution terms, including the following:

- The U.S. Attorney's Office for the Southern District of New York (Office) agreed not to prosecute the company for any non-tax crimes related to its participation in the campaign contribution, to the extent the company admitted such participation.
- The company, in turn, agreed to:
    - Truthfully and completely disclose information to the Office;
    - Cooperate with the Office and any other law enforcement entity;
    - Attend any meetings or court proceedings requested by the Office and secure the attendance of current and former staff;
    - Provide documents; and
    - Commit no crimes.

---

39 *See* Criminal Resource Manual § 719 (U.S. Dep't of Justice 2018), https://www.justice.gov/archives/usam/criminal-resource-manual-719-informal-immunity-distinguished-formal-immunity.

40 *Id.*

41 Letter from Robert Khuzami, Acting U.S. Attorney, S.D.N.Y., to Charles A. Stillman & James A. Mitchell, Ballard Spahr LLP (Sept. 20, 2018), https://www.justice.gov/usao-sdny/press-release/file/1119501/download.

- If the company committed additional crimes or the Office determined that false, incomplete, or misleading testimony or information had been provided by the company or its staff, the Office reserved the right to prosecute it, and the company agreed the information it had previously provided to the Office could be used to prosecute it.[42]

The following chart summarizes some of the key takeaways from the discussion above. "Witness" is used to describe the person entering into the relevant agreement or subject to the relevant order, even if that person has also been charged as a defendant:

WITNESS'S CONSENT NECESSARY	WITNESS PLEADS GUILTY	BINDS OTHER PROSECUTORS	LIMITS ON USING INFORMATION AGAINST WITNESS	LIKELY DEFENSE ARGUMENT IF WITNESS TESTIFIES
COOPERATION AGREEMENT				
Yes	Yes	No, but other offices may choose to honor as a matter of practice.		Witness currying favor for sentencing consideration.
PROFFER AGREEMENT				
Yes	No	No, but may prohibit sharing of information unless receiving agency agrees to be bound by any use restrictions on that information.	Cannot use information at trial unless defendant-witness's testimony is inconsistent with proffer statements / defendant's counsel makes arguments directly contrary to proffer statements.	
IMMUNITY ORDER				
No	No	Yes	Cannot use information directly or indirectly against witness. *Kastigar* v. *United States*, 406 U.S. 441, 460 (1972).	Witness not being held accountable.

42 *Id.*

WITNESS'S CONSENT NECESSARY	WITNESS PLEADS GUILTY	BINDS OTHER PROSECUTORS	LIMITS ON USING INFORMATION AGAINST WITNESS	LIKELY DEFENSE ARGUMENT IF WITNESS TESTIFIES
NON-PROSECUTION AGREEMENT				
Yes	No, but witness may be required to disgorge ill-gotten gains/ pay back taxes.	No		Witness not being held accountable.
NO AGREEMENT				
No, but witness may invoke Fifth Amendment and refuse to testify; better practice to ensure witness with exposure has access to counsel.	No	No	May be ethical issues under Rule of Professional Conduct 4.3 (dealing with unrepresented persons) if witness has criminal exposure and is unrepresented; witness could also argue there was implicit understanding that incriminating information would not be used against him, or that information was given in the course of plea bargaining. *See* FED. R. EVID. 410(a)(4).	Witness not being held accountable; may be argument that witness was the beneficiary of an implicit non-prosecution agreement.

B. *Grand Jury*

In the federal system, a person subpoenaed to testify before the grand jury does not receive immunity and prosecutors may introduce hearsay evidence, upon which the jurors may rely to find probable cause.[43] Federal grand juries typically have eighteen-month terms—a period of time that can be extended—and nationwide subpoena power over people and documents, with compliance enforced by the district court's contempt powers.[44] The contempt powers include the ability to civilly jail people who refuse to testify or to provide documents (unless there is a valid invocation of their Fifth Amendment right not to incriminate themselves).[45] That incarceration is designed to coerce compliance with the subpoena, and ends when the grand jury with oversight over the investigation is dissolved.

State grand jury practice varies. In at least one state, compelling a witness to testify before the grand jury provides that witness with transactional immunity[46] and hearsay testimony is not permitted.[47] Other states rarely, if ever, use grand juries to charge. In states where grand jury practice is common, prosecutors should explore requiring immunized witnesses who are likely to be hostile to the government to testify before the grand jury. Whether to require a witness with a non-prosecution agreement or an immunized witness who is not expected to be hostile to testify before the grand jury is very much a judgment call.

---

43 John C. Jeffries, Jr. & John Gleeson, *The Federalization of Organized Crime: Advantages of Federal Prosecution*, 46 Hastings L.J. 1095, 1109 (1995).

44 *Id.* State grand juries do not enjoy this same nationwide jurisdiction, however, and prosecutors will likely need to use the Uniform Act to Secure the Attendance of Witnesses from Without a State in Criminal Proceedings in cases that include witnesses and/or evidence from other states. For a list of state statutes enacting, and guidance about using, that Uniform Act, see Darrell E. White II, *Subpoenaing Out-of-State Witnesses in Criminal Proceedings: A Step-by-Step Guide*, Attorney Gen. J. (May 18, 2021), https://www.naag.org/criminal-law/attorney-general-journal/subpoenaing-out-of-state-witnesses/. Note that many state courts have concluded that the Uniform Act can also be used to obtain documents, as well as evidence. See *id.*

45 *Id.*

46 N.Y. Crim. Proc. L. § 190.40 (Consol. 2020).

47 *Id.* § 190.30.

As described elsewhere in this Manual, information obtained though the grand jury is typically confidential, and prosecutors should take care to comply with secrecy requirements.[48]

III. Selected Legal Issues

Certain legal issues may be more likely to arise in investigations of police officers than in other types of corruption cases. Those issues include: (1) for officers who are also subject to administrative proceedings, complying with *Garrity* v. *New Jersey*; (2) conflicts of interest for prosecutors, particularly those who work directly with the officers in question; and (3) defense counsel conflicts of interest, particularly if those attorneys are retained by a police union or representing multiple defendants. Finally, while this issue does not relate directly to a case against a corrupt police officer, prosecutors should be mindful of potential discovery or disclosure obligations that may arise in cases that relied upon the corrupt officer.

A. Garrity

In *Garrity* v. *New Jersey*, the Supreme Court held that the Fourteenth Amendment prohibits use in subsequent criminal proceedings of statements obtained under threat of removal from office.[49] As explained elsewhere in this Manual,[50] courts have further required prosecutors to show that statements compelled by a threat of termination were not used to obtain evidence to prosecute the speaker.[51] The Supreme Court has also protected officers' rights to assert the Fifth Amendment before commissions investigating police corruption, requiring the reinstatement of an officer who was discharged for doing just that.[52]

---

48 The improper distribution of grand jury material may even lead to prosecution in some states. *See* Chapter 1.2. For additional discussion of grand jury secrecy requirements, see, e.g., Chapter 2.8, Part III(B)(1), Chapter 5.3, Part I.

49 Garrity v. New Jersey, 385 U.S. 493, 500 (1967) (explaining that the rule applies "to all, whether they are policemen or other members of our body politic").

50 *See* Chapter 2.8, Part III(B), Chapter 6.1, Part III(I).

51 Kastigar v. United States, 406 U.S. 441, 442 (1972).

52 Gardner v. Broderick, 392 U.S. 273, 276-79 (1968) (reinstating police officer who was discharged after asserting his Fifth Amendment right not to testify before a commission that

B. *Prosecutor Conflicts of Interest*

The institutional distance between federal authorities and local law enforcement has historically imbued federal corruption investigations with greater independence than similar investigations carried out by local prosecutors. While a local prosecutor who works closely with allegedly corrupt officers may have the purest of intentions, a case charged (or not charged) by a prosecutor who has relied upon the officers' testimony in other cases has legal and optical risks. An alternative to relying on federal authorities to root out local corruption is relying instead on the state attorney general's office or local prosecutors in other jurisdictions. Creating some distance between the investigators and the subjects of the investigation can help assure the public that preexisting relationships are not leading to unduly lenient—or unduly harsh—treatment.

As the final report from the 1970s Knapp Commission, discussed below, noted:

> The close relationship between prosecutors and police also affects public confidence in the district attorneys' willingness to prosecute policemen. Whether or not the district attorneys are in fact reluctant to conduct such prosecutions, large segments of the public believe that they are and this inhibits some people from reporting allegations of police corruption to them.[53]

That acknowledgment was one factor leading the Knapp Commission to recommend that a Special New York Deputy Attorney General, with staff including investigators with no ties to the police department, be empowered to prosecute corruption-related crimes and to "spot[] patterns of corruption."[54]

C. *Defense Counsel Conflicts of Interest*

In some jurisdictions, police unions retain and provide counsel to individual officers.[55] This can pose conflict of interest issues, given the counsel's

---

was investigating police corruption).

53 Knapp Comm'n Report on Police Corruption 256 (1972), http://digitallibrary.usc.edu/cdm/ref/collection/p15799coll69/id/3986.

54 *Id.* at 262.

55 *See, e.g.*, Pirillo v. Takiff, 341 A.2d 896, 904-06 (Pa. 1975) (Fraternal Order of Police providing attorneys to multiple police officers who were subpoenaed to appear before a grand jury).

potentially divided loyalties between the interests of the union—which may, as an example, prefer that an officer not cooperate with the government if that cooperation implicated other officers—and the interests of an individual officer, who may have a more favorable resolution to his case if he cooperates. To protect the right to conflict-free counsel, and to protect the record for the likely appeal if an officer is convicted, prosecutors should be mindful that the attorney representing a police officer may well be provided by a police union or fraternal organization, and should not hesitate to raise that issue with defense counsel and, if necessary, to the court.

There may also be instances where the same lawyer represents multiple officers. The Federal Rules of Criminal Procedure require courts to "promptly inquire about the propriety of joint representation and must personally advise each defendant of the right to the effective assistance of counsel, including separate representation."[56] The presumption is that a conflict will arise. The rule thus further provides "[u]nless there is good cause to believe that no conflict of interest is likely to arise, the court must take appropriate measure to protect each defendant's right to counsel."[57] At least some states have similar statutes.[58]

The American Bar Association warns defense counsel against undertaking such representation, providing that "[e]xcept where necessary to secure counsel for preliminary matters such as initial hearings or applications for bail, a defense counsel (or multiple counsel associated in practice) should not undertake to represent more than one client in the same criminal case."[59]

Defense attorney conflicts of interest also have constitutional dimensions. The U.S. Supreme Court has "recognized that multiple representation of criminal defendants engenders special dangers of which a court must be aware."[60] While allowing one attorney to represent codefendants "is not per se violative of constitutional guarantees of effective assistance of counsel," the Court has concluded that trial judges confronted with the prospect of joint representation must take adequate steps to ascertain whether the conflicts warrant

56 Fed. R. Crim. P. 44(c).

57 *Id.*

58 *See, e.g.*, Del. Sup. Ct. Crim. R. 44(c); Fla. R. Crim. P. 3.150(c).

59 ABA Standards for Criminal Justice: Defense Function s. 4-1.7(d) (Am. Bar Ass'n 2017), https://www.americanbar.org/groups/criminal_justice/standards/DefenseFunctionFourthEdition/.

60 Wheat v. United States, 486 U.S. 153, 159-60 (1988).

separate counsel.[61] The Court has identified some of the issues that can arise, noting that "joint representation of conflicting interests is suspect because of what it tends to prevent the attorney from doing."[62] Specifically, joint representation may "prevent an attorney from challenging the admission of evidence prejudicial to one client but perhaps favorable to another, or from arguing at the sentencing hearing the relative involvement and culpability of his clients in order to minimize the culpability of one by emphasizing that of another."[63] While defendants can waive potential conflicts of interest, these waivers must be knowing, voluntary, and intelligent.[64]

Similar conflicts may arise when a defendant's counsel also represents witnesses in the matter. Courts have, at times, addressed these conflicts of interest by disqualifying counsel, finding that a conflict of interest was not waivable, and reversing convictions. For example, the Pennsylvania Supreme Court precluded attorneys retained by the Fraternal Order of Police from representing multiple law enforcement witnesses before a grand jury.[65] More recently, after officers were convicted in federal court of the brutal assault on Abner Louima, the Second Circuit Court of Appeals concluded that even though the district court held a hearing to advise the defendants of their rights to conflict-free counsel, at which hearing they waived their rights to such counsel, the conflict was unwaivable.[66] Notably, at the district court level, federal prosecutors took the position that the conflict was not waivable, but the trial court disagreed and permitted defense counsel to continue representing the officers through trial.[67]

The Second Circuit concluded the conflict in the Louima case was not waivable because: (1) the law firm had a ten-million-dollar retainer with the Patrolmen's Benevolent Association (PBA); (2) the PBA was facing a civil suit by Louima, the defense of which could shape how the firm represented the defendant in the criminal case; and (3) and the firm had a strong incentive to curry favor with the PBA, given the terms of that retainer.[68] This actual conflict,

---

61 *Id.* at 159-60; *see also* Cuyler v. Sullivan, 446 U.S. 335, 345-47 (1980); Holloway v. Arkansas, 435 U.S. 475, 482 (1978).

62 *Holloway*, 435 U.S. at 490-91.

63 *Id.* at 489-90.

64 *See id.* at 483 n.5.

65 Pirillo v. Takiff, 341 A.2d 896, 906 (Pa. 1975).

66 United States v. Schwarz, 283 F.3d 76, 83 (2d Cir. 2002).

67 *Id.* at 83.

68 *Id.* at 91, 86.

combined with the "lapse in representation" created by the fact the defendant alleged a "plausible alternative defense strategy or tactic [that] might have been pursued" that was "inherently in conflict with or not undertaken due to the" firm's loyalties to the PBA, required a reversal of the conviction.[69]

While prosecutors should consult the case law in their jurisdiction and discuss with a supervisor any motions for a hearing to permit the defendant to waive conflicts of interest or for disqualification of defense counsel, "[i]n appropriate circumstances, a prosecutor may suggest that the defendant's rights are being prejudiced by a common representation."[70] Because of the potentially dire appellate consequences of not inquiring into conflicts,[71] offices should strongly consider establishing standard practices or policies to address defense attorney conflicts of interest. If these do not exist, the head of that office may wish to consider meeting with the bench and the bar to discuss implementing them, as it is in the interest of justice to ensure that defendants are aware of their rights to conflict-free representation. Retrials required by unwaived, or unwaivable, conflicts are not in the interest of courts, defense attorneys, prosecutors, victims, or witnesses.

D. *Disclosure Obligations in Other Cases*

While an in-depth exploration of this issue is outside of the scope of this chapter, prosecutors should also be aware that disclosure obligations may arise in past cases in which a corrupt officer previously testified.[72]

---

69 *Id.* at 92 (quoting United States v. Levy, 25 F.3d 146, 157 (2d Cir. 1994)).

70 Restatement (Third) of the Law Governing Lawyers § 129 cmt. c (Am. Law Inst. 2000); United States v. Curcio, 680 F.2d 881, 885 (2d Cir. 1982) (right to counsel of one's own choice permits defendants to make knowing waiver of conflict). *See also* United States v. Flanagan, 679 F.2d 1072, 1075-76 (3d Cir.1982) (no error to disqualify joint counsel even where defendants understood problem and wanted to waive conflict where defendants were group of police officers accused of misconduct whose stories were likely inconsistent and lawyer might have to cross-examine witnesses differently on behalf of each), *rev'd with directions to dismiss appeal on other grounds*, 465 U.S. 259 (1984) (decision to disqualify lawyer not final, appealable order).

71 *See, e.g.*, Lewis v. State, 757 A.2d 709, 720 (Del. 2000) (reversing conviction where defendants were represented by same attorney, no conflict waiver hearing was held, and there was an actual conflict of interest because, among other things, the quantum of evidence against each defendant differed).

72 *See* Brady v. Maryland, 373 U.S. 83, 87 (1963); Giglio v. United States, 405 U.S. 150, 154 (1972).

In some cases, and in some states, ethical rules may require disclosing information about a corrupt officer to those connected to cases in which he provided important testimony or material evidence. Rule 3.8(g)(1) of the Model Rules of Professional Conduct requires a prosecutor who learns of "new, credible and material evidence creating a reasonable likelihood that a convicted defendant did not commit an offense" for which he was convicted to "promptly disclose that evidence to an appropriate court or authority."[73] If the conviction was obtained in the prosecutor's jurisdiction, the prosecutor is further obligated to "promptly disclose that evidence to the defendant unless a court authorizes delay" and to further investigate if the defendant was convicted of an offense that he did not commit.[74]

Notably, the first requirement to disclose the evidence extends beyond the prosecutor's own jurisdiction, meaning that if—for example—a prosecutor in jurisdiction *A* learned during the course of prosecuting a police officer who previously worked in jurisdiction *B* that the officer had serious credibility issues, the Model Rules might require that prosecutor to notify the "appropriate court or authority" in jurisdiction *B* if that officer's testimony was relied upon to convict a defendant.

Rule 3.8(h) of the Model Rules also requires that if a prosecutor "knows of clear and convincing evidence establishing that a defendant in the prosecutor's jurisdiction" was convicted of an offense he did not commit, the prosecutor "shall seek to remedy the conviction."[75]

As of July 2020, nineteen states had a version of 3.8(g) or 3.8(h), or both, in their rules of professional conduct.[76]

---

73 Model Rules of Prof'l Conduct r. 3.8(g)(1) (Am. Bar Ass'n 2020).

74 *Id.* at r. 3.8(g)(2).

75 *Id.* at r. 3.8(h).

76 Bruce A. Green & Ellen Yaroshefsky, *Should Criminal Justice Reformers Care About Prosecutorial Ethics Rules?*, 58 Duq. L. Rev. 249, 270 n.105 (2020) (Alaska, Arizona, California, Colorado, Delaware, Hawaii, Idaho, Illinois, Massachusetts, Michigan, New Mexico, New York, North Carolina, North Dakota, Tennessee, Washington, West Virginia, Wisconsin, and Wyoming).

IV. Commissions and Consent Decrees

Discrete instances of police corruption can be investigated using the tools, and bearing in mind the potential ethical issues, described above. Rampant police corruption, however, may warrant the use of commissions with powers to engage in broader investigations, to recommend systemic reforms, and to enter into consent decrees that provide for ongoing oversight and assistance. Unlike the commencement of a criminal investigation of a specific target or set of targets, the appropriateness of either of these tools is typically a political decision.

A. *New York City Commissions*

New York City's police department has had several police corruption panels since its formation in the mid-nineteenth century.[77] The three most recent, from the 1970s and 1990s, are summarized below.

1. Knapp Commission: 1970s

The Commission to Investigate Allegations of Police Corruption, which was led by Whitman Knapp—and thus became known as the Knapp Commission—was established by a 1970 Executive Order to:

> 1) investigate the extent of alleged police corruption in the city and any relationship of such alleged corruption to crime and law enforcement; 2) inquire into and evaluate the existing procedures for investigating specific allegations of corruption and present practices designed to prevent corruption and ascertain whether these procedures provide the public with adequate assurance that charges of police corruption are dealt with vigorously, promptly and fairly; 3) recommend improvements in these procedures, additional steps to provide stronger safeguards against corruption, and any improvements in methods of law enforcement which will tend to eliminate police corruption.[78]

---

77 Bob Hennelly, *New York City's Cycle of Police Corruption: Do Reforms Stick, and Does It Matter?*, City & State N.Y. (July 17, 2016), https://www.cityandstateny.com/articles/politics/new-york-city/new-york-city%e2%80%99s-cycle-of-police-corruption-and-reform-do-reforms-stick,-and-does-it-matter.html.

78 Fahy v. Comm'n to Investigate Allegations of Police Corruption, 319 N.Y.S.2d 242, 245

The Knapp Commission followed an April 1970 *New York Times* exposé that detailed allegations of widespread corruption in the New York Police Department, which were shared with reporters by officers who went to the media because "city officials had been remiss in investigating corruption."[79] The article, and others that followed, prompted the mayor to appoint a committee that included the NYPD Police Commissioner, two district attorneys, and two other high-ranking city officials.[80] That committee then recommended that the mayor appoint a commission to "carry forward this investigation," given "magnitude of the task and the difficulties of properly performing the investigation in light of the demanding responsibilities upon the members in connection with their respective offices."[81]

After surviving a legal attack arguing that the mayor did not have the power to appoint it,[82] the Knapp Commission held hearings that revealed the scope of corruption in the police force, led to prosecutions and discipline of some corrupt officers,[83] and resulted in significant reforms.[84] In a lengthy report issued in 1972, it detailed recommendations intended to reduce the opportunities for corrupt activities and to increase the risks of punishment for those who nonetheless strayed.[85] It also described the misconduct and corruption it found, and suggested—as noted above—the creation of a Special Deputy Attorney General position to carry on its work prosecuting corrupt officers and identifying new patterns of corruption.[86] That position was later created by the governor and resulted in several successful prosecutions.[87]

(N.Y. Sup. Ct. 1971); *see also* Kiernan v. New York, 315 N.Y.S.2d 74, 77 (N.Y. Sup. Ct. 1970) (quoting full text of executive order and local law that created the Knapp Commission).

79 David Burnham, *Graft Paid to Police Here Said to Run Into Millions*, N.Y. Times (Apr. 25, 1970), https://www.nytimes.com/1970/04/25/archives/graft-paid-to-police-here-said-to-run-into-millions-survey-links.html.

80 *Kiernan*, 315 N.Y.S.2d at 76-78.

81 *Id.*

82 *Id.* at 80.

83 *See, e.g.*, People v. Archer, 68 A.D.2d 441, 442 (N.Y. App. Div. 1979) (assistant district attorney convicted of accepting bribes after Knapp Commission-related investigation); Gallagher v. Cawley, 43 A.D.2d 931, 931 (N.Y. App. Div. 1974) (suspension of officer who accepted small bribe).

84 Barbara Davidson, *The Knapp Commission Didn't Know It Couldn't Be Done*, N.Y. Times (Jan. 9, 1972), https://www.nytimes.com/1972/01/09/archives/the-knapp-commission-didnt-know-it-couldnt-be-done-the-knapp.html.

85 Knapp Comm'n Report, *supra* note 53, at 17.

86 *Id.* at 262.

87 Ross Galin, *Hon. John F. Keenan, U.S. District Judge for the Southern District of New York*,

2. Mollen Commission: 1990s

The Commission to Investigate Allegations of Police Corruption and the Anti-Corruption Procedures of the Police Department was headed by Milton Mollen,[88] and—perhaps predictably—became known as the Mollen Commission. This commission began twenty years after the Knapp Commission published its report and was given the mandate "to investigate allegations of corruption, the effectiveness of the police department procedures to prevent and detect corruption and to recommend improvements and reforms in the existing procedures."[89]

Like the Knapp Commission before it, the Mollen Commission survived a legal attack on its right to exist,[90] resulted in charges against corrupt officers,[91] and issued a comprehensive report that recommended certain reforms.[92]

In its report, the Mollen Commission found the 1990s corruption was different than what Whitman Knapp and his team found in the 1970s: "Unlike the situation a generation ago . . . the vast majority of New York City police officers are honest and hard-working."[93] However, the corruption that did exist was "more serious and threatening than ever before."[94] The Mollen Commission reported that corruption

---

The Federal Lawyer 21, 23 (June 2016), https://www.fedbar.org/wp-content/uploads/2019/10/Keenan-Hon-John-F-pdf-2.pdf; Leslie Maitland, *Second Deputy Inspector Indicted by Jury Studying Bribery of Police*, N.Y. Times (Mar. 9, 1977), https://www.nytimes.com/1977/03/09/archives/second-deputy-inspector-indicted-by-jury-studying-bribery-of-police.html. *But see* People v. Di Falco, 44 N.Y.2d 482, 486-88 (N.Y. 1978) (concluding grant of authority for deputy attorney general was limited, and dismissing indictment of matter outside of that authority because deputy attorney general was not authorized to appear before the grand jury under New York law).

88 Joseph P. Fried, *Milton Mollen, 97, Dies; Investigated Police Corruption in New York*, N.Y. Times (Aug. 15, 2017), https://www.nytimes.com/2017/08/15/nyregion/milton-mollen-dead-investigated-police-corruption-in-new-york-city.html.

89 Kelly v. Dinkins, 590 N.Y.S.2d 166, 167 (N.Y. Sup. Ct. 1992) (concluding Mollen Commission was within mayor's power to create).

90 *Id.* at 168.

91 *See, e.g.*, United States v. DiLorenzo, No. 94 Cr. 303 (AGS), 1995 U.S. Dist. LEXIS 4539, *4 n.1 (S.D.N.Y. Apr. 10, 1995).

92 Milton Mollen, Comm'n to Investigate Allegations of Police Corruption and the Anti-Corruption Procedures of the Police Dep't, City of New York, Comm'n Rep. 110-11 (1994), https://archive.org/details/MollenCommissionNYPD.

93 *Id.* at 1.

94 *Id.* at 1-2.

> flourished in parts of our City not only because of opportunity and greed, but because of a police culture that exalts loyalty over integrity; because of the silence of honest officers who fear the consequences of 'ratting' on another cop no matter how grave the crime; because of willfully blind supervisors who fear the consequences of a corruption scandal more than corruption itself; because of the demise of the principle of accountability that makes all commanders responsible for fighting corruption in their commands; because of a hostility and alienation between the police and community in certain precincts which breeds an 'Us versus Them' mentality; and because for years the New York City Police Department abandoned its responsibility to insure the integrity of its members.[95]

Rather than taking bribes to look the other way, the Mollen Commission wrote, corrupt officers were themselves "acting as criminals, especially in connection with the drug trade," and leaders in the police department were more concerned with bad press if these misdeeds were uncovered than with actually rooting out the corrupt officers preying on the communities they had promised to serve.[96] The Commission "determined that the NYPD's corruption controls had virtually collapsed and that the NYPD had mostly abandoned its responsibility to police itself."[97] It recommended, among other things, a permanent, independent police commission with subpoena power that would continue investigating any police corruption.[98]

---

95 *Id.* at 2.

96 *Id.* at 2-6. A successful civil case brought around the time of the Mollen Commission by an officer who was harassed by other officers after she reported corruption describes what might happen to those who breach the "blue wall of silence." White-Ruiz v. New York, 983 F. Supp. 365, 368-69 (S.D.N.Y. 1997) (detailing slashed tires, shunning, graffiti, and directives from the precinct commander not to report "minor misconduct" committed by other officers and to transfer to a new precinct because of the hostility she faced after reporting another officer's misdeeds).

97 Mayor of New York v. Council of New York, 696 N.Y.S.2d 761, 763 (N.Y. Sup. Ct. 1999), *rev'd*, 280 A.D.2d 380 (N.Y. App. Div. 2001).

98 *Id.*

3. New York City Commission to Combat Police Corruption: Ongoing

Less than a year after the Mollen Commission's final report was issued, the mayor of New York issued an executive order creating the New York City Commission to Combat Police Corruption.[99] Since 1995, the Commission has monitored all aspects of NYPD corruption control policies and procedures.[100] It has the power to review NYPD documents and, as of spring 2021, issued annual reports as well as twenty-five substantive reports that look more closely at specific areas of concern.[101] All reports are made available to the public through the Commission's website.[102] The substantive reports address a variety of topics, including how the NYPD handles disciplinary cases;[103] deaths in custody;[104] the NYPD policies on false statements;[105] and how the NYPD completes background screening of new applicants.[106]

The various commissions that have been used in the New York City area—including the ongoing work and analysis by the New York City Commission to Combat Police Corruption—may provide a useful precedent for

---

99 *About the Commission*, NYC Comm'n to Combat Police Corruption, https://www1.nyc.gov/site/ccpc/about/about.page (llast visited Apr. 15, 2021). *See also* New York City Charter §§ 450-58 (July 2004), http://www.nyc.gov/html/records/pdf/section%201133_citycharter.pdf.

100 *Commission Mandate*, NYC Comm'n to Combat Police Corruption, https://www1.nyc.gov/site/ccpc/about/mandate.page (last visited Apr. 15, 2021).

101 *Id.*

102 *Id.*

103 Richard J. Davis, Comm'n to Combat Police Corruption, City of New York, New York City Police Dep't's Prosecution of Disciplinary Cases (2000), https://www1.nyc.gov/assets/ccpc/downloads/pdf/The-NYPD-s-Prosecution-of-Disciplinary-Cases-July-2000.pdf.

104 Mark Pomerantz, Comm'n to Combat Police Corruption, City of New York, Police Reporting in "Death in Custody" Cases (2004), https://www1.nyc.gov/assets/ccpc/downloads/pdf/Police-Reporting-in-Death-In-Custody-Cases-November-2004.pdf.

105 Richard J. Davis, Comm'n to Combat Police Corruption, City of New York, New York City Police Dep't's Disciplinary System: A Review of the Dep't's December 1996 False Statement Policy (1999), https://www1.nyc.gov/assets/ccpc/downloads/pdf/The-NYPDs-Disciplinary-System-A-Review-of-the-Departments-False-Statement-Policy-August-1999.pdf.

106 Mark Pomerantz, Comm'n to Combat Police Corruption, City of New York, Review of the Background Screening Process of New Recruits (2005), https://www1.nyc.gov/assets/ccpc/downloads/pdf/Review-of-the-Background-Screening-Process-of-New-Recruits-February-2005.pdf.

addressing systemic issues that might allow for or contribute to corruption in a police department.

B. *Illinois Attorney General Office's Consent Decree: 2018*

While it is more common for the USDOJ to enter consent decrees with state and local government entities, at least one AGO has entered into a consent decree with a local police department, and two others have sought injunctive relief to address systemic misconduct by police.[107]

In 2018, the Illinois AGO and the Chicago Police Department agreed the department would implement significant reforms.[108] The history leading up to the decree is perhaps unique. On January 13, 2017, the USDOJ issued a report that found "systemic abuses by the Chicago Police Department against minorities" and called for courts to oversee changes to the department's practices and policies.[109] Under a new administration, however, the USDOJ policy on entering consent decrees changed.[110]

---

107 *See* Chapter 6.2, Part II, which describes cases brought by the Pennsylvania and New York AGOs. Pennsylvania v. Porter, 659 F.2d 306, 311 (3d Cir. 1981) (en banc); New York v. Town of Wallkill, 01-Civ-0364 (CM), 2001 U.S. Dist. LEXIS 13364, at *9 (S.D.N.Y. Mar. 16, 2001).

108 *Consent Decree Documents*, Chi. Police Consent Decree, https://chicagopoliceconsentdecree.org/resources/ (last visited Apr. 15, 2021); *Chicago Police Announce Path Forward in Fulfilling Consent Decree, But Do Not Address Complaints About Missed Deadlines*, CBS Chi. (Aug. 10, 2020), https://chicago.cbslocal.com/2020/08/10/chicago-police-announce-path-forward-in-fulfilling-consent-decree-but-do-not-address-complaints-about-missed-deadlines/. For additional discussion of this case, *see* Chapter 6.2, Part II(C).

109 *Chicago Police Announce Path Forward*, *supra* note 108; Julie Bosman & Mitch Smith, *Chicago Police Routinely Trampled on Civil Rights, Justice Dept. Says*, N.Y. Times (Jan. 13, 2017), https://www.nytimes.com/2017/01/13/us/chicago-police-justice-department-report.html; U.S. Dep't of Justice Civil Rights Div. & U.S. Att'y's Office, N. Dist. of Ill., Investigation of the Chi. Police Dep't (2017), https://www.justice.gov/opa/file/925846/download.

110 Sheryl Gay Stolberg & Eric Lichtblau, *Sweeping Federal Review Could Affect Consent Decrees Nationwide*, N.Y. Times (Apr. 3, 2017), https://www.nytimes.com/2017/04/03/us/justice-department-jeff-sessions-baltimore-police.html. That change in policy was described in a memorandum, which reflected then-Attorney General Jeff Sessions's long-held views about consent decrees. Memorandum from the U.S. Attorney General to Heads of Civil Litigating Components, U.S. Attorneys (Nov. 7, 2018), https://www.justice.gov/opa/press-release/file/1109681/download; Jacey Fortin, *Jeff Sessions Limited Consent Decrees. What About the Police Departments Already Under Reform?*, N.Y. Times (Nov. 15, 2018), https://www.nytimes.com/2018/11/15/us/sessions-consent-decrees-police.html.

In late August 2017, the Illinois AGO filed a lawsuit against the Chicago Police Department that sought to require the department to implement the changes recommended in the USDOJ report issued earlier that year.[111]

In early 2019, a consent decree was entered by the federal judge overseeing the litigation. The 236-page document addressed issues including community policing; use of force; recruitment, hiring, and promotion; officer wellness; and training and supervision.[112] It provided for the appointment of an independent monitor to carry out the duties, responsibilities, and authority conferred by the consent decree, which included reviewing policies and procedures.[113] The monitor would report to the court and conduct the reviews, audits, and assessments contemplated by the decree, and, with his or her team, have a budget of up to $2.85 million per year.[114]

In addition to the consent decree, the parties entered into a separate Memorandum of Agreement (MOA) with community organizations.[115] The monitor was required to, among other things, meet with the community organizations who were part of the MOA, and to hold public meetings to explain the reports and hear "community perspectives on police interactions."[116]

The Illinois AGO established a website, chicagopoliceconsentdecree.org, to provide access to the consent decree, describe the monitor selection process, and provide information of interest to the public.[117] The monitor also established a website that provides information about the oversight process, including the actual reports filed by the monitor.[118]

---

111 Mitch Smith, *Illinois Attorney General Sues Chicago Over Police Practices*, N.Y. Times (Aug. 29, 2017), https://www.nytimes.com/2017/08/29/us/chicago-police-consent-decree.html.

112 Consent Decree at i-vi, Illinois v. Chicago, No. 17-cv-6260 (N.D. Ill. Jan. 31, 2019), https://www.chicago.gov/content/dam/city/depts/cpb/supp_info/ConsentDecreeComplete.pdf.

113 *Id.* at 186, 194-95.

114 *Id.* at 186, 189.

115 *Id.* at 203; Memorandum of Agreement Between the Office of the Illinois Attorney General and the City of Chicago and *Campbell v. City of Chicago* Plaintiffs and *Communities United v. City of Chicago* Plaintiffs (Mar. 2018), http://chicagopoliceconsentdecree.org/wp-content/uploads/2019/05/Executed_MOA.pdf.

116 Consent Decree at 203, *Illinois*, No. 17-cv-6260.

117 *Reforming Chicago's Police Dep't*, Chicago Police Consent Decree, http://chicagopoliceconsentdecree.org/ (last visited Apr. 15, 2021).

118 *Independent Monitoring Team*, Chicago Police Dep't Consent Decree, https://cpdmonitoringteam.com/ (last visited Apr. 15, 2021). For more on monitors, see Chapter 1.6, Part III(B).

In appropriate circumstances where widespread corruption or other policing issues are present in a police department, other AGOs may wish to consider the precedent set by the Illinois AGO. The publicly-available materials provide a roadmap for such offices to use in assessing whether this approach is right for them.

Conclusion

Police corruption can be investigated with many of the tools used in other corruption cases, some of which provide useful leverage to break the so-called "blue wall of silence." Prosecutors should be aware of the opportunities and limitations when using various means to secure the testimony of officers and conspirators.

Given the important role officers play in investigating other criminal cases, prosecutors should be sensitive about conflicts of interest and the potential appearance of impropriety if officers with whom they work are alleged to be corrupt. Local prosecutors should be willing to recuse and refer to another prosecutor—including the state AGO—when referrals are more likely to maintain public trust in the process. Particularly in areas where police unions provide attorneys for their members, prosecutors should be aware of defense counsel conflicts of interest and seek waivers or, when necessary, disqualification.

Finally, systemic corruption may call for a systemic solution. Commissions and consent decrees may be useful tools to explore when individual cases alone appear to be insufficient to address pervasive police corruption.

Section Two

Investigating Corruption Cases

This section looks closely at the investigation of corruption cases, with tools and tips that are equally useful for other complex cases.[1] As in Section One, the chapters overlap, and some authors touch on the same concepts.

The section starts with a chapter by Steve Solow, who was one of the authors of the American Bar Association's Criminal Justice Standards for Prosecutorial Investigations, and Johnjerica Hodge. These authors describe those standards, discuss the role of the prosecutor in a corruption prosecution, and note the utility of a thoughtful investigative plan. Next, Carrie Cohen provides more detailed guidance about how to think through the covert and overt stages of a corruption investigation. In two detailed chapters, Wesley Cheng and Michael Chu discuss legal and practical requirements for obtaining wiretaps and online evidence—powerful tools that can generate important proof at trial but require careful use. In the next chapter, Dan Cort and Stacy Aronowitz discuss the utility of covert actors like undercover officers and informants, as well as some of the potential legal and ethical issues that can arise in undercover operations.

Next, Robert Shapiro and Daniel Pietragallo describe how, in appropriate circumstances, investigators and prosecutors from multiple jurisdictions can

---

1 One area that we do not cover in this Manual that may be important to state prosecutors is the Uniform Act to Secure the Attendance of Witnesses from Without a State in Criminal Proceedings, which provides a mechanism to require an out-of-state witness to testify at grand jury or court proceedings. NAAG has published guidance on the state enactments of this Act on its website. Darrell E. White II, *Subpoenaing Out-of-State Witnesses in Criminal Proceedings: A Step-by-Step Guide*, Attorney Gen. J. (May 18, 2021), https://www.naag.org/criminal-law/attorney-general-journal/subpoenaing-out-of-state-witnesses/.

work together on corruption cases. Christine Hoffman then provides a comprehensive overview of the government-affiliated entities that are available to assist state investigators through training, technical assistance, or other resources. The last chapter, by Brian Kane and Brenda Bauges, discusses concurrent proceedings and analyzes the government's powers, obligations, and challenges when engaging in multiple cases arising out of the same underlying facts.

These chapters contemplate prosecutors overseeing, shaping, or directing investigations. Prosecutors should be aware that actions taken during an investigation are entitled only to qualified—rather than absolute—immunity,[2] and litigation has occurred as to whether prosecutors may ethically oversee undercover operations involving deception.[3] Despite these risks, this approach has been encouraged by the ABA and has been a part of federal prosecutors' typical practice for years.[4] It is the best way to ensure that investigations are effective, lawful, and efficient. Not every bad act by a politician will violate a statute, and prosecutors can refocus, or end, an investigation that is going down a path that will not lead to charges. Prosecutors are also sensitive to legal issues and can shape investigations to reduce the risk of improperly infringing on targets' constitutional rights. Prosecutors can address potential admissibility issues as the investigation progresses, so that the evidence gathered will be available to introduce at an eventual trial. Overseeing the investigation also makes sense as a matter of strategy: Nothing prepares a prosecutor for trial like being part of the team that built the case.

---

2 *See* Chapter 2.1, Part II.
3 *See* Chapter 2.5, Part V.
4 *See* Chapter 2.1, Part I.

Chapter 2.1

The Prosecutor's Role in Anticorruption Investigations

Steven P. Solow, Johnjerica Hodge

Steven P. Solow is a partner in the litigation practice at Baker Botts LLP. He represents organizations and individuals in complex white collar and civil cases, internal investigations, compliance assessments, and corporate governance matters. He previously served as Chief of the Environmental Crimes Section at the United States Department of Justice, and before that was a prosecutor with the New York State Organized Crime Task Force. He has also been a law professor at both the University of Maryland School of Law and at the Elisabeth Haub School of Law at Pace University. In addition to his work as a litigator, he serves as a court-appointed monitor over a multinational corporation.

Johnjerica Hodge is a partner on the appeals and critical motions team at Katten Muchin Rosenman LLP. She concentrates her practice on internal and government investigations, corporate compliance, and appellate litigation. Prior to joining Katten, she served as a clerk for Chief Judge Carl E. Stewart of the Fifth Circuit Court of Appeals.

The authors note with appreciation the contributions of Leslie Couvillion, an attorney at Baker Botts LLP, in the preparation of this chapter.

Introduction

This chapter offers the prosecutor engaged in the important work of anticorruption prosecutions two guides: first, practical guidance for the investigative phase of a matter; and second, a brief overview of potential individual civil liability for prosecutors involved in the investigation.[1] Particularly in complex cases, prosecutors are often involved at the earliest phases of these investigations.[2] The prosecutor's involvement is often legally mandated—for example, when seeking the use of investigative tools such as search warrants. But more importantly, the prosecutor also provides legal and ethical guidance to support decision making during the investigation. Doing so both supports the investigation and serves to maintain the broad legitimacy of the criminal justice system. Equally true, the failure to fulfill this role appropriately can reduce the likelihood of the investigation's success, undermine the public's trust in the justice system, and increase the risk of individual civil liability for the prosecutor.

I. The Role of Prosecutors Involved in Anticorruption Investigations

Those who commit corruption offenses work hard to keep their crimes a secret. Victims of these crimes frequently do not even know that they have

---

1 As discussed below, prosecutors involved in an investigation may have only qualified immunity from civil lawsuits, unlike absolute immunity during the judicial phase of a criminal case. In 2020 and 2021, the United States Congress began considering legislation that may substantially change the qualified immunity doctrine. *See* George Floyd Justice in Policing Act of 2021, H.R. 1280, 117th Cong. (as passed, Mar. 3, 2021); Ending Qualified Immunity Act, H.R. 7085, 116th Cong. (as introduced, June 4, 2020).

2 This interchange during the oral argument in *Pottawattamie County* v. *McGhee*, 558 U.S. 1103 (2010), between the esteemed Supreme Court litigator Paul Clement and Justice Samuel Alito shows that the United States Supreme Court understands the modern role of prosecutors:

> MR. CLEMENT: And in a lot of cases prosecutors don't even get involved until after probable cause, until after there have been arrests, something like that. And in those cases --
>
> JUSTICE ALITO: That's an entirely false picture of the way any sophisticated prosecution is handled today, completely false.

Transcript of Oral Argument at 32, Pottawattamie County v. McGhee, 558 U.S. 1103 (2010) (No. 08-1065), https://www.supremecourt.gov/oral_arguments/argument_transcripts/2009/08-1065.pdf.

been victimized. Corruptly awarded government contracts may be invisible, but the harm to the public is real—from overpaying for a bridge, to receiving shoddy work or goods—and, when the wrongdoing is revealed, it undermines public trust and confidence in government. For these reasons, and others, anti-corruption work is vital to the public and can be deeply satisfying work for a prosecutor.

During the judicial stage of a criminal matter, as the Supreme Court in *Berger* v. *United States* explained, a prosecutor is "the representative not of an ordinary party to a controversy, but of a sovereignty whose obligation to govern impartially is as compelling as its obligation to govern at all."[3] Therefore, the prosecutor's interest is not in winning a case, but in ensuring "that justice shall be done."[4] One problem with this guidance from the Supreme Court is that it is somewhat scant on specifics.[5] The American Bar Association, through its *Standards for Criminal Justice: Prosecutorial Investigations* (the Standards), seeks to extend the Supreme Court's message to the investigative stage and to provide more specific guidance as to how to seek justice.[6] The Standards are aimed at maximizing the positive role the prosecutor can play in an investigation, while managing the challenges and risks of that role.

That this guidance applies to the investigative stage of a criminal matter is crucial, for the justice seeking role of the prosecutor is of even greater importance at that stage. As Justice Robert H. Jackson explained, the "most dangerous power of the prosecutor" is the investigative power because it lacks judicial oversight and is susceptible to abuse.[7] A prosecutor can abuse the investigative power by choosing "some person whom he dislikes or desires to embarrass, or select[ing] some group of unpopular persons and then look[ing] for an offense."[8] Justice requires a prosecutor to work in the opposite direction, by first

---

3 Berger v. United States, 295 U.S. 78, 88 (1935) (holding that defendant was entitled to a new trial based on the cumulative effects of prosecutor's misconduct).

4 *Id.*

5 David Alan Sklansky, *The Nature and Function of Prosecutorial Power*, 106 J. Crim. L. & Criminology 473, 479-80 (2016) (observing that, while the words of the *Berger* opinion are "hallowed texts," they are not "paragons of specificity").

6 *See* ABA Standards for Criminal Justice: Prosecutorial Investigations 5 (Am. Bar Ass'n 2014).

7 Robert H. Jackson, *The Federal Prosecutor*, 31 J. Crim. L. & Criminology 3, 5 (1940). This short speech by Justice Jackson should be required reading for every prosecutor, and not just federal ones. *See id.*

8 *Id.*

identifying that a crime has occurred and "then looking for the man who has committed it."[9] The investigating prosecutor "is not a member of the adversary process and should perform a radically different role" from that performed by an adversary.[10] "During the investigation . . . [t]he role of the investigating attorney is not that of an advocate but that of a neutral fact finder."[11]

The introduction to the Standards explains that "we do not expect prosecutors to be typical advocates. We expect them to hold truth, justice, and mercy more sacred than winning."[12] Prosecutors, particularly during the investigation, serve "the public, not victims and not the police."[13] That obligation to the public drives "what cases they bring and how they investigate and prosecute them."[14] As discussed in the following sections, in order to maximize the benefits of prosecutorial involvement in criminal investigations and minimize the risks of such involvement, the Standards provide guidance as to managing relationships with law enforcement and other parties, strategically considering which investigative tools to use, and how to solve problems as they arise in an investigation.

A. *A Prosecutor Manages Relationships with Law Enforcement, Other Parties, and the Public*

In all phases of a matter, "[t]he prosecutor's client is the public, not particular government agencies or victims."[15] Moreover, it is the prosecutor's duty to seek to ensure that a criminal investigation is not based upon premature beliefs as to guilt or innocence, and that investigations are not prompted by improper political or discriminatory considerations.[16] To help make these ideals a working reality, the Standards provide practical approaches. For example, consistent with the National District Attorneys Association's *National*

---

9 *Id.*

10 Roberta K. Flowers, *A Code of Their Own: Updating the Ethics Codes to Include the Non-Adversarial Roles of Federal Prosecutors*, 37 B.C. L. Rev. 923, 934 (1996).

11 *Id.*

12 ABA Standards for Criminal Justice: Prosecutorial Investigations 1 (Am. Bar Ass'n 2014).

13 *Id.*

14 *Id.*

15 *Id.* at s. 26-1.2(b).

16 *Id.* at s. 26-1.2(d)(ii) (listing improper discriminatory considerations as including race, ethnicity, religion, gender, sexual orientation, political beliefs, age, and economic status).

Prosecution Standards,[17] the Standards discuss the role prosecutors should play in providing and facilitating training for police and investigators, as well as the value of developing an investigative plan.[18]

1. Investigative Plans

An investigative plan in an anticorruption investigation can be a key tool for the prosecutor. The development of such a plan helps provide clarity as to the approach to the investigation, and can provide a statement of the methods and means to be used, as well as an agreement to evaluate the status of the investigation regularly.[19] The Standards discuss whether the creation of such a plan creates a discoverable document, and ways in which the process of developing a search warrant or Title III affidavit can serve as a substitute for a written investigative plan.[20]

The Standards identify four basic steps for developing an investigative plan.[21] The first step is to discuss the investigative predicate—that is, to assess the basis for conducting the investigation.[22] This can include a review of information from various sources, including law enforcement, public records, databases and elsewhere.[23] The second step is to establish the goals of the investigation, which may include prosecution, but also may include asset recovery,[24] use of civil remedies,[25] development of informants,[26] or identification of structural or institutional changes to limit the vulnerability to future criminal conduct.[27] The third, and most difficult, step is to assess potential investigative approaches.[28] Various approaches to pursuing the investigation should be con-

---

17 Nat'l Dist. Att'ys Ass'n, National Prosecution Standards ss. 2-5.3, 2-5.4, 3-1.1 to 3-1.6 (3d ed. 2009).

18 ABA Standards on Prosecutorial Investigations s. 26-1.3.

19 *Id.*

20 *Id.* s. 26-1.3(e) cmt. & n.47.

21 *Id.* s. 26-1.3(e) cmt.

22 *Id.*

23 *Id.*

24 For further discussion see Chapter 6.4.

25 For further discussion see Chapter 6.2.

26 For further discussion see Chapter 2.5.

27 ABA Standards on Prosecutorial Investigations s. 26-1.3(e) cmt. For discussion of structural and institutional changes, see *infra* note 53 and accompanying text. For discussion of systemic reforms in the context of police corruption, see Chapter 1.8, Part IV.

28 ABA Standards on Prosecutorial Investigations s. 26-1.3(e) cmt. This may also include thinking about the timing of covert and overt stages of the investigation. For a closer look at these issues, see Chapter 2.2.

sidered, as well as the likely results of each approach and the resources they may require.[29] Finally, the fourth step is to consider legal issues likely to arise during the investigation.[30] Completing these four steps is not the end of the planning process, however. Any investigative plan requires constant review and revision as the investigation proceeds.[31]

Investigative plans and planning can play a further role in formalizing internal communication between the prosecutor and investigators about the progress and challenges that arise in a complex anticorruption investigation.[32] Prosecutors engaged in a complex investigation may face challenges in managing the relationship with investigators. Even an experienced prosecutor may be paired with investigators who bring more years of experience to bear. Moreover, investigators almost always work at the direction of their agency and may not consider the prosecutor's views as controlling over their actions.

With the many time demands on all involved in law enforcement work, critical pathways of communication can be lost. This may lead to a loss of goodwill with colleagues. More seriously, it can lead to wasted effort, imprudent investigative steps, and significant problems. The investigative plan, and its regular review, can provide the structure to enhance the likelihood of effective communication within the investigative team.

2. Status of Victims, Witnesses, Subjects, and Targets in the Anticorruption Investigation

The inward looking aspects of the Standards discussed above are coupled with guidance on outward facing roles, including those related to relationships with and towards those identified as potential victims, witnesses, subjects, and targets, as well as contacts with people represented by counsel. The Standards recognize that, in the course of an investigation, a person may be an offender, a victim, and a witness.[33] Choosing someone's status is a complex endeavor. A constant theme throughout the Standards is the recommendation that the prosecutor engaged in an investigation should seek counsel and advice from

---

29 ABA Standards on Prosecutorial Investigations s. 26-1.3(e) cmt.
30 *Id.*
31 *Id.*
32 *Id.* s. 26-1.3(f) & cmt.
33 *Id.* s. 26-1.4(a), (b) & cmt.

supervisors and other trusted sources when making significant investigation decisions.[34]

Particularly in the context of anticorruption investigations, the public may be aware of and interested in the case. As the Standards state: "At times it is unavoidable that a victim, witness, or target will be identified [publicly] by the investigative process. But prosecutorial press conferences during investigations can be avoided entirely, and leaks by the government are abhorrent."[35] The Standards also note that, in limited circumstances, a prosecutor may make a statement "to remove unfair stigma . . . [or to] announce that an investigation has concluded and no charges will be brought."[36]

B. *A Prosecutor Strategically Considers Investigative Tools*

As addressed in Part II of the Standards,[37] a prosecutor carefully considers specific investigative techniques to use or avoid.[38] These include undercover agents, informants, subpoenas, arrests, grand juries, electronic surveillance, and technologically assisted physical surveillance, among other techniques.[39] The office of the prosecutor may also provide training, oversight, and other means of communication to enhance the role of the prosecutor in investigations.[40] The prosecutor considers carefully the costs and benefits of particular investigative tools and techniques as well as the costs and benefits of the entire investigation in light of "among other things, the nature of the criminal activity

---

34 *Id.* ss. 26-1.2(e) & cmt., 26-2.15.

35 *Id.* s. 26-1.5(a)-(b) cmt.

36 *Id.* The decision of then-FBI Director James Comey to state publicly that he had reopened an investigation into the private email server Hillary Clinton used as Secretary of State is a notable example of a failure to consider the Standards' admonition that, in most instances while an investigation is ongoing, "the government seek to do its work in confidence until . . . public adversarial proceedings begin." *See id.*; *see also* Greg Price, *James Comey Not "Biased" in Clinton Investigation But "Dramatically Departed from FBI Norms," DOJ IG Report Concludes*, NEWSWEEK (June 14, 2018), https://www.newsweek.com/comey-biased-clinton-doj-ig-977266. For further discussion of media relations, see Chapter 5.3.

37 *See* ABA STANDARDS ON PROSECUTORIAL INVESTIGATIONS ss. 26-2.1 to 26-2.18.

38 *See id.* s. 26-2.2.

39 *Id.* ss. 26-2.3 to 26-2.12. These techniques are also discussed in this Manual. *See* Chapter 2.5 (undercover agents and informants), Chapter 1.8, Part II(B) (grand jury), Chapter 2.3 (electronic surveillance).

40 ABA STANDARDS ON PROSECUTORIAL INVESTIGATIONS s. 26-2.15 & cmt.

as well as the impact of conducting the investigation on other enforcement priorities and resources."[41]

This guidance about weighing costs and benefits of the entire investigation captures a theme of the Standards. In commencing an investigation, prosecutors should "be considering the costs of their actions to all members of the public they serve,"[42] and should "be explicit and think more broadly in their assumptions, goals, and cost assessments."[43] Thus, while Part II of the Standards contains much useful guidance on specific investigative techniques and tools, the overriding message for the prosecutor is that the decision to pursue one investigation is a decision, tacitly, not to pursue others.[44] Given the intense demands in time and other resources in an anticorruption case, Part II seeks to help the prosecutor evaluate whether a particular investigation is worthy of initiation and pursuit.

C. *A Prosecutor Resolves Potential Misconduct and Other Problems*

Prosecutors also have the difficult, but critical, responsibility to address and resolve instances of misconduct on the part of those around them. As in many other areas where concerns about misconduct are raised, the Standards make clear that, consistent with the broader duty to report misconduct,[45] prosecutors who have reason to suspect misconduct should promptly notify their supervisors.[46] The commentary to the Standard on suspected law enforcement misconduct seeks to assure line prosecutors that, when in doubt, and without hesitation, they should notify and seek guidance from supervisors when they have questions about any investigation activity.[47] Consistent with the obligations of a prosecutor, decisions regarding concerns about law enforcement misconduct must be made "without regard to adverse consequences on pending cases or investigations."[48] Similarly, prosecutors should report suspected mis-

41 *Id.* s. 26-2.1(c)(vi).

42 Rory K. Little, *Proportionality as an Ethical Precept for Prosecutors in Their Investigative Role*, 68 Fordham L. Rev. 723, 759 (1999).

43 *Id.* at 758-59.

44 *See* ABA Standards on Prosecutorial Investigations s. 26-2.1(c)(vi).

45 *Id.* s. 26-3.1. *See also* Chapter 5.1, Part I.

46 ABA Standards on Prosecutorial Investigations s. 26-3.1.

47 *Id.* s. 26-3.1 cmt.

48 *Id.* s. 26-3.1(f).

conduct by other prosecutors, judges, witnesses, informants, and jurors, as well as reporting suspected evidence that may have been illegally obtained, whether by law enforcement or private parties.[49]

Two additional issues of significant concern in anticorruption investigations may become the prosecutor's obligation to resolve. First, a prosecutor may need to respond to political pressure and consider the impact of criminal investigations on the political process.[50] Second, the prosecutor may need to review and oversee criminal investigations by government agencies and officials.[51] The Standards state unequivocally that the prosecutor should not allow political pressure to influence the conduct, focus, duration, or outcome of a criminal investigation.[52]

While each anticorruption case must be evaluated on its own, the prosecutor who investigates complex cases is uniquely positioned to identify the institutional flaws and practices that may (even unintentionally) facilitate corruption offenses or make certain institutions or programs vulnerable to corruption. In addition to the guidance provided by the Standards, the prosecutor engaged in anticorruption cases may consider whether and how to shift from being a sophisticated investigator and prosecutor of individual cases, to being one who takes the "lead in developing and implementing strategies for crime control."[53] While this chapter began by noting the satisfaction that can come from pursuing corruption offenses, even successful efforts at prosecuting corruption cases may be inadequate to the task of controlling some systemic criminal activity.[54] Beyond seeking justice in just one case, the prosecutor may be uniquely positioned to identify the regulatory changes, structural changes, or changes in public reporting and monitoring that may lead to long-term or systemic solutions to corruption-related problems.[55]

---

49 *Id.* ss. 26-3.1 to 26-3.5.

50 *See id.* s. 26-3.6.

51 *See id.* s. 26-3.7.

52 *Id.* s. 26-3.6(a).

53 Ronald Goldstock, *The Prosecutor as Problem Solver*, *in* HANDBOOK OF ORGANIZED CRIME IN THE UNITED STATES 431, 440 (Robert J. Kelly et al. eds., 1994). In a short but useful article, the former director of the New York State Organized Crime Task Force, Ronald Goldstock, lays out the basis for the prosecutor developing and implementing strategies for long-term crime control. *Id.* at 440-44. For further discussion of systemic reforms in the context of police corruption, see Chapter 1.8, Part IV.

54 Goldstock, *supra* note 53, at 431.

55 *See* RONALD GOLDSTOCK, N.Y. STATE ORGANIZED CRIME TASK FORCE, CORRUPTION

D. *Overall Benefits and Risks of Prosecutor Involvement in Investigations*

The Standards are premised on the belief that the role of the prosecutor provides clear benefits in complex criminal investigations.[56] The prosecutor's involvement in an investigation can increase the likelihood that:

- Investigations will be conducted in a manner consistent with applicable legal rules, such that evidence obtained will be legally admissible;
- The administration of justice will be fair and impartial; and
- If a prosecution is brought, the evidence will be sufficient to obtain, and sustain, a conviction.[57]

The Standards also recognize that involvement at the investigative phase of a criminal matter also presents risk for the prosecutor to manage.[58] These risks include:

- That the investment of time and resources at the investigative phase will lead to premature or inaccurate conclusions as to guilt or innocence;
- That the potential notoriety of an anticorruption case will inappropriately influence the desire to push a case forward; and
- That, despite a good faith belief in the valid ends of addressing corruption, various pressures and complexities of the investigation can create

---

and Racketeering in the New York City Construction Industry 1 (1990). Among other things, public reporting and efforts by the New York State Organized Crime Task Force led to the creation of the New York City School Construction Authority (NYCSCA). *See* Selwyn Raab, *52 Companies Banned from School Construction Bids,* N.Y. Times (Aug. 27, 1991), https://www.nytimes.com/1991/08/27/nyregion/52-companies-banned-from-school-construction-bids.html. Rather than bringing individual corruption cases, the NYCSCA was able to eliminate problematic bidders for lucrative public contracts. For example, the NYCSCA banned fifty-two companies from bidding for contracts based upon, among other things, connections to organized crime groups. *See id.* For further discussion of bid rigging and union corruption, see Chapters 1.3 and 1.6, respectively.

56 *See* ABA Standards on Prosecutorial Investigations 1.

57 *Id.*

58 *Id.*

a risk that some members of the investigation team will resort to invalid means.[59]

Because anticorruption investigations may involve matters of strong, even extraordinary, public interest and awareness, the role and judgment of the prosecutor may be subject to intense scrutiny. Defense counsel in such cases may be attorneys who are former prosecutors (if not former anticorruption prosecutors). They may have experience and perspective equal to or greater than the prosecutors, and may well believe that their best defense is an offense that puts the government's case (and conduct of the investigation) on trial.[60] The approaches outlined above are designed to help prosecutors successfully navigate their way in this important work.

II. Limits on Prosecutor Civil Liability Under 42 U.S.C. § 1983: Absolute and Qualified Immunity

The second part of this chapter addresses the potential for the prosecutor to face personal civil liability, and is designed to help a prosecutor operate in a manner that limits such potential liability. As detailed below, a prosecutor's risk of personal civil liability differs during the judicial and investigative phases of a case. In the judicial phase, prosecutors have absolute immunity from claims under 42 U.S.C. § 1983.[61] However, this absolute immunity does not extend to

---

59 *See id.* at 1-2.

60 For further discussion of defenses, see Chapter 4.3.

61 Section 1983 states:

> Every person who, under color of any statute, ordinance, regulation, custom, or usage, of any State or Territory or the District of Columbia, subjects, or causes to be subjected, any citizen of the United States or other person within the jurisdiction thereof to the deprivation of any rights, privileges, or immunities secured by the Constitution and laws, shall be liable to the party injured in an action at law, suit in equity, or other proper proceeding for redress, except that in any action brought against a judicial officer for an act or omission taken in such officer's judicial capacity, injunctive relief shall not be granted unless a declaratory decree was violated or declaratory relief was unavailable. For the purposes of this section, any Act of Congress applicable exclusively to the District of Columbia shall be considered to be a statute of the District of Columbia.

42 U.S.C. § 1983 (2018). Note, however, that at least some states provide prosecutors with only qualified immunity even at the judicial phase of a case. *See, e.g.*, Reed v. City & Cty. of Honolulu, 873 P.2d 98, 105 (Haw. 1994) (citing Orso v. City & Cty. of Honolulu, 534 P.2d 489 (Haw. 1975)).

the investigative phase, where investigative prosecutors, like other members of the investigative team, currently have only qualified immunity.

A. *Absolute Immunity: Judicial Phase*

A long line of Supreme Court decisions provides absolute immunity to prosecutors from claims under 42 U.S.C. § 1983 for their conduct related to presenting evidence or argument in court during the judicial phase of a criminal case.[62] These decisions stem from the belief that allowing § 1983 claims for misconduct "threatens to undermine the necessary independence and integrity of the prosecutorial decision making process," and an accompanying belief that the adversarial process (with oversight by defense counsel, judges, and juries), as well as the public nature of criminal proceedings, will protect the justice system against misconduct.[63] Thus, the Supreme Court relies upon "checks on prosecutorial misconduct, including the criminal law and professional discipline" to justify absolute immunity.[64]

As a result, prosecutors' conduct that is "intimately associated with the judicial phase of the criminal process,"[65] "even when they act maliciously, wantonly or negligently,"[66] is insulated from personal civil liability under § 1983. For example, prosecutors are entitled to absolute immunity for personal liability even if they knowingly use false testimony before a grand jury and at trial.[67]

---

62 *See* Imbler v. Pachtman, 424 U.S. 409, 431 (1976). *See also* Van De Kamp v. Goldstein, 555 U.S. 335, 344-45 (2009) (expanding immunity to claims that supervisory prosecutors had failed to properly train or supervise prosecutors as being actions "intimately associated with the judicial phase of the criminal process").

63 *Van De Kamp*, 555 U.S. at 349; Burns v. Reed, 500 U.S. 478, 485 (1991) ("Specifically, there was concern that harassment by unfounded litigation would cause a deflection of the prosecutor's energies from his public duties, and the possibility that he would shade his decisions instead of exercising the independence of judgment required by his public trust." (internal quotation marks and citation omitted)).

64 *See Burns*, 500 U.S. at 486 (citing *Imbler*, 424 U.S. at 429).

65 Loupe v. O'Bannon, 824 F.3d 534, 538 (5th Cir. 2016) (internal quotation marks and citation omitted).

66 *Id.* at 539 (internal quotation marks and citation omitted).

67 *Burns*, 500 U.S. at 485, 489-90.

B. *Qualified Immunity: Investigative Phase*

The Supreme Court does not extend this absolute immunity to acts related to the investigative phase of a case.[68] As noted in the discussion of the ABA Standards above, during the investigative phase, the prosecutor has a broader obligation than at the judicial phase to engage as a non-adversarial fact finder. The possibility of individual civil liability links that obligation to a personal risk. Consistent with these obligations at the investigation stage, the Supreme Court has reasoned that a grant of qualified immunity is needed to deter misconduct by all those engaged in investigative activities, including the prosecutor.[69]

Qualified immunity, as the name suggests, is limited. It covers prosecutors for conduct that does not violate clearly established statutory or constitutional rights a reasonable person would have known.[70] Thus, in assessing whether qualified immunity is applicable, courts first evaluate whether the plaintiff has alleged a constitutional violation, and then examine whether the right was clearly established when the alleged violation occurred.[71] Although not as broad as absolute immunity, the Supreme Court describes qualified immunity as "protecting all but the plainly incompetent or those who knowingly violate the law."[72] A prosecutor can raise the qualified immunity defense irrespective of whether the prosecutor's alleged mistake was factual or legal.[73]

Ultimately, the application of qualified immunity presents a challenge to the criminal justice system. The limit on a prosecutor's immunity during the investigative phase is a judicial determination that, outside of the court-supervised judicial stages of a case, potential liability is appropriate for several purposes. First, it treats prosecutors in the same way it treats the law enforcement officers in a criminal investigation.[74] As noted above, and for both

---

68 Buckley v. Fitzsimmons, 509 U.S. 259, 273 (1993) ("A prosecutor's administrative duties and those investigatory functions that do not relate to an advocate's preparation for the initiation of a prosecution or for judicial proceedings are not entitled to absolute immunity.").

69 *See Burns*, 500 U.S. at 485-86, 492-93, 496.

70 *Buckley*, 509 U.S. at 268.

71 Gavitt v. Born, 835 F.3d 623, 640 (6th Cir. 2016) (internal quotation marks and citation omitted).

72 *Id.*

73 *Id.* at 641.

74 Notably, some states and Congress are reassessing the appropriateness of qualified immunity. *See* Felicia Sonmez & Colby Itkowitz, *House Passes Expansive Policing Overhaul Bill*

prosecutors and law enforcement officers, limited immunity is presumed to have a deterrent effect on misconduct. Second, prosecutors play a vital role in the criminal justice system, and it is critical that prosecutors not be deterred from carrying out their duties because of the possibility of a lawsuit from a criminal defendant or another party involved in the criminal proceeding. If a lawsuit challenges the prosecutor's actions during an investigation, qualified immunity may allow the prosecutor to end such a claim during its early stages.[75] But, to ensure that this defense is available, prosecutors should ensure that their conduct is the type that qualified immunity protects.

C. *Conduct Not Protected by Qualified Immunity*

Of course, certain conduct is not protected by qualified immunity, and that is equally true even if that conduct falls within the judicial phase of a case.[76] This includes the destruction of evidence at any time (as opposed to wrongful withholding of evidence).[77] Prosecutors who engage in intentionally malicious behavior outside the bounds of legal conduct face criminal and civil liability as well as sanctions by the bar.[78]

Named in Honor of George Floyd, WASH. POST (Mar. 3, 2021), https://www.washingtonpost.com/politics/george-floyd-police-reform-bill-vote/2021/03/03/5ea9ba3a-7c6c-11eb-85cd-9b7fa90c8873_story.html; Hailey Fuchs, *Qualified Immunity Protection for Police Emerges as Flash Point Amid Protests*, N.Y. TIMES (June 23, 2020), https://www.nytimes.com/2020/06/23/us/politics/qualified-immunity.html (noting that state legislatures are reevaluating the appropriateness of qualified immunity). Although at least some of those reforms appear limited to policing, it remains to be seen how those changes may impact the qualified immunity afforded prosecutors (if at all).

75 *Gavitt*, 835 F.3d at 640.

76 *See* Fields v. Wharrie, 740 F.3d 1107, 1111-12 (7th Cir. 2014) (holding that a prosecutor who fabricated evidence during the investigative phase of a case cannot then avail himself of the protection of absolute immunity by introducing the manufactured evidence at trial). In denying that claim, Judge Richard Posner noted that by such conduct the prosecutor "has not demonstrated an entitlement to absolute immunity—nor to qualified immunity for the fabrication, either." *Id.* at 1114.

77 Yarris v. County of Delaware, 465 F.3d 129, 143 (3d Cir. 2006) (holding that detectives were not entitled to qualified immunity based on allegations they failed to preserve evidence).

78 *See* Imbler v. Pachtman, 424 U.S. 409, 427-29 (1976).

D. *Determining if Absolute or Qualified Immunity Applies*

1. The Supreme Court's "Functional Approach"

The Supreme Court has instructed courts to use a "functional approach" when assessing whether a prosecutor is entitled to absolute or qualified immunity.[79] Under the functional approach, courts examine the activity at issue, rather than when the person engaged in the activity.[80] For example, "acts undertaken by a prosecutor in preparing for the initiation of judicial proceedings or for trial" fall within the scope of absolute immunity if the prosecutor is acting as an advocate while performing those acts.[81] Thus, a prosecutor will not be limited to qualified immunity simply because a prosecutor's conduct occurred before judicial proceedings are initiated.[82] Consequently, like most fact-intensive inquiries, the qualified immunity assessment can differ based on the facts of the case. One useful construct, while not definitive, may be to think about whether the conduct is viewed as finding evidence versus using evidence.[83]

However, the line between a prosecutor's investigative functions and advocacy functions is blurred and often difficult to assess. The difficulty arises, in part, because a prosecutor's "role as advocate for the State involve[s] actions preliminary to the initiation of a prosecution and actions apart from the courtroom."[84] Prosecutors should therefore take special care when assisting with investigations, especially considering that they bear the burden of establishing that they are entitled to immunity.[85] Moreover, because of the breadth of absolute immunity, courts have been cautious in granting prosecutors absolute immunity.[86]

---

79 Buckley v. Fitzsimmons, 509 U.S. 259, 269, 277 (1993).

80 *Id.* at 269.

81 *Id.* at 273.

82 Brunson v. Murray, 843 F.3d 698, 704-05 (7th Cir. 2016); Burns v. Reed, 500 U.S. 478, 495 (1991) (noting that the determining factor is "whether the prosecutor's actions are closely associated with the judicial process").

83 *See* Bianchi v. McQueen, 917 F. Supp. 2d 822, 828 (N.D. Ill. 2013) (citing *Buckley*, 509 U.S. at 273, 276), *aff'd* 818 F.3d 309 (7th Cir. 2016).

84 *Burns*, 500 U.S. at 486 (internal citation omitted).

85 *Id.*

86 *Id.* at 486-87 ("The presumption is that qualified rather than absolute immunity is sufficient to protect government officials in the exercise of their duties.").

2. Examples

As an initial matter, it is important to remember that a court need not delve into whether a prosecutor is entitled to qualified immunity if the plaintiff cannot establish a constitutional violation.[87] For example, in *Bianchi* v. *McQueen*, the plaintiff alleged that the prosecutor fabricated evidence to support the charges brought against the plaintiff.[88] However, the plaintiff's claims failed because the plaintiff was unable to show that his rights had been violated.[89] Because the plaintiff was never jailed or convicted of the allegations, the court held that the plaintiff suffered no deprivation of liberty to support a due process claim against the prosecutor.[90] Thus, the court found no need to analyze whether the prosecutor's conduct occurred in the role of an advocate or investigator.[91]

When the plaintiff can establish a constitutional violation, however, the question of whether a prosecutor is entitled to absolute or qualified immunity is critical. Courts have held the following actions to be investigative, and thus subject to qualified immunity analysis: authorizing a warrantless wiretap,[92] swearing to the facts in an affidavit used to obtain an arrest warrant,[93] colluding with police officers "to fabricate false charges against" a defendant,[94] speaking to the press,[95] and fabricating evidence.[96]

Seemingly similar conduct can be subjected to differing immunity analyses. For instance, preparing and acting on a charging document can involve both investigative and advocacy related activities. Courts have held that prosecutors are not entitled to absolute immunity when they swear to false facts in the charging document because that is considered to be an investigative activity

---

87 Bianchi v. McQueen, 818 F.3d 309, 319 (7th Cir. 2016).

88 *Id.*

89 *Id.*

90 *Id.* at 320 ("Because the plaintiffs suffered no liberty deprivation, they suffered no due process violation.").

91 *Id.*

92 *Burns*, 500 U.S. at 495-96 (citing Mitchell v. Forsyth, 472 U.S. 511, 524 (1985)).

93 Foreman v. Wadsworth, 844 F.3d 620, 624 (7th Cir. 2016) (citing Kalina v. Fletcher, 522 U.S. 118, 129 (1997)).

94 *Id.* at 626 n.2 (citing *Burns*, 500 U.S. at 496).

95 Buckley v. Fitzsimmons, 509 U.S. 259, 277-78 (1993).

96 Buchanan v. Metz, 647 F. App'x 659, 668-69 (6th Cir. 2016).

protected only by qualified immunity.[97] Conversely, a prosecutor may initiate a prosecution based on a false charging document without losing the protection of absolute immunity because the initiation of the case is considered to be an advocacy-related activity.[98]

Courts have rejected attempts by plaintiffs to use a prosecutor's participation in an investigation as a means of bypassing absolute immunity when the plaintiff's claim challenges the prosecution, not the investigation.[99] In *Buchanan* v. *Metz*, for example, the plaintiff alleged, among other things, that the prosecutor's failure to disclose exculpatory evidence was an investigatory action.[100] However, the plaintiff lacked any facts demonstrating that the failure to disclose related to the underlying investigation.[101] Rather, the plaintiff merely alleged that the prosecutor decided to bring charges, and that the investigator's testimony mirrored the prosecutor's theory of the case.[102] The court concluded that when the alleged nondisclosure of facts is not connected to the underlying investigation, the failure to disclose is "prosecutorial in function and remains within the ambit of absolute immunity."[103]

Prosecutors have also been sued on the basis that they brought charges before conducting a proper investigation. When faced with claims that prosecutors should have conducted additional investigation before bringing charges based on police reports, courts have viewed the prosecutor's role in question as the case-initiating role, in which the prosecutor acts as an advocate and thus granted absolute immunity.[104] Courts have also extended qualified immunity protection to prosecutors when new developments in investigatory techniques reveal that a past investigation was flawed.[105]

---

97 Olson v. Champaign County, 784 F.3d 1093, 1102-03 (7th Cir. 2015).

98 Brunson v. Murray, 843 F.3d 698, 704-05 (7th Cir. 2016).

99 *Buchanan*, 647 F. App'x at 669 ("Because prosecutors are almost always involved with the police's investigation of crimes, the claimant would need only to reframe every claim to attack the preparation instead of the absolutely immune actions themselves." (internal quotations and citations omitted)).

100 *Id.*

101 *Id.*

102 *Id.* at 668-69.

103 *Id.* at 669.

104 Brunson v. Murray, 843 F.3d 698, 705 (7th Cir. 2016) ("The prosecutor's choice to accept the police report and go forward with the prosecution without seeking further investigation by the state police was not an investigative act. It was a deliberate decision not to interfere with the investigation.").

105 Gavitt v. Born, 835 F.3d 623, 646 (6th Cir. 2016) ("While their investigation and

E. *The Future of Qualified Immunity*

A 2020 dissent by Justice Clarence Thomas suggests there may be some support for revising the qualified immunity doctrine.[106] After reviewing the evolution of qualified immunity, Justice Thomas cast doubt on several aspects of the doctrine, such as the "objective inquiry into clearly established law."[107] He instead proposed that courts revert to "asking whether immunity was historically accorded the relevant official in an analogous situation at common law."[108] Justice Thomas's dissent does not necessarily portend the death of qualified immunity, especially since no other Justice joined the dissent, but it suggests that there is at least some support for changes to qualified immunity.

Regardless of whether qualified immunity is ultimately eliminated or merely restricted, the way prosecutors handle anticorruption investigations may be impacted. Although not an anticorruption case, the Fourth Circuit Court of Appeals decision in *Nero* v. *Mosby* may be instructive.[109] There, the court reversed a district court's denial of immunity for a prosecutor's decision to file charges for police misconduct and to hold a press conference announcing those charges.[110] As the court found, the officers charged in the case had "transform[ed] [their] resentment at being prosecuted into the ascription of improper and malicious actions to the State's advocate."[111] Following the logic of *Imbler*, the Fourth Circuit cautioned that failing to provide prosecutors immunity for exercising their discretion to bring charges could stifle the exercise of their crucial role in the criminal justice system.[112]

Again, although *Nero* was not an anticorruption investigation, it is another example of judicial concern about the impact on prosecutors having to defend against such claims, even with the protection of immunity. That

---

interpretation of their findings now appear to have been flawed, they also appear to have been consistent with generally accepted methods and standards at the time.").

106 Baxter v. Bracey, 590 U.S. ___, 140 S. Ct. 1862, 1862 (2020) (Thomas, J., dissenting).

107 *Id.* at 1864.

108 *Id.* (citation and internal quotation marks omitted).

109 890 F.3d 106 (4th Cir. 2018).

110 *Id.* at 113-14.

111 *Id.* at 117 (citation and internal quotation marks omitted).

112 *Id.* at 132 (Wilkinson, J., concurring) ("One of the dangers against which *Imbler* warned was the use of hindsight . . . to give rise to a § 1983 action or something akin to a state malicious prosecution claim . . . [T]he vigorous and fearless performance of the prosecutor's duty would be eroded along with robust public discourse." (citation and internal quotation marks omitted)).

said, the increasing scrutiny of the law enforcement function generally, and anticorruption investigations in particular, raises the likelihood that past considerations may give way to legislative or judicial efforts to cabin or even abolish qualified immunity.

Conclusion: What Does This Mean for Me?

Those who read this book are likely doing so because they seek to perform at the highest level of their profession. Most readers may not be able to imagine approaching, much less crossing, the line where liability could attach. But immunity does not exist only to be used by prosecutors who have engaged in questionable conduct. Even when a prosecutor has handled the investigation and subsequent prosecution with the intent to fulfill the mandates of *Berger*[113] and Justice Jackson's famous speech,[114] the prosecutor may nonetheless become embroiled in litigation from a criminal suspect, defendant, or third-party witness.[115] Even if the legal requirements to establish liability are high at the present time, the barriers to filing and pursuing a civil claim under § 1983 are far lower. Simply being accused and having to defend such a claim, particularly in a corruption case, can be personally devastating, as well as damaging to the justice system the prosecutor represents.[116]

The reality is that prosecutors face a minimal risk of personal liability.[117] That low level of risk has fed concerns about undeterred prosecutorial

---

113 *See supra* text accompanying notes 3-4.

114 *See supra* text accompanying note 7.

115 *See* Garmon v. County of Los Angeles, 828 F.3d 837, 843-44 (9th Cir. 2016).

116 Although the prosecutors were not formally sanctioned, the news coverage on the prosecutors under investigation for misconduct due to their handling of the corruption trial of former Senator Ted Stevens shows the high stakes of prosecutorial misconduct allegations in a public integrity case. *See, e.g.*, John Bresnahan, *Report Blasts Stevens Prosecutors*, Politico (Mar. 15, 2012), https://www.politico.com/story/2012/03/report-blasts-prosecutors-in-stevens-case-074056; Charlie Savage, *Stevens Case Prosecutor Kills Himself*, N.Y. Times (Sept. 27, 2010), https://www.nytimes.com/2010/09/28/us/politics/28stevens.html. *See also* Chapter 5.1, Part III(C).

117 Malia N. Brink, *A Pendulum Swung Too Far: Why The Supreme Court Must Place Limits On Prosecutorial Immunity*, 4 Charleston L. Rev. 1, 2 (2009) ("The legal landscape has also changed; evidence shows that prosecutorial misconduct is often not the subject of disciplinary proceedings or criminal charges . . . .").

misconduct in the media,[118] in the legal community,[119] as well as in prior scholarly analysis of the prosecution function.[120] Personal and political interference with the public prosecutor further undermines confidence in the impartiality of the criminal justice system.[121] At the same time, many throughout the country have called for reform of the qualified immunity doctrine and reckoning with mass incarceration.[122]

This convergence of concerns is beyond what Justice Jackson envisioned when he warned of an individual prosecutor abusing the investigative power.[123] Simply falling back on a notion of vigorously executing their duties may not be enough to insulate prosecutors from litigation and calls for legislative reform. Prosecutors may still have an opportunity to address these concerns on their own terms through support of criminal justice reforms and by following the practices recommended in the ABA Standards, among other ways.[124] If they do not do so, however, prosecutors may face more stringent external constraints over their exercise of discretion,[125] and heightened individual risks.

---

118 Alexa Van Brunt, *Prosecutors Shouldn't Have Immunity from Their Unethical—Or Unlawful—Acts*, The Guardian (Feb. 5, 2015), https://www.theguardian.com/commentisfree/2015/feb/05/prosecutors-immunity-unethical-unlawful-acts.

119 Erin Miller, *Rethinking Prosecutorial Immunity*, SCOTUSblog (Nov. 5, 2009), https://www.scotusblog.com/2009/11/what-would-prosecutors-do/.

120 Bennett L. Gershman, *The Most Dangerous Power of the Prosecutor*, 29 Pace L. Rev. 1, 27-28 (2008).

121 *See* Katie Benner et al., *Fearful of Trump's Attacks, Justice Dept. Lawyers Worry Barr Will Leave Them Exposed*, N.Y. Times (Feb. 15, 2020), https://www.nytimes.com/2020/02/15/us/politics/trump-barr-justice-department.html (reporting on career prosecutors' concern that the president was undermining their reputation for upholding the law "without favor or political bias").

122 Fuchs, *supra* note 74; David Lat, *How Tough-on-Crime Prosecutors Contribute to Mass Incarceration*, N.Y. Times (Apr. 8, 2019), https://www.nytimes.com/2019/04/08/books/review/emily-bazelon-charged.html (reviewing Emily Bazelon, Charged: The New Movement to Transform American Prosecution and End Mass Incarceration (2019)) ("Bazelon argues that . . . prosecutors[] . . . bear much of the responsibility for over-incarceration, conviction of the innocent and other serious problems of the criminal justice system.").

123 *See* Jackson, *supra* note 7, at 5.

124 *See* David Alan Sklansky, *The Progressive Prosecutor's Handbook*, 50 U.C. Davis L. Rev. Online 25, 28-40 (2017).

125 *See* Note, *The Paradox of "Progressive Prosecution,"* 132 Harv. L. Rev. 748, 750-52 (2018).

CHAPTER 2.2

Timing of Covert & Overt Aspects of the Investigation

Carrie H. Cohen

Carrie H. Cohen is a partner in the Investigations & White Collar Defense practice group of the New York office of Morrison & Foerster LLP and chair of its Workplace Investigations Misconduct Task Force. She formerly served as Chief of the Public Corruption Unit in the Criminal Division of the New York State Attorney General's Office and as an Assistant U.S. Attorney for the Southern District of New York, where she prosecuted public corruption and securities fraud cases. Carrie is an adjunct professor at the University of Pennsylvania Law School where she teaches a seminar on Public Corruption and the Law.

Lauren M. Gambier, an associate in the litigation department of the New York office of Morrison & Foerster LLP, contributed to the writing of this chapter.

INTRODUCTION

Proper timing of the covert and overt aspects of public corruption investigations is essential to obtain the best quality evidence and maintain the integrity of the investigation. Public corruption is different from other crimes that an attorney general's office typically investigates in that both the crime and the investigation of the crime have serious public trust implications. Thus, an AGO must avoid giving the impression that it is acting for partisan reasons, seeking to influence the outcome of an election, or harassing public officials in the absence of sufficient evidence of misconduct.[1] That said, an AGO also needs to protect the public's confidence in public officials and institutions by ensuring that public corruption is brought to light and prosecuted. Although public corruption investigations uniquely impact the public trust, traditional investigative tools more commonly associated with violent or street crime are equally applicable to the investigation of public corruption offenses. But given the high profile nature of many public corruption cases and the serious collateral consequences to a corruption target who may not ultimately be charged, these traditional investigative tools must be deployed prudently, and the transition from covert to overt stages of an investigation must be handled with care.

A well-timed covert investigation enables an AGO to gather high-quality evidence while avoiding appearances of partisanship or other impropriety. Appropriately timing when to go overt[2] with an investigation further helps an AGO to preserve and obtain relevant evidence and affords the AGO some control with respect to the public and media narrative surrounding the investigation.

I. The Covert Investigation

Evidence obtained through covert investigation can be of particular value in public corruption cases. Covert investigative techniques allow for the collection of documents or other physical evidence before it can be destroyed or altered. Covert investigative techniques also allow for physical or electronic surveillance of suspects, collaborators, or witnesses without them altering or concealing their behavior from investigators. Potential cooperating witnesses may be less likely to be intimidated or deterred from speaking with investigators if the investigation is covert. Covert investigations often provide evidence of the crime as it is taking place and also have the benefit of being conducted

1 *See* Chapter 1.7, Part III (timing of investigations of election crimes); Chapter 5.1, Part I (inappropriate for prosecutors to use partisan or political considerations when determining whether to file charges).

2 "Going overt" means doing anything that may lead to disclosure of the existence of an investigation. Daniel Small, *Overt Investigations, in* Prosecution of Public Corruption Cases 145, 147 (U.S. Dep't of Justice 1988), https://www.ncjrs.gov/pdffiles1/Digitization/110010-110033NCJRS.pdf.

away from the public eye, thus preventing any rush to judgment or any criticism of how the investigation is conducted.

The timing of the various elements of the covert investigation will depend on the specific facts and circumstances of the case and also on the relevant legal framework governing investigative techniques. Some covert investigative techniques create some risk of exposing the investigation, so that risk should also be taken into account. An investigation does not necessarily proceed in a linear fashion. As the investigation reveals new leads or forecloses certain theories, investigative techniques may need to change to follow these new paths.

A. *Investigation Strategy*

Before commencing an investigation, it is essential to develop an investigation strategy. The strategy should take into account what the investigation seeks to prove, what kinds of evidence will be needed, what sources may yield the needed evidence, what methods of investigation will be used, and what resources—in terms of both money and people—are available for the investigation. Any plan for the investigation should also be sufficiently flexible to allow for updating as new information is discovered and as new leads are generated.

While the order of operations in any given investigation is likely to be flexible, many elements of the investigation will require advance planning and consideration. For example, if the investigation may eventually require a wiretap, investigators should gather evidence to support the warrant application and make plans to exhaust other investigative means.[3] If the investigation plan includes issuing subpoenas for certain documents or records, or attempts to interview certain witnesses or informants, the AGO must consider whether any of the subpoenas or the witnesses might compromise the covert nature of the investigation. As an example, sending a subpoena to a national bank may well pose little to no risk that the target will learn that the investigation exists; however, careful consideration must be given to whether and when to send a subpoena to a local bank affiliated with the target or known to inform account holders upon receipt of a subpoena. A well-planned investigation strategy will help to ensure that evidence to support future stages of the investigation is

---

3 For an in-depth discussion of using a wiretap in public corruption cases, *see* Chapter 2.3.

being gathered at the outset and help to avoid pitfalls such as premature exposure of the investigation.

B. *Public Source Information*

In the digital age, a trove of publicly available information is mere clicks away from being discovered. One of the very first steps in any investigation is to obtain information available on the internet by, for example, conducting internet searches on individuals and companies, searching public databases for relevant filings or incorporation papers, and reading social media posts and blogs by relevant individuals. Indeed, the internet and publicly available information should be mined repeatedly during the investigation both to capture new information and to investigate new leads and information.[4]

C. *Subpoenas*

A valuable early step for any investigation is the ability to collect documentary evidence in order to preserve it and create leads without the target's knowledge. Accordingly, the ability to subpoena documents is a crucial tool to obtain information at the early stages of a corruption investigation. When little is known about the nature of the target's activity or who else may be involved in such activity, documentary evidence can provide a starting point. Documents may lead to a money trail to follow, can inform investigators about other possible participants or beneficiaries of the corrupt scheme, and may provide leads on future targets for physical or electronic surveillance. Documents to consider obtaining via subpoena include phone records, IP addresses, toll records, business records, tax returns, credit card records, bank records, and other financial or asset-related information.[5]

---

4 While prosecutors may be able to search for some of this information themselves, prosecutors cannot be used as witnesses to introduce, for example, a screenshot that reflects a particular social media message a target posted on a certain day. *See* Model Rules of Prof'l Conduct r. 3.7(a) (Am. Bar Ass'n 2020). An agent or investigator should, at a minimum, recreate such a search while the page or entry still exists and document any information that might be used at trial. (Alternatively, a search warrant can be obtained, but if an entry is deleted and not maintained by the service provider, a contemporaneous screenshot or a preservation request/order may be necessary to preserve the evidence. For more on this, see Chapter 2.4, Part I.)

5 A search warrant or other process may be required for certain of these documents. *See* Carpenter v. United States, 138 S. Ct. 2206, 2220-21 (2018); State v. Walton, 324 P.3d 876, 906-08 (Haw. 2014).

Obtaining documents during the covert stage of the investigation is ideal insofar as it minimizes the risk that documents will be altered or destroyed by the target or his or her coconspirators. However, subpoenaing documents may lead to a target or witness learning of the investigation well in advance of plans for the investigation to become overt. Investigators should become familiar with local and state laws as well as industry practices about whether third parties will notify individuals when their records are sought by or provided to law enforcement. Thus, the value of any particular type of documentary evidence at the early stages of the investigation must be weighed against the risk that obtaining such documents may result in undesired exposure of the existence of the investigation.

D. *Physical Surveillance*

Physical surveillance is a broad term that describes many forms of monitoring and gathering evidence relating to targets of the corruption investigation. It can include everything from physically following and photographing or video recording suspects, to reviewing the outside of their mail and searching through their trash. Physical surveillance is particularly valuable at the early stages of a covert investigation as it can provide concrete proof of the conduct being investigated and generate further investigative leads as other individuals or entities that may be involved in the corruption scheme are discovered.

Because officials engaged in public corruption are likely to try to avoid leaving a paper trail, physical surveillance can be an ideal way to obtain direct evidence of misconduct that cannot be easily established through documents. Physical surveillance enables an investigator to see evidence of the many different forms that public corruption can take. It may provide insight into whether conduct is suspicious, which cannot always be determined from documentary evidence alone. For example, documents obtained via subpoena may reveal what appear to be legitimate financial records for a business affiliated with one of the targets of the investigation, but physical surveillance of the business location may reveal that it is a front rather than a legitimate business.

Corruption sometimes can be conducted via middlemen and lower-level associates of the corrupt public official. Physical surveillance also affords the opportunity to see the target's apparent collaborators, which in turn can help reveal the mechanics of the corrupt scheme and provide further leads for investigation. Learning who else is involved in or is benefitting from the corrupt scheme is crucial to identifying potential cooperating witnesses or confidential informants.

E. *Cooperating Witnesses or Confidential Informants*

Cooperating witnesses and confidential informants can be another source of valuable information during the covert investigation stage. They may directly inform investigators of things they have seen, heard, or done, or may assist in obtaining information or admissions from the investigation target and his or her coconspirators by, for example, making recorded consensual telephone calls (although state consent laws vary).[6] The use of confidential informants is complicated and must be handled appropriately.[7] In addition, potential informants are often reluctant to cooperate for a multitude of reasons, including fear of retaliation, a desire to avoid getting involved in a potential scandal, reluctance to implicate friends or colleagues, or fear that they themselves may be implicated in a crime.

Given these potential factors, the process of identifying and cultivating cooperators or informants should start as soon as practicable in the investigation. Discussions with potential confidential informants or cooperating witnesses, however, can result in the existence of the investigation being leaked to the target. It is thus essential to consider carefully whether a potential witness is likely, for reasons of loyalty, profit, complicity, or otherwise, to inform the target of the investigation before approaching them about the possibility of cooperating with the AGO.

---

6 According to a 2018 law review article, thirty-eight states and D.C. require only one-party consent; eleven states require all parties to consent for a communication to be recorded. Rauvin Johl, *Reassessing Wiretap and Eavesdropping Statutes: Making One-Party Consent the Default*, 12 Harv. L. & Pol'y Rev. 177, 180 (2018) (citation omitted).

7 A separate chapter in this Manual addresses the use of confidential informants and cooperating witness in corruption cases. *See* Chapter 2.5; *see also* Chapter 1.8, Part II(A) (discussing cooperation agreements, non-prosecution agreements, and immunity orders). For additional issues to consider in managing the use of confidential informants, *see generally* Stephen S. Trott, *The Successful Use of Informants and Criminals as Witnesses for the Prosecution in a Criminal Case*, *in* Prosecution of Public Corruption Cases 115 (U.S. Dep't of Justice 1988), https://www.ncjrs.gov/pdffiles1/Digitization/110010-110033NCJRS.pdf.

F. *Electronic Surveillance*

Given the covert nature of public corruption, electronic surveillance of telephone calls or emails can be an invaluable tool for gathering evidence of corruption. Electronic surveillance also has the further advantage of allowing prosecutors to show the jury the crime as it is taking place in real time. But the legal standards for obtaining authorization for electronic surveillance are stringent, and maintaining such surveillance is resource intensive.[8] It is also likely that any wiretapping warrant will be challenged by the defendant when the corruption case ultimately goes to trial. It is thus crucial to secure wiretapping warrants at the appropriate time that meet all necessary legal requirements.

Not only is the requisite showing of probable cause required, but federal law and many state laws require that in order to receive a warrant for electronic eavesdropping, the authority seeking the warrant demonstrate that it has exhausted other investigative techniques or that other investigative techniques would fail to reveal necessary evidence or would compromise the investigation.[9] Seeking a wiretap warrant too early in the investigation, prior to attempting other investigative procedures, can result in denial of the warrant or risk the suppression of evidence obtained through the wiretap for failure to comply with the statutory requirements.[10] As discussed at greater length in Chapter 2.3, suppression motions based on alleged failures to adhere to the legal requirements for obtaining the wiretap warrant are likely to be contentious, especially given how damaging wiretap evidence (both telephone and email) can be to the defendant at trial.

Apart from concerns regarding the legal sufficiency of the warrant, seeking a warrant too early in an investigation also creates the risk that the wiretap covers the wrong individuals, too many individuals, or too few individuals and thus will not obtain relevant evidence. Corruption, like other crimes, is often conducted through middlemen or lower-level collaborators, who may not have been identified at the earlier stages of the investigation. Electronic surveillance also is both labor intensive and costly and so ideally should be narrowly tailored

---

8 For a more in-depth discussion of using wiretaps in corruption cases, see Chapter 2.3.

9 *See* Chapter 2.3, Part III (discussing legal requirements for wiretaps).

10 *See* United States v. Lilla, 699 F.2d 99, 104-05 (2d Cir. 1983) (suppressing wiretap that did not conform to statutory requirements).

to monitor only those telephone numbers or email addresses most likely to provide evidence of the crime taking place.

II. The Overt Investigation

One of the most consequential decisions to be made in public corruption investigations is when to make the investigation overt. Once the investigation is overt, not only will the subject of the investigation and any of his or her coconspirators likely become aware of the investigation, but the public also may learn about the investigation, and a public reaction to it is likely. Managing both the public and media response to the investigation and the new challenges presented by the fact that the target is aware of the investigation can be a considerable challenge.[11] The timing of an overt investigation thus should be carefully considered.

A. *When to Make the Investigation Overt?*

There are many factors to take into account in deciding when to go overt with an investigation. An AGO loses some degree of control over the investigation once it becomes overt and so must be prepared for the changing needs of the investigation. The office also must consider the potential risks associated with making an investigation overt.[12]

A potentially overlooked, but very important, consideration is whether, logistically, the AGO is prepared for the investigation to become overt. Steps to consider taking in advance of making the investigation overt may include the following:

- Finalizing research on any relevant evidentiary or legal issues;
- Preparing investigative staff for a rapidly increased pace of work;

---

11 For additional guidance on media issues in corruption cases, see Chapter 5.3.

12 For further discussion of considerations in making an investigation overt, see Small, *supra* note 2, at 147.

- Determining what search warrants or witness subpoenas may be necessary;
- Obtaining and being prepared to execute warrants and witness subpoenas;
- Preparing for other legal mechanisms, such as asset freezing, that may be necessary;
- Planning for when and how to search for and seize evidence and interview witnesses, including the target;
- Creating a plan for cooperating witnesses or informants to, at law enforcement's direction and control, meet or speak with the target or coconspirators;
- Strategizing about any press coverage and avoiding leaks; and
- Drafting charging documents so that, if necessary, they can be quickly finalized and used.

To determine whether the investigation should become overt, another factor to consider is whether all information that can be obtained from the covert investigation has in fact been obtained. Once an investigation is known to the targets, there is some risk that documents or other evidence may be altered or destroyed. It should also be expected that the targets will be much more careful in what they say and to whom. Accordingly, it is ideal to obtain as much evidence as possible before the targets learn of the investigation. Safety of witnesses also must always be considered.

The AGO may be able to control how a target becomes aware of the investigation, as well as controlling how much information the target learns about the investigation. The target may be informed by a witness or informant, may be confronted directly by investigators for an interview, may find their home or office being searched pursuant to a warrant, may be told by a third party who receives a subpoena for information about the target, may learn of the investigation from the news, or may learn of it through some other means.

How much the target knows and how he or she comes by that knowledge will likely affect how the target responds to learning of the investigation. Depending on the facts and circumstances of the particular case, it may be best for the target to learn the full extent of the investigation immediately, it may be best for the target to learn only a small amount of information, or it may be preferable for the target to be misdirected about the nature and scope of the investigation. The decision of how much the target should learn of the investigation once it becomes overt should take into consideration what knowledge an AGO wants the target to have about the investigation at the outset, including its assessment of what the target is likely to do as a result of learning that information.

Once a target learns of the investigation, it is essential to act quickly in order to prevent the alteration or destruction of evidence, collusion between witnesses, and hiding of assets and—whenever possible—to have cooperating witnesses, informants, and surveillance operations in place in order to capture incriminating discussions the target may have with others regarding the investigation. While targets may be more careful about discussing the crime, they may discuss the investigation, which can result in relevant admissions.

B. *Components of the Overt Investigation*

While an overt investigation can pose challenges that a covert investigation does not, it also affords additional opportunities for evidence gathering and strengthening a case. Once freed from the burden of keeping an investigation secret, other tools, such as search warrants and a broader array of witness interviews, become available. Valuable evidence of corruption that does not amount to cash bribes—for example, certain kinds of favorable treatment—can be obtained through searches of the target's home or office, or the homes or places of business of his or her family members, colleagues, or coconspirators. After the investigation becomes overt, it also is essential to follow up on leads that were not exhausted during the covert phase of the investigation, including checking on witnesses' explanations for questionable activity or conduct and exploring any alternative, non-corrupt bases for income, gifts, or other potential fruits of corruption.[13]

---

13 This can be important both to ensure that the potential charges have merit and to preempt potential defenses at trial.

The freedom to interview witnesses who may have compromised the secrecy of the investigation had they been interviewed earlier is another potential benefit of the overt phase of the investigation. Such witness interviews can, in turn, generate new leads for other individuals to interview or surveil, or other places to search for relevant evidence. Simultaneous execution of search warrants and interviews of witnesses also can ensure that witnesses' homes or places of business can be searched before they have the opportunity to alter or destroy any evidence.

C. *Media Considerations*

While an AGO may exercise some control regarding when an investigation becomes overt and what information about it is initially made known, it is likely that additional information will leak as witnesses or others discuss the investigation. Cases involving public officials accused of corruption are likely to receive significant attention once they become publicly known. Given the aforementioned concerns regarding the perception of integrity and propriety of the investigation, AGOs should have a plan to deal with media coverage of an investigation.[14]

A planned strategy can include the following: (1) whether to designate a single spokesperson; (2) whether to confirm or deny the existence of the investigation (assuming no grand jury or confidentiality issues); and (3) how much information to reveal about the nature and scope of the investigation, including the identity of the targets of the investigation. In making such decisions, it is important to bear in mind the consequences that such revelations can have on the investigation and on its subjects. Confirming to the media the identity of targets may cause significant personal and professional harm to these individuals, may invite charges that the attorney general is acting in an improperly political manner, and may violate the state Rules of Professional Conduct.[15] But widespread public knowledge of the investigation may also encourage others with knowledge to come forward or may put pressure on the targets or others to cooperate. What is revealed to the media, and when to reveal that information, should thus be the subject of careful planning, especially given grand jury

---

14 For additional guidance in this area, see Chapter 5.3; Robert C. Bonner, *Media Relations*, *in* Prosecution of Public Corruption Cases 249 (U.S. Dep't of Justice 1988), https://www.ncjrs.gov/pdffiles1/Digitization/110010-110033NCJRS.pdf.

15 *See* Model Rules of Prof'l Conduct rr. 3.6, 3.8(f) (Am. Bar Ass'n 2020).

secrecy requirements, policies against disclosing anything about the existence of an investigation, and ethical rules.

Conclusion

While public corruption investigations often are complex and difficult, the use of covert and overt traditional investigative techniques can yield valuable evidence. The timing of the use of such techniques is equally complex, but planning and forethought can help ensure a fair, neutral, and thorough investigation.

Chapter 2.3

A Practitioner's Guide to Wiretaps in Public Corruption Investigations

Wesley Cheng

Wesley Cheng has served as an Assistant District Attorney for the Manhattan District Attorney's Office, an Assistant Attorney General in the New York Attorney General's Office, and an Associate General Counsel for the Office of the Metropolitan Transit Authority Inspector General. He has also been an adjunct instructor of Trial Advocacy at the Benjamin N. Cardozo School of Law and Co-Director of the Criminal Prosecution Clinic at New York Law School.

NAAG thanks the Center for the Advancement of Public Integrity (CAPI) at Columbia Law School and the Laura and John Arnold Foundation for their permission to reprint this chapter, a previous draft of which was originally published as a paper on the CAPI website.

Introduction

The nonconsensual interception of wire, oral, or electronic communications of targets in criminal investigations is a powerful law enforcement tool that can be used to great effect in many cases, including public corruption cases. Indeed, particularly in cases where wrongful behavior is covert—as is often the case when public officials are involved—there is great value to evidence that allows prosecutors to use the defendant's own recorded words against him in the courtroom. But prosecutors should consider many factors before using this labor-intensive, long-term tool in a corruption investigation, and once prosecutors decide to seek a wiretap, several legal issues may arise.

This chapter sets forth some factors a prosecutor should take into account when considering a wiretap and precautions a prosecutor should take to ensure the best possible position for litigation following the wiretap, especially as it relates to a public corruption case.[1]

I. Is this the Right Case for a Wiretap?

Before discussing the legal issues relating to wiretaps, it is necessary to assess whether a wiretap is appropriate for this particular investigation. In doing so, ask the following questions.

A. *Do We Have the Money?*

Sufficient financial resources must be available to support a wiretap, and to ensure that the agency can continue the investigation in the event of an extension of the initial wiretap. On June 30, 2020, the United States Courts system released its annual wiretap report for the previous year.[2] The average

---

1 The requirements described in this paper are the federal requirements under Title III of the Wiretap Act. The Wiretap Act is more formally known as the Omnibus Crime Control and Safe Streets Act of 1968, Pub. L. No. 90-351, 82 Stat. 197 (1968). It has been amended numerous times and is codified at 18 U.S.C. §§ 2510-22 (2018). For the most part, the requirements for a wiretap application at the state law level are very similar, if not identical, to the requirements enumerated in the federal wiretapping statute. *See, e.g.*, United States v. Lilla, 699 F.2d 99, 102 (2d Cir. 1983) ("For practical purposes the federal and New York statutory requirements are the same."). However, some states narrow the scope of situations in which law enforcement officials can obtain a wiretap. For example, in Alaska and several other states, law enforcement officials can receive permission for a wiretap only when probable cause for specific enumerated crimes has been shown. *See, e.g.*, Alaska Stat. § 12.37.010 (2020) (listing murder, kidnapping, some felony drug offenses, sex trafficking, and human trafficking offenses). This is in contrast to the availability of a wiretap for any crime that the federal statute permits (although the requirement for probable cause remains). Even more of an outlier, the state of Vermont does not have a state wiretap law. *See* Rauvin Johl, *Reassessing Wiretap and Eavesdropping Statutes: Making One-Party Consent the Default*, 12 Harv. L. & Pol'y Rev. 177, 180 (2018) (citation omitted). Prosecutors seeking to obtain a wiretap in Vermont must do so under the federal statute in federal court.

2 *See 2019 Wiretap Report*, U.S. Courts (June 30, 2020), https://www.uscourts.gov/news/2020/06/30/2019-wiretap-report-orders-and-convictions-increase.

cost of a wiretap was $75,160, which includes the cost of installing intercept devices and monitoring communications.[3] Overall, 3,225 wiretaps were authorized in federal and state courts, and 2,528 extensions were requested and authorized.[4]

B. *Do We Have the Manpower?*

An eavesdropping investigation involves a team of investigators that will need to monitor the wiretapped phone lines at all times. That means that someone will always need to be at the location where conversations are intercepted and recorded. Simultaneously, an investigative team will need to be in the field performing physical surveillance for at least some of the time the wiretap is live. Monitoring a phone twenty-four hours a day for thirty days at a time consumes significant manpower. An agency must have enough investigators to carry on an investigation like this. These issues become even more important if a foreign language is involved and translators are required.

C. *Is This Case Worthy of a Wiretap?*

Of the 3,225 wiretaps issued in 2019, approximately seventy-six percent were for narcotics cases.[5] Conspiracy, homicide, and assault were the next most frequently cited crimes in wiretap applications. So, for the most part, wiretap cases are used to investigate major offenses.[6] In deciding whether to engage in a wiretap investigation, think of whether the amount of resources being used to investigate is worthy of the crime or target that will eventually be prosecuted. In a public corruption case, this may be an easy call with an elected official, but it should be considered, particularly in cases involving lower-level public officials or employees.

---

3 *Id.*
4 *Id.*
5 *Id.*
6 *Id.*

II. Legal Framework

If a wiretap is practical in a particular public corruption investigation, then the prosecutor should consider the legal foundation of an eavesdropping warrant. Eavesdropping warrants are a variant of general search warrants and are thus governed by the limitations of a search warrant.[7] Title III of the Wiretap Act requires, as with a general search warrant, that an eavesdropping warrant only be issued upon a showing of probable cause.[8] It goes several steps further by requiring or authorizing the following:

- The application must include the name of the target (if known), the type of communication that will be intercepted,[9] and the time period for eavesdropping.[10]
- The statute enumerates the investigative, judicial, and enforcement agencies that are authorized to seek, review, and execute eavesdropping warrants.[11]

---

7 The statute states:

(3) Upon such application the judge may enter an ex parte order, as requested or as modified, authorizing or approving interception of wire, oral, or electronic communications within the territorial jurisdiction of the court in which the judge is sitting (and outside that jurisdiction but within the United States in the case of a mobile interception device authorized by a Federal court within such jurisdiction), if the judge determines on the basis of the facts submitted by the applicant that--

(a) there is probable cause for belief that an individual is committing, has committed, or is about to commit a particular offense enumerated in section 2516 of this chapter [18 U.S.C. § 2516];

(b) there is probable cause for belief that particular communications concerning that offense will be obtained through such interception;

. . .

(d) except as provided in subsection (11), there is probable cause for belief that the facilities from which, or the place where, the wire, oral, or electronic communications are to be intercepted are being used, or are about to be used, in connection with the commission of such offense, or are leased to, listed in the name of, or commonly used by such person.

18 U.S.C. § 2518 (2018).

8 *Id.*

9 *See id.* § 2518(4)(a), (c).

10 *See id.* § 2518(1)(d).

11 *See id.* § 2518(4)(d).

- The affiant is required to state how "normal investigative procedures have been tried and have failed or reasonably appear unlikely to succeed if tried or to be too dangerous."[12]

- The authorizing judge has discretion to direct investigators to update the judge on the investigation at whatever intervals the judge requires.[13]

- The statute states that eavesdropping can continue beyond the originally authorized period, but only under certain circumstances.[14]

These requirements apply to all wiretap applications, not just those in public corruption investigations. As discussed in greater detail below, however, given the likely publicity that a public corruption case will generate, a corruption prosecutor will want to follow these requirements scrupulously and to be ready to defend investigative actions every step of the way. Litigation over adherence to these requirements is more likely to occur and to be more contentious in a corruption case than in an average wiretap case.

Once a judge has authorized an eavesdropping warrant, there are several other requirements to keep in mind:

- The statute specifies how intercepted conversations are to be preserved, safeguarded, and stored.[15]

- The statute states what investigators must do in the case of intercepting a non-pertinent conversation, commonly referred to as minimization.[16]

- The statute states the circumstances under which intercepted conversations may be disclosed or used as evidence.[17]

---

12 *See id.* § 2518(3)(c). Courts have criticized prosecutors for not spelling out investigative efforts in sufficient detail and have suggested that similarly insufficient efforts would result in the suppression of future wiretaps. United States v. Concepcion, 579 F.3d 214, 220 (2d Cir. 2009); *see also* United States v. Lilla, 699 F.2d 99, 104-05 (2d Cir. 1983) (suppressing state-authorized wiretap that did not conform to federal and state statutory requirements because it did not reflect that standard investigative procedures had been properly exhausted or shown to be reasonably unlikely to succeed).

13 *See* 18 U.S.C. § 2518(6).

14 *See id.* § 2518(5).

15 *See id.* § 2518(8)(a).

16 *See id.* § 2518(5).

17 *See id.* § 2518(9).

- The statute lays out notice requirements for interceptees.[18]

Again, a prosecutor will want to ensure strict adherence to each of these requirements in a corruption investigation.

III. Legal Considerations

Litigation arising from wiretaps comes from various areas of the statute. This part outlines some of the most important statutory requirements.

A. *Exhaustion/Necessity*

Every eavesdropping warrant is required to describe other investigative techniques used prior to the submission of the wiretap according to 18 U.S.C. § 2518(1)(c).[19] The description must include why the procedures tried have failed, why they reasonably appear to be unlikely to succeed if tried, or why they are too dangerous to try.[20] Investigative techniques to exhaust before an eavesdropping warrant becomes necessary include:[21]

Physical surveillance
Public record checks
Pen registers
Trap and traces
GPS tracking
Analysis of toll records
Trash seizures
Financial investigation
Undercover agents
Search warrants
Controlled purchases
Confidential informants
Covert cameras
Tracking devices
Subscriber information
Mail cover[22]

18 *See id.* § 2518(8)(d).

19 *See id.* § 2518(1)(c).

20 *Id.*

21 *See generally* United States v. Penaloza-Romero, No. 14-289(8) (SRN/JSM), 2015 U.S. Dist. LEXIS 76913, at *68-69 (D. Minn. May 5, 2015).

22 "Mail cover" is an investigative technique where law enforcement officials request that postal workers record information from the outside of letters and parcels before they are delivered. *See* United States v. Hinton, 222 F.3d 664, 674 (9th Cir. 2000); Ron Nixon, *U.S. Postal Service Logging All Mail for Law Enforcement*, N.Y. Times (July 3, 2013), https://www.nytimes.com/2013/07/04/us/monitoring-of-snail-mail.html.

It is important that statements of necessity not become "boilerplate assertions . . . unsupported by specific facts relevant to the particular circumstances of this case."[23] This was the holding from the Ninth Circuit Court of Appeals, which suppressed an eavesdropping warrant on these grounds in *United States* v. *Blackmon.*[24] In that case, investigators began eavesdropping on a target, and through this wiretap developed probable cause to begin eavesdropping on the defendant's phone.[25] However, the necessity section of the eavesdropping warrant for the defendant's phone was, apart from a few alterations, "a duplicate" of the initial target's necessity section.[26] The *Blackmon* court specifically noted that "no further investigative efforts were attempted in between the application" for the initial wiretap and the defendant's wiretap.[27] Thus, the Court suppressed the wiretap because the necessity section of the eavesdropping warrant contained "generalized statements that would be true of any narcotics investigation."[28]

B. *Official Must Authorize the Application*

Sections 2518(4)(d) and 2516(1) of Title 18 require all applications to name the identity of the authorizing individual in a wiretap, and also limit the pool of United States Department of Justice officials who are empowered to authorize the application.[29] This was the subject of litigation in *United States* v. *Giordano.*[30] In this case, investigators obtained an eavesdropping warrant on a narcotics trafficker, which was not authorized by the attorney general or one of his designated assistants.[31] Instead, the attorney general's executive assistant authorized the eavesdropping warrant.[32] In suppressing evidence from the wiretap, the Supreme Court held that an executive assistant's authorization was inconsistent with the language and legislative history of Title III.[33]

---

23 United States v. Blackmon, 273 F.3d 1204, 1210 (9th Cir. 2001); *accord* United States v. Lilla, 699 F.2d 99, 104-05 (2d Cir. 1983).

24 *Blackmon*, 273 F.3d at 1210-11.

25 *Id.* at 1206.

26 *Id.*

27 *Id.*

28 *Id.* at 1211.

29 18 U.S.C. §§ 2516(1), 2518(4)(d) (2018).

30 416 U.S. 505, 512-23 (1974).

31 *Id.* at 508-09.

32 *Id.* at 510.

33 *Id.* at 523.

C. *Minimizing Non-Pertinent and Privileged Calls*

1. Pertinent v. Non-Pertinent

The target of an eavesdropping investigation will have both pertinent and non-pertinent conversations over the wiretapped device. Title III only authorizes the interception of calls that are pertinent to the criminal investigation.[34] Section 2518(5) of Title 18 accounts for this by requiring that an investigation be "conducted in such a way as to minimize the interception of communications not otherwise subject to interception under this chapter."[35] There is no specific bright-line rule on proper minimization, which has led to substantial litigation over this part of the statute.

In *Scott* v. *United States,*[36] investigators intercepted conversations about a conspiracy to import and distribute narcotics.[37] Approximately forty percent of the intercepted calls related to narcotics.[38] However, investigators listened to all calls, which included non-pertinent conversations between the target and her mother.[39] In ruling that suppression was not appropriate in this case, the Court declined to assess the subjective intent of the investigator, instead ruling that there would need to be an "objective assessment of the officer's actions in light of the facts and circumstances confronting him at the time," without regard to his underlying intent or motivation.[40] Objectively, the Court ruled, each recorded call could contain evidence of criminality, and this analysis would need to be done on a case-by-case basis.[41]

United States v. *North*[42] was a case where the Fifth Circuit Court of Appeals used an objective analysis to suppress evidence on the grounds that investigators did not follow minimization requirements.[43] In *North*, prior to eavesdropping on the defendant's phone, investigators were given minimization instructions to listen initially to the conversation to determine whether it was

---

34 18 U.S.C. § 2518(5).
35 *Id.*
36 436 U.S. 128 (1978).
37 *Id.* at 131.
38 *Id.* at 132.
39 *Id.* at 132, 142.
40 *Id.* at 136.
41 *Id.* at 139-40.
42 735 F.3d 212 (5th Cir. 2013).
43 *Id.* at 216.

pertinent or non-pertinent.[44] If it was deemed non-pertinent, the investigator was to cease monitoring the call, and then spot check the call to determine whether or not the conversation had veered toward criminality.[45] In one intercepted call, the defendant admitted more than an hour into the conversation that he had narcotics hidden in his car; however, the defendant did not have any narcotics-related conversations before that point, and investigators had minimized only eight times for an average of less than one minute each time.[46] Based on this information, investigators arrested the defendant and charged him with possession of cocaine.[47] In ruling to suppress the evidence derived from the wiretap, the court held that it was not objectively reasonable for agents to listen in for nearly one hour to a conversation that did not turn to criminal matters until the last few minutes.[48]

2. Privileged Communications

A subcategory of non-pertinent conversations is privileged communications, such as those between attorneys and clients, parishioners and clergymen, doctors and patients, and husbands and wives. Perhaps the most important of these categories in public corruption investigations is attorney-client communications, because so many public officials are lawyers themselves, and frequently consult lawyers in connection with their professional duties. The consequences of improper minimization of these kinds of communications were specifically addressed in *United States* v. *Renzi*.[49] In that case, investigators were given the following instructions regarding attorney-client communications:

> Unless otherwise addressed in this memorandum, never knowingly listen to or record a confidential conversation between a person and his or her attorney when other parties are not present. Anytime that an attorney or law office employee is a party to a conversation, call the agent supervising the interception . . . If it is determined that a conversation involving an attorney constitutes confidential legal consultation of any kind, notify the agent supervising the interception, shut off the monitor and stop recording.[50]

44 *Id.*
45 *Id.*
46 *Id.*
47 *Id.* at 214.
48 *Id.* at 216.
49 722 F. Supp. 2d 1100 (D. Ariz. 2010).
50 *Id.* at 1107 (alterations in original).

In *Renzi*, investigators failed to minimize thirty-seven attorney-client conversations, which the district court held went beyond the scope of what was authorized by the wiretap.[51] The court also took issue with the government concealing from the court in its reports that they were recording these kinds of conversations, even if the conversations were subject to privilege review by agents and lawyers not otherwise involved in the investigation.[52] Investigators also failed to identify as privileged and seal attorney-client calls that it inadvertently intercepted during the wiretap in violation of the USDOJ's *Electronic Surveillance Manual*.[53] The court, viewing the conduct in its totality, suppressed the entire wiretap as opposed to merely suppressing the privileged calls.[54]

In a different case, dealing with the spousal privilege, the court decided against suppressing the whole wiretap. In *United States* v. *Goffer*,[55] investigators on a securities fraud wiretap investigation were given a minimization packet, which included the following instructions:

> There is also a privilege concerning communications between spouses. You are to discontinue monitoring if you discover that you are intercepting a personal communication solely between husband and wife. If it appears that a third person is present during this communication, however, the communication is not privileged. So, too, if the communication deals not with private matters between husband and wife, but instead with ongoing as opposed to past violations of law, it is not a privileged communication.[56]

The district court found that eighteen conversations between the defendant and his wife were not properly minimized.[57] Of these eighteen, three specifically stood out to the court as "particularly egregious," bordering on "voyeuristic," where investigators listened to deeply personal and intimate discussions about their marriage.[58] The court characterized the lack of minimization in relation to these calls "disgraceful," yet declined to suppress the entire

---

51 *Id.* at 1108.

52 *Id.* at 1109.

53 *Id.*; *see also* Electronic Surveillance Manual 27-31 (U.S. Dep't of Justice 2005), https://www.justice.gov/sites/default/files/criminal/legacy/2014/10/29/elec-sur-manual.pdf.

54 *Renzi*, 722 F. Supp. 2d at 1111.

55 756 F. Supp. 2d 588 (S.D.N.Y. 2011).

56 *Id.* at 591.

57 *Id.* at 594.

58 *Id.*

wiretap.[59] The court found that, on the whole, the wiretap was professionally conducted and generally well executed, and that later in the investigation, calls between the defendant and his spouse were minimized within the first ten seconds of the conversation.[60]

Thus, if investigators do not minimize properly, the use of all or part of the wiretap at trial may be in jeopardy. Instructing monitoring agents in this area—and reviewing line sheets to check for compliance—is key to avoiding these problems.

D. *Sealing Requirements*

Immediately upon expiration of the authorized wiretapping period, 18 U.S.C. § 2518(8)(a) requires the recording be made available to the judge and sealed under his directions in order to preserve the integrity of the evidence.[61] In a case where the recording has not been properly placed under seal, the government must provide a "satisfactory explanation" for its failure to comply with the sealing requirement.[62] In *United States* v. *Cline*,[63] the government had a one-week delay in sealing recordings in a narcotics trafficking case because of the judge's court schedule.[64] In upholding the defendant's conviction, the Tenth Circuit Court of Appeals found that there was no evidence of bad faith, tampering, or an attempt by the government to use the delay to gain a tactical advantage.[65]

E. *Notice Requirements*

Section 2518(8)(d) of Title 18 requires that named interceptees, as well as parties to intercepted communications in the judge's discretion, be given notice that their calls were intercepted within ninety days.[66] A violation of this part of the statute does not necessarily result in suppression of the wiretap, however. In *United States* v. *Principie*,[67] investigators arrested several targets

59 *Id.* at 595.
60 *Id.* at 596-98.
61 18 U.S.C. § 2518(8)(a) (2018).
62 *Id.*
63 349 F.3d 1276 (10th Cir. 2003).
64 *Id.* at 1283.
65 *Id.* at 1284.
66 18 U.S.C. § 2518(8)(d).
67 531 F.2d 1132 (2d Cir. 1976).

as a result of an eavesdropping investigation into forged United States savings bonds.[68] The government did not provide notice to the named target, Ralph Principie, or to an unnamed target, Dawn Slomka.[69] In declining to suppress the wiretap, the Second Circuit Court of Appeals held that, on top of showing notice was not properly served within ninety days, there must be a showing of actual prejudice to the defendant.[70] Principie could make no such showing.[71] As it related to Slomka, the court ruled that since Slomka was not a named target to any of the eavesdropping warrants, notice was not required under § 2518(8)(d).[72] Instead, it was up to the judge's discretion, and the court found that not supplying notice to Slomka, who played a minor role in the conspiracy, was not an abuse of discretion.[73]

Nearly forty years after the *Principie* decision, the New York State Court of Appeals issued a similar decision. In *People* v. *Rodriguez*,[74] the court similarly held that suppression was not warranted after investigators failed to properly notify defendant of the warrant until more than ninety days after it expired in violation of section 700.50(3) of the New York Criminal Procedure Law, a similar statute to § 2518(8)(d).[75] The court held that the defendant received notice of the warrant at arraignment, and there was no showing of prejudice as a result of not being notified prior to arraignment.[76]

IV. Strategic Issues to Consider in Public Corruption Wiretaps

Even after prosecutors have fulfilled the necessity and exhaustion requirements, there are numerous strategic issues specifically related to wiretaps in public corruption cases to consider before moving forward with an application. First, a prosecutor needs to decide whose calls to intercept. In

---

68 *Id.* at 1134-36.
69 *Id.* at 1141, 1143.
70 *Id.* at 1141-42.
71 *Id.*
72 *Id.* at 1143.
73 *Id.*
74 970 N.E.2d 816 (N.Y. 2012).
75 *Id.* at 818-19.
76 *Id.* at 819-20.

many wiretap investigations, the ultimate target may be the obvious choice to intercept, but that may not be true in a corruption case for a variety of reasons. For one, in many corruption cases the target will be a politician or other high-ranking government official and many such people are lawyers, raising the possibility of privilege and minimization issues. Second, a high-ranking official target may be more careful about talking on the phone in an inculpatory manner than someone else in the target's circle would be, making a wiretap on the underling's phone more fruitful. Third, it is not uncommon for the person at the top of a criminal conspiracy to let others do the dirty work for him—this is as true for public officials as it is for drug kingpins—meaning the official's phone may not be the best choice because he is not personally handling all of the negotiations and transactions involved in the crime.

For example, in the investigation of New York State Senate Majority Leader Dean Skelos, prosecutors intercepted a phone used by Adam Skelos (Dean's son) and a phone used by Dean.[77] As it turned out, the charged scheme centered around Dean's solicitation of bribes in the form of money and employment for Adam, and Adam's phone captured vital evidence about that scheme.[78] In addition, Adam was much less careful about what he said on the phone than Dean was,[79] and prosecutors did not have to worry as much about privileged calls in connection with that interception because Adam was not a lawyer.

When a lawyer's phone is targeted, extra care is required. Agents and prosecutors must make certain to identify all individuals who call the phone or who are called by the phone, to ensure that minimization is done properly. In advance, agents will have to identify all numbers that the targeted lawyer is likely to call that might create privilege problems, e.g., phone numbers at the target's law firm if he works at a firm, his own lawyer's numbers if he is represented, and his clients' numbers. And as with all cases, prosecutors will have to repeatedly emphasize the importance of proper minimization to all agents and officers monitoring the wire, should themselves review line sheets to ensure compliance with those requirements—or, if there are concerns about the lead prosecutor being tainted, perhaps have a different prosecutor review the line

77 *See* United States v. Skelos, 15 CR 317 (KMW), 2015 U.S. Dist. LEXIS 142485, at *12-13, 16-17 (S.D.N.Y. Oct. 20, 2015).

78 *See id.* at *17-18.

79 *See, e.g.*, James T. Madore, *Wiretaps in Court Show Dean Skelos' Power, Influence in Albany*, Newsday (June 21, 2018), https://www.newsday.com/news/new-york/skelos-retrial-albany-corruption-1.19341752.

sheets. It also may be challenging to tell the difference between legal and political advice when a politician is consulting with his or her counsel, or when a politician's chief of staff is also a lawyer. These complications make monitoring the wire even more important than in the average case.

Another issue that arises with targets who are public officials is the importance of ensuring that the investigation is not, and does not appear to be, politically motivated. As far as the wiretap goes, that means that monitoring agents will need to be particularly careful of conversations between the target and other elected or high-ranking officials, and consider aggressively minimizing political conversations that are not obviously criminal. Regardless of the prosecutor's office involved in the case—U.S. Attorney's Office, state attorney general's office, or local prosecutor's office—no prosecutor will want to face allegations that a case is politically motivated, and listening in too freely to a public official's conversations about political matters may add fuel to that fire.

For all these reasons, it is essential to acknowledge any minimization mistakes in the regular reports to the court and in any requests to extend the wire. If litigation over the wiretap occurs (which should be expected in a public corruption case), the prosecutor will want to have established diligence in fixing any problems with monitoring promptly and completely. Disclosure of everything to the judge as soon as practicable and before asking for an extension may demonstrate that diligence.

Conclusion

Eavesdropping continues to be one of the most effective ways of investigating and prosecuting cases in the United States, and can provide highly valuable evidence in a public corruption case. But corruption cases have unique challenges, so prosecutors should remember the above practical and legal considerations before using this kind of investigative tool.

Chapter 2.4

Tools for Obtaining Online Evidence

Michael Chu

Michael Chu serves as the International Computer Hacking & Intellectual Property Attorney Advisor for Internet Fraud & Public Health for the United States Department of Justice.[1] *Since 2007, Mr. Chu has prosecuted computer and intellectual property crimes as the Computer Hacking & Intellectual Property Coordinator first at the U.S. Attorney's Office in Las Vegas and then in Houston. Before joining the USDOJ, Mr. Chu was a litigator in private practice where he was named a Texas Rising Star. While in private practice, he created a pro bono asylum program which won the Human Rights Initiative of North Texas's Angel of Freedom Award. He frequently speaks on corporate data thefts and intellectual property issues and has taught at numerous USDOJ/State Department programs.*

Introduction

Any effective conspiracy requires coordination with multiple participants. The same online services that make it easy to stay in touch with friends or share files with family also make it easy for conspirators to orchestrate crimes. As technology advances quickly, law enforcement is responding quickly to keep up with advancing criminal tactics. This chapter introduces some basic approaches to obtaining evidence to bring online conspirators to justice.

---

1 Although the author will attempt to keep his views consistent with the policies of the USDOJ, if any views inadvertently deviate from those policies, they are purely his own.

For example, if a whistleblower has reported that the target of an investigation is anonymously directing the criminal conspiracy from behind an easily disposable email account, such as Burner@fakemail.com, investigators and prosecutors can use that one piece of information to uncover further evidence. Preliminarily, investigators seek to verify that this email account exists and is active by obtaining basic subscriber information. Next, investigators may learn who else is communicating with this account, and ultimately may obtain the contents of the emails being sent to and from this account. Achieving each step requires time and legal process, so issuing a request to preserve the contents of this account is the very first step.

I. Preservation Requests: Preserving the Status Quo

A. *Preservation Requests and How to Serve Them*

Issuing a request to a provider that directs it to preserve the content of an account is fairly straightforward. No court order is required. The provider is obligated to preserve evidence upon "request of a governmental entity."[2] The statute, discussed in Part II(A) below, does not specify what form this request should take. As discussed below, some providers that receive a large volume of requests have streamlined the process by asking investigators to fill in an online form.

Other providers may receive requests far less frequently and may not have an online form. In this case, a request can usually be served on the provider by email. Experience suggests that these preservation requests should generally:

- Be on official letterhead to minimize questions as to the request's authenticity;
- List the account identifiers (e.g., email address, username, Facebook user ID) so that the provider can identify the account you wish to preserve;

---

2 18 U.S.C. § 2703(f)(1) (2018). This includes both federal and state governments. 18 U.S.C. § 2711(4).

- List the categories of items you want preserved with reasonable particularity; and

- Provide the contact information for you and your agent to help the provider track the request or in case the provider has any questions.

By statute, providers must preserve the items requested for ninety days.[3] The statute also provides for one ninety-day extension.[4] If an extension is requested, providers will generally retain what was originally preserved, not make a second snapshot of the account as of the date of that second request.

B. *Effects and Risks of Preservation Request*

A preservation request is only a preliminary step that should accompany quick action to begin the legal process to obtain this evidence. It is necessary because electronic evidence can rapidly disappear, whether due to intentional deletion with a touch of a button or automatic overwriting as companies make room for new information by deleting old records on a rolling basis. Although a preservation request will maintain the status quo for ninety days, the evidence needed to prove the case is not necessarily preserved by the initial request. The preservation request likely covers only the initial clues that will lead to other evidence several links down the chain.

For example, since email accounts are often free, criminals often hide behind temporary accounts, which can easily be created and discarded, to commit crimes anonymously. Nonetheless, searching the contents of the temporary account may yield clues as to the user's identity and location. Emails sent to and from that account, as well as any recovery email addresses, may provide leads back to other accounts used by the criminal to conduct his personal business. Because this downstream evidence is not covered by the initial preservation request, legal process must be quickly obtained to acquire evidence that comprises the next link in the chain.

Despite their benefits, it should be noted that preservation requests carry the risk of exposing a covert investigation. The statute that governs this

---

3 18 U.S.C. § 2703(f)(2).

4 *Id.*

area, the Electronic Communications Privacy Act (ECPA),[5] does not provide for non-disclosure of preservation requests—only for non-disclosure of legal process. Some internet service providers may notify customers of preservation requests.[6] Alternatively, the investigation's target may be running a private server, in which case sending a preservation request will alert him to the investigation.

C. *Preserving Foreign Evidence with the High Tech Crime 24/7 Network*

If online evidence is being kept by a foreign service provider, the High Tech Crime 24/7 Network can help request preservation of evidence in other countries. If the foreign service provider is located in a member country and if the member country and foreign service provider are not likely to alert the account holder, then the USDOJ can contact that member country's representative, which in turn will issue the preservation request.[7] Once that evidence is preserved, a variety of tools exist to obtain the evidence through legal process.[8] For the United States, the High Tech Crime 24/7 Network is administered by the USDOJ's Computer Crimes & Intellectual Property Section (CCIPS) and requests to preserve foreign evidence can be made either by contacting the USDOJ CCIPS duty attorney or by contacting your nearest U.S. Attorney's Office and asking to speak to the Office's Computer Hacking/Intellectual Property Coordinator.[9]

---

5 The part of the ECPA discussed in this chapter is also known as the Stored Communications Act, codified at 18 U.S.C. §§ 2701-2712, enacted as Title II of the ECPA. For discussion of the Wiretap Act, 18 U.S.C. §§ 2501-2522, see Chapter 2.3.

6 For a discussion of non-disclosure orders in the context of legal process, see Part V(A) below.

7 *See* Albert Rees, *24/7 High Tech Crime Network*, Computer Crime & Intellectual Property Section, Criminal Division, U.S. Dep't of Justice (Apr. 2007), http://www.oas.org/juridico/english/cyb20_network_en.pdf.

8 *See, e.g.*, Michael Chu, *International Cooperation: A Primer of the Tools and Resources Available When Your Investigation Takes You Overseas*, 62 U.S. Att'ys' Bull. 23, 24-29 (Mar. 2014), https://www.justice.gov/sites/default/files/usao/legacy/2014/04/11/usab6202.pdf.

9 *See About CCIPS*, U.S. Dep't of Justice (May 26, 2015), https://www.justice.gov/criminal-ccips/about-ccips.

II. Legal Process to Obtain Electronic Evidence

A. *Overview of the Electronic Communications Privacy Act*

After a domestic service provider's data has been preserved, the next step is to obtain this information within the ninety-day time period. In the context of electronic evidence, the ECPA governs attempts to obtain information from an entity when it acts as either an "electronic communication service" or a "remote computing service."[10] As its name suggests, the ECPA focuses on the balance between our society's privacy rights with our society's needs for effective law enforcement.

Under the ECPA:

- A "remote computing service" "means the provision to the public of computer storage or processing services by means of an electronic communications system."[11] Examples include a cloud storage provider like DropBox or Amazon's EC2 (elastic cloud computing) service, which rents out computing processing power.

- An "electronic communication service" "means any service which provides to users thereof the ability to send or receive wire or electronic communications."[12] Unlike the definition of a remote computing service, this definition is not limited to services provided "to the public," so it also applies to services being privately provided by, for example, employers.[13] In turn, both "wire communication" and "electronic communication" are broadly defined.[14] Examples include email providers like Yahoo! or Google (Gmail).

If either of these definitions apply to the service provider holding the information being sought, then producing that information is a federal violation unless (1) legal process (discussed below) has been provided, or (2) an exception—such as an emergency involving the danger of death or serious

10 18 U.S.C. § 2702(a) (2018).

11 *Id.* § 2711(2).

12 *Id.* §§ 2510(15), 2711(1).

13 *See id.* § 2711(2).

14 *See* 18 U.S.C. § 2510(1), (12) (wire communications and electronic communications, respectively).

physical injury—applies that allows the service provider to voluntarily provide the information you seek.[15]

As its name implies, the Electronic Communications Privacy Act protects the public's privacy by increasing the level of judicial scrutiny as increasingly private information is sought. Discussed below are three categories of legal process to obtain evidence. The most private category of evidence—contents—is subject to the most judicial scrutiny and requires a search warrant. The middle ground—"other" information—requires an order under 18 U.S.C. § 2703(d). The least private category of evidence—basic subscriber information—is subject to the least judicial scrutiny and requires a subpoena.

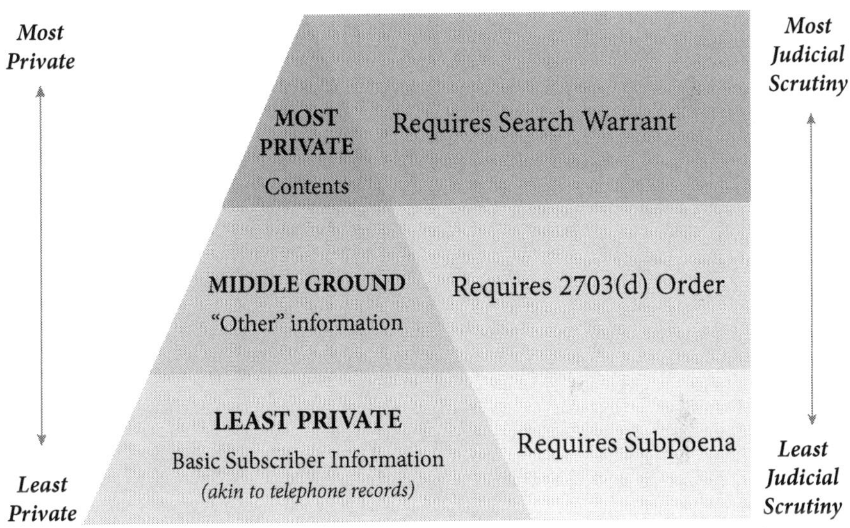

B. *Least Private: Basic Subscriber Information Only Requires Subpoena*

Returning to the example above, early in the investigation, investigators may want to check if the email address Burner@fakemail.com was active during the relevant time period. This kind of basic subscriber information,

15 18 U.S.C. § 2702(b), (c).

which is the least private type of information and the equivalent of phone records, is obtainable with a subpoena.[16]

Under 18 U.S.C. § 2703(c)(2), a federal or state subpoena can be used to obtain the following account information:

> (A) name;
> (B) address;
> (C) local and long distance telephone connection records, or records of session times and durations;
> (D) length of service (including start date) and types of service utilized;
> (E) telephone or instrument number or other subscriber number or identity, including any temporarily assigned network address [such as an IP address assigned to the user when the account was accessed]; and
> (F) means and source of payment for such service (including any credit card or bank account number) [Gmail is a free service, but a user may have listed a credit card to pay for other Google services such as Google Voice or Google Play (the name of its app store)].[17]

When obtaining information, it is helpful to distinguish between two types of information: (1) information created by the provider versus (2) information supplied by the user. Information like times and dates of service or activity is created by the provider to keep its service running, and thus, is less able to be falsified by the user (who is often the target of the investigation). On the other hand, information provided by the user is rarely verified, and thus, can be falsified by the user. That said, user provided information can sometimes lead to important clues as to the user's identity. For example, the author once convicted someone who created an email address derived from the name of a fictional mafia boss from the television show *Wiseguy.* A key part of the case was identifying who had used that email account. As it turned out, the

---

16 *See* 18 U.S.C. § 2703(c)(2)(A)-(F). Alternatively, if enough evidence exists to satisfy the higher standard for obtaining a 2703(d) order or a search warrant for the account (discussed below), then obtaining basic subscriber information may be included in those types of legal processes. *See id.* (noting that you can obtain this information with a subpoena "or any means available under paragraph (1)").

17 18 U.S.C. § 2703(c)(2).

defendant was not just a fan of the show, but he had also been charged in his youth with a killing as a mafia enforcer. This, combined with other clues, led to his eventual unmasking and conviction.

Means of payment and IP addresses, obtainable through a subpoena, may seem innocuous, but may lead to additional clues. Payment information may lead to the identity of the target or may be a stolen credit card bought on the dark web. IP addresses may be the true IP address assigned by your target's real internet service provider or it may lead to evidence showing intent to mask his true address and identity. Alone, payment and IP information may not be conclusive proof, but they can make for promising leads.

C. *2703(d) Orders: More than a Subpoena, Less than a Search Warrant*

Continuing with the example above, basic subscriber information for Burner@fakemail.com may have yielded useful leads but not enough evidence to obtain a search warrant. As suggested in the diagram above, between those two ends of the continuum—subpoena for subscriber information (least judicial scrutiny) and search warrant for substantive content (most scrutiny)—a wide category of useful evidence may be obtained through an order under 18 U.S.C. § 2703(d). For example, so called "envelope" information, which would show what email addresses are corresponding with Burner@fakemail.com and when the messages are sent, is in this category of information. Envelope information can be obtained through an order under 18 U.S.C. § 2703(d), which is often called a 2703(d) order.[18]

To be clear, contents of those messages (including the subject lines) cannot be obtained without a search warrant.[19] A 2703(d) order, however, is not just limited to envelope information. Many types of information, short of contents of an account, are obtainable, such as:

---

18 *See id.* § 2703(b), (c), (d).

19 *See id.* § 2510(8) ("'contents,' when used with respect to any wire, oral, or electronic communication, includes any information concerning the substance, purport, or meaning of that communication"); Computer Crime and Intellectual Property Section, Criminal Division, U.S. Dep't of Justice, Searching and Seizing Computers and Obtaining Electronic Evidence in Criminal Investigations 122-23 (2009); Orin S. Kerr, *A User's Guide to the Stored Communications Act, and a Legislator's Guide to Amending It*, 72 Geo. Wash. L. Rev. 1208, 1228 (2004).

- List from Apple's App Store of applications purchased by a target;
- List of other accounts from that same provider (in the example, Gmail) linked by browser cookie to the target's account (here, Burner@fakemail.com);
- List of other accounts that had been accessed by the same IP address around the same time/date that your target's account (Burner@fakemail.com) had logged into email services (usually, providers limit this information to a twenty-four hour period);
- Records of devices owned by a suspect including Media Access Control addresses, Unique Device Identifiers, or other identifiers that might be compared to devices seized during a physical search warrant (assuming that the provider tracks that information); and
- The precise physical location of a certain computer server to determine where it is (e.g., within a state in the United States or overseas).

To obtain a 2703(d) order, the government must file an application with the court that provides (1) specific and articulable facts that (2) show that there are reasonable grounds to believe that (3) the information sought is relevant and material to (4) an ongoing criminal investigation.[20] A 2703(d) order can issue from any "court of competent jurisdiction" which includes "a court of general criminal jurisdiction of a State authorized by the law of that State to issue search warrants."[21]

A court may refuse to issue a 2703(d) order under some circumstances. If state law otherwise prohibits issuing the order, a court may refuse to grant it.[22] The service provider may move to quash if complying with the 2703(d) order would cause an undue burden on the provider.[23] Also, unlike a search warrant, the statute does not require an affidavit from the agent, but a court may choose to decline to grant the 2703(d) order without one. Within these confines, a

---

20 18 U.S.C. § 2703(d).
21 *Id.* § 2711(3)(B).
22 *Id.* § 2703(d).
23 *Id.*

2703(d) order can be a useful tool for obtaining information short of the content of online communications.

D. *Search Warrants: Obtaining Communications, Contents of Online Accounts, and Location*

1. Warrants are Required to Search the Contents of Online Accounts

Returning to the example above, after further investigation of subscriber information and envelope information for Burner@fakemail.com, an investigator may seek to review the contents of emails to and from this account, as well as any documents or pictures attached to these emails or otherwise stored in this account. Even temporary accounts often contain clues as to the user's true identity and location—or can lead to clues as to other email accounts that may hold more evidence. For example, in one case where a perpetrator hid behind a temporary email account, the author worked with a talented Federal Bureau of Investigation investigator to find evidence of another email account used by the target. Although that too turned out to be a temporary account, investigators kept working back, obtaining search warrants for the target's other email accounts, until finally locating the target's long-term personal email account. That personal email account helpfully contained evidence of the target's identity, including a scan of his passport, documentation of his finances, personal photographs, and correspondence with his family.

A search warrant is required to obtain these contents.[24] Requiring a warrant also makes intuitive sense as contents are at the most private end of the spectrum, and thus, require the most judicial scrutiny. These search warrants can be obtained from any "court of competent jurisdiction," which, as noted above, includes state courts that are empowered to issue warrants. Thus, state warrants can be obtained if they are "issued using State warrant procedures."[25]

---

24 *Id.* § 2703(a), (b). Subsections 2703(a) & (b) also state that contents can be obtained without a warrant under certain circumstances (for example, where an email has gone unopened for more than 180 days, the equivalent of being abandoned). However, in *United States v. Warshak*, 631 F.3d 266, 274 (6th Cir. 2010), the Sixth Circuit Court of Appeals held that a warrant was required to obtain contents of an online account, a holding that most providers have since followed. As a practical matter, only a warrant will obtain contents.

25 18 U.S.C. § 2703(a), (b).

Despite the higher burdens, warrants for the contents of an online account can yield a treasure trove of evidence. One of the most difficult burdens for white collar prosecutors is to prove mens rea, a defendant's knowledge and intent. The frank, unvarnished email correspondence between conspirators can establish that intent. Even better, this correspondence is sometimes written in real time as the crime is being committed. In one of the author's cases, a search warrant obtained the archived chats between a hacker and his buyer. In those chats, the hacker described the progress of his intrusion in real time, including the point that system administrators had kicked him out of the network—as well as the point, several hours later, when he found a way back in.

Notably, these principles apply to more than just emails, as companies like Facebook, Google, Yahoo!, and Microsoft increasingly offer more than just email services. For example, Facebook stores not just user posts, but also member-to-member instant messages.[26] Similarly, Gmail users can store documents and archive Google's instant messages in the Google Drive cloud storage account associated with a Gmail email address. A search warrant for a Google or iCloud account could even yield otherwise encrypted and inaccessible data, such as messages through WhatsApp, an encrypted point-to-point messaging service that does not itself have access to the private decryption keys. Some smartphones prompt their users to link their phones to Gmail accounts (for Android phones) or iCloud (for iPhone), so some data from encrypted services like WhatsApp can often be obtained via search warrants.[27]

2. Location Records Require Search Warrant

Until recently, the legal process required to obtain location information collected by a provider was determined by whether the investigator sought prospective location information, which required a warrant, or historical location records, which did not.[28] That changed in June 2018 when the U.S. Supreme Court handed down *Carpenter* v. *United States*, which generally requires a

---

26 *See, e.g.*, United States v. Recio, 884 F.3d 230, 233 (4th Cir. 2018) (holding that song lyrics posted on Facebook page were admissions adopted by defendant under Federal Rule of Evidence 801(d)(2)(A)).

27 *See About Google Drive Backups*, WhatsApp, https://faq.whatsapp.com/android/chats/about-google-drive-backups/?lang=fb (last visited Apr. 19, 2021) ("Media and messages you back up aren't protected by WhatsApp end-to-end encryption while in Google Drive.").

28 *See In re* Historical Cell Site Data, 724 F.3d 600, 605-15 (5th Cir. 2013).

search warrant for records of even historical cell tower location information, absent exigent circumstances.[29]

3. Practice Tips for Obtaining ECPA Search Warrants

First, a search warrant affidavit should describe not just the sufficiency of probable cause to believe that a crime was committed, but also of probable cause to believe that evidence will be found within the account to be searched (e.g., Burner@fakemail.com).

This may involve attempting to prove that the evidence you seek is likely still in the account to be searched and has not been deleted. The investigator's training and experience can establish that conspirators often retain these kinds of records. Why would conspirators preserve incriminating evidence? As investigators have found, often the conspirators want to memorialize who did what to resolve any later disputes as to who was owed what when it comes time to divide the proceeds of their conspiracy.

Another rationale that investigators can articulate in their search warrant affidavits is to describe how users generally tend to retain electronic information. Companies like Google and Yahoo! have, for years, expressly encouraged people to never delete their emails and other information by offering increasingly more email storage.[30] As investigators have found, criminals have often responded to these companies' incentives by not deleting anything from their accounts. If these facts are within your investigator's training and experience, then consider describing these experiences in the search warrant affidavit.

---

29 Carpenter v. United States, 138 S. Ct. 2206, 2221 (2018).

30 *See* Matthew Panzarino, *Yahoo Mail Gets Cross-Platform Themes, 1 TB of Storage, 'Mail Plus' Features For All and Better 'Conversations'*, TECH CRUNCH (Oct. 8, 2013), https://techcrunch.com/2013/10/08/yahoo-updates-mail-on-all-platformswith-new-design-that-mirrors-award-winning-weather-ios-app/.

III. How to Serve ECPA Search Warrants, 2703(d) Orders, and Subpoenas

A. *Practice Tips*

Most service providers publish law enforcement guides that describe how to serve legal process on them quickly and efficiently. It may help to remember that from the providers' perspective, the goal is generally to comply with legal process as efficiently and cost-effectively as possible. Serving legal process by fax has often given way to email, which has now increasingly been replaced by law enforcement-specific online portals. Many guides also describe what kinds of information can be obtained. Common examples of these law enforcement guides are listed in the footnotes.[31]

B. *Microsoft Issues: Domestic Service Providers Must Produce Information Even If Outside the United States*

Currently, service providers that are subject to U.S. law are required to comply with ECPA's obligations, regardless of whether the information at issue is stored inside or outside the United States. Until March 2018, service providers had balked at producing information that they stored outside the United States. The so-called *Microsoft* issue first arose when Microsoft Corporation successfully objected to a search warrant that compelled it to produce emails that it retained outside the United States.[32] After that Second Circuit Court of Appeals decision, every district court (and magistrate judge) to consider the

---

31 *See, e.g.*, *Information for Law Enforcement Authorities*, Facebook, https://www.facebook.com/safety/groups/law/guidelines/ (last visited Apr. 19, 2021); *Requests for User Information FAQs*, Google, https://support.google.com/transparencyreport/answer/7381738?hl=en (last visited Apr. 19, 2021); *Legal Process Guidelines*, Apple, https://www.apple.com/legal/privacy/law-enforcement-guidelines-us.pdf (last visited Apr. 19, 2021); *Guidelines for Law Enforcement*, Twitter, https://help.twitter.com/en/rules-and-policies/twitter-law-enforcement-support (last visited Apr. 19, 2021); *ISP List*, SEARCH, http://www.search.org/resources/isp-list/ (last visited Apr. 19, 2021).

32 *In re* Warrant to Search a Certain E-Mail Account Controlled & Maintained by Microsoft Corp., 829 F.3d 197, 209-10, 222 (2d Cir. 2016), *en banc review denied*, 855 F.3d 53 (2d Cir. 2017).

issue disagreed with the *Microsoft* ruling.[33] Given the prospect of an imminent circuit split, USDOJ asked the Supreme Court to take up the issue.[34]

While the case was pending before the Supreme Court, on March 23, 2018, Congress passed the Clarifying Lawful Overseas Use of Data (CLOUD) Act.[35] That act clarifies that ECPA's obligations apply to all data within a service provider's possession, custody, or control, "regardless of whether such communication, record, or other information is located within or outside of the United States."[36]

IV. Authenticating Records Using Record Certifications

Recently, the Federal Rules of Evidence's provisions for self-authenticating evidence were amended to ease the admission of electronic evidence. (Although these are federal rules, many states' evidence rules are similar, and it seems likely that states may adopt these new provisions as litigants in those jurisdictions increasingly present electronic evidence.)

Rule 902(11) has long permitted authentication of records of regularly conducted activities by certification.[37] In 2017, Federal Rule of Evidence 902(13) was added to allow authentication of certain electronic evidence by certification.[38] This certification process still leaves room for certain defense

---

33 *See, e.g.*, *In re* Search Warrant No. 16-960-M-1 to Google, 275 F. Supp. 3d 605, 619 (E.D. Pa. 2017); *In re* Search of Content Stored at Premises Controlled by Google Inc., 16-mc-80263-RS, 2017 U.S. Dist. LEXIS 129068, at *3 (N.D. Cal. Aug. 14, 2017); *In re* Search of Info. Associated with [redacted]@gmail.com that is Stored at Premises Controlled by Google, Inc., 16-mj-00757 (BAH), 2017 U.S. Dist. LEXIS 130153, at *13 (D.D.C. July 31, 2017).

34 *See* United States v. Microsoft Corp., 138 S. Ct. 1186, 1187 (2018). Thirty-six attorneys general filed an amicus brief in support of USDOJ. Brief for the State of Vermont, et al., as Amici Curiae Supporting Petitioners, *Microsoft Corp.*, 138 S. Ct. 118 (No. 17-2) (July 27, 2017).

35 The CLOUD Act was passed as part of the Consolidated Appropriations Act, 2018, Pub. L. 115-141, and amends the Stored Communications Act, 18 U.S.C. §§ 2701-2712 (2018). *Microsoft Corp.*, 138 S. Ct. at 1187-88.

36 18 U.S.C. § 2713.

37 Fed. R. Evid. 902(11).

38 *Id.* 902(13).

challenges.[39] Nonetheless, certification is useful in eliminating many common challenges as to admissibility, leaving courts to rule on more focused challenges.

Every state's evidence rules differ in some respects, but the Federal Rules of Evidence generally require advanced written notice to defendants of an intention to use these certifications to introduce evidence.[40] They may also require the proponent to make the record and certification available for inspection in order to determine in advance if there are legitimate challenges to authenticity. As state courts increasingly face these issues, state legislatures may consider adopting similar provisions.

V. Non-Disclosure Orders, 18 U.S.C. § 2705(b): Avoid Tipping Off Your Target

A. *Obtaining a Non-Disclosure Order*

A service provider normally has no obligation to avoid notifying the account holder (i.e., its customer) that it has been served with legal process. Although some providers will voluntarily respect an investigator's written request to avoid notifying account holders that legal process has been served, the safest course is to obtain a non-disclosure order. Under 18 U.S.C. § 2705(b), a court shall enter a non-disclosure order if there is reason to believe that notification would result in:

1. endangering the life or physical safety of an individual;
2. flight from prosecution;
3. destruction of or tampering with evidence;

39 *See id.* 902(13) advisory committee's note to 2017 amendments ("Similarly, a certification authenticating a computer output, such as a spreadsheet, does not preclude an objection that the information produced [by the spreadsheet software] is unreliable—the authentication establishes only that the output came from the computer.").

40 *Id.* ("[T]he expense and inconvenience of producing a witness to authenticate an item of electronic evidence is often unnecessary . . . the adversary either stipulates authenticity before the witness is called or fails to challenge the authentication testimony once it is presented.").

4. intimidation of potential witnesses; or

5. otherwise seriously jeopardizing an investigation or unduly delaying a trial.[41]

USDOJ policy requires federal applications for non-disclosure to be limited to a period of one year or less and to be tailored to the facts of each case.[42] Although federal internal policies do not, of course, bind state authorities, service providers may attempt to resist any state court order that attempts to impose a longer period of non-disclosure.

B. *Practice Tip: Determine If the Provider Will Respect Legal Process*

As a practical matter, most mainstream providers will honor a non-disclosure order from the court. However, if the provider does not have a written law enforcement guide, consider first investigating whether the provider is likely to notify your targets. Obviously, if the target or a conspirator hosts the requested emails on a small private server, a non-disclosure order will not be effective. Similarly, some providers can be openly hostile to authority of any sort.

Conclusion

As online services are increasingly used to orchestrate crimes and conspiracies of all stripes, the techniques and processes outlined above will help obtain evidence to solve cases and bring criminals to justice.

---

41 18 U.S.C. § 2705(b)(1)-(5).

42 *See* Justice Manual § 9-13.700 (U.S. Dep't of Justice 2020), https://www.justice.gov/jm/jm-9-13000-obtaining-evidence#9-13.700.

Chapter 2.5

Working Effectively with an Undercover Officer, Confidential Informant, or Cooperating Witness

Daniel G. Cort, Stacy P. Aronowitz

Daniel G. Cort serves as First Deputy Commissioner of the New York City Department of Investigation, which is New York City's Inspector General, with independent oversight of city government. From March 2014 to December 2018, Mr. Cort was the chief of the Public Integrity Bureau of the New York Attorney General's Office. Prior to that, he was an assistant district attorney at the New York County District Attorney's Office for nineteen years, most recently serving as chief of that office's Public Integrity Unit.

Stacy P. Aronowitz serves as Counsel to the Criminal Division of the New York Attorney General's Office. She joined the office in 2004 and served as the Deputy Chief of the Public Integrity Bureau from 2007 to 2019. In 2019, she became Counsel to the Criminal Division. Earlier in her career, she worked in the litigation department at Schulte Roth & Zabel, LLP.

Introduction

Deception is a loaded term filled with negative connotations. It is not something that lawyers, and especially prosecutors, should usually engage in or direct others to engage in while doing their jobs. But deception is, by definition, required during undercover investigations. The inherent contradiction between the usual expectation of honesty and truthfulness in law enforcement and the need to be less than forthright when using undercover officers, confidential informants, and cooperating witnesses makes this topic complex. It is an area where prosecutors and investigators can be incredibly creative. The possibilities of creating scenarios to catch criminals is limited only by the imagination of law enforcement and, of course, the law. Because of the balance between the need for deception and the need to follow the law, prosecutors should exercise care and caution when using this law enforcement technique.

I. Background

A. *Definitions*

For the purposes of this chapter, the following definitions will apply:

- An *undercover officer* (UC) is an employee of a law enforcement organization who uses an assumed name or assumed identity to engage in investigative activity.[1]
- A *confidential informant* (CI) is someone who provides information to law enforcement regarding criminal activities.[2] The police may have agreed with the CI that the CI's identity will not be disclosed, and the identity of the CI may be unknown to the prosecutor. A CI may have a range of motivations, and law enforcement personnel should generally try to assess a witness's true motivation, which may include revenge, greed, power, some payment or benefit, good citizenship, and avoiding criminal prosecution or jail.

---

1 This definition is adapted from the U.S. Department of Justice Guidelines on FBI Undercover Operations. *See* Attorney General's Guidelines on FBI Undercover Operations 1 (U.S. Dep't of Justice 2002), https://www.justice.gov/sites/default/files/ag/legacy/2013/09/24/undercover-fbi-operations.pdf.

2 *See* Attorney General's Guidelines Regarding the Use of Confidential Informants 2 (U.S. Dep't of Justice), https://fas.org/irp/agency/doj/fbi/dojguidelines.pdf (last visited Apr. 19, 2021).

- A *cooperator* or cooperating witness is a person who is criminally culpable and has agreed to cooperate with law enforcement in exchange for consideration on a pending criminal case.[3]

This article will refer to UCs, CIs, and cooperators collectively as *covert actors* and their actions assisting law enforcement as *undercover operations*.

B. *History of Covert Actors in the Courts*

The Supreme Court has a long history of approving undercover operations. In *Grimm* v. *United States*[4] and *Andrews* v. *United States*,[5] the Supreme Court permitted the tactic of postal inspectors assuming false identities to investigate individuals mailing obscene material. Since those decisions, the Supreme Court has made clear that "[c]riminal activity is such that stealth and strategy are necessary weapons in the arsenal of the police officer."[6]

II. Deciding Whether to Work with a Covert Actor

There are both benefits and pitfalls to working with covert actors and the prosecutor must always balance them when deciding whether to use these law enforcement tools.

A. *Potential Drawbacks to Working with a Covert Actor*

It is important to consider the downsides of working with a covert actor. Use of deception may carry some potential ethical risks.[7] The most serious issue is the risk of entrapping otherwise innocent individuals who are not predisposed to engaging in criminal activity.[8] Prosecutors who supervise covert actors must always be mindful of this risk. The purpose of undercover operations is to gather evidence of criminal conduct, not to create it.

---

3 *See id.* For an explanation of cooperation agreements, see Chapter 1.8, Part II(A).

4 156 U.S. 604, 609-10 (1895).

5 162 U.S. 420, 423 (1896).

6 Sherman v. United States, 356 U.S. 369, 372 (1958).

7 *See* Model Rule of Prof'l Conduct r. 8.4(c) (Am. Bar Ass'n 2020). *See infra* Part V(C).

8 *See infra* Part V(A); *see also* Chapter 4.3, Part IV.

Similarly, when using deception, those in law enforcement must be careful to prevent their activities from causing an increase in criminal activity. This is especially true for long term operations when law enforcement creates illegal business, such as a fictitious fencing operation, or participating in the purchasing of narcotics.

Undercover operations can be time consuming and complicated, with no guarantee of success. Likewise, using covert actors can be resource intensive and create potential safety issues. Only those offices or departments with sufficient resources should utilize these law enforcement techniques. It may be necessary for smaller offices and departments to coordinate with federal partners or other, larger law enforcement agencies.[9]

B. *Potential Benefits of Working with a Covert Actor*

On the other hand, using covert actors offers significant benefits. Covert actors can provide law enforcement with invaluable information. Sometimes, the use of undercover operations is the only way to investigate and prosecute secretive and consensual crimes where no direct participant wants the crimes detected. These include public corruption matters like bribery, where the public is the victim but has no way of discovering the harm, as well as many types of white collar crime, narcotics and gambling operations, organized crime, and terrorism.

C. *Factors to Consider When Deciding Whether to Use a Covert Actor*

A primary consideration is whether the specific covert actor will be effective in obtaining necessary evidence. Not everyone can be effective at using deception. Research reported in the *Journal of Nonverbal Behavior* found that convincing lying is associated with good social skills, such as an ability to control your words as well as controlling nonverbal communication. The researchers studied lying by adolescents and found that those with the highest level of social competence were the most talented liars. They were able to verbalize untruths while controlling their nonverbal behavior, including facial expression, vocal pitch and mannerisms, posture, and eye contact. Those with

9 For discussion of partnering with federal authorities and using forensic resources, see Chapter 2.6 and Chapter 2.7 respectively.

the poorest social skills had the most trouble controlling their nonverbal behavior when lying.[10]

Another consideration is whether the subject of the criminal investigation is likely to provide false, misleading, or self-serving statements because he is aware that the other person is a covert actor or that the conversation is being recorded. Research shows that most people's ability to detect lies is no more accurate than chance, and this finding generally holds true across different types of people.[11] Research also shows, however, that skilled liars are better at detecting lying by others, and that the capacity to detect lies is associated with the ability to effectively deceive others.[12] In a small study of teenage offenders and teenage non-offenders, the findings demonstrated that the offenders were significantly more accurate in their ability to detect deception than the non-offenders. [13] The authors suggest that experience in a criminal environment may mean that teenage offenders frequently lie and are lied to and thus develop greater skill than non-offenders in effectively lying and detecting lies.[14] Taken together, these studies suggest that even a skillful UC or CI may still find it challenging to ensnare a sophisticated corrupt official or other bad actor, but—as the large number of successful cases developed through undercover operations attests—may nonetheless find success.

In addition to being effective, a prosecutor must consider whether the covert actor is reliable. Will the CI be available when needed? Will he or she follow instructions? Will he or she meet with police officers when asked to do so? Should the operation require more than a few days, will the CI be available for the duration of the operation?

An effective undercover operation requires significant resources. While an isolated controlled call may not be particularly time consuming, many

---

10 Robert S. Feldman et al., *Nonverbal Deception Abilities and Adolescents' Social Competence: Adolescents with Higher Social Skills are Better Liars*, 23 J. Nonverbal Behav. 237, 237-49 (1999).

11 Charles F. Bond, Jr., & Bella M. DePaulo, *Accuracy of Deception Judgments*, 10 Personality & Soc. Psychol. Rev. 214, 230-34 (2006).

12 Gordon R. T. Wright et al., *"You Can't Kid a Kidder": Association Between Production and Detection of Deception in an Interactive Deception Task*, Frontiers in Hum. Neuroscience 1, 6 (2012).

13 Louise Jupe et al., *Teenage Offenders' Ability to Detect Deception in Their Peers*, 30 Applied Cognitive Psychol. 401, 401 (2016).

14 *Id.*

undercover operations will only be effective over a longer period of time, and the investigative team must be willing to invest in an operation that may last weeks or months. In addition to an effective covert actor, appropriate staffing is critical, including whatever personnel is needed to protect the identity and safety of the covert actor. Proper technology is also important, often including high-tech recording devices.

Before committing to the time and expense of an undercover operation, a prosecutor should consider whether other ways of gathering the evidence may be more effective. Building a document case may be less costly and require fewer people. Making use of electronic eavesdropping, while costly and personnel intensive,[15] may be less risky. Both of these other methods can, of course, be used in conjunction with an undercover operation.

Other factors to consider include:

- Whether the undercover operation will constitute an unnecessary intrusion or invasion into personal privacy of innocent people connected to the target, such as unwitting spouses, significant others, and children;
- Whether the target of the operation is represented by counsel;[16] and
- Whether the illegal conduct of the covert actor might be too offensive to a jury and might therefore adversely impact the jury's view of a case (e.g., firearms trafficking, narcotics sales).

III. Practical Issues

A. *The Need for a Predicate*

An undercover operation should not be a fishing expedition. Before committing resources to an undercover operation, and given the risks of such an undertaking, prosecutors should make sure that they have reason to believe a

---

15 See Chapter 2.3 for a discussion of the requirements and costs associated with obtaining a wiretap.

16 *See infra* Part V(B).

crime occurred, is occurring, or will occur. Predicates, which are articulable reasons for conducting an undercover operation, are necessary to counter a later entrapment argument. A predicate may be established in a number of ways, including from surveillance, a citizen's complaint, an anonymous tip, a tip from an informant, a newspaper article, data mining, or information gleaned from a separate investigation.

B. *Planning*

Planning is imperative. Prior to commencing an undercover operation, the prosecutor should identify the target or targets, determine potential costs, ensure adequate staffing, and plan for the time the operation will take. All prosecutor's offices that plan to oversee undercover operations should ensure that they or their investigative partners have the appropriate equipment and devices available so that such an operation can be instituted quickly and on little notice. When possible, prosecutors should make use of the covert actor in the planning. Covert actors likely know the target and the scheme better than anyone else, so it is helpful to ask them about possible scenarios, and brainstorm with them about approaches and techniques. Note, however, that care should be taken not to appear to make a CI or cooperator a junior agent; while a target's coconspirator may have the best insights into aspects of the target's likely expectations and behavior, criminals are never members of the law enforcement team.[17]

C. *What to Tell Your Covert Actor*

For CIs and cooperators, information about the case generally flows only one way: from the covert actor to law enforcement. The American Bar Association recommends developing policies for handing CIs and cooperators that include "a rule that investigative information obtained from other sources should not be provided to the confidential informant unless doing so would

---

17 Two cautionary tales from long-term informants associated with the FBI provide worst-case scenarios for failing to maintain professional distance from informants. *See generally* United States v. Salemme, 91 F. Supp. 2d 141 (D. Mass. 1999) (discussing relationship between informant James "Whitey" Bulger and his corrupt FBI Special Agent handler); U.S. Dep't of Justice Office of the Inspector General, A Review of the FBI's Handling and Oversight of FBI Asset Katrina Leung (U) (2006), https://fas.org/irp/agency/doj/oig/leung.pdf (describing informant, and double agent, Katrina Leung and the FBI Special Agent handler who had a sexual relationship with her).

materially advance the investigation."[18] Prosecutors thus need not, and generally should not, keep the CI or cooperator informed about the developments or progress in the case. (This general rule does not apply if the CI or cooperator's safety may be at risk.) Remember that one effective cross-examination technique at trial is to highlight any close relationship between CIs or cooperators and their law enforcement handlers. Maintaining a businesslike and professional relationship between an informant and prosecutor is essential for the case and for any later challenges to the prosecutor's ethics.

When prosecutors are working with UCs, however, they should explain the potential crimes to the UCs. A UC should read the statute, go through the elements of the crime, discuss what evidence would be helpful, and make sure to discuss the principles of entrapment. Certain offices' policies may require certain protocols with a CI or cooperator, so prosecutors should become familiar with their office policy.

D. *Exercise Caution with Your CI or Cooperator*

Prosecutors should investigate potential CIs and cooperators, and research their criminal and social history, financial status, employment, associates, and motivations. This information should be in a format that will be easy to provide to the target's defense attorney if the target is charged and the CI or cooperator testifies against the target.

It is essential to determine if the CI is represented by counsel. If the CI is represented, the prosecutor will need the consent of his attorney or a court order to communicate with him about the subject of that representation.[19] In some jurisdictions, if a CI is not represented and has legal exposure, the prosecutor may request court-appointed counsel to represent an indigent CI.[20]

---

18 ABA Standards for Criminal Justice: Prosecutorial Investigations s. 26-2.4(f)(i) (Am. Bar Ass'n 2014), https://www.americanbar.org/content/dam/aba/publications/criminal_justice_standards/Pros_Investigations.pdf.

19 Model Rules of Prof'l Conduct r. 4.2 (Am. Bar Ass'n 2020) ("In representing a client, a lawyer shall not communicate about the subject of the representation with a person the lawyer knows to be represented by another lawyer in the matter, unless the lawyer has the consent of the other lawyer or is authorized to do so by law or a court order.").

20 *Accord id.* r. 4.3 ("The lawyer shall not give legal advice to an unrepresented person, other than the advice to secure counsel, if the lawyer knows or reasonably should know that the interests of such a person are or have a reasonable possibility of being in conflict with the interests of the client.").

Make sure the CIs and cooperators follow instructions. Loose cannons and cowboys do not make good covert actors. The prosecutor should endeavor to corroborate, as much as reasonably possible, any information that a CI or cooperator provides to investigators.

E. *Protect the Covert Actor*

A prosecutor should consider the safety of a covert actor. In some instances, there may be no real danger and thus no need for special protection, but in those cases where safety may be an issue, a prosecutor should endeavor to ensure that the prosecutor's office, the investigators, or the police do what they can to provide for the safety of the covert actor. Frequently, investigators or police are responsible for assessing risks to a covert actor's physical security, but, at a minimum, the prosecutor should make sure someone is handling that part of the operation. Protection of a UC is almost always a concern of fellow officers and investigators and usually does not involve the prosecutor. Likewise, protection of CIs and cooperators is in the investigators' domain, but the prosecutor may need to become involved, depending on what is required to keep those individuals safe. If all that is required is a squad car circling the residential block where a cooperator lives or armed protection for a cooperator to get to the courthouse to testify, then obviously the prosecutor does not need to be involved. But if more elaborate protection is required, such as providing the CI or cooperator with temporary or permanent relocation or a new identity, the prosecutor will likely need to help guide the process.[21] Although providing a new identity for a witness may be beyond the power of an attorney general's office, the federal Witness Security Program may be available to some witnesses in state or local cases.[22]

Introducing a UC into the case may enhance safety for cooperators and CIs and may strengthen the case. The UC can provide safety by creating distance between the witness and the target. While a cooperator or CI may be necessary to provide access to the targets, safety may require a cooperator or CI

---

21 The federal Witness Security Program requires a "request by a government attorney" for a witness to be considered for the program. JUSTICE MANUAL § 9-21.100 (U.S. DEP'T OF JUSTICE 2020), https://www.justice.gov/jm/jm-9-21000-witness-security#9-21.100.

22 *Id.* at § 9-21.140. Local or state authorities will need to work with the U.S. Attorney's Office in their district to submit an application for the Witness Security Program and the state will be required to reimburse the United States for costs. *Id.* For more information about this process, see Chapter 1.6, Part II(A).

to be removed from a situation. Additionally, cooperators typically have criminal liability and may, as a result, be viewed as less credible witnesses. Having the cooperator introduce a UC may alleviate the cooperator's need to testify. If the cooperator is still a necessary witness, the UC may then be able to corroborate at least some aspects of the cooperator's testimony. Although this requires some thought and planning, it can significantly strengthen a case. To further reduce the likelihood that members of the criminal conspiracy will learn the identity of a cooperator, it may be helpful to have the UC, in turn, introduce another UC.[23]

F. *Use Technology*

Absent corroboration, juries generally are skeptical of cooperators and CIs.[24] If feasible, every dealing that a cooperator has with targets of criminal activity should be audio recorded. Even better, if possible, record every meeting on video. Technology has advanced so that audio recording devices can be hidden effectively in very small, everyday items. Likewise, video recording devices can be concealed in a shirt button or in another inconspicuous article of clothing. Unfortunately, these items can fail. Therefore, redundant recording devices should be utilized and surveillance, if possible, should be conducted of every meeting.

Prior to the meeting, a so-called "header" should be placed on each recording. This pre-meeting recording should be narrated by the case officer and should contain the officer's name; the date; the time; the names of the witness and the person who is expected to be recorded; the approximate location; the clear, oral consent of the covert actor (in one-party consent states); any required court authorization; and any other relevant information.

It is important to stress to the investigator the importance of maintaining the proper chain of custody of all recordings. A lost recording can be fatal to a case. It is excellent fodder for the defense and may result in an adverse inference charge by the trial judge.

---

23 Of course, prosecutors will still need to comply with any discovery or disclosure requirements in their jurisdiction, which may require disclosure of information that would reveal the identity of the informant or cooperator.

24 For more on corroborating cooperators and CIs, see Chapter 4.3, Part I(B).

The recording device should only be controlled by an investigator or the UC. In only the most unusual cases should the cooperator or informant be given the ability to turn on or off the device. The assigned prosecutor should listen to every recording as soon as possible. Informants and cooperators (and even UCs) may describe a recording as more incriminating than the prosecutor might find it to be. It is important for the prosecutors to make their own judgment about the recording to understand the strength of the case and to give the covert actor guidance for future meetings.

G. *Use Multiple Investigative Tools*

No investigation should rely on only one investigative tool. While recorded face-to-face meetings are a very effective technique, other equally important methods can advance an investigation. For example, wiretaps,[25] search warrants, and surveillance are all techniques that prosecutors should consider. When practicable, it is a good idea to use these investigative tools in conjunction with the use of cooperators.

Cooperators and CIs should be treated as inherently untrustworthy. If practicable, monitoring phone calls can provide a level of insurance for investigators that cooperators and CIs are following law enforcement's direction. If a cooperator or CI already works for or has been placed inside a business, search warrants can be an effective way to seize incriminating evidence without running afoul of the Fourth Amendment protections against unlawful search and seizure; prosecutors should avoid calling the cooperator as a witness to introduce seized evidence. A so-called "sneak and peek" search warrant should be considered in appropriate cases, where permitted, in order to view evidence inside a target's home or business without giving notice of the search.[26] Surveillance is often crucial in any investigation, including one with a covert actor.

---

25 See Chapter 2.3 for a discussion of wiretaps. While they are a powerful tool in the right case, they have strict legal and often heavy resource requirements.

26 *See* U.S. Dep't of Justice, Delayed Notice Search Warrants: A Vital and Time-Honored Tool for Fighting Crime 1 (2004), https://www.justice.gov/sites/default/files/dag/legacy/2008/10/17/patriotact213report.pdf (explaining that such searches may be necessary in certain circumstances where there is both an urgent need to conduct a search and a pressing concern to maintain confidentiality of an ongoing investigation).

H. *Be Creative*

Even with a cooperator, it often requires creativity to obtain evidence of criminality. Cooperators and CIs may have valuable suggestions as to how to gather incriminating evidence. Sometimes, investigators are faced with a situation where the crime has already been committed. An undercover operation can still be useful by providing the target with an opportunity to admit past illegal activity. One often-used technique to encourage the target to discuss past illegal conduct is to instruct the cooperator to tell the target that the cooperator was approached by law enforcement and ask the target what he should do. That type of conversation between targets and cooperators can lead to incriminating evidence. It could also reveal evidence of witness tampering, destruction of evidence, or obstruction of justice.

Another investigative avenue is to have the cooperator suggest that the target continue with past illegal dealings. If that tack is taken, the investigator and prosecutor need to be especially mindful of entrapment laws in their jurisdiction.[27] In the case of certain ongoing schemes or crimes, a cooperator or CI can introduce a UC to the target, with the UC playing the role of potential new victim of the crime.

When investigating a bribery case, deciding on the inducement may require creativity. Sometimes that will be easy; the target may ask for cash. Other times, the person soliciting the bribe will not take cash. In those situations, the investigator should consider using other things of value, such as event tickets, gift cards, a trip, or even the promise of a job for the person or a family member. Note that a particularly grand inducement may, however, be grounds for an entrapment defense or an allegation of outrageous government conduct.[28]

---

27 *See infra* Part V(A); *see also* Chapter 4.3, Part IV.

28 These arguments are rarely successful, at least in federal court. A federal appeals court considered whether an informant's offer of $250,000 to a defendant who recruited a team to launch missiles at an air force base and bomb synagogues was relevant for entrapment and outrageous government conduct defenses. United States v. Cromitie, 727 F.3d 194, 211 (2d Cir. 2013). The court concluded, over a strong dissent that focused on non-monetary factors, *id.* at 227-30, that the defendant had not been entrapped. *Id.* at 211, 215. It held that the "amount of money that might constitute a due process violation should be measured in relation to the inducement available for a particular criminal act from non-governmental sources and the nature of the act itself." *Id.* at 221. Given the seriousness of the offense, the court concluded that "only an offer significantly higher would require us to consider whether due process limits had been exceeded." *Id.*

Another creative use of undercovers and cooperators is to start a business. This type of business is sometimes called "a proprietary," which is a "sole proprietorship, partnership, corporation, or other business entity operated on a commercial basis, which is owned, controlled, or operated wholly or in part on behalf of the [law enforcement agency], and whose relationship with the [law enforcement agency] is concealed from third parties."[29] Other agencies may call such businesses "undercover storefront operations."[30] The classic example of this would be a fencing operation set up by the police. In this type of undercover sting operation, the police put the word out on the street that a certain garage or car repair business is willing to purchase stolen vehicles. The police then wait for criminals to bring in stolen merchandise, which they purchase. In the corruption context, a well-known and controversial example is the Abscam operation where the FBI set up a phony company called Abdul Enterprises and used that company and a cooperator to find government officials, including a senator and several congressmen, willing to accept bribes.[31]

One potential problem with opening a proprietary is that it can create crime that did not previously exist. For example, before opening a fencing operation, there may have not been a market for stolen vehicles. By starting such a business, the police might create a market and might inadvertently cause car thefts to increase.[32]

Proprietaries can be as simple or complicated as needed. They may simply consist of an office with a secretary, or they may involve opening an actual business. It may not be necessary for law enforcement to open its own business.

---

29 Council of the Inspectors Gen. on Integrity and Efficiency, Guidelines on Undercover Operations 2 (2013), https://www.ignet.gov/sites/default/files/files/guidelines-undercover-operations-june-2013.pdf.

30 Office of Inspector Gen. Oversight & Review Div. 16-06, U.S. Dep't of Justice, A Review of ATF's Undercover Storefront Operations 1 (2016), https://oig.justice.gov/reports/2016/o1606.pdf [hereinafter ATF Storefront Report].

31 *See ABSCAM*, Fed. Bureau of Investigation, https://www.fbi.gov/history/famous-cases/abscam (last visited Apr. 19, 2021).

32 *Accord* John Diedrich & Raquel Rutledge, *ATF's Milwaukee Sting Operation Marred by Mistakes, Failures*, J. Sentinel (Jan. 29, 2013), http://archive.jsonline.com/watchdog/watchdogreports/atfs-milwaukee-sting-operation-marred-by-mistakes-failures-mu8akpj-188952581.html (detailing storefront sting intended to obtain guns and drugs but that instead resulted in an ATF machine gun landing on the streets of Milwaukee and $35,000 in merchandise being stolen from the store, and may have led to increased crime); *see also infra* Part V(B)(4).

Sometimes, businesses friendly with law enforcement, or a cooperator's own business, can be used for an undercover operation. In the garbage carting case prosecuted in New York City in the 1990s, the New York County District Attorney's Office used a large downtown office building owned by someone friendly with law enforcement to employ an undercover detective as a building manager who dealt with members of a commercial garbage carting cartel.[33]

In some instances, it may be possible to introduce a covert actor as an employee of a target business. This can be used in all types of criminal cases, including investigations into organized crime or public corruption. When introducing a covert actor into a target business, it is important to understand the capabilities and limitations of the person. For example, if you send in a covert actor with no office skills to pose as an administrative assistant in a target business, the operation is at risk.

When law enforcement places a covert actor inside a business or other location, Fourth Amendment issues may arise. That a covert actor is present with the unwitting permission of the target does not confer blanket permission to search and seize evidence in the entire location.

IV. Anatomy of a Covert Operation

Prosecutors use covert actors to catch criminals, gather evidence, induce further cooperation (flip the target), and potentially save time, money, and other resources in the long run, including by building a strong case that is likely to induce defendants to plead guilty. Undercover operations can be potentially expensive, dangerous, and time consuming. For those reasons, it is important to make sure that every such operation is successful.

A. *Maximize Benefits*

To maximize the benefits of the undercover operation, prosecutors should, when possible, have the undercover officer:

---

33 Merrill Goozner, *N.Y. Trying to Trash Mob Hold on Waste-Hauling*, Chi. Trib. (Dec. 6, 1996), https://www.chicagotribune.com/news/ct-xpm-1996-12-06-9612060216-story.html.

1. Use clearly incriminating language. Clear language strengthens the evidence and helps prevent an argument that the target was entrapped. Note, however, that sometimes this will not be possible. Language that is ideal for purposes of proof may well compromise an operation if the target becomes suspicious of efforts to spell out a criminal scheme. As an example, a covert actor who asks a sophisticated target, "Will you accept a bribe?" is likely to be ineffective.

2. Minimize the use of coded language. Sometimes such language cannot be avoided if it is simply the way the members of the criminal enterprise communicate. If possible, a covert actor should use language that generally mirrors statutory requirements, without raising red flags for the target.

3. Confirm the criminality of the conversation. In some circumstances, a covert actor may be able to elicit evidence of consciousness of guilt. As an example, the covert actor might say something like "I hope we don't get caught doing this because I don't want to go to jail," if that is unlikely to spook the target. If the target agrees that criminal liability is a concern, the prosecutor can introduce that statement at trial to show that the target knew that what was going on was illegal.

4. Cover all of the elements of the crime. For example, in a bribery investigation, the covert actor should make reasonable efforts to describe the quid pro quo.

5. Record as much of the transaction as possible. Whenever the covert actor pays or receives money, it should be counted out loud, if that will not raise suspicions, or shown on video. While a gap in the conversation can be explained on the witness stand by the government witness as being the time that cash was exchanged, it is much more powerful for the recording to clearly show the money exchange.

6. Let the target speak. Often the best covert actors are intelligent, good conversationalists who can put other people at ease. Unfortunately, those are the same people who like to talk. It is important to instruct the covert actor that his or her primary goal is to let the targets speak. The more the targets speak, the better the evidence. A recording of a target merely agreeing with the government witness

and answering monosyllabically may increase the risk of an entrapment defense or create proof issues at trial.

As noted above, most people are bad at detecting lies.[34] Therefore, investigators and prosecutors who are supervising undercover operations should encourage covert actors not to be distracted by fearing that targets will suspect they are being recorded. While it is essential to always be aware of the danger of detection—both to the viability of the ongoing investigation and, more importantly, to any physical risk to those participating—the covert actor should do his best to make it clear that the target is agreeing to commit a crime.

B. *Anticipate Defenses*

Defense counsel tend to use certain defenses when faced with an incriminating recorded conversation. Generally, they fall into the following categories:

1. It did not happen the way the covert actor says it did;
2. There was some misunderstanding or misinterpretation;
3. The recording does not tell the whole story;
4. There are unrecorded conversations that provide an innocent explanation or support an entrapment defense;
5. The recordings are inaudible or unintelligible; or
6. The target was entrapped either because he had no predisposition (no preexisting intent) or the government induced the target to commit the crime.

Items one through three can be countered, in large part, by making sure that the recorded conversations are clearly incriminating. If the recorded conversations are clear, the defendant will not be able to argue that the criminal transaction did not happen the way the cooperator said it did. Nor will the

---

34 Maria Hartwig & Charles F. Bond, Jr., *Why Do Lie-Catchers Fail? A Lens Model Meta-Analysis of Human Lie Judgments*, 137 Psychol. Bull. 643, 643 (2011).

target be able to argue that there was a misunderstanding, misinterpretation, or that the recording does not tell the whole story.

Item four can be countered if investigators successfully direct covert actors to have no contact with targets unless they are set up to record any conversations that might result. Item five is the responsibility of the investigators—to make sure that, to the extent possible, the best equipment is used in as quiet an environment as possible. It may be as simple as instructing the government witness to avoid a loud restaurant. If possible, covert actors should be given an opportunity to use the equipment in a practice run to enable them to hear and understand what makes for an audible conversation.

As for the last item, entrapment, it is important for investigators and prosecutors running undercover operations to always be aware of this defense and to direct covert actors to talk less, listen more, and, as much as possible, let the target demonstrate a willingness and ability to commit the crime.

V. Legal and Ethical Issues

A. *Entrapment*

Law enforcement should not "incite" "and create crime for the sole purpose of prosecuting and punishing it."[35] Some states and the *Model Penal Code* treat whether a defendant was entrapped as a legal question using an objective standard, and consider only if there was improper government conduct.[36] In those states, the burden of proof typically remains with the defendant.[37] More states follow the lead of the Supreme Court and federal courts by treating

---

35 Sorrells v. United States, 287 U.S. 435, 444 (1932); Butts v. United States, 273 F. 35, 38 (8th Cir. 1921). For a longer discussion of entrapment, see Chapter 4.3, Part IV.

36 Paul Marcus, The Entrapment Defense § 1.05A (Matthew Bender, 2020 ed.); *see also, e.g.*, People v. Connolly, 591 N.W.2d 340, 342 (Mich. Ct. App. 1998) (describing a "two-pronged test" for entrapment assessing "whether (1) the police engaged in impermissible conduct that would induce a law-abiding person to commit a crime in similar circumstances, or (2) the police engaged in conduct so reprehensible that it cannot be tolerated."); Model Penal Code § 2.13, LexisNexis (Am. Law Inst. 2020).

37 Marcus, *supra* note 36, at § 5.05 (concluding that burden of proof typically remains with the defense in objective standard states).

entrapment as a factual question in which the trier of fact must decide both if the government improperly induced the defendant to commit a crime and if the defendant was predisposed to commit that crime.[38] In most of those subjective standard jurisdictions, if a defendant presents "substantial evidence of entrapment, the State must produce evidence to show the defendant's predisposition to commit the crime."[39] Put another way, in states using the objective test, courts consider only "how much and what manner of persuasion, pressure, and cajoling are brought to bear by law enforcement officials to induce persons to commit crimes."[40] In jurisdictions employing the subjective standard, juries are typically charged with assessing both whether there was improper government inducement and, if so, whether the government proved that defendant was predisposed to commit the crime.[41]

Thus, in both subjective and objective standard states, the conduct of covert actors will be scrutinized to determine if they improperly induced or encouraged the crime. Was the defendant pressured to commit the crime? What, if any, inducements did the police use in order to get the defendant to act? Merely soliciting a target to commit a crime is not improper,[42] but repeated and persistent solicitation may constitute entrapment in objective standard states and may require the prosecution to prove predisposition in subjective standard states.[43]

---

38 *See id.* at § 2.01 & n.10; *Sorrells*, 287 U.S. at 451 (reasoning that the defense is meant to prevent "otherwise innocent" people from being improperly lured into committing a crime). For further discussion of entrapment and other defenses, see Chapter 4.3.

39 Marcus, *supra* note 36, at § 4.05C (citation and internal quotation marks omitted) (discussing courts' approach to burden of proof in subjective standard states and the federal government, which typically requires "[r]elatively little" from the defense to shift the burden of proof to the prosecution).

40 People v. Barraza, 591 P.2d 947, 954 (Cal. 1979).

41 Marcus, *supra* note 36, at § 4.05C.

42 *See Sorrells*, 287 U.S. at 441, 451.

43 *Id.* at 451 (explaining that entrapment doctrine forbids punishment of an "otherwise innocent" person whose "alleged offense" is "the product of the creative activity" of government officials). Inducement is the opportunity plus something else making entrapment more likely. *See* United States v. Gendron, 18 F.3d 955, 961 (1st Cir. 1994). That something else is generally "excessive pressure by the government upon the defendant or the government's taking advantage of an alternative, non-criminal type of motive." *Id.* The *Gendron* case discusses examples of government overreaching being considered prohibited inducement. *Id.* at 961-62 (listing separate examples as including intimidation and threats against a defendant's family; calling every day, threatening the defendant; engaging in forceful solicitation and dogged insistence until defendant capitulated; playing upon defendant's sympathy for informant's common narcotics experience and withdrawal symptoms; using repeated suggestions, which succeeded only when

The USDOJ *Guidelines for FBI Undercover Operations* reflect the federal subjective approach, and provide that, "[e]ntrapment occurs when the Government implants in the mind of a person who is not otherwise disposed to commit the offense the disposition to commit the offense and then induces the commission of that offense in order to prosecute."[44] Under these guidelines, no undercover activity involving an inducement to an individual can be authorized unless:

1. The illegal nature of the activity is reasonably clear to potential subjects;

2. The nature of any inducement offered is justifiable in view of the character of the illegal transaction in which the individual is invited to engage;

3. There is a reasonable expectation that offering the inducement will reveal illegal activity; and

4. One of the two following limitations is met:

   i. There is reasonable indication that the subject is engaging, has engaged, or is likely to engage in the illegal activity proposed or in similar illegal conduct; or

   ii. The opportunity for illegal activity has been structured so that there is reason to believe that any persons drawn to the opportunity, or brought to it, are predisposed to engage in the contemplated illegal conduct.[45]

If the police officers, covert actors, and others involved in the operation avoid certain conduct, a successful entrapment defense may be less likely.

---

defendant had lost his job and needed money for his family's food and rent, and claimed to be suicidal).

44 Guidelines on FBI Undercover Operations, *supra* note 1, at 16. While the guidelines are written for the FBI, the USDOJ requires all of its law enforcement components to follow them. ATF Storefront Report, *supra* note 30, at 1.

45 Guidelines on FBI Undercover Operations, *supra* note 1, at 16.

Officers should not pressure a target to commit a crime through promises of excessive profits.[46] A graduating series of offers, from innocent to criminal, may be viewed as entrapment.[47] Pursuing the target repeatedly for an extended period of time may be viewed as entrapment.[48] Threats, coercion, or appeals to innocent motives may be viewed as entrapment.[49] Finally, falsely telling the target that what she is doing is legal may provide the defense known as "entrapment by estoppel."[50] This defense is available when a government agent authorizes a defendant to engage in otherwise criminal conduct and the defendant, relying thereon, commits forbidden acts in the mistaken but reasonable, good faith belief that he has in fact been authorized to do so.[51]

B. *Fourth Amendment, Fifth Amendment, Sixth Amendment, and Ethical Anti-Contact Issues*

Prosecutors supervising undercover operations need to be cognizant of Fourth, Fifth, and Sixth Amendment requirements. Some of the common considerations are described in this part. Line prosecutors should always consult with supervisors prior to initiating any undercover operation and should never themselves engage in undercover activity.[52]

1. Fourth Amendment Considerations

The Fourth Amendment protects against unreasonable searches and seizures.[53] Courts have generally concluded that undercover actors do not

---

46 Grossman v. State, 457 P.2d 226, 230 (Alaska 1969); *see also* State v. Lively, 921 P.2d 1035, 1046-47 (Wash. 1996) (discussing a due process violation based on outrageous government conduct); People v. Isaacson, 378 N.E.2d 78, 84 (N.Y. 1978) (same). *See also* Chapter 4.3, Part IV(B) (describing United States v. Barta, 776 F.3d 931, 937 (7th Cir. 2015), a case where the court concluded that the defendant was entrapped as a matter of law).

47 *Gendron*, 18 F.3d at 964 (relying on Jacobson v. United States, 503 U.S. 540, 543-47 (1992) in which the government graduated its solicitations from innocent lure to frank offer).

48 *See Jacobson*, 503 U.S. at 543-47 (describing how the defendant ordered child pornography after twenty-six months of repeated mailings and communications).

49 *See* United States v. Dennis, 826 F.3d 683, 690 (3d Cir. 2016) ("[T]he defendant must show that law enforcement engaged in conduct that takes the form of persuasion, fraudulent representation, threats, coercive tactics, harassment, promises of reward or pleas based on need, sympathy or friendship." (internal quotes and citations omitted)).

50 *See, e.g.*, United States v. W. Indies Transp., Inc., 127 F.3d 299, 313 (3d Cir. 1997).

51 United States v. Gil, 297 F.3d 93, 107 (2d Cir. 2002).

52 *See infra* Part V(C).

53 U.S. Const. amend. IV.

violate the Fourth Amendment by concealing their status as police agents,[54] or being invited into target's home or business under false pretenses.[55] This is because targets have no reasonable expectation of privacy in a location into which they invite others, even if those invitees are concealing their motives for being there.[56] As a result, the Supreme Court has repeatedly held that undercover actors do not violate the Fourth Amendment by having discussions with targets—even in targets' hotel rooms, offices, or homes—as long as they are permitted to be there.[57]

However, covert actors who are acting as government agents will violate the Fourth Amendment if they venture outside of locations where they are invited to be.[58] Much as they do for determining the scope of a consent search, courts will apply an "objective reasonableness" standard to determine if a covert actor trespassed into an unauthorized location.[59] This is often a fact-sensitive inquiry. For example, an informant who has been invited to a target's apartment may not have permission to enter the bedroom and look under the bed in that same apartment.[60] The government can mitigate this risk somewhat by instructing covert actors not to stray into locations they do not have permission to enter.[61]

2. Fifth Amendment Considerations

The Fifth Amendment guarantees several rights, including the right against compelled self-incrimination and the right to due process.[62] While it has concluded that informants obtaining inculpatory statements from defendants

---

54 *See, e.g.*, United States v. White, 401 U.S. 745, 752 (1971).

55 United States v. Baldwin, 621 F.2d 251, 252-53 (6th Cir. 1980).

56 United States v. Jacobsen, 466 U.S. 109, 117 (1984) ("It is well settled that when an individual reveals private information to another, he assumes the risk that his confidant will reveal that information to the authorities, and if that occurs the Fourth Amendment does not prohibit governmental use of that information.").

57 *See, e.g.*, *White*, 401 U.S. at 746-47, 749-51 (home); Hoffa v. United States, 385 U.S. 293, 301-03 (1966) (hotel); Lopez v United States, 373 U.S. 427, 438-39 (1963) (office).

58 *See, e.g.*, United States v. Bennett, 709 F.2d 803, 805-06 (2d Cir. 1983).

59 *See* Florida v. Jimeno, 500 U.S. 248, 251 (1991) ("The standard for measuring the scope of a suspect's consent under the Fourth Amendment is that of 'objective' reasonableness—what would the typical reasonable person have understood by the exchange between the officer and the suspect?").

60 *Bennett*, 709 F.2d at 805-06.

61 *Id.* at 806.

62 U.S. Const. amend. V.

do not violate the right against compelled self-incrimination,[63] the Supreme Court has recognized that the conduct of undercover agents could conceivably be "so outrageous that due process principles would absolutely bar the government from invoking judicial processes to obtain a conviction."[64] Defendants thus have argued that undercover operations violate their right to due process.[65] Courts have concluded that the government's conduct in an undercover operation must "shock the conscience" to violate a defendant's due process rights—a standard unmet by defendants in federal courts of appeals for over forty years.[66]

3. Sixth Amendment and Rule of Professional Conduct 4.2 Considerations

Among the Sixth Amendment guarantees to a defendant are the right to assistance of counsel,[67] which attaches at indictment and at all "critical" stages of criminal proceedings.[68] After the right to counsel has attached, courts have concluded that "indirect and surreptitious interrogations as well as those conducted in the jailhouse" are not permitted.[69] Thus, prosecutors may not direct covert actors—or anyone, for that matter—to have contact with an indicted defendant about the charged case.

---

63 Hoffa v. United States, 385 U.S. 293, 303-04 (1966).

64 United States v. Russell, 411 U.S. 423, 431-32 (1973).

65 *See, e.g.*, United States v. Carpentier, 689 F.2d 21, 26-27 (2d Cir. 1982); United States v. Jannotti, 673 F.2d 578, 606-10 (3d Cir. 1982). Both cases were unsuccessful appeals of convictions obtained through the Abscam operation. In one, the Third Circuit Court of Appeals reversed a dismissal by the district court, which concluded that the defendant's Fifth Amendment Due Process rights had been violated by the government's aggressive undercover operation. United States v. Jannotti, 501 F. Supp. 1182, 1189-93, 1205 (E.D. Pa. 1980), *rev'd*, 673 F.2d 578, 611 (3d Cir. 1981) (en banc), *cert. denied*, 457 U.S. 1106 (1982).

66 *See, e.g.*, United States v. Cromitie, 727 F.3d 194, 217-21 (2d Cir. 2013) (denying due process claim where informant planned crime, provided weapons, promised $250,000, and "exploited" the defendant's religious views). "Only a divided panel of the Third Circuit has ruled that government conduct violated due process limits, *see* United States v. Twigg, 588 F.2d 373 (3d Cir. 1978) and that Circuit has since ruled that the rationale of *Twigg* had been limited by *Hampton*." *Id.* at 218 (citing United States v. Beverly, 723 F.2d 11, 12 (3d Cir. 1983) and Hampton v. United States, 425 U.S. 484 (1976)).

67 U.S. Const. amend. VI.

68 Missouri v. Frye, 566 U.S. 134, 140 (2012).

69 United States v. Henry, 447 U.S. 264, 276 (1980) (quoting United States v. Massiah, 377 U.S. 201, 206 (1964)). *See also Massiah*, 377 U.S. at 205 ("Any secret interrogation of the defendant, from and after the finding of the indictment, without the protection afforded by the presence of counsel, contravenes the basic dictates of fairness in the conduct of criminal causes and the fundamental rights of persons charged with crime." (citation omitted)).

Even before the commencement of formal legal proceedings, targets may have hired counsel. The *Model Rules of Professional Conduct* provide instruction on lawyers' obligations to represented persons.[70] Specifically, Model Rule 4.2 provides that "[i]n representing a client, a lawyer shall not communicate about the subject of the representation with a person the lawyer knows to be represented by another lawyer in the matter, unless the lawyer has the consent of the other lawyer or is authorized to do so by law or a court order."[71]

Some courts have concluded that Rule 4.2 provisions apply before the commencement of formal criminal proceedings and restrict prosecutors from directing covert actors to have contact with targets who are represented by counsel;[72] others, however, have concluded that this rule does not apply to preindictment criminal investigations, as they are "authorized by law."[73] Even courts in the first category recognize that targets should not be able to inoculate themselves against undercover operations by hiring "house counsel," and analyze if the target is represented "in conjunction with the criminal matter in which he is held suspect, and the government has knowledge of that fact."[74] This is because the right to counsel is offense specific.[75] As a result, the Sixth Amendment does not prohibit, as an example, an undercover operation targeting a represented defendant in an entirely separate scheme from a crime for which he has already been indicted.[76] However, the ABA views its non-contact requirements more broadly than the Sixth Amendment, opining in the notes to Rule 4.2 that "[t]he fact that a communication does not violate a state or federal constitutional right is insufficient to establish that the communication is permissible under this Rule."[77] As a result, it is possible that contacts that are not proscribed by the Constitution or by case law would nonetheless be forbidden by the state bar.

---

70 Model Rules of Prof'l Conduct r. 4.2 (Am. Bar Ass'n 2020).

71 *Id.*

72 United States v. Hammad, 858 F.2d 834, 838 (2d Cir. 1988).

73 United States v. Balter, 91 F.3d 427, 436 (3d Cir. 1996) (agreeing with five other circuits that "[r]ule 4.2 is inapplicable to contacts made by prosecutors or their agents with criminal suspects in the course of a pre-indictment investigation").

74 *Hammad*, 858 F.2d at 839.

75 McNeil v. Wisconsin, 501 U.S. 171, 175 (1991).

76 *Id.* at 181; *see also* Texas v. Cobb, 532 U.S. 162, 174 (2001) (holding there was no Sixth Amendment right for defendant represented on charged burglary to have counsel present when he was questioned about murder that occurred during the course of that burglary).

77 Model Rules of Prof'l Conduct r. 4.2 cmt. 5 (Am. Bar Ass'n 2020).

When a prosecutor directs a law enforcement operation, the covert actors are agents of the prosecutor.[78] Before approving an undercover operation, prosecutors should thus determine (1) if the target is represented by counsel on the matter that is being investigated, if possible, and (2) if it is nonetheless permissible under *both* the case law and rules of professional conduct in their jurisdiction to direct a covert actor to interact with the target. This is an area in which it is important to consult with supervisors and to research ethics rules and case law very carefully. If the target of the operation is represented in the matter under investigation and the prosecutor directs the covert actor to communicate with the target, the prosecutor may violate the bar's rules of professional conduct, the target's right to counsel, or both.

4. Application to Proprietaries or Undercover Storefront Operations

As previously discussed, in some cases, prosecutors may wish to consider placing a covert actor inside a target business or using an undercover proprietary storefront operation. When constructed and managed carefully, these operations can provide valuable evidence of wrongdoing.[79]

A placement in an existing business is generally constitutionally permissible,[80] as long as the covert actor does not intrude into areas in which he or she is not authorized to be.[81] Thus, if it is not reasonable for a receptionist to be rummaging through the business's computer systems or the back offices, then it is safer for the prosecutor to obtain a search warrant before conducting those kinds of searches.[82] To avoid due process concerns, the operation

---

78 *See, e.g.*, *Hammad*, 858 F.2d at 837 (quoting United States v. Hammad, 678 F. Supp. 397, 399 (E.D.N.Y. 1987)).

79 For a useful analysis of successful and unsuccessful ATF storefront firearms purchasing operations, see generally ATF Storefront Report, *supra* note 30. While some aspects of that analysis may not be germane for a white collar operation, lessons can be learned about some of the general pros—like the ability to gather high-quality recorded evidence and to introduce UCs (rather than relying on CIs) into a location to interact with targets—and cons—including the high expenditure of time and money to run a successful operation, and challenges with attracting high-value targets—of storefront operations. *Id.* at 64-66.

80 *See* Lewis v. United States, 385 U.S. 206, 211 (1966) ("A government agent, in the same manner as a private person, may accept an invitation to do business and may enter upon the premises for the very purposes contemplated by the occupant.").

81 United States v. Scherer, 673 F.2d 176, 182 (7th Cir. 1982).

82 *See* Gouled v. United States, 255 U.S. 298, 304-06 (1921) (finding the Fourth Amendment

itself—whether it includes placement of a covert actor in an existing business or a proprietary—should not employ tactics that "shock the conscience."[83] Finally, if a target is represented by counsel, special care should be taken to thoroughly research the Sixth Amendment case law in the jurisdiction and the no-contact rules established by the state bar to which the prosecutor belongs.

C. *Attorney Misrepresentations*

Rule 8.4(c) of the Model Rules of Professional Conduct provides that it is professional misconduct for a lawyer to "engage in conduct involving dishonesty, fraud, deceit or misrepresentation."[84] Prosecutors must not themselves pose as covert actors. Discipline has been imposed for violations of Rule 8.4(c) on a prosecutor in Colorado who pretended to be a defense attorney in an effort to apprehend a fugitive murder suspect,[85] and on a prosecutor in Ohio who used a fake Facebook page to investigate an alibi himself by suggesting to a defendant's girlfriend that the defendant was having an affair.[86]

Prosecutors' oversight of undercover operations is a surprisingly murky area. While undercover operations do not, per se, violate a defendant's constitutional rights,[87] a few jurisdictions have suggested that prosecutors who supervise undercover operations may violate Rule 8.4(c). For example, in 2017, undercover investigations across the state of Colorado were halted after the state's office of attorney regulation counsel suggested that a prosecutor may have violated Colorado's version of Rule 8.4(c) by supervising an undercover investigation.[88] As a result of litigation brought by the Colorado Attorney General's Office, the rule was amended to explicitly permit lawyers to "advise, direct, or supervise others, including clients, law enforcement officers, or investigators, who participate

---

violated where business acquaintance, at federal agents' instruction, obtained entry into petitioner's office by falsely representing that he intended to pay only a social visit, but secretly ransacked the office).

83 *See* United States v. Cromitie, 727 F.3d 194, 217-21 (2d Cir. 2013).

84 Model Rules of Prof'l Conduct r. 8.4(c) (Am. Bar Ass'n 2020).

85 *In re* Pautler, 47 P.3d 1175, 1179-81 (Colo. 2002).

86 Disciplinary Counsel v. Brockler, 48 N.E.3d 557, 558-60 (Ohio 2016). *See also* Office of Disciplinary Counsel v. Miller, No. 32DB2017 (Pa. Feb. 8, 2019), www.pacourts.us/assets/opinions/DisciplinaryBoard/out/32DB2017-Miller.pdf.

87 *See supra* Part V(B).

88 Amie Ely, *Ethics Corner: Survey of "Ethics Gurus" in AG Office Reveals Priorities*, Nat'l Ass'n of Att'ys Gen. (Nov. 17, 2017), https://www.naag.org/ethics/attorney-general-journal/survey-of-ethics-gurus-in-attorney-general-offices-reveals-priorities/.

in lawful investigative activities."[89] In *In re Gatti*, the Oregon Supreme Court rejected calls by a chorus of prosecutors to recognize an exception to the rule against deception for prosecutors supervising undercover activities.[90] As a result of that decision, the Rules of Professional Conduct in Oregon were later amended to explicitly permit attorneys to "supervise lawful covert activity in the investigation of violations of civil or criminal law or constitutional rights, provided the lawyer's conduct is otherwise in compliance with these Rules of Professional Conduct."[91] Federal courts have typically approved of prosecutors overseeing undercover investigations,[92] and the ABA recommends it.[93]

Some state bars explicitly allow such supervision. As noted, in Colorado and Oregon it is now permitted for a lawyer to supervise others involved in lawful investigative activity.[94] Likewise, Florida expressly permits lawyers to advise law enforcement in undercover operations: "[I]t shall not be professional misconduct for a lawyer for a criminal law enforcement agency or regulatory agency to advise others about or to supervise another in an undercover investigation, unless prohibited by law or rule . . . ."[95] Other jurisdictions have issued ethics rulings favorable to attorneys engaged in covert operations in the course of their official duties.[96]

---

89 Joseph G. Michaels, *"Lawful Investigative Activities" and Rule 8.4(c)*, Colo. Lawyer 36, 36-37 (June 2019), https://www.cobar.org/Portals/COBAR/TCL/2019/June/CL_Features_Ethics.pdf.

90 8 P.3d 966, 976 (Or. 2000) (noting also that the court lacked authority to read in an exception that the statute did not contain).

91 Or. Rules of Prof'l Conduct r. 8.4(b) (2020).

92 Ely, *supra* note 88.

93 For a discussion of a prosecutor's role in an investigation, see Chapter 2.1.

94 Or. Rules of Prof'l Conduct r. 8.4(b) (2020); Co. Rules of Prof'l Conduct r. 8.4(c) (2019).

95 Rules Regulating the Fl. Bar r. 4-8.4(c) (2020).

96 *See, e.g.*, D.C. Bar Legal Ethics Comm., Op. 323 (2004) ("Lawyers employed by government agencies who act in a non-representational official capacity in a manner they reasonably believe to be authorized by law do not violate Rule 8.4 if, in the course of their employment, they make misrepresentations that are reasonably intended to further the conduct of their official duties."); Utah State Bar Ethics Advisory Op. Comm., Op. No. 02-05 (2002) ("A governmental lawyer who participates in a lawful covert governmental operation that entails conduct employing dishonesty, fraud, misrepresentation or deceit for the purpose of gathering relevant information does not, without more, violate the Rules of Professional Conduct."); Va. State Bar Standing Comm. on Legal Ethics, Op. 1765 (2003) ("[W]hen an attorney . . . uses lawful methods . . . as part of his intelligence or covert activities, those methods cannot be seen as reflecting adversely on his fitness to practice law.").

D. *Other Ethical Issues*

While obtaining evidence of criminal activity is important, it is equally important to protect your job as a prosecutor, your career as a lawyer, and your personal reputation. To that end, any agreements with cooperators should be memorialized in writing.[97] Cooperators have flipped once against their previous associates, and they might flip against the unwary law enforcement official. Prosecutors should never make promises they cannot keep, and they should direct law enforcement handlers they supervise not to make such promises to CIs or cooperators.

A prosecutor should avoid being alone with a CI or cooperator, even for a short time. It is best to have a law enforcement officer present as a witness rather than two prosecutors; if there becomes a need to testify about the contents of a conversations, the officer can be called to the stand. If a cooperator is represented by counsel and counsel is willing to waive his or her presence to allow you to meet—for example, to prepare for trial—that waiver should be in writing. At all times, a prosecutor should act as if he or she is being recorded. Any benefit provided to a cooperator—even a simple proffer agreement—must eventually be disclosed to the defense.[98] For that reason, it is imperative that the prosecutor and other law enforcement officials keep meticulous records reflecting any agreements, understandings, or benefits that are given to a CI or cooperator. The prosecutor must ensure that any funds expended on behalf of the CI or cooperator, including for meals, hotels, or the like, are tracked and eventually disclosed.[99]

---

97 For more on cooperation agreements, see Chapter 1.8, Part II(A).

98 For an explanation of proffer agreements, see Chapter 1.8, Part II(A). For a useful list of potential benefits to disclose, see JUSTICE MANUAL § 9-5.002, Part I(B)(7) (U.S. DEP'T OF JUSTICE 2020), https://www.justice.gov/jm/jm-9-5000-issues-related-trials-and-other-court-proceedings.

99 *See, e.g.*, People v. Colon, 918 N.E.2d 936, 940 (N.Y. 2009) (finding that the "benefits conferred on a witness by a prosecutor provide a basis for the jury to question the veracity of a witness . . . [and] it is important that witnesses provide truthful testimony when questioned about the receipt of such benefits, and the People must be vigilant to avoid misleading the court or jury").

Conclusion

The use of covert actors is one of the most powerful tools available to law enforcement to combat hidden crime. With such power, however, comes much responsibility. To effectively use these techniques, prosecutors must be thoroughly prepared, must be willing to think creatively, must be bold, and, most importantly, must be aware of the potential legal and ethical pitfalls.

Chapter 2.6

Cooperation with Federal & Local Partners: Considerations for Attorney General Offices Investigating & Prosecuting Public Corruption

Robert Shapiro, Daniel Pietragallo

Robert Shapiro serves as First Assistant Attorney General, Special Prosecutions Unit, at the Colorado Attorney General's Office, Denver, Colorado.

Daniel Pietragallo serves as Senior Assistant Attorney General, Financial Fraud Unit, at the Colorado Attorney General's Office, Denver, Colorado.

Introduction

This chapter introduces state prosecutors and investigators to some of the diverse resources available to prosecute corruption throughout the various levels of government. In appropriate cases, multiple jurisdictions can work together to comprehensively and effectively investigate and prosecute public corruption. As most attorneys general do not have jurisdiction over every criminal matter in their state,[1] this chapter will also discuss how jurisdictional

---

1 Criminal jurisdiction ranges from complete (e.g., Alaska, Delaware, and Rhode Island), to little, to practically no jurisdiction at the trial level (e.g., Connecticut and West Virginia). Chris Toth, et al., *Criminal Justice*, *in* State Attorneys General Powers & Responsibilities 359,

challenges may limit the role an attorney general's office can play in a joint investigation, and suggest creative ways to ensure that corruption defendants are appropriately held accountable for the full scope of their crimes. Even offices with limited jurisdiction can benefit from harnessing a wide array of diverse resources and building partnerships. Prosecutors should learn about the resources available in their states, establish relationships with potential partners, and proactively seek opportunities to work together when cases merit a collaborative approach.

As explained in this chapter, collaboration with other law enforcement partners in corruption cases can be beneficial, but at times may be cumbersome. As the chief law enforcement officer in the state, an attorney general may be uniquely positioned to leverage the most effective complement of resources from federal, other state, and local partners to achieve the most meaningful results. Like federal prosecutors, prosecutors in an AGO are generally not as entrenched in local politics and can often devote more resources to complex, long-term investigations and prosecutions. But like local prosecutors, state-level prosecutors are not subject to federalism concerns,[2] have state statutes at their disposal,[3] and may be more attuned to local concerns than their federal counterparts. The attorney general's role thus permits thoughtful joint investigations with trustworthy partners and, in appropriate cases, prosecutions of corrupt state and local officials through the state courts.

I. Jurisdiction and Authority of State Attorneys General

Before determining whether to partner with other state and federal authorities, an AGO must determine whether it should initiate an investigation at all or whether it should leave that decision to the local authorities. Typically, our criminal justice system is localized, with primary jurisdiction resting with the local authorities and only limited or discretionary authority resting with

---

370-72 (Emily Myers ed., 4th ed. 2018).

2 *See* Kelly v. United States, 140 S. Ct. 1565, 1571-72 (2020) ("[F]ederal fraud law leaves much public corruption to the States (or their electorates) to rectify."); McDonnell v. United States, 136 S. Ct. 2355, 2373 (2016) (quoting McNally v. United States, 483 U.S. 350, 360 (1987)).

3 For a discussion of state corruption statutes, see Chapters 3.1 to 3.4.

the attorney general.[4] That said, some states vest more authority in the attorney general, but those AGOs still exercise their discretion sparingly.[5] State law varies widely with respect to AGO criminal jurisdiction, breaking into seven categories of jurisdiction: (1) complete; (2) concurrent; (3) limited to specific areas; (4) upon own initiative; (5) upon request; (6) only advisory; and (7) no criminal jurisdiction.[6] States typically grant their AGO authority to investigate and prosecute public corruption (including local corruption), and other related offenses, such as election fraud and tax fraud.[7]

Even in public corruption cases, a state-level prosecutor may choose to partner with local authorities based on a wide variety of factors, including the existing relationship with the local authorities, whether local authorities are the target of the investigation, and whether initially involving local authorities would avoid future conflict with them. Because corruption matters raise concerns with public trust in government, prosecutors and investigators may wish to consider practical, non-legal factors when building a case. Being familiar with the affected community and local political atmosphere may help determine if bringing in federal assistance is desirable. Knowing economic conditions in the community as well as any cultural differences can help determine how best to build an investigation. This knowledge may be gained by partnering with local law enforcement.

II. The Foundation and Case for State Attorney General Leadership

State-level prosecutors are well equipped to lead joint investigations of public corruption matters not just because they have legal authority, but because they may be seen as more impartial than local or federal authorities, and they are more likely than local prosecutors to have broad access to funding and resources. Because the state attorney general often is elected separately from the state governor, he or she is arguably more politically independent

---

4 Rachel E. Barkow, *Federalism & Criminal Law: What the Feds Can Learn from the States*, 109 Mich. L. Rev. 519, 545 (2011) ("In almost every state, a conscious choice has been made to defer to local prosecutors.").

5 *Id.* at 551-55, 561-65.

6 Toth, *supra* note 1, at 359.

7 Barkow, *supra* note 4, at 546; Toth, *supra* note 1, at 361.

than the federal attorney general, a presidential appointee.[8] Being elected at a state-wide level rather than a local level may make a state attorney general more impartial than local authorities in matters of public corruption. A reputation for independence may incline potential partners in federal or local government to respect a state-level prosecutor's leadership. Other factors that may bolster a state attorney general's assertion of leadership in state or local corruption cases include a proven track record of fair and effective courtroom success, an active role as a teacher for peers in the legal and law enforcement communities, and serving on professional committees and task forces.

Equally as important as attorney generals' reputations are their access to other law enforcement entities and their leaders. Federal and state lawmakers have both identified corruption as an area appropriate for centralized prosecution, so state-level prosecutors are likely to have ongoing working relationships with federal corruption authorities and to have developed expertise in a complex legal area.[9] AGOs may also be able to centralize and coordinate efforts with any specialized state unit dedicated to public integrity violations.[10] Finally, high-stakes public corruption matters are defended with a unique intensity and require a centralized, well-funded prosecution because they frequently threaten the career and reputation of powerful, well-connected figures.[11]

III. Partnering with Federal Authorities

A state AGO may consider both positive and negative consequences of partnering with federal authorities in a state corruption matter. On the positive side, partnering with federal authorities offers expanded resources and diverse levels of expertise. On the negative side, coordinating requires communicating

---

8 Barkow, *supra* note 4, at 538-39 ("[A]lmost all state attorneys general are separately elected from the governor and may not even be a member of the same party as the governor."); Emily Myers, *Status in State Government*, *in* State Attorneys General Powers & Responsibilities 46, 46 (Emily Myers ed., 4th ed. 2018). Prosecutors should not make decisions about an investigation or case based on political considerations. *See* Chapter 5.1, Part I.

9 Barkow, *supra* note 4, at 570-71.

10 *Accord U.S. Anti-Corruption Oversight: A State-by-State Survey*, Ctr. for the Advancement of Pub. Integrity, Columbia L. Sch., https://web.law.columbia.edu/capi-map (last visited Apr. 19, 2021) (providing an interactive map of state-level oversight institutions).

11 See Chapter 4.3 for a discussion of the intensity of public corruption defenses.

among the different authorities, establishing clearly defined roles, and protecting confidential information. Multi-agency investigations can also pose complications for prosecutors when complying with discovery and disclosure obligations, particularly if the other agencies are part of the "prosecution team" for *Brady* imputation purposes.[12]

A. *Tax Authorities*

With many state corruption matters centering on an official's abuse of power for some form of gain, including monetary gain, state-level prosecutors and investigators may consider teaming with state and federal tax authorities to trace the flow of corrupt money. The federal Internal Revenue Service Criminal Investigation unit particularly focuses on investigating tax evasion and money laundering.[13] Federal income tax information is typically confidential,[14] but state tax investigators may request federal tax records from the IRS for certain enforcement actions[15] and prosecutors typically have broader authority to seek tax records from third parties.[16] Tax records can provide important evidence, particularly if prosecutors wish to prove that a defendant has unexplained wealth and wish to argue that the funds came from the corrupt endeavor. However, unauthorized disclosure of federal tax returns or return information by a state employee is punishable by up to five years in federal prison, so prosecutors, investigators, and staff must take care that the returns are used only for the purpose for which they were provided.[17] Even sharing those returns with

---

12 *See* Chapter 2.8, Part II(B); Chapter 5.1, Part III.

13 *See* Internal Revenue Serv., Crim. Investigation Ann. Rep. 2020 6, 21 (2020), https://www.irs.gov/pub/irs-pdf/p3583.pdf.

14 26 U.S.C. § 6103(a) (2018).

15 Federal law permits disclosure only to certain state officials, for certain purposes, and using specific procedures. *See generally* 26 U.S.C. § 6103(d). For example, "any disclosure by an Internal Revenue Service (IRS) official to a state taxing authority be made pursuant to a request in writing from the state taxing authority." Fedele v. Harris, No. 1:14-cv-559 (GLS/CFH), 2018 U.S. Dist. LEXIS 122019, at *13 (N.D.N.Y. July 20, 2018). "Courts have held that an agreement between a state taxing authority and the IRS will satisfy this written request requirement if such agreement: (i) requests tax information; (ii) is signed by the head of the state agency; and (iii) designates those authorized to receive the information." *Id.* (citing Smith v. United States, 964 F.2d 630, 633 (7th Cir. 1992)).

16 Trump v. Vance, 941 F.3d 631, 641 (2d Cir. 2019), *aff'd* 140 S. Ct. 2412, 2431 (2020).

17 26 U.S.C. § 7213(a)(2). Unlawful disclosure of tax return information can also lead to civil liability and require the discloser to pay the taxpayer's attorneys' fees and court costs. 26 U.S.C. § 7431(c).

contractors who are assisting the investigation may result in criminal liability unless certain conditions are met.[18]

B. *Offices of Inspector General*

Within each federal agency, the an inspector general possesses specialized authority and may be another valuable resource for state authorities.[19] As a representative example, if a state corruption investigation involves allegations of mortgage or bank fraud, the state investigator may partner with various IGs affiliated with federal entities such as the Department of Housing and Urban Development,[20] the Small Business Administration,[21] or the Federal Housing Finance Agency.[22] If school loan fraud or wage-related fraud are part of a broader state corruption investigation, the IGs affiliated with the federal Department of Education[23] or the Department of Labor[24] may assist the investigation. IGs throughout the federal government may be valuable sources of information in a wide range of state public corruption investigations.

C. *Cyber Fraud Task Force*

An AGO investigating public corruption should also consider partnering with the U.S. Secret Service Cyber Fraud Task Force (CFTF),[25] which can assist with a criminal investigation and offer various benefits to taskforce participants. The CFTF focuses on preventing and combatting complex cyber-enabled

---

18 26 U.S.C. § 6103(b)(5)(B)(iii).

19 Inspector General Act of 1978, P.L. No. 95-452, 92 Stat. 1101, 5 U.S.C. app. § 2 (2018) (Offices of Inspector General within separate federal agencies promote economy, efficiency, and effectiveness and prevent fraud and abuse within that agency). For discussion of other resources to assist with investigations, see Chapter 2.7.

20 U.S. Dep't of Housing and Urban Dev., Off. of Inspector Gen., https://www.hudoig.gov/ (last visited Apr. 19, 2021).

21 U.S. Small Bus. Admin., Off. of Inspector Gen., https://www.sba.gov/office-of-inspector-general (last visited Apr. 19, 2021).

22 Fed. Housing Fin. Agency, Off. of Inspector Gen., https://www.fhfaoig.gov/ (last visited Apr. 19, 2021).

23 U.S. Dep't of Educ., Off. of Inspector Gen., https://www2.ed.gov/about/offices/list/oig/index.html (last visited Apr. 19, 2021).

24 U.S. Dep't of Labor, Off. of Inspector Gen., https://www.oig.dol.gov/ (last visited Apr. 19, 2021).

25 *Secret Service Announces the Creation of the Cyber Fraud Task Force*, U.S. Secret Serv. (July 9, 2020), https://www.secretservice.gov/newsroom/releases/2020/07/secret-service-announces-creation-cyber-fraud-task-force.

financial crimes.[26] CFTF investigations draw on strategic partnerships with private sector technical experts in both cyber and financial sectors.[27]

D. *Federal Bureau of Investigations and Other Federal Agencies*

The Federal Bureau of Investigation, including the FBI Cyber Investigative Joint Task Force,[28] is another likely partner for an AGO investigating corruption. The FBI's top criminal investigative priority is public corruption.[29] Potential benefits of partnering with the FBI include its ability to fund and manage electronic surveillance, wiretaps, and other high-value, but high-cost, investigative techniques.[30] For example, the FBI includes a high-tech cell-site mapping unit known as the Cellular Analysis and Survey Team.[31] Cell-site mapping evidence may be useful in establishing the investigative target's approximate location at a particular time.[32] Federal authorities may have greater familiarity with and resources to address witness safety issues, including through the formal witness protection program administered by the U.S. Marshals Service.[33]

---

26 *Id.*

27 *Id.*

28 *National Cyber Investigative Joint Task Force*, Fed. Bureau of Investigation, https://www.fbi.gov/investigate/cyber/national-cyber-investigative-joint-task-force (last visited Apr. 19, 2021).

29 *What We Investigate: Public Corruption*, Fed. Bureau of Investigation, https://www.fbi.gov/investigate/public-corruption (last visited Apr. 19, 2021).

30 Barkow, *supra* note 4, at 572 n.281.

31 *See* Fed. Bureau of Investigation, Cellular Analysis Survey Team Policy Guide 11 (Jan. 5, 2018), https://vault.fbi.gov/cellular-analysis-survey-team-policy-guide-0997pg/cellular-analysis-survey-team-policy-guide-0997pg-part-01-of-01/view.

32 Tom Jackman, *Experts Say Law Enforcement's Use of Cellphone Records Can be Inaccurate*, Wash. Post (Jun. 27, 2014), https://www.washingtonpost.com/local/experts-say-law-enforcements-use-of-cellphone-records-can-be-inaccurate/2014/06/27/028be93c-faf3-11e3-932c-0a55b81f48ce_story.html?utm_term=.16eb21152c54.

33 For more information about federal witness relocation and protection, see 18 U.S.C. §§ 3521-30 (2018). State governments can request witness protection, but will be required to, among other things, reimburse the federal government for expenses. 18 U.S.C. § 3526(b)(1). *See also* Chapter 1.6, Part II(A); Chapter 2.5, Part III(E).

Conclusion

AGOs are vital to investigating and prosecuting public corruption crimes. Respecting local authorities and drawing on federal resources can help state-level investigators and prosecutors enforce centralized standards of public integrity without raising federalism concerns that might arise when federal authorities prosecute state officials. Because the federal government gives considerable priority and allocates significant resources to monitoring, investigating, and prosecuting possible abuses of public trust, AGOs may wish to request the support of federal authorities to assist with corruption investigations.

Chapter 2.7

Forensic Assistance Resources

Christine A. Hoffman

Christine A. Hoffman serves as Acting Gloucester County Prosecutor at the New Jersey Attorney General's Office. She previously served as the Assistant Attorney General and Deputy Director of the New Jersey Division of Criminal Justice, Chief of the Division's Corruption Bureau, Deputy Chief of the Division's Major Crimes Bureau, and Assistant Prosecutor with the Burlington County Prosecutor's Office. She is also a faculty member of the New Jersey Attorney General's Advocacy Institute and an adjunct law professor at Rutgers Law School.

Introduction

Investigations into public corruption may involve discovering and examining highly complex and deliberately surreptitious financial dealings all while avoiding detection by the investigation's target as well as the public and press. Performing such complex investigations can exceed resources typically available to law enforcement. Training and equipment are costly, both in dollars and staffing time. Investigators of public corruption may need to seek out assistance and maximize alternative resources. Moreover, even if a law enforcement agency has staffing and equipment in these areas, complexities in an individual case may still require additional outside assistance. The following chapter is a guide to the resources and assistance available to law enforcement agencies carrying out complex financial investigations.

I. Financial Analysis

Theft and money laundering are often at the core of corruption schemes. Stolen government money or bribes can be moved through a variety of financial transactions to disguise the source. For this reason, sophisticated financial analysis is integral to conducting corruption investigations.

A. *Regional Information Sharing Systems (RISS)*

RISS organization serves thousands of member law enforcement agencies in their efforts to successfully further criminal investigations and prosecutions.[1] Agency membership is typically open to all levels of law enforcement, as well as multijurisdictional task forces and regulatory agencies with law enforcement or criminal investigative authority.[2] RISS provides event deconfliction, information and intelligence-sharing resources, investigative support and analytical services, and training and publications.[3]

RISS Investigative Support Services will directly assist investigators.[4] RISS intelligence staff can access dozens of research tools, specialized databases, public record information, criminal justice information, and other data.[5] They are able to search, compile, and provide a report of their findings to officers in need of quick information.[6] RISS analysts also develop specialized analytical products for investigators and prosecutors.[7] These products include financial analysis reports, as well as other reports and charts that may be useful such as complex flowcharts and link-analysis charts.[8] Staff will also testify as expert witnesses at trial if needed.[9]

---

1 *About the RISS Program*, Reg'l Info. Sharing Sys. (RISS), https://www.riss.net/about-us/ (last visited Apr. 19, 2021).

2 *Id.*

3 *Id.*

4 *Investigative Support Services*, Reg'l Info. Sharing Sys. (RISS) https://www.riss.net/investigative-support-services/ (last visited Apr. 19, 2021).

5 *Id.*

6 *Id.*

7 *Id.*

8 *Id.*

9 *Id.*

RISS receives congressional funding and is administered by the U.S. Department of Justice's Bureau of Justice Assistance (BJA).[10] The centralized RISS Technology Support Center supports six regional centers encompassing the entire country: MAGLOCLEN (Middle Atlantic-Great Lakes Organized Crime Law Enforcement Network); MOCIC (Mid-States Organized Crime Information Center); NESPIN (New England State Police Information Network); RMIN (Rocky Mountain Information Network); ROCIC (Regional Organized Crime Information Center); and WSIN (Western States Information Network).[11]

B. *National White Collar Crime Center (NW3C)*

NW3C provides law enforcement support through information sharing and a case pointer system, investigative services, limited funding for cases, original research and white paper publications, and training.[12] Like RISS, NW3C is funded by USDOJ's BJA.[13] Its membership includes thousands of member agencies across the United States and the world.[14] Member agencies include all levels of law enforcement and certain regulatory agencies, and key partners include academic institutions.[15]

The NW3C analysis unit offers direct support in investigations involving complex schemes with voluminous financial transactions among multiple accounts over a significant period of time.[16] To reduce time spent on data entry, bank and credit card statements can be submitted to a NW3C support team member who then will use financial software to create a single, comprehensive database for analysis. Separately or in conjunction with this service, NW3C can assist with the following: examination of bank records and financial

---

10 *About the RISS Program*, *supra* note 1.

11 *RISS Centers*, Reg'l Info. Sharing Sys., https://riss.net (RISS Centers menu lists the six regions) (last visited Apr. 19, 2021).

12 *About Us*, The Nat'l White Collar Crime Ctr. (NW3C), https://www.nw3c.org/about (last visited Apr. 19, 2021); Bureau of Justice Assistance, The National White Collar Crime Center: Helping America Fight Economic Crime 3 (Apr. 2002), https://www.ncjrs.gov/pdffiles1/bja/184958.pdf.

13 *About Us*, The Nat'l White Collar Crime Ctr. (NW3C), https://www.nw3c.org/about (last visited Apr. 19, 2021).

14 *Id.*

15 *Key Partnerships*, The Nat'l White Collar Crime Ctr., https://www.nw3c.org/about/key-partnerships (last visited Apr. 19, 2021).

16 Bureau of Justice Assistance, *supra* note 12, at 3.

documents; analysis of transaction patterns; preparation of charts showing links between criminals and their activities; and analysis of qualitative data and trends.[17] Additionally, NW3C offers useful training courses in financial investigations practical skills and financial records examination and analysis.[18]

C. *Financial Crimes Enforcement Network (FinCEN)*

FinCEN is a bureau within the Treasury Department that obtains and maintains financial transactions data, and analyzes and disseminates that data for law enforcement purposes.[19] FinCEN uses counter-money laundering laws such as the Bank Secrecy Act (BSA) to require data collection and reporting by banks and other financial institutions.[20] This recordkeeping preserves a financial trail for investigators to follow as they track criminals and their assets.[21] FinCEN researches and analyzes BSA information in combination with a variety of other government, intelligence, and public databases.[22] FinCEN is one of the largest repositories of information available to law enforcement and regularly discloses that information to its law enforcement partners.[23] FinCEN also provides a wide range of support, including training and materials, to the law enforcement community to educate them about financial mechanisms that are susceptible to financial crimes.[24]

FinCEN partners with law enforcement agencies at all levels. Through Project Gateway, FinCEN works with law enforcement officials across the country to provide online access to FinCEN's databases and financial information.[25] Law enforcement agencies can directly search certain information collected

---

17 *Id.*

18 *Id.* at 2.

19 *What We Do*, Fin. Crimes Enf't Network, https://www.fincen.gov/what-we-do (last visited Apr. 19, 2021).

20 *FinCEN's Mandate from Congress*, Fin. Crimes Enf't Network, https://www.fincen.gov/resources/statutes-regulations (last visited Apr. 19, 2021).

21 *What We Do*, Fin. Crimes Enf't Network, https://www.fincen.gov/what-we-do (last visited Apr. 19, 2021).

22 *Id.*

23 *Law Enforcement Overview*, Fin. Crimes Enf't Network, https://www.fincen.gov/resources/law-enforcement-overview (last visited Apr. 19, 2021).

24 *Support of Law Enforcement*, Fin. Crimes Enf't Network, https://www.fincen.gov/resources/law-enforcement/support-law-enforcement (last visited Apr. 19, 2021).

25 *Frequently Asked Questions*, Fin. Crimes Enf't Network, https://www.fincen.gov/frequently-asked-questions (last visited Apr. 19, 2021) (under "Who are FinCEN's Customers?").

and analyzed by FinCEN. These agencies may also make direct requests to FinCEN for assistance in developing and running complex searches and performing specialized analysis of BSA and other records.[26] In 2021, Congress passed legislation that requires a beneficial owner of a corporation to disclose its identity.[27] State and local enforcers are required to obtain authorization from a court of competent jurisdiction to obtain beneficial ownership information that would assist their civil or criminal investigations.[28]

FinCEN information is often useful in identifying and obtaining key information such as personal identifiers, bank accounts, criminal associations, internal or regulatory investigations of financial institutions, or other financial intelligence. Direct dissemination of certain BSA documents is limited, even for criminal discovery, and prosecutors should research and discuss with a supervisor how to fulfill their discovery and disclosure obligations without violating federal law.[29]

D. *Other Resources and Training*

The Federal Law Enforcement Training Center (FLETC) is run by the U.S. Department of Homeland Security (DHS) and is the nation's largest provider of law enforcement training.[30] In addition to training federal law

26 *Support of Law Enforcement*, Fin. Crimes Enf't Network, https://www.fincen.gov/resources/law-enforcement/support-law-enforcement (last visited Apr. 19, 2021).

27 As part of the National Defense Authorization Act for Fiscal Year 2021, Congress enacted the Anti-Money Laundering Act of 2020. National Defense Authorization Act for Fiscal Year 2021, Pub. L. No. 116-283, §§ 6001-6511 (2021).

28 *Id.* § 6403 (to be codified at 31 U.S.C. § 5336(B)(i)(II)) ("FinCEN may disclose beneficial ownership information reported pursuant to this section only upon receipt of . . . a request, through appropriate protocols . . . from a State, local, or Tribal law enforcement agency, if a court of competent jurisdiction, including any officer of such a court, has authorized the law enforcement agency to seek the information in a criminal or civil investigation").

29 Suspicious Activity Reports (SARs) are protected from disclosure by statute, 31 U.S.C. § 5318(g)(2)(A)(ii), and unauthorized disclosure is a federal criminal offense. *See* Fin. Crimes Enforcement Network, Unauthorized Disclosure of Suspicious Activity Reports (Aug. 18, 2004), https://www.fincen.gov/sites/default/files/guidance/unauthorizeddisclosureofbanksar.pdf; Press Release, U.S. Attorney's Office for the N. Dist. of Cal., Internal Revenue Service Analyst Pleads Guilty to Making Unauthorized Disclosure of Suspicious Activity Reports (Aug. 15, 2019), https://www.justice.gov/usao-ndca/pr/internal-revenue-service-analyst-pleads-guilty-making-unauthorized-disclosure. *But cf.* United States v. Holihan, 248 F. Supp. 2d 179, 186–87 (W.D.N.Y. 2003) (holding SARs supporting documentation is not protected).

30 *Learn About FLETC*, Fed. Law Enf't Training Ctrs., https://www.fletc.gov/learn-about

enforcement, FLETC provides tuition-free and low-cost training to state and local law enforcement agencies.[31] Programs are conducted across the United States and are normally hosted by a local law enforcement agency.[32] Training is also conducted at several FLETC facilities located across the nation.[33] A number of courses are available covering financial analysis, economic crimes, and money laundering.[34]

The Federal Bureau of Investigations (FBI) Law Enforcement Enterprise Portal (LEEP) is an electronic gateway to a number of law enforcement services and resources.[35] Users have a single sign-on process to access many different services and online resources.[36]

State resources, such as New Jersey's Anti-Money Laundering Task Force, may also offer trainings.[37]

E. *Partnerships*

Traditional partnerships for public corruption investigations include federal agencies such as FBI or DHS, as discussed above. However, other federal authorities may also be good resources. For example, within many federal agencies, an office of the inspector general acts as an independent unit to combat waste, fraud, and abuse in the programs, and may be able to assist with public corruption investigations.[38] These units typically have auditors on staff to assist with their audits and investigations. If the subject matter of a corruption investigation overlaps with an inspector general's area of responsibility,

-fletc (last visited Apr. 19, 2021).

31 *State, Local & Tribal Law Enforcement Training*, Fed. Law Enf't Training Ctrs, https://www.fletc.gov/state-local-tribal-law-enforcement-training (last visited Apr. 19, 2021).

32 *Id.*

33 *Id.*

34 *See, e.g.*, *Money Laundering & Asset Forfeiture Training Program*, Fed. Law Enf't Training Ctrs, https://www.fletc.gov/training-program/money-laundering-asset-forfeiture-training-program (last visited Apr. 19, 2021).

35 *Law Enforcement Enterprise Portal*, Fed. Bureau of Investigation, https://www.fbi.gov/services/cjis/leep (last visited Apr. 19, 2021).

36 *Id.*

37 *Cf. Financial and Cyber Crimes Bureau*, N.J. Off. of the Att'y Gen., https://www.nj.gov/oag/dcj/financial-computer.htm (last visited Apr. 19, 2021).

38 *See* Inspector General Act of 1978, P.L. No. 95-452, 92 Stat. 1101, 5 U.S.C. app. § 2 (2018) (Offices of Inspector General within separate federal agencies promote economy, efficiency, and effectiveness and prevent fraud and abuse within that agency).

such as housing or education, that unit within the relevant agency may be able to partner and provide assistance. The U.S. Postal Inspection Service[39] and the U.S. Secret Service[40] may both assist state and local agencies with certain types of financial investigations.

F. *Professional Organizations or Associations*

Numerous professional organizations or associations assist law enforcement with policies, standards, analysis, training, and education.

The Association of Certified Fraud Examiners (ACFE) is the world's largest anti-fraud organization, with tens of thousands of members.[41] Membership is open to all levels of experience and to all industries, but many members are Certified Fraud Examiners.[42] ACFE provides training courses covering financial and computer fraud.[43]

The Association of Certified Anti-Money Laundering Specialists (ACAMS) is the largest international membership organization dedicated to fighting financial crimes.[44] ACAMS has members in 175 countries across the public and private sector.[45] ACAMS provides training and certification, and also runs conferences and forums.[46] Its Certified Anti-Money Laundering Specialist (CAMS) credential and other advanced certifications are recognized as gold standards in anti-money laundering certifications.[47]

---

39 Federal Postal Inspectors work closely with law enforcement agencies and prosecutors investigating crimes that adversely affect or fraudulently use the mail. U.S. Postal Inspection Serv., *A Law Enforcement Guide to Postal Crimes*, Homeland Security Dig. Library, Pub. 146 (Jun. 2004), https://www.hsdl.org/?view&did=453162; *see also What We Do*, U.S. Postal Inspection Serv., https://www.uspis.gov/about/what-we-do/ (last visited Apr. 19, 2021).

40 The Secret Service's investigative mission is to safeguard the payment and financial systems of the United States. *Our Investigative Mission*, U.S. Secret Serv., https://www.secretservice.gov/investigation/ (last visited Apr. 19, 2021).

41 *Who We Are*, Ass'n of Certified Fraud Exam'rs, https://www.acfe.com/who-we-are.aspx (last visited Apr. 19, 2021).

42 *Membership Categories*, Ass'n of Certified Fraud Exam'rs, https://www.acfe.com/getting-started-categories.aspx (last visited Apr. 19, 2021).

43 *Events, Training & Products*, Ass'n of Certified Fraud Exam'rs, https://www.acfe.com/training-events.aspx (last visited Apr. 19, 2021).

44 ACAMS, https://www.acams.org/ (last visited Apr. 19, 2021).

45 *About ACAMS*, ACAMS, https://www.acams.org/en/about (last visited Apr. 19, 2021).

46 *Id.*

47 *The Gold Standard*, ACAMS, https://www.acams.org/en/certifications/cams-certification

The International Association of Financial Crimes Investigators (IAFCI) is another large association with thousands of members worldwide.[48] The membership is about one-third law enforcement, one-third banking, and one-third retail and service.[49] IAFCI also offers trainings and its own certification programs, including both financial and digital analysis.[50]

The Association of Law Enforcement Intelligence Units (LEIU) is an agency-based membership organization consisting of hundreds of local, state, and federal agencies across the nation.[51] LEIU maintains a criminal intelligence clearinghouse, holds an annual conference with certified training, and provides technical assistance in the formation and organization of an agency's intelligence function.[52] LEIU is a good resource for identifying possible assistance with financial analysis from other law enforcement agencies.

LEIU works with the International Association of Law Enforcement Intelligence Analysts (IALEIA). IALEIA has grown to be the largest non-profit, professional organization in the world representing law enforcement analysts.[53] IALEIA is based in the United States, but supports regional chapters throughout the world.[54] IALEIA has supporting agencies (including several federal and state agencies and all RISS regional centers).[55] IALEIA also has a certification program for analysts and offers training for analysts.[56]

(last visited Apr. 19, 2021).

48 *Benefits of Membership*, IAFCI, https://www.iafci.org/Public/About_IAFCI/Benefits_of_Membership/Public/About_IAFCI/Benefits_of_Membership.aspx (last visited Apr. 19, 2021); *About IAFCI*, IAFCI, https://www.iafci.org/Public/About_IAFCI/Public/About_IAFCI/ About_IAFCI.aspx (last visited Apr. 19, 2021).

49 *About IAFCI*, IAFCI, https://www.iafci.org/Public/About_IAFCI/Public/About_IAFCI/About_IAFCI.aspx (last visited Apr. 19, 2021).

50 *IAFCI Certifications*, IAFCI, https://www.iafci.org/Public/Certifications/Public/About_IAFCI/IAFCI_Certifications.aspx (last visited Apr. 19, 2021).

51 *About LEIU*, Law Enf't Intelligence Units, http://www.leiu.org/about (last visited Apr. 19, 2021).

52 *Id.*

53 *Mission*, Int'l Ass'n of Law Enf't Intelligence Analysts, https://www.ialeia.org/mission.php (last visited Apr. 19, 2021).

54 *Id.*

55 *Our Partner Organizations*, Int'l Ass'n of Law Enf't Intelligence Analysts, https://www.ialeia.org/our_partner_organizations.php (last visited Apr. 19, 2021).

56 *Certification Process*, Int'l Ass'n of Law Enf't Intelligence Analysts, https://www.ialeia.org/certification_process.php (last visited Apr. 19, 2021); *Training*, Int'l Ass'n of Law Enf't Intelligence Analysts, https://www.ialeia.org/training.php (last visited Apr. 19, 2021).

The Association of Certified Financial Crime Specialists (ACFCS) is a professional organization with members from both financial institutions and law enforcement.[57] ACFCS provides trainings, including webinars on a range of financial and corruption topics.[58] ACFCS also offers a certification program.[59]

G. *Time-Saving Equipment*

To reduce the amount of time spent on voluminous financial analysis, public corruption investigators may use software to capture and organize financial data. For example, Actionable Intelligence Technologies Inc.'s software, Comprehensive Financial Investigative Solution (CFIS), assists with financial investigations and forensic accounting.[60] CFIS automatically processes paper and electronic financial documents; records data into a centralized database; provides data analysis, including flow of funds tracing; and displays financial transactional patterns.[61]

II. High-Tech Forensic Assistance

Beyond financial forensic analysis, investigative technology can enable investigators to track cell phones or vehicles, recover emails or texts among coconspirators, break encryption or otherwise recover digital information, and de-anonymize criminals attempting to use cryptocurrency. For law enforcement agencies that may need digital forensic or surveillance technology when investigating public corruption, a number of resources are discussed below.[62]

---

57 *About*, Ass'n of Certified Fin. Crime Specialists, https://www.acfcs.org/about (last visited Apr. 19, 2021).

58 *Live & On Demand Financial Crime Prevention Training*, Ass'n of Certified Fin. Crime Specialists, https://www.acfcs.org/training (last visited Apr. 19, 2021).

59 *CFCS Certification*, Ass'n of Certified Fin. Crime Specialists, https://www.acfcs.org/certification/ (last visited Apr. 19, 2021).

60 *About CFIS*, Comprehensive Fin. Investigative Solution, http://www.aitcfis.com/about/ (last visited Apr. 19, 2021).

61 *Id.*

62 For a discussion of legal considerations of using electronic surveillance and obtaining online evidence, see Chapters 2.3 and 2.4.

A. *Regional Computer Forensics Laboratory (RCFL)*

In 2000, the FBI established a national program for the creation and operation of Regional Computer Forensics Laboratories (RCFLs).[63] An RCFL is a full-service forensics laboratory and training center devoted solely to the examination of digital evidence to support criminal investigations.[64] The RCFL's duties include seizing and collecting digital evidence at a crime scene, conducting an impartial examination of submitted computer evidence, and testifying as required.[65] The current service areas cover the entire country and are as follows: Chicago, Greater Houston, Heart of America, Intermountain West, Kentucky, New England, New Jersey, New Mexico, North Texas, Northwest, Orange County (California), Philadelphia, Rocky Mountain, San Diego, Silicon Valley, Tennessee Valley, and Western New York.[66]

More specifically, the RCFL can provide pre-seizure consultations for search warrants by advising on computer-related language.[67] The RCFL can also provide on-site assistance, sending examiners out to assist with the seizure and collection of electronic media.[68] Because examinations are typically conducted on copies of the original evidence to avoid evidence contamination, examiners will either duplicate the evidence on-site or bring the evidence back to the laboratory for duplication.[69] Examiners will conduct an examination of the digital evidence and convert it to a usable format for the investigator.[70] The examiners are available to testify in court as to how they conducted the examination and what they discovered.[71]

The RCFL also has a Cell Phone Investigative Kiosk, which allows law enforcement officers to immediately extract data from a cell phone, put it into a

---

63 *About*, Reg'l Comput. Forensics Lab., https://www.rcfl.gov/about (last visited Apr. 19, 2021).

64 Reg'l Comput. Forensics Lab., https://www.rcfl.gov/ (last visited Apr. 19, 2021).

65 *Service Offerings*, Reg'l Comput. Forensics Lab., https://www.rcfl.gov/services (last visited Apr. 19, 2021).

66 *Service Areas*, Reg'l Comput. Forensics Lab., https://www.rcfl.gov/service-areas (last visited Apr. 19, 2021).

67 *Service Offerings*, Reg'l Comput. Forensics Lab., https://www.rcfl.gov/services/services (last visited Apr. 19, 2021).

68 *Id.*

69 *Id.*

70 *Id.*

71 *Id.*

report, and make a copy of the report.[72] Similarly, the RCFL has a Loose Media Kiosk, which allows law enforcement officers to immediately review evidentiary data found on devices like thumb drives, flash media, and CDs/DVDs.[73]

B. *Cyber Crimes Center (C3)*

DHS created the Homeland Security Investigations (HSI) Cyber Crimes Center (C3) to combat crimes committed on, or facilitated by, the internet.[74] C3 operates a computer forensics laboratory, which provides subject matter expertise on new technologies and emerging threats, along with continuing education for computer forensics agents and analysts.[75] Also, DHS computer forensics agents and analysts are located throughout the country and are trained to perform forensic examinations of seized digital devices and media.[76]

C. *RISS*

In addition to the forensic financial services discussed above, the RISS program offers a variety of specialized analytical products and equipment.[77] Similar to the RCFL, RISS will conduct digital forensic examinations and also assist with analyzing the resulting data.[78] Services include analysis of call detail records (also known as toll billing records); audio and video enhancements to identify suspects; and lending surveillance equipment such as body-wire receivers, global positioning systems, cameras, video recorders, specialized lenses, night-vision goggles, and ground-penetrating radar systems.[79]

---

72 *Id.*

73 *Id.*

74 *HSI Cyber Crimes Center*, U.S. Immigr. & Customs Enf't, https://www.ice.gov/cyber-crimes (last visited Apr. 19, 2021).

75 *Id.*

76 Dep't of Homeland Sec. Science & Tech. Directorate, Cyber Security Division Cyber Security Forensics Project (2017), https://www.dhs.gov/sites/default/files/publications/FactSheet_Cybersecurity%20Forensics%20One%20Pager%20FINAL_508.PDF.

77 *Investigative Support Services*, *supra* note 4.

78 *Id.*

79 *Id.*

D. *NW3C*

NW3C offers a number of free training opportunities on how to conduct cyber investigations, process digital evidence, and investigate network intrusions.[80]

E. *Other Resources and Training*

As discussed above, DHS's FLETC provides training to law enforcement agencies. FLETC training not only covers complex financial investigations, but also other types of digital investigation and electronic surveillance.[81] Similarly, FBI's LEEP offers services and resources for the law enforcement community relating generally to cybercrime.[82]

The National Computer Forensic Institute (NCFI) is a federally-funded training center that instructs state and local investigators, prosecutors, and even judges in digital evidence and cybercrime investigations.[83] Opened in 2008, NCFI is run by the U.S. Secret Service's Criminal Investigation Division and the Alabama Office of Prosecution Services, and has trained law enforcement from hundreds of agencies nationwide.[84] The training, including travel, is completely covered by NCFI.[85] In some of the courses, NCFI issues investigators free hardware, software, and licenses necessary to conduct forensic investigations, which they keep for continued use after the training.[86]

The Law Enforcement Cyber Center (LECC) is a collaborative project led by the International Association of Chiefs of Police (IACP) and funded

---

80 *See generally* NW3C Course Catalog (Jan. 2020), https://www.nw3c.org/docs/training/nw3c-training-catalog.pdf.

81 *See, e.g.*, *Digital Evidence Acquisition Specialist Training*, Fed. Law Enf't Training Ctrs., https://www.fletc.gov/training-program/digital-evidence-acquisition-specialist-training (last visited Apr. 19, 2021); *Covert Electronic Surveillance Program*, Fed. Law Enf't Training Ctrs., https://www.fletc.gov/training-program/covert-electronic-surveillance-program (last visited Apr. 19, 2021).

82 *Law Enforcement Enterprise Portal*, Fed. Bureau of Investigation, https://www.fbi.gov/services/cjis/leep (last visited Apr. 19, 2021).

83 *About*, Nat'l Comput. Forensics Inst., https://www.ncfi.usss.gov/ncfi/pages/about.xhtml (last visited Apr. 19, 2021).

84 *Id.*

85 *Id.*

86 *Id.*

by USDOJ's BJA. [87] The Cyber Center was developed to be a national resource for law enforcement and related public safety entities.[88] It is intended to assist in educating and building the capacity of these entities for cybercrime investigations, digital forensics, and information systems security.[89] The website has links to other resources and partners that provide training and other resources.[90]

F. *Partnerships*

Important partnerships in this area include the FBI Cyber Investigative Joint Task Force[91] and the U.S. Secret Service Cyber Fraud Task Force,[92] both of which can assist with a criminal investigation and offer various benefits to taskforce participants. As discussed above, DHS controls the Cyber Crimes Center as well as a Computer Forensics Unit, which manages the Computer Forensics Laboratory.[93] Additionally, states may have resources available to aid in investigating and prosecuting cybercrimes. For example, within its Office of Homeland Security and Preparedness, New Jersey has a Cybersecurity and Communications Integration Cell (NJCCIC) for information sharing, threat analysis, and incident reporting.[94]

---

87 *About the Cyber Center*, IACP Law Enf't Cyber Ctr., http://www.iacpcybercenter.org/about-the-cyber-center/ (last visited Apr. 19, 2021) (noting that the Cyber Center is a collaboration among IACP, NW3C, and the Police Executive Research Forum).

88 *Id.*

89 *Id.*

90 *See, e.g., Training*, Law Enf't Cyber Ctr., https://www.iacpcybercenter.org/topics/training-2/ (last visited Apr. 19, 2021); *Resources*, Law Enf't Cyber Ctr., https://www.iacpcybercenter.org/prosecutors/resources/ (last visited Apr. 19, 2021).

91 *National Cyber Investigative Joint Task Force*, Fed. Bureau of Investigation, https://www.fbi.gov/investigate/cyber/national-cyber-investigative-joint-task-force (last visited Apr. 19, 2021).

92 Secret Service Announces the Creation of the Cyber Fraud Task Force, U.S. Secret Serv., https://www.secretservice.gov/newsroom/releases/2020/07/secret-service-announces-creation-cyber-fraud-task-force (July 9, 2020).

93 *HSI Cyber Crimes Center*, U.S. Immigrations & Customs Enf't, https://www.ice.gov/partnerships-centers/cyber-crimes-center (last visited Apr. 19, 2021).

94 *Defending New Jersey's Digital Density*, N.J. Cybersecurity & Commc'ns Integration Cell, https://www.cyber.nj.gov/about (last visited Apr. 19, 2021).

G. *Professional Organizations or Associations*

The High Technology Crime Investigation Association (HTCIA) is a non-profit association formed to provide education and collaboration to law enforcement and industry members for the prevention and investigation of high-tech crimes.[95] HTCIA focuses on networking and training opportunities.[96]

The National Cyber-Forensics & Training Alliance (NCFTA) is another non-profit association focused on identifying, mitigating, and neutralizing cybercrime threats. NCFTA conducts real-time information sharing and analysis with experts in the public, private, and academic sectors.[97]

SEARCH, the National Consortium for Justice Information and Statistics, is a non-profit membership organization that supports information sharing, interoperability, communications, information technology, and high-tech crime investigative needs of law enforcement.[98] SEARCH provides trainings for high-tech crime investigations, public safety and emergency communication, and information, and also assists local and state agencies with technical, policy, and operational matters.[99]

Conclusion

Public corruption cases can be complicated, but many sources offer high quality training and expertise at no or low cost. Prosecutors and investigations who fight public corruption should take advantage of these resources to improve their own investigative skills and to use existing expertise to assist with ongoing investigations.

---

95 *About*, High Tech. Crime Investigation Ass'n, https://htcia.org/about/ (last visited Apr. 19, 2021).

96 *Id.*

97 *About Us*, Nat'l Cyber-Forensics & Training All., https://www.ncfta.net/home-2/about-us/ (last visited Apr. 19, 2021).

98 *Company Background*, SEARCH, https://www.search.org/about-search/company-background/ (last visited Apr. 19, 2021).

99 *Get Help*, SEARCH, https://www.search.org/get-help/ (last visited Apr. 19, 2021); *Assistance*, SEARCH, https://www.search.org/get-help/assistance (last visited Apr. 19, 2021).

Chapter 2.8

Concurrent Investigations Involving Criminal, Civil, & Administrative Authorities

Brian Kane, Brenda Bauges

Brian Kane serves as Idaho Chief Deputy Attorney General.

Brenda Bauges is the Associate Dean for Student Affairs and Inclusion at the University of Idaho College of Law and former Idaho Deputy Attorney General.

Introduction

An attorney general's broad authority typically includes administrative, civil, and criminal enforcement powers, as well as a responsibility to defend the state and its agencies in civil suits. One single instance of wrongdoing, or a course of related conduct, may be subject to all three types of authority, and could result in cases involving multiple government entities. If different legal matters arise with respect to the same underlying facts, they are called parallel or concurrent proceedings.[1]

---

1 In this chapter, the term "concurrent proceedings" will be used. This term is intended to describe what are often referred to as "parallel proceedings," but better reflects the potential intersections among different types of proceedings. *See, e.g.*, David A. Hyman, *When Rules Collide: Procedural Intersection and the Rule of Law*, 71 Tul. L. Rev. 1389, 1394 n.10 (1997).

Concurrent proceedings draw on the same underlying facts. These underlying facts may form the basis of a criminal prosecution, a civil lawsuit, or an administrative proceeding, and these proceedings may unfold concurrently with one another. In these concurrent proceedings, government attorneys typically use different investigative tools to gather those facts, and then present those facts in different types of proceedings that may result in criminal, civil, or employment consequences to the defendant. Government attorneys seeking to coordinate these efforts must still comply with their respective professional rules of conduct and statutory authority, and they must maintain proper boundaries as they exercise the power of their office. Having a system in place across an attorney general's office ensures effective communication, compartmentalization, and coordination during the investigative, charging, and trial phases of concurrent proceedings.

This chapter will first explain what concurrent investigations are and in what contexts they can arise. Next, it will explore the complications that may manifest during the course of a concurrent investigation. It will finally focus on the most effective ways to manage concurrent investigations in light of these complications.

I. Definition and Examples of Concurrent Investigations

The ultimate result of concurrent investigations could be one criminal proceeding, one civil litigation, one civil regulatory proceeding, or some other combination of proceedings. The same office might occupy different—even adversarial—roles across these concurrent proceedings, and multiple jurisdictions could be involved.

In considering the propriety of concurrent investigations involving the same government enforcing both civil and criminal statutes, the Supreme Court has held that these investigations do not violate the due process clause, unless the enforcers act in bad faith.[2] "Bad faith" includes bringing "a civil action

2 *See* United States v. Kordel, 397 U.S. 1, 6, 11-12 (1970). State Supreme Courts have also approved of concurrent proceedings. *See, e.g.*, State v. Kobrin Sec., Inc., 544 A.2d 833, 837-38 (N.J. 1988).

solely to obtain evidence for . . . criminal prosecution;" failing "to advise the defendant in its civil proceeding that it contemplates his criminal prosecution; . . . [or] any other special circumstances that might suggest the unconstitutionality or even the impropriety of th[e] criminal prosecution."[3] Thus, while concurrent investigations and proceedings are not prohibited, government attorneys should think carefully about whether and how to share information. Additional complications can arise when the same office represents adversarial interests.

An unfortunately common example of a situation that could give rise to concurrent investigations is a corrections officer who is alleged to have had sexual contact with an inmate in a state prison.[4] This set of facts may result in a number of proceedings:

- A criminal investigation against the guard,[5] by an AGO prosecutor or by a prosecutor outside of the AGO;
- An administrative personnel investigation,[6] where an AGO lawyer represents an administrative board considering whether to terminate the guard's employment;
- Civil litigation by the inmate-victim against the prison, where the AGO represents the defendant-prison, and may interact directly with the guards who are under investigation.

These concurrent investigations will involve multiple teams of attorneys, and their interests may or may not be generally aligned. This scenario will be examined throughout this chapter. In corruption cases, concurrent proceedings

---

3 *Kordel*, 397 U.S. at 11-12.

4 The federal Prison Rape Elimination Act of 2003 (PREA), 34 U.S.C. §§ 30301-30309 (2018), requires the Bureau of Justice Statistics to collect data and report on the incidence of sexual victimization in federal, state, and county correctional facilities. *Id.* at § 30303(a). Reports of allegations of sexual victimization in recent years have increased, not necessarily due to an increase in incidents, but due to an improvement in data collection and reporting. *See* Jessica Stroop, Bureau of Justice Statistics, U.S. Dep't of Justice, PREA Data Collection Activities, 2018 1 (June 2018), https://www.bjs.gov/content/pub/pdf/pdca18.pdf.

5 *See* Idaho Code § 18-6110(1), (4) (2020) ("It is a felony for any employee of the Idaho department of correction . . . to have sexual contact with a prisoner . . . punishable by imprisonment in the state prison for a term not to exceed life.").

6 *See id.* § 50-1604(4) (listing reasons for removing a public civil servant).

may arise where the same conduct violates both civil and criminal statutes, or where multiple authorities are investigating an event or a target.[7]

II. Complications in Conducting Concurrent Investigations

When multiple investigations are conducted regarding the same set of facts, complications can arise. For example: ethical conflicts can exist; the timing of or tools used in one investigation can be detrimental to the other; an attorney's professional conduct obligations may be triggered; and, in some limited circumstances, resolving one proceeding may bar the other.

A. *Concurrent Proceedings Require a Broad Perspective*

Rules of professional conduct do not specifically exclude representation by the AGO of more than one interest in a case.[8] In fact, the rules of professional conduct acknowledge that an AGO will often be able to represent multiple interests in situations where a private attorney could not.[9] In the example of a

7 For example, a public official alleged to have misused a charitable foundation in connection with personal expenses or campaign finance could face a personal criminal investigation into misconduct in office or campaign finance violations while the charitable organization and leadership could face related civil or criminal investigations of violations of laws governing charities. If tax issues were to arise, state and federal tax authorities could also bring related civil or criminal investigations.

8 *See* Model Rules of Prof'l Conduct, Preamble and Scope cmt. 18 (Am. Bar Ass'n 2020). This chapter refers to the American Bar Association Model Rules of Professional Conduct because every state has adopted similar rules. *Alphabetical List of Jurisdictions Adopting Model Rules*, Am. Bar Ass'n (Mar. 28, 2018), https://www.americanbar.org/groups/professional_responsibility/publications/model_rules_of_professional_conduct/alpha_list_state_adopting_model_rules/ (listing every state but California and most territories); Order re Request for Approval of Proposed Amendments to the Rules of Professional Conduct of the State Bar of California, No. S240991 (Cal. May 10, 2018), http://www.calbar.ca.gov/Portals/0/documents/Supreme%20Court%20Order%202018-05-09.pdf (adopting rules of professional conduct based on the ABA Model Rules, although maintaining a number of rules distinct from the ABA rules). Each state's rules may vary.

9 Model Rules, Preamble and Scope cmt. 18 ("[L]awyers under the supervision of these officers may be authorized to represent several government agencies in intragovernmental legal controversies in circumstances where a private lawyer could not represent multiple private clients. These Rules do not abrogate any such authority."). *Accord* People v. Waterstone, 783 N.W.2d 314, 314 (Mich. 2010) (reversing decision disqualifying attorney general's office from

corrections officer's sexual misconduct against an inmate, the AGO may criminally prosecute the officer while defending the state department of corrections in a civil lawsuit brought by the victim. The state department of corrections is a client of the AGO represented by civil defense counsel, while separate prosecution counsel from the office's criminal division investigates and charges the officer who committed the offense. The prosecutor's goal would be to prove that the officer engaged in improper conduct that violated the law, while the attorney representing the prison in the civil case may conclude that his obligation to zealously represent his client requires minimizing the seriousness of the assault.

These potentially divergent obligations can create challenges. The prosecutor could make statements in connection with a criminal investigation or case that could be used against the government in related civil proceedings. Similarly, a civil government attorney could obtain information from or provide assurances to the corrections officer that that officer could argue prohibits him from being prosecuted by another member of the same office.[10]

When the office represents interests that are arguably adverse, imposing conflict walls between the teams that represent those separate interests and keeping clear records of those walls may be useful to counter arguments that a defendant's rights have been violated and to ensure that there is no appearance of impropriety.[11] Even if no true conflict of interest exists in this situation under

---

acting as a special prosecutor in related case against judge that same office represented in a related civil proceeding), Att'y Gen. v. Pub. Serv. Comm'n, 625 N.W.2d 16, 29, 33 (Mich. Ct. App. 2000) (collecting cases and concluding that while "in most instances, an attorney general may represent adverse state agencies in intragovernmental disputes," a "conflict of interest arises when the Attorney General intervenes as a party in opposition to a state agency that she represents as counsel").

10 In one case, the AGO represented prison guards in a civil suit and later appointed a special prosecutor to investigate the same incident, which resulted in the guards being charged. *See* Michael Rezendes, *Bridgewater Guards to Stand Trial in Patient's Death*, Bos. Globe (Dec. 3, 2017), https://www.bostonglobe.com/metro/2017/12/03/guards-will-soon-stand-trial-years-after-death-patient-bridgewater-state-hospital/Rf8TA61y7CJrscVWSnE50K/story.html. The defendants argued that information the civil assistant attorney general encouraged them to provide was later used to prosecute them. *Id.* The court deferred its decision on the motion to dismiss the case due to the alleged conflict of interest until after the trial. *Id.* As the defendants were acquitted, no decision appears to have been entered. Tom Relihan, *Judge Clears 3 Former Guards in Death of Patient at Bridgewater State Hospital*, MetroWest Daily News (Dec. 12, 2017), https://www.metrowestdailynews.com/news/20171211/judge-clears-3-former-guards-in-death-of-patient-at-bridgewater-state-hospital.

11 *See, e.g.*, *Att'y Gen.*, 625 N.W.2d at 24 (detailing conflict wall procedure in AGO that

rules of professional conduct, a government attorney's actions in one matter may, as a practical matter, affect a related concurrent matter.

Issues can also arise if the government attorneys represent interests that are not obviously adverse, such as when the government pursues administrative, civil, or criminal cases against the same defendant. While "[t]here is nothing improper about the government undertaking simultaneous criminal and civil investigations,"[12] prosecutors and civil attorneys should think carefully about whether, when, and how to share information. In some cases, attorneys may and should discuss each team's goals, resources, and timing. But if one team has power to, as an example, compel a statement by threatening adverse employment action, sharing that statement with another team may imperil any case that results.

B. *Rules of Professional Conduct and Imputation Issues*

1. Conflicts of Interest

The American Bar Association Model Rules recognize that government attorneys' offices, unlike private law firms, may be authorized to represent clients whose interests are adverse.[13] In fact, sometimes state constitutions and statutes specifically assign representation of certain governmental clients to the AGO, which may mean that the office is obligated to represent potentially adverse clients. However, some conflicts rules still apply to government attorneys.[14] Model Rule 1.11 addresses special conflicts of interest for former and current government lawyers.[15] Government attorneys are subject to rules pertaining to current client conflicts and former client conflicts, but conflicts held by one individual government attorney are not automatically imputed to

---

represented both appellant and appellee in civil case, and noting that no person in the office—including the attorney general—"has access to the files and records of both parties"); People v. Tennessen, 2009 Guam 3, ¶ 46-50 (Guam 2009) (concluding that AGO did not show that wall was maintained throughout case where conflicted attorney general had been disqualified from overseeing investigation), *overruled in part by* Barrett-Anderson v. Camacho, 2018 Guam 20, ¶ 19 (Guam 2018).

12 United States v. Stringer, 535 F.3d 929, 933 (9th Cir. 2008).

13 Model Rules, Preamble and Scope cmt. 18.

14 *Id.* (noting that government attorneys may have the authority held by the client in the private attorney-client relationship).

15 *Id.* r. 1.11.

other associated government officers or employees.[16] Nevertheless, ensuring lawyers working on potentially adverse related matters do not have access to each other's files and setting up discrete chains of command for each litigation team is prudent.[17] Although deputy attorneys general from the same office can typically be involved in concurrent investigations and subsequent proceedings, they should be aware of their own state's statutes, rules, office policies, and any ethics decisions regarding whether screening is required.

The goals and interests of different governmental teams in concurrent investigations and proceedings may be aligned; however, this is not always the case. Deputy attorneys general should be aware of their professional obligations if a situation arises where their team's interests—for example, to reach a resolution that potentially impedes the concurrent investigation—are not aligned with the other team's interests. For some cases, it may be prudent to make it clear at the initial stages of the investigations that each team's obligations to represent its client may require investigating, charging, or resolving a case in a manner that is not optimal for the interests of another team. Protocols regarding communication should be instituted in such scenarios to insure there are no inopportune surprises that would detrimentally affect the other proceeding.

Courts have distinguished between AGOs representing government interests on both sides of a case—which they permit, with walls—and a situation where "the Attorney General is an actual party to the litigation." [18] At least some courts have concluded that in the second category of cases, "independent counsel should be appointed for the state agency in order to remedy the ethical impediment to the Attorney General's position as a party."[19] But such situations should be carefully examined to insure that the attorney general is not being sued as a strategic block to representation, for example. In instances where opposing parties have attempted to disqualify an AGO or a particular government lawyer, courts typically scrutinize the facts of each particular case, the loyalties at issue, the interests and identities of the parties, and the standing of the litigant seeking disqualification.[20]

---

16 *Id.* r. 1.11 cmt. 2. *Accord Att'y Gen.*, 625 N.W.2d at 24.

17 Model Rules r. 1.11 cmt. 2.

18 State *ex rel.* Comm'r of Transp. v. Eagle, 63 S.W.3d 734, 773 (Tenn. Ct. App. 2001).

19 *Id. See also Att'y Gen.*, 625 N.W.2d at 30 (collecting cases that conclude 'that the Attorney General may represent opposing state agencies also provide that the Attorney General may do so only 'where he or she is not an actual party' in the dispute").

20 *See, e.g.*, Rogers v. Office of the Att'y Gen., 16-cv-00429-RL-MGG, 2017 U.S. Dist. LEXIS

2. Confidentiality Obligations

Civil government attorneys' ability to share information with other teams may be limited by their confidentiality obligations to their clients. For private attorneys, the confidentiality requirements are generally clear: A lawyer representing a private client is prohibited from revealing information relating to the representation of that client, with limited exceptions;[21] the loyalties of a lawyer representing an organizational client lie with the organization, not any one individual employed by it.[22] However, the Model Rules explicitly disclaim any role in identifying the "client" of a government attorney.[23] Thus, civil government attorneys should be prepared to consult state statutes, case law, and ethics decisions by their state bar to determine the identity of their client and limitations on information sharing with other government attorneys.[24] Even if interests between the teams appear aligned, confidentiality obligations may still limit the information that may be shared.

3. Ethical and Constitutional Obligations to Disclose Exculpatory and Impeachment Evidence

An additional consideration for prosecutors collaborating with civil government attorneys on concurrent investigations is prosecutors' obligation

---

22935, *5-6 (N.D. Ill. Feb. 17, 2012); Prisco v. New York, 804 F. Supp. 518, 520-22 (S.D.N.Y. 1992).

21 Model Rules r. 1.6.

22 *See id.* r. 1.13 & cmt. 2.

23 *Id.* r. 1.13 cmt. 9 ("Defining precisely the identity of the client and prescribing the resulting obligations of such lawyers may be more difficult in the government context and is a matter beyond the scope of these Rules.").

24 Kathleen Clark, *Government Lawyers and Confidentiality Norms*, 85 Wash. U. L. Rev. 1033, 1037-38 (2007) ("There is no single answer to the question of client identity for government lawyers. Instead, one must examine the structure of authority within government to identify which of several possible entities is actually the client."); Justin G. Davids, *State Attorneys General and the Client-Attorney Relationship: Establishing the Power to Sue State Officers*, 38 Colum. J.L. & Soc. Probs. 365, 373-75 (2005) (observing that defining the attorney general's "client" is not a simple task).

Note that discipline has been imposed on an attorney who represented an entity but, perhaps unintentionally, caused individuals employed by that entity to believe she was representing them. In Pennsylvania, the general counsel of a state college testified before a grand jury about information that individual employees provided her. Off. Disc. Counsel v. Baldwin, 225 A.3d 817, 848-49 (Pa. 2020). Even though she later argued that her representation was of the college, and not the individuals, the state supreme court concluded that it was reasonable for the individual employees to believe that she was acting as their personal counsel and, as a result, she violated the state's rule of professional conduct 1.6. *Id.*

to disclose exculpatory or impeachment information to the accused. Under ethical rules, a prosecutor is required to "make timely disclosure to the defense of all evidence or information known to the prosecutor that tends to negate the guilt of the accused or mitigates the offense."[25] In connection with a defendant's sentencing, a prosecutor must also disclose "all unprivileged mitigating information known to the prosecutor, except when the prosecutor is relieved of this responsibility by a protective order of the tribunal."[26] Thus, prosecutors have an expansive ethical obligation to disclose exculpatory information they know, which would apply to information shared with them by others working on other concurrent cases.

The government's constitutional obligations to provide exculpatory or impeachment information to a defendant are broader than an individual prosecutor's ethical disclosure obligations, as they extend to any information known by the prosecution team—not just information actually known by the prosecutors themselves.[27] If those involved in concurrent investigations collaborate closely, courts may conclude that the civil enforcers are also members of the prosecution team for *Brady* imputation purposes, and require the disclosure of exculpatory or impeachment information known by civil enforcers to a criminal defendant.[28] Some of the factors that courts are likely to consider when determining if a team working on a concurrent investigation should be treated as member of the prosecution team for *Brady* imputation purposes include:

- Whether the two teams coordinated their investigations or shared resources by, for example,
    - discussing strategy,
    - making charging decisions together,

---

25 Model Rules r. 3.8(d); *see also, e.g.*, Giglio v. United States, 405 U.S. 150, 154 (1972); Justice Manual §§ 9-5.001 to 9-5.100 (U.S. Dep't of Justice 2020), https://www.justice.gov/jm.

26 Model Rules r. 3.8(d).

27 *See, e.g.*, Kyles v. Whitley, 514 U.S. 419, 437 (1995) (The prosecution has "a duty to learn of any favorable evidence known to others acting on the government's behalf in the case, including the police.").

28 Justice Manual § 9-5.002. Note that the Manual suggests that federal prosecutors "err on the side of inclusiveness when identifying the members of the prosecution team for discovery purposes. Carefully considered efforts to locate discoverable information are more likely to avoid future litigation over *Brady* and *Giglio* issues and avoid surprises at trial." *Id.*

    - conducting arrests or searches together, or
    - interviewing witnesses together.

- Whether the civil team has access to the information that the prosecution team gathered, and vice versa.[29]

Finally, at least some courts have concluded that exculpatory or impeachment information known by one prosecutor in an office is imputed to all prosecutors in that same office.[30] If this analysis is applied broadly, it could require the provision of any exculpatory or impeachment information known by any member of an AGO, regardless of whether that person is a member of the prosecution team. Using our original example, that could mean that exculpatory or impeachment information known by any attorney may be imputed to a prosecutor in the same office. This could be particularly tricky if that information is in the hands of an attorney defending the prison in a lawsuit—who has differing and arguably somewhat adversarial obligations than those held by the team prosecuting the defendant-guard. This is another area where attorneys should research the law in their state for guidance. Given that sharing such information could also implicate the civil attorney's privilege obligations, if the caselaw in the relevant state suggests that imputation will be construed broadly, attorneys should consult with their supervisors and with ethics experts in their office. To the extent that the information is considered "confidential" under the rules of professional conduct, attorneys should be aware that lawyers are permitted to "reveal information related to the representation of a client . . . to comply with other law or court order."[31] In some circumstances, they may wish to consider seeking ex parte guidance from the court overseeing the criminal or civil cases, or both.

---

29 *Accord id.*

30 *In re* Sealed Case, 185 F.3d 887, 896 (D.C. Cir. 1999) ("The United States Attorney's Office for the District of Columbia prosecutes cases in both the federal District Court and the local Superior Court, and the prosecutor is responsible (at a minimum) for all *Brady* information in the possession of that office."); State v. Williams, 896 A.2d 973, 990 (Md. 2006) ("[I]n deciding the coverage area of the *Brady* obligation, it is proper to consider the State's Attorney Office as a single entity.").

31 Model Rules r. 1.6(b)(6).

4. Public Statements

Ethical requirements guiding the making of public statements may also be implicated in concurrent proceedings.[32] Ethics rules require lawyers who participate in the investigation or litigation of a matter not to "make an extrajudicial statement that [they] know[] or reasonably should know will be disseminated by means of public communication and will have a substantial likelihood of materially prejudicing an adjudicative proceeding in the matter."[33] This restriction also applies to every other lawyer in the same "government agency" as the lawyer investigating or litigating the matter.[34]

Prosecutors have additional duties to "refrain from making extrajudicial comments that have a substantial likelihood of heightening public condemnation of the accused."[35] They are also required to "exercise reasonable care to prevent" others "associated with the prosecutor"—including employees, investigators, and law enforcement personnel—from making such comments.[36] If the civil enforcers work closely enough with the prosecutors to be part of the prosecution team, they should also avoid making extrajudicial comments the prosecutor would not be permitted to make.

C. *Bars to Subsequent Proceedings*

If the government is pursuing a criminal prosecution as well as a civil proceeding for the same offense and an opportunity for a settlement arises in either matter, the Double Jeopardy clause of the Fifth Amendment may complicate settlement efforts.[37] A court may construe any settlement broadly enough to encompass all government-initiated actions, whether civil or criminal. Although double jeopardy only applies to criminal punishments, a penalty for conduct found in a civil statute may be barred as double jeopardy if two conditions are met.[38]

---

32 For further discussion of media relations in public corruption cases, see Chapter 5.3.

33 MODEL RULES r. 3.6(a).

34 *Id.* r. 3.6(d).

35 *Id.* r. 3.8(f).

36 *Id.*

37 *See* U.S. CONST. amend. V ("No person shall . . . be subject for the same offen[s]e to be twice put in jeopardy of life or limb.").

38 *See* Hudson v. United States, 522 U.S. 93, 99-100 (1997).

First, the criminal prosecution and the civil proceeding must be for the "same offense" under the test set forth in *Blockburger* v. *United States.* If the criminal prosecution and the civil proceeding each require the government to prove at least one element that is not required by the other, then the two actions do not seek to penalize the same offense, and double jeopardy will not bar either action.[39]

If the two actions do seek redress for the "same offense," a remedy that is described as civil may, in limited circumstances, be so punitive that a court concludes it is, in fact, a criminal penalty. While courts will give some weight to a legislative description of a penalty as civil, a statutory scheme that is sufficiently punitive in purpose or effect will be considered a criminal penalty for purposes of a double jeopardy analysis.[40] The factors a court will review to determine whether the penalty is punitive enough to create a double jeopardy issue are:

1. Does the sanction involve an affirmative disability or restraint?
2. Has it historically been regarded as punishment?
3. Does it come into play only with a finding of scienter?
4. Does it promote retribution and deterrence?
5. Is the behavior it applies to already a crime?
6. Is there an alternative purpose to which it may be connected?
7. Does it appear excessive in relation to that alternative purpose?[41]

Any one of these factors by itself will not be determinative, but each must be considered based on the totality of the circumstances. Additionally, even when using these factors, "only the clearest proof" will override legislative intent that the penalty be civil.[42]

---

39 *See, e.g., id.* at 107-08 (Stevens, J., concurring and applying *Blockburger v. United States,* 284 U.S. 299 (1932) and progeny).

40 *Id.* at 99-100.

41 *Id.* (citing Kennedy v. Mendoza-Martinez, 372 U.S. 144, 168-69 (1963)).

42 *Hudson*, 522 U.S. at 100; *Kennedy*, 372 U.S. at 209 (Stewart, J., dissenting). *See also* Mary

III. Effective Management of Concurrent Investigations: Communication, Compartmentalization, and Coordination

Regardless of the potential difficulties mentioned above, concurrent investigations and proceedings are often appropriate;[43] likewise, "coordination and sharing between the lawyers and agents on the criminal prosecution team, on the one hand, and [a civil enforcer], on the other, is, in itself, unexceptional and unproblematic."[44] AGOs may thus wish to develop a method by which to undertake their effective administration.[45] Subject to the laws and procedures in effect in each state, teams conducting concurrent investigations may consider the importance of communication, compartmentalization, and coordination.

A. *Communication*

When an incident may warrant redress in a combination of criminal, civil, regulatory, or administrative fora, attorneys who are responsible for those different types of enforcement often should open the lines of communication. Topics that may be discussed during initial conversations include:

M. Cheh, *Constitutional Limits on Using Civil Remedies to Achieve Criminal Law Objectives: Understanding and Transcending the Criminal-Civil Law Distinction*, 42 Hastings L.J. 1325, 1374 (1991) (noting that courts have concluded that the following were not criminal in nature: "involuntary civil commitment proceedings; disciplinary proceedings against prisoners affecting their release date; civil contempt proceedings; civil paternity actions; civil lawsuits recovering treble damages or punitive damages; and proceedings to suspend or terminate government employment, a government contract, or a license to engage in profession or business" (citations omitted)).

43 *See* United States v. Kordel, 397 U.S. 1, 11 (1970) (holding that to require governmental agencies to choose between forgoing criminal prosecutions in favor of civil proceedings, or staying civil proceedings until the conclusion of the criminal proceedings, would "stultify enforcement of . . . law"); United States v. Stringer, 535 F.3d 929, 933 (9th Cir. 2008) (stating that "[t]here is nothing improper about the government undertaking simultaneous criminal and civil investigations").

44 United States v. Rhodes, No. 18-CR-887 (JMF), 2019 U.S. Dist. LEXIS 118564, at *11 (S.D.N.Y. July 16, 2019).

45 In the federal government, the Justice Manual recommends that every U.S. Attorney's Office and every litigating component "should have policies and procedures for appropriate coordination of the government's criminal, civil, regulatory, and administrative remedies" which should "stress early, effective, and regular communication between criminal, civil, and agency attorneys to the fullest extent appropriate to the case and permissible by law." Justice Manual § 1-12.000 (U.S. Dep't of Justice 2020), https://www.justice.gov/jm/jm-1-12000-coordination-parallel-criminal-civil-regulatory-and-administrative-proceedings.

1. Whether simultaneous investigations are appropriate under the circumstances;

2. Appropriate methods of preserving information gathered during the investigation;

3. The boundaries of coordination and information sharing;

4. Whether one team has primary jurisdiction or responsibility over the case; and

5. How the particular facts of the case are likely to implicate various ethical rules and obligations, including the rules of professional conduct and constitutional issues mentioned above.

The powers of administrative, civil, and criminal enforcers to obtain information are not coextensive; their obligations to disclose information can also differ. In some cases, enforcers may be statutorily permitted to share information.[46] While non-adverse government enforcers can often ethically collaborate on investigations and cases, and some information can be shared among different types of enforcers, there are some dangers to avoid. Certain information compelled by one enforcer could, if shared with another, violate ethics rules or laws, or imperil either or both cases. At the same time, as noted earlier, if the teams are working together closely, exculpatory or impeachment information known by administrative or civil enforcers could be imputed to the prosecution team for *Brady* and *Giglio* purposes.

When possible, discussions about whether these issues are likely to arise and, if so, how to properly segregate information and teams may prevent problems. If the relevant state courts provide limited guidance, enforcers may wish to look to federal caselaw—particularly decisions involving matters that were investigated civilly by the SEC and criminally by federal prosecutors—to analyze how best to structure relationships between civil, criminal, and administrative enforcement teams. Public guidance from the U.S. Department of Justice, including that in the Justice Manual, may also be of use.

---

46 *See, e.g.*, 15 U.S.C. § 77t(b) (2018) (SEC may transmit evidence "concerning such [apparently illegal] acts or practices to the Attorney General who may, in his discretion, institute the necessary criminal proceedings under this title").

It may be prudent for enforcement teams to decide whether to work together as closely as legally and ethically permitted (and consider the civil/administrative team to be a part of the prosecution team, with attendant disclosure obligations) or to erect barriers between the teams. As discussed in the next part, even if the teams determine it is appropriate to work together as much as possible, legal and professional obligations may limit what information is appropriate to communicate between investigative teams.

B. *Compartmentalization*

Serious complications can arise when concurrent investigations are not properly compartmentalized. One court has described parallel investigations as "side-by-side train tracks that never intersect."[47] While investigators often can coordinate to share information they obtain, there are some areas where sharing information can be problematic. Those engaging in concurrent investigations should treat their investigations as proceeding alone, with any other investigation simply being viewed as another potential source of information. Criminal investigators should not encourage civil investigators to deviate from their normal investigative practices to facilitate obtaining information on behalf of the criminal investigation and vice versa.

While the examples below are not exhaustive, they address some potential issues that can arise if information is not compartmentalized. They are useful to consider and discuss even at the initial stages of concurrent investigations. Government attorneys should, of course, consult the caselaw and ethics rules in their jurisdiction.

1. Information Obtained by Prosecutors

If prosecutors use the grand jury to obtain evidence or testimony, that evidence or testimony cannot typically be shared with other enforcers unless a court order explicitly permits other enforcers to see it.[48] This is true even if the

---

47 United States v. Scrushy, 366 F. Supp. 2d 1134, 1139 (N.D. Ala. 2005) (noting that, as a factual matter, the SEC's civil investigation merged with the USDOJ's criminal investigation in that case).

48 Many states and the federal government prohibit the disclosure of grand jury information, even to other government attorneys, except for circumstances expressly permitted by law. *See* Fed. R. Crim. P. 6(e); Chapter 5.3, Part I. Inappropriately sharing secret grand jury information carries steep penalties. *See, e.g.*, Jess Bidgood, *Pennsylvania's Attorney General Is Convicted on*

civil or administrative authority is in the same office as the prosecuting authority, as can be the case in many AGOs.[49] Federal guidance thus recommends that if a decision is made to proceed with concurrent investigations, prosecutors consider seeking evidence using investigative tools—such as search warrants or administrative subpoenas issued by their law enforcement partners—that will not prevent them from sharing evidence with other enforcers if it is otherwise appropriate to do so.[50] While it is undoubtedly appropriate to consider whether to bring a criminal or a civil case—or both—an office should not use the possibility of criminal enforcement to seek unfair additional civil or administrative monetary penalties.[51]

2. Information Obtained by Civil Enforcers

A civil investigation may not be conducted solely to obtain information for a criminal case as such conduct would violate due process.[52] Jurisdictions may vary in terms of what conduct will show that a civil action was brought solely to obtain evidence for a criminal proceeding. Some examples of conduct that could so indicate are the civil investigation being opened after the criminal case, the civil case being dismissed after obtaining necessary evidence for the criminal case, and the normal investigative procedures of the civil team not

---

All Counts, N.Y. Times (Aug. 15, 2016), https://www.nytimes.com/2016/08/16/us/trial-kathleen-kane-pennsylvania-attorney-general.html (Pennsylvania's Attorney General Kathleen Kane was convicted of leaking secret grand jury documents to news media to discredit a political rival). For further discussion of the Kathleen Kane case, see Chapter 1.2.

49 *See* Fed. R. Crim. P. 6(e)(3)(E) (listing grounds for courts to authorize disclosures); N.Y. Penal Law § 215.70 (Consol. 2020) (designating unlawful grand jury disclosure as a felony). *See also* Trump v. Vance, 140 S. Ct. 2412, 2427 (2020) ("[T]he federal system and most states have adopted statutes or court rules" that "impose sharp restrictions on the extent to which matters occurring before a grand jury may be divulged" to outside persons.) (quoting Sara S. Beale & William C. Bryson, Grand Jury Law & Practice § 5:1, at 5-3 (2d ed. 2018)).

50 Justice Manual § 1-12.000 ("During the investigation, attorneys should consider investigative strategies that maximize the government's ability to share information among criminal, civil, and agency administrative teams, including the use of investigative means other than grand jury subpoenas for documents or witness testimony . . . ."); Organization & Functions Manual § 27 (U.S. Dep't of Justice 2012), https://www.justice.gov/jm/organization-and-functions-manual-27-parallel-proceedings (suggesting using "administrative subpoenas, search warrants, consensual monitoring, [and] interviews" to obtain evidence without the use of a grand jury subpoena).

51 *Accord* Justice Manual § 1-12.100.

52 United States v. Stringer, 535 F.3d 929, 939 (9th Cir. 2008) (citing United States v. Kordel, 397 U.S. 1, 11-12 (1970)).

being followed.[53] On the other hand, factors that can indicate the civil investigation was pursued appropriately—and thus the information obtained can be shared with and used by the prosecution—include advising a suspect in the civil investigation that prosecution could be contemplated, subjects or targets having counsel to advise them during the civil investigation, and no affirmative misrepresentations on the part of the civil investigators.[54]

If information being sought in connection with a civil investigation will be provided to prosecutors, it may be prudent to acknowledge that the information may be shared.[55] Federal appeals courts have suggested that the Fourth and Fifth Amendments could be violated if a defendant was "led through trickery or deceit to turn over documentary or physical evidence in their possession . . . ."[56] Courts have thus considered motions to suppress evidence in a criminal case on the grounds that consent to provide evidence in connection with a concurrent civil enforcer's case was obtained by trickery or deceit because that civil enforcer did not disclose the possibility or existence of a criminal case.[57] Federal district courts have suppressed evidence obtained through civil or administrative proceedings that the courts concluded were pretextual efforts to build a criminal case; however, as long as no affirmative misrepresentations were made, those motions have generally been unsuccessful at the circuit level.[58]

State courts, too, have considered concurrent criminal and civil cases, and some have "expressed concern that the civil discovery process not be used

---

53 *See id.* at 939.

54 *Id.* at 940-41.

55 *Id.* at 934-35 (citing SEC form that accompanied subpoena, which advised that the information obtained by the SEC may be made available to federal or state prosecutors and noted that the recipient could "refuse, in accordance with the rights guaranteed to you by the Fifth Amendment of the Constitution of the United States, to give any information that may tend to incriminate you or subject you to fine, penalty, or forfeiture"); United States v. Carriles, 541 F.3d 344, 356 (5th Cir. 2008) (approving of government's warnings in immigration interview regarding the risks of self-incrimination, perjury, and that statement could be used in another proceeding). Both *Stringer* and *Carriles* were reversals of district court decisions dismissing indictments for what those trial courts concluded was the improper use of civil (*Stringer*) or administrative (*Carriles*) procedures to build a criminal case.

56 *Stringer*, 535 F.3d at 940 (collecting cases).

57 *See, e.g., id.*; United States v. Tweel, 550 F.2d 297, 299 (5th Cir. 1977) (holding that an IRS agent's failure to tell a taxpayer "of the obvious criminal nature of this investigation was a sneaky deliberate deception by the agent . . . and a flagrant disregard for [the taxpayer's] rights" and that records obtained through that deception should have been suppressed).

58 *Stringer*, 535 F.3d at 940.

to compel a defendant to provide information in support of the State's case in a parallel criminal proceeding," and "concluded that the use of information so obtained would constitute 'such unfairness and want of consideration for justice as to require reversal.'"[59] In *State* v. *Melendez*, the New Jersey Supreme Court considered whether a defendant's answer to a civil forfeiture complaint should have been admitted in a related criminal trial against him.[60] In that case, officers seized several thousand dollars when they arrested the defendant.[61] After he was charged in the criminal case and had counsel appointed, the defendant alone was served with a civil forfeiture complaint seeking to forfeit the seized cash, which he later answered without the benefit of an attorney.[62] Statements that he made in that answer were then used against him in his criminal trial.[63] The New Jersey Supreme Court concluded that "claimants in a civil forfeiture action who are defendants in a parallel criminal case also face an untenable choice: to forfeit their property or incriminate themselves."[64] The court concluded that the statements in the forfeiture answer were not truly voluntary, and thus were improperly admitted in the defendant's criminal trial.[65]

3. Statements Compelled by Administrative Enforcers

Administrative enforcers may have the power to require state employees to comply with an investigation or face termination. In *Garrity* v. *New Jersey*, the U.S. Supreme Court concluded that such statements were not truly voluntary, as they required employees "either to forfeit their jobs or incriminate themselves."[66] These compelled statements should not be provided to prosecutors because "a government employee who has been threatened with an adverse employment action by her employer for failure to answer questions put to her by her employer receives immunity from the use of her statements or their fruits in subsequent criminal proceedings . . . ."[67]

---

59 State v. P.Z., 703 A.2d 901, 917 (N.J. 1997) (quoting State v. Kobrin Secs., Inc., 544 A.2d 833, 838 (N.J. 1988)).

60 State v. Melendez, 222 A.3d 639, 641-42 (N.J. 2020).

61 *Id.* at 641.

62 *Id.*

63 *Id.*

64 *Id.* at 647.

65 *Id.*

66 Garrity v. New Jersey, 385 U.S. 493, 497 (1967). See Chapter 6.1, Part III(I) for additional discussion of this issue, including potential warnings that can be given by administrative bodies.

67 *See* Sher v. U.S. Dep't of Veterans Affairs, 488 F.3d 489, 501 (1st Cir. 2007). *Accord* State v. Burris, 187 A.3d 830, 170 N.H. 802, 811-12 (N.H. 2018). At least one state has held that

In *Kastigar* v. *United States*, the Supreme Court considered how to treat testimony compelled under 18 U.S.C. § 6002, which requires a witness to testify but provides that "no testimony or other information compelled under the order (or any information directly or indirectly derived from such testimony or other information) may be used against the witness in any criminal case, except a prosecution for perjury, giving a false statement, or otherwise failing to comply with the order."[68] The Court held that because any subsequent use by prosecutors of a defendant's compelled statement is unconstitutional, the government has the burden of proving that "the evidence it proposes to use is derived from a legitimate source wholly independent of the compelled testimony."[69]

A number of federal and state courts have applied *Kastigar* to statements that are compelled under *Garrity*.[70] They have provided use immunity to statements provided by an employee who faced termination. If those statements were provided to the prosecution team, prosecutors were required to prove that they did not use those statements or "any information derived from such statements" to investigate or prosecute the defendant.[71]

C. *Coordination*

Knowing the appropriate bounds of information sharing, teams can coordinate their investigative efforts. While this does not mean asking agents in one investigation to do tasks normally assigned to the other, it can involve aligning investigative strategies and efforts. For example, prosecutors can endeavor to use mechanisms other than the grand jury to obtain statements and evidence to facilitate sharing of that information. Similarly, if the civil team has the most effective methods to obtain information, the teams might decide that the civil investigation proceeds before the criminal investigation to best

---

its state constitution "requires transactional immunity to supplant the privilege against self-incrimination, even in the context of public employment." Carney v. Springfield, 532 N.E.2d 631, 635-36 (Mass. 1988). Under that interpretation, if an employee is required to provide information upon pain of termination during an administrative hearing, prosecutors may be unable to later charge him for crimes associated with the topic of his compelled testimony. *See id.*

68 18 U.S.C. § 6002 (2018); Kastigar v. United States, 406 U.S. 441, 442 (1972).

69 *Kastigar*, 406 U.S. at 460. *See also* Chapter 6.1, Part III(I).

70 United States v. Connolly, No. 16 Cr. 0370 (CM), 2019 U.S. Dist. LEXIS 76233, at *51 (S.D.N.Y. May 2, 2019) (collecting cases).

71 United States v. Pendergrass, 648 F. App'x 29, 32 (2d Cir. 2016).

facilitate the gathering of that information. So long as the investigations remain separate, such coordination may be appropriate.

Using our example of a correctional officer who was accused of having sexual contact with an inmate, assume that he was the subject of a prosecution and a personnel investigation for potential termination of employment. If the officer is required to cooperate with the internal investigation or face termination, a prosecutor cannot in the criminal case use the compelled internal investigation material and should not request it to avoid *Garrity/Kastigar* issues. Screening the criminal investigation from this information would be prudent. If the prosecutor obtains information using a grand jury subpoena, that information should typically not be provided to the team undertaking the personnel investigation, unless a court order permits that sharing. However, if the prosecution team obtained information using another mechanism—perhaps a voluntary interview—it may be permissible to share that information with the team considering whether the officer should face employment consequences.

The limitations on coordination imposed by *Garrity* do not mean that coordination should be completely abandoned in such cases. Rather, both sides of a concurrent investigation may communicate to discuss the mechanics of coordination without sharing the substance of what each team has learned. In one case, the civil penalties may provide sufficient redress even if they require immunity from criminal prosecution. In another case, a just resolution may require prosecuting a government employee while also working to terminate him, even if that requires precautions and screens between the prosecution team and the personnel team. Where concurrent investigations are appropriate, an early decision about coordination may guide the course of the investigations and may allow both teams to anticipate whether civil enforcers will be considered members of the prosecution team for *Brady* imputation or other purposes.

Whatever the case may be, knowing the limits of coordination can allow each investigation to work successfully within those boundaries. Only by communicating, compartmentalizing, and coordinating can attorneys general offices determine how best to represent the public interest when determining whether and how to pursue concurrent cases.

IV. Stays

One issue that can arise in concurrent proceedings is whether to seek or permit a stay of one of the cases—typically, a civil case—until the conclusion of the other—typically, a criminal case. Notably, the Constitution "does not ordinarily require a stay of civil proceedings pending the outcome of criminal proceedings . . . ."[72] However, depending on the circumstances, it may be appropriate to request, accede to, or object to a stay of a civil proceeding, the postponement of civil discovery, or the imposition of protective orders and conditions, particularly when one of the concurrent cases is criminal.[73] This is because if the noncriminal proceeding is not deferred, it "might undermine the party's Fifth Amendment privilege against self-incrimination, expand rights of criminal discovery beyond the limits of [the criminal discovery rules, which are typically less expansive than civil discovery], expose the basis of the defense to the prosecution in advance of criminal trial, or otherwise prejudice the case."[74] In determining the appropriateness of a stay, courts also consider the public interest and may deny a stay if, for example, it would cause an ongoing danger to the public.[75] Whether to grant a stay is typically left to the discretion of the trial court,[76] and the burden is on the party requesting the stay.[77]

---

72 Kashi v. Gratsos, 790 F.2d 1050, 1057 (2d Cir. 1986) (quoting SEC v. Dresser Indus., 628 F.2d 1368, 1372 (D.C. Cir. 1980) (en banc)).

73 *Dresser Indus.*, 628 F.2d at 1375; Jiaxing Brother Fastener Co. v. United States, 179 F. Supp. 3d 1156, 1168 (Ct. Int'l Trade 2016) (overruling government's objection to defendant's request to stay).

74 *Dresser Indus.*, 628 F.2d at 1376.

75 *See, e.g.*, *id.* at 1380 (explaining that staying the SEC's civil enforcement action "might well defeat its purpose," which is to prevent false or misleading corporate statements from infecting the financial markets, in contrast to IRS tax collection, which can be postponed until after a criminal proceeding without seriously injuring the public).

76 *See Kashi*, 790 F.2d at 1057. *See also* United States v. Kordel, 397 U.S. 1, 12 n.27 (1970) (noting that courts may "defer[] civil proceedings pending the completion of parallel criminal prosecutions when the interests of justice seem[] to require such action").

77 Clinton v. Jones, 520 U.S. 681, 708 (1997); *see also* SEC v. Shkreli, No. 15-CV-7175 (KAM) (RML), 2016 U.S. Dist. LEXIS 36734, at *10-21 (E.D.N.Y. Mar. 22, 2016) (granting federal prosecutors' request to stay civil SEC action after applying six factors often considered by courts in the Second Circuit Court of Appeals); SEC v. Balwani, No. 5:18-cv-01603-EJD, 2019 U.S. Dist. LEXIS 100335, at *7-12 (N.D. Cal. June 14, 2019) (denying federal prosecutors' request to stay civil SEC action after applying six factors considered by courts in the Ninth Circuit Court of Appeals).

Conclusion

Particularly in complex matters like anticorruption efforts, coordination among criminal, civil, and administrative authorities may most effectively serve the public interest. However, the involved authorities must carefully consider, at every stage of the case, whether working together is legally and ethically permissible, and, if so, whether it is a strategic benefit. If each team is aware of the potential complications and manages the concurrent investigations with communication, compartmentalization, and coordination, the individual teams and the office as a whole will be in the best position to vindicate the public's interest.

Practice Tips for Concurrent Investigations

- Communicate
    - Identify potential concurrent matters as early in the process as practical, and whether they are likely to result in civil, criminal, or administrative actions.
    - If possible, determine for enforcement matters which one is of highest priority. If only one matter can be completed, which one would it be?
    - Recognize whether a global resolution is possible and pursuable.
    - Determine how to document communication and coordination among teams and compartmentalization within a team.
- Compartmentalize
    - Understand and communicate the effects of and limitations on information sharing.
    - Carefully evaluate whether and when to use the grand jury to obtain evidence, and abide by limitations on sharing that information.

  - Determine whether the teams should coordinate as closely as legally allowed with the understanding that those involved in related civil or administrative matters may be considered part of the prosecution team for *Brady* imputation purposes.

- Coordinate

  - Identify, usually based on which matter has priority, who the lead team or attorney will be.

  - Do not use powers available to only one enforcer solely to obtain information for another (e.g., do not use the grand jury to gather information for civil enforcers or depose a target in a civil case solely to gather evidence to charge him with a crime).

Section Three

Criminal Corruption Statutes

Federal law leaves much public corruption to the states to rectify.[1] While federal prosecutions may reach some state and local corruption, particularly bribery and various forms of fraud, each state may look to its own state law in order to prevent and control public corruption within its borders. While each state's laws pertaining to public corruption are unique, some commonalities exist across states.

Section Three categorizes and catalogues the various state laws that may be used to prosecute different forms of public corruption. Using the federal laws as a guide, this section examines crimes of illegal influence, such as bribery and extortion; crimes of misuse of office and misuse of public money; crimes arising from attempts to thwart transparency obligations; and crimes relating to conflicts of interest. This section makes clear that many states already have adequate legal bases for policing public corruption within their own borders, even if those laws have not been used extensively, whereas other states may lack adequate public corruption laws and may consider encouraging their legislatures to create new laws.

1 Kelly v. United States, 140 S. Ct. 1565, 1571-72 (2020).

CHAPTER 3.1

Bribery & Illegal Influence Crimes

Ann Ratnayake Macy

Ann Ratnayake Macy is the Executive Director of the National Center for Child Abuse Statistics and Policy. She began her career at the American Prosecutors Research Institute at the National District Attorney's Association. She is co-chair of the Victim's Committee in the American Bar Association's Criminal Justice Section, Equal Justice Division, and she was a Presidential Leadership Scholar in 2018.

Special thanks to Charlotte Janovyak for her comprehensive work gathering related state corruption statutes.

INTRODUCTION

When does giving cash, loans, gifts, and other benefits to a sitting public official become illegal? This chapter discusses illegal influence in civic life. When a public official does not provide her honest services by exercising independent judgment to maximize the benefit for the people she represents, jurisdictions lose tax dollars and potential benefits. Legislatures have drawn a line between legitimate constituent relations and criminal activity through several types of statutes: bribery, gratuity, kickbacks/fraudulent contracts, extortion, and gifts.

This chapter is divided into three parts: Part I defines various types of illegal influence crimes; Part II describes specific federal laws and how the courts have interpreted them; and Part III examines state statutes addressing illegal influence.

I. Overview of Illegal Influence Crimes

A. *Bribery*

This chapter will mostly focus on bribery statutes. Bribery is "[t]he corrupt payment, receipt, or solicitation of a private favor for official action."[1] Not every gift, contribution, or favor constitutes illegal bribery.[2] Bribery occurs only if the benefit is coupled with a particular criminal intent to trade a benefit in return for payment.[3] Statutes prohibiting bribery generally have the following elements:

1. A thing of value,

2. Corrupt intent/intent to influence,

3. A public official, and

4. An official act.[4]

The wording of the statutes varies among the states and the federal government.

B. *Gratuity*

While bribery is forward looking (the briber buys an action), gratuities are backward looking (giving thanks for an act already done).[5] Statutes that criminalize gratuities typically do not require prosecutors to prove that the gratuity caused the performance of the act in question.[6] While bribery requires

---

1 *See Bribery*, Black's Law Dictionary 236 (11th ed. 2019).

2 12 Am. Jur. 2d *Bribery* § 6 (2020) (citing United States v. Harvey, 532 F.3d 326 (4th Cir. 2008)).

3 *Id.*

4 *See* discussion *infra* Parts II(C) and III(B).

5 Criminal Resource Manual § 2043 (U.S. Dep't of Justice 2020), https://www.justice.gov/usam/criminal-resource-manual; United States v. Brewster, 506 F.2d 62, 72 (D.C. Cir. 1974). Note that the U.S. Department of Justice appears to be treating the Criminal Resource Manual as an archived document.

6 *Brewster*, 506 F.2d at 72. *See also* United States v. Sun-Diamond Growers of Cal., 526 U.S. 398, 405 (1999).

specific intent and quid pro quo, gratuities do not.[7] Bribery and gratuities are banned to various extents by federal and state laws.

C. *Kickbacks*

Kickbacks and contract fraud are often found with bribery and other quid pro quo schemes. A common form of kickback is where a public employee or contractor pays (or "kicks back") a portion of his or her salary or contract payment to the public official who hired the employee or contractor. Many states have statutes prohibiting public officials from trading appointments made while in public office for any form of benefit.[8] Many states also prohibit kickbacks specifically in connection with government contracts or employment.[9]

D. *Extortion*

Extortion by a public official is related to soliciting a bribe. It generally involves a public official obtaining property or money by threatening to take or withhold official action or by demanding money or property "under color of official right."[10]

II. Federal Law

Congress has passed statutes to address illegal influence crimes by federal public servants.[11] Courts have additionally interpreted other statutes to

---

7 *Brewster*, 506 F.2d at 72.

8 *See, e.g.*, Idaho Code Ann. § 18-1358; 5 Ill. Comp. Stat. 430/5-30; Miss. Code Ann. § 97-11-53; Nev. Rev. Stat. Ann. § 197.050; Wash. Rev. Code Ann. § 9A.68.040; W. Va. Code § 61-5A-7. Unless otherwise indicated, all statutes cited in this chapter refer to the version of the statute current at the time of publication of this Manual.

9 *See, e.g.*, N.M. Stat. Ann. § 30-41-1; Vt. Stat. Ann. tit. 13 § 1106; Wyo. Stat. Ann. § 6-5-117. For further discussion of bid rigging in public contracts, see Chapter 1.4.

10 *See* Criminal Resource Manual § 2404 (discussing phrase "under color of official right" as used in the Hobbs Act, 18 U.S.C. § 1951, and noting that the Supreme Court called common law extortion by a public official the "rough equivalent" of what we now call taking a bribe (citing Evans v. United States, 504 U.S. 255, 260-61 (1992)). Some state statutes use similar language in prohibiting extortion by a public official. *See, e.g.*, Cal. Penal Code § 518; Okla. Stat. tit. 21, § 1481.

11 18 U.S.C. §§ 201, 1341, 1343 (prohibiting bribery, frauds and swindles, and wire fraud).

assist with the prosecution of bribery. Both the Hobbs Act extortion statute and "honest services" statute prohibit public officials—both state and federal—from soliciting or accepting bribes in return for being influenced in their official acts.[12] An assortment of other federal statutes prohibit bribery and other forms of illegal influence in specific situations.[13]

A. *Honest Services*

The honest services doctrine originated in court decisions holding that the mail and wire fraud statutes prohibited schemes to deprive the state of the intangible right of "honest services" from an official, and that concept was later codified.[14] Actions of an official not providing her "honest services" by exercising independent judgment on official matters could fall within the federal mail or wire fraud statutes.[15] The government must show that (1) the defendant perpetrated a scheme to defraud, (2) with intent to defraud, (3) using mails, wires, or the internet in furtherance of the scheme, and (4) that the result did or would have caused the government to lose money, property, or honest services.[16] The Supreme Court has construed the honest services fraud statute to criminalize only schemes to defraud involving bribes and kickbacks.[17]

B. *Hobbs Act*

The federal Hobbs Act defines extortion as "obtaining of property from another, with his consent . . . under the color of official right."[18] The Supreme Court explained "[a]t common law, extortion was an offense committed by a public official who took 'by colour of his office' money that was not due to him

---

12 *Id.* §§ 1341, 1343, 1346, 1951(b)(2).

13 *See, e.g.*, 29 U.S.C. § 186 (prohibiting certain payments made in the labor relations context). *See also* United States v. Sun-Diamond Growers of Cal., 526 U.S. 398, 408-09 (1999).

14 18 U.S.C. § 1346; Brian H. Connor, Comment, *The Quid Pro Quo Quark: Unstable Elementary Particle of Honest Services Fraud*, 65 CATH. U.L. REV. 335, 337 (2015). Congress enacted § 1346 in response to the Supreme Court's decision in *McNally v. United States*, which—as the Court itself later put it—"stopped the development of the [honest services fraud's] intangible rights doctrine in its tracks." Skilling v. United States, 561 U.S. 358, 401 (2010) (citing McNally v. United States, 483 U.S. 350, 360 (1987)).

15 Connor, *supra* note 14, at 337.

16 18 U.S.C. §§ 1341, 1343, 1346. *See* Kyle Boynton & Anna Majestro, *Mail & Wire Fraud*, 53 AM. CRIM. L. REV. 1505, 1507 (2016).

17 *Skilling*, 561 U.S. at 404 (narrowing 18 U.S.C. § 1346 to avoid constitutional issues).

18 18 U.S.C. § 1951.

for the performance of his official duties."[19] It was "the rough equivalent of what we would now describe as 'taking a bribe'"[20] Force is not an element of Hobbs Act extortion because "the coercive element is provided by the public office itself."[21] The Hobbs Act applies to both state and federal officials.[22]

C. *Bribery*

The federal bribery statute is broken into three subsections. Subsection (a) defines terms.[23] Subsection (b) delineates the crimes of giving and receiving bribes.[24] Subsection (c) delineates analogous crimes of accepting and giving illegal gratuities.[25]

---

19 Evans v. United States, 504 U.S. 255, 260-61 (1992).

20 *Id.*

21 *Id.* at 266; United States v. Margiotta, 688 F.2d 108, 130-31 (2d Cir. 1982) ("The public officer's misuse of his office supplies the necessary element of coercion . . . .").

22 *See, e.g.*, Criminal Resource Manual § 2404 (U.S. Dep't of Justice 2020), https://www.justice.gov/usam/criminal-resource-manual; McDonnell v. United States, 136 S. Ct. 2355, 2367-71 (2016) (reviewing former Virginia governor's conviction under federal statutes).

23 18 U.S.C. § 201(a).

24 The portion of the statute pertaining to the giver of a bribe applies to:

> (b) Whoever—
>
> (1) directly or indirectly, corruptly gives, offers or promises anything of value to any public official or person who has been selected to be a public official, or offers or promises any public official or any person who has been selected to be a public official to give anything of value to any other person or entity, with intent--
>
> (A) to influence any official act; or
>
> (B) to influence such public official or person who has been selected to be a public official to commit or aid in committing, or collude in, or allow, any fraud, or make opportunity for the commission of any fraud, on the United States; or
>
> (C) to induce such public official or such person who has been selected to be a public official to do or omit to do any act in violation of the lawful duty of such official or person.

Id. § 201(b)(1).

The portion of the statute pertaining to the receiver of a bribe applies to:

> (b) Whoever . . .
>
> (2) being a public official or person selected to be a public official, directly or indirectly, corruptly demands, seeks, receives, accepts, or agrees to receive or accept anything of value personally or for any other person or entity, in return for:
>
> (A) being influenced in the performance of any official act;
>
> (B) being influenced to commit or aid in committing, or to collude in, or allow, any fraud, or make opportunity for the commission of any fraud, on the United States; or
>
> (C) being induced to do or omit to do any act in violation of the official duty of such official or person.

Id. § 201(b)(2).

25 *Id.* § 201(c).

To prove a charge of bribery for the giver, the government must prove: (1) anything of value was corruptly given, offered, or promised with (2) intent to influence, to a present or future (3) public official, for an (4) "official act."[26] When prosecuting the receiver, the government must prove: (1) a public official, with (2) intent to be influenced in performance of (3) an official act, received (4) anything of value.[27]

1. Anything of Value

The courts have interpreted "anything of value" broadly to include pecuniary benefits as well as intangible and other benefits such as promises of future employment, overseas travel, sexual acts, illegal immigration documents, shares of stock, life insurance policies, and unsecured loans, among other things.[28] Even items that do not have commercial worth, but that the recipient subjectively places value on, meet the definition.[29]

2. Intent

The Supreme Court has read the "intent to influence" or "intent to be influenced" language in 18 U.S.C. § 201 to mean "quid pro quo—a specific intent to give or receive something of value in exchange for an official act."[30] Lower court decisions suggest the intent requirement is not satisfied by vague hopes of benefit or campaign contributions that are not tied to a specific official

---

26 United States v. Sun-Diamond Growers of Cal., 526 U.S. 398, 404 (1999); Erin Choi et al., *Public Corruption*, 53 Am. Crim. L. Rev. 1619, 1622 (2016) (citing United States v. Valle, 538 F.3d 341, 344 (5th Cir. 2008)); Daniel Hayes Lowenstein, *Political Bribery & the Intermediate Theory of Politics*, 32 UCLA L. Rev. 784, 795-96 (1985)).

27 *See Federal Corruption Statutes—Bribery—Definition of "Official Act"* —McDonnell v. United States, 130 Harv. L. Rev. 467, 468-69 (2016).

28 Flynn Burke et al., *Public Corruption*, 50 Am. Crim. L. Rev. 1371, 1375 (2013).

29 *Id.* at 1376.

30 *Sun-Diamond Growers of Cal.*, 526 U.S. at 404-05.

act.[31] The existence of an agreement and the defendant's participation in the agreement may be proven with circumstantial evidence.[32]

3. Public Official

The federal statute applies to any public official, which the statute defines as a "Member of Congress, Delegate ... or an officer or employee or person acting on or behalf of the United States, or any department, agency or branch of Government thereof... in any official function," as well as witnesses, jurors, and persons who have been selected to be public employees.[33] Whether the person is a public official under this statute depends on if she occupies a "position of public trust with official federal responsibilities";[34] she also must "possess some degree of responsibility for carrying out a federal program or policy."[35] State or local officials with no federal responsibilities are not subject to prosecution under § 201.[36] Prosecutors do not need to prove that an official is actually able to undertake the objective of the person making the bribe to prove a violation of § 201.[37]

4. Official Act

The statute defines official act as:

---

31 United States v. Harvey, 532 F.3d 326, 335 (4th Cir. 2008) ("Not every gift, favor or contribution to a government or political official constitutes bribery... bribery occurs only if the gift is coupled with a particular criminal intent.") (citations omitted); United States v. Jennings, 160 F.3d 1006, 1013 (4th Cir. 1998) ("[A] goodwill gift to an official to foster a favorable business climate, given simply with the 'generalized hope or expectation of ultimate benefit on the part of the donor,' does not constitute a bribe."); United States v. Tomblin, 46 F.3d 1369, 1379 (5th Cir. 1995) ("Intending to make a campaign contribution does not constitute bribery, even though many contributors hope that the official will act favorably because of their contributions.").

32 *See* United States v. US Infrastructure, Inc., 576 F.3d 1195, 1203 (11th Cir. 2009); United States v. Carpenter, 961 F.2d 824, 827 (9th Cir. 1992).

33 18 U.S.C. § 201(a).

34 Dixson v. United States, 465 U.S. 482, 496 (1984) ("[T]he proper inquiry is not simply whether the person had signed a contract with the United States or agreed to serve as the Government's agent, but rather whether the person occupies a position of public trust with official federal responsibilities").

35 *Id.* at 499.

36 *Id.*

37 Choi, *supra* note 26, at 1626-27 (citing United States v. Gjieli, 717 F.2d 968, 976-77 (6th Cir. 1983) and United States v. Analytis, 687 F. Supp. 87, 89-92 (S.D.N.Y. 1988)).

> [A]ny decision or action on any question, matter, cause, suit, proceeding or controversy, which may at any time be pending, or which may by law be brought before any public official, in such official's official capacity, or in such official's place of trust or profit.[38]

In *McDonnell* v. *United States*, the Supreme Court interpreted "official act" to require a public official to use or agree to use a formal exercise of government power.[39] A formal exercise of power is analogous to a "lawsuit before a court, a determination before an agency, or a hearing before a committee."[40] "It must also be something specific and focused that is 'pending' or 'may by law be brought' before a public official."[41] Under this definition, setting up meetings, without any other action or pressure, in exchange for pecuniary benefit is not bribery under 18 U.S.C. § 201.[42]

In reaching this conclusion, the Court used the doctrine *noscitur a sociis*, which means a word is known by the company it keeps.[43] The Court compared the phrase "any question or matter" to its neighboring words "cause, suit, proceeding or controversy."[44] Using the presumption "that statutory language is not superfluous," the Court concluded that "'question' and 'matter' may be understood to refer to a formal exercise of governmental power" even if that exercise "does not necessarily fall into one of th[e] prescribed categories."[45]

a. Question, Matter, Cause, Suit, Proceeding or Controversy

The statute requires that an official action occur within a "question or matter," which the Court interprets to mean something focused and concrete, involving a formal exercise of governmental power that is similar in nature to a lawsuit, administrative determination, or hearing. The Court explains that

---

38 18 U.S.C. § 201(a)(3).

39 McDonnell v. United States, 136 S. Ct. 2355, 2367-72 (2016). While McDonnell was charged with honest services fraud, 18 U.S.C. §§ 1343, 1346, and violating the Hobbs Act, 18 U.S.C. § 1951, prosecutors and defense attorneys had agreed they would define key terms in each statute by reference to Section 201's "official act" definition. *Id.* at 2365. For more on *McDonnell*-based defenses, see Chapter 4.3, Part II.

40 *Id.* at 2369. *See also* Federal Corruption Statutes, *supra* note 27, at 469.

41 *McDonnell*, 136 S. Ct. at 2372.

42 *Id.* (internal quotations omitted).

43 *Id.* at 2368-69.

44 *Id.* at 2369.

45 *Id.*

"pending" suggests "the kind of thing that can be put on an agenda, tracked for progress, and then checked off as complete."[46]

b. Any Decision or Action

When defining "any decision or action," the *McDonnell* Court looked to *United States* v. *Sun-Diamond Growers of California*, 526 U.S. 398 (1999).[47] In *Sun-Diamond,* the Court narrowly construed the federal gratuities statute to avoid "absurdities" of convicting individuals on corruption charges for engaging in routine behaviors, such as the President hosting a championship sports team at the White House.[48] The *McDonnell* Court concluded that *Sun-Diamond* meant "that hosting an event, meeting with other officials, or speaking with interested parties is not, standing alone, a 'decision or action'" even if it "is related to a pending question or matter."[49] "Instead, something more is required: § 201(a)(3) specifies that the public official must make a decision or take an action *on* that question or matter, or agree to do so."[50]

D. *Gratuity*

The same statute also prohibits illegal gratuity:

> Whoever—
>
> (1) otherwise than as provided by law for the proper discharge of official duty—
>
> > (A) directly or indirectly gives, offers, or promises anything of value to any public official, former public official, or person selected to be a public official, for or because of any official act performed or to be performed by such public official, former public official, or person selected to be a public official; or

46 *Id.* at 2369.
47 *Id.* at 2370.
48 *Id.*
49 *Id.*
50 *Id.*

> (B) being a public official, former public official, or person selected to be a public official, otherwise than as provided by law for the proper discharge of official duty, directly or indirectly demands, seeks, receives, accepts, or agrees to receive or accept anything of value personally for or because of any official act performed or to be performed by such official or person.[51]

While the gratuity and the bribery subsections are somewhat analogous, key differences exist. Bribery involves giving things of value to influence government action.[52] Gratuities involve giving things of value "for or because of any official act performed."[53] To prove a violation of the gratuity statute, prosecutors need only show a linkage between the benefit and official act, rather than the formal quid pro quo required for bribery.[54] The maximum sentence for a gratuity conviction is much less severe than for a bribery conviction. A person may be imprisoned up to fifteen years for bribery, whereas a violation of the illegal gratuity statute may be punished by up to two years imprisonment.[55]

The Supreme Court has provided guidance about the degree of linkage between a gratuity and an official act. In *Sun-Diamond*, an association gave gifts of over five thousand dollars to the Secretary of Agriculture.[56] The Secretary had discretion over two matters in which the association had an interest in obtaining favorable treatment.[57] However, the government's theory of the case did not allege the gifts were given "for or because of an official act" to be performed by the Secretary, but rather because of the Secretary's general position.[58] The Court held that the government "must prove a link between a thing of value conferred upon a public official and a specific 'official act' for or because of which it was given."[59] The government needs to prove more than that a gift was given "to build a reservoir of goodwill," and must specify the acts in question.[60]

---

51 18 U.S.C. § 201(c).
52 *Id.* § 201(b).
53 *Id.* § 201(c).
54 United States v. Sun-Diamond Growers of Cal., 526 U.S. 398, 404-05 (1999).
55 *Id.*
56 *Id.* at 401.
57 *Id.*
58 *Id.* at 403-04.
59 *Id.* at 414.
60 *Id.* at 404.

III. State Bribery Laws

State bribery statutes vary widely in their wording, but typically share the same elements of: (1) act, (2) thing of value, (3) intent, and (4) governmental official.[61]

A. *Structure of State Bribery Statutes*

As discussed above, the federal bribery statute sets forth two pairs of parallel crimes: one for the government official receiving the benefit, and one for the giver of the bribe.[62] It includes both the bribery and gratuity prohibitions in one statute. Most states do not have one statute outlawing both bribery and gratuity. Some states have a single statute that prohibits bribery for both government officials and the giver of the bribe, but does not discuss gratuities.[63] Other states have two parallel statutes with one prohibiting the act of bribing the government official, and the other prohibiting the receipt of the bribe.[64]

B. *Variance in State Bribery Statute Elements*

1. Thing of Value

The federal bribery statute uses the terminology "anything of value" to describe a benefit given to a public official in a bribery deal.[65] Some states use similar terminology to describe the benefit given, but other states use different terms of art as follows:

- Anything of value;[66]
- Benefit;[67]

---

61 *See, e.g.*, Mass. Gen. Laws ch. 268A, § 3; Scaccia v. State Ethics Comm'n, 727 N.E.2d 824, 828 (Mass. 2000).

62 18 U.S.C. § 201(b)(1) (briber); *id.* § 201(b)(2) (bribee).

63 *E.g.*, Ariz. Rev. Stat. Ann. § 13-2602; Colo. Rev. Stat. Ann. § 18-8-302; Fla. Stat. Ann. § 838.015.

64 *E.g.*, Conn. Gen. Stat. §§ 53a-147, 53a-148; Del. Code Ann. tit. 11, §§ 1201, 1203.

65 18 U.S.C. § 201(b).

66 Ala. Code § 13A-10-61; D.C. Code § 22-712; La. Rev. Stat. Ann. § 14:118; Mass. Gen. Laws ch. 268A, § 2; N.M. Stat. Ann. § 30-24-1; N.C. Gen. Stat. § 14-217; N.D. Cent. Code § 12.1-12-01; 1 N. Mar. I. Code §§ 8551(b), 8552.

67 Alaska Stat. § 11.56.100; Am. Samoa Code Ann. §§ 46.4701, 46.4702; Ariz. Rev.

- Bribe;[68]
- Compensation, gift, gratuity, reward, or money;[69] and
- Unauthorized property.[70]

2. Intent

Similar to the federal statute, many states use "intent to influence" in their bribery statutes.[71] Other terms of art used are "intent to control the per-

---

Stat. Ann. § 13-2602; Ark. Code Ann. § 5-52-101; Conn. Gen. Stat. Ann. § 53A-147; Del. Code Ann. tit. 11, § 1201; Colo. Rev. Stat. § 18-8-302; Fla. Stat. Ann. § 838.015; Ga. Code Ann. § 16-10-2; 9 Guam Code Ann. §§ 49.20, 49.30; Haw. Rev. Stat. Ann. § 710-1040; Idaho Code Ann. § 18-1352; Iowa Code § 722.1 ("with the understanding that the [bribe] . . . will influence"); Kan. Stat. Ann. § 21-6001 ("intent to improperly influence"); Ky. Rev. Stat. Ann. § 521.020; 17-A Me. Rev. Stat. Ann. § 602; Minn. Stat. Ann. § 609.42; Mo. Rev. Stat. § 576.010; Mont. Code Ann. § 45-7-101; Neb. Rev. Stat. Ann. § 28-917; N.H. Rev. Stat. Ann. § 640-2; N.J. Stat. Ann. § 2C:27-2; N.Y. Penal Law § 200.12; Ohio Rev. Code Ann. § 2921.02 ("with purpose to corrupt a public servant or party official, or improperly to influence"); Or. Rev. Stat. § 162.015; 18 Pa. Cons. Stat. Ann. § 4701; P.R. Laws Ann. tit. 33, §§ 4890, 4891; Tenn. Code Ann. § 39-16-102; Tex. Penal Code § 36.02; Utah Code Ann. § 76-8-103; Wash. Rev. Code Ann. § 9A.68.010; Wyo. Stat. § 6-5-102.

68 Cal. Penal Code § 67; Md. Code Ann., Crim. Law § 9-201; Okla. Stat. Ann. tit. 21, § 265; S.D. Codified Laws § 22-12A-11.

69 Mich. Comp. Laws § 750.117; Miss. Code Ann. § 97-11-11; Nev. Rev. Stat. Ann. § 197.010; R.I. Gen. Laws § 11-7-4; S.C. Code Ann. § 16-9-210; V.I. Code Ann. tit. 14, §§ 403, 406; Va. Code Ann. §§ 18.2-438, 18.2-439, 18.2-447; Vt. Stat. Ann. tit. 13, §§ 1101, 1102; W. Va. Code § 61-5-4.

70 720 Ill. Comp. Stat. 5/33-1; Ind. Code Ann. § 35-44.1-1-2; Wis. Stat. § 946.10.

71 Alaska Stat. § 11.56.100; Ariz. Rev. Stat. Ann. § 13-2602; Cal. Penal Code §§ 67, 92; Colo. Rev. Stat. Ann. § 18-8-302; Del. Code Ann. tit. 11, § 1207; Ga. Code Ann. § 16-10-2 ("purpose of influencing"); Haw. Rev. Stat. Ann. § 710-104; 720 Ill. Comp. Stat. 5/33-1; Iowa Code § 722.1 ("with the understanding that the promise or thing of value or benefit will influence"); Ky. Rev. Stat. Ann. § 521.020; La. Rev. Stat. Ann. § 14:118; Me. Rev. Stat. Ann. tit. 17-A, § 602; Md. Code Ann., Crim. Law § 9-201 ("bribe . . . to influence"); Mass. Gen. Laws Ch. 268a, § 2; Mich. Comp. Laws Ann. § 750.117; Minn. Stat. § 609.42; Miss. Code Ann. § 97-11-11; Neb. Rev. Stat. Ann. § 28-917; Nev. Rev. Stat. Ann. § 197.010; N.H. Rev. Stat. Ann. § 640-2 ("with the purpose of influencing"); N.M. Stat. Ann. § 30-24-1; N.Y. Penal Law § 200.12; Okla. Stat. Ann. tit. 21, § 265; Or. Rev. Stat. § 162.015; S.C. Code Ann. § 16-9-210; S.D. Codified Laws § 22-12a-11; Tenn. Code Ann. § 39-16-102; Utah Code Ann. § 76-8-103; Vt. Stat. Ann. tit. 13, § 1101; V.I. Code Ann. tit. 14, § 406; Va. Code Ann. § 18.2-438; W. Va. Code Ann. § 3-9-12; Wis. Stat. Ann. § 946.10; Wyo. Stat. Ann. § 6-5-102.

formance,"[72] "corruptly"[73] and "purposefully or knowingly,"[74] as well as the following:

- Intent to secure result;[75]
- Knowingly;[76]
- Intent to improperly influence;[77]
- Understanding;[78] and
- No intent specified, but bribe offered "as consideration."[79]

3. Government Official

States prohibit bribery of officials acting for or on behalf of the state in a manner analogous to how § 201 makes it a federal crime to bribe a "public official."[80] However, state statutes describe and define which officials are covered in different ways. The most prevalent statutory type applies bribery statutes to "public servants" and defines public servant in broad terms.[81] Some states also broaden the bribery statutes to prohibit bribery of private citizens and election

---

72 Ind. Code Ann. § 35-44.1-1-2.

73 Ala. Code. § 13A-10-61; D.C. Code § 22-712; R.I. Gen. Laws §§ 11-7-3, -4, -5.

74 Mont. Code Ann. § 45-7-101.

75 Wash. Rev. Code Ann. § 9A.68.010.

76 Am. Samoa Code Ann. §§ 46.4701, 46.4702; Fla. Stat. Ann. § 838.015; Mo. Rev. Stat. § 576.010; N.D. Cent Code § 12.1-12-01; Tex. Penal Code § 36.02.

77 Kan. Stat. Ann. § 21-6001; Ohio Rev. Code Ann. § 2921.02.

78 Ark. Code Ann. § 5-52-101; N.C. Gen. Stat. § 14-217; 1 N. Mar. I. Code §§ 8551(b); P.R. Laws Ann. tit. 33, §§ 4890, 4891.

79 Ark. Code Ann. § 5-52-101; Conn. Gen. Stat. § 53A-147, 53A-148; 9 Guam Code Ann. §§ 49.20, 49.30; Idaho Code Ann. § 18-1352; N.J. Stat. Ann. § 2C:27-2 (defining "benefit as consideration" as "any benefit not authorized by law"); 18 Pa. Cons. Stat. Ann. § 4701.

80 *E.g.*, Ga. Code Ann. § 16-10-2.

81 Ala. Code. §§ 13A-10-1, 13A-10-61; Alaska Stat. Ann. §§ 11.81.900, 11.56.100; Ariz. Rev. Stat. Ann. § 13-2602; Ark. Code Ann. §§ 5-52-101, 5-52-105; Am. Samoa Code Ann. §§ 46.4701, 46.4702; Colo. Rev. Stat. Ann. §§ 18-8-302, 18-8-306; Conn. Gen. Stat. §§ 53A-146, 53A-147; Del. Code Ann. tit. 11 §§ 1201, 1203; Fla. Stat. Ann. § 838.015; 9 Guam Code Ann. § 49.30; Haw. Rev. Stat. Ann. § 710-1040; Idaho Code Ann. §§ 18-1351, 18-1352; Ind. Code Ann. § 35-44.1-1-2; Ky. Rev. Stat. Ann. § 521.020; Me. Rev. Stat. Ann. tit. 17-A, § 602; Mont. Code Ann. § 45-7-101; N.D. Cent. Code Ann. § 12.1-12-01; Neb. Rev. Stat. Ann. § 28-917; N.H. Rev. Stat. Ann. § 640-2; N.J. Stat. Ann. § 2C:27-10; N.Y. Penal Law § 200.12; Ohio Rev. Code Ann. § 2921.02; Or. Rev. Stat. Ann. §§ 162.015, 162.025; 18 Pa. Cons. Stat. Ann. § 4701; Tenn. Code Ann. § 39-16-102; Utah Code Ann. § 76-8-105; Wyo. Stat. Ann. § 6-5-102.

officials.[82] Other states may narrow the scope of the term "public official" or "public servant" but still prohibit bribery of a broad range of various public servants through different statute sections.[83] Descriptions of covered government officials include the following:

- Any person acting for or on behalf of the state;[84]
- Public employee, public officer, or public servant;[85]
- Public officer, public official, person holding office, or officer of any branch of government;[86]
- Executive officers;[87]
- Judicial officers and jurors;[88]

---

82 *E.g.*, Miss. Code Ann. § 97-11-11 ("any officer, agent or trustee, either public or private").

83 *E.g.*, Cal. Penal Code §§ 67, 67.5, 92, 165.

84 Ga. Code Ann. § 16-10-2.

85 Ala. Code §§ 13A-10-1, 13A-10-61; Alaska Stat. Ann. §§ 11.81.900, 11.56.100; Ariz. Rev. Stat. Ann. § 13-2602; Ark. Code Ann. § 5-52-105; Am. Samoa Code Ann. § 46.4701; Colo. Rev. Stat. Ann. § 18-8-306; Conn. Gen. Stat. §§ 53a-146, 53a-147; Del. Code Ann. tit. 11 § 1203; D.C. Code § 22-712; Fla. Stat. Ann. § 838.015; 9 Guam Code Ann. § 49.30; Haw. Rev. Stat. Ann. § 710-1040; Idaho Code §§ 18-1351, 18-1352; 720 Ill. Comp. Stat. 5/33-1; Ind. Code Ann. § 35-44.1-1-2; Iowa Code § 722.1; Ky. Rev. Stat. Ann. § 521.020; Me. Rev. Stat. Ann. tit. 17-A, § 602; Md. Code Ann., Crim. Law § 9-201; Mass. Ann. Laws ch. 268A, §§ 2, 3; Mo. Rev. Stat. § 576.010; Mont. Code Ann. § 45-7-101; N.H. Rev. Stat. Ann. § 640-2; N.J. Stat. Ann. § 2C:27-10; Neb. Rev. Stat. Ann. § 28-917; N.Y. Penal Law § 200.12; N.D. Cent. Code Ann. § 12.1-12-01; 1 N. Mar. I. Code §§ 8551(b), 8552; Ohio Rev. Code Ann. § 2921.02; Or. Rev. Stat. Ann. §§ 162.015, 162.025; 18 Pa. Cons. Stat. Ann. § 4701; P.R. Laws Ann. tit. 33, §§ 4890, 4891; Tenn. Code Ann. § 39-16-102; Utah Code Ann. § 76-8-105; V.I. Code Ann. tit. 14, §§ 403, 406; Wash. Rev. Code Ann. § 9A.68.010; Wyo. Stat. Ann. § 6-5-102.

86 Cal. Penal Code § 67.5; Kan. Stat. Ann. § 21-6001; La. Rev. Stat. Ann. § 14:118; Mich. Comp. Laws § 750.117; Minn. Stat. § 609.42; Miss. Code Ann. § 97-11-11; N.M. Stat. Ann. §§ 30-24-1, 30-24-2; Nev. Rev. Stat. Ann. §§ 197.020, 197.040; N.C. Gen. Stat. § 14-217; Okla. Stat. Ann. tit. 21, § 381; R.I. Gen. Laws § 11-7-4; S.C. Code Ann. §§ 16-9-210, 16-9-220; S.D. Codified Laws § 22-12A-7; Va. Code Ann. §§ 18.2-438, 18.2-439; Vt. Stat. Ann. tit. 13, §§ 1101, 1102; W. Va. Code §§ 61-5-4, 61-5-5; Wis. Stat. § 946.10.

87 Cal. Penal Code § 67; Idaho Code § 18-2701; Nev. Rev. Stat. Ann. § 197.010; Okla. Stat. Ann. tit. 21, § 265.

88 Cal. Penal Code § 92; Iowa Code §§ 722.1, 722.2; Idaho Code Ann. §§ 18-1301, 18-1302; La. Rev. Stat. Ann. § 14:118; R.I. Gen. Laws § 11-7-1; S.D. Codified Laws § 22-12a-11; Tex. Penal Code § 36.02; Va. Code Ann. § 18.2-441; Vt. Stat. Ann. tit. 13, § 1101; W. Va. Code § 61-5-7.

- Members of a legislative body;[89]
- Electors;[90] and
- Local officials.[91]

4. Act

In the federal statute, "official act" is defined as "any decision or action on any question, matter, cause, suit, proceeding or controversy, which may at any time be pending, or which may by law be brought before any public official . . . ."[92] The District of Columbia, Georgia, Massachusetts, North Carolina, and North Dakota use the term "official act" in their bribery statutes.[93] Other states' bribery statutes use varying terminology, sometimes listing various examples of types of official action,[94] sometimes including "exercise of discretion" in such a list,[95] and sometimes more broadly referring to any conduct in relation to the official's position, employment, or duty.[96]

---

89 Cal. Penal Code §§ 85, 86; Ga. Code Ann. § 16-10-4; Idaho Code §§ 18-4703, 18-4704; Miss. Code Ann. § 97-7-55; Nev. Rev. Stat. Ann. § 198.010; N.Y. Pub Off. Law § 75; S.D. Codified Laws § 22-12A-4.

90 Idaho Code Ann. § 18-2320; Miss. Code Ann. § 97-13-1; Wis. Stat. § 12.11.

91 Cal. Penal Code § 165; Ga. Code Ann. § 16-10-4.

92 18 U.S.C. § 201(a)(3).

93 D.C. Code § 22-712; Ga. Code Ann. § 16-10-2; Mass. Ann. Laws ch. 268A, § 2; N.C. Gen. Stat. § 14-217; N.D. Cent. Code Ann. § 12.1-12-01. *See also* 9 Guam Code Ann. §§ 49.20, 49.30 ("official function").

94 Ark. Code Ann. § 5-52-101; Cal. Penal Code § 67; Conn. Gen. Stat. § 53A-147; Iowa Code § 722.1; Nev. Rev. Stat. Ann. §§ 197.010, 197.020; N.J. Stat. Ann. § 2C:27-2; Okla. Stat. Ann. tit. 21, § 265; P.R. Laws Ann. tit. 33, §§ 4890, 4891; S.C. Code Ann. §§ 16-9-210, -220; Tex. Penal Code § 36.02; V.I. Code Ann. tit. 14, §§ 403, 406.

95 Ala. Code § 13A-10-61; Alaska Stat. § 11.56.100; Am. Samoa Code Ann. §§ 46.4701, 46.4702; Ariz. Stat. § 13-2602; Colo. Rev. Stat. § 18-8-302; Del. Code Ann. tit. 11 § 1201; Fla. Stat. Ann. § 838.015; Haw. Rev. Stat. Ann. § 710-1040; Idaho Code Ann. § 18-1352; Ky. Rev. Stat. Ann. § 521.020; 17-A Me. Rev. Stat. Ann. § 602; Mo. Rev. Stat. § 576.010; Mont. Code Ann. § 45-7-101; Neb. Rev. Stat. Ann. § 28-917; N.H. Rev. Stat. Ann. § 640-2; N.Y. Penal Law § 200.12; Or. Rev. Stat. § 162.015; 18 Pa. Cons. Stat. Ann. § 4701; Tenn. Code Ann. § 39-16-102; Utah Code Ann. § 76-8-103; Va. Code Ann. §§ 18.2-438, 18.2-439, 18.2-447; Vt. Stat. Ann. tit. 13, §§ 1101, 1102; Wash. Rev. Code Ann. § 9A.68.010; Wyo. Stat. § 6-5-102.

96 720 Ill. Comp. Stat. 5/33-1; Ind. Code Ann. § 35-44.1-1-2; Kan. Stat. Ann. § 21-6001; La. Rev. Stat. Ann. § 14:118; Md. Code Ann., Crim. Law § 9-201; Mich. Comp. Laws § 750.117; Minn. Stat. § 609.42; N.M. Stat. Ann. §§ 1-20-11, 1-20-12, 30-24-1; 1 N. Mar. I. Code §§ 8551(b), 8552; Ohio Rev. Code Ann. § 2921.02; R.I. Gen. Laws §§ 11-7-3, -4, -5; W. Va. Code § 61-5-4; Wis. Stat. § 946.10.

State statutes with "official act" language that is substantially similar to the federal law may be construed consistently with the Supreme Court's *McDonnell* decision, particularly if the state court has "look[ed] to [f]ederal law for guidance in construing" a § 201 cognate in the past.[97] Otherwise, states have "the prerogative to regulate the permissible scope of interactions between state officials and their constituents" and are not subject to "the [f]ederal [g]overnment [] setting standards of good government for local and state officials."[98]

C. *Punishment for Bribery*

All states have felony bribery statutes with imprisonment severity ranging from two years to life imprisonment.[99]

Table 3.1-1—Maximum Classification of Bribery Offense

Alabama	Class C felony Maximum 10 years imprisonment
Alaska	Class B felony Maximum 10 years imprisonment
American Samoa	Class D felony Maximum five years imprisonment (AM. SAMOA CODE ANN. §§ 46.2301, 46.4701, 46.4702)
Arizona	Class 4 felony Maximum 3.75 years imprisonment
Arkansas	Felony Severity varies based on amount of benefit

97 Scaccia v. State Ethics Comm'n, 727 N.E.2d 824, 828 (Mass. 2000) (explaining that Massachusetts courts look to federal caselaw interpreting § 201(c)(1)(A) for guidance in construing the state's gratuities statute, as the legislature adopted the same language). *See also* Chapter 4.3, Part II(A).

98 McDonnell v. United States, 136 S. Ct. 2355, 2373 (2016) (citations omitted).

99 Mark Quiner, *Ethics and Public Corruption Laws: Penalties*, NAT'L CONFERENCE OF STATE LEGISLATURES (Mar. 2, 2021), http://www.ncsl.org/research/ethics/50-state-chart-criminal-penalties-for-public-corr.aspx. Statutes for states and territories that were not included in the National Conference of State Legislature's chart are cited within this table.

Table 3.1-1—Maximum Classification of Bribery Offense

California	Felony Maximum 4 years imprisonment
Colorado	Class 3 felony Maximum 12 years imprisonment
Connecticut	Class C felony Maximum 10 years imprisonment
Delaware	Class E felony Maximum 5 years imprisonment
District of Columbia	Felony Maximum 10 years imprisonment
Florida	Felony of the second degree Maximum 15 years imprisonment
Georgia	Maximum 20 years imprisonment
Guam	Third degree felony Maximum 5 years imprisonment
Hawaii	Class B felony Maximum 10 years imprisonment
Idaho	Felony Maximum 5 years imprisonment
Illinois	Class 2 felony Maximum 7 years imprisonment
Indiana	Level 5 felony Maximum 6 years imprisonment
Iowa	Class D felony Maximum 5 years imprisonment
Kansas	Severity level 7, nonperson felony

Table 3.1-1—Maximum Classification of Bribery Offense

State	Classification
Kentucky	Class C felony Maximum 10 years imprisonment
Louisiana	Felony Maximum 5 years imprisonment
Maine	Class C crime Maximum 5 years imprisonment
Maryland	Misdemeanor Maximum 12 years imprisonment
Massachusetts	Felony Maximum 10 years imprisonment
Michigan	Felony Maximum 10 years imprisonment
Minnesota	Maximum 10 years imprisonment
Mississippi	Felony Maximum 10 years imprisonment
Missouri	Class E felony Maximum 4 years imprisonment
Montana	Felony Maximum 10 years imprisonment
Nebraska	Class IV felony Maximum 2 years imprisonment
Nevada	Class C felony Maximum 5 years imprisonment
New Hampshire	Class B felony Maximum 7 years imprisonment
New Jersey	Felony Severity varies based on amount of benefit

Table 3.1-1—Maximum Classification of Bribery Offense

New Mexico	Third degree felony Maximum 3 years imprisonment
New York	Class A felony Maximum life imprisonment
North Carolina	Class F felony Sentences vary based on statutory factors.
North Dakota	Class C felony Maximum 5 years imprisonment
Northern Mariana Islands	Felony Maximum 5 years imprisonment (6 N. Mar. I. Code § 3201)
Ohio	Third degree felony Maximum 36 months imprisonment
Oklahoma	Felony Maximum 10 years imprisonment
Oregon	Class B felony Maximum 10 years imprisonment
Pennsylvania	Third degree felony Maximum 7 years imprisonment
Puerto Rico	Second degree felony Maximum 15 years imprisonment
Rhode Island	Felony Maximum 20 years imprisonment
South Carolina	Felony Maximum 10 years imprisonment
South Dakota	Class 4 felony Maximum 10 years imprisonment

Table 3.1-1—Maximum Classification of Bribery Offense

Tennessee	Class B felony Maximum 30 years imprisonment
Texas	Second degree felony Maximum 20 years imprisonment
Utah	Second degree felony Maximum 15 years imprisonment
Vermont	Felony Maximum 10 years imprisonment
Virginia	Class 4 felony Maximum 10 years imprisonment (VA. CODE ANN. § 18.2-10(4))
Virgin Islands	Felony Maximum 5 years imprisonment (V.I. CODE ANN. tit. 14, §§ 403, 406)
Washington	Class B felony Maximum 10 years imprisonment
West Virginia	Felony Maximum 10 years imprisonment
Wisconsin	Class H felony Maximum 6 years imprisonment
Wyoming	Felony Maximum 10 years imprisonment

D. *Possible Defenses in State Bribery Statutes*

1. Affirmative Defenses

Several states allow bribery-specific affirmative defenses. Delaware, Hawaii, Kentucky, New York, and Oregon have specific statutes stating that extortion by a public servant is an affirmative defense.[100] Other states have statutes listing a campaign contribution as an affirmative defense to bribery.[101] By contrast, Illinois has a set of statutes criminalizing solicitation of campaign contributions by an executive branch employee from "a person engaged in a business or activity" over which that executive branch employee "has regulatory authority."[102]

2. Not a Defense to Prosecution

In some states, including New Jersey, defendants are statutorily forbidden from claiming extortion as an affirmative defense to bribery.[103] In Arkansas, it is not a defense that the "decision, opinion, recommendation, vote or use of discretion, except for the benefit, was otherwise proper."[104] Many statutes state "it is not a defense . . . that the person sought to be influenced was not qualified to act in the desired way."[105]

E. *Gratuities and Kickbacks*

State gratuity statutes rarely are similar to the federal gratuity statute. An example of a state gratuity statute is "Every judicial officer who asks or receives any emolument, gratuity or reward, or any promise thereof, except such as may be authorized by law, for doing any official act, is guilty of a misdemeanor."[106]

---

100 Del. Code Ann. tit. 11, § 1202; Haw. Rev. Stat. Ann. § 710-1040; Ky. Rev. Stat. Ann. § 521.020; N.Y. Penal Law § 200.05; Or. Rev. Stat. § 162.035.

101 *E.g.*, Tex. Penal Code Ann. § 36.02(d); Colo. Rev. Stat. Ann. § 18-8-305; Utah Code Ann. § 76-8-102.

102 720 Ill. Comp. Stat. 5/33-3.1. For further discussion of defenses in corruption cases, see Chapter 4.3.

103 N.J. Stat. Ann. § 2C:27-2 ("In any prosecution under this section of an actor who offered, conferred or agreed to confer, or who solicited, accepted or agreed to accept a benefit, it is no defense that he did so as a result of conduct by another constituting theft by extortion or coercion or an attempt to commit either of those crimes.").

104 Ark. Code Ann. § 5-52-101.

105 *E.g.*, Alaska Stat. Ann. § 11.56.100; N.J. Stat. Ann. § 2C:27-2; Utah Code Ann. § 76-8-105.

106 Idaho Code § 18-1303. *See also, e.g.*, Cal. Penal Code § 70; Del. Code Ann., tit. 11, § 1206; Fla. Stat. Ann. § 838.016; 9 Guam Code Ann. §§ 49.60, 49.70; Idaho Code § 18-1354; Me. Rev. Stat. Ann. tit. 17-A, § 604; N.H. Rev. Stat. Ann. § 640-4; N.Y. Penal Law §§ 200.30, 200.35; Okla. Stat. Ann. tit. 21, § 269; S.D. Codified Laws §§ 22-12A-1, 22-12A-2.

In addition to prohibiting gratuities, some states specifically prohibit kickbacks for awarding government employment or contracts.[107]

F. *Extortion*

Many states prohibit extortion by a public official, which is similar to soliciting a bribe. Most statutes prohibit obtaining property of another by threatening to take or withhold action as a public servant.[108] Other states echo the language of the Hobbs Act[109] and prohibit obtaining property of another under color of official right or because of official authority.[110] Still other states have statutes prohibiting extortion by a public official but the conduct prohibited is more akin to soliciting improper fees or compensation without connection to any particular official action.[111]

Conclusion

When a public official does not exercise her independent judgment to maximize the benefit for the people she represents, jurisdictions lose tax dollars and potential benefits. Citizens can also lose trust in government. While statutes vary, every state has some scheme to regulate illegal influence crimes that criminalizes at least some forms of appealing to a public official's personal desire for pecuniary gain in order to influence an official action.

---

107 *See, e.g.*, N.M. Stat. Ann. § 30-41-1; Vt. Stat. Ann. tit. 13, §§ 1106, 1107. *See also* Chapter 3.4(III), (IV).

108 *See* Alaska Stat. § 11.41.520; Ariz. Rev. Stat. § 13-1804; Conn. Gen. Stat. § 53a-119; Del. Code Ann. tit. 11, § 846; Ga. Code Ann. § 16-8-16; Haw. Rev. Stat. § 707-764; Idaho Code § 18-2403; 720 Ill. Comp. Stat. 5/12-6; Ind. Code § 35-45-2-1; Iowa Code § 711.4; Ky. Rev. Stat. Ann. § 514.080; Mass. Gen. Laws ch. 265, § 25; Mo. Rev. Stat. §§ 105.452, 105.478; Mont. Code Ann. § 45-7-103; Neb. Rev. Stat. § 28-513; N.H. Rev. Stat. § 637:5; N.J. Stat. Ann. § 2C:20-5; N.M. Stat. Ann. § 10-16-3; N.Y. Penal Law § 135.60; Or. Rev. Stat. § 164.075; 18 Pa. Cons. Stat. § 3923; S.D. Codified Laws § 22-30A-4; Tenn. Code Ann. § 39-11-106; Utah Code Ann. § 76-6-406; Wash. Rev. Code §§ 9A.56.130, 9A.04.110(28)(h); Wyo. Stat. Ann. § 6-5-104.

109 18 U.S.C. § 1951.

110 *See* Cal. Penal Code § 518; D.C. Code § 22-3251; Miss. Code Ann. § 97-3-82; Okla. Stat. tit. 21, § 1481; 11 R.I. Gen. Laws § 11-42-1.1; Wis. Stat. § 946.12(5); Tex. Penal Code Ann. § 31.03.

111 *See* Ark. Code Ann. § 21-6-103; Fla. Stat. Ann. § 839.11; Nev. Rev. Stat. § 197.170. For further discussion of soliciting improper fees, see Chapter 3.4(III), (IV).

Chapter 3.2

Misuse of Public Office & Public Money

Marissa G. Walker

Marissa G. Walker is Program Counsel for the Center for Ethics & Public Integrity, National Attorneys General Training & Research Institute, National Association of Attorneys General.

Introduction

Federal and state laws protect the integrity of public funds and the power of public office. Rooted in the common law concepts of malfeasance, nonfeasance, embezzlement, theft, fraud, and conversion, these laws ensure that public power and money are used in the manner intended by the public and lawmakers. Unlike the bribery laws, these laws do not criminalize the use of money as an incentive to change official behavior. Instead, these laws apply to situations where officials are using public money or office in improper ways. They are based on the idea that the public should be able to trust officials and other people with great power and access to taxpayers' money to use that power and access in an honest, responsible manner. While these laws do not necessarily require that the wrongdoer personally benefit from the misuse, they generally do not criminalize good-faith mistake either. Public servants entrusted with money and power need not be perfect, but they must not deliberately abuse the public's trust or subvert expectations.

I. State Law Official Misconduct

All of public corruption—including misuse of public funds—can be considered broadly to be a type of official misconduct, but "[i]t is probably impossible and certainly impracticable to express all the duties of public offices in statutes."[1] While many different, specific laws require public officials to preserve the integrity of their offices and not personally profit from their positions of power, the common law crime of official misconduct has been codified in many states as a catch-all provision.[2] No single federal offense of official misconduct is based on this common law concept, although various federal criminal laws may apply to instances of official misconduct so long as strict federal requirements are met.[3]

State official misconduct statutes are used to prosecute officials whose conduct is clearly unlawful, but not necessarily contrary to any other, more specific state statutes. Official misconduct is broadly defined as a public official committing an improper act or failing to take a required action relating to his

---

1 *See* State v. Green, 376 A.2d 424, 427 (Del. Super. Ct. 1977).

2 *See, e.g., id.* (explaining that the Delaware statute relating to official misconduct is in part "the modern, codified version of the common law offense of nonfeasance in office").

3 For example, in the "Bridgegate" scandal in New Jersey, federal authorities prosecuted two public servants working for the governor of New Jersey for colluding to close an access lane to the George Washington Bridge in order to snarl traffic in Fort Lee, New Jersey, as political retribution for the Fort Lee mayor's refusal to endorse the governor for reelection. The two public officials were initially convicted under 18 U.S.C. § 666(a)(1)(A), discussed *infra* Part II(B), for intentionally misapplying property of an organization receiving federal benefits, and were convicted of federal wire fraud, under 18 U.S.C. § 1343. *See* Kelly v. United States, 140 S. Ct. 1565, 1568 (2020). The Supreme Court, reversing the convictions, interpreted both federal statutes to require the government to show that the object of the state officials' fraud was money or property. *Id.* at 1568-69. "That requirement . . . prevents these statutes from criminalizing all acts of dishonesty by state and local officials." *Id.* at 1571. The Court specifically referred to New Jersey's official misconduct statute in explaining that "federal fraud law leaves much public corruption to the States (or their electorates) to rectify." *Id.* at 1571-72 (citing to N.J. Stat. Ann. § 2C:30-2). "Federal prosecutors may not use property fraud statutes to set standards of disclosure and good government for local and state officials." *Id.* at 1574 (quotation and citation omitted). If federal prosecutors cannot show that the object of a government official's fraud is money or property, the conduct may be left to state authorities to prosecute under the state official misconduct statute. *See id.* at 1571-72. Relating to the Bridgegate scandal, a private citizen attempted to lodge state official misconduct charges against the governor in connection with the same scheme, but New Jersey state prosecutors declined to pursue the case. *See* Abbott Koloff, *Bergen Prosecutor Won't Pursue Christie Complaint*, NorthJersey.com (Jan. 27, 2017), https://www.northjersey.com/story/news/2017/01/27/bergen-county-prosecutor-wont-pursue-christie-complaint/97156082/.

or her public office to benefit the public official or harm someone else. While statutory elements may differ somewhat, the elements under the common law concept of misconduct are typically: (1) A public official, (2) in relation to his or her office or under the color of his or her authority, (3) commits an unauthorized act or fails to take a required action, (4) with the required two-fold intent of (a) knowing that the act or omission is unauthorized and (b) intending to obtain a benefit or cause harm.

A. *States and Territories that Have Codified the Common Law Formulation*

The states and territories listed in the table below have codified some version of the common-law formulation of official misconduct. While these states and territories have more specific statutes and ethical standards relating to how a public official should behave in carrying out official duties, the statute sections below are broadly worded to capture any misfeasance or nonfeasance in office that is not otherwise expressly prohibited by statute.[4] Typically, states classify the crime as a misdemeanor, although some states classify it as a felony or modify the severity depending on the amount of money at issue.[5]

4 Unless otherwise indicated, all citations to statutes in this chapter refer to the version current at the time of publishing.

5 Mark Quiner, *Ethics and Public Corruption Laws: Penalties*, Nat'l Conf. of State Legislatures (Mar. 2, 2021), http://www.ncsl.org/research/ethics/50-state-chart-criminal-penalties-for-public-corr.aspx.

Table 3.2-1—Official Misconduct

State	Statutory Excerpt	Maximum Classification
Alaska	(a) A public servant commits the crime of official misconduct if, with intent to obtain a benefit or to injure or deprive another person of a benefit, the public servant (1) performs an act relating to the public servant's office but constituting an unauthorized exercise of the public servant's official functions, knowing that that act is unauthorized; or (2) knowingly refrains from performing a duty which is imposed upon the public servant by law or is clearly inherent in the nature of the public servant's office. ALASKA STAT. § 11.56.850.	Class A Misdemeanor
Arkansas	(a) A person commits the offense of abuse of office if, being a public servant . . . and with the purpose of benefiting in a pecuniary fashion or obtaining a sexual favor for himself or herself or another person or of harming another person, the person knowingly: (1) Commits an unauthorized act which purports to be an act of his or her office; or (2) Omits to perform a duty imposed on him or her by law or clearly inherent in the nature of his or her office. ARK. CODE ANN. § 5-52-107.	Class B Felony

Table 3.2-1—Official Misconduct

State	Statutory Excerpt	Maximum Classification
Colorado	(1) A public servant commits first degree official misconduct if, with intent to obtain a benefit for the public servant or another or maliciously to cause harm to another, he or she knowingly: (a) Commits an act relating to his office but constituting an unauthorized exercise of his official function; or (b) Refrains from performing a duty imposed upon him by law; or (c) Violates any statute or lawfully adopted rule or regulation relating to his office. COLO. REV. STAT. § 18-8-404. Note: In Colorado, there are two degrees of official misconduct, which differ only in the intent to harm or benefit aspect. Second degree official misconduct differs in that it requires only that the public servant "knowingly, arbitrarily, and capriciously" violates a statute or rule relating to his or her office or refrains from performing a legal duty. *Compare* COLO. REV. STAT. § 18-8-404 *with* COLO. REV. STAT. § 18-8-405.	Class 2 Misdemeanor

Table 3.2-1—Official Misconduct

State	Statutory Excerpt	Maximum Classification
Delaware	A public servant is guilty of official misconduct when, intending to obtain a personal benefit or to cause harm to another person: (1) The public servant commits an act constituting an unauthorized exercise of official functions, knowing that the act is unauthorized; or (2) The public servant knowingly refrains from performing a duty which is imposed by law or is clearly inherent in the nature of the office; or (3) The public servant performs official functions in a way intended to benefit the public servant's own property or financial interests under circumstances in which the public servant's actions would not have been reasonably justified in consideration of the factors which ought to have been taken into account in performing official functions; or (4) The public servant knowingly performs official functions in a way intended to practice discrimination on the basis of race, creed, color, sex, age, handicapped status or national origin. DEL. CODE ANN. tit. 11, § 1211.	Class A Misdemeanor
Guam	A public servant commits a misdemeanor if, with intent to benefit himself or another person or to harm another person or to deprive another person of a benefit: (a) he commits an act relating to his office but constituting an unauthorized exercise of his official functions, knowing that such act is unauthorized; or (b) he knowingly refrains from performing a duty which is imposed upon him by law or is clearly inherent in the nature of his office. 9 GUAM CODE ANN. § 49.90.	Misdemeanor

Table 3.2-1—Official Misconduct

State	Statutory Excerpt	Maximum Classification
Illinois	(a) A public officer or employee or special government agent commits misconduct when, in his official capacity or capacity as a special government agent, he or she commits any of the following acts: (1) Intentionally or recklessly fails to perform any mandatory duty as required by law; or (2) Knowingly performs an act which he knows he is forbidden by law to perform; or (3) With intent to obtain a personal advantage for himself or another, he performs an act in excess of his lawful authority; or (4) Solicits or knowingly accepts for the performance of any act a fee or reward which he knows is not authorized by law. 720 ILL. COMP. STAT. 5/33-3.	Class 3 Felony
Indiana	A public servant who knowingly or intentionally: (1) commits an offense in the performance of the public servant's official duties; . . . commits official misconduct. IND. CODE § 35-44.1-1-1.	Level 6 Felony
Iowa	Any public officer or employee, or any person acting under color of such office or employment, who knowingly does any of the following, commits a serious misdemeanor: . . . 4. By color of the person's office and in excess of the authority conferred on the person by that office, requires any person to do anything or to refrain from doing any lawful thing. . . . 6. Fails to perform any duty required of the person by law. IOWA CODE § 721.2.	Serious Misdemeanor

Table 3.2-1—Official Misconduct

State	Statutory Excerpt	Maximum Classification
Kentucky	[A public servant commits official misconduct when he:] (a) Commits an act relating to his office which constitutes an unauthorized exercise of his official functions; or (b) Refrains from performing a duty imposed upon him by law or clearly inherent in the nature of his office; or (c) Violates any statute or lawfully adopted rule or regulation relating to his office. KY. REV. STAT. ANN. §§ 522.020-522.030. Note: Official misconduct in the first degree requires that the official knowingly commit the above actions with intent to confer a benefit or injure another person, whereas official misconduct in the second degree does not require the intent to benefit or injure.	Class A Misdemeanor
Louisiana	A. Malfeasance in office is committed when any public officer or public employee shall: (1) Intentionally refuse or fail to perform any duty lawfully required of him, as such officer or employee; or (2) Intentionally perform any such duty in an unlawful manner; or (3) Knowingly permit any other public officer or public employee, under his authority, to intentionally refuse or fail to perform any duty lawfully required of him, or to perform any such duty in an unlawful manner. LA. REV. STAT. ANN. § 14.134.	Felony

Table 3.2-1—Official Misconduct

State	Statutory Excerpt	Maximum Classification
Maine	A person is guilty of official oppression if, being a public servant and acting with the intention to benefit himself or another or to harm another, he knowingly commits an unauthorized act which purports to be an act of his office, or knowingly refrains from performing a duty imposed on him by law or clearly inherent in the nature of his office. ME. REV. STAT. ANN. tit. 17-A, § 608.	Class E Crime
Minnesota	A public officer or employee who does any of the following, for which no other sentence is specifically provided by law, [commits misconduct] . . . : (1) intentionally fails or refuses to perform a known mandatory, nondiscretionary, ministerial duty of the office or employment within the time or in the manner required by law; or (2) in the capacity of such officer or employee, does an act knowing it is in excess of lawful authority or knowing it is forbidden by law to be done in that capacity; or (3) under pretense or color of official authority intentionally and unlawfully injures another in the other's person, property, or rights . . . . MINN. STAT. § 609.43.	Misdemeanor

Table 3.2-1—Official Misconduct

State	Statutory Excerpt	Maximum Classification
Montana	(1) A public servant commits the offense of official misconduct when in an official capacity the public servant commits any of the following acts: (a) purposely or negligently fails to perform any mandatory duty as required by law or by a court of competent jurisdiction; (b) knowingly performs an act in an official capacity that the public servant knows is forbidden by law; [or] (c) with the purpose to obtain a personal advantage or an advantage for another, performs an act in excess of the public servant's lawful authority. MONT. CODE ANN. § 45-7-401. Note: Subsections (d) and (e) of this statute specifically prohibit soliciting or accepting an improper fee or reward and knowingly conducting a meeting of a public agency unlawfully. MONT. CODE ANN. § 45-7-401(d), (e).	Misdemeanor
Nebraska	(1) A public servant commits official misconduct if he knowingly violates any statute or lawfully adopted rule or regulation relating to his official duties. NEB. REV. STAT. § 28-924.	Class II Misdemeanor
New Hampshire	A public servant . . . is guilty of a misdemeanor if, with a purpose to benefit himself or another or to harm another, he knowingly commits an unauthorized act which purports to be an act of his office; or knowingly refrains from performing a duty imposed on him by law or clearly inherent in the nature of his office. N.H. REV. STAT. ANN. 643:1.	Misdemeanor

Table 3.2-1—Official Misconduct

State	Statutory Excerpt	Maximum Classification
New Jersey	A public servant is guilty of official misconduct when, with purpose to obtain a benefit for himself or another or to injure or to deprive another of a benefit: a. He commits an act relating to his office but constituting an unauthorized exercise of his official functions, knowing that such act is unauthorized or he is committing such act in an unauthorized manner; or b. He knowingly refrains from performing a duty which is imposed upon him by law or is clearly inherent in the nature of his office. N.J. Stat. Ann. § 2C:30-2. Note: New Jersey has a separate section for committing a "pattern of official misconduct" for two or more acts of official misconduct even if the acts were not part of a common scheme or plan. *See* N.J. Stat. Ann. § 2C:30-7. New Jersey also requires enhanced penalties upon conviction of a public employee or officer for specific crimes that involve or touch upon the office, including official misconduct. N.J. Stat. Ann. § 2C:43-6.5.	Second Degree Crime
New York	A public servant is guilty of official misconduct when, with intent to obtain a benefit or deprive another person of a benefit: 1. He commits an act relating to his office but constituting an unauthorized exercise of his official functions, knowing that such act is unauthorized; or 2. He knowingly refrains from performing a duty which is imposed upon him by law or is clearly inherent in the nature of his office. N.Y. Penal Law § 195.00. Note: New York also criminalizes rewarding official misconduct and receiving a reward for official misconduct. *See* N.Y. Penal Law §§ 200.20, 200.22, 200.25, 200.27.	Class A Misdemeanor

Table 3.2-1—Official Misconduct

State	Statutory Excerpt	Maximum Classification
North Carolina	If any . . . official of any of the State institutions, or of any county, city or town, shall willfully omit, neglect or refuse to discharge any of the duties of his office, for default whereof it is not elsewhere provided that he shall be indicted, he shall be guilty of a Class 1 misdemeanor. N.C. Gen. Stat. § 14-230(a).	Class 1 Misdemeanor
Northern Mariana Islands	Every person who, being a public official, does any illegal act under the color of office, or willfully neglects to perform the duties of his or her office as provided by law, is guilty of misconduct in public office . . . . 6 N. Mar. I. Code § 3202.	Misdemeanor
Oregon	(1) A public servant commits the crime of official misconduct in the first degree if: (a) With intent to obtain a benefit or to harm another: (A) The public servant knowingly fails to perform a duty imposed upon the public servant by law or one clearly inherent in the nature of office; or (B) The public servant knowingly performs an act constituting an unauthorized exercise in official duties . . . . Or. Rev. Stat. § 162.415. Note: Oregon also criminalizes official misconduct in the second degree, regardless of whether there is an intent to obtain a benefit or harm. Or. Rev. Stat. § 162.405.	Class A Misdemeanor

Table 3.2-1—Official Misconduct

State	Statutory Excerpt	Maximum Classification
Tennessee	(a) A public servant commits an offense who, with intent to obtain a benefit or to harm another, intentionally or knowingly: (1) Commits an act relating to the public servant's office or employment that constitutes an unauthorized exercise of official power; (2) Commits an act under color of office or employment that exceeds the public servant's official power; (3) Refrains from performing a duty that is imposed by law or that is clearly inherent in the nature of the public servant's office or employment; (4) Violates a law relating to the public servant's office or employment; or (5) Receives any benefit not otherwise authorized by law. TENN. CODE ANN. § 39-16-402.	Class E Felony
Texas	(a) A public servant commits an offense if, with intent to obtain a benefit or with intent to harm or defraud another, he intentionally or knowingly: (1) violates a law relating to the public servant's office or employment . . . . TEX. PENAL CODE ANN. § 39.02.	Class A Misdemeanor
Utah	A public servant is guilty of a class B misdemeanor if, with an intent to benefit himself or another or to harm another, he knowingly commits an unauthorized act which purports to be an act of his office, or knowingly refrains from performing a duty imposed on him by law or clearly inherent in the nature of his office. UTAH CODE ANN. § 76-8-201.	Class B Misdemeanor

Table 3.2-1—Official Misconduct

State	Statutory Excerpt	Maximum Classification
Washington	(1) A public servant is guilty of official misconduct if, with intent to obtain a benefit or to deprive another person of a lawful right or privilege: (a) He or she intentionally commits an unauthorized act under color of law; or (b) He or she intentionally refrains from performing a duty imposed upon him or her by law. WASH. REV. CODE § 9A.80.010. Note: Washington also makes it a misdemeanor if a public officer neglects to perform a duty. WASH. REV. CODE § 42.20.100.	Gross Misdemeanor
Wisconsin	Any public officer or public employee who does any of the following is guilty of [official misconduct]: (1) Intentionally fails or refuses to perform a known mandatory, nondiscretionary, ministerial duty of the officer's or employee's office or employment within the time or in the manner required by law; or (2) In the officer's or employee's capacity as such officer or employee, does an act which the officer or employee knows is in excess of the officer's or employee's lawful authority or which the officer or employee knows the officer or employee is forbidden by law to do in the officer's or employee's official capacity; or (3) Whether by act of commission or omission, in the officer's or employee's capacity as such officer or employee exercises a discretionary power in a manner inconsistent with the duties of the officer's or employee's office or employment or the rights of others and with intent to obtain a dishonest advantage for the officer or employee or another . . . . WIS. STAT. § 946.12.	Class I Felony

Table 3.2-1—Official Misconduct

State	Statutory Excerpt	Maximum Classification
Wyoming	(a) A public servant commits [official misconduct] . . . , if, with intent to obtain a pecuniary benefit or maliciously to cause harm to another, he knowingly: (i) Commits an act relating to his official duties that the public servant does not have the authority to undertake; (ii) Refrains from performing a duty imposed upon him by law; or (iii) Violates any statute relating to his official duties. (b) [Or] . . . if he intentionally fails to perform a duty in the manner and within the time prescribed by law. WYO. STAT. ANN. § 6-5-107.	Misdemeanor

B. *Elements of the Common Law Formulation*

1. Public Official

In most cases, whether the defendant is a public official is beyond dispute. Depending on the state, the statute may define the term "public official" or "public servant,"[6] or it may be a matter for the court to determine based on case law.[7] On occasion, a court must consider whether temporary, lower level or contracted positions would be subject to prosecution for official misconduct.[8] In

6 *See, e.g.*, N.H. REV. STAT. ANN. §§ 640:2, 643:1 (defining "public servant" for purposes of official misconduct); N.J. STAT. ANN. § 2C:27-1(g) (defining "public servant").

7 *See* People v. Coutu, 589 N.W.2d 458, 459 Mich. 348, 354-55 (Mich. 1999) (listing factors to determine whether a position constituted public office).

8 *See* State v. Morrison, 151 A.3d 561, 564 (N.J. 2016) (holding that a volunteer EMT working for a private, non-profit first-aid squad was not a public servant for purposes of official misconduct); *Coutu*, 459 Mich. at 354-55 (finding that a deputy sheriff is a public official for purposes of misconduct in office).

such instances, whether the individual exercises governmental authority may determine whether the individual is considered an official.[9]

2. Relating to Public Office or Under Color of Authority

Some statutes require that the public official be acting in an official capacity rather than in a personal capacity. A broadly worded statute may allow prosecution for misconduct committed by an official while not strictly carrying out official functions.[10] Under many state statutes, public officials may not knowingly refrain from performing a duty "clearly inherent in the nature of the office."[11] That phrase has been interpreted as meaning "those unspecified duties that are so essential to the accomplishment of the purposes for which the office was created."[12] Even where the statute requires the official to act within his or her "official capacity," it may reach not only those "express duties set out by statute or rule for a public official but more broadly to all the duties and responsibilities a public official or employee has in serving the public interest in a particular public office."[13] In determining whether alleged misconduct relates to official duties, courts may consider whether the misconduct renders an official incapable of performing the duties of his or her office.[14] Sometimes, courts

---

9 *See* State v. Perez, 883 A.2d 367, 368-69 (N.J. 2005) (finding that an employee of a privatized Department of Motor Vehicles location was a public servant for purposes of official misconduct despite not being a state employee); State v. Vickery, 646 A.2d 1159, 1162 (N.J. Super. Ct. Law Div. 1994) (finding that members of the Society for the Prevention of Cruelty to Animals who had power to investigate reports of animal cruelty, to make arrests and seizures, and to sue for and collect fines were within the definition of public servant); State v. Quezada, 953 A.2d 1206, 1210 (N.J. Super. Ct. App. Div. 2008) (finding that a volunteer firefighter is a public servant for purposes of official misconduct because firefighting is a government function).

10 *See* Howell v. State, 421 A.2d 892, 897 (Del. 1980) (noting that the broad language of the Delaware statute (1) extends the common-law crime of nonfeasance to include a public servant's personal gain from knowing failure to perform a duty "clearly inherent in the nature of his office," and (2) does not confine such duties to the official functions of a public servant).

11 As listed in the table above, states with the "clearly inherent" language include Alaska, Arkansas, Delaware, Guam, Kentucky, Maine, New Hampshire, New Jersey, New York, Oregon, Tennessee, and Utah.

12 State v. Green, 376 A.2d 424, 428 (Del. Super. Ct. 1977) (finding that the duty of avoiding an unspecified conflict of interest or other ethical violation is not clearly inherent in serving as an officer of a state bank).

13 *See* State v. Ford, 397 N.W.2d 875, 879-80 (Minn. 1986) (finding that an assistant principal at a public school had committed official misconduct by granting favors to students in exchange for sexual contact).

14 *See* Hynes v. Hogan, 558 N.W.2d 35, 38–39 (Neb. 1997) (finding that a county attorney did not commit official misconduct by residing in the wrong county, even though that did

may also consider whether the alleged misconduct occurs because of the office held or because of an opportunity afforded by that office.[15]

3. Improper Act or Omission

In determining whether an official committed an act of misconduct, courts may consider whether the act is contrary to a law, rule, regulation, or policy that applies to the defendant in his or her official capacity, even if such a rule does not contain an independent penal clause.[16]

Official misconduct statutes have been subject to constitutional challenges for vagueness. A statute is unconstitutionally vague if it fails to provide sufficient notice for an ordinary person to understand what conduct it prohibits or if it does not include standards to prevent arbitrary and discriminatory enforcement.[17] Since official misconduct statutes typically do not describe the specific criminal conduct they are intended to reach, it may be prudent for prosecutors to use "extra caution" to make clear exactly how the defendant is alleged to have exceeded his or her lawful authority.[18] Courts look to facts of the particular case and the specificity of the indictment to determine if a defendant is adequately informed of the nature of charges against him.[19]

Because official misconduct statutes apply to a broad range of public officials undertaking many different types of actions, examples of acts constituting official misconduct are extremely varied.[20]

---

disqualify him from serving as county attorney).

15 State v. Saavedra, 117 A.3d 1169, 1181 (N.J. 2015).

16 People v. Weber, 479 N.E.2d 382, 384 (Ill. App. Ct. 1985).

17 *See* City of Chicago v. Morales, 527 U.S. 41, 56 (1999).

18 People v. Davis, 668 N.E.2d 119, 124 (Ill. App. Ct. 1996).

19 *Id.* at 124-25; People v. Goldswer, 368 N.Y.S.2d 323, 324 (N.Y. App. Div. 1975) (finding the New York statute not vague because "the language clearly apprises a reasonable man of the nature of the acts prohibited and of what conduct is required of him").

20 *See, e.g.*, People v. Price, 589 N.E.2d 192, 194-95 (Ill. App. Ct. 1992) (meat inspector committed misconduct in shooting a hog in a slaughterhouse with a pistol despite being aware of proper slaughtering procedure); People v. Larsen, 808 P.2d 1265, 1266-67 (Colo. 1991) (district attorney committed misconduct in failing to turn in or prosecute his wife and receptionist for possession of less than one ounce of marijuana); Howell v. State, 421 A.2d 892, 894-95, 897 (Del. 1980) (president of board of education committed misconduct in unreasonably delaying for two years reimbursing school district for materials and labor spent on president's personal home).

4. Mens Rea

Two mens rea requirements ensure that good faith mistakes in public office do not risk criminal prosecution.[21] First, the defendant must undertake an act or omission that he or she knows to be unlawful.[22] Second, the defendant must do so intending to obtain a benefit for him- or herself or to cause a harm to someone else.[23]

Some statutes require the public official to know that the act is unauthorized by law, or to know there is a duty to perform an act, but to fail to perform it.[24] An official's knowledge may be proven circumstantially based on, for example, that official's obligation to know the law, rules, regulations, and standards relating to his or her office.[25] Where the statutes require that the public servant refuses or fails to perform or intentionally performs in an unlawful manner, "mere inadvertence or negligence, or even criminal negligence, will not support a violation . . . ."[26]

The typical formulation of official misconduct does not require that the defendant actually gain a benefit or inflict harm but requires only that the unauthorized action is undertaken with the intent to do so.[27] The concept of "benefit" or "harm" may be broadly interpreted. Although monetary benefit is certainly included, the concept of "benefit" may be broader than graft or financial advantage, assuming the statute does not explicitly require monetary gain.[28]

---

21 People v. Feerick, 714 N.E.2d 851, 856 (N.Y. 1999).

22 *Id.*

23 *Id.*

24 *See, e.g.*, DEL. CODE ANN. tit. 11, § 1211(1), (2).

25 *See* State v. Saavedra, 117 A.3d 1169, 1181-82 (N.J. 2015); People v. Price, 589 N.E.2d 192, 194-95 (Ill. App. Ct. 1992) (finding that a meat inspector had requisite knowledge of a regulation forbidding shooting animals because of its presence in his employment manual for fifteen years as well as other factors).

26 State v. Petitto, 59 So. 3d 1245, 1254 (La. 2011).

27 *See Saavedra*, 117 A.3d at 1181.

28 *Feerick*, 714 N.E.2d at 856. For example, a volunteer firefighter was convicted of official misconduct for calling in false fire alarms for the "benefit" of the joy or gratification in responding to the call. State v. Quezada, 953 A.2d 1206, 1208 (N.J. Super. Ct. App. Div. 2008). A bus driver was convicted for pinching a passenger's buttocks for the "benefit" of "momentary sexual titillation." People of Guam v. Camacho, 103 F.3d 863, 866 (9th Cir. 1996) (applying Guam law).

C. *Some Statutes Expressly Require More Specific Acts or Omissions*

Some states criminalize more specific acts or omissions under the name official misconduct. For example, falsifying or tampering with official records is official misconduct in several states.[29] Misusing non-public information is sometimes characterized as official misconduct.[30] A variety of other more specific acts may be considered official misconduct.[31]

D. *Few States Continue to Recognize Common Law Misconduct*

In Maryland, common law misconduct in office is defined as corrupt behavior by a public officer in the exercise of the duties of his or her office or while acting under color of office.[32] Although this crime is not codified, it was used in 2015 by the Maryland State Attorney for Baltimore City to charge six police officers who were also charged with murder and manslaughter in the arrest and death of Freddie Gray.[33]

In Michigan, a statute section incorporates common law indictable offenses not otherwise codified into statute, which includes the common law crime of misconduct in office.[34] Michigan common law defines misconduct in

29 *See, e.g.*, FLA. STAT. § 838.022(1)(a); IND. CODE 35-44.1-1-1(4) (failing to deliver public records); IOWA CODE § 721.1(2).

30 *See, e.g.*, KAN. STAT. ANN. § 21-6002(a)(3).

31 *See, e.g.*, IOWA CODE § 721.2; KAN. STAT. ANN. § 21-6002; MO. REV. STAT. § 576.040; NEV. REV. STAT. ANN. §§ 197.110, 197.180; VT. STAT. ANN. tit. 13, §§ 3006, 3007, 3008; W. VA. CODE § 61-5-28.

32 *See* Pinheiro v. State, 225 A.3d 495, 506 (Md. App. 2020); Maryland Mun. League, *Ethics, Conduct, and Disclosure*, http://www.mdmunicipal.org/DocumentCenter/Home/View/262 (last visited Apr. 20, 2021) (noting that misconduct in office is a misdemeanor).

33 *See* Alan Blinder & Richard Perez-Pena, *6 Baltimore Police Officers Charged in Freddie Gray Death*, N.Y. TIMES (May 1, 2015), https://www.nytimes.com/2015/05/02/us/freddie-gray-autopsy-report-given-to-baltimore-prosecutors.html?_r=0. No convictions resulted from these charges. Kevin Rector, *Charges Dropped, Freddie Gray Case Concludes with Zero Convictions Against Officers*, BALT. SUN (July 27, 2016), https://www.baltimoresun.com/news/crime/bs-md-ci-miller-pretrial-motions-20160727-story.html.

34 *See* People v. Coutu, 459 Mich. 348, 353-54 (Mich. 1999) (referring to MICH. COMP. LAWS § 750.505).

office as "corrupt behavior by an officer in the exercise of the duties of his office or while acting under color of his office."[35] Under the statute, it is a felony.[36]

II. Public Money: Federal Laws Pertaining to Embezzlement and Misapplication

One type of misconduct federal and state statutes frequently address is misconduct with respect to public money, often referred to as embezzlement, theft, or misapplication of public funds.

The United States Department of Justice Public Integrity Section investigates and prosecutes corruption at all levels of government.[37] The USDOJ's jurisdiction and interest extends to all state and local agencies that receive large amounts of federal funds.[38] Two key federal statutes aimed at protecting integrity of federal funds distributed to state and local agencies are 18 U.S.C. §§ 641 and 666.[39] Section 641 is the general theft statute, prohibiting embezzlement, stealing, purloining, and knowing conversion of any thing of value of the United States.[40] Section 666 applies to state and local government agencies, as well as private organizations and Indian tribal governmental agencies, that receive $10,000 or more annually in federal assistance, and prohibits embezzlement, stealing, theft, fraud, conversion, and intentional misapplication of property or money by an agent of such agency regardless of whether the money or property stolen or misapplied is specifically federal money or property.[41]

---

35 People v. Redmond, No. 261458, 2006 Mich. App. LEXIS 3322, at *8-9 (Mich. Ct. App. Nov. 14, 2006) (quoting People v. Perkins, 662 N.W.2d 727 (Mich. 2003)).

36 Mich. Comp. Laws § 750.505.

37 U.S. Dep't of Justice, Public Integrity Section, https://www.justice.gov/criminal/pin (last visited Apr. 20, 2021).

38 *See* Criminal Resource Manual § 1002 (U.S. Dep't of Justice 2020), https://www.justice.gov/usam/criminal-resource-manual-1002-theft-and-bribery-federally-funded-programs. Note that the USDOJ appears to be treating the *Criminal Resource Manual* as an archived document.

39 *Id.*; 18 U.S.C. §§ 641, 666 (2018). Numerous other statutory provisions prohibit specific types of misuse or theft of public funds. *See, e.g.*, *id.* §§ 643, 644, 648, 649, 650, 651, 652, and 653.

40 18 U.S.C. § 641.

41 18 U.S.C. § 666(a)(1)(A); Criminal Resource Manual § 1002. For a discussion of bribery generally, refer to Chapter 3.1.

Notably, cases that may be subject to federal prosecution under §§ 641 and 666 may also be subject to prosecution under state laws, and may raise federalism concerns.[42] Federal prosecution of state officials for embezzlement or theft raises two possible problems: first, the federal government has limited authority to prosecute crimes that are traditionally local in nature; and second, the federal government has limited ability to regulate officials of a separate sovereign.[43] The Supreme Court has repeatedly refused to involve the federal government in setting standards of good government for local and state officials beyond what Congress clearly legislates.[44]

A. *Federal Protection of Public Money: 18 U.S.C. § 641*

Section 641 prohibits theft of federal property or money.[45] It applies to any person, not just a federal government official or agent, who "embezzles, steals, purloins, or knowingly converts to his use or the use of another, or without authority, sells, conveys or disposes of any record, voucher, money, or thing of value of the United States . . . ."[46] To support a conviction under 18 U.S.C. § 641, the government must establish that the defendant (1) knowingly (2) stole or converted to the use of another (3) something of value of the United States.[47]

1. Offense Conduct

Section 641 broadly lists four overlapping larceny-type offenses—"embezzlement, stealing, purloining and knowing conversion"—into one offense in order to reach all possible instances of a person obtaining wrongful advantages from the government's property.[48] The offenses included under the statute range from specific to broad. The most specific offense is embezzlement, which is defined as "fraudulent appropriation of property by a person to whom such property has been entrusted, or into whose hands it has lawfully come."[49] The

42 *See* Peter J. Henning, The Prosecution and Defense of Public Corruption: The Law and Legal Strategies § 1.03 (Matthew Bender, 2020 ed.).

43 *Id.* (citing Peter J. Henning, *Federalism and the Federal Prosecution of State and Local Corruption*, 92 Ky. L. Rev. 75, 80–81 (2003)).

44 *See* Kelly v. United States, 140 S. Ct. 1565, 1574 (2020); McDonnell v. United States, 136 S. Ct. 2355, 2373 (2016); McNally v. United States, 483 U.S. 350, 360 (1987).

45 18 U.S.C. § 641.

46 *Id.*

47 United States v. Hall, 549 F.3d 1033, 1038 (6th Cir. 2008).

48 Morissette v. United States, 342 U.S. 246, 271-72 (1952).

49 Moore v. United States, 160 U.S. 268, 269 (1895).

offense of embezzlement is different from other theft or larceny-type crimes in that the original possession or control over the money is lawful, but restricted to an authorized purpose.[50] In other larceny-type crimes, such as stealing and purloining, the initial taking is itself unlawful.[51] Knowing conversion broadly may include misuse or abuse of property, or use in an unauthorized manner of property placed in one's custody for limited use—it is like embezzlement without the appropriation to one's own benefit.[52]

2. Property Protected

Section 641 broadly protects property including "any record, voucher, money, or thing of value of the United States or any department or agency thereof, or any property made or being made under contract for the United States or any department or agency thereof . . . ."[53] A key question in determining whether the property is protected by § 641 is whether the federal government's interest in the property is sufficient. If it is sufficient, federal jurisdiction attaches, but if it is not sufficient, the prosecution is deferred to state and local authorities.[54]

3. Intent

The intent required for a conviction under § 641 is intent to appropriate government property for a use inconsistent with the owner's rights and benefits.[55] Two recurring issues arise around intent. First, intent to take government property only temporarily will suffice under a theory of embezzlement or knowing conversion of property.[56] It is not a defense to embezzlement if the defendant intends to keep the property only temporarily and return it at some future time.[57] Second, courts typically do not require a prosecutor to prove

---

50 *See* United States v. Powell, 294 F. Supp. 1353, 1355 (E.D. Va. 1968) *as cited by* Criminal Resource Manual § 1638 (U.S. Dep't of Justice 2020), https://www.justice.gov/usam/criminal-resource-manual-1638-embezzlement-government-property-18-usc-641.

51 *See* Criminal Resource Manual § 1639 (explaining that the terms steal or purloin refer generally to the crime of larceny and include all forms of larceny, including by trick).

52 *Morissette*, 342 U.S. at 271-72.

53 18 U.S.C. § 641 (2018).

54 *See* Criminal Resource Manual § 1643; Henning, *supra* note 42, at § 3.02[2].

55 United States v. Jones, 217 F. App'x 333, 336 (5th Cir. 2007).

56 *See* United States v. Powell, 294 F. Supp. 1353, 1355 (E.D. Va. 1968).

57 *See id.*

that the defendant knows the property belongs to the government in order to convict under § 641.[58]

B. *Federal Protection of Programs Receiving Federal Funds: 18 U.S.C. § 666(a)(1)(A)*

Section 666(a)(1)(A) allows for federal prosecution of anyone who unlawfully takes money or property having a value of $5,000 or more from state and local governments that receive more than $10,000 in federal funds annually.[59] Congress created § 666 to protect the integrity of the federal funds administered through state and local organizations, even in cases where prosecution through § 641 would encounter problems, for example, in establishing the federal nature of the property.[60] Because state agencies and programs receive federal funds, § 666 may be a federal statutory vehicle for prosecuting instances of state misconduct, so long as that misconduct is a fraud to obtain money or property.[61] Congress intended that § 666 may be used "to root out public corruption."[62]

1. Offense Conduct

In all prosecutions under 18 U.S.C. § 666(a)(1)(A), the United States must prove the following general elements: (1) "that the defendant is an agent of an organization or of a state, local, or Indian Tribal government;" (2) "that the organization, government, or agency receives benefits in excess of $10,000 in a one-year period pursuant to a Federal program involving a grant, a contract, a subsidy, a loan, a guarantee, insurance, or another form of Federal assistance;" (3) that the object of the fraud was property or money (whether the fraud was

---

58 *See* United States v. Jeffery, 631 F.3d 669, 677-78 (4th Cir. 2011).

59 18 U.S.C. § 666(a)(1)(A).

60 Criminal Resource Manual § 1002 (U.S. Dep't of Justice 2020), https://www.justice.gov/usam/criminal-resource-manual-1002-theft-and-bribery-federally-funded-programs.

61 *See* Kelly v. United States, 140 S. Ct. 1565, 1573 (2020) (explaining that a state's fraudulent exercise of regulatory power does not constitute property fraud, but a "government's right to its employees' time and labor, by contrast, can undergird a property fraud prosecution" and collecting "home-and-garden examples" of misuse of property).

62 United States v. Willis, 844 F.3d 155, 165 (3d Cir. 2016). *See also* United States v. Pabey, 664 F.3d 1084, 1089 (7th Cir. 2011) (affirming conviction of mayor who used deception to have "on-the-clock city workers" renovate his daughter's new home); United States v. Delano, 55 F.3d 720, 723 (2d Cir. 1995) (affirming conviction of city parks commissioner who induced his employees into doing gardening work for political contributors).

embezzlement, theft, conversion, misapplication, or otherwise); (4) that the property had a value of $5,000 or more; and (5) that the property "was owned by or under the care, custody, or control of such organization, government, or agency."[63] Beyond these elements, the government must prove the elements of the underlying theft offense charged.[64]

The statute requires proof that the defendant embezzled, stole, obtained by fraud, knowingly converted, or intentionally misapplied the property at issue.[65] Embezzlement, theft, and fraud are included in § 666 with their usual common law definitions.[66]

2. Who is Subject to the Statute—Definition of "Agent"

The statute requires that the defendant be "an agent of an organization, or of a State, local, or Indian tribal government, or any agency thereof."[67] Subsection (d)(1) defines "agent" as "a person authorized to act on behalf of another person or a government and, in the case of an organization or government, includes a servant or employee, and a partner, director, officer, manager, and representative."[68] Consistent with the statute's broad purpose of protecting the integrity of federal programs, this definition of "agent" goes beyond just government officials or employees. Courts have construed "agent" to include consultants and independent contractors.[69]

3. Intent

Section 666 encompasses several different underlying common law crimes, all of which have varying intent requirements. The exact criminal intent required for any particular case will depend on the prosecution's theory about

---

63 Criminal Resource Manual § 1004. *See also Kelly*, 140 S. Ct. at 1572 (explaining that the object of the fraud must be property and that the cost of implementing an exercise of regulatory power does not satisfy that requirement).

64 Criminal Resource Manual § 1004.

65 18 U.S.C. § 666(a)(1)(A) (2018).

66 *See* Henning, *supra* note 42, at § 4.06[2] (citing to common law definitions of conversion); United States v. Abu-Shawish, 507 F.3d 550, 556 n.5 (7th Cir. 2007) (using interchangeably "fraud," "fraudulently," and "stole" with "embezzle," "steal," "fraudulently obtain," "knowingly convert," and "intentionally misapply property").

67 18 U.S.C. § 666(a)(1).

68 *Id.* § 666(d)(1).

69 United States v. Vitillo, 490 F.3d 314, 322-23 (3d Cir. 2007).

the underlying common law crime—embezzlement, theft, fraud, conversion, or misapplication.[70]

4. Must the Funds Taken be Federal?

Under the plain language of the statute, the federal government can prosecute the theft of any money or property taken from an organization receiving more than $10,000 in federal funds. The stolen money or property need not be federal in nature, nor have been acquired with federal funds.[71] But "to avoid prosecutions for minor kickbacks and limit violations to cases of outright corruption," charges under § 666 may only be brought if the property in question is worth at least $5,000.[72] According to the U.S. Department of Justice Criminal Resource Manual, the "advisability of a Federal prosecution under 18 U.S.C. § 666(a)(1)(A) should be carefully weighed against the likelihood that State prosecution will be sufficient to protect Federal interests."[73]

III. Public Money: State Laws Pertaining to Embezzlement and Misapplication

State statutes designed to protect public money from misuse are generally based on the common law concept of embezzlement. In common law, embezzlement involves a person in a position of trust or control improperly taking money or property for his own benefit.[74] Embezzlement differs from general

---

70 *See* Criminal Resource Manual §§ 1005-1009 (U.S. Dep't of Justice 2020), https://www.justice.gov/archives/jm/criminal-resource-manual-1001-1199 (explaining different intent requirements for each offense); United States v. De La Cruz, 469 F.3d 1064, 1068-69 (7th Cir. 2006) (explaining that ratification of an action will not be a complete defense if criminal intent is otherwise established).

71 Sabri v. United States, 541 U.S. 600, 604-06 (2004); United States v. Kranovich, 401 F.3d 1107, 1111-12 (9th Cir. 2005).

72 *See* United States v. Abbey, 560 F.3d 513, 522 (6th Cir. 2009).

73 Criminal Resource Manual § 1001; *see also* Kelly v. United States, 140 S. Ct. 1565, 1571-72 (2020) ("The upshot is that federal fraud law leaves much public corruption to the States (or their electorates) to rectify.").

74 *See* Medley v. State, 600 So. 2d 957, 960-61 (Miss. 1992) ("[E]mbezzlement is the wrongful conversion of property lawfully possessed by the person charged."). *See also* Brown v. State, 178 So. 3d 1234, 1261 n.17 (Miss. 2015) (citing Morissette v. United States, 342 U.S. 246, 272 (1952) and explaining that conversion may include misuse or abuse of property "where the initial possession by the converter was entirely lawful").

theft or larceny because with embezzlement the breach of trust is exceeding an otherwise permissible use of money or property.[75] While statutes criminalizing general business embezzlement may also apply to public officials who steal or misuse public funds,[76] this section focuses on state laws specifically aimed at protecting public funds that are controlled by public officials or agents for the benefit of the public. Misuse of public funds may also be considered official misconduct, which is discussed above.[77]

Laws designed specifically to punish corrupt officials who steal or misuse public funds differ from general embezzlement in a few key ways. These statutes usually enumerate more than one offense (for example embezzlement, conversion, fraudulent accounting, and unauthorized misuse), so the elements of the crime depend on the specific statute that is charged. These statutes do not necessarily require the defendant to have personally benefitted from the offense, although personal benefit is an element of the offense in some states. In some jurisdictions, the defendant may be presumed to know his conduct violates the law based on his official position.[78]

A. *Offense Conduct*

While the state statutes protecting public funds vary greatly in their language and specific offenses, the behavior prohibited can broadly be categorized as falling into three categories: embezzlement or conversion; accounting fraud and other irregularities; or misuse or misapplication.

---

75 *See* State v. Scott, 497 S.E.2d 735, 737-38 (S.C. Ct. App. 1998) (distinguishing a breach of trust from larceny on the grounds that larceny requires the defendant to gain possession of the property unlawfully, whereas with a breach of trust, the defendant has lawful possession of the property in the beginning, but exceeds the bounds of that lawful possession).

76 *See, e.g.*, R.I. Gen. Laws § 11-41-3 (general embezzlement statute); State v. Lough, 899 A.2d 468, 471 (R.I. 2006) (police officer embezzling public property charged under general embezzlement law).

77 *See, e.g.*, Howell v. State, 421 A.2d 892, 897 (Del. 1980) (finding that a board of education president profiting personally from the services and property of the department of education constituted official misconduct).

78 Under the Kentucky public trust statute, for example, a public servant is presumed to "know any legal obligation relative to his or her criminal liability." *See* Ky. Rev. Stat. Ann. § 522.050(2)(a).

1. Embezzlement or Conversion

Most statutes prohibit embezzlement or conversion by a public official or other person responsible for the safekeeping of public funds. As defined in the statutes, embezzlement generally consists of (1) being entrusted with money or property by virtue of the defendant's position, (2) appropriating that money or property to defendant's own use or the use of another person, and (3) thereby depriving the owner of the use of the property or money.[79] Some statutes expressly include the conduct of loaning the money or property or otherwise making a profit from the money or property.[80]

2. Accounting Irregularities

Many states specifically prohibit accounting irregularities or fraud, whether the accounting irregularities are stand-alone offenses or whether they give rise to the presumption of embezzlement.[81]

3. Misuse

Beyond prohibiting embezzlement and conversion to the defendant's own benefit as well as accounting fraud, the statutes may prohibit using public funds for any purpose not authorized by law, including refusing or omitting to pay money when lawfully due. This broad concept is expressed in various ways and may or may not involve a personal benefit to the defendant.[82]

---

79 The following statutes are examples of laws that express the general formulation of embezzlement: Cal. Penal Code § 424(a)(1); Colo. Rev. Stat. § 18-8-407; Idaho Code § 18-5701(1), (10); Ky. Rev. Stat. Ann. § 522.050(1); Mich. Comp. Laws § 750.175; Miss. Code Ann. § 97-11-25; Nev. Rev. Stat. Ann. § 197.210; P.R. Laws Ann. tit. 33, § 4895; S.C. Code Ann. § 16-13-210(A); Utah Code Ann. § 76-8-402(2)(a); V.I. Code Ann. tit. 14, § 1662(1); Wash. Rev. Code § 42.20.070(1); Wyo. Stat. § 6-5-110.

80 *E.g.*, Cal. Penal Code § 424(a)(2); Idaho Code § 18-5701(2).

81 *E.g.*, Cal. Penal Code § 424(a)(3), (4); Idaho Code § 18-5701(3), (4), (5), (6); Ind. Code 35-44.2-2-2(1), (2), (3); Ky. Rev. Stat. § 522.050(2)(b)(1), (2)(b)(2); Miss. Code Ann. § 97-11-29; Nev. Rev. Stat. Ann. § 204.030(1)(a), (1)(b); P.R. Laws Ann. tit. 33, § 4895(c); R.I. Gen. Laws §§ 11-28-1, 11-28-2; S.C. Code Ann. § 16-13-220; Utah Code Ann. § 76-8-402(2)(e), (f); V.I. Code Ann. tit. 14, § 1662(5), (6), (7); Wash. Rev. Code § 42.20.070(2), (3).

82 *See, e.g.*, Cal. Penal Code § 424(a)(2), (5), (6), (7); Colo. Rev. Stat. § 18-8-407(1); Idaho Code § 18-5701(2), (7), (8), (9), (10); Kan. Stat. Ann. § 21-6005(a); Mich. Comp. Laws § 750.490a; Minn. Stat. § 609.445; Miss. Code Ann. §§ 97-11-25, -27, -29, -31; Nev. Rev. Stat. Ann. §§ 204.010, 204.020, 204.030; N.J. Stat. Ann. § 2C:27-12; P.R. Laws Ann. tit. 33, § 4895(b), (d), (e); Utah Code Ann. § 76-8-402(2)(c), (d), (g), (h), (i); V.I. Code Ann. tit. 14, § 1662(2),

Misuse of public funds does not require that the defendant have actual custody of the public funds. Misuse can be committed by taking actions to authorize the expenditure of public moneys for nonpublic purposes.[83]

B. *Intent Issues*

Each statute pertaining to safekeeping of public money is worded and framed differently with respect to the exact prohibited conduct, as well as the required mental state. Statutes use common terms such as "knowingly," "fraudulently," and "willfully," which must be interpreted according to each state's statute and case law. A recurrent issue is mistake. Reasonable, good-faith mistakes made in handling public money are not criminalized, but establishing that a mistake is reasonable may be more difficult for public officials or other people specifically entrusted with public money than for non-officials.[84]

1. Unauthorized or Unlawful Use

Some statutes refer to an official or person in a position of trust making an unauthorized or unlawful use of public money. Where the presence or absence of legal authorization or obligation is an element of the offense, the prosecution must show that the defendant knew or should have known that his use of public money was not permitted.[85] This may be understood as actual knowledge or criminal negligence in failing to know that the act is unauthorized. In the context of public officials, a reasonable, good-faith mistake could mean that the defendant lacked the required intent.[86] Public officials are expected to know and embrace the duties imposed on them by law, however, and mistake defenses may be less successful for them than for less sophisticated defendants.[87]

---

(3), (4), (8), (9), (10); Wash. Rev. Code §§ 42.20.060; 42.20.070(4); Wyo. Stat. Ann. § 6-5-111.

83 *See, e.g.*, People v. Groat, 24 Cal. Rptr. 2d 15, 18 (Cal. Ct. App. 1993).

84 *See* Stark v. Superior Court, 257 P.3d 41, 55 (Cal. 2011) ("Limiting the requirement to actual knowledge would operate to shield those whose efforts at determining their duties does not comport with the significant public responsibility these individuals bear.").

85 *Stark*, 257 P.3d at 57-59.

86 *Id.* at 59.

87 *Id.* at 60.

2. "Knowingly" Committing an Offense

The word "knowingly," without reference to authorization of law, means simply knowledge of the facts.[88] Mental state requirements, such as knowledge, may be defined by statutory law.[89] Again, reasonable, good-faith mistake of fact can negate the "knowledge" element of offenses that require a knowing conversion or embezzlement.[90]

3. Willfulness

A "willful" mental state is typically understood as having the same meaning as general intent, which is having the conscious objective or desire to engage in the conduct or cause the result.[91] It excludes inadvertence or mistake, and generally means the same as "knowingly" or "intentionally."[92]

C. *Punishment*

State statutes that specifically address embezzlement or misuse of public funds often classify those offenses as either felonies or misdemeanors, depending on the amount of public money or property involved, and most disqualify the defendant from public office.[93] Some state statutes provide that a public

---

88 *Id.* at 63; State v. Olsen, 386 P.3d 908, 913 (Idaho 2016) (citing section 18-101(5) of the Idaho Code and explaining that "knowingly" requires "knowledge that the facts exist which bring the act or omission within the provisions of this code").

89 *See, e.g.*, WASH. REV. CODE § 9A.08.010 (defining "knowledge" as "aware[ness] of a fact, facts, or circumstances or result described by a statute defining an offense" or having "information which would lead a reasonable person in the same situation to believe that facts exist which facts are described by a statute defining an offense"); KAN. STAT. ANN. § 21-5202(i) (defining "knowingly" as with awareness of "the nature of such person's conduct or that the circumstances exist").

90 *See* Logan v. State, 951 So. 2d 630, 633 (Miss. Ct. App. 2007) (arguing unsuccessfully that defendant mistakenly believed that he had permission to take the embezzled property); People v. Fick, No. 276770, 2008 Mich. App. LEXIS 1427, at *9 (Mich. Ct. App. 2008) (explaining that "knowingly" in the Michigan embezzlement of public money statute "was intended to exclude from the definition of the offense mistakes of fact, accidents, such as the loss of the money by fire or other casualty, or inadvertent appropriations" and that "felonious intent is not an element of the crime").

91 *See, e.g.*, UTAH CODE ANN. § 76-2-103.

92 State v. Bell, 370 P.2d 508, 510 (Idaho 1962).

93 *See, e.g.*, CAL. PENAL CODE §§ 424, 425 (felony for embezzlement, falsification of accounts, and neglecting to pay over public moneys); COLO. REV. STAT. § 18-8-407 (embezzlement of public property is a felony); IDAHO CODE § 18-5702(1), (2), (3) (felony for public officer or employee

official may be disqualified from holding public office specifically for misuse of public money.[94]

Conclusion

Public officials have unique power and access to public money, both of which must be used honestly and for authorized, legal purposes. The ways that public officials can potentially abuse that power and access are too numerous and diverse to be comprehensively prohibited by a neat set of specific statutes. The state misconduct statutes and the state and federal statutes relating to misuse of public funds ensure that no abuse of power or access—no matter how creative or unusual—is immune from prosecution.

---

who is charged with safekeeping of public moneys or for any public officer or employee for an amount over $300); Kan. Stat. Ann. § 21-6005(b) (felony for crimes involving more than $1,000, but misdemeanor for less than $1,000); Ky. Rev. Stat. Ann. § 522.050(3) (abuse of public trust is a felony with varying severity depending on the amount); Mich. Comp. Laws §§ 750.175, 750.490a (felony for embezzlement, but misdemeanor for purchase by employee upon public credit for private use); Nev. Rev. Stat. Ann. §§ 197.210, 204.010, 204.020, 204.030, 204.050 (felony for crimes involving $650 or more, but misdemeanor for crimes involving less than $650); N.J. Stat. Ann. § 2C:27-12 (corruption of public resources may be a crime of the first, second, third, or fourth degree, depending on the value and purpose of the public resource); P.R. Laws Ann. tit. 33, § 4895 (felony); 11 R.I. Gen. Laws §§ 28-1, -2 (failure to pay state funds into treasury may result in imprisonment up to five years and fines of varying amounts); S.C. Code Ann. §§ 16-13-210(B), 16-13-230 (felony for embezzlement of any amount or breach of trust over $2,000; misdemeanor for breach of trust with fraudulent intention if the amount is $2,000 or less); Utah Code Ann. § 76-8-402 (misuse of public money is a felony with varying severity depending on the amount); Wash Rev. Code §§ 42.20.060; 42.20.070 (felony for misappropriation and falsification of accounts and for misappropriation by a treasurer, but misdemeanor for falsely auditing and paying claims); Wyo. Stat. Ann. §§ 6-5-110; 6-5-111 (felony for failure or refusal to account for, deliver and pay over public property, but misdemeanor for wrongful appropriation).

94 *E.g.*, Cal. Penal Code § 424(a); Colo. Rev. Stat. § 18-8-407(1); Idaho Code § 18-5702(5)(c); Kan. Stat. Ann. § 21-6005(b)(2); Ky. Rev. Stat. Ann. § 522.050(4); N.J. Stat. Ann. § 2C:51-2(d); S.C. Code Ann. § 16-13-210(C); Utah Code Ann. § 76-8-404; V.I. Code Ann. tit. 14, §§ 1662-63. For more about removal or disqualification from holding office, see Chapter 6.3, Part I.

CHAPTER 3.3

Political Transparency & Disclosure

Marissa G. Walker

Marissa G. Walker is Program Counsel for the Center for Ethics & Public Integrity, National Attorneys General Training & Research Institute, National Association of Attorneys General.

INTRODUCTION

Involvement in the political process is "central to the meaning and purpose of the First Amendment,"[1] but federal and state laws regulating campaign finance also protect the governmental interest in preventing corruption and the appearance of corruption.[2] Campaign finance and lobbying disclosure requirements protect the public's interest in knowing the identity and interests of those involved in political spending.[3] "Otherwise the voice of the people may all too easily be drowned out by the voice of special interest groups seeking favored treatment while masquerading as proponents of the public weal."[4] Disclosure requirements do not prohibit seeking to influence the political process, but they ask "who is being hired [to attempt to influence the political process], who is putting up the money, and how much."[5] In this way, laws regulating political

1 *See* Citizens United v. Fed. Election Comm'n, 558 U.S. 310, 329 (2010).

2 *Id.* at 345 (citing Buckley v. Valeo, 424 U.S. 1, 25 (1976)).

3 *See id.* at 366-67.

4 United States v. Harriss, 347 U.S. 612, 625 (1954) (upholding lobbying disclosure requirements as constitutionally valid).

5 *Id.*

spending and influence maintain the integrity of the basic governmental process.[6] Knowing and willful violation of these requirements carries serious criminal penalties.[7]

I. Campaign Finance

Federal and state laws regulate how candidates obtain and spend money in campaigns for public office in order to limit "the disproportionate influence of wealthy individuals and special interest groups" on our elective system of government, and in order to "[d]eter abuses by mandating public disclosure of campaign finances."[8] Size limitations on contributions preserve "the integrity of our system of representative democracy" because large contributions may be "given to secure political quid pro quos from current and potential office holders."[9] Moreover, size limits and disclosure requirements prevent the "appearance of corruption" by reducing "opportunities for abuse" and by informing the public about who is seeking to influence an election.[10]

A. *First Amendment Considerations*

The First Amendment prohibits any law "abridging the freedom of speech."[11] "When the government attempts to regulate the financing of political campaigns and express advocacy through contribution limits, therefore, it must have a countervailing interest that outweighs the limit's burden on the exercise of First Amendment rights."[12] The Supreme Court has recognized that the gov-

---

6 *Id.*

7 *See infra* Parts I(B), II(C).

8 *See* Fed. Election Comm'n, The FEC and the Federal Campaign Finance Law (2004, updated 2019), https://transition.fec.gov/pages/brochures/fecfeca.shtml.

9 Buckley v. Valeo, 424 U.S. 1, 26-27 (1976). FECA violations do not require proof of a quid pro quo, but accepting campaign contributions may violate the Hobbs Act, 18 U.S.C. § 1951, if accepted in exchange for a specific requested exercise of official authority. Evans v. United States, 504 U.S. 255, 268 (1992); McCormick v. United States, 500 U.S. 257, 273 (1991).

10 *Buckley*, 424 U.S. at 27; Citizens United v. Fed. Election Comm'n, 558 U.S. 310, 367-69 (2010).

11 U.S. Const. amend. I.

12 SpeechNow.org v. Fed. Election Comm'n, 599 F.3d 686, 692 (D.C. Cir. 2010).

ernment's interest in preventing corruption or the appearance of corruption is sufficiently important to outweigh First Amendment interests.[13]

In *Buckley* v. *Valeo*,[14] the Supreme Court upheld disclosure requirements and limits on campaign contributions of the Federal Election Campaign Act (FECA),[15] explaining that while disclosing money given to candidates is beneficial, "disclosure was only a partial measure, and that contribution ceilings were a necessary legislative concomitant to deal with the reality or appearance of corruption inherent in a system permitting unlimited financial contributions . . . ."[16] The Court distinguished independent expenditures from contributions and held that the anticorruption justification falls short with respect to independent expenditures.[17] "The absence of prearrangement and coordination of an expenditure with the candidate or his agent not only undermines the value of the expenditure to the candidate, but also alleviates the danger that expenditures will be given as a quid pro quo for improper commitments from the candidate."[18] Later, in *First National Bank* v. *Bellotti*,[19] the Court struck down a state law prohibition on corporate independent expenditures with respect to referenda issues, ruling that the First Amendment does not allow political speech restrictions based on a speaker's corporate identity, but it did not opine on "the quite different context of participation in a political campaign for election to public office."[20]

In *Citizens United*, the Supreme Court ruled that there is no anticorruption interest in limiting independent expenditures of individuals or corporations who wish to engage in political speech.[21] The Court emphasized that the government "may not suppress political speech on the basis of the

---

13 *Id.*

14 424 U.S. 1 (1976).

15 52 U.S.C. §§ 30101-30146 (2018).

16 *Buckley*, 424 U.S. at 27-28.

17 *Id.* at 45. An independent expenditure is money spent by a person "expressly advocating the election or defeat of a clearly identified candidate" and "that is not made in concert or cooperation with or at the request or suggestion of such candidate, the candidate's authorized political committee, or their agents, or a political party committee or its agents." 52 U.S.C. § 30101(17).

18 *Buckley*, 424 U.S. at 47.

19 435 U.S. 765 (1978).

20 *Id.* at 784, 787-88 n.26.

21 Citizens United v. Fed. Election Comm'n, 558 U.S. 310, 357 (2010).

speaker's corporate identity."[22] When expenditures are independent, the Court held, any government restrictions on those expenditures violate the First Amendment because the government has no legitimate interest in regulating them.[23] The lack of coordination between the money and the candidate shows that the voters retain ultimate power. "The fact that a corporation, or any other speaker, is willing to spend money to try to persuade voters presupposes that the people have the ultimate influence over elected officials," and insulates elected officials from the corrupting influence of the corporate expenditure, no matter how large.[24] Disclaimer and disclosure requirements, however, were constitutional because the government did have a legitimate interest in those regulations: (1) disclaimer requirements avoided confusion by making it clear ads were not funded by a political party or a candidate and (2) disclosure requirements fulfilled the public's interest in knowing who was speaking about a candidate.[25] Under *Citizens United*, laws restricting contributions to organizations that engage only in independent expenditures[26] and state laws restricting or prohibiting corporate expenditures have been invalidated.[27] However, restrictions and limits on contributions as well as disclosure and disclaimer requirements have been consistently upheld as based on a governmental interest in providing the public with information about the sources of campaign funds, as well as the interest in deterring corruption and the appearance of corruption.[28]

B. *Criminal Violations of Campaign Finance Laws*

Federal law criminalizes both willfully false disclosures and contributions or expenditures knowingly and willfully made in violation of its restrictions.[29] FECA limits the size of contributions based on donor type and recipient, prohibits contributions from certain potentially corrupting

---

22 *Id.* at 365.

23 *See id.* at 357-58.

24 *Id.* at 360.

25 *Id.* at 366-69.

26 SpeechNow.org v. Fed. Election Comm'n, 599 F.3d 686, 696 (D.C. Cir. 2010).

27 Am. Tradition P'ship v. Bullock, 567 U.S. 516, 516-17 (2012) (striking down Montana's century-old prohibition on corporate expenditures despite a history of corporate corruption in that state).

28 *SpeechNow.org*, 599 F.3d at 696 (citing Buckley v. Valeo, 424 U.S. 1, 66 (1976)).

29 52 U.S.C. § 30109(d) (2018). False disclosures may also violate the federal False Statement Statute, 18 U.S.C. § 1001 (2018), or may amount to a conspiracy to defraud the United States, 18 U.S.C. § 371 (2018).

entities—such as corporations, unions, banks, and foreign nationals—and imposes strict disclosure requirements on the campaign finance process.[30] To prevent circumvention of its restrictions, it also prohibits a person from making a contribution in the name of another by, for example, giving funds to a straw donor so that the straw donor's name would be disclosed and the true source of the funds concealed.[31]

The states and territories have campaign finance laws and regulations that are, in many aspects, similar to the federal laws, although each state's law is unique. The National Conference of State Legislatures comprehensively analyzes and summarizes the campaign finance laws of all fifty states.[32]

1. Willful Mens Rea

Criminal violations of federal campaign financing laws require proof that the conduct was committed knowingly and willfully.[33] "The word 'willfully' is sometimes said to be 'a word of many meanings' whose construction is often dependent on the context in which it appears."[34] In the context of "overwhelmingly complex" laws like tax laws, the word requires proof that the defendant actually knew of the complex law at issue in order to avoid criminalizing and chilling otherwise intuitively lawful conduct.[35] However, because "campaign contribution laws are not so complex or surprising that the average citizen would likely be trapped by them," a violation only requires the government to prove that defendants "intended to violate the law (whatever the law was); but it need not prove [d]efendants' awareness of the specific law's commands."[36]

All states and territories criminalize knowing and willful violations of campaign finance laws, although those campaign finance laws may differ. A

---

30 U.S. Dep't of Justice, Federal Prosecution of Election Offenses 122 (Richard C. Pilger ed., 2017).

31 *See* 52 U.S.C. § 30122.

32 *See Campaign Finance*, Nat'l Conf. of State Legislatures (Oct. 15, 2020), https://www.ncsl.org/research/elections-and-campaigns/ncsl-s-campaign-finance-webpages.aspx.

33 52 U.S.C. § 30109(d).

34 United States v. Danielczyk, 788 F. Supp. 2d 472, 487 (E.D. Va. 2011) (citing Bryan v. United States, 524 U.S. 184, 191 (1998)), *rev'd on other grounds*, 683 F.3d 611 (4th Cir. 2012), *and reconsideration denied by* 917 F. Supp. 2d 573 (E.D. Va. 2013).

35 *Id.*

36 *Id.* at 490-91; United States v. Whittemore, 776 F.3d 1074, 1080-81 (9th Cir. 2015).

majority of states and territories categorize these violations as misdemeanors, although felony prosecution is possible in some jurisdictions.[37]

2. Criminal Avoidance of Limits and Disclosure Requirements

If a candidate or campaign accepts a benefit or service tantamount to a contribution and fails to disclose it (or if its value exceeds contribution limits), it may be a prosecutable offense. Whether a benefit amounts to a "contribution" and "expenditure" is governed by statute, which includes definitions as well as examples of monetary exchanges that are not regulated as contributions or expenditures.[38] Federal law requires candidate committees, party committees, and political action committees (PACs) to file periodic reports disclosing the money they raise and spend.[39] All states have unique disclosure requirements that require different participants in an election (candidates, parties, PACs, possibly donors) to disclose contributions, expenditures, sometimes debts, and sometimes independent expenditures in a specified manner and at a specified time.[40] While the minutiae of those disclosure requirements are beyond the

---

37 *E.g.*, Ala. Code § 17-5-19 (felony possible); Alaska Stat. § 15.56.012; Am. Samoa Code Ann. § 6.1723; Ariz. Rev. Stat. Ann. § 16-943; Ark. Code Ann. § 7-6-202; Cal. Gov. Code § 91000; Colo. Rev. Stat. § 1-13-107; Conn. Gen. Stat. § 9-623 (felony); 15 Del. Code Ann. § 8043; D.C. Code § 1-1163.35(c) (imprisonment up to 5 years); Fla. Stat. § 106.19; Ga. Code Ann. § 21-5-9; 3 Guam Code Ann. § 8102; Haw. Rev. Stat. § 11-412; Idaho Code § 67-6625; 10 Ill. Comp. Stat. 5/9-26; Ind. Code §§ 3-14-1-1 to 3-14-1-17; Iowa Code § 68A.701; Kan. Stat. Ann. §§ 25-4168, 25-4171; Ky. Rev. Stat. Ann. § 121.990 (felony); La. Rev. Stat. § 18:1505.6; Me. Stat. tit. 21-A, § 1004-A (monetary penalties); Md. Code Ann., Election Law § 13-603; Mass. Gen. Laws ch. 55, § 2; Mich. Comp. Laws § 169.252; Minn. Stat. §§ 10A.022, 211A.11; Miss. Code Ann. § 23-15-811; Mo. Rev. Stat. § 130.081; Mont. Code Ann. § 13-35-103; Neb. Rev. Stat. § 49-1472; Nev. Rev. Stat. § 294A.100 (felony possible); N.H. Rev. Stat. Ann. § 664:21; N.J. Stat. Ann. § 19:44A-21; N.M. Stat. Ann. § 1-19-36; N.Y. Elec. Law § 14-126; N.C. Gen. Stat. § 163-278.27; N.D. Cent. Code § 16.1-08.1-03.3; 1 N. Mar. I. Code § 6428; Ohio Rev. Code Ann. § 3599.40; Okla. Stat. tit. 21, §§ 187, 187.1, 187.2 (felony possible); Or. Rev. Stat. § 260.993 (felony possible); 25 Pa. Cons. Stat. § 3543; P.R. Laws Ann. tit. 16, § 633d; R.I. Gen. Laws § 17-25-13; S.C. Code Ann. § 8-13-1520; S.D. Codified Laws § 12-27-22; Tenn. Code Ann. § 2-10-308 (civil penalty); Tex. Elec. Code Ann. § 253.004; Utah Code Ann. § 20A-1-609; Vt. Stat. Ann. tit. 17, § 2903; V.I. Code Ann. tit. 18, § 911; Va. Code Ann. § 24.2-953; Wash. Rev. Code Ann. § 42.17A.750; W. Va. Code § 3-8-5d; Wis. Stat. § 11.1401 (felony possible); Wyo. Stat. Ann. § 22-26-112. Unless otherwise indicated, all citations to statutes in this chapter refer to the version current at the time of publishing.

38 *See* 52 U.S.C. § 30101(8), (9) (2018).

39 *See id.* § 30104.

40 The National Conference of State Legislatures has compiled state disclosure and reporting

scope of this chapter, failure to disclose required information or making a false statement in a disclosure could result in a criminal violation.[41] For example, if a supporter or associate of a candidate for office pays money to someone in exchange for that person not making public damaging allegations against the candidate, that payment may be considered tantamount to a campaign contribution and, if not disclosed or if larger than the statutory limit, could be criminal.[42]

3. Prohibited Types of Contributions and Attempts to Evade Prohibitions

Certain types of contributions—particularly corporate and foreign contributions—are prohibited by state and federal law. Evading such prohibitions may result in two prosecutable offenses: the underlying violation itself and the use of the evasion tactic, such as use of a conduit or straw donor or an illegal reimbursement scheme.

a. Ban on Corporate and Foreign Contributions

Federal law prohibits contributions and expenditures by certain individuals and organizations, including corporations[43] and foreign nationals.[44] Regarding corporations, a federal law was passed in 1907 to prohibit them from contributing directly to candidates for office.[45] The current federal statute prohibits corporations from making a contribution or expenditure in connection with certain federal elections, but permits "the establishment, administration, and solicitation of contributions to a separate segregated fund to be utilized for political purposes" through a PAC.[46] PACs must register and disclose their activities but may make contributions and expenditures in connection

---

requirements. *See Disclosure and Reporting Requirements*, NAT'L CONF. OF STATE LEGISLATURES (July 17, 2015), https://www.ncsl.org/research/elections-and-campaigns/disclosure-and-reporting-requirements.aspx.

41 *See* 52 U.S.C. § 30109(d).

42 *See, e.g.*, Information at 11-18, United States v. Cohen, No. 18 Cr. 602 (S.D.N.Y. Aug. 21, 2018) (charging violations of contribution limits and corporate contribution prohibition); Indictment at 2-4, United States v. Edwards, No. 11 Cr. 161-1 (M.D.N.C. June 3, 2011) (charging violations of contribution limits, conspiracy, and false statements).

43 52 U.S.C. § 30118(a).

44 52 U.S.C. § 30121.

45 FEC v. Beaumont, 539 U.S. 146, 149 (2003).

46 *Id.*; 52 U.S.C. § 30118(b)(2)(C).

with federal elections using contributions received from employees of the corporation.[47]

Many states also ban corporate contributions.[48] For example, under Massachusetts law, corporations may not make any contributions to a candidate or to a candidate's committee, may not establish or administer a PAC, and may not contribute to a PAC that is not an independent expenditure PAC, but they may make unlimited independent expenditures, subject to certain disclosure requirements and may also make unlimited contributions to independent expenditure PACs.[49]

Foreign nationals are prohibited by federal law from contributing or donating in connection with federal, local, and state elections, from making independent expenditures to expressly advocate the election or defeat of a candidate, and from donating to outside groups that would contribute to candidates or finance express-advocacy expenditures.[50]

b. Evasion of Prohibitions

Contributing in another person's name or under a false name is prohibited to prevent attempts to thwart prohibitions, disclosure requirements, and contribution limits.[51] The prohibition on using a false name also prohibits using a straw donor to make an indirect contribution, whether accomplished by advancement or by reimbursement, because using a straw donor conceals the

---

47 *Beaumont*, 539 U.S. at 149.

48 Twenty-two states ban corporate contributions. Nat'l Conf. of State Legislatures, State Limits on Contributions to Candidates, 2019-2020 Election Cycle (June 2019), at https://www.ncsl.org/Portals/1/Documents/Elections/Contribution-Limits-to-Candidates-2019-2020.pdf. As of June 2019, the states that prohibit corporate contributions were Alaska, Arizona, Arkansas, Colorado, Connecticut, Iowa, Kentucky, Massachusetts, Michigan, Minnesota, Missouri, Montana, North Carolina, North Dakota, Ohio, Oklahoma, Pennsylvania, Rhode Island, Texas, West Virginia, Wisconsin, and Wyoming. *Id.*

49 1A Auto, Inc. v. Dir. of the Office of Campaign & Political Fin., 105 N.E.3d 1178, 1180 (Mass. 2018) (rejecting a First Amendment challenge to the law), *cert. denied* __ U.S. __, 139 S. Ct. 2613 (2019).

50 52 U.S.C. § 30121; *see also* Bluman v. Fed. Election Comm'n, 800 F. Supp. 2d 281, 287 (D.D.C. 2011) ("The government may exclude foreign citizens from activities intimately related to the process of democratic self-government." (quotation and citation omitted)), *aff'd*, 565 U.S. 1104 (2012).

51 *See* 52 U.S.C. § 30122.

true origin of the funds.[52] State statutes similarly prohibit use of a false name, straw donor, or reimbursement contributions.[53] Some states may classify an intentional violation of the straw donor prohibition involving a certain minimum amount of money as a felony.[54]

4. Illegal Coordination May Trigger Contribution Restrictions

"[A]lthough the First Amendment protects truly independent expenditures for political speech, the government is entitled to regulate coordination between candidates' campaigns and purportedly independent groups."[55] Coordination between a candidate and a purportedly independent group would hamper laws requiring campaigns to disclose donors and limit contributions.[56] The Supreme Court has not determined what coordination means,[57] and FECA does not define coordination, but federal regulations define coordination as "made in cooperation, consultation or concert with, or at the request or

---

52 United States v. O'Donnell, 608 F.3d 546, 549 (9th Cir. 2010); Mariani v. United States, 212 F.3d 761, 775 (3d Cir. 2000).

53 *See, e.g.*, FLA. STAT. § 106.08(5)(a) ("A person may not make any contribution through or in the name of another, directly or indirectly, in any election."). In 2017, Michael Grieco, then the Miami Beach Commissioner and mayoral candidate, pleaded no contest to a state law violation of Florida's prohibition on straw donors for accepting money that originated from a foreign source. *Grieco Resigns as Miami Beach Commissioner, Accepts Plea Deal*, CBS MIAMI (Oct. 24, 2017), https://miami.cbslocal.com/2017/10/24/michael-grieco-resign-criminal-charge-2/. The Miami-Dade State Attorney at the time commented that "You cannot give money through a straw donor. It makes perfect sense. The whole purpose is for contributions to a PAC or a campaign is to have open transparency on who is giving to whom." *Id.*

54 *See, e.g.*, N.C. GEN. STAT. § 163-278.14(a) ("No individual, political committee, or other entity shall make any contribution anonymously or in the name of another."); *id.* at § 163-278.27(c) ("A person who intentionally violates [the straw donor prohibition] and the unlawful contributions total more than ten thousand dollars ($10,000) per election is guilty of a Class I felony."). In North Carolina, "no statute of limitations bars prosecution of a felony." State v. Gates, 781 S.E.2d 883, 888 (N.C. Ct. App. 2016) (citing State v. Johnson, 167 S.E.2d 274, 279 (N.C. 1969)).

55 O'Keefe v. Chisholm, 769 F.3d 936, 941 (7th Cir. 2014). *See also* Statement of Facts 3-5, United States v. Harber, No. 1:14-CR-373-LO (E.D. Va. Feb. 12, 2015); Press Release, U.S. Att'y's Office, E. Dist. of Va., U.S. Dep't of Justice, Alexandria Man Sentenced to 24 Months in Prison for Coordinated Campaign Contributions and False Statements (June 12, 2015), https://www.justice.gov/usao-edva/pr/alexandria-man-sentenced-24-months-prison-coordinated-campaign-contributions-and-false (announcing "the first criminal prosecution in the United States based upon the coordination of campaign contributions between political committees").

56 *O'Keefe*, 769 F.3d at 941.

57 *Id.*

suggestion of, a candidate, a candidate's authorized committee, or a political party committee."[58] State statutes, regulations, or case law may similarly determine what contacts between a candidate and a purportedly independent entity are permissible.[59] Like federal law, state laws may similarly mandate that if a candidate's committee coordinates campaign activities with a supposedly independent group, spending by that group must be treated as a campaign contributions subject to reporting laws.[60]

5. Digital Advertising Disclosure

An emerging area of state campaign finance regulation relates to digital advertising. For example, the State of Washington requires advertisers in any medium—print, broadcast, or online—to maintain accurate records of sponsors of political advertisements in state and local elections,[61] and has enforced that requirement against social media companies.[62] The purpose of such a requirement is to allow the public to understand the source of political advertisements.[63] Other states have enacted or have attempted to enact similar laws.[64]

---

58 11 C.F.R. § 109.20(a) (2020).

59 *See, e.g.*, Archer v. Chisholm, 191 F. Supp. 3d 932, 939 (E.D. Wis. 2016) (citing Wis. Coal. for Voter Participation, Inc. v. Wisc. Elections Bd., 605 N.W.2d 654, 659-60 (Wis. Ct. App. 1999)).

60 *Id.*

61 Wash. Rev. Code § 42.17A.345.

62 Stipulation and Agreed Judgment, State v. Twitter, Inc., No. 20-2-15134-3 (Wash. Super. Ct. Oct. 12, 2020), https://agportal-s3bucket.s3.amazonaws.com/Signed%20Twitter%20Judgment.pdf; Stipulation and Judgment, State v. Google, Inc., No. 18-2-14130-3 SEA (Wash. Super. Ct. Dec. 18, 2018), https://agportal-s3bucket.s3.amazonaws.com/GoogleJudgment-20181218_0.pdf; Stipulation and Judgment, State v. Facebook, Inc., No. 18-2-14129-0 SEA (Wash. Super. Ct. Dec. 18, 2018), https://agportal-s3bucket.s3.amazonaws.com/FacebookJudgment-20181218_0.pdf.

63 *See* Press Release, Wash. State Office of the Att'y Gen., AG Ferguson Releases Statement After Defeating Facebook's Attempt to Dismiss Campaign Fin. Lawsuit (Aug. 7, 2020), https://www.atg.wa.gov/news/news-releases/ag-ferguson-releases-statement-after-defeating-facebook-s-attempt-dismiss.

64 *See Digital Political Ads*, Nat'l Conf. of State Legislatures (Aug. 31, 2020), https://www.ncsl.org/research/elections-and-campaigns/digital-political-ads.aspx (discussing various legislative attempts to regulate digital political advertising, including successful efforts in California, Maryland, New York, and Virginia).

II. Lobbying

The First Amendment protects lobbying, which is essentially "petition[ing] the government for a redress of grievances."[65] One scholar characterizes "the social function of lobbying [a]s to take money and turn it into political power . . . through the production of information and the careful use of influence."[66] Because of the inherent exchange of money and power in lobbying, federal and state laws regulate lobbying through registration and regular reporting of lobbying activities. Additionally, many of the criminal laws pertaining to bribery and conflicts of interest restrict how an official may interact with lobbyists, among other people.[67]

A. *What Behavior Triggers Registration and Reporting Requirements*

1. Federal Law

The federal Lobbying Disclosure Act (LDA)[68] requires lobbyists to register and report on their activities. An individual is a lobbyist for a particular client if he or she makes more than one lobbying contact for that client and if "lobbying activities" constitute at least twenty percent of the individual's time in services for that client during a calendar quarter. In addition to the time threshold, a monetary amount threshold must also be met before triggering registration and reporting requirements.[69]

---

65 U.S. Const. amend. I.

66 Zephyr Teachout, Corruption in America 144 (2014).

67 *See* Chapters 3.1, 3.4.

68 2 U.S.C. §§ 1601-1614 (2018).

69 The federal LDA requires that lobbying firms must file a registration for each lobbying client that produces income for the firm of at least $3,000 per quarter. 2 U.S.C. § 1603(a); Sec'y of the S. & Clerk of the H.R., Lobbying Disclosure Act Guidance 2 (Jan. 31, 2017), https://lobbyingdisclosure.house.gov/ldaguidance.pdf (updating registration threshold). State laws may have similar time and money thresholds. *See, e.g.*, Conn. Gen. Stat. § 1-91(12) (compensation or expenditures of $3,000 or more in any calendar year); Me. Stat. tit. 3, § 312-A(10) (more than eight hours in any calendar month); Mass. Gen. Laws ch. 3, § 39 (threshold of twenty-five hours or more than $2,500 during the reporting period). *See also* Memorandum Op. and Order at 16 n.9, *In re* Search of Information, No. 20-gj-35 (BAH) (D.D.C. Aug. 28, 2020), https://www.dcd.uscourts.gov/sites/dcd/files/20gj35%20Partial%20Unsealing%20Order.pdf (noting the potential difficulty of proving the time and money thresholds in a criminal case). Note that in 2021, Congress began considering legislation that would change the federal lobbying laws in significant ways. For the People Act of 2021, H.R. 1, S. 1, 117th Cong. (2021).

Assuming that the time and compensation thresholds are met, whether an activity constitutes a "lobbying contact" is defined under federal law as "any oral or written communication" to statutorily defined executive or legislative branch officials made on behalf of a client with regard to:

> (i) the formulation, modification, or adoption of Federal legislation (including legislative proposals);
>
> (ii) the formulation, modification, or adoption of a Federal rule, regulation, Executive order, or any other program, policy, or position of the United States Government;
>
> (iii) the administration or execution of a Federal program or policy (including the negotiation, award, or administration of a Federal contract, grant, loan, permit, or license); or
>
> (iv) the nomination or confirmation of a person for a position subject to confirmation by the Senate.[70]

The LDA further lists nineteen examples of what does not constitute lobbying contacts.[71] "Lobbying activities" means the four categories outlined above "and efforts in support of such contacts."[72] A "client" is "any person or entity that employs or retains another person for financial or other compensation to conduct lobbying activities on behalf of that person or entity."[73]

2. State Laws

State laws vary in terms of what types of activities require registration and reporting.[74] A handful of state laws narrowly define lobbying activity

---

70 2 U.S.C. § 1602(8)(A)(i)-(iv).

71 *Id.* § 1602(8)(B).

72 *Id.* § 1602(7).

73 *Id.* § 1602(2).

74 The Council on Governmental Ethics Laws produces a comprehensive annual guide to state lobbying laws, including changes to legislation and recent litigation concerning lobbying issues. *See generally* KENNETH A. GROSS, COGEL BLUE BOOK: 2020 LOBBYING UPDATE ON LITIGATION AND LEGISLATION, U.S. & CANADA (2020) (categorizing and summarizing state lobbying laws). The National Conference of State Legislatures also summarizes what conduct triggers registration and reporting requirements in each state. *See How States Define Lobbying and Lobbyist*, NAT'L CONF. OF STATE LEGISLATURES (Sept. 8, 2020), https://www.ncsl.org/

as attempting to influence legislation only.[75] Some state laws further include attempts to influence legislation as well as administrative action or rulemaking.[76] The remainder of the state laws, like the federal law, also regulate attempts to influence administration of a program or policy, possibly including awarding of contracts.[77] Some states define lobbying to include indirect communications with public officials, known as grassroots lobbying.[78]

B. *What Must be Disclosed?*

While the details of registration and reporting requirements vary by jurisdiction, lobbyist registration may require disclosure of the registrant's identity, the client, the business or activities of each, and the names and backgrounds of the registrant's employees expected to work for the client.[79] Additionally, the registrant may be required to identify any organization that contributes money to fund the lobbying activities or that actively participates in lobbying activities.[80] Registration also typically requires disclosure of the general issue areas that the registrant expects to address or has already addressed on behalf of the client.[81]

Under federal law, registration also must disclose any foreign entity that holds at least twenty percent equitable ownership in the client or any contributing organization, or that directly or indirectly, in whole or in major part, plans, supervises, controls, directs, finances, or subsidizes the activities of the client or any contributing organization; or is an affiliate of the client or any contributing organization and has a direct interest in the outcome of the lobbying activity.[82]

Regular lobbying reports occur at statutorily required intervals and typically require reporting of any changes or updates since the original registration,

---

research/ethics/50-state-chart-lobby-definitions.aspx.

75 *See, e.g.*, ME. STAT. tit. 3, § 312-A.

76 *See, e.g.*, ALASKA STAT. § 24.45.011; COLO. REV. STAT. § 24-6-301(3.5).

77 *See, e.g.*, ALA. CODE § 36-25-1.1; ARIZ. REV. STAT. ANN. § 41-1231(11).

78 *See, e.g.*, CAL. GOV'T CODE § 82045(e); CONN. GEN. STAT. § 1-91(11); ME. STAT. tit. 3, § 312-A(7-B); WASH. REV. CODE § 42.17A.640.

79 *See* 2 U.S.C. § 1603(b); *Lobbyist Registration Requirements*, NAT'L CONF. OF STATE LEGISLATURES (Sept. 8, 2020), https://www.ncsl.org/research/ethics/50-state-chart-lobbyist-registration-requirements.aspx.

80 *See* 2 U.S.C. § 1603(b).

81 *See id.*

82 *Id.* § 1603(b)(4).

as well as income received from the client and expenses incurred.[83] Federal registrants and registered lobbyists are also required to file periodic disclosures of campaign contributions and certification of compliance with gift rules.[84]

C. *Penalties*

The LDA has both civil and criminal penalties. A civil penalty of up to $200,000 may be imposed for knowingly failing to remedy a defective filing after notice of such defect or for knowingly failing to comply with any other provision of the LDA.[85] Imprisonment of up to five years and a criminal fine may be imposed for knowingly and corruptly failing to comply with any provision of the LDA.[86] "Knowingly and corruptly" failing to comply requires proof of a "consciousness of wrongdoing."[87]

In some states, intentional violation of lobbying laws may be categorized as a misdemeanor.[88] In other states, it may be penalized as a felony.[89]

Conclusion

Transparency laws protect the integrity of representative government by limiting corruption and the appearance of corruption, and by providing information to the public about the identity and interests of those who seek to influence public officials through campaign contributions and lobbying. These requirements enable citizens to hold their officials accountable and engender confidence in our government.

---

83 *Id.* § 1604(b). *See also 50 State Chart: Lobbyist Activity Report Requirements*, Nat'l Conf. of State Legislatures (May 15, 2018), https://www.ncsl.org/research/ethics/50-state-chart-lobbyist-report-requirements.aspx.

84 2 U.S.C. § 1604(d).

85 *Id.* § 1606(a).

86 *Id.* § 1606(b). *See also* Press Release, U.S. Att'y's Office, N. Dist. of Cal., U.S. Dep't of Justice, Lobbyist Jack Abramoff and CEO Rowland Marcus Andrade Charged With Fraud in Connection With $5 Million Initial Coin Offering Of Cryptocurrency AML Bitcoin (June 25, 2020), https://www.justice.gov/usao-ndca/pr/lobbyist-jack-abramoff-and-ceo-rowland-marcus-andrade-charged-fraud-connection-5 (announcing the "first ever known prosecution of a lobbyist for a criminal violation of the [LDA]").

87 Arthur Andersen LLP v. United States, 544 U.S. 696, 705-06 (2005) (interpreting mens rea for a different statute that also required knowing, corrupt intent).

88 *See, e.g.*, Cal. Gov't Code § 91000; Colo. Rev. Stat. § 24-6-309.

89 *See, e.g.*, Ala. Code § 36-25-27; Conn. Gen. Stat. § 1-100.

Chapter 3.4

Criminal Conflicts of Interest

Marissa G. Walker

Marissa G. Walker is Program Counsel for the Center for Ethics & Public Integrity, National Attorneys General Training & Research Institute, National Association of Attorneys General.

Introduction

Conflict of interest laws aim to prevent a public official from putting himself in a position to be tempted to take unfair personal advantage of his official position.[1] Conflicts of interest are criminalized under federal law adjacent to the more infamous offense of bribery.[2] Although bribery laws focus on com-

---

1 United States v. Miss. Valley Generating Co., 364 U.S. 520, 549-50 (1961) (explaining that conflict of interest rules "attempt[] to prevent honest government agents from succumbing to temptation by making it illegal for them to enter into relationships which are fraught with temptation").

2 18 U.S.C. §§ 201-227. Beyond these criminal statutes, an extensive set of federal regulations apply to government officials and employees. *See generally* 5 C.F.R. §§ 2635.101-2635.902. Unless otherwise indicated, all statutes cited in this chapter refer to the version of the statute current at the time of publication.

pensation offered as a quid pro quo for an official act, conflict of interest laws are "prophylactic" in nature.[3] Conflict of interest rules are:

> directed at an evil which endangers the very fabric of a democratic society, for a democracy is effective only if the people have faith in those who govern, and that faith is bound to be shattered when high officials and their appointees engage in activities which arouse suspicions of malfeasance and corruption.[4]

In other words, a public official may violate conflict of interest rules without necessarily committing any actual harm or deriving any personal benefit.[5]

States and territories take a variety of approaches to preventing conflicts of interest and penalizing violations. In order to consider these various state conflict of interest laws and concepts in an organized way, this chapter uses the federal criminal laws pertaining to conflicts of interest as a guide to understanding analogous state laws that may reach the same underlying conduct. The chapter covers official conduct affecting a personal financial interest, nepotism, representing another interest in a particular matter before government, receiving money from third parties not relating to a particular matter, activity after government service, financial disclosure obligations, and restrictions on confidential information.

I. Official Conduct Affecting Personal Financial Interest

Section 208 of title 18 of the United States Code prohibits current federal government employees from:

---

3 Crandon v. United States, 494 U.S. 152, 158-59 (1990).

4 *Miss. Valley Generating Co.*, 364 U.S. at 562. *See also* Peter J. Henning, The Prosecution and Defense of Public Corruption: The Law and Legal Strategies, § 9.05[1] (Matthew Bender, 2020 ed.) (quoting *Miss. Valley Generating Co.* and thoroughly analyzing the federal laws pertaining to conflicts of interest).

5 *Id.* at 549; *Crandon*, 494 U.S. at 164 ("Congress appropriately enacts prophylactic rules that are intended to prevent even the appearance of wrongdoing and that may apply to conduct that has caused no actual injury to the United States.").

> participat[ing] personally and substantially . . . through decision, approval, disapproval, recommendation, the rendering of advice, investigation, or otherwise, in a judicial or other proceeding, application, request for a ruling or other determination, contract, claim, controversy, charge, accusation, arrest, or other particular matter in which, to his knowledge, he, his spouse, minor child, general partner, organization in which he is serving as officer, director, trustee, general partner or employee, or any person or organization with whom he is negotiating or has any arrangement concerning prospective employment, has a financial interest . . . .[6]

State governments have enacted various similar statutes in order to "remove from public officials the temptation to take advantage of their official positions to 'feather their own nests' by letting to themselves or to firms or corporations in which they are interested contracts for services, materials, supplies, or the like."[7] Based on the concept that "[n]o man can serve two masters," these laws "enforce a well-recognized and salutary principle, both of the moral law and of public policy, that he who is entrusted with the business of others cannot be allowed to make such business an object of pecuniary profit to himself."[8]

A. *Personal and Substantial Participation in a Particular Matter*

The nature of the participation prohibited by the federal statute is potentially broad, but the statutory language requires the government employee to be directly and significantly involved in a particular matter. It prohibits participation "personally and substantially as a Government officer or employee, through decision, approval, disapproval, recommendation, the rendering of advice, investigation, or otherwise . . . ."[9] Further, under the federal statute, the government action in which the employee may not participate must be a "particular matter."[10] That concept, as defined by federal regulation, encompasses "only matters that involve deliberation, decision, or action that is focused upon the interests of specific persons, or a discrete and identifiable class of persons" and does not include "the consideration or adoption of broad policy options

---

6 18 U.S.C. § 208(a).
7 Lexington Insulation Co. v. Davidson Cty., 90 S.E.2d 496, 497-98 (N.C. 1955).
8 *Id.* (citation omitted).
9 18 U.S.C. § 208(a).
10 *Id.*

that are directed to the interests of a large and diverse group of persons."[11] The term "particular matter" is used throughout the federal conflict of interest laws with the purpose of limiting "application of the laws to actions focusing upon particular, distinct, and identifiable sets of facts with reasonably measurable implications and consequences."[12]

Some state laws similarly require that the public servant exercise judgment or some level of discretion in a particular matter in order for the involvement to trigger the need to disclose a conflict of interest.[13] This may include "any person acting as an advisor or consultant to the government in performing a governmental function" and may prohibit anyone "who is exercising his or her judgment and choice on a matter material to any government contract, purchase, payment, or other pecuniary transaction from owning directly or indirectly a substantial portion of any nongovernmental entity involved in that government contract, purchase, payment, or pecuniary transaction."[14]

Some states approach the issue more broadly and without requiring participation in a particular matter by simply prohibiting any use of official position for personal gain. Such statutes do not require that the official undertake an official action that results in personal gain. Rather, "[i]t is enough that employees use their 'official position' for personal gain or to seek employment."[15] Other state statutes focus more specifically on contracts or transactions, rather than the more general "matter."[16]

B. *Financial Interest*

The "financial interest" sufficient for a violation of the federal statute need not be a realized gain or loss. Rather, the federal statute is designed to prevent even the appearance of impropriety. A "financial interest exists on the part of a part[y] to a [§] 208 action where there is a real possibility of gain or loss as a

---

11 United States v. Stadd, 636 F.3d 630, 637 (D.C. Cir. 2011) (quoting 5 C.F.R. § 2635.402(b)(3)).

12 Van Ee v. EPA, 202 F.3d 296, 303 (D.C. Cir. 2000) (quoting U.S. Department of Justice's Office of Legal Counsel).

13 *See, e.g.*, ALA. CODE § 13A-10-62 ("exercises any substantial discretionary function in connection with a government contract, purchase, payment or other pecuniary transaction").

14 Vaughn v. State, 880 So. 2d 1178, 1197 (Ala. Crim. App. 2003).

15 Skvorc v. State, 996 P.2d 1192, 1200 (Alaska 2000).

16 *See, e.g.*, N.D. CENT. CODE § 12.1-13-03.

result of developments in or resolution of a matter."[17] "All that is required is that there be a real, as opposed to a speculative, possibility of benefit or detriment."[18] This includes the possibility of "prospective employment."[19]

State laws prohibiting public officials from using public office for personal gain often specify that the prohibited gain must be direct and personal, affecting the official as an individual or as a member of a small group, but not simply having a beneficial effect on a class of which the official happens to be a member.[20] "Any broader view . . . would seriously impair not only the ability of [the government] to attract and retain qualified officials, but also [the officials'] ability to deal with fiscal problems generally."[21] In states requiring a pecuniary benefit, that benefit typically must amount to some private financial gain, rather than a benefit that is political in nature.[22] If a political benefit were sufficient, there would be "a conflict of interest on every dais, at each parade, and at every ribbon-cutting, given that the very nature of seeking to satisfy one's constituents and secure re-election all but requires the taking of official action to secure intangible political gains."[23]

Particularly where the state conflict-of-interest statute carries a criminal penalty, a court may require that "a public official must have a non-speculative, non-remote pecuniary or proprietary interest in the decision at issue."[24] Where a statute precludes a state official or employee from making a contract that would benefit the official or his family members, it may include nepotism situations, such as employment agreements benefiting the official's family members as well as subsequent employment decisions affecting the family member.[25]

---

17 United States v. Gorman, 807 F.2d 1299, 1303 (6th Cir. 1986) (noting further that "[g]ain or loss need not be probable for the prohibition against official action to apply").

18 *Id.*

19 18 U.S.C. § 208(a).

20 Lambert v. Wilcox Cty. Comm'n, 623 So. 2d 727, 730 (Ala. 1993) (interpreting section 36-25-5(a) of the Alabama Code and finding that a county commissioner who was also a bus driver did not obtain any direct and personal gain from voting on a measure that increased funding for public education).

21 *Id.*

22 Commonwealth v. Veon, 150 A.3d 435, 448 (Pa. 2016).

23 *Id.* at 447-48 (finding such a "criminalization of politics [to be] a bridge too far").

24 *See, e.g.*, Hughes v. Jorgenson, 50 P.3d 821, 824 (Ariz. 2002) (finding that the interest was too remote and not pecuniary or proprietary where a sheriff was involved in the decision of whether to press charges against his sister for drug possession).

25 *See, e.g.*, State v. Hunter, Nos. C-140684, C-140704, C-140717, 2016 Ohio App. LEXIS 96, at ¶ 18 (Ohio Ct. App. Jan. 15, 2016).

C. *General Intent*

Federal § 208 is a general intent crime, but the government employee must know of the financial interest.[26] Knowledge does not apply to the other aspects of the crime,[27] although "participating" in a matter is commonly understood to be done knowingly and intentionally.[28]

State laws typically require a knowledge or awareness of the potential conflict of interest in order to sustain a criminal conviction.[29] It may not be necessary that the public official know that his conduct is unlawful, but knowledge of the financial interest that creates the conflict of interest may be sufficient.[30]

D. *Disclosure or Other Exemption*

Under the federal statute, government employees may participate in government action in which they have an interest if the interest is both insubstantial and properly disclosed,[31] or too remote or inconsequential to affect the integrity of the government, as determined by regulation.[32] As shown in the table below, some state laws similarly allow disclosure of some types of financial interests to enable participation in a matter affecting that interest.

The table below excerpts the relevant statutory language prohibiting having a personal interest in a government transaction.[33] A response of "yes" in the column titled "Disclosure Component" does not mean that simple disclosure of the conflict will avoid criminal or civil liability. Rather, it means that disclosure may be required and may begin a process of curing the conflict, depending on the particular law and facts.

---

26 18 U.S.C. § 208(a) ("to his knowledge").

27 United States v. Hedges, 912 F.2d 1397, 1402 (11th Cir. 1990).

28 United States v. Bouchey, No. 91-3120, 1992 U.S. App. LEXIS 15117, at *5 (D.C. Cir. 1992).

29 *See, e.g.*, Vaughn v. State, 880 So. 2d 1178, 1201-02 (Ala. Crim. App. 2003).

30 *See, e.g.*, State v. Pinkney, 522 N.E.2d 555, 561-62 (Ohio 1988).

31 18 U.S.C. § 208(b)(1).

32 18 U.S.C. § 208(b)(2). Section 208 also has narrow exemptions for special government employees (18 U.S.C. § 208(b)(3)) and for financial interests resulting solely from birthrights in an Indian tribe (18 U.S.C. § 208(b)(4)).

33 The text in the table does not necessarily capture all aspects or every detail of the quoted statutes.

Table 3.4-1—Conduct Affecting Personal Financial Interest

State	Statutory Excerpt	Disclosure Component	Maximum Offense Classification
Alabama	(a) A public servant commits the crime of failing to disclose a conflict of interest if he exercises any substantial discretionary function in connection with a government contract, purchase, payment or other pecuniary transaction without advance public disclosure of a known potential conflicting interest in the transaction. ALA. CODE § 13A-10-62.	Yes	Misde-meanor
	(a) No public official or public employee shall use or cause to be used his or her official position or office to obtain personal gain for himself or herself.... ALA. CODE §§ 36-25-5, 36-25-27.	No	Felony
Alaska	(a) A public officer may not use, or attempt to use, an official position for personal gain, and may not intentionally secure or grant unwarranted benefits or treatment for any person. (b) A public officer may not: ... (4) take or withhold official action in order to affect a matter in which the public officer has a personal or financial interest.... ALASKA STAT. §§ 39.52.120, 39.52.440. *See also* ALASKA STAT. § 39.52.150.	No	Civil Penalty

Table 3.4-1—Conduct Affecting Personal Financial Interest

State	Statutory Excerpt	Disclosure Component	Maximum Offense Classification
Arizona	A. Any public officer or employee of a public agency who has, or whose relative has, a substantial interest in any contract, sale, purchase or service to such public agency shall make known that interest in the official records of such public agency and shall refrain from voting upon or otherwise participating in any manner as an officer or employee in such contract, sale or purchase. B. Any public officer or employee who has, or whose relative has, a substantial interest in any decision of a public agency shall make known such interest in the official records of such public agency and shall refrain from participating in any manner as an officer or employee in such decision. ARIZ. REV. STAT. ANN. §§ 38-503, 38-510.	Yes	Felony
Arkansas	(a) A legislator who is required to take an action in the discharge of his or her official duties that may affect his or her financial interest . . . which is distinguishable from the effects of the action on the public generally or a broad segment of the public, shall: [disclose the conflict in writing]. ARK. CODE ANN. §§ 21-8-803, 21-8-903. *See also* ARK. CODE ANN. §§ 21-8-1001, 21-8-1004.	Yes	Misde-meanor
California	No public official at any level of state or local government shall make, participate in making or in any way attempt to use his official position to influence a governmental decision in which he knows or has reason to know he has a financial interest. CAL. GOV'T CODE §§ 87100-87105, 91000. *See also* CAL. GOV'T CODE §§ 1090, 8920, 8926, 87407, 87450.	No	Misde-meanor

Table 3.4-1—Conduct Affecting Personal Financial Interest

State	Statutory Excerpt	Disclosure Component	Maximum Offense Classification
Colorado	A public servant commits failing to disclose a conflict of interest if he exercises any substantial discretionary function in connection with a government contract, purchase, payment, or other pecuniary transaction without having given seventy-two hours' actual advance written notice to the secretary of state and to the governing body of the government which employs the public servant of the existence of a known potential conflicting interest of the public servant in the transaction with reference to which he is about to act in his official capacity. COLO. REV. STAT. § 18-8-308. *See also* COLO. REV. STAT. §§ 24-18-105, 24-18-107, 24-18-108.5, 24-18-109.	Yes	Misdemeanor
Connecticut	No public official or state employee shall, while serving as such, have any financial interest in, or engage in, any business, employment, transaction or professional activity, which is in substantial conflict with the proper discharge of his duties or employment in the public interest and of his responsibilities as prescribed in the laws of this state . . . [or] . . . shall accept other employment which will . . . impair his independence of judgment as to his official duties or employment . . . . CONN. GEN. STAT. §§ 1-84(a), (b), 1-85, 1-89.	No	Felony
Delaware	No state employee. . . may participate on behalf of the State in the review or disposition of any matter pending before the State in which [he or she] . . . has a personal or private interest . . . . DEL. CODE ANN. tit. 29, § 5805(a)(1). *See also* DEL. CODE ANN. tit. 29, § 1002(a).	Yes	Misdemeanor
District of Columbia	No employee shall use his or her official position or title, or personally and substantially participate . . . in a . . . particular matter . . . in a manner that the employee knows is likely to have a direct and predictable effect on the employee's financial interests . . . . D.C. CODE §§ 1-1162.23(a), 1162.21.	Yes	Civil Penalty

Table 3.4-1—Conduct Affecting Personal Financial Interest

State	Statutory Excerpt	Disclosure Component	Maximum Offense Classification
Florida	A state public officer may not vote on any matter that the officer knows would inure to his or her special private gain or loss. . . . No county, municipal, or other local public officer shall vote in an official capacity upon any measure which would inure to his or her special private gain or loss . . . No appointed public officer shall participate in any matter which would inure to the officer's special private gain or loss. FLA. STAT. §§ 112.3143(2), (3), (4), 112.317.	Yes	Civil Penalty
Georgia	(1) It shall be unlawful for any full-time public official who has state-wide powers, for himself or on behalf of any business, or for any business in which such public official or member of his family has a substantial interest to transact any business with any agency. (2) It shall be unlawful for any public official who has limited powers for himself or on behalf of any business, or for any business in which such public official or member of his family has a substantial interest to transact any business with the agency for which such public official serves. GA. CODE ANN. §§ 45-10-22(a), 45-10-28.	No	Civil Penalty
Guam	No employee shall take any official action directly affecting . . . (1) business or other undertaking in which the employee has a financial interest . . . . 4 GUAM CODE ANN. §§ 15205(a), 15211.	No	Civil Reme-dies

Table 3.4-1—Conduct Affecting Personal Financial Interest

State	Statutory Excerpt	Disclosure Component	Maximum Offense Classification
Hawaii	(a) No employee shall take any official action directly affecting . . . (1) [a] business or other undertaking in which the employee has a substantial financial interest; or (b). . . shall acquire financial interests in any business or other undertaking which the employee has reason to believe may be directly involved in official action to be taken by the employee. HAW. REV. STAT. ANN. §§ 84-14, 84-19, 84-15.	No	Civil Reme-dies
Idaho	No public servant shall . . . [b]e interested in any contract made by him in his official capacity . . . . IDAHO CODE §§ 18-1359(1)(d), 18-1360.	No	Misde-meanor
Illinois	No person holding any office, either by election or appointment under the laws or Constitution of this State, may be in any manner financially interested directly in his own name or indirectly in the name of any other person, association, trust, or corporation, in any contract or the performance of any work in the making or letting of which such officer may be called upon to act or vote. . . . . 50 ILL. COMP. STAT. ANN. 105/3, 105/4.	Yes	Felony
Indiana	(a) A state officer . . . may not participate in any decision or vote, or matter relating to that decision or vote, if the state officer . . . has knowledge that [he] has a financial interest in the outcome of the matter . . . . IND. CODE §§ 4-2-6-9, 4-2-6-12.	Yes	Civil Penalty

Table 3.4-1—Conduct Affecting Personal Financial Interest

State	Statutory Excerpt	Disclosure Component	Maximum Offense Classification
Indiana	A public servant who knowingly or intentionally: (1) has a pecuniary interest in; or (2) derives a profit from; a contract or purchase connected with an action by the governmental entity served by the public servant commits conflict of interest, a Level 6 felony. IND. CODE § 35-44.1-1-4(b).	Yes	Felony
Iowa	Any officer or employee of the state . . . who is directly or indirectly interested in any contract to furnish anything of value to the state . . . where such interest is prohibited by statute commits a serious misdemeanor. This section shall not apply to any contract awarded as a result of open, public and competitive bidding. IOWA CODE § 721.11.	No	Misde-meanor
Kansas	No state officer or employee shall . . . be substantially involved in the preparation of or participate in the making of a contract with any person or business by which such officer or employee is employed or in whose business such officer or employee or any member of such officer's or employee's immediate family has a substantial interest . . . . KAN. STAT. ANN. §§ 46-233(a)(1), 46-243(a).	No	Misde-meanor
Kentucky	A public servant shall not knowingly act as a representative or agent for the Commonwealth or any agency in the transaction of any business or regulatory action with himself, or with any business in which he or a member of his family has any interest greater than five percent (5%) of the total value thereof. KY. REV. STAT. ANN. §§ 11A.040(3); 11A.990. *See also* KY. REV. STAT. §§ 6.731; 6.761; 45A.340(2), 45A.990.	No	Felony

Table 3.4-1—Conduct Affecting Personal Financial Interest

State	Statutory Excerpt	Disclosure Component	Maximum Offense Classification
Louisiana	A. No public servant . . . shall participate in a transaction [involving the governmental entity] in which he has a personal substantial economic interest of which he may be reasonably expected to know [or] B. . . . [of which he has] actual knowledge [of] any of the following persons ha[ving] a substantial economic interest: (1) Any member of his immediate family. (2) Any person in which he has a substantial economic interest of which he may reasonably be expected to know. (3) Any person of which he is an officer, director, trustee, partner, or employee. (4) Any person with whom he is negotiating or has an arrangement concerning prospective employment. (5) Any person who is a party to an existing contract with such public servant . . . . LA. STAT. ANN. §§ 42:1112; 42:1153.	No	Civil Penalty
Maine	An executive employee may not have any direct or indirect pecuniary interest in or receive or be eligible to receive, directly or indirectly, any benefit that may arise from any contract made on behalf of the State when the state entity that employs the executive employee is a party to the contract. ME. REV. STAT. tit. 5, § 18-A. *See also* ME. REV. STAT. tit. 30-A, § 2605.	Yes	Contract is Void

Table 3.4-1—Conduct Affecting Personal Financial Interest

State	Statutory Excerpt	Disclosure Component	Maximum Offense Classification
Maryland	[A]n official or employee may not participate in a matter if: (1) the official or employee or a qualifying relative of the official or employee has an interest in the matter and the official or employee knows of the interest; or (2) any of [a list of specified affiliates] is a party to the matter . . . . MD. CODE ANN., GEN. PROV. §§ 5-501(a); 5-502; 5-904.	Yes	Sanction
Massachusetts	A state employee who has a financial interest, directly or indirectly, in a contract made by a state agency, in which the commonwealth or a state agency is an interested party, of which interest he has knowledge or has reason to know, shall be punished . . . . MASS. GEN. LAWS ch. 268A, §7. *See also* MASS. GEN. LAWS ch. 268A, §§ 23, 26.	Yes	Felony
Michigan	[A] public servant shall not be a party, directly or indirectly, to any contract between himself or herself and the public entity of which he or she is an officer or employee . . . . MICH. COMP. LAWS § 15.322, 15.327. *See also* MICH. COMP. LAWS §§ 15.302, 15.308, 15.342.	No	Misde-meanor
Minnesota	(a) A public official . . . who in the discharge of official duties would be required to take an action or make a decision that would substantially affect the official's financial interests . . . (1) must [disclose the potential conflict]. MINN. STAT. §§ 10A.07, 10A.34. *See also* MINN. STAT. § 43A.38(5), 43A.39.	Yes	Civil Penalty

Table 3.4-1—Conduct Affecting Personal Financial Interest

State	Statutory Excerpt	Disclosure Component	Maximum Offense Classification
Mississippi	No public servant shall be interested, directly or indirectly . . . in any contract with the state . . . authorized by any law passed or order made by any board of which he may be or may have been a member. MISS. CODE ANN. §§ 25-4-105(2), 25-4-109.	No	Civil Penalty
Missouri	1. No elected or appointed official or employee of the state or any political subdivision thereof shall: . . . (4) Favorably act on any matter that is so specifically designed so as to provide a special monetary benefit to such official or his spouse or dependent children, including but not limited to increases in retirement benefits, whether received from the state of Missouri or any third party by reason of such act. . . . (5) Use his decision-making authority for the purpose of obtaining a financial gain which materially enriches himself, his spouse or dependent children by acting or refraining from acting for the purpose of coercing or extorting from another anything of actual pecuniary value. MO. REV. STAT. §§ 105.452, 105.478.	No	Felony
Montana	. . . [A] public officer . . . may not acquire an interest in any business or undertaking that the officer . . . has reason to believe may be directly and substantially affected to its economic benefit by official action to be taken by the officer's . . . agency. . . . MONT. CODE ANN. §§ 2-2-105(2), 2-2-103.	No	Civil Penalty

Table 3.4-1—Conduct Affecting Personal Financial Interest

State	Statutory Excerpt	Disclosure Component	Maximum Offense Classification
Nebraska	Except as provided in [other sections], no officer may have an interest in any contract to which his or her governing body, or anyone for its benefit, is a party. The existence of such an interest in any contract shall render the contract voidable by decree of a court of competent jurisdiction as to any person who entered into the contract or took assignment of such contract with actual knowledge of the prohibited conflict. NEB. REV. STAT. §§ 49-14,103.01(2), 49-14,103.04. *See also* NEB. REV. STAT. §§ 49-1498, 49-1499, 49-1499.02.	Yes	Misdemeanor
Nevada	A public officer or employee shall not participate as an agent of government in the negotiation or execution of a contract between the government and . . . any business entity in which the public officer or employee has a significant pecuniary interest or any person to whom the public officer or employee has a commitment in a private capacity. NEV. REV. STAT. §§ 281A.400(3), 281A.420, 281A.430, 281A.790.	Yes	Civil Penalty
New Hampshire	No person holding a public office . . . shall, by contract or otherwise, except by open competitive bidding, buy real estate, sell or buy goods, commodities, or other personal property of a value in excess of $200 at any one sale to or from the state or political subdivision under which he holds his public office. N.H. REV. STAT. ANN. §§ 95:1, 95:2.	No	Misdemeanor
New Jersey	A public servant commits a crime of the fourth degree if, while performing his official functions on behalf of a governmental entity, the public servant knowingly transacts any business with himself, a member of his immediate family, or a business organization in which the public servant or an immediate family member has an interest. N.J. STAT. ANN. §§ 2C:27-9, 2C:43-6.5. *See also* N.J. STAT. ANN. § 52:13D-23(e).	No	Felony

Table 3.4-1—Conduct Affecting Personal Financial Interest

State	Statutory Excerpt	Disclosure Component	Maximum Offense Classification
New Mexico	A. It is unlawful for a public officer or employee to take an official act for the primary purpose of directly enhancing the public officer's or employee's financial interest or financial position . . . B. A public officer or employee shall be disqualified from engaging in any official act directly affecting the public officer's or employee's financial interest, except a public officer or employee shall not be disqualified from engaging in an official act if the financial benefit of the financial interest to the public officer or employee is proportionately less than the benefit to the general public. C. No public officer during the term for which elected and no public employee during the period of employment shall acquire a financial interest when the public officer or employee believes or should have reason to believe that the new financial interest will be directly affected by the officer's or employee's official act. N.M. Stat. Ann. § 10-16-4. *See also* N.M. Stat. Ann. §§ 10-16-7; 10-16-9(A); 30-23-6.	No	Felony
New York	No officer or employee of a state agency, member of the legislature or legislative employee should have any interest, financial or otherwise, direct or indirect, or engage in any business or transaction or professional activity or incur any obligation of any nature, which is in substantial conflict with the proper discharge of his or her duties in the public interest. NY Pub. Off. Law § 74(2).	No	Civil Penalty
North Carolina	No public officer or employee who is involved in making or administering a contract on behalf of a public agency may derive a direct benefit from the contract . . . . N.C. Gen. Stat. § 14-234(a)(1). *See also* N.C. Gen. Stat. §§ 138A-31, 138A-35.	No	Misde-meanor

Table 3.4-1—Conduct Affecting Personal Financial Interest

State	Statutory Excerpt	Disclosure Component	Maximum Offense Classification
North Dakota	Every public servant authorized to sell or lease any property, or to make any contract in his official capacity, alone or in conjunction with other public servants, who voluntarily becomes interested individually in the sale, lease, or contract, directly or indirectly, is guilty of a class A misdemeanor. N.D. Cent. Code § 12.1-13-03(1).	Yes	Misdemeanor
Northern Mariana Islands	(a) A public official or public employee shall not participate in a transaction involving the public official or employee's governmental entity: (1) In a manner or under circumstances that the public official or public employee knows or reasonably should know that the public official or public employee's participation in the transaction may substantially influence the transaction; (2) If the public official or public employee has actual knowledge that a person with whom the public official or employee has a familial, personal, financial, or other nonbusiness relationship has a substantial economic interest in the transaction. 1 N. Mar. I. Code §§ 8533, 8572. *See also* 1 N. Mar. I. Code § 8532.	No	Misdemeanor
Ohio	No public official shall knowingly . . . [a]uthorize . . . any public contract in which the public official . . . has an interest . . . . Ohio Rev. Code Ann. § 2921.42(A)(1).	No	Felony
Oklahoma	In the event a state officer or employee: . . . knows that a particular matter involving specific parties is likely to have a direct and predictable effect on [his] material financial interests . . . the state officer or employee shall not participate in the matter . . . . Okla. Ethics Comm'n Rules rr. 4.7(1), 6.13.	Yes	Civil Penalty

Table 3.4-1—Conduct Affecting Personal Financial Interest

State	Statutory Excerpt	Disclosure Component	Maximum Offense Classification
Oregon	[A] public official may not use or attempt to use official position or office to obtain financial gain or avoidance of financial detriment . . . . OR. REV. STAT. §§ 244.040(1), 244.350(1)(c).	No	Civil Penalty
Pennsylvania	(a) No public official or public employee shall engage in conduct that constitutes a conflict of interest. (f) No public official . . . shall enter into any contract valued at $ 500 or more with the governmental body with which the public official . . . is associated . . . unless the contract has been awarded through an open and public process . . . . 65 PA. CONS. STAT. §§ 1103, 1109.	No	Felony
Puerto Rico	Any public officer or employee who, by reason of his/her office, directly or through third party, promotes, authorizes or executes a contract, bid or any other operation in which he/she has an interest without having a dispensation or authorization allowed by the law shall incur a fourth degree felony. P.R. LAWS ANN. tit. 33, § 4884. *See also* P.R. LAWS ANN. tit. 3, §§ 1857a(g), 1857f.	Yes	Felony
Rhode Island	No person subject to this code of ethics shall have any interest, financial or otherwise, direct or indirect, or engage in any business, employment, transaction, or professional activity, or incur any obligation of any nature, which is in substantial conflict with the proper discharge of his or her duties or employment in the public interest and of his or her responsibilities as prescribed in the laws of this state . . . . 36 R.I. GEN. LAWS §§ 36-14-5(a), 36-14-19.	No	Misdemeanor

Table 3.4-1—Conduct Affecting Personal Financial Interest

State	Statutory Excerpt	Disclosure Component	Maximum Offense Classification
South Carolina	(A) No public official, public member, or public employee may knowingly use his official office, membership, or employment to obtain an economic interest for himself . . . (B) No public official, public member, or public employee may make, participate in making, or in any way attempt to use his office, membership, or employment to influence a governmental decision in which he, a family member, an individual with whom he is associated, or a business with which he is associated has an economic interest . . . . S.C. CODE ANN. §§ 8-13-700; 8-13-735; 8-13-775; 8-13-1520.	Yes	Misde-meanor
South Dakota	No elected or appointed member of a state authority, board, or commission may have an interest in. . . any contract . . . with the state . . . . S.D. CODIFIED LAWS §§ 3-23-1, 3-23-3, 3-23-5.	Yes	Misde-meanor
Texas	An elected or appointed officer . . . who has a personal or private interest in a measure, proposal, or decision pending before the board or commission shall publicly disclose the fact . . . [and] may not vote or otherwise participate in the decision. TEX. GOV'T CODE ANN. § 572.058(a).	Yes	Civil Penalty/ Removal
Utah	[I]t is an offense for a public officer . . . to: . . . use or attempt to use his official position to . . . further substantially the officer's or employee's personal economic interest . . . . UTAH CODE ANN. §§ 67-16-4(1)(c); 67-16-9; 67-16-12.	No	Felony
Vermont	No senator shall be permitted to vote upon any question in which he or she is directly or immediately interested. VT. SENATE R. 71. *See also* VT. HOUSE R. 75; VT. EXEC. CODE OF ETHICS § III.A; VT. STAT. ANN. tit. 24, § 1984.	No	

Table 3.4-1—Conduct Affecting Personal Financial Interest

State	Statutory Excerpt	Disclosure Component	Maximum Offense Classification
Virgin Islands	No territorial officer or employee shall: (1) be financially interested in any contract made or negotiated by him in his official capacity, or by any public agency of which he is a member. (2) be a purchaser at any sale or a vendor at any purchase made by him in his official capacity. (3) have any interest, financial or otherwise, direct or indirect, or engaged in any business or transaction or professional activity, or incur any obligation of any nature, which is in substantial conflict with the proper discharge of his duties in the public interest and of his responsibilities as prescribed in the laws of the Virgin Islands. (4) accept other employment which will either impair his independence of judgment as to his official duties or require him, or induce him, to disclose confidential information acquired by him in the course of and by reason of his official duties. V.I. CODE ANN. tit. 3 §§ 1102, 1108.	No	Felony
Virginia	No officer or employee of a state or local government or advisory agency shall: . . . Accept any money, loan, gift, favor, service, or business or professional opportunity that reasonably tends to influence him in the performance of his official duties. VA. CODE ANN. §§ 2.2-3103(5), 2.2-3120.	No	Misdemeanor
Washington	No state officer or state employee may have an interest, financial or otherwise, direct or indirect, or engage in a business or transaction or professional activity, or incur an obligation of any nature, that is in conflict with the proper discharge of the state officer's or state employee's official duties. WASH. REV. CODE §§ 42.52.020, 42.52.490. *See also* WASH. REV. CODE §§ 42.52.030; 42.52.190.	No	Civil Penalty

Table 3.4-1—Conduct Affecting Personal Financial Interest

State	Statutory Excerpt	Disclosure Component	Maximum Offense Classification
West Virginia	[N]o elected or appointed public official or public employee or member of his or her immediate family or business with which he or she is associated may be a party to or have an interest in the profits or benefits of a contract which the official or employee may have direct authority to enter into, or over which he or she may have control . . . . W. VA. CODE §§ 6B-2-4, 6B-2-5(d).	Yes	Civil Penalty
Wisconsin	(1) Any public officer or public employee who does any of the following is guilty of a Class I felony: (a) In the officer's or employee's private capacity, negotiates or bids for or enters into a contract in which the officer or employee has a private pecuniary interest, direct or indirect, if at the same time the officer or employee is authorized or required by law to participate in the officer's or employee's capacity as such officer or employee in the making of that contract or to perform in regard to that contract some official function requiring the exercise of discretion on the officer's or employee's part; or (b) In the officer's or employee's capacity as such officer or employee, participates in the making of a contract in which the officer or employee has a private pecuniary interest, direct or indirect, or performs in regard to that contract some function requiring the exercise of discretion on the officer's or employee's part. WIS. STAT. § 946.13. *See also* WIS. STAT. §§ 19.45; 19.46.	No	Felony
Wyoming	A public official, public member or public employee shall not make an official decision or vote on an official decision if the public official, public member or public employee has a personal or private interest in the matter . . . . WYO. STAT. ANN. §§ 9-13-106, 9-13-109. *See also* WYO. STAT. ANN. §§ 6-5-106; 6-5-118.	No	Misdemeanor

II. Nepotism

Nepotism occurs when a public official hires or appoints a family member to a position because of the personal relationship between that person and the public official. Some jurisdictions prohibit nepotism through laws specifically prohibiting government officials from making personnel decisions pertaining to relatives. Other jurisdictions rely on more general conflict of interest laws, like those discussed above, to prohibit nepotism.

Under the federal law, the criminal conflict of interest statute, 18 U.S.C. § 208(a), which prohibits a government official from participating personally and substantially in a decision "or other particular matter in which" he has a financial interest, applies to personal and substantial participation in employment decisions or contracts of a relative.[34] The Civil Service Reform Act of 1978 provides complementary civil penalties.[35]

States that do not have a stand-alone nepotism statute may disallow instances of nepotism through the use of general conflict of interest statutes that prohibit personal involvement in a decision or contract in which an official has a personal interest, using public office for personal gain, or using public office to bestow unwarranted privileges or benefits on oneself or another person. States and territories that lack an express prohibition on nepotism but that have an applicable conflict of interest statute include: California,[36] Colorado,[37] Connecticut,[38] Guam,[39] Hawaii,[40] Illinois,[41] Massachusetts,[42] Michigan,[43]

---

34 United States v. Lund, 853 F.2d 242, 244, 249 (4th Cir. 1988) (quoting 18 U.S.C. § 208(a)).

35 5 U.S.C. §§ 2302(b)(7), 3110(b), (c); *Lund*, 853 F.2d at 247 (rejecting defendant's argument that the Civil Service Reform Act provisions specifically addressing nepotism "somehow limit[] any application of the more general federal conflict-of-interest statute"). The federal anti-nepotism statute does not apply to presidential appointments in the White House Office. Application of the Anti-Nepotism Statute to a Presidential Appointment in the White House Office, 41 Op. O.L.C. 1, 2017 OLC LEXIS 1, at *1 (Jan. 20, 2017) (determining that "the President's special hiring authority in 3 U.S.C. § 105(a) exempts positions in the White House Office from [§] 3110").

36 Cal. Gov't Code § 8920.

37 Colo. Rev. Stat. § 24-18-201.

38 Conn. Gen. Stat. §§ 1-84, 1-85.

39 4 Guam Code Ann. §§ 15204, 15205.

40 Haw. Rev. Stat. § 84-13.

41 5 Ill. Comp. Stat. 420/3-202; 50 Ill. Comp. Stat. Ann. 105/3.

42 Mass. Gen. Laws ch. 268A, § 6.

43 Mich. Comp. Laws §15.342.

Minnesota,[44] New York,[45] Northern Mariana Islands,[46] Ohio,[47] Pennsylvania,[48] Rhode Island,[49] South Dakota,[50] Washington,[51] West Virginia,[52] and Wisconsin.[53]

State prohibitions on nepotism vary in terms of the degree of relationship between the public official and the relative, in terms of what exactly is prohibited (hiring for any type of public employment, hiring for employment within the public official's own agency, directly supervising the relative, or some other employer-employee relationship), and in terms of whether unpaid positions are also prohibited, as listed below. States with an express prohibition on nepotism may also have a general conflict of interest statute that would apply to nepotism.[54]

Table 3.4-2—Nepotism

State	Nepotism Statute(s)	Prohibited Action
Alabama	Ala. Code § 41-1-5	Employment in any position, supervising
Alaska	Alaska Stat. §§ 24.60.090, 39.90.020	Legislative: hiring (1) during the legislative session in the house in which the legislator is a member, (2) by an agency of the legislature, (3) in either house during the interim between sessions, or (4), whether for compensation or not, by the committee. Direct supervision prohibited. Executive: Employment in same agency
Arizona	Ariz. Rev. Stat. Ann. § 38-481	Employment in same agency

44 Minn. Stat. §§ 10A.07, 43A.38.
45 N.Y. Pub. Off. Law §74(3)(d).
46 1 N. Mar. Code §§ 8145, 8531.
47 Ohio Rev. Code Ann. §2921.42.
48 65 Pa. Cons. Stat. § 1103.
49 36 R.I. Gen. Laws § 36-14-5(d).
50 S.D. Codified Laws § 3-23-1.
51 Wash. Rev. Code §§ 42.52.020, 42.52.070.
52 W.Va. Code § 6B-2-5(b).
53 Wis. Stat. §§ 19.45(2), 19.59(1)(a).
54 *See, e.g.*, Ky. Rev. Stat. Ann. § 11A.020; Me. Stat. tit. 1, § 1014; Md. Code Ann., Gen. Prov. § 5-501.

Table 3.4-2—Nepotism

State	Nepotism Statute(s)	Prohibited Action
Arkansas	Ark. Code Ann. §§ 21-8-101; 25-16-1001 to 1007	Employment in same agency
District of Columbia	D.C. Code § 1-618.04	Employment in same agency
Florida	Fla. Stat. § 112.3135	Employment in same agency
Georgia	Ga. Code Ann. § 45-10-80	Employment in any position
Idaho	Idaho Code § 18-1359(1)(e)	Employment in any position
Indiana	Ind. Code § 4-2-6-16	Employment in same agency
Iowa	Iowa Code § 71.1	Employment in same agency
Kansas	Kan. Stat. Ann. § 46-246a	Employment in any position, any action relating to employment or discipline
Kentucky	Ky. Rev. Stat. Ann. § 6.754	Employment in same branch
Louisiana	La. Stat. Ann. § 42:1119	Employment in same agency
Maine	Me. Stat. tit. 5, § 7051(3)	Employment final decision
Maryland	Md. Code Ann., State Gov't § 2-107	Employment in same branch (legislative)
Mississippi	Miss. Code Ann. § 25-1-53	Employment in any position
Missouri	Mo. Const. art. VII, § 6	Employment in any position
Montana	Mont. Code Ann. §§ 2-2-301 to 2-2-304	Employment in any position
Nebraska	Neb. Rev. Stat. § 49-1499.07	Employment in any position
Nevada	Nev. Rev. Stat. § 281.210	Employment in any position
New Hampshire	N.H. Rev. Stat. Ann. § 21-G:26-a	Employment in any position
New Jersey	N.J. Stat. Ann. §§ 52:11-5.1, 52:13D-21.2	Various
New Mexico	N.M. Stat. Ann. § 10-1-10	Employment in same office

Table 3.4-2—Nepotism

State	**Nepotism Statute(s)**	**Prohibited Action**
North Carolina	N.C. GEN. STAT. § 138A-40	Employment in a supervised or managed position
North Dakota	N.D. CENT. CODE § 44-04-09	Employment in any position or supervising
Oklahoma	OKLA. STAT. tit. 21, §§ 481–487	Employment in any position
Oregon	OR. REV. STAT. ANN. § 244.177	Employment in public body the official serves or controls
Puerto Rico	P.R. LAWS ANN. tit. 3, § 1857a(h)	Employment in any position
South Carolina	S.C. CODE ANN. § 8-13-750	Employment in position that relative supervises or manages
Tennessee	TENN. CODE ANN. §§ 3-1-203, 8-31-101 to -107	Supervising
Texas	TEX. GOV'T CODE ANN. §§ 573.041-573.044	Employment in any position
Utah	UTAH CODE ANN. §§ 52-3-1 to -4	Direct supervision
Virginia	VA. CODE ANN. § 2.2-3106	The Virginia statute against personal interest in government contracts expressly allows employment contracts of relatives, unless the public employee exercises control over the employment or activities of the relative.
Wyoming	WYO. STAT. ANN. § 9-13-104	Employment in any position

III. Representing Another Interest in a Particular Matter Before Government

State and federal laws prohibit a government official or employee from using the prestige, contacts, or knowledge from their government position in order to profit in their off-duty "moonlighting" hours, representing private interests before agencies of the very government with which they are associated.[55] Like other conflict of interest statutes, these rules are based on the "moral principle . . . that no man may serve two masters . . . a maxim which is especially pertinent if one of the masters happens to be economic self-interest."[56]

The laws prohibiting a government official from representing a private interest in a particular matter vary by jurisdiction. Two federal statutes focus on preventing divided loyalty in a situation where a federal employee becomes involved in a particular matter in which the government has an interest, but does so in order to represent a different or adverse interest in that matter. The first statute, 18 U.S.C. § 203, prohibits compensation for representational services in a matter in which the government has an interest, and the second statute, 18 U.S.C. § 205, prohibits acting as an agent or attorney in any matter in which the government has an interest, regardless of compensation.[57] The state statutes vary in terms of whether compensation is required and exactly what type of representation is prohibited.

A. *Receiving Compensation in Exchange for Representational Services*

Of the two relevant federal statutes, one (§ 203) requires that compensation be received as an element of the offense and the other (§ 205) does not. Section 203 prohibits covered federal employees from receiving "any compensation for any representational services, as agent or attorney or otherwise . . . in relation to any proceeding . . . or other particular matter in which the United States is a party or has a direct and substantial interest . . . ."[58] Section 205, however, does not require compensation but was intended to criminalize "situations in which a private party seeking a governmental benefit enlists the representational assistance of a federal employee, who potentially could use confidential information or abuse his office or position to assist such a party" and "the governmental decision at stake is focused on conferring a benefit, imposing a sanction, or otherwise having a discernable effect on the financial or similarly concrete interests of discrete and identifiable persons or entities."[59]

55 *In re* Determination of Exec. Comm'n on Ethical Standards, 561 A.2d 542, 547 (N.J. 1989).

56 *See* United States v. Miss. Valley Generating Co., 364 U.S. 520, 548-49 (1961).

57 18 U.S.C. §§ 203, 205 (2018).

58 18 U.S.C. § 203(a)(1)(B) (2018).

59 Van Ee v. EPA, 202 F.3d 296, 302-03 (D.C. Cir. 2000). Section 205(a)(1) also prohibits

Section 203 is broader than § 205 in that it reaches any representational services "as agent or attorney or otherwise," but narrower in that the representation must be compensated.[60] The representational relationships covered are broader than formal agency or attorney-client relationships, and include informal contacts such as lobbying and influencing.[61] It also covers representation "personally or by another,"[62] which includes a possible "two-step arrangement in which an officer, for compensation, personally influences another officer to influence the department."[63] Section 205, however, broadly reaches uncompensated representation, but narrowly requires the representational services to be limited to acting "as agent or attorney" without the broadening "or otherwise" language.[64]

These aspects of the federal statutes—scope of the representation and whether compensation is paid—may similarly arise in the various state statutes prohibiting representation by a government official. Additionally, many state statutes prohibit a government lawyer from representing a private interest in a matter before only the government agency or body for which the lawyer works, rather than prohibiting the government lawyer from representing a private interest before any governmental body. The idea behind that distinction between the government at large and the specific government agency parallels the question of identifying a governmental lawyer's client as either one specific agency or the government as a whole.[65] Still, some state statutes are phrased more broadly.

---

covered employees from serving as an agent or attorney in "prosecuting any claim against the United States, or receiv[ing] any gratuity, or any share of or interest in any such claim . . . ." 18 U.S.C. § 205(a)(1).

60 18 U.S.C. §§ 203(a), 205(a)(2).

61 United States v. Wallach, 979 F.2d 912, 920 (2d Cir. 1992), *analyzed in* HENNING, *supra* note 4, at § 9.02[4] (discussing the scope of prohibited representational services).

62 18 U.S.C. § 203(a)(1).

63 *Wallach*, 979 F.2d at 920.

64 18 U.S.C. §§ 203(a), 205(a).

65 Gray v. R.I. Dep't of Children, Youth & Families, 937 F. Supp. 153, 158-59 (D.R.I. 1996) (comparing and contrasting the federal law prohibiting government officials from representing private interests with the analogous Rhode Island state statute).

B. *Particular Matter*

To be within either federal statute, the compensation received must relate to a particular matter in which the government has an interest.[66] While the list of possible particular matters is open ended, it includes a "proceeding, application, request for a ruling or other determination, contract, claim, controversy, charge, accusation, arrest, or other particular matter in which the United States is a party or has a direct and substantial interest."[67] Additionally, the particular matter must be federal in nature and must take place "before any department, agency, court, court-martial, officer, or any civil, military, or naval commission."[68] For the federal statute that reaches uncompensated representational services, the law does not apply to a federal employee's volunteer activities on behalf of political organizations except in very unusual situations because the influencing of policy does not constitute involvement in a particular matter.[69]

State statutes prohibiting a government official or employee from representing private interests before the government typically focus on representation in a particular matter, similar to the federal statutes. The term "matter," may include "any case, proceeding, application, determination, issue, or question, but does not include the proposal, consideration, or enactment of statutes, rules, ordinances, resolutions, or charter or constitutional amendments."[70]

---

66 United States v. Williams, 705 F.2d 603, 622 (2d Cir. 1983) (discussing § 203). Section 205 refers either to "a private party's claim against the United States," or a "covered matter," which is defined as "any judicial or other proceeding, application, request for a ruling or other determination, contract, claim, controversy, investigation, charge, accusation, arrest, or other particular matter." 18 U.S.C. § 205(a)(1), (a)(2), (h).

67 18 U.S.C. § 203(a)(1)(B). *See also* 18 U.S.C. § 205(h) ("any judicial or other proceeding, application, request for a ruling or other determination, contract, claim, controversy, investigation, charge, accusation, arrest, or other particular matter").

68 18 U.S.C. § 203(a)(1)(B); *see also* United States v. Biaggi, 853 F.2d 89, 98-99 (2d Cir. 1988).

69 Van Ee v. EPA, 202 F.3d 296, 308 (D.C. Cir. 2000). Note, however, that certain employees of the federal government, including many in the executive branch, are also subject to the Hatch Act, 5 U.S.C. §§ 7321-7326, which regulates their participation in partisan political activities.

70 *See, e.g.*, Royer v. Dillow, No. 13 CA 71, 2014-Ohio-53, 2014 Ohio App. LEXIS 47, ¶ 11 (Ohio Ct. App. Jan. 9, 2014).

C. *Intent*

The intent required under the federal statutes is general intent, rather than "corrupt" intent.[71] For the federal offense of receiving compensation in exchange for an official act, a court has explained that it is not a lesser-included offense of bribery because of a "critical difference going to intent."[72] Bribery requires receiving "corruptly" and "in return for being influenced" whereas the improper compensation law prohibits receipt of compensation "otherwise than as provided by law for the proper discharge of official duties."[73]

Table 3.4-3—Representing Another Interest in a Particular Matter

State	Statutory Language	Prohibit Only Compensated Representation?	Limited to Agency for Which the Employee Works?	Maximum Offense Classification
Alabama	If a public official or public employee, or family member of the public employee or family member of the public official, or a business with which the person is associated, represents a client or constituent for a fee before any quasi-judicial board or commission, regulatory body, or executive department or agency, notice of the representation shall be given . . . . No member of the Legislature shall for a fee, reward, or other compensation represent any person, firm, or corporation before the Public Service Commission or the State Board of Adjustment. ALA. CODE §§ 36-25-10, 36-25-27.	Yes	No	Felony

71 United States v. Alexandro, 675 F.2d 34, 43 (2d Cir. 1982) (involving an immigration official charged with receiving a bribe in violation of 18 U.S.C. § 201(c), conflict of interest in violation of 18 U.S.C. § 203, and conspiracy to receive bribes in violation of 18 U.S.C. § 371).

72 *Id.*

73 *Id.*

Table 3.4-3—Representing Another Interest in a Particular Matter

State	Statutory Language	Prohibit Only Compensated Representation?	Limited to Agency for Which the Employee Works?	Maximum Offense Classification
Alaska	(a) A public officer may not represent, advise, or assist a person in any matter pending before the administrative unit that the officer serves, if the representation, advice, or assistance is (1) for compensation, unless the representation, advice, assistance, and compensation are required by statute, regulation, or court rule, or is otherwise customary; or (2) without compensation, but rendered to benefit a personal or financial interest of the public officer. ALASKA STAT §§ 39.52.160, 39.52.440.	No	Yes	Civil Penalty
Arizona	A public officer or employee shall not represent another person for compensation before a public agency . . . concerning any matter with which the officer or employee was directly concerned and in which the officer or employee personally participated . . . by a substantial and material exercise of administrative discretion. ARIZ. REV. STAT. ANN. §§ 38-504(A), 38-510.	Yes	Yes	Felony
	No public officer or employee may receive or agree to receive directly or indirectly compensation other than as provided by law for any service rendered or to be rendered by him personally in any case, proceeding, application, or other matter which is pending before the public agency of which he is a public officer or employee. ARIZ. REV. STAT. ANN. §§ 38-505, 38-510.	Yes	Yes	Felony

Table 3.4-3—Representing Another Interest in a Particular Matter

State	Statutory Language	Prohibit Only Compensated Representation?	Limited to Agency for Which the Employee Works?	Maximum Offense Classification
California	A Member of the Legislature shall not . . . [a]ccept or agree to accept, or be in partnership with any person who accepts or agrees to accept, any employment, fee, or other thing of monetary value, or portion thereof, in consideration of his or her appearing, agreeing to appear, or taking any other action on behalf of another person before any state board or agency. CAL. GOV'T CODE §§ 8920(b)(3), 8926.	Yes	No	Misdemeanor (Felony for Conspiracy)
Connecticut	No public official or state employee . . . shall agree to accept . . . any employment, fee or other thing of value, or portion thereof, for appearing, agreeing to appear, or taking any other action on behalf of another person before [various state departments] . . . . CONN. GEN. STAT. §§ 1-84(d), 1-89.	Yes	No	Felony
Delaware	No state employee, state officer or honorary state official may represent or otherwise assist any private enterprise with respect to any matter before the state agency with which the employee, officer or official is associated by employment or appointment. DEL. CODE ANN. tit. 29, § 5805(b)(1).	No	Yes	Misdemeanor
	No state officer may represent or otherwise assist any private enterprise with respect to any matter before the State. DEL. CODE ANN. tit. 29, § 5805(b)(2).	No	No	Misdemeanor

Table 3.4-3—Representing Another Interest in a Particular Matter

State	Statutory Language	Prohibit Only Compensated Representation?	Limited to Agency for Which the Employee Works?	Maximum Offense Classification
Guam	No employee shall assist any person or business or act in a representative capacity before any territorial agency for any compensation in any transaction involving the Territory. 4 GUAM CODE ANN. §§ 15205(c), 15211.	Yes	No	Action Void-able
	No employee shall assist any person or business or act in a representative capacity for a fee or other compensation to secure passage of a bill or to obtain a contract, claim, or other transaction or proposal in which the employee has participated or will participate as an employee, nor shall the employee assist any person, or business, or act in a representative capacity for a fee or other compensation on such bill, contract, claim, or other transaction or proposal before the Legislature or territorial agency of which the individual is an employee. 4 GUAM CODE ANN. §§ 15205(d), 15211.	Yes	Yes	Action Void-able
	No employee shall assist any person or business or act in a representative capacity before a territorial agency for a fee or other compensation, on any bill, contract, claim, or other transaction or proposal involving official action by the agency if the employee has official authority over that agency . . . . 4 GUAM CODE ANN. §§ 15205(e), 15211.	Yes	Yes	Action Void-able

Table 3.4-3—Representing Another Interest in a Particular Matter

State	Statutory Language	Prohibit Only Compensated Representation?	Limited to Agency for Which the Employee Works?	Maximum Offense Classification
Hawaii	No legislator or employee shall assist any person or business or act in a representative capacity before any state or county agency for a contingent compensation in any transaction involving the State. HAW. REV. STAT. §§ 84-14(c); 84-19.	Yes	No	Action Void-able
	No legislator or employee shall assist any person or business or act in a representative capacity for a fee or other compensation to secure passage of a bill or to obtain a contract, claim, or other transaction or proposal in which the legislator or employee has participated or will participate as a legislator or employee, nor shall the legislator or employee assist any person or business or act in a representative capacity for a fee or other compensation on such bill, contract, claim, or other transaction or proposal before the legislature or agency of which the legislator or employee is an employee or legislator. HAW. REV. STAT. §§ 84-14(d); 84-19.	Yes	Yes	Action Void-able
	No employee shall assist any person or business or act in a representative capacity before a state or county agency for a fee or other consideration on any bill, contract, claim, or other transaction or proposal involving official action by the agency if the employee has official authority over that state or county agency . . . . HAW. REV. STAT. §§ 84-14(e); 84-19.	Yes	Yes	Action Void-able

Table 3.4-3—Representing Another Interest in a Particular Matter

State	Statutory Language	Prohibit Only Compensated Representation?	Limited to Agency for Which the Employee Works?	Maximum Offense Classification
Idaho	A public servant commits a misdemeanor if he solicits, accepts or agrees to accept compensation for advice or other assistance in preparing or promoting a bill, contract, claim, or other transaction or proposal as to which he knows that he has or is likely to have an official discretion to exercise. IDAHO CODE § 18-1357(1).	Yes	No	Misdemeanor
Illinois	No legislator may accept or participate in any way in any representation case . . . before (1) the Court of Claims of this State or (2) before the Illinois Workers' Compensation Commission, when the State of Illinois is the respondent. 5 ILL. COMP. STAT. 420/2-104; 420/2-105. *See also* 5 ILL. COMP. STAT. 420/3-105, 50 ILL. COMP. STAT. 105/3.	No	No	Misdemeanor
Kansas	No state officer or employee shall accept employment in any representation case, unless such officer or employee has properly filed the disclosure statement . . . . KAN. STAT. ANN. §§ 46-239(a), 46-226, 46-240, 46-276.	Yes	No	Misdemeanor

Table 3.4-3—Representing Another Interest in a Particular Matter

State	Statutory Language	Prohibit Only Compensated Representation?	Limited to Agency for Which the Employee Works?	Maximum Offense Classification
Kentucky	A person is guilty of unlawful compensation for assistance in public matters when . . . [w]hile a public servant, he solicits, accepts or agrees to accept compensation for advice or other assistance in preparing a bill, contract, claim or other transaction or proposal as to which he knows that he is likely to have an official discretion to exercise. KY. REV. STAT. ANN. § 521.040. *See also* KY. REV. STAT. ANN. §§ 6.757(b), 45A.340(2), 45A.990(3).	Yes	N/A	Misdemeanor
Louisiana	(1) No public servant . . . shall receive or agree to receive any thing of economic value for assisting a person in a transaction, or in an appearance in connection with a transaction, with the agency of such public servant . . . . LA. STAT. ANN. §§ 42:1111(E), 42:1153.	Yes	Yes	Civil Penalty
Maine	A person is guilty of improper compensation for services if . . . [b]eing a public servant, he solicits, accepts or agrees to accept any pecuniary benefit in return for advice or other assistance in preparing or promoting a bill, contract, claim or other transaction or proposal as to which he knows that he has or is likely to have an official discretion to exercise . . . . ME. STAT. tit. 17-A, § 606.	Yes	Yes	Misdemeanor (Class E Crime)

Table 3.4-3—Representing Another Interest in a Particular Matter

State	Statutory Language	Prohibit Only Compensated Representation?	Limited to Agency for Which the Employee Works?	Maximum Offense Classification
Maryland	[A]n official or employee may not, for contingent compensation, assist or represent a party in any matter before or involving any unit of the State or a political subdivision of the State . . . . MD. CODE ANN., GEN. PROV. §§ 5-504(a)(2), 5-902, 5-904. *See also* MD. CODE ANN., GEN. PROV. §§ 5-504(b)(1).	Yes	No	Civil Penalty
Massachusetts	(a) No state employee shall otherwise than as provided by law for the proper discharge of official duties, directly or indirectly receive or request compensation from anyone other than the commonwealth or a state agency, in relation to any particular matter in which the commonwealth or a state agency is a party or has a direct and substantial interest . . . (c) No state employee shall, otherwise than in the proper discharge of his official duties, act as agent or attorney for anyone other than the commonwealth or a state agency for prosecuting any claim against the commonwealth or a state agency, or as agent or attorney for anyone in connection with any particular matter in which the commonwealth or a state agency is a party or has a direct and substantial interest. MASS. GEN. LAWS ch. 268A, § 4.	Yes	No	Felony

Table 3.4-3—Representing Another Interest in a Particular Matter

State	**Statutory Language**	**Prohibit Only Compensated Representation?**	**Limited to Agency for Which the Employee Works?**	**Maximum Offense Classification**
Minnesota	A public official who represents a client for a fee before an individual, board, commission, or agency that has rulemaking authority in a hearing conducted under chapter 14, must disclose the official's participation in the action to the board within 14 days after the . . . appearance. MINN. STAT. §§ 10A.08, 10A.34; 43A.38(5)(c).	Yes	No	Civil Penalty
Missouri	No elected or appointed official or employee . . . shall . . . Perform any services during the time of his or her office or employment for any consideration . . . by which service he or she attempts to influence a decision of any agency of the state, or of any political subdivision in which he or she is an officer or employee or over which he or she has supervisory power. MO. REV. STAT. §§ 105.454(1)(4), 105.478.	Yes	Yes	Felony

Table 3.4-3—Representing Another Interest in a Particular Matter

State	Statutory Language	Prohibit Only Compensated Representation?	Limited to Agency for Which the Employee Works?	Maximum Offense Classification
Montana	(1) A public servant in any department or agency exercising regulatory function . . . may not solicit, accept, or agree to accept any pecuniary benefit from a person known to be subject to the regulation . . . . (2) A public servant having any discretionary function to perform in connection with . . . pecuniary transactions of the government may not solicit, accept, or agree to accept any pecuniary benefit from any person known to be interested in or likely to become interested in any . . . transaction. (3) A public servant having judicial or administrative authority . . . may not solicit, accept, or agree to accept any pecuniary benefit from a person known to be interested in or likely to become interested in any matter before the public servant or tribunal . . . . (4) A legislator . . . may not solicit, accept, or agree to accept any pecuniary benefit from a person known to be interested in or likely to become interested in any matter before the legislature . . . . MONT. CODE ANN. § 45-7-104. *See also* MONT. CODE ANN. § 2-2-121(2).	Yes	Yes	Misdemeanor

Table 3.4-3—Representing Another Interest in a Particular Matter

State	Statutory Language	Prohibit Only Compensated Representation?	Limited to Agency for Which the Employee Works?	Maximum Offense Classification
Nevada	If a public officer or employee serves in a state agency of the Executive Department or an agency of any county, city or other political subdivision, the public officer or employee: Shall not accept compensation from any private person to represent or counsel the private person on any issue pending before the agency in which that public officer or employee serves, if the agency makes decisions . . . . NEV. REV. STAT. ANN. § 281A.410(1)(a).	Yes	Yes	Civil Penalty
New Hampshire	A person is guilty of a misdemeanor if . . . [b]eing a public servant, he solicits, accepts, or agrees to accept any pecuniary benefit in return for advice or other assistance in preparing or promoting a bill, contract, claim, or other transaction or proposal as to which he knows that he has or is likely to have an official discretion to exercise. N.H. REV. STAT. ANN. § 640:6(I).	Yes	Yes	Misde-meanor
New Jersey	No special State officer or employee . . . shall represent . . . any person or party other than the State in connection with any cause, proceeding, application or other matter pending before the particular office . . . in which such special State officer or employee holds office or employment. N.J. STAT. ANN. §§ 52:13D-16(a), 52:13D-21.	No	Yes	Civil Penalty

Table 3.4-3—Representing Another Interest in a Particular Matter

State	Statutory Language	Prohibit Only Compensated Representation?	Limited to Agency for Which the Employee Works?	Maximum Offense Classification
New Mexico	A legislator shall not appear for, represent or assist another person in a matter before a state agency, unless without compensation or for the benefit of a constituent, except for legislators who are attorneys or other professional persons engaged in the conduct of their professions and, in those instances, the legislator shall refrain from references to the legislator's legislative capacity . . . . N.M. Stat. Ann. §§ 10-16-9(B); 10-16-17.	Yes	No	Misdemeanor

Table 3.4-3—Representing Another Interest in a Particular Matter

State	Statutory Language	Prohibit Only Compensated Representation?	Limited to Agency for Which the Employee Works?	Maximum Offense Classification
New York	No statewide elected official, or state officer or employee, other than in the proper discharge of official state or local governmental duties, or member of the legislature or legislative employee, or political party chairman shall receive, directly or indirectly, or enter into any agreement express or implied for, any compensation, in whatever form, for the appearance or rendition of services by himself, herself or another in relation to any case, proceeding, application or other matter before a state agency where such appearance or rendition of services is in connection with: (i) the purchase, sale, rental or lease of real property, goods or services, or a contract therefor, from, to or with any such agency; (ii) any proceeding relating to rate making; (iii) the adoption or repeal of any rule or regulation having the force and effect of law; (iv) the obtaining of grants of money or loans; (v) licensing; or (vi) any proceeding relating to a franchise provided for in the public service law. N.Y. Pub. Off. § 73(7)(a). *See also* N.Y. Pub. Off. § 73(2), (7)(b).	Yes	No	Misdemeanor

Table 3.4-3—Representing Another Interest in a Particular Matter

State	Statutory Language	Prohibit Only Compensated Representation?	Limited to Agency for Which the Employee Works?	Maximum Offense Classification
North Dakota	A public servant is guilty of a class A misdemeanor if he solicits, accepts, or agrees to accept a thing of pecuniary value from nongovernmental sources: a. As compensation for advice or other assistance in preparing or promoting a bill, contract, claim, or other matter which is or is likely to be subject to his official action; b. As compensation for omitting or delaying official action; or c. As a fee or compensation for services not rendered or to which he was not legally entitled. N.D. CENT. CODE § 12.1-12-03(1).	Yes	Yes	Misde-meanor
Northern Mariana Islands	A nonelected public official or public employee shall not appear as the advocate of another person before a Commonwealth governmental entity. A public official or public employee shall not appear as an attorney for another person before a Commonwealth governmental entity. A public official or public employee shall not provide formal or informal representation for a client, constituent, or other person whom the public official or public employee has represented for a fee or other consideration in a matter within the preceding 12 months. 1 N. MAR. I. CODE §§ 8536, 8537, 8538, 8572.	No	No	Misde-meanor

Table 3.4-3—Representing Another Interest in a Particular Matter

State	Statutory Language	Prohibit Only Compensated Representation?	Limited to Agency for Which the Employee Works?	Maximum Offense Classification
Ohio	No present or former public official or employee shall . . . represent a client or act in a representative capacity for any person on any matter in which the public official or employee personally participated as a public official or employee through . . . substantial exercise of administrative discretion. OHIO REV. CODE ANN. §§ 102.03(A)(1), 102.99(B).	No	Yes	Misde-meanor
Oklahoma	No state officer or employee shall receive or agree to receive compensation to represent or assist another individual or other entity in any transaction involving the state . . . . No state officer or employee shall represent another individual or other entity as an attorney in any matter before the Commission, nor shall any state officer or employee represent another individual or other entity in any matter before the agency that employs the state officer or employee, unless authorized by law. OKLA. ETHICS COMM'N RULE 4.18, 4.19, 6.13.	Yes	No	Civil Penalty
Oregon	A person may not attempt to represent or represent a client for a fee before the governing body of a public body of which the person is a member. OR. REV. STAT. §§ 244.040(6), 244.350.	Yes	Yes	Civil Penalty

Table 3.4-3—Representing Another Interest in a Particular Matter

State	Statutory Language	Prohibit Only Compensated Representation?	Limited to Agency for Which the Employee Works?	Maximum Offense Classification
Puerto Rico	(a) No public servant shall represent any private person or business, either directly or indirectly, with respect to an official action, if he/she, a member of his/her family unit, relative, partner or housemate has participated, shall participate or will probably participate in the disposition of said official action. . . . (b) No public servant shall represent any private person or business before an agency with regard to any official action in which the appointing authority is his/her relative, member of his/her family unit, partner or housemate. (c) No public servant shall, in his/her private capacity, represent or counsel, either directly or indirectly, a private person or business before any agency, in cases or matters involving a conflict of interests or public policy between the Government and the interests of such a private person or business. (d) No full-time public servant shall, during working hours, represent, advise or serve as an expert for a private person or business in trials, public hearings or in any other case or matter before a court of justice, quasi judicial body or an agency. P.R. Laws Ann. tit. 3, §§ 1857c, 1857f.	No	No	Civil Penalty

Table 3.4-3—Representing Another Interest in a Particular Matter

State	Statutory Language	Prohibit Only Compensated Representation?	Limited to Agency for Which the Employee Works?	Maximum Offense Classification
Rhode Island	No person subject to this code of ethics shall: (1) Represent him or herself before any state or municipal agency of which he or she is a member or by which he or she is employed . . . (2) Represent any other person before any state or municipal agency of which he or she is a member or by which he or she is employed. (3) Act as an expert witness before any state or municipal agency of which he or she is a member or by which he or she is employed with respect to any matter the agency's disposition of which will or can reasonably be expected to directly result in an economic benefit or detriment to him or herself. . . . 36 R.I. GEN. LAWS §§ 36-14-5(e), 36-14-19.	No	Yes	Misdemeanor
South Carolina	No person may offer or pay to a public official . . . or public employee . . . for advice or assistance given in the course of his employment as a public official, public member, or public employee. S.C. CODE ANN. §§ 8-13-720, 8-13-1520.	Yes	No	Misdemeanor
	A public official . . . may not knowingly represent another person before a governmental entity . . . [and] may not knowingly represent another person before the same unit or division of the governmental entity for which the public member has official responsibility. . . . S.C. CODE ANN. §§ 8-13-740; 8-13-1520. *See also* S.C. CODE ANN. § 8-13-745.	No	Yes	Misdemeanor

Table 3.4-3—Representing Another Interest in a Particular Matter

State	Statutory Language	Prohibit Only Compensated Representation?	Limited to Agency for Which the Employee Works?	Maximum Offense Classification
Texas	A member of the legislature may not, for compensation, represent another person before a state agency in the executive branch of state government unless [exceptions apply]. TEX. GOV'T CODE ANN. § 572.052.	Yes	No	Misde-meanor
Utah	[I]t is an offense for a public officer or public employee to receive or agree to receive compensation for assisting any person or business entity in any transaction involving an agency unless the public officer or public employee files a sworn, written [disclosure] statement . . . . UTAH CODE ANN. §§ 67-16-6(1), 67-16-14.	Yes	No	Dis-missal Void con-tract
Washington	Except in the course of official duties or incident to official duties, no state officer or state employee may assist another person, directly or indirectly, whether or not for compensation, in a transaction involving the state: (a) In which the state officer or state employee has at any time participated; or (b) If the transaction involving the state is or has been under the official responsibility of the state officer or state employee within a period of two years preceding such assistance. WASH. REV. CODE §§ 42.52.040(1), 42.52.490.	No	Yes	Civil Penalty

Table 3.4-3—Representing Another Interest in a Particular Matter

State	Statutory Language	Prohibit Only Compensated Representation?	Limited to Agency for Which the Employee Works?	Maximum Offense Classification
West Virginia	No . . . public official or public employee shall . . . represent a client or act in a representative capacity with or without compensation on behalf of any person in a contested case . . . or other particular matter involving a specific party or parties which arose during his or her period of public service or employment and in which he or she personally and substantially participated in a decision-making, advisory or staff support capacity, unless the appropriate government agency, after consultation, consents to such representation. W. Va. Code §§ 6B-2-5(f), 6B-2-10.	No	Yes	Misdemeanor
Wisconsin	No state public official . . . may represent a person for compensation before a department or any employee thereof, except: 1. In a contested case which involves a party other than the state with interests adverse to those represented by the state public official; or 2. At an open hearing at which a stenographic or other record is maintained; or 3. In a matter that involves only ministerial action by the department; or 4. In a matter before the department of revenue or tax appeals commission that involves the representation of a client in connection with a tax matter. Wis. Stat. §§ 19.45(7)(a), 19.58.	Yes	No	Misdemeanor

IV. Receiving Money from Third Parties Not Relating to a Particular Matter

Conflict of interest rules reach all types of personal enrichment from third parties that fall short of bribery and gratuities (for lack of a quid pro quo character), but that still threaten to taint the public official's independent judgment and full loyalty to the public interest. Forms of personal enrichment include salary supplementation, gifts, honoraria, and reimbursement of expenses. Because the public officials cannot reciprocate without endangering the public interest, the receipt of gifts and other ostensibly free benefits from third parties is restricted by law.[74]

The relevant federal law, 18 U.S.C. § 209, is different from other conflict-of-interest rules because the prohibited payments need not relate to any particular matter or governmental action. It prohibits giving or receiving "any salary, or any contribution to or supplementation of salary, as compensation for his services as an officer or employee . . . from any source other than the Government of the United States . . . ."[75] Even more than other conflicts rules, § 209 is a "rule prohibiting two payrolls and two paymasters for the same employee on the same job."[76] Three rationales underlie this prohibition:

> First, the outside payor has a hold on the employee deriving from his ability to cut off one of the employee's economic lifelines. Second, the employee may tend to favor his outside payor even though no direct pressure is put on him to do so. And, third, because of these real risks, the arrangement has a generally unwholesome appearance that breeds suspicion and bitterness among fellow employees and other observers.[77]

In part because of these three bases for the rule, § 209 does not apply to payments that occur before a person becomes a government employee, such

---

74 State v. Ross, 151 P.3d 1261, 1265 (Ariz. Ct. App. 2007) (explaining that, under Arizona conflict-of-interest laws, accepting gifts is prohibited "even if there is no direct link between what is given and what is expected in return" and that "so long as the source and nature of the valuable thing or benefit manifests a substantial and improper influence on the officer's duties").

75 18 U.S.C. § 209 (2018).

76 Crandon v. United States, 494 U.S. 152, 165 (1990).

77 *Id.*

as severance payments by an employer when the employee leaves to join the government.[78]

Many states prohibit receipt of money from a third party as compensation for official duties. State statutes also prohibit gifts and other forms of personal enrichment from third parties not tied to any particular act.[79]

Under federal law and typically under state law, the intent of the payor determines whether the payment is made as compensation for the payee's government services. Section 209 does not require a specific intent, unlike bribery, but to "conclude that a payment was made 'as compensation,' one must determine the intent of the payor."[80] This intent requirement avoids "criminalizing otherwise innocent conduct."[81] State laws similarly typically prohibit receipt of compensation for performance of official duties as a public officer.[82] If the public employee receives compensation in exchange for an act already required by his public duties, it is irrelevant that he may have performed those duties while on leave from his government job.[83]

---

78 *Id.* at 159. *See also* HENNING, *supra* note 4, at § 9.06 (analyzing § 209 in detail).

79 *See* Skvorc v. State, 996 P.2d 1192, 1201-02 (Alaska 2000) (explaining that compensation is not limited to salary-type pay arrangements, but may include "any money, thing of value, or economic benefit conferred on or received by a person in return for services rendered or to be rendered by the person for another").

80 United States v. Project on Gov't Oversight, 616 F.3d 544, 550 (D.C. Cir. 2010).

81 *Id.* ("Without the requirement of an intent element, a parent's monthly checks to a child who works for the government could be construed as violating § 209(a): only the parent's intent distinguishes payments to help cover the rent from payments to subsidize what the parent regards as an insufficient public-sector salary.").

82 *See, e.g.*, State v. Ross, 151 P.3d 1261, 1266-67 (Ariz. Ct. App. 2007) (construing the Arizona statute and finding that "the conflict of interest statute requires an action related to the officer's official duties as a public officer"); Bott v. State, 492 So. 2d 722, 723 (Fla. Dist. Ct. App. 1986) ("an essential element of the offenses of bribery and unlawful compensation for official behavior [is] that the act or omission sought to be influenced be in the official capacity of the public servant").

83 *See Skvorc*, 996 P.2d at 1202.

Table 3.4-4—Receiving Money from Third Parties Not Relating to a Particular Matter

State	Statutory Language	Maximum Offense Classification
Alabama	No lobbyist, or subordinate of a lobbyist or principal shall offer or provide a thing of value to a public employee or public official or to a family member of the public employee or family member of the public official; and no public employee or public official or family member of the public employee or family member of the public official shall solicit or receive a thing of value from a lobbyist, subordinate of a lobbyist or principal. Notwithstanding the foregoing, a lobbyist or principal may offer or provide and a public official, public employee, or candidate may solicit or receive items of de minimis value. ALA. CODE §§ 36-25-5.1(a), 36-25-27.	Felony
Alaska	A public officer may not . . . accept, receive, or solicit compensation for the performance of official duties or responsibilities from a person other than the state. ALASKA STAT. §§ 39.52.120 (b)(2), 39.52.130, 39.52.440.	Civil Penalty
Arizona	A public officer or employee shall not use or attempt to use the officer's or employee's official position to secure any valuable thing or valuable benefit for the officer or employee that would not ordinarily accrue to the officer or employee in the performance of the officer's or employee's official duties if the thing or benefit is of such character as to manifest a substantial and improper influence on the officer or employee with respect to the officer's or employee's duties. ARIZ. REV. STAT. ANN. §§ 38-504(C), 38-510.	Felony
Arkansas	A person commits the offense of soliciting unlawful compensation if he or she requests a benefit for the performance of an official action as a public servant knowing that he or she is required to perform that action: (1) Without compensation, other than authorized salary or allowances; or (2) At a level of compensation lower than that requested. ARK. CODE ANN. § 5-52-104. *See also* ARK. CODE ANN. §§ 21-8-801(a)(1), 5-52-108.	Misdemeanor

Table 3.4-4—Receiving Money from Third Parties Not Relating to a Particular Matter

State	Statutory Language	Maximum Offense Classification
California	A Member of the Legislature shall not . . . [r]eceive or agree to receive, directly or indirectly, any compensation, reward, or gift from any source except the State of California for any service, advice, assistance or other matter related to the legislative process . . . . CAL. GOV'T CODE §§ 8920(b)(4), 8926.	Misdemeanor
Colorado	A public servant commits a class 2 misdemeanor if he requests a pecuniary benefit for the performance of an official action knowing that he was required to perform that action without compensation or at a level of compensation lower than that requested. COLO. REV. STAT. § 18-8-304. *See also* COLO. REV. STAT. § 24-18-104(1)(b).	Misdemeanor
Connecticut	(j) No public official, state employee or candidate for public office, or a member of any such person's staff or immediate family shall knowingly accept any gift . . . from a person known to be a registrant or anyone known to be acting on behalf of a registrant. (k) No public official, spouse of the Governor or state employee shall accept a fee or honorarium . . . (m) No public official or state employee shall knowingly accept, directly or indirectly, any gift . . . from any person the public official or state employee knows or has reason to know: (1) Is doing business with or seeking to do business with the department or agency in which the public official or state employee is employed; (2) is engaged in activities which are directly regulated by such department or agency . . . . CONN. GEN. STAT. §§ 1-84, 1-89.	Felony
District of Columbia	An employee shall not receive any compensation . . . or any other thing of value from a source other than the District government for the employee's performance of official duties. D.C. CODE §§ 1-1162.23(d)(1), 1-1162.21.	Civil Penalty

Table 3.4-4—Receiving Money from Third Parties Not Relating to a Particular Matter

State	Statutory Language	Maximum Offense Classification
Florida	It is unlawful for . . . a public servant, to knowingly and intentionally request, solicit, accept, or agree to accept, any pecuniary or other benefit not authorized by law, for the past, present, or future performance, nonperformance, or violation of any act or omission . . . either within the official discretion of the public servant, in violation of a public duty, or in performance of a public duty. FLA. STAT. § 838.016(1). *See also* FLA. CONST. art. II, § 8(e).	Felony
Georgia	If any person who has been elected to any office shall sell or farm out said office; or if any person shall purchase or agree to give any money or thing of value to a person elected for the privileges of exercising the duties of said office . . . he shall be guilty of a felony . . . . GA. CODE ANN. § 45-11-2.	Felony
Idaho	No public servant shall . . . [s]olicit, accept or receive a pecuniary benefit as payment for services, advice, assistance or conduct customarily exercised in the course of his official duties . . . . IDAHO CODE §§ 18-1359(1)(b), 18-1360.	Misde-meanor
Illinois	No legislator may accept compensation, other than that provided by law for members of the General Assembly, for performance of his official legislative duties. 5 ILL. COMP. STAT. ANN. 420/2-103.	Petty Offense
Kansas	No state officer or employee shall accept compensation for performance of official duties. KAN. STAT. ANN. § 46-235.	Misde-meanor
Kentucky	A public servant shall not knowingly accept compensation, other than that provided by law for public servants, for performance of his official duties without the prior approval of the commission. KY. REV. STAT. ANN. §§ 11A.040(5), 11A.990.	Felony

Table 3.4-4—Receiving Money from Third Parties Not Relating to a Particular Matter

State	Statutory Language	Maximum Offense Classification
	A public servant is guilty of soliciting unlawful compensation when he requests a pecuniary benefit for the performance of an official action knowing that he was required to perform that action without compensation or at a level of compensation lower than that requested. KY. REV. STAT. ANN. § 521.030.	Misdemeanor
Louisiana	No public servant shall receive anything of economic value, other than compensation and benefits from the governmental entity to which he is duly entitled, for the performance of the duties and responsibilities of his office or position . . . . LA. STAT. ANN. §§ 42:1111, 42:1153.	Civil Penalty
Maine	A person is guilty of improper gifts to public servants if . . . [b]eing a public servant that person solicits, accepts or agrees to accept any pecuniary benefit from a person if the public servant knows or reasonably should know that the purpose of the donor in making the gift is to influence the public servant in the performance of the public servant's official duties or vote . . . . ME. STAT. tit. 17-A, § 605.	Misdemeanor (Class E Crime)
Massachusetts	No current officer or employee of a state, county or municipal agency shall knowingly, or with reason to know: . . . solicit or receive anything of substantial value . . . because of the officer or employee's official position. MASS. GEN. LAWS ch. 268A, §§ 23(b)(2), 26.	Felony
Michigan	A public officer or employee shall not solicit or accept a gift or loan of money, goods, services, or other thing of value for the benefit of a person or organization, other than the state, which tends to influence the manner in which the public officer or employee or another public officer or employee performs official duties. MICH. COMP. LAWS § 15.342(4).	Civil Penalty

Table 3.4-4—Receiving Money from Third Parties Not Relating to a Particular Matter

State	Statutory Language	Maximum Offense Classification
Minnesota	Whoever is a public officer or public employee and under color of office or employment intentionally asks, receives, or agrees to receive a fee or other compensation in excess of that allowed by law or where no such fee or compensation is allowed, is guilty of a misdemeanor. MINN. STAT. § 609.45. *See also* MINN. STAT. §§10A.071, 43A.38(5)(a).	Misdemeanor
Mississippi	No public servant shall use his official position to obtain, or attempt to obtain, pecuniary benefit for himself other than that compensation provided for by law . . . . MISS. CODE ANN. § 25-4-105(1).	Civil Penalty
Missouri	No elected or appointed official or employee . . . shall: (1) Perform any service for any agency of the state . . . for receipt or payment of any compensation, other than of the compensation provided for the performance of his or her official duties . . . . MO. REV. STAT. §§ 105.454(1)(1), 105.478.	Felony

Table 3.4-4—Receiving Money from Third Parties Not Relating to a Particular Matter

State	Statutory Language	Maximum Offense Classification
Montana	(1) A public servant in any department or agency exercising regulatory function . . . may not solicit, accept, or agree to accept any pecuniary benefit from a person known to be subject to the regulation . . . . (2) A public servant having any discretionary function to perform in connection with . . . pecuniary transactions of the government may not solicit, accept, or agree to accept any pecuniary benefit from any person known to be interested in or likely to become interested in any . . . transaction. (3) A public servant having judicial or administrative authority . . . may not solicit, accept, or agree to accept any pecuniary benefit from a person known to be interested in or likely to become interested in any matter before the public servant or tribunal . . . . (4) A legislator . . . may not solicit, accept, or agree to accept any pecuniary benefit from a person known to be interested in or likely to become interested in any matter before the legislature . . . . MONT. CODE ANN. § 45-7-104. *See also* MONT. CODE ANN. §§ 2-2-104, 2-2-111, 2-2-121, 2-2-136.	Misdemeanor
Nevada	A public officer or employee shall not accept any salary, retainer, augmentation, expense allowance or other compensation from any private source for the performance of the public officer's or employee's duties as a public officer or employee. NEV. REV. STAT. § 281A.400(4).	Civil Penalty
New Hampshire	A person is guilty of a misdemeanor if: I. Being a public servant he solicits, accepts or agrees to accept any pecuniary benefit from a person who is or is likely to become subject to or interested in any matter or action pending before or contemplated by himself or the governmental body with which he is affiliated; or II. He knowingly gives, offers, or promises any pecuniary benefit prohibited by paragraph I. N.H. REV. STAT. ANN. § 640:5.	Misdemeanor

Table 3.4-4—Receiving Money from Third Parties Not Relating to a Particular Matter

State	Statutory Language	Maximum Offense Classification
New Jersey	No State officer or employee . . . shall solicit, receive or agree to receive, whether directly or indirectly, any compensation, reward, employment, gift, honorarium, out-of-State travel or subsistence expense or other thing of value from any source other than the State of New Jersey, for any service . . . related to the officer, employee, or member's official duties, except as authorized in this section. N.J. Stat. Ann. §§ 52:13D-24. 52:13D-21.	Civil Penalty
New Mexico	No legislator, public officer or employee may request or receive an honorarium for a speech or service rendered that relates to the performance of public duties. N.M. Stat. Ann. §§ 10-16-4.1, 10-16-17.	Misde-meanor
New York	A member of the legislature or any officer or employee of the legislature who asks or receives or consents or agrees to receive any emolument, gratuity or reward or any promise of emolument, gratuity or reward or any money, property or thing of value or of personal advantage, except such as may be authorized by law, for doing or omitting to do any official act . . . shall be guilty of a felony . . . . N.Y. Pub. Off. Law § 77. *See also* N.Y. Pub. Off. Law § 74(3)(a).	Felony
North Carolina	A public servant or legislative employee shall not solicit or receive personal financial gain . . . for acting in the public servant or legislative employee's official capacity, or for advice or assistance given in the course of carrying out the public servant's or legislative employee's duties. N.C. Gen. Stat. §§ 138A-33; 138A-45.	Disci-pline

Table 3.4-4—Receiving Money from Third Parties Not Relating to a Particular Matter

State	Statutory Language	Maximum Offense Classification
Northern Mariana Islands	(a) No person shall give to any public official or public employee . . . any anonymous gift. (b) No person shall give or offer to give to any public official . . . anything of value . . . based upon any explicit or implicit mutual understanding that the votes, official actions, decisions or judgments of any official, employee, or Commonwealth contractor concerning the business of the Commonwealth would be influenced thereby . . . . 1 N. MAR. I. CODE §§ 8551, 8552, 8553, 8572.	Misdemeanor
Ohio	[With limited exception], no person elected or appointed to an office of or employed by the general assembly or any department . . . of the state, excluding the courts, shall receive or agree to receive directly or indirectly compensation other than from the agency with which he serves for any service rendered or to be rendered by him personally in any case, proceeding, application, or other matter that is before the general assembly or any department, division, institution, instrumentality, board, commission, or bureau of the state, excluding the courts. OHIO REV. CODE ANN. §§ 102.04(A), 102.99.	Misdemeanor
	No public servant shall knowingly solicit or accept, and no person shall knowingly promise or give to a public servant . . . [a]ny compensation . . . to perform the public servant's official duties . . . . OHIO REV. CODE ANN. § 2921.43(A).	Misdemeanor
Oklahoma	No state officer or employee shall accept any gift for himself or herself or for his or her family member from any vendor or vendor's agent that is selling or attempting to sell goods or services to the state officer or employee's agency if the state officer or employee is engaged in purchasing decisions . . . . OKLA. ETHICS COMM'N RULE r. 4.8-4.16, 6.13.	Civil Penalty

Table 3.4-4—Receiving Money from Third Parties Not Relating to a Particular Matter

State	Statutory Language	Maximum Offense Classification
Puerto Rico	(b) No public servant shall accept or keep a job or contractual relations from which he/she obtains undue advantage with a private person or business that is regulated by or has contractual business or financial relations with the government agency for which he/she works, when the public servant is empowered to decide or influence the official actions of the agency with regard to such private person or business. P.R. LAWS ANN. tit. 3, §§ 1857b, 1857f.	Felony
Rhode Island	No person subject to this code of ethics shall accept other employment which will either impair his or her independence of judgment as to his or her official duties or employment or require him or her, or induce him or her, to disclose confidential information acquired by him or her in the course of and by reason of his or her official duties. 36 R.I. GEN. LAWS §§ 36-14-5(b), 36-14-19.	Misdemeanor
South Carolina	A public official, public member, or public employee . . . who receives, accepts, or takes, directly or indirectly, from a person, anything of value worth twenty-five dollars or more in a day and anything of value worth two hundred dollars or more in the aggregate in a calendar year must report . . . the thing of value from: (1) a person, if there is reason to believe the donor would not give the thing of value but for the public official's public member's, or public employee's office or position; (2) a person, or from an officer or director of a person, if the public official, public member, or public employee has reason to believe the person: (a) has or is seeking to obtain contractual or other business or financial relationships with the public official's, public member's, or public employee's governmental entity; (b) conducts operations or activities which are regulated by the public official's, public member's, or public employee's governmental entity. S.C. CODE ANN. §§ 8-13-710, 8-13-1520. *See also* S.C. CODE ANN. § 8-13-715.	Misdemeanor

Table 3.4-4—Receiving Money from Third Parties Not Relating to a Particular Matter

State	Statutory Language	Maximum Offense Classification
Tennessee	It is an offense for any member of the general assembly, member-elect of the general assembly, governor, member of the governor's staff, secretary of state, treasurer, or comptroller of the treasury to knowingly receive a fee, commission or any other form of compensation for consulting services from any person or entity, other than compensation paid by the state, a county or municipality. TENN. CODE ANN. § 2-10-123.	Misdemeanor
Texas	(a) A public servant in an agency performing regulatory functions or conducting inspections or investigations commits an offense if he solicits, accepts, or agrees to accept any benefit from a person the public servant knows to be subject to regulation, inspection, or investigation by the public servant or his agency. [Sections (b)-(g) list different types of public servants and persons who might be subject to the public servant's power, and prohibits the public servant from accepting a benefit from that person.] TEX. PENAL CODE ANN. § 36.08. *See also* TEX. PENAL CODE ANN. § 36.07.	Misdemeanor
Utah	[With limited exception,] it is an offense for a public officer or public employee to knowingly receive, accept, take, seek, or solicit, directly or indirectly for himself or another a gift of substantial value or a substantial economic benefit tantamount to a gift . . . that would tend improperly to influence a reasonable person in the person's position to depart from the faithful and impartial discharge of the person's public duties . . . [or] if the public officer or public employee recently has been, is now, or in the near future may be involved in any governmental action directly affecting the donor or lender, unless a disclosure of the gift, compensation, or loan and other relevant information has been made . . . . UTAH CODE ANN. §§ 67-16-5; 67-16-12.	Felony

Table 3.4-4—Receiving Money from Third Parties Not Relating to a Particular Matter

State	Statutory Language	Maximum Offense Classification
Vermont	If a member of the Public Utility Commission or the clerk of such Commission receives pay for any service from any party other than the State, or for neglect of any service, he or she shall be imprisoned not more than six months or fined not more than $1,000.00, or both. This section shall not be construed to prevent the clerk of such Commission from receiving the usual fees for copies of records or papers in his or her office. VT. STAT. ANN. tit. 13, § 1105.	Misdemeanor
Virgin Islands	No territorial officer or employee shall: . . . accept other employment which will either impair his independence of judgment as to his official duties . . . . V.I. Code Ann. §§ 1102(4), 1108.	Felony
Virginia	No officer or employee of a state or local governmental or advisory agency shall . . . [s]olicit or accept money or other thing of value for services performed within the scope of his official duties . . . . VA. CODE ANN. §§ 2.2-3103(1), 2.2-3120. *See also* VA. CODE ANN. § 30-103.	Misdemeanor
Washington	A public servant is guilty of requesting unlawful compensation if he or she requests a pecuniary benefit for the performance of an official action knowing that he or she is required to perform that action without compensation or at a level of compensation lower than that requested. WASH. REV. CODE ANN. § 9A.68.020.	Felony
	A person is guilty of receiving . . . unlawful compensation if . . . [b]eing a public servant, he or she requests, accepts, or agrees to accept compensation for advice or other assistance in preparing a bill, contract, claim, or transaction regarding which he or she knows he or she is likely to have an official discretion to exercise . . . . WASH. REV. CODE ANN. §§ 9A.68.030. *See also* WASH. REV. CODE ANN. §§ 42.52.110-42.52.140.	Felony

Table 3.4-4—Receiving Money from Third Parties Not Relating to a Particular Matter

State	Statutory Language	Maximum Offense Classification
West Virginia	(a) It shall be unlawful: (1) For any public servant in any department . . . exercising regulatory functions, or conducting inspections or investigations, or carrying on civil or criminal litigation on behalf of the government, or having custody of prisoners, to solicit, accept or agree to accept, directly or indirectly, any gift or gratuity from a person known by such public servant to be subject to such regulation, inspection, investigation or custody, or against whom such litigation is known by such public servant to be pending or contemplated. [Subsections (2)-(4) list different types of public servants and persons who might be subject to the public servant's power, and prohibits the public servant from accepting gifts from that person.] W. VA. CODE §§ 61-5A-6, 61-5A-9(d). *See also* W. VA. CODE §§ 6B-2-5(c), 6B-2-10.	Misdemeanor
Wisconsin	No person may offer or give to a state public official, directly or indirectly, and no state public official may solicit or accept from any person, directly or indirectly, anything of value if it could reasonably be expected to influence the state public official's vote, official actions or judgment, or could reasonably be considered as a reward for any official action or inaction on the part of the state public official. This subsection does not prohibit a state public official from engaging in outside employment. WIS. STAT. §§ 19.45(3), 19.58.	Misdemeanor
Wyoming	A public servant commits soliciting unlawful compensation if he solicits, accepts or agrees to accept a pecuniary benefit for the performance of an official action knowing that he was required to perform that action without compensation or at a level of compensation lower than that requested. WYO. STAT. ANN. § 6-5-104.	Felony

V. Activity After Government Service

The idea of the revolving door is that many government officials and employees enter public service knowing that at some point in the future—possibly as soon as the next change of administration—they will be seeking employment in the private sector, so it is a conflict between the faithful government employee and his future self. That knowledge may influence a government employee's judgment in favor of those private interests while serving the public.[84] On the other hand, the government must "draw upon America's entire reservoir of talent and skill to help conduct our . . . most important business—the public business."[85] "[O]ffering the opportunity to move from private to public employment and back again may enable the government to secure the services of skilled people who are unwilling to devote their careers to public service at current rates of pay."[86] To balance these concerns, ethics rules at the federal and state level generally focus not on prohibiting employment after public service, but on limiting the types of matters the former government employee may work on after leaving public service.

Revolving door laws "place certain restrictions on public officials and employees with respect to the relationship that may exist between a public official or employee, and the government, and the private sector."[87] The relevant federal law and state laws generally agree on the basic "ethical requirement that . . . a public employee may not, upon retirement, act on behalf of a private client in any matter upon which he was engaged in the public interest."[88] But laws vary significantly in how they restrict public employees' post-employment involvement in government-related matters.

---

84 *See* United States v. Medico Indus., Inc., 784 F.2d 840, 843 (7th Cir. 1986).

85 Crandon v. United States, 494 U.S. 152, 166-67 (1990) (quoting President John F. Kennedy's Message from the President of the United States Relative to Ethical Conduct in the Government, H.R. Doc. No. 145, 87th Cong., 1st Sess., 2 (1961)).

86 *Medico*, 784 F.2d at 843.

87 State v. Nipps, 419 N.E.2d 1128, 1132 (Ohio Ct. App. 1979).

88 *In re* Biederman, 307 A.2d 595, 597 (N.J. 1973) (discussing a lawyer's ethical obligation and stating that "[t]he same principle is reflected in" the conflict of interest statute). *See also* 18 U.S.C. § 207(a).

The relevant federal statute, 18 U.S.C. § 207, has two main types of restrictions: a permanent restriction and a two-year restriction.[89] The permanent restriction prohibits a former officer or employee of the executive branch from knowingly making, with the intent to influence, any communication to or appearance before any department, agency, or court, in connection with a particular matter where (A) the government is a party or has a direct and substantial interest, (B) the person participated in the matter personally and substantially as an officer or employee, and (C) the matter involved a specific party or specific parties at the time of the person's participation.[90] The two-year restriction prohibits the same conduct, but instead of matters the former employee personally and substantially participated in, it pertains to matters "such person knows or reasonably should know [were] actually pending under his or her official responsibility as such officer or employee within a period of 1 year before the termination of his or her service or employment with the United States" and applies for only two years after leaving government service.[91]

Some states similarly have both permanent and temporary restrictions that differ in terms of the nature of the government employee's activity and the type of activity that is prohibited after leaving government employment.[92] Other states may have just one type of restriction.[93] Others have a variety of restrictions and timeframes.[94] Key features of revolving door laws are what role the government employee played while employed by the government (whether it must be personal and substantial participation or supervisory responsibility),[95] whether the restriction flows from involvement in a particular matter with

89 18 U.S.C. § 207(a). Additionally, § 207 has various other specific restrictions. *Id.* § 207(b)-(g).

90 *Id.* § 207(a)(1).

91 *Id.* § 207(a)(2).

92 *See, e.g.*, Fla. Stat. § 112.3185(3), (4).

93 *See, e.g.*, Del. Code Ann. tit. 29, § 5805(d).

94 *See, e.g.*, Or. Rev. Stat. § 244.045.

95 The permanent federal restriction requires that the former employee participated in the matter personally and substantially, which the statute defines as "an action taken as an officer or employee through decision, approval, disapproval, recommendation, the rendering of advice, investigation, or other such action." 18 U.S.C. § 207(i)(2).

specific parties or from general involvement as a government employee,[96] and whether the law has an intent requirement.[97]

The table below summarizes relevant state statutes into what level of prior involvement disqualifies future action ("If the public employee has"), what the scope of the subsequent prohibited activity is ("Then he or she cannot"), the duration of the prohibition, and the offense classification.

Table 3.4-5—Activity After Government Service

State & Statute	If the public employee has
Alabama ALA. CODE § 36-25-13	Served as a member of a board, agency, commission, department, or legislative body or worked for such body pursuant to an arrangement such as a consulting agreement, agency transfer, loan, or similar agreement, or been elected to a term of office
Alaska ALASKA STAT. §§ 39.52.180(a), 39.52.440	Participated personally and substantially through the exercise of official action on a matter that was under consideration by the administrative unit served by that public officer
ALASKA STAT. § 39.52.180 (d)	Held a position listed in the subsection

96 Under the federal statute, both the permanent and two-year restriction apply only to situations that involve a "particular matter," which must involve "specific parties" at the time it was pending. Under the statutory definition, "particular matter" "includes any investigation, application, request for a ruling or determination, rulemaking, contract, controversy, claim, charge, accusation, arrest, or judicial or other proceeding." 18 U.S.C. § 207(i)(3).

97 The federal statute has two intent requirements for both the permanent restriction and the two-year restriction. It prohibits a former government employee from knowingly making certain types of communications or appearances with the intent to influence. 18 U.S.C. § 207(a)(1). Some state laws similarly prohibit representation or communications with the intent to influence a decision or prohibit serving as a lobbyist. *E.g.*, ALASKA STAT. § 39.52.180 (d); CAL. GOV'T CODE § 87406.

Then he or she cannot	Duration	Maximum Offense Classification
Serve for a fee as a lobbyist or otherwise represent clients, including his or her employer before that body	2 years	Felony Note: Further specific restrictions also apply.
Represent, advise, or assist a person for compensation regarding that matter	2 years	Civil Penalty
Engage in activity as a lobbyist	1 year	Civil Penalty

Table 3.4-5—Activity After Government Service

State & Statute	If the public employee has
ALASKA STAT. § 39.52.180 (e)	Served as a former head of a principal department in the executive branch or as a former employee of the Office of the Governor in a policy-making position
Arizona ARIZ. REV. STAT. ANN. §§ 38-504(A), 38-510	Personally participated in any matter by a substantial and material exercise of administrative discretion
California CAL. GOV'T CODE §§ 87401, 87402, 91000	Participated in a proceeding
CAL. GOV'T CODE § 87406	Served as a member of the legislature or was an elected state officer
Colorado COLO. REV. STAT. § 24-18-105(3)	Been directly involved in matters during his employment
Connecticut CONN. GEN. STAT. §§ 1-84b(a), 1-89	Participated personally and substantially while in state service in a particular matter
CONN. GEN. STAT. §§ 1-84b(b), 1-89	Served in a department, agency, board, commission, council or office

Then he or she cannot	Duration	Maximum Offense Classification
Serve on the governing board of a company, organization, or other entity that was regulated by that department or with which the former department head worked as part of an official duty	1 year	Civil Penalty
Represent another person concerning that same matter for compensation before a public agency by which she/he was employed	1 year	Felony
For compensation act as agent or attorney for, or otherwise represent, aid, advise, counsel, consult, or assist any other person before any court or state administrative agency or any officer or employee thereof by making any formal or informal appearance, or by making any oral or written communication with the intent to influence, in connection with that proceeding in which the State of California is a party or has a direct and substantial interest.	Permanent	Misdemeanor
For compensation, act as agent or attorney for, or otherwise represent, any other person by making any formal or informal appearance, or by making any oral or written communication, before (for legislators) the Legislature, any committee or subcommittee thereof, any present Member of the Legislature, or any officer or employee thereof, or (for other elected officers) any state administrative agency, or any officer or employee thereof, if the appearance or communication is made for the purpose of influencing legislative action	1 year	Misdemeanor
Obtain employment in which he will take direct advantage, unavailable to others, of those matters	6 months	Guide to Conduct
Represent anyone other than the state in that particular matter in which the state has a substantial interest	Permanent	Felony
Represent anyone other than the state for compensation before that body concerning any matter in which the state has a substantial interest	1 year	Felony

Table 3.4-5—Activity After Government Service

State & Statute	If the public employee has
Delaware DEL. CODE ANN. tit. 29, § 5805(d)	Has given an opinion, conducted an investigation or otherwise was directly and materially responsible for a matter in the course of official duties as a state employee, officer or official
Florida FLA. STAT. § 112.3185(3)	Participated personally and substantially while an employee in a contract through decision, approval, disapproval, recommendation, rendering of advice, or investigation
FLA. STAT. § 112.3185(4)	Had a contract for services within his or her responsibility while an employee
FLA. CONST. art. II, § 8(e)	Served as a member of the legislature or statewide elected officer
Guam 4 GUAM CODE ANN. § 15210(b)	Served in an agency that has taken official action in a matter
Hawaii HAW. REV. STAT. ANN. § 84-18, 84-19	Participated on matters involving official action by the particular state agency or subdivision thereof with which the former employee had actually served
Illinois 5 ILL. COMP. STAT. ANN. 430/5-45, 430/50-5	During the year immediately preceding termination of State employment, participated personally and substantially in the award of State contracts, or the issuance of State contract change orders, with a cumulative value of $25,000 or more to the person or entity, or its parent or subsidiary, in making a regulatory or licensing decision that directly applied to the person or entity, or its parent or subsidiary

Then he or she cannot	Duration	Maximum Offense Classification
Represent or otherwise assist any private enterprise on that matter involving the State	2 years	Misdemeanor
Have or hold any employment or contractual relationship with any business entity in connection with that contract	Permanent	Civil Penalty
Have or hold any employment or contractual relationship with any business entity with that contract for services	2 years	Civil Penalty
Personally represent another person or entity for compensation before the government body or agency of which the individual was an officer	2 years	Civil Penalty
Assist any person or business, or act in a representative capacity for a fee or other consideration, on that matter	1 year	Action Voidable
Represent any person or business for a fee or other consideration on that matter	1 year	Action Voidable
Knowingly accept employment or receive compensation or fees for services from a person or entity	1 year	Misdemeanor

Table 3.4-5—Activity After Government Service

State & Statute	If the public employee has
Indiana IND. CODE §§ 4-2-6-11(b), 4-2-6-12	Engaged in negotiation or administration of a contract or made a regulatory or licensing decision
IND. CODE § 4-2-6-11(b)	Served as a state officer, employee, or special state appointee
IND. CODE § 4-2-6-11(c)	Personally and substantially participated in a matter
IND. CODE §§ 4-2-6-11(d), 4-2-6-12	Served as a state officer, employee, or special state appointee
IND. CODE § 35-44.1-1-5(b)	As a public servant approved, negotiated, or prepared on behalf of the agency the terms or specifications of a contract or purchase
Iowa IOWA CODE §§ 68B.7, 68B.32D	Been directly concerned and personally participated in any case, proceeding, or application
Kansas KAN. STAT. ANN. §§ 46-233(a)(2), 46-276	Participated as a state officer or employee in the making of any contract with any person or business
Kentucky KY. REV. STAT. ANN. §§ 11A.040(6)-(10), 11A.990	Various rules and time frames

Then he or she cannot	Duration	Maximum Offense Classification
Accept or receive compensation from an employer that has had that contract or regulatory or licensing decision	1 year	Civil Penalty
Accept employment or compensation as a lobbyist	1 year	Civil Penalty
Represent or assist a person in that particular matter	Permanent	Civil Penalty
Accept employment or compensation that would lead a reasonable person to believe that: (1) employment; or (2) compensation; is given or had been offered for the purpose of influencing the former state officer, employee, or special state appointee in the performance of the individual's duties or responsibilities while a state officer, an employee, or a special state appointee	Permanent	Civil Penalty
Obtain a pecuniary interest in that contract or purchase with an agency	1 year	Felony
Receive compensation for any services for any entity in relation to that case, proceeding, or application	2 years	Civil Penalty
Accept employment with such person or business as an employee, independent contractor or subcontractor	2 years	Misdemeanor

Table 3.4-5—Activity After Government Service

State & Statute	If the public employee has
Louisiana LA. STAT. ANN. §§ 42:1121; 42:1153	Participated in a transaction involving the governmental entity by which he was formerly employed
Maine ME. STAT. tit. 1, § 1024	Served as a legislator
Maryland MD. CODE ANN., GEN. PROV. §§ 5-504(d), 5-904	Participated significantly in a case, a contract, or any other specific matter as an official or employee
Massachusetts MASS. GEN. LAWS ch. 268A, §§ 5(a), 12(a), 18(a)	Participated as a state employee in any particular matter in which the commonwealth or a state agency is a party or has a direct and substantial interest
MASS. GEN. LAWS ch. 268A, §§ 5(b), 12(b), 18(b)	Had official responsibility as a state employee at any time within a period of two years prior to the termination of his employment over any particular matter in which the commonwealth or a state agency is a party or has a direct and substantial interest
Mississippi MISS. CODE ANN. § 25-4-105(2)	Served as a member of any board that passed a law or made an order authorizing any contract with the state, or any district, county, city or town thereof
Missouri MO. REV. STAT. §§ 105.454(1)(5), 105.478	Served as an officer or employee in an agency or had supervisory power over an agency
MO. REV. STAT. §§ 105.454(1)(6), 105.478	Directly concerned or personally participated during the period of his or her service or employment in any case, decision, proceeding or application

Then he or she cannot	Duration	Maximum Offense Classification
Assist another person, for compensation, in that transaction, or in an appearance in connection with that transaction	2 years	Civil Penalty
Engage in compensated lobbying	1 year	Civil Penalty
Assist or represent a party, other than the State, in that matter involving the government for compensation	Permanent	Civil Penalty
Act as agent or attorney for, or receive compensation directly or indirectly from anyone other than the commonwealth or a state agency, in connection with such particular matter	Permanent	Felony
Appear personally before any court or agency of the commonwealth as agent or attorney for anyone other than the commonwealth in connection with such particular matter	1 year	Felony
Be interested, directly or indirectly, in such contract	1 year	Civil Penalty
Perform any service for consideration by which he or she attempts to influence a decision of that agency	1 year	Felony
Perform any service for any consideration for any person, firm or corporation in relation to such case, decision, proceeding or application	Permanent	Felony

Table 3.4-5—Activity After Government Service

State & Statute	If the public employee has
Montana Mont. Code Ann. §§ 2-2-105(3), 2-2-136	Been directly involved in matters during a term of office or during employment
Nevada Nev. Rev. Stat. Ann. §§ 281A.410; 281A.550 (various specific rules)	Served in a state agency of the Executive Department or an agency of any county, city, or other political subdivision
New Jersey N.J. Stat. Ann. § 52:13D-17	Made any investigation, rendered any ruling, given any opinion, or been otherwise substantially and directly involved in a matter at any time during the course of his office or employment
New Mexico N.M. Stat. Ann. §§ 10-16-8(B), 10-16-17	Participated in a matter personally and substantially while a public officer or employee
N.M. Stat. Ann. §§ 10-16-8(D), 10-16-17	Served or worked for a state agency or local government agency
New York N.Y. Pub. Off. Law § 73(8)(a)(i)	Served as a state officer or employee
N.Y. Pub. Off. Law § 73(8)(a)(ii)	Served as a state officer or employee and was directly concerned and personally participated in or had under his or her active consideration a case, proceeding, application or transaction during the period of his or her service or employment

Then he or she cannot	Duration	Maximum Offense Classification
Obtain employment in which the officer or employee will take direct advantage, unavailable to others, of involvement in those matters	1 year	Civil Penalty
Represent or counsel for compensation a private person upon any issue which was under consideration by the agency during the public officer's or employee's service	1 year	Civil Penalty
Represent, appear for, negotiate on behalf of, or provide information not generally available to members of the public or services to any person or party other than the State in connection with that matter	Permanent	Misdemeanor
Represent a person in dealings with the government on that matter	Permanent	Misdemeanor
Represent for pay a person before the state agency or local government agency at which the employee worked	1 year	Misdemeanor
Appear or practice before such state agency or receive compensation for any services rendered by such former officer or employee on behalf of any person, firm, corporation or association in relation to any case, proceeding or application or other matter before such agency	2 years	Misdemeanor
Appear, practice, communicate or otherwise render services before any state agency or receive compensation for any such services rendered by such former officer or employee on behalf of any person, firm, corporation or other entity in relation to any such case, proceeding, application or transaction	Permanent	Misdemeanor

Table 3.4-5—Activity After Government Service

State & Statute	If the public employee has
N.Y. Pub. Off. Law § 73(8)(a)(iii)	Served as a member of the legislature
N.Y. Pub. Off. Law § 73(8)(a)(iii)	Served as a legislative employee
N.Y. Pub. Off. Law § 73(8)(a)(iv)	Served as an officer or employee in the executive chamber of the governor
North Carolina N.C. Gen. Stat. § 120C-304	Served as a legislator or public servant
North Dakota N.D. Cent. Code § 54-66-13	Served as an elected public official
Northern Mariana Islands 1 N. Mar. I. Code §§ 8543(a), 8572	Participated personally and substantially in the proceeding during his term of public office or public employment
1 N. Mar. I. Code §§ 8543(b), 8572	Participated personally and substantially in the subject matter of the transaction during his term of public legal authority
1 N. Mar. I. Code §§ 8543(b), 8572	Participated personally and substantially in a contract
Ohio Ohio Rev. Code Ann. §§ 102.03(A)(4), 102.99(B)	Personally participated as a public official or employee in any matter

Then he or she cannot	Duration	Maximum Offense Classification
Receive compensation for any services on behalf of any person, firm, corporation or association to promote or oppose, directly or indirectly, the passage of bills or resolutions by either house of the legislature.	2 years	Misdemeanor
Receive compensation for any services on behalf of any person, firm, corporation or association to appear, practice or directly communicate before either house of the legislature to promote or oppose the passage of bills or resolutions by either house of the legislature	2 years	Misdemeanor
Appear or practice before any state agency	2 years	Misdemeanor
Register as a lobbyist	6 months	Void registration
Be a lobbyist	2 years	Misdemeanor
Assist or represent any person other than the Commonwealth in any judicial, legislative, or administrative proceeding involving the Commonwealth or any of its agencies	Permanent	Misdemeanor
Assist or represent any person in any business transaction involving the Commonwealth	1 year	Misdemeanor
Assist or represent any person in that contract	Permanent	Misdemeanor
Represent a client or act in a representative capacity for any person on that matter	1 year	Misdemeanor

Table 3.4-5—Activity After Government Service

State & Statute	If the public employee has
Oklahoma OKLA. CONST. art. V, § 23	Served as a member of the legislature
Oregon OR. REV. STAT. §§ 244.045, 244.350	Various specific rules and timeframes
Pennsylvania 65 PA. CONS. STAT. § 1103(g). *See also* 65 PA. CONS. STAT. § 1103(i)	Been associated with a governmental body
Puerto Rico P.R. LAWS ANN. tit. 3, §§ 1857e(a), 1857f	Intervened in matters or official actions while working as a public servant
P.R. LAWS ANN. tit. 3, §§ 1857e(b), 1857f	Worked for an agency
P.R. LAWS ANN. tit. 3, §§ 1857e(c), 1857f	Taken official action over an agency, private person, or business
Rhode Island 36 R.I. GEN. LAWS §§ 36-14-5(e)(4), 36-14-19	Employed by a state or municipal agency
South Carolina S.C. CODE ANN. §§ 8-13-755, 8-13-1520. *See also* S.C. CODE ANN. § 8-13-760	Directly and substantially participated in a matter during his public service or employment

Then he or she cannot	Duration	Maximum Offense Classification
Be interested, directly or indirectly, in any contract with the state, or any county or other subdivision thereof, authorized by law passed during the term for which he was elected	2 years	
		Civil Penalty
Represent a person, with promised or actual compensation, on any matter before that governmental body	1 year	Misdemeanor
Provide information, intervene, cooperate, advise in any way or represent in any capacity, either directly or indirectly, a private person, business or public entity, in those official actions or matters	Permanent	Civil Penalty
Provide information, intervene, cooperate, advise in any way or represent directly or indirectly a private person, business or public entity before that agency	2 years	Civil Penalty
Hold an office, have monetary interest or contract, directly or indirectly, with that agency, private person, or business	1 year	Civil Penalty
Represent himself, represent any other person, or act as an expert witness before that agency (unless it is a matter of public record in a court of law)	1 year	Misdemeanor
Serve as a lobbyist or represent clients before the agency or department on which he formerly served in that matter or accept employment from a person who is regulated by the agency or department on which he formerly served if the employment involves that matter	1 year	Misdemeanor

Table 3.4-5—Activity After Government Service

State & Statute	If the public employee has
South Dakota S.D. Codified Laws § 2-12-8.2	Served as elected officer, department or agency head, or division director, or the highest paid employee reporting to such person
Tennessee Tenn. Code Ann. §§ 3-6-304, 3-6-306	Served as member of the general assembly, elected official in the executive branch, member of the governor's cabinet, or cabinet level staff within the governor's office
Texas Tex. Gov't Code Ann. § 572.054(a)	Served as member of the governing body or executive head of a regulatory agency
Tex. Gov't Code Ann. § 572.054(b)	Served as state officer or employee of a regulatory agency and participated during the period of state service or employment, either through personal involvement or because the case or proceeding was a matter within the officer's or employee's official responsibility
Utah Utah Code Ann. § 67-24-103	Served as state official
Vermont Vt. Stat. Ann. tit. 2, §§ 266(b), 268	Served as legislator or executive officer
Virginia Va. Code Ann. §§ 2.2-3104, 2.2-3120. *See also* Va. Code Ann. § 30-103(7)	Been an officer or employee of an agency that promulgated legislation, executive orders, or regulations

Then he or she cannot	Duration	Maximum Offense Classification
Register as a lobbyist, other than a public employee lobbyist	2 years	Misdemeanor
Be a lobbyist	1 year	Civil Penalty
Make any communication to or appearance before an officer or employee of the agency in which the member or executive head served if the communication or appearance is made: (1) with the intent to influence; and (2) on behalf of any person in connection with any matter on which the person seeks official action	2 years	Misdemeanor
Represent any person or receive compensation for services rendered on behalf of any person regarding such a particular matter	Permanent	Misdemeanor
Become a lobbyist or engage in lobbying that would require registration as a lobbyist	1 year	
Be a lobbyist	1 year	Civil Penalty
Before the agency of which he was an officer or employee, represent a client or act in a representative capacity on behalf of any person or group, for compensation, on matters related to that legislation, executive orders, or regulations	1 year	Misdemeanor

Table 3.4-5—Activity After Government Service

State & Statute	If the public employee has
Washington	In the two years prior to termination,
WASH. REV. CODE ANN. §§ 42.52.080(1), 42.52.490	- engaged in the negotiation or administration on behalf of government of one or more contracts with a potential employer - been in a position to make discretionary decisions affecting the outcome of such negotiation or the nature of such administration and - the contract had a total value of more than $10,000
WASH. REV. CODE ANN. §§ 42.52.080 (2), 42.52.490	Participated in specific legislative or executive action that expressly authorized or funded a contract or grant
WASH. REV. CODE ANN. §§ 42.52.080 (5), 42.52.490	Participated during state employment in a transaction involving the state
West Virginia W. VA. CODE §§ 6B-2-5(f), 6B-2-10	Served as an elected or appointed public official or public employee and personally and substantially participated in a decision-making, advisory or staff support capacity in a contested case, rate-making proceeding, license or permit application, regulation filing or other particular matter involving a specific party or parties which arose during his or her period of public service or employment
W. VA. CODE §§ 6B-2-5(g), 6B-2-10	Served as elected or appointed public official or full-time staff attorney or accountant with a governmental entity authorized to hear contested cases or promulgate or propose rules
Wisconsin WIS. STAT. §§ 19.45(8), 19.579, 19.58	Associated with a governmental department
WIS. STAT. §§ 19.45(8), 19.579, 19.58	Had a proceeding under his responsibility as a public official
WIS. STAT. §§ 19.45(8), 19.579, 19.58	Participated personally and substantially in a proceeding as a public official

Then he or she cannot	Duration	Maximum Offense Classification
Accept employment or receive compensation from an employer that would include fulfilling or implementing, in whole or in part, the provisions of that contract	1 year	Civil Penalty
Have a direct or indirect beneficial interest in that contract or grant	2 years	Civil Penalty
Assist another person, whether or not for compensation, with that transaction	Permanent	Civil Penalty
Represent a client or act in a representative capacity with or without compensation on behalf of any person in such a matter	Permanent	Misdemeanor
Appear in a representative capacity before the governmental entity in which he or she serves or served or is or was employed in specific enumerated matters	1 year	Misdemeanor
For compensation, on behalf of any person other than a governmental entity, make any formal or informal appearance before, or negotiate with, any officer or employee of the department with which he was associated	1 year	Misdemeanor
For compensation, on behalf of any person other than a governmental entity, make any formal or informal appearance before, or negotiate with, any officer or employee of a department in connection with that proceeding	1 year	Misdemeanor
For compensation, act on behalf of any party other than the state in connection with that proceeding	Permanent	Misdemeanor

VI. Other Measures to Prevent Conflicts

A. *Financial Disclosure*

Like the federal government, almost all states and territories have financial disclosure requirements for some types of government officials.[98] Filing these reports is a safeguard against government misconduct and conflicts of interest by holding public officials accountable for their outside financial interests before any possible conflicts arise.[99] While details regarding who must file, what must be disclosed, and penalties vary by jurisdiction, the laws typically require government officials, candidates for elected office, and employees to disclose sources of income, private business affiliations and positions, assets, liabilities, gifts, awards, and transactions. Failure to file or late filing of a statement may result in a daily automatic penalty up to a specified maximum amount. Intentionally filing false information may be a more serious offense. Details may be found in the particular statutes listed below.

Table 3.4-6—Financial Disclosure

State	Statute Section	Maximum Offense Classification
Alabama	Ala. Code § 36-25-14	Misdemeanor
Alaska	Alaska Stat. §§ 39.50.010-39.50.200	Misdemeanor
American Samoa	None	
Arizona	Ariz. Rev. Stat. Ann. §§ 18-444, 38-541 to 38-545	Misdemeanor
Arkansas	Ark. Code Ann. §§ 21-8-701 to 21-8-704, 21-8-403	Misdemeanor

98 Idaho and Michigan do not have annual filing requirements. *See* Liz Essley Whyte & Ryan J. Foley, *Conflicted Interests*, The Center for Public Integrity (Dec. 14, 2017), https://publicintegrity.org/state-politics/conflicted-interests-state-lawmakers-often-blur-the-line-between-the-publics-business-and-their-own/. American Samoa appears to lack a generally applicable financial disclosure requirement. Lauvo v. Am. Samoa Gov't, 1 Am. Samoa 3d 224, 226 (Am. Samoa 1997).

99 Pub. Citizen, Personal Financial Disclosure Requirements for Public Officials 1 (2019), https://www.citizen.org/sites/default/files/personal-financial-disclosures-june2011.pdf.

Table 3.4-6—Financial Disclosure

State	Statute Section	Maximum Offense Classification
California	Cal. Gov't Code §§ 87200 et seq., 91000, 91013	Misdemeanor
Colorado	Colo. Rev. Stat. §§ 24-6-201 to 24-6-203	Misdemeanor
Connecticut	Conn. Gen. Stat. § 1-83	Felony
Delaware	Del. Code Ann. §§ 5811-5816	Misdemeanor
District of Columbia	D.C. Code §§ 1-1162.24, 1-1162.25, 1-1162.21	Civil Penalty
Florida	Fla. Const. Art. II, § 8; Fla. Stat. § 112.3144	Civil Penalty
Georgia	Ga. Code Ann. §§ 45-10-26, 45-10-28	Civil Penalty
Guam	4 Guam Code Ann. §§ 13101-13106	Misdemeanor
Hawaii	Haw. Rev. Stat. § 84-17	Civil Penalty
Idaho	None	
Illinois	5 Ill. Comp. Stat. §§ 420/4A-101 to 420/4A -108	Misdemeanor
Indiana	Ind. Code § 4-2-6-8	Class A Infraction
Iowa	Iowa Code § 68B.35	Civil Penalty
Kansas	Kan. Stat. Ann. § 46-247 to 46-252	Misdemeanor
Kentucky	Ky. Rev. Stat. Ann. §§ 6.787, 6.797, 11A.050	Misdemeanor
Louisiana	La. Rev. Stat. §§ 42:1114, 42:1124.1	Misdemeanor
Maine	Me. Stat. tit. 1, § 1016-G	Misdemeanor (Class E Crime)
Maryland	Md. Code Ann., Gen. Prov. §§ 5-601 to 5-611; Crim. Law § 9-101	Misdemeanor
Massachusetts	Mass. Gen. Laws ch. 268B, § 5	Felony
Michigan	None	
Minnesota	Minn. Stat. § 10A.09	Civil Penalty
Mississippi	Miss. Code Ann. §§ 25-4-25 to 25-4-31	Felony
Missouri	Mo. Rev. Stat. §§ 105.483 to 105.492	Misdemeanor

Table 3.4-6—Financial Disclosure

State	Statute Section	Maximum Offense Classification
Montana	Mont. Code Ann. §§ 2-2-106, 2-2-136	Civil Penalty
Nebraska	Neb. Rev. Stat. §§ 49-1493 to 49-1497; 49-14,134	Felony
Nevada	Nev. Rev. Stat. §§ 281.556-281.581	Civil Penalty
New Hampshire	N.H. Rev. Stat. Ann. §§ 14-B:8 to 14-B:10; 15-A:1 to 15-A:9	Misdemeanor
New Jersey	N.J. Stat. Ann. § 52:13D-21(i), (n) N.J. Exec. Order No. 2 (Jan. 17, 2018)	Civil Penalty
New Mexico	N.M. Stat. Ann. §§ 10-16A-1 to 10-16A-8	Misdemeanor
New York	N.Y. Pub. Off. Law § 73-a	Misdemeanor
North Carolina	N.C. Gen. Stat. §§ 138A-21 to 138A-28	Felony
North Dakota	N.D. Cent. Code §§ 16.1-09-01 to 16.1-09-07	Misdemeanor
Northern Mariana Islands	1 N. Mar. I. Code §§ 8511-8523	Misdemeanor
Ohio	Ohio Rev. Code Ann. §§ 102.02, 102.99	Misdemeanor
Oklahoma	Okla. Ethics Comm'n Rules 3.13-3.16, 6.13	Civil Penalty
Oregon	Or. Rev. Stat. §§ 244.050-244.115, 244.350	Civil Penalty
Pennsylvania	65 Pa. Cons. Stat. §§ 1104, 1105, 1109	Misdemeanor
Puerto Rico	P.R. Laws Ann. tit. 3, §§ 1858-1858i	Felony
Rhode Island	R.I. Gen. Laws §§ 36-14-16 to 36-14-21	Misdemeanor
South Carolina	S.C. Code Ann. §§ 8-13-1110, 8-13-1510	Misdemeanor
South Dakota	S.D. Codified Laws §§ 3-1A-1 to 3-1A-6	Misdemeanor
Tennessee	Tenn. Code Ann. §§ 8-50-501 to 8-50-506, 3-6-205	Civil Penalty
Texas	Tex. Gov't Code Ann. §§ 572.001-572.034	Misdemeanor
Utah	Utah Code Ann. §§ 20A-11-1601 to 20A-11-1606	Misdemeanor

Table 3.4-6—Financial Disclosure

State	Statute Section	Maximum Offense Classification
Vermont	Vt. Stat. Ann. tit. 17, § 2414, tit. 3, § 1211	No Penalty
Virgin Islands	V.I. Code Ann. tit. 3, §§ 1105, 1108	Felony
Virginia	Va. Code Ann. §§ 2.2-3113 to -3118.2, 30-109 to -129	Misdemeanor
Washington	Wash. Rev. Code §§ 42.17A.700 to -.715, 42.17A.750	Civil Penalty
West Virginia	W. Va. Code §§ 6B-2-6, 6B-2-8, 6B-2-10	Misdemeanor
Wisconsin	Wis. Stat. §§ 19.43, 19.44, 19.47, 19.58	Misdemeanor
Wyoming	Wyo. Stat. Ann. §§ 9-13-108, 9-13-109	Misdemeanor

B. *Restrictions on Use or Disclosure of Confidential Information*

Like the federal government,[100] many states regulate conflicts of interest through criminalizing the misuse of nonpublic information gained in the course of public employment. While each state statute is unique, four types of prohibitions recur, as summarized in the table below:

1. Some states prohibit any disclosure of confidential information.

2. Some states prohibit disclosure or use of confidential information for personal benefit or pecuniary gain.

---

100 Federal regulation prohibits federal employees from engaging "in a financial transaction using nonpublic information, . . . [or] allow[ing] the improper use of nonpublic information to further his own private interest or that of another . . . ." 5 C.F.R. § 2635.703(a). The regulation prohibits giving advice, recommendation, and knowing unauthorized disclosure. *Id.* Nonpublic information is "information that the employee gains by reason of Federal employment and that he knows or reasonably should know has not been made available to the general public." *Id.* § 2635.703(b). In addition to the regulations, 18 U.S.C. § 1905 criminalizes disclosure of certain forms of confidential information by federal officers and employees. Misuse of nonpublic information could also amount to a violation of a separate, specific statute, such as the securities statutes, 18 U.S.C. § 1348, and statutes pertaining to bidding on public contracts, 41 U.S.C. § 2102.

3. Some states prohibit acquiring a pecuniary interest, speculating, or wagering in reliance on confidential information.

4. Some states prohibit accepting employment or engaging in business or professional activities that would likely require use or disclosure of confidential information.

Table 3.4-7—Confidential Information Restrictions

State	Statute Excerpt	Type of Prohibition (See Above)	Maximum Offense Classification
Alabama	No public official, public employee, former public official or former public employee . . . shall use or disclose confidential information . . . in any way that could result in financial gain . . . . ALA. CODE §§ 36-25-8, 36-25-27.	2	Felony
	A public servant commits the crime of misuse of confidential information if in contemplation of official action by himself or by a governmental unit with which he is associated, or in reliance on information to which he has access in his official capacity and which has not been made public, he: (1) Acquires a pecuniary interest in any property, transaction or enterprise which may be affected by such information or official action; (2) Speculates or wagers on the basis of such information or action; or (3) Aids another to do any of the foregoing. ALA. CODE § 13A-10-82.	3	Misde-meanor

Table 3.4-7—Confidential Information Restrictions

State	Statute Excerpt	Type of Prohibition (See Above)	Maximum Offense Classification
Alaska	A person who is or has been a public servant commits the crime of misuse of confidential information if the person (1) learns confidential information through employment as a public servant; and (2) while in office or after leaving office, uses the confidential information for personal gain or in a manner not connected with the performance of official duties other than by giving sworn testimony or evidence in a legal proceeding in conformity with a court order. ALASKA STAT. § 11.56.860.	2	Misde-meanor
	A current or former public officer may not disclose or use information gained in the course of, or by reason of, the officer's official duties that could in any way result in the receipt of any benefit for the officer or an immediate family member, if the information has not also been disseminated to the public [or if it is] information acquired in the course of official duties that is confidential by law. ALASKA STAT. §§ 39.52.140, 39.52.440.	1, 2	Civil Penalty
American Samoa	A public servant commits the crime of misuse of official information if, in contemplation of official action . . . or in reliance on information to which he has access in his official capacity and which has not been made public, he knowingly: (1) acquires a pecuniary interest . . . (2) speculates or wagers . . . or (3) aids, advises, or encourages another to do any of the foregoing . . . . AM. SAMOA CODE ANN. § 46.4705.	2, 3	Misde-meanor

Table 3.4-7—Confidential Information Restrictions

State	Statute Excerpt	Type of Prohibition (See Above)	Maximum Offense Classification
Arizona	During the period of a public officer's or employee's employment or service and for two years thereafter, a public officer or employee shall not disclose or use for the officer's or employee's personal profit, without appropriate authorization, any information acquired by the officer or employee in the course of the officer's or employee's official duties which has been clearly designated to the officer or employee as confidential . . . . ARIZ. REV. STAT. ANN. §§ 38-504(B), 38-510.	1, 2	Felony
Arkansas	A public servant commits the offense of misuse of confidential information if, in contemplation of official action by himself or herself or a governmental unit with which he or she is associated or in reliance on information to which he or she has access in his or her official capacity and which has not been made public, the public servant: (1) Acquires or aids another to acquire a pecuniary interest in any property, transaction, or enterprise that may be affected by the information; or (2) Speculates or aids another to speculate on the basis of the information. ARK. CODE ANN. § 5-52-106.	3	Misdemeanor
	No public servant shall accept employment or engage in any public or professional activity while serving as a public official which he or she might reasonably expect would require or induce him or her to disclose any information acquired by him or her by reason of his or her official position that is declared by law or regulation to be confidential. ARK. CODE ANN. §§ 21-8-304(b), 21-8-302, 21-8-801(a)(2).	4	Misdemeanor

Table 3.4-7—Confidential Information Restrictions

State	Statute Excerpt	Type of Prohibition (See Above)	Maximum Offense Classification
	No public servant shall disclose any such information gained by reason of his or her position, nor shall he or she otherwise use such information for his or her personal gain or benefit. ARK. CODE ANN. §§ 21-8-304(c), 21-8-302, 21-8-801(a)(2).	1, 2	Misdemeanor
California	A Member of the Legislature shall not . . . (1) Accept other employment which he has reason to believe will . . . require him, or induce him, to disclose confidential information acquired by him in the course of and by reason of his official duties. (2) Willfully and knowingly disclose, for pecuniary gain, to any other person, confidential information acquired by him in the course of and by reason of his official duties or use any such information for the purpose of pecuniary gain. CAL. GOV'T CODE §§ 8920(b)(1), (2); 8926.	 4 2	Misdemeanor (Felony for Conspiracy)

Table 3.4-7—Confidential Information Restrictions

State	Statute Excerpt	Type of Prohibition (See Above)	Maximum Offense Classification
Colorado	Any public servant, in contemplation of official action by himself or by a governmental unit with which he is associated or in reliance on information to which he has access in his official capacity and which has not been made public, commits misuse of official information if he: (a) Acquires a pecuniary interest in any property, transaction, or enterprise which may be affected by such information or official action; or (b) Speculates or wagers on the basis of such information or official action; or (c) Aids, advises, or encourages another to do any of the foregoing with intent to confer on any person a special pecuniary benefit. COLO. REV. STAT. § 18-8-402. *See also* COLO. REV. STAT. §§ 24-18-103(2), 24-18-104(1)(a).	2, 3	Felony
Connecticut	(b) No public official or state employee shall accept other employment which will . . . require him, or induce him, to disclose confidential information acquired by him in the course of and by reason of his official duties. (c) No public official or state employee shall wilfully [sic] and knowingly disclose, for financial gain, to any other person, confidential information acquired by him in the course of and by reason of his official duties or employment . . . . CONN. GEN. STAT. §§ 1-84(b), (c); 1-89.	4 2	Felony
Delaware	No person shall disclose any information required to be maintained confidential by [law]. DEL. CODE ANN. tit. 29, § 5805(e).	1	Misde-meanor

Table 3.4-7—Confidential Information Restrictions

State	Statute Excerpt	Type of Prohibition (See Above)	Maximum Offense Classification
Florida	Any public servant who . . . in reliance on information to which she or he has access in her or his official capacity and which has not been made public, commits any of the following acts: (1) Acquisition of a pecuniary interest . . . which may be affected by such information . . . (2) Speculation or wagering on the basis of such information . . . . shall be guilty of a misdemeanor of the first degree . . . . FLA. STAT. § 839.26.	2, 3	Misdemeanor
Guam	A public servant commits a misdemeanor if, in contemplation of official action by himself or by a governmental unit with which he is associated, or in reliance on information to which he has or has had access in his official capacity and which has not been made public he: (a) acquires or divests himself of a pecuniary interest in any property, transaction or enterprise which may be affected by such information or official action; (b) speculates or wagers on the basis of such information or official action; or (c) aids another to do any of the foregoing, while in office or after leaving office with the intent of using such information. 9 GUAM CODE ANN. § 49.80.	3	Misdemeanor
	No former employee shall disclose any information which by law is not available to the public and which the employee acquired in the course of official duties or use the information for personal gain or the benefit of anyone. 4 GUAM CODE ANN. §§ 15210(a), 15203.	2	Civil Penalty

Table 3.4-7—Confidential Information Restrictions

State	Statute Excerpt	Type of Prohibition (See Above)	Maximum Offense Classification
Hawaii	No legislator or employee shall disclose information which by law or practice is not available to the public and which the legislator or employee acquires in the course of the legislator's or employee's official duties, or use the information for the legislator's or employee's personal gain or for the benefit of anyone . . . . HAW. REV. STAT. ANN. §§ 84-12, 84-18, 84-19.	1, 2	Action Void-able
Idaho	No public servant shall . . . [u]se or disclose confidential information . . . with the intent to obtain a pecuniary benefit . . . or with the intent to harm the government[] . . . . IDAHO CODE §§ 18-1359(1)(c), 18-1360.	2	Misde-meanor
Illinois	No legislator in order to further his own economic interest, or those of any other person may disclose or use confidential information acquired in the course of his official duties. 5 ILL. COMP. STAT. ANN. 420/3-104.	2	Guide to Con-duct
Indiana	A public servant who knowingly or intentionally: . . . (3) acquires or divests himself or herself of a pecuniary interest in any property, transaction, or enterprise or aids another person to do so based on information obtained by virtue of the public servant's office that official action that has not been made public is contemplated; . . . commits official misconduct, a Level 6 felony. IND. CODE § 35-44.1-1-1(3).	3	Felony

Table 3.4-7—Confidential Information Restrictions

State	Statute Excerpt	Type of Prohibition (See Above)	Maximum Offense Classification
	A current state officer, employee, or special state appointee may not knowingly . . . [a]ccept employment or engage in business or professional activity that would require the individual to disclose confidential information . . . . IND. CODE §§ 4-2-6-5.5(a)(2), 4-2-6-12.	4	Civil Penalty
Iowa	A public officer or employee who, by reason of the officer's or employee's employment, has access to any public record, or to any file, dossier, or accumulation of information of any kind, and who gives or transfers to any person, in exchange for anything of value other than fees authorized by law, any such record, file, dossier, or accumulation of information, or any part thereof, or who imparts to any person any information contained therein, in exchange for anything of value other than fees authorized by law, commits a serious misdemeanor. IOWA CODE § 721.10.	2	Serious Misde-meanor
Kansas	No state officer or employee shall disclose or use confidential information acquired in the course of his or her official duties in order to further his or her own economic interest or those of any person. KAN. STAT. ANN. § 46-241.	2	Misde-meanor
Kentucky	A public servant, in order to further his own economic interests, or those of any other person, shall not knowingly disclose or use confidential information acquired in the course of his official duties. KY. REV. STAT. ANN. §§ 11A.040(1), 11A.990.	2	Felony

Table 3.4-7—Confidential Information Restrictions

State	Statute Excerpt	Type of Prohibition (See Above)	Maximum Offense Classification
Kentucky	A public servant is guilty of misuse of confidential information when, in contemplation of official action by himself or by a governmental unit with which he is associated, or in reliance on information to which he has access in his official capacity and which has not been made public, he: (a) Accepts or agrees to accept a pecuniary interest in any property, transaction or enterprise which may be affected by such information or official action; or (b) Speculates or wagers on the basis of such information or official action; or (c) Aids another to do any of the foregoing. Ky. Rev. Stat. Ann. § 522.040.	3	Felony
Louisiana	No public servant shall receive any thing of economic value for any service, the subject matter of which . . . [d]raws substantially upon official data or ideas which have not become part of the body of public information. La. Stat. Ann. §§ 42.1111(C), 42.1153.	4	Civil Penalty
Maine	A person is guilty of misuse of information if, being a public servant and knowing that official action is contemplated, or acting in reliance on information which he has acquired by virtue of his office or from another public servant, he: A. Acquires or divests himself of a pecuniary interest in any property, transaction or enterprise that may be affected by such official action or information; B. Speculates or wagers on the basis of such official action or information; or C. Knowingly aids another to do any of the things described in paragraphs A and B. Me. Stat. tit. 17-A, § 609.	2, 3	Misdemeanor (Class E Crime)

Table 3.4-7—Confidential Information Restrictions

State	Statute Excerpt	Type of Prohibition (See Above)	Maximum Offense Classification
Maryland	[A]n official or employee may not disclose or use confidential information acquired by reason of the official's or employee's public position and not available to the public: (1) for personal economic benefit; or (2) for the economic benefit of another. MD. CODE ANN., GEN. PROV. § 5-507.	2	Civil Penalty
Massachusetts	No current or former officer or employee of a state, county or municipal agency shall knowingly, or with reason to know . . . accept employment or engage in any business or professional activity which will require him to disclose confidential information which he has gained by reason of his official position or authority. MASS. GEN. LAWS ch. 268A, § 23(c).	4	Civil Penalty
Michigan	A public officer or employee shall not divulge to an unauthorized person[] confidential information acquired in the course of employment in advance of the time prescribed for its authorized release to the public. MICH. COMP. LAWS § 15.342(1).	1	Civil Penalty
Minnesota	An employee in the executive branch shall not use confidential information to further the employee's private interest, and shall not accept outside employment or involvement in a business or activity that will require the employee to disclose or use confidential information. MINN. STAT. § 43A.38.	2, 4	Civil Penalty

Table 3.4-7—Confidential Information Restrictions

State	Statute Excerpt	Type of Prohibition (See Above)	Maximum Offense Classification
Mississippi	No person may intentionally use or disclose information gained in the course of or by reason of his official position or employment as a public servant in any way that could result in pecuniary benefit . . . if the information has not been communicated to the public or is not public information. MISS. CODE ANN. § 25-4-105(5).	2	Civil Penalty
Missouri	1. A public servant commits the offense of misuse of official information if . . . in reliance on information to which he or she has access in his or her official capacity and which has not been made public, he or she knowingly: (1) Acquires a pecuniary interest in any property, transaction, or enterprise which may be affected by such information . . . ; or (2) Speculates or wagers on the basis of such information . . . ; or (3) Aids, advises or encourages another to do any of the foregoing with purpose of conferring a pecuniary benefit on any person. MO. REV. STAT. § 576.050.	3	Misde-meanor
Montana	A person commits the offense of misuse of confidential criminal justice information if the person . . . purposely or knowingly: (a) accesses the criminal justice information network for personal use or financial gain; or (b) disseminates information accessed from the criminal justice information network to any person who is not authorized to receive confidential criminal justice information . . . . MONT. CODE ANN. § 45-7-601.	1, 2	Misde-meanor

Table 3.4-7—Confidential Information Restrictions

State	Statute Excerpt	Type of Prohibition (See Above)	Maximum Offense Classification
Nebraska	Any public servant . . . in reliance on information to which he has access in his official capacity and which has not been made public, commits misuse of official information if he: (a) Acquires pecuniary interest in any property, transaction, or enterprise which may be affected by such information . . . ; or (b) Speculates or wagers on the basis of such information . . . ; or (c) Aids, advises, or encourages another to do any of the foregoing with intent to confer on any person a special pecuniary benefit . . . . NEB. REV. STAT. § 28-925.	3	Misdemeanor
Nevada	If a public officer or employee acquires, through the public officer's or employee's public duties or relationships, any information which by law or practice is not at the time available to people generally, the public officer or employee shall not use the information to further a significant pecuniary interest of the public officer or employee or any other person or business entity. NEV. REV. STAT. § 281A.400(5).	2	Civil Penalty
New Hampshire	A public servant . . . is guilty of a misdemeanor if, . . . in reliance on information which he has acquired by virtue of his office or from another public servant, he: I. Acquires or divests himself of a pecuniary interest in any property, transaction or enterprise which may be affected by such . . . information; or II. Speculates or wagers on the basis of such . . . information; or III. Knowingly aids another to do any of the foregoing. N.H. REV. STAT. ANN. § 643:2.	2, 3	Misdemeanor

Table 3.4-7—Confidential Information Restrictions

State	Statute Excerpt	Type of Prohibition (See Above)	Maximum Offense Classification
New Jersey	A person commits a crime if, . . . in reliance on information to which he has or has had access in an official capacity and which has not been made public, he: a. Acquires a pecuniary interest in any property, transaction or enterprise which may be affected by such information . . . ; or b. Speculates or wagers on the basis of such information . . . ; or c. Aids another to do any of the foregoing, while in office or after leaving office with a purpose of using such information. N.J. STAT. ANN. § 2C:30-3.	3	Felony (Crime of Second Degree)
	No State officer or employee . . . shall willfully disclose to any person, whether or not for pecuniary gain, any information not generally available to members of the public . . . . No State officer or employee . . . shall use for the purpose of pecuniary gain, whether directly or indirectly, any information not generally available to members of the public . . . . N.J. STAT. ANN. §§ 52:13D-25.	1, 2	Civil Penalty
New Mexico	No legislator or public officer or employee shall use or disclose confidential information acquired by virtue of the legislator's or public officer's or employee's position with a state agency or local government agency for the legislator's, public officer's or employee's or another's private gain. N.M. STAT. ANN. §§ 10-16-6, 10-16-17.	2	Misdemeanor
New York	No officer or employee . . . should accept employment or engage in any business or professional activity which will require him to disclose confidential information which he has gained by reason of his official position or authority. N.Y. PUB. OFF. LAW § 74(3)(b).	4	Civil Penalty

Table 3.4-7—Confidential Information Restrictions

State	Statute Excerpt	Type of Prohibition (See Above)	Maximum Offense Classification
	No officer or employee . . . should disclose confidential information acquired by him in the course of his official duties nor use such information to further his personal interests. N.Y. PUB. OFF. LAW § 74(3)(c).	2	Civil Penalty
North Carolina	It is unlawful for any officer or employee . . . in reliance on information which was made known to him in his official capacity and which has not been made public, to . . . (1) Acquire a pecuniary interest in any property, transaction, or enterprise or gain any pecuniary benefit which may be affected by such information . . . ; or (2) Intentionally aid another to do any of the above acts. N.C. GEN. STAT. § 14-234.1. *See also* N.C. GEN. STAT. § 138A-34.	3	Misde-meanor
North Dakota	A person is guilty of a class A misdemeanor if during employment as a public servant, or within one year thereafter, . . . in reliance on information to which he has or had access only in his capacity as a public servant, he: a. Acquires a pecuniary interest in any property, transaction, or enterprise which may be affected by such information . . . ; b. Speculates or wagers on the basis of such information . . . ; or c. Aids another to do any of the foregoing. N.D. CENT. CODE § 12.1-13-02(1). *See also* N.D. CENT. CODE § 12.1-13-01.	3	Misde-meanor
Northern Mariana Islands	A public official or public employee or a former public official or former public employee shall not disclose or use for the[ir] . . . own economic benefit or that of another person confidential information acquired by the public position or employment that is not generally available to the public. 1 N. MAR. I. CODE § 8532(b).	2	Sanc-tions

Table 3.4-7—Confidential Information Restrictions

State	Statute Excerpt	Type of Prohibition (See Above)	Maximum Offense Classification
Ohio	No present or former public official or employee shall disclose or use, without appropriate authorization, any information acquired by the public official or employee in the course of the public official's or employee's official duties that is confidential . . . . Ohio Rev. Code Ann. §§ 102.03(B), 102.99.	1	Misdemeanor
Oregon	A public servant commits the crime of misuse of confidential information if . . . in reliance on information to which the public servant has access in an official capacity and which has not been made public, the public servant acquires or aids another in acquiring a pecuniary interest in any property, transaction or enterprise which may be affected by such information . . . . Or. Rev. Stat. §§ 162.425; 244.040(4).	3	Misdemeanor
Pennsylvania	A public servant commits a misdemeanor of the second degree if, in contemplation of official action by himself or by a governmental unit with which he is associated, or in reliance on information to which he has access in his official capacity and which has not been made public, he: (1) acquires a pecuniary interest in any property, transaction or enterprise which may be affected by such information or official action; (2) speculates or wagers on the basis of such information or official action; or (3) aids another to do any of the foregoing. 18 Pa. Cons. Stat. § 5302.	3	Misdemeanor

Table 3.4-7—Confidential Information Restrictions

State	Statute Excerpt	Type of Prohibition (See Above)	Maximum Offense Classification
Puerto Rico	Any public officer, employee, former officer or former employee who uses for his/her own benefit or for the benefit of a third party any information or data that could have been known solely by reason of his/her office, employment or assignment shall incur a fourth degree felony. P.R. LAWS ANN. tit. 33, § 4881.	2	Felony
Rhode Island	No person subject to this code of ethics shall willfully and knowingly disclose, for pecuniary gain, to any other person, confidential information acquired by him or her in the course of and by reason of his or her official duties or employment or use any information for the purpose of pecuniary gain. 36 R.I. GEN. LAWS §§ 36-14-5(c), 36-14-19.	2	Misde-meanor
South Carolina	A public official, public member, or public employee may not use or disclose confidential information gained in the course of or by reason of his official responsibilities in a way that would affect an economic interest held by him, a member of his immediate family, an individual with whom he is associated, or a business with which he is associated. S.C. CODE ANN. §§ 8-13-725(A), 8-13-1520.	2	Misde-meanor

Table 3.4-7—Confidential Information Restrictions

State	Statute Excerpt	Type of Prohibition (See Above)	Maximum Offense Classification
Texas	(a) A public servant commits an offense if, in reliance on information to which the public servant has access by virtue of the person's office or employment and that has not been made public, the person: (1) acquires or aids another to acquire a pecuniary interest in any property, transaction, or enterprise that may be affected by the information; (2) speculates or aids another to speculate on the basis of the information . . . . (b) A public servant commits an offense if with intent to obtain a benefit or with intent to harm or defraud another, he discloses or uses information for a nongovernmental purpose that: (1) he has access to by means of his office or employment; and (2) has not been made public. . . . . TEX. PENAL CODE ANN. § 39.06.	3	Felony
Utah	[I]t is an offense for a public officer, public employee, or legislator to . . . accept employment or engage in any business or professional activity that he might reasonably expect would require or induce him to improperly disclose controlled information that he has gained by reason of his official position . . . [or disclose or improperly use . . . protected information . . . in order to further substantially the officer's or employee's personal economic interest . . . . UTAH CODE ANN. §§ 67-16-4(1)(a), (b); 67-16-12.	2, 4	Felony
Virgin Islands	No territorial officer or employee shall: . . . (4) accept other employment which will . . . require him, or induce him, to disclose confidential information . . . [or] (5) willfully and knowingly disclose . . . confidential information . . . or use any information for the purpose of pecuniary gain. V.I. CODE ANN. tit. 3, §§ 1102(4), (5); 1108.	2, 4	Felony

Table 3.4-7—Confidential Information Restrictions

State	Statute Excerpt	Type of Prohibition (See Above)	Maximum Offense Classification
Virginia	No officer or employee of a state or local governmental or advisory agency shall . . . [u]se for his own economic benefit or that of another party confidential information that he has acquired by reason of his public position and which is not available to the public. VA. CODE ANN. §§ 2.2-3103(4), 2.2-3120. *See also* VA. CODE ANN. § 30-103.	2	Misdemeanor
Washington	(1) No state officer or state employee may accept employment or engage in any business or professional activity that . . . would require or induce him or her to make an unauthorized disclosure of confidential information . . . . (2) No state officer or state employee may make a disclosure of confidential information . . . or otherwise use the information for his or her personal gain or benefit . . . . (3) No state officer or state employee may disclose confidential information to any person not entitled or authorized to receive the information. WASH. REV. CODE ANN. §§ 42.52.050, 42.52.490.	1, 2, 4	Civil Penalty
West Virginia	No present or former public official or employee may knowingly and improperly disclose any confidential information . . . nor use such information to further his or her personal interests or the interests of another person. W. VA. CODE §§ 6B-2-5(e), 6B-2-10.	1, 2	Misdemeanor

Table 3.4-7—Confidential Information Restrictions

State	Statute Excerpt	Type of Prohibition (See Above)	Maximum Offense Classification
Wisconsin	No state public official may intentionally use or disclose information . . . in any way that could result in the receipt of anything of value for himself or herself . . . if the information has not been communicated to the public or is not public information. WIS. STAT. §§ 19.45(4), 19.579, 19.58.	2	Misdemeanor

CONCLUSION

Conflict of interest laws acknowledge the truism that "power tends to corrupt" by aiming to prevent public corruption before it occurs.[101] A functioning democracy requires that the people must have faith that their public officials are working for the public good. Prohibiting certain conflicts and requiring the disclosure of others serve that end.[102] In addition to avoiding actual self-enrichment, public officials and employees must avoid situations that, by law, are considered too likely to lead to the temptation to enrich oneself.[103] While states take different approaches to preventing this temptation, most seek to prevent conflicts between a public official's interest in personal profit and in serving the public by preventing disloyalty in a particular government matter, disloyalty upon leaving government service, disloyalty arising from an obligation to repay, and misuse of confidential information. By reducing even the appearance of impropriety, these laws contribute to increasing public confidence in state government.

---

101 Letter from Lord Acton to Archbishop Mandell Creighton (Apr. 5, 1887), http://oll.libertyfund.org/titles/acton-acton-creighton-correspondence ("Power tends to corrupt and absolute power corrupts absolutely. . . . There is no worse heresy than that the office sanctifies the holder of it.").

102 *See* United States v. Miss. Valley Generating Co., 364 U.S. 520, 562 (1961).

103 *Id.* at 549; Crandon v. United States, 494 U.S. 152, 164 (1990) ("Congress appropriately enacts prophylactic rules that are intended to prevent even the appearance of wrongdoing and that may apply to conduct that has caused no actual injury to the United States.").

Section Four

The Corruption Trial & Common Defenses

This section contains chapters that address two areas that are likely to be of particular interest in corruption trials: jury addresses and the presentation of complex data. While it is outside of the scope of this Manual to provide a comprehensive discussion of general trial practice, jury addresses may pose special challenges in corruption cases, given the rhetorical temptation to draw sweeping parallels between a defendant on trial and the jury's opportunity to "send a message" to corrupt politicians everywhere. (This is a temptation that should be fought.) Given that many corruption cases involve sometimes-complicated financial and other data, this section also includes a discussion of how best to present that data. One area that we do not cover that may be important to state prosecutors is the Uniform Act to Secure the Attendance of Witnesses from Without a State in Criminal Proceedings, which provides a mechanism to require an out-of-state witness to testify at court proceedings. NAAG has published guidance on using this Act, including cites to the statutes in every state and territory that enacted it, on its website.[1]

The other topic covered by this chapter is common defenses. Law professor Peter Henning, who is the author of *The Prosecution and Defense of Public Corruption* and a former prosecutor himself, details many of the common defenses in corruption cases. This chapter provides an overview of the types of issues that can arise after a case has been charged, and can help a prosecutor structure an investigation to reduce the risk of successful defenses. Some aspects of this chapter intersect with topics discussed elsewhere in the Manual—for example, Howard Master also discusses legislative privilege in Chapter 1.3, and Dan Cort and Stacey Aronowitz also discuss entrapment and other issues that can arise with undercover operations in Chapter 2.5.

---

1 Darrell E. White II, *Subpoenaing Out-of-State Witnesses in Criminal Proceedings: A Step-by-Step Guide*, Attorney Gen. J. (May 18, 2021), https://www.naag.org/criminal-law/attorney-general-journal/subpoenaing-out-of-state-witnesses/.

Chapter 4.1

Addressing the Jury in a Public Corruption Trial

Amie N. Ely

Amie N. Ely is the Director of the Center for Ethics & Public Integrity, National Attorneys General Training & Research Institute, National Association of Attorneys General.

Introduction

A corruption trial is the culmination of extensive investigation, analysis, and preparation. Remarks to the jury should be clear and effective. The opening statement should provide a roadmap of the trial to come. The closing argument should weave together the evidence the jury heard, the reasonable inferences to be drawn from that evidence, and the law to explain why the jury should convict.

Prosecutors should take care not to jeopardize their case by making inappropriate statements or arguments to the jury. Prosecutors should also become intimately familiar with ethical rules and appellate opinions on proper jury addresses in their jurisdictions.[1] Public corruption trials potentially present special challenges because of the intangible nature of the harm of corruption

---

1 Nat'l Dist. Att'ys Ass'n, National Prosecution Standards ss. 6-8.1, 6-8.2 & cmt. (3d ed. 2009).

crimes. Members of the jury may more readily identify themselves as victims of the defendant's alleged corruption and prosecutors may see themselves as participating in a broader campaign to defend the government's integrity. This chapter identifies inappropriate arguments to avoid in any criminal jury trial, but especially a public corruption trial.

I. The Prosecutor's Interest is in Pursuing Justice

Unlike other lawyers who represent individual clients, the prosecutor is obligated to represent "a sovereignty" that has an "obligation to govern impartially"[2] and is required to "seek justice."[3] This means that the prosecutor is not seeking to win at all costs, but must see "that justice shall be done."[4] Justice has "the twofold aim" that "guilt shall not escape or innocence suffer."[5] While recognizing the prosecutor's duty to "prosecute with earnestness and vigor," the Supreme Court has explained that "while [the prosecutor] may strike hard blows, he is not at liberty to strike foul ones. It is as much his duty to refrain from improper methods calculated to produce a wrongful conviction as it is to use every legitimate means to bring about a just one."[6] As discussed below, prosecutor's jury addresses must argue facts that will be, or were, evidence and reasonable inferences without infringing on constitutional rights of the accused, without vouching for witness credibility or sharing the prosecutor's personal opinion, and without seeking to inflame passions or prejudices of the jury.

---

2 Berger v. United States, 295 U.S. 78, 88 (1935).

3 *See, e.g.*, Amie N. Ely, Note, *Prosecutorial Discretion as An Ethical Necessity: The Ashcroft Memorandum's Curtailment of the Prosecutor's Duty to "Seek Justice"*, 90 Cornell L. Rev. 237, 241 (2004) ("The duty to seek justice is the 'long-understood role of the prosecutor in every jurisdiction' . . . ." (citation omitted)).

4 *Berger*, 295 U.S. at 88; *see also* Donnelly v. DeChristoforo, 416 U.S. 637, 648-649 (1974) (Douglas, J., dissenting) ("The function of the prosecutor under the Federal Constitution is not to tack as many skins of victims as possible to the wall. His function is to vindicate the right of people as expressed in the laws and give those accused of crime a fair trial."); NDAA Prosecution Standards ss. 1-1.1 to 1-1.2.

5 *Berger*, 295 U.S. at 88.

6 *Id.*

II. Opening Statements

Opening statements are the prosecutor's opportunity to set forth a roadmap of what she expects to introduce at trial. They provide an opportunity to:

- Introduce the themes of the trial to come;
- Summarize what the witnesses will likely say and the evidence will likely show;
- "Pull the sting" on areas that may be confusing to the jury—like the fact that information may be introduced in a fragmentary fashion, given the rules of evidence—or things like unsavory aspects of a witness's character that a defense attorney may highlight; and
- Ask the jurors to pay close attention to the facts and the law, and to use their common sense when reaching a verdict.

While missteps during closing arguments are typically more likely to result in reversal, opening statements also present some risks. First, prosecutors should take care not to argue facts that they do not reasonably believe will be introduced into evidence.[7] This includes referencing the testimony of witnesses they do not intend to call to testify. However, as the Supreme Court has recognized, "[m]any things might happen during the course of the trial which

---

7 Opening statements should explain legal and factual issues and should be limited to evidence that "will be available and admitted into evidence at trial." NDAA Prosecution Standards ss. 6-4.1 to 6-4.2. "It is improper for an attorney to refer to any testimony or to assert any facts in his opening statement unless, in good faith, he reasonably believes that supporting evidence will be offered and admitted at trial." State v. Bernier, 486 A.2d 147, 149 (Me. 1985); *see also* Michael G. Walsh, Annotation, *Prosecutor's Reference in Opening Statement to Matters Not Provable or Which He Does Not Attempt to Prove as Ground for Relief*, 16 A.L.R.4th 810 (2020). In addition to imperiling your case, this could also result in censure. *See* State v. Torres, 744 A.2d 699, 709 (N.J. Super. Ct. App. Div. 2000) (referring matter of assistant prosecutor's inappropriate opening statement to the state attorney general for potential punishment). *Accord* ABA Standards for Criminal Justice: Prosecution Function s. 3-6.5(b) (Am. Bar Ass'n 2017), https://www.americanbar.org/groups/criminal_justice/standards/ProsecutionFunctionFourthEdition/ ("The prosecutor's opening statement at trial should be confined to a fair statement of the case from the prosecutor's perspective, and discussion of evidence that the prosecutor reasonably believes will be available, offered and admitted to support the prosecution case.").

would prevent the presentation of all the evidence described in advance."[8] If an expected witness becomes unavailable or a prosecutor elects to—in good faith—not call that witness to the stand, the damage to the case will likely be at trial rather than appeal, as the defense attorney may comment on the promise unmet and the prosecution may lose the opportunity to introduce valuable evidence. If a prosecutor thinks that a judge may not admit a piece of evidence, it is a good practice to file a motion in limine to request a pretrial ruling if she wishes to discuss it during her opening.

Second, prosecutors must not comment on whether the defendant will, or will not, testify.[9] In cases where a defendant's statement will be introduced into evidence, prosecutors may reference that statement but should make clear that a statement *was* made, and not use loose language that might imply that the defendant *will* testify.[10] This issue is discussed at greater length in the part on closing arguments.

Third, while prosecutors may thank the jury for its service, they cannot invite jurors to "send a message" or to protect the community by convicting the defendant.[11]

A few additional primarily strategic notes about openings are relevant for the corruption prosecutor. Depending on the jurisdiction, it may be permissible to show the actual evidence expected to be admitted—perhaps the photo of the defendant accepting that cash bribe, if you are so lucky to have

---

8 Frazier v. Cupp, 394 U.S. 731, 736 (1969); *see also* State v. Rainey, 580 A.2d 682, 686-87 (Me. 1990) (holding that there was no error in a prosecutor's reference during opening statements to a fact later found to be inadmissible when "the prosecutor had a reasonable belief that the testimony would be offered and admitted at trial").

9 *Accord* Griffin v. California, 380 U.S. 609, 615 (1965) (closing); ABA STANDARDS FOR THE PROSECUTION FUNCTION s. 3-6.5(c) ("The prosecutor should scrupulously avoid [during an opening statement] any comment on a defendant's right to remain silent.").

10 Simpson v. State, 112 A.3d 941, 949-50 (Md. 2015) (reversing conviction where prosecutor said "defendant will tell you" because even though prosecutor was referring to defendant's written statement, her remarks were "reasonably susceptible of the inference by the jury that [p]etitioner had an obligation to testify and, if he did not, the jury should view that as evidence of his guilt"). *See also* State v. Turner, 433 A.2d 397, 400-02 (Me. 1981) (reversing conviction where prosecutor said during opening statement that the defendant "will tell you," even though prosecutor argued he intended to refer to a post-arrest statement that was admitted at trial rather than the defendant's potential testimony).

11 Hill v. State, 734 A.2d 199, 202 (Md. 1999).

that as evidence.[12] Unless it is clear that the court will permit this, however, it is safer to request a pretrial ruling on the display of evidence during an opening statement.

Prosecutors should take care not to "overpromise" in the opening statement and may wish to describe expected witness testimony more generally to avoid potential discrepancies between what was predicted in the opening and what a witness actually says on the stand. While appropriate witness preparation can mitigate the risk of a witness saying something unexpected on the witness stand, it is generally safer to avoid unnecessary precision. That said, if a prosecutor expects that, for example, a defendant's written statement will be introduced at trial, it may be both effective and safe to quote it during an opening statement.

Finally, the opening *statement* is just that—a statement. It is not an argument, and if it is presented as one, the likely defense objections will, at best, disrupt your flow and make your opening less persuasive; at worst, an argumentative opening provides grounds for appeal or a bar complaint.[13]

As discussed below, it appears that more caselaw has developed addressing errors and alleged errors during closing arguments. Prosecutors would be safe to assume that anything not permitted during a closing argument is, *ipso facto*, equally proscribed for an opening statement.[14]

---

12 *See* People v. Wash, 861 P.2d 1107, 1133 (Cal. 1993) ("The purpose of the opening statement 'is to prepare the minds of the jury to follow the evidence and to more readily discern its materiality, force and effect', and the use of matters which are admissible in evidence, and which are subsequently in fact received in evidence, may aid this purpose." (citations omitted)).

13 State v. Lynch, 357 P.3d 119, 127-28 (Ariz. 2015), *rev'd on other grounds*, 136 S. Ct. 1818 (2016); *In re* Martinez, 462 P.3d 36, 42-43, 46 (Ariz. 2020) (concluding prosecutor in *Lynch* violated Ariz. Rule of Prof'l Conduct 8.4(d) by making comments prejudicial to the administration of justice in his jury address).

14 Wilhelm v. State, 326 A.2d 707, 713-14 (Md. 1974) ("[A]lthough opening statements in a jury trial cannot be equated with closing arguments made to the jury, there is sufficient similarity of the issues involved in both to permit generally the application of common principles.").

III. Closing Arguments

Closing arguments provide the opportunity to tie together the evidence introduced during trial and argue that the evidence is sufficient to prove the defendant's guilt. A commentator described them as often "the most important part of the trial, providing the attorneys with their last opportunity to convince the jury of the defendant's guilt or innocence."[15]

In addition to allowing the prosecutor to provide a cohesive narrative of the trial, closings provide an opportunity to point out how witnesses are corroborated by other evidence—perhaps how two witnesses' statements interlock, or how cellphone records introduced through a document custodian corroborate a cooperating witness's description of frequent telephone contact with a defendant. In cases where the loss or gain amount is an element, a prosecutor can "do the math" for the jury in the closing argument.[16]

Prosecutors should be prepared to display evidence throughout the closing, through embedding exhibits in, for example, a PowerPoint presentation; displaying them using a projector; or holding them up for the jury to view in person. Most states permit juries to take notes,[17] so including the exhibit number in your presentation will allow them to request an exhibit—if exhibits are not sent back with the jury for deliberations—and will also make your record clearer on appeal.

Depending on the jurisdiction and the judge, a prosecutor may be able to discuss the law at length during the argument.[18] For more complicated

---

15 Michael Lyon, *Issues in the Third Circuit: Avoiding the Woodshed: The Third Circuit Examines Prosecutorial Misconduct in Closing Argument in* United States v. Wood, 53 Vill. L. Rev. 689, 689 (2008).

16 Chapter 3.2, n.93 & Chapter 3.4, Table 3.4-5—Activity After Government Service list some state corruption-related statutes that require prosecutors to prove a loss, gain, or contract amount.

17 *See* Maureen A. Howard & Jeffrey C. Barnum, *Bringing Demonstrative Evidence in From the Cold: The Academy's Role in Developing Model Rules*, 88 Temp. L. Rev. 513, 538 nn.121-24 (2016) (concluding that at least 45 states permit or require judges to allow juries to take notes).

18 Craig Lee Montz, *Why Lawyers Continue to Cross the Line in Closing Argument: An Examination of Federal and State Cases*, 28 Ohio N.U.L. Rev. 67, 82 (2001) (concluding that "in most jurisdictions, counsel may read from the jury instructions during closing argument") (citations omitted). However, the author of this chapter was interrupted midway through a closing by a federal judge who objected to seeing language from the jury instructions on a

cases—such as those involving racketeering or other complex charges—explaining how the evidence fulfills the elements may be necessary, and a prosecutor may wish to ask for permission outside of the jury's presence to discuss legal concepts. Prosecutors should not hesitate to note that instructions on the law are the judge's purview, which may reduce the chance of an objection from opposing counsel or a complaint from the bench.

As discussed briefly in the next part, rebuttal arguments are almost always permitted after the defense's closing argument.[19] These give the prosecutor an opportunity to respond to the defense attorney's closing argument. As a matter of strategy, prosecutors should generally map out the arguments they intend to make to the jury and should think carefully about which belong best in the closing argument, as well as which should be "saved" for rebuttal.[20]

While closing arguments provide prosecutors with the important opportunity to explain their case to the jury and can be the most rewarding part of a trial, they also provide perhaps the greatest opportunity for error.[21] Some of the limitations on closing arguments that are likely to be most relevant to corruption prosecutors are discussed below.

A. *Argue Facts in Evidence and Reasonable Inferences*

A foundational limitation is that any argument to a jury must "be fair and accurate in the discussion of the law, the facts, and the reasonable inferences that may be drawn from the facts."[22] To ensure that the closing argument accurately summarizes the evidence in the record, the prosecutor should review

---

PowerPoint slide; the judge permitted some discussion of the application of the law to the facts, but did not like seeing "her charge" presented to the jury by the government.

19 In the federal system, rebuttals are explicitly required by statute. Fed. R. Crim. P. 29.1(3). *See also* John B. Mitchell, *Why Should the Prosecutor Get the Last Word?*, 27 Am. J. Crim. L. 139, 140 n.2 (2000) (noting that in Florida, if a defendant does not present a case, the prosecutor is not entitled to a rebuttal argument).

20 Note, however, that it may be improper to advance a new theory in a rebuttal argument. United States v. Taylor, 728 F.2d 930, 936-37 (7th Cir. 1984); People v. Burrell, 592 N.E.2d 453, 462 (Ill. App. Ct. 1992).

21 *Accord* Alex J. Grant, *Mirroring the Trial: Making Sense of the Law of Closing Argument in Criminal Cases*, 41 W. New Eng. L. Rev. 7, 8 (2019) (noting "the federal and state case reports in every jurisdiction continue to collect criminal cases in which convictions are overturned, or nearly overturned, by what is said during closing argument" (footnote omitted)).

22 Nat'l Dist. Att'ys Ass'n, National Prosecution Standards s. 6-8.1 (3d ed. 2009).

the trial transcript prior to summation, to the extent that time and resources permit.[23] The prosecutor should not misstate the evidence in the record or argue inferences that are not supported in the record.[24]

B. *Do Not Make Impermissible Arguments*

1. Argument May Not Jeopardize Constitutional Rights of the Accused

A potential foul blow a prosecutor must avoid striking is making a statement that jeopardizes the constitutional rights of the accused.[25] The Fifth Amendment prohibits prosecutors from commenting in any way on the defendant's exercise of the right to remain silent, whether post arrest or during the trial.[26] While this rule seems straightforward, applying it is difficult where the prosecutor may be attempting to draw reasonable inferences from testimony of defense witnesses.[27] If the defense chooses to put on a case that does not include the defendant's testimony and the prosecution chooses to comment on that case, it must scrupulously avoid commenting on any lack of trial testimony from the accused[28] and should be careful not to shift the burden of proof to the defense.[29] Similarly, the prosecution cannot use post-arrest silence to attempt to

---

23 *Accord* ABA Standards for Criminal Justice: Prosecution Function s. 3-6.8(a) (Am. Bar Ass'n 2017), https://www.americanbar.org/groups/criminal_justice/standards/ProsecutionFunctionFourthEdition/ (recommending prosecutor "review the evidence in the record").

24 *Id.*

25 *See* Berger v. United States, 295 U.S. 78, 88 (1935) (noting that while the prosecutor "may strike hard blows, he is not at liberty to strike foul ones").

26 *See* U.S. Const. amend. V ("No person . . . shall be compelled in any criminal case to be a witness against himself . . . ."); United States v. Sepulveda, 15 F.3d 1161, 1186 (1st Cir. 1993) (calling the prohibition on commenting on the right to remain silent a "bedrock" rule).

27 *Sepulveda*, 15 F.3d at 1186-88.

28 *Id.* at 1186-87.

29 Prosecutors may be able to thread this needle by prefacing a discussion of the defense case with something like "to be clear, the defendant has no burden during this trial, but because he elected to call witnesses, you should scrutinize the testimony of each of those witnesses much as you scrutinize the testimony of any other witness." Note that some affirmative defenses may be a defendant's burden to prove; the proscription against burden-shifting may not apply to aspects of a prosecutor's closing argument that address such a defense. Prosecutors should research the applicable statutes and caselaw to determine if a defense is an affirmative defense that is the defendant's burden to prove before treating it as such, however, and should not forget that proving each element of a crime remains the government's burden. *See, e.g.*, Patterson v. New York, 432 U.S. 197, 205-06, 210 (1977) (concluding that "affirmative defenses" cannot shift to the

impeach a defense explanation presented during trial.[30] The prosecution must also refrain from commenting on the defendant's exercise of his Sixth Amendment right to a trial.[31]

The risk of burden-shifting warrants additional discussion. In any criminal matter, the prosecution alone bears the burden of proving guilt beyond a reasonable doubt.[32] Whether a statement constitutes impermissible burden shifting depends on context and phrasing.[33] For example, a prosecutor may not argue that a defendant is guilty because he or she failed to establish a compelling theory of the case.[34] Another way impermissible burden shifting may occur is by arguing that in order to acquit the defendant, the jury would have to find that prosecution witnesses were lying.[35] A jury could acquit based on reasonable doubt while still finding that prosecution witnesses were truthful and accurate.[36]

2. Argument May Not Vouch for Credibility or Give Personal Opinion

Beyond constitutional limits on prosecution comments, other boundaries constrain the manner in which the prosecution may wield the tremendous power of its position. The prosecution may not vouch for the credibility of a government witness by referencing the attorney's personal knowledge or other information outside of trial evidence.[37] Not only does the vouching violate the basic principle that arguments to the jury must be limited to facts presented

---

defendant the burden of disproving an element of the offense). For further discussion of defenses, see Chapter 4.3.

30 Wainwright v. Greenfield, 474 U.S. 284, 291 (1986) (explaining the fundamental unfairness of implicitly assuring a suspect that his or her silence will not be used against him or her and then using that silence to impeach at trial).

31 *See* U.S. Const. amend. VI ("In all criminal prosecutions, the accused shall enjoy the right to a speedy and public trial, by an impartial jury of the State and district wherein the crime shall have been committed . . . ."); Cunningham v. Zant, 928 F.2d 1006, 1019-20 (11th Cir. 1991).

32 *See* Steven N. Gosney, *Trial Techniques for a Florida Prosecutor—A Positive Prescription for Ethical Closing Arguments*, 42 Am. J. Trial Advoc. 151, 165 (2018).

33 United States v. Cornett, 232 F.3d 570, 574 (7th Cir. 2000).

34 *See* United States v. Roberts, 119 F.3d 1006, 1015 (1st Cir. 1997).

35 *Cornett*, 232 F.3d at 574 (citations omitted); United States v. Vargas, 583 F.2d 380, 387 (7th Cir. 1978).

36 *Cornett*, 232 F.3d at 574; *Vargas*, 583 F.2d at 387.

37 United States v. Berrios, 676 F.3d 118, 133 (3rd Cir. 2012).

at trial and reasonable inferences,[38] it violates that principle in a unique and significant way. Because the prosecuting attorney is in the role of representing the sovereign and seeking justice,[39] the rule against vouching prevents the prosecution from using that authority to bolster its own witnesses.[40] Vouching for government witnesses risks improperly inducing the jury to believe the government's judgment rather than its own analysis of the evidence.[41] That said, a prosecutor can make arguments about a witness's incentives to tell the truth that rely on the facts in the record and the jury's common sense. For example, if a prosecutor elicited from a cooperating witness that he expected that his sentence would be no different if the defendant was convicted or acquitted, but that he could face additional prosecution if he lied under oath, the prosecutor could certainly argue that these facts provided an incentive for the cooperating witness to tell the truth about the defendant's actions.[42]

Similarly, while it is appropriate to argue that the evidence points to the defendant's guilt, the prosecution should avoid making statements to the jury that appear to convey the prosecutor's personal belief that the defendant is guilty.[43] Again, given the special role of the prosecutor, this rule prevents her from "add[ing] the weight of [her] own—or the government's—thumb to the scales of justice" as well as preventing reference to facts outside the trial record.[44] The prosecution must, of course, urge the jury to find the defendant guilty, but it should "predicate[] these entreaties *explicitly* and *exclusively* on reasonable inferences yielded by the evidence."[45] Especially in the context of public corruption, where sometimes what is illegal and corrupt may seem to a lay person only technically distinct from what is considered politics as usual,[46]

---

38 *See* Nat'l Dist. Att'ys Ass'n, National Prosecution Standards s. 6-8.1 (3d ed. 2009).

39 Berger v. United States, 295 U.S. 78, 88 (1935).

40 *See Berrios*, 676 F.3d at 133; NDAA Prosecution Standards s. 1-1.1.

41 United States v. Walker, 155 F.3d 180, 184 (3d Cir. 1998); *Berrios*, 676 F.3d at 133.

42 United States v. Carr, 424 F.3d 213, 228-29 (2d Cir. 2005).

43 *See* United States v. Smith, 982 F.2d 681, 684 (1st Cir. 1993).

44 *See* United States v. Farnkoff, 535 F.2d 661, 668 (1st Cir. 1976) (quoting United States v. Cotter, 425 F.2d 450, 453 (1st Cir. 1970)).

45 *Smith*, 982 F.2d at 684; ABA Standards for Criminal Justice: Prosecution Function s. 3-6.8(b) (Am. Bar Ass'n 2017), https://www.americanbar.org/groups/criminal_justice/standards/ProsecutionFunctionFourthEdition/ ("The prosecutor should not argue in terms of counsel's personal opinion, and should not imply special or secret knowledge of the truth or of witness credibility.").

46 *See* McDonnell v. United States, 136 S. Ct. 2355, 2372 (2016) ("The basic compact underlying representative government *assumes* that public officials will hear from their

a prosecutor may be tempted to convey to the jury that he or she has personal knowledge of the degree of defendant's misconduct. However, a corruption prosecutor should rely solely on facts and reasonable inferences to prove guilt and should explain the law objectively and without personal opinion.

3. Argument May Not Seek to Inflame Passions or Prejudices of the Jury

One type of disallowed argument that might prove tempting in public corruption prosecutions is the appeal to emotion, passions, or prejudices of the jury. This category of argument improperly diverts the jury's focus from the evidence, the law, and the question of whether this particular defendant committed the crime at issue in this particular case.[47] Appeals to the jury to act as the community conscience may not automatically be prohibited, but they may prejudice the defendant's right to a fair trial if they are calculated to incite passions of the jurors "wholly irrelevant to any facts or issues in the case."[48]

Arguments to the jury in a corruption case may tend to draw on concepts of harm and integrity outside of the factual elements subject to proof at trial. As one court explained, corruption "cannot properly be seen as a victimless crime," because it "threatens the foundation of democratic government" and "tears at the general belief of the citizenry that government officials will carry out their duties honestly . . . ."[49] But those types of concepts may be outside of the factual proof at trial. An analogous situation arises in drug cases where prosecutors have argued that a particular case is part of the "ongoing drug war."[50] Where the prosecution has urged a jury to help solve a pressing social issue through a guilty verdict in a particular case, courts have found such an argument to be improperly inciting passions.[51]

---

constituents and act appropriately on their concerns . . . ."); United States v. Tomblin, 46 F.3d 1369, 1379 (5th Cir. 1995) ("Intending to make a campaign contribution does not constitute bribery, even though many contributors hope that the official will act favorably because of their contributions.").

47 *See* ABA Standards for the Prosecution Function s. 3-6.8(c).

48 *See* United States v. Solivan, 937 F.2d 1146, 1151 (6th Cir. 1991).

49 United States v. Hayes, 762 F.3d 1300, 1309 (11th Cir. 2014) (addressing bribery); United States v. Rosen, 716 F.3d 691, 694 (2d Cir. 2013) ("The corruption of elected officials undermines public confidence in our democratic institutions.").

50 *See Solivan*, 937 F.2d at 1152.

51 *See id.* at 1153; United States v. Monaghan, 741 F.2d 1434, 1441 (D.C. Cir. 1984); United States v. Barlin, 686 F.2d 81, 93 (2d Cir. 1982) (finding that the improper argument did not

Similarly, while the prosecution may communicate the seriousness and gravity of corruption, it should avoid hyperbole inducing the jury to identify themselves as victims of the crime.[52] In other contexts, where the victim of the crime is more concrete and specific, prosecutors should not appeal to juror emotions and sympathies with the victim.[53] In the public corruption context, where jurors are, in a sense, among the public victims of the corruption, it may be prudent to avoid inducing jurors to feel personally aggrieved by the defendant.[54]

Finally, it is important to note that arguments that do not result in reversal of a conviction may nonetheless imperil a prosecutor's license to practice

---

warrant reversal because of overwhelming evidence of guilt and proper jury instruction); James Joseph Duane, *What Message Are We Sending to Criminal Jurors When We Ask Them to "Send a Message" With Their Verdict?*, 22 Am. J. Crim. L. 565, 580 n.40 (1995) (collecting state appellate court cases concluding it was inappropriate for prosecutors to ask jurors to "send a message" by finding a defendant guilty). In a press conference announcing the indictment of New York State Assembly Speaker Sheldon Silver, the United States Attorney commented that the indictment makes clear that "the show-me-the-money culture of Albany has been perpetuated and promoted at the very top of the political food chain." Preet Bharara, U.S. Att'y S.D.N.Y., *U.S. v. Sheldon Silver*, Prepared Remarks 2 (Jan. 22, 2015), https://www.justice.gov/sites/default/files/usao-sdny/legacy/2015/02/23/remarks.pdf. Similarly, in announcing the indictment of New York State Senate Majority Leader Dean Skelos, the same United States Attorney commented that "First, public corruption is a deep-seated problem in New York State. It is a problem in both chambers; it is a problem on both sides of the aisle. And second, we are deadly serious about tackling that problem." Press Release, Dep't of Justice, U.S. Att'y's Off. S.Dist. of N.Y., New York State Senate Majority Leader Dean Skelos and Son Arrested on Corruption Charges (May 4, 2015), https://www.justice.gov/usao-sdny/pr/new-york-state-senate-majority-leader-dean-skelos-and-son-arrested-corruption-charges. While these comments were made to the public in connection with indictments, rather than to a jury during trial, they reflect the temptation to characterize a particular corruption case as part of an effort to cure a societal harm. The trial court later criticized these and other similar comments about Silver, finding that the U.S. Attorney improperly "bundle[d] together unproven allegations regarding the Defendant with broader commentary on corruption and a lack of transparency in certain aspects of New York State politics" in a manner that could have been understood "as a commentary on the character or guilt of the Defendant." United States v. Silver, 103 F. Supp. 3d 370, 373, 378-79 (S.D.N.Y. 2015). While the defendant did not obtain the relief he sought—the dismissal of the indictment—the decision is a reminder about the danger of tying allegations about individual defendants to broader statements about good government.

52 *See* United States v. Dominguez, 835 F.2d 694, 700-01 (7th Cir. 1987) (finding that, in a drug case, referring to the threat of drugs to society generally was permissible, but referring to threats to specific friends or family members was not permissible).

53 *See* United States v. Berrios, 676 F.3d 118, 135 (3d Cir. 2012) (criticizing prosecutor for reading poem about victim during closing argument).

54 *See Dominguez*, 835 F.2d 700-01.

law. In Arizona, a prosecutor was reprimanded by the state bar for arguments that appealed to the jury's emotions that the state's supreme court characterized as "'prosecutorial misconduct' that did not rise to the level requiring reversal of criminal convictions."[55] The state supreme court distinguished what it characterized as an error by a prosecutor—including misconduct or simple mistakes—"that may necessitate a new trial and a prosecutor's conduct that violates the ethics rules."[56] The court concluded that the prosecutor's "repetitious misconduct in addressing jurors in trial in a manner inconsistent with established case law" warranted a reprimand, and required him to pay costs and expenses of the disciplinary proceeding.[57]

IV. Rebuttal Closing Arguments

The prosecution is almost always permitted to respond to the defense's closing argument because it has the burden of proof. This rebuttal argument should not be a repeat of the first closing argument, but may echo some of the themes developed in that argument and can provide an important opportunity to correct misimpressions left by the defense. If a "defense summation makes arguments and allegations against the government"—which may be even more likely in corruption cases— "the prosecutor may respond to them in rebuttal."[58]

A good practice is to predict, as much as possible, what the defendant is likely to argue in closing and be prepared to rebut it—even by scripting out potential points ahead of time. As one example, it is common for defense attorneys to argue that proof "beyond a reasonable doubt" is an all-but-impossible burden; if permitted in their jurisdiction, prosecutors may wish to be prepared to point out that while this burden is—and should be—weighty, it is the same one applied by juries across the country, and one that has been met by the government in this case. (This then permits another brief recap of the strongest prosecution evidence already summarized in the closing.)

While prosecutors must, just as in a closing, avoid personally vouching for a witness, they can still respond to defense arguments attacking a witness's

---

55 *In re* Martinez, 462 P.3d 36, 40 (Ariz. 2020).

56 *Id.* at 47.

57 *Id.* at 49-50.

58 United States v. Tocco, 135 F.3d 116, 130 (2d Cir. 1998).

credibility. One common, and typically effective, approach is to point out that a witness who was lying to curry favor with the government would have told a better story.[59] As an example, if a witness testifies about paying a defendant a small bribe, and the defendant's attorney argues that witness is lying in an effort to frame his or her client, a prosecutor might argue that a witness who was lying to get a defendant in trouble or curry favor with the government likely would have claimed to pay a larger bribe.[60]

In a public corruption trial, it may be particularly tempting for the defense to make jury nullification arguments.[61] Prosecutors should object to such arguments and be prepared to respond to them in rebuttal if necessary. They may be given more leeway to make arguments necessary to respond to improper defense arguments.[62]

Conclusion

Justice Robert H. Jackson, while serving as the Attorney General of the United States, noted:

> The qualities of a good prosecutor are . . . elusive . . . . A sensitiveness to fair play and sportsmanship is perhaps the best protection against the abuse of power, and the citizen's safety lies in the prosecutor who tempers zeal with human kindness, who seeks truth

---

59 *See* United States v. Vázquez-Larrauri, 778 F.3d 276, 283 (1st Cir. 2015) (noting that one "proper credibility argument is that a witness would have told a better, more consistent story if the witness had been lying").

60 As always, the prudent prosecutor will do research in his or her own jurisdiction to determine the limits of argument about witness credibility. *See, e.g.*, Irick v. United States, 565 A.2d 26, 35 (D.C. 1989) ("Despite decisions in the dozens, the law governing what a prosecutor may or may not say about the credibility of a [witness] is not always easy to discern or apply.").

61 Defendants are not entitled to these arguments. "[A]lthough jurors possess the raw power to set an accused free for any reason or for no reason, their duty is to apply the law as given to them by the court." United States v. Sepulveda, 15 F.3d 1161, 1190 (1st Cir. 1993).

62 R. Collin Mangrum, *I Believe, the Golden Rule, Send a Message, and Other Improper Closing Arguments*, 48 Creighton L. Rev. 521, 523 n.4 (2015) (collecting cases); *accord* State v. Rawlins, 932 S.W.2d 449, 454 (Mo. Ct. App. 1996) (holding in case where defense counsel's closing argument asked the jury to nullify, "[a] defendant may not provoke a reply to his or her own argument and then claim error").

and not victims, who serves the law and not factional purposes, and who approaches his task with humility.[63]

These qualities may be even more important in the corruption prosecutor. When arguing directly to a jury that a fellow public servant has abused the privilege of public office and broken the public's trust, a prosecutor should scrupulously adhere to the rules designed to guarantee due process and fair play. By doing so, the prosecutor will help to restore trust in the government, ensure that any conviction is fair and insulated from reversal on appeal, and maintain her bar license and reputation.

63 Robert H. Jackson, Att'y Gen. of the U.S., The Federal Prosecutor, Address at the Second Annual Conf. of U.S. Att'ys 7 (Apr. 1, 1940), https://www.justice.gov/sites/default/files/ag/legacy/2011/09/16/04-01-1940.pdf.

Chapter 4.2

Introducing Complex Data at Trial

Steve Grimes, Jeff Perconte

Steve Grimes is a former federal prosecutor and currently a partner at Winston & Strawn LLP in Hong Kong and Chicago.

Jeff Perconte is a former federal prosecutor and former partner at Drinker Biddle & Reath LLP (now Faegre Drinker Biddle & Reath LLP). He currently is assistant general counsel for the Major League Baseball Players Association.

Introduction

Public corruption prosecutions often include voluminous and complex records, such as bank and telephone records. This chapter focuses on two tools prosecutors may employ to present these types of records to a jury concisely and effectively: (1) summary charts and (2) demonstrative aids. This chapter explains the rules of evidence addressing each of these tools, potential objections the defense may raise to each tool, and the potential advantages and disadvantages of each tool.

I. Summary Charts

Federal Rule of Evidence 1006 allows for succinctly and effectively presenting complex data at trial. The rule permits the use of a summary of "the contents of voluminous writings . . . that cannot be conveniently examined in court."[1] A summary under Rule 1006 can be used in lieu of or in addition to the underlying records and is admissible as evidence to prove a fact in issue. Prosecutors have used Rule 1006 summaries in corruption cases to present compilations of financial records, records of communications, and various other types of voluminous data.[2] Like a demonstrative aid, a Rule 1006 summary or chart allows a prosecutor to condense large amounts of sophisticated or complex data into a digestible format for the jury. A summary or chart may also help to maintain the jury's attention and ensure that the jury understands the underlying evidence.

A Rule 1006 summary differs from a merely demonstrative aid in a number of ways. First, and most importantly, the Rule 1006 summary itself may be admitted into evidence and examined by the jury during its deliberations while a demonstrative aid is not admissible.[3] Second, while Rule 1006 requires that the underlying sources of the summary be admissible, the sources do not actually have to be admitted, unlike the sources of a demonstrative aid.[4] The rule essentially provides for an exception to the best evidence rule, which would ordinarily require a party offering a summary exhibit to admit the original

---

1 Fed. R. Evid. 1006. The following states and territory have Rules 1006 that are similar or identical to Federal Rule of Evidence 1006: Alaska, Arizona, Arkansas, Colorado, Delaware, Florida (as Rule 90.956, which adds a notice provision), Hawaii, Idaho, Iowa, Kentucky, Louisiana, Maine, Michigan, Minnesota, Mississippi, Montana, Nebraska, Nevada, New Hampshire, New Mexico, North Carolina, North Dakota, Ohio, Oklahoma (as Rule 3006), Oregon, Puerto Rico (as Rule 72), Rhode Island, South Dakota (as Rule 19-18-6), Tennessee, Texas, Utah, Vermont, Washington, West Virginia, Wisconsin (as Rule 910.06), and Wyoming. Art of Advocacy: Demonstrative Evidence, Chapter 9, § 9.05 n.19 (Matthew Bender, 2020 ed.). *See also* Pamela H. Bucy, *The Poor Fit of Traditional Evidentiary Doctrine and Sophisticated Crime: An Empirical Analysis of Health Care Fraud Prosecutions*, 63 Fordham L. Rev. 383, 415 n.158 (1994).

2 *See, e.g.*, United States v. Whitfield, 590 F.3d 325, 364-65 (5th Cir. 2009) (affirming admission of summary exhibit of bank records and checks in bribery case against judges and attorney); United States v. Massey, 89 F.3d 1433, 1441 (11th Cir. 1996) (affirming use of Rule 1006 summary chart in racketeering bribery case to present evidence showing relationship between attorney's payment of county judge's lunch bills and attorney's appointment as a special assistant public defender).

3 *See* United States v. Milkiewicz, 470 F.3d 390, 396-98 (1st Cir. 2006); United States v. Janati, 374 F.3d 263, 272-73 (4th Cir. 2004).

4 *See Janati*, 374 F.3d at 272-73 (noting that Rule 1006 does not require that the underlying documentation actually be introduced into evidence); *but see* United States v. Citron, 783 F.2d 307, 316 (2d Cir. 1986) ("Courts have long required that district courts ascertain that summary charts 'fairly represent and summarize the evidence upon which they are based.'" (citations omitted)).

source documents in evidence.[5] However, a summary exhibit must be an accurate and neutral representation of the underlying records. While an exhibit can be created based on evidence most favorable to one party, its ability to argue or persuade is limited by its underlying sources. A demonstrative exhibit is not so limited and can be used more liberally to argue to and persuade the jury.

A prosecutor seeking to admit a Rule 1006 summary of complex data should anticipate a number of objections from defense counsel. These objections often stem from Rule 1006's foundational requirements and may include:

- *The summary is unnecessary because the underlying data is not voluminous.* According to Rule 1006, the proponent of a summary must demonstrate that the data is sufficiently voluminous and that in-court examination of the underlying materials would be inconvenient. Defense counsel can therefore object that the summary is unnecessary because the sources are not voluminous. However, to overcome this objection, the proponent simply must demonstrate that it would be time-consuming, inconvenient, or difficult to examine the data in court, not that it would be impossible to do so.[6]

- *The underlying materials were not available to the defense.* This objection can take many forms. Defense counsel may argue that the materials supporting the summary were not produced within a reasonable time before trial. Or, defense counsel may argue the summary itself was not turned over within sufficient time to allow the defense to review the summary for accuracy. However, courts typically construe this foundational requirement liberally. If the prosecutor can show that the underlying material was available to the defense within a reasonable amount of time before trial, the fact that the summaries are proffered during trial typically will not bar the evidence, though the judge may require a delay in

5 *See* Fed. R. Evid. 1002; *Milkiewicz*, 470 F.3d at 396.

6 *See* United States v. Evans, 910 F.2d 790, 800 (11th Cir. 1990) (affirming admission of Rule 1006 summary in extortion case against county commissioner that summarized sixty payments of $100 over a five-year period).

its use to allow the defense to review it.[7] Similarly, this objection can be overcome by offering the underlying documents as evidence at trial.[8]

- *The underlying materials are not admissible.* Another objection to a Rule 1006 summary is that the underlying materials are not admissible. That the underlying materials are inadmissible hearsay is the most common objection to summary exhibits. Therefore, a prosecutor should carefully consider how he or she will lay the foundation for the appropriate hearsay exception at trial. If the materials are business records under Federal Rule of Evidence 803(6), for example, affidavits of the appropriate custodians of record may satisfy Rule 803(6).[9]

- *The summary is inaccurate, misleading, or argumentative.* This objection could be brought under Rule 1006 or Rule 403. Each of these arguments boils down to the rule that charts and summaries are inadmissible if they contain information that is not present in the underlying materials.[10] With that tenet in mind, it is permissible to present only those facts favorable to one party's position in a Rule 1006 summary as long as those facts appear in the summary's sources.[11] Additionally, an objection that an exhibit is inaccurate goes to the weight of the evidence, not its admissibility.[12]

---

7 *See* United States v. Dukes, 242 F. App'x 37, 49-50 (4th Cir. 2007) (affirming admission of summary exhibit when government made it available after trial had begun where underlying documents were available at reasonable place and time prior to trial and evidence was presented out of order to allow defendant time to review summary exhibit). *See also* United States v. Isaacs, 593 F.3d 517, 527-28 (7th Cir. 2010) (finding that requirement to make underlying records available was satisfied when records produced three days before trial, where underlying data had been produced fifteen months earlier).

8 *See* United States v. Solis, 299 F.3d 420, 442 (5th Cir. 2002) (affirming admission of summaries that relied upon previously admitted evidence).

9 *See* United States v. Oros, 578 F.3d 703, 708-10 (7th Cir. 2009) (holding that summary charts of telephone and bank records should not have been admitted in bribery case when government failed to lay the foundation for business records exception to hearsay rule, but that admission was harmless error).

10 *See* United States v. Drougas, 748 F.2d 8, 25 (5th Cir. 1984).

11 *See* United States v. Swanquist, 161 F.3d 1064, 1072-73 (7th Cir. 1998) ("A party is not obligated . . . to include within its charts or summaries its opponent's version of the facts." (citation omitted)).

12 *See* United States v. Masiarczyk, 1 F. App'x 199, 208-09 (4th Cir. 2001) (noting that objections that a summary exhibit may contain inaccuracies, ambiguities, or omissions go to the weight and not the admissibility of the evidence).

- *The summary has not been properly authenticated.* Authenticating a Rule 1006 summary usually requires testimony of a witness with personal knowledge of the summary's compilation.[13] It is therefore important that the authenticating witness has previously reviewed the underlying materials that form the basis of the summary, especially if the witness did not personally create the summary.

In conclusion, prosecutors may consider using a summary or chart under Rule 1006 when they want the jury to have access to the data during deliberations and when the data is sufficiently complex that a summary would save time or clarify the evidence.

II. Demonstrative Exhibits

There is a second option for a prosecutor who needs to summarize complex evidence or voluminous documents for a jury: a demonstrative aid.[14] The rules governing summary exhibits and demonstratives are "are not always mutually exclusive, and so it is unsurprising that confusion sometimes arises . . . over the appropriate basis for admitting a particular summary."[15] "When considering the admissibility of exhibits of this nature, it is critical to distinguish between charts or summaries *as evidence* and charts or summaries *as pedagogical devices*."[16]

As discussed above, "[c]harts and summaries as evidence are governed by Federal Rule of Evidence 1006, which permits the introduction of charts, summaries, or calculations 'of voluminous writings, recordings, or photographs which cannot conveniently be examined in court.'"[17] "In contrast, charts

---

13 *See* United States v. Bray, 139 F.3d 1104, 1112 (6th Cir. 1998) (noting no dispute as to authenticity where summary was authenticated by testimony of postal inspector who prepared the summary).

14 *See* United States v. White, 737 F.3d 1121, 1134-36 (7th Cir. 2013); United States v. Milkiewicz, 470 F.3d 390, 395, 397 (1st Cir. 2006).

15 *Milkiewicz*, 470 F.3d at 395.

16 Pierce v. Ramsey Winch Co., 753 F.2d 416, 431 (5th Cir. 1985). *See also* Baugh v. Cuprum S.A. de C.V., 730 F.3d 701, 707 (7th Cir. 2013); United States v. Wood, 943 F.2d 1048, 1053 (9th Cir. 1991).

17 *Wood*, 943 F.2d at 1053 (quoting Fed. R. Evid. 1006).

or summaries of testimony or documents already admitted into evidence are merely pedagogical devices and are not evidence themselves."[18]

A trial judge may allow the use of a demonstrative exhibit as a pedagogical device under Federal Rule of Evidence 611(a), which gives the trial court "control over the mode . . . [of] presenting evidence."[19] A demonstrative exhibit is most frequently used as a pedagogical device to "clarify and simplify complex testimony or other information and evidence or to assist counsel in the presentation of argument to the court or jury."[20]

A demonstrative exhibit used as a "pedagogical device" is:

> [A]n illustrative aid such as information presented on a chalkboard, flip chart, or drawing, and the like, that (1) is used to summarize or illustrate evidence, such as documents, recordings, or trial testimony, that has been admitted in evidence; (2) is itself not admitted into evidence; and (3) may reflect to some extent, through captions or other organizational devices or descriptions, the inferences and conclusions drawn from the underlying evidence by the summary's proponent.[21]

"This type of exhibit is 'more akin to argument than evidence since [it] organizes the jury's examination of testimony and documents already admitted in evidence.'"[22] When the term "pedagogical device" is used this way, "demonstrative exhibits are meant 'to illustrate or clarify a party's position,' and they are by definition 'less neutral in [their] presentation' and thus are not properly considered evidence."[23] Generally, a demonstrative exhibit used as a pedagogical device should be accompanied by a limiting instruction that informs the jury of the exhibit's purpose and that it is not itself evidence.[24]

---

18 *Id.* (citing *Pierce*, 753 F.2d at 431).

19 *Milkiewicz*, 470 F.3d at 397 (quoting Fed. R. Evid. 611(a)).

20 *Id.* (quoting United States v. Bray, 139 F.3d 1104, 1111 (6th Cir. 1998)).

21 *Bray*, 139 F.3d at 1111; *see Milkiewicz*, 470 F.3d at 397.

22 *Bray*, 139 F.3d at 1111 (quoting United States v. Paulino, 935 F.2d 739, 753 (6th Cir. 1991), *superseded by statute on other grounds*, U.S. Sentencing Guidelines § 3B1.1 (U.S. Sentencing Comm'n 1993), *as recognized in* United States v. Caseslorente, 220 F.3d 727, 734 (6th Cir. 2000)). *See* Baugh v. Cuprum S.A. de C.V., 730 F.3d 701, 707 (7th Cir. 2013).

23 *Baugh*, 730 F.3d at 707 (quoting *Milkiewicz*, 470 F.3d at 396-98.)

24 *Bray*, 139 F.3d at 1111 (quoting Gomez v. Great Lakes Steel Div. Nat'l Steel Corp., 803 F.2d 250, 257-58 (6th Cir. 1986)).

Accordingly, demonstrative exhibits that are not admitted into evidence because they are used as pedagogical devices should not go to the jury during deliberation.[25] As the Seventh Circuit Court of Appeals noted in *Baugh* v. *Cuprum S.A. de C.V.*:

> We would not allow a lawyer to accompany the jury into the deliberation room to help the jurors best view and understand the evidence in the light most favorable to her client. The same goes for the objects or documents used only as demonstrative exhibits during trial.[26]

Nonetheless, courts have noted that the lines between exhibits offered *as evidence* and exhibits offered *as pedagogical devices* are "easily blurred."[27] Specifically, "a summary that is admissible under Rule 1006 . . . could properly be offered under Rule 611(a) if the supporting material has been admitted into evidence."[28] Furthermore, "a chart that originally was offered as a jury aid to assist with review of voluminous underlying documents already in evidence—and which accurately summarizes those documents—alternatively could be admitted under Rule 1006 if the court conclude[s] that the supporting documents could not be examined conveniently in court."[29] "[A] court also has discretion under Rule 703 to provide the jury in some circumstances with the 'facts or data' underlying an expert's opinion, and such material may be presented in the form of a summary chart."[30]

---

25 *Baugh*, 730 F.3d at 708.

26 *Id. But see* Big John, B.V. v. Indian Head Grain Co., 718 F.2d 143, 148 (5th Cir. 1983) ("The submission of [demonstrative exhibits] whether or not admitted in evidence, to the jury during deliberations, accompanied by careful cautionary instructions as to their use and limited significance, is within the discretion accorded the district court in order that it may guide and assist the jury in understanding the factual controversy." (citation omitted)); United States v. Downen, 496 F.2d 314, 321 (10th Cir. 1974) ("[W]e hold that the submission of papers, documents or articles, whether or not admitted in evidence, to the jury for view during trial or jury deliberations, accompanied by careful cautionary instructions as to their use and limited significance, is within the discretion accorded the Trial Court in order that it may guide and assist the jury in understanding and judging the factual controversy.").

27 United States v. White, 737 F.3d 1121, 1135 (7th Cir. 2013) (quoting *Milkiewicz*, 470 F.3d at 397).

28 *Id.* (quoting *Milkiewicz*, 470 F.3d at 397).

29 *Id.* (quoting *Milkiewicz*, 470 F.3d at 397).

30 *Milkiewicz*, 470 F.3d at 397-98 (citing Fed. R. Evid. 703; United States v. Janati, 374 F.3d 263, 273 (4th Cir. 2004)).

Courts have identified the "key difference" between these approaches as "the purpose for which the summaries are offered."[31] Exhibits admitted "under Rule 1006 are explicitly intended to reflect the contents of the documents they summarize and typically are substitutes in evidence for the voluminous originals."[32] Thus, they must be "accurate and nonprejudicial."[33] Alternatively, exhibits admitted under Rule 611(a) as a pedagogical aid to illustrate a party's position, or under Rule 703 to assist an expert's testimony, may be "less neutral" in their presentation.[34] Such exhibits may reflect the inferences and conclusions the proponent wishes the jury to draw from the underlying evidence they summarize.[35] "In some cases, however, such pedagogical devices may be sufficiently accurate and reliable that they, too, are admissible in evidence, even though they do not meet the specific requirements of Rule 1006."[36]

Demonstrative exhibits used as pedagogical tools to help persuade a jury or the court are not considered substantive evidence, but they are subject to a number of evidentiary objections.[37] Specifically, because these exhibits are not themselves admissible as evidence, they need not meet the standards required for the admission of substantive evidence, and they do not have to be "completely accurate."[38] However, the exhibits can be excluded under Rule 403 if they are so inaccurate that they are misleading or if they present a significant risk of jury confusion.[39] Additionally, since the exhibits are generally used to summarize admissible evidence, a party may seek to exclude the exhibits by objecting to the admissibility of the underlying information.[40]

Though they are inadmissible as evidence, demonstrative aids allow prosecutors to create a visual aid during trial that may assist the jury in following

---

31 *Milkiewicz*, 470 F.3d at 398.

32 *Id.*

33 *Id.* (quoting United States v. Bray, 139 F.3d 1104, 1111 (6th Cir. 1998)); Gomez v. Great Lakes Steel Div. Nat'l Steel Corp., 803 F.2d 250, 257 (6th Cir. 1986)).

34 *Milkiewicz*, 470 F.3d at 398.

35 *Id.* (citing *Bray*, 139 F.3d at 1111; *Janati*, 374 F.3d at 273).

36 *Id.* (citing *Bray*, 139 F.3d at 1112; 6 Jack B. Weinstein & Margaret A. Berger, Weinstein's Federal Evidence, § 1006.04(2) (Mark S. Brodin, ed., Matthew Bender 2d ed. 2020)).

37 *See, e.g.*, Wilbon v. Plovanich, No. 12 C 1132, 2016 U.S. Dist. LEXIS 95369, at *8 (N.D. Ill. July 21, 2016).

38 *Id.* (citing Roland v. Langlois, 945 F.2d 956, 963 (7th Cir. 1991)).

39 *Id.*

40 *See Bray*, 139 F.3d at 1110-11.

and processing complicated or potentially confusing evidence. Demonstrative aids are not, however, limited merely to summarizing or otherwise presenting complex or voluminous data or documents. For example, a public corruption prosecution may involve surveillance of several meetings between the defendant and others engaged in the allegedly corrupt activity. Because trials are presented witness-by-witness rather than chronologically or fact-by-fact, the storyline can appear fragmented to a jury. If the case involves several meetings or transactions over a period of time, one law enforcement witness may not be able to testify regarding all of the surveillance conducted during the investigation. Recorded telephone conversations that precede or follow meetings may be introduced through yet a different witness and may further impact the jury's ability to follow exactly what date, meeting, or transaction a witness is discussing.

One way to reorganize and simplify this evidence is for the prosecutor or a witness to create a demonstrative exhibit for each particular meeting or transaction that lists and provides a short summary of the surrounding calls and surveillance in what essentially amounts to a timeline. A prosecutor may create this type of demonstrative as witnesses are testifying by simply adding summaries of meetings or calls on a white board, a flip book, or a computer screen that includes one entry for each different meeting or transaction.

While the jury may not be able to take this type of demonstrative exhibit to the jury room during deliberations, it will assist jurors in following the evidence introduced at trial. By turning attention to the timeline and entries for a particular transaction or meeting, the prosecutor: (1) alerts the jury that the witness is now going to talk about a specific transaction or meeting that took place on the particular date; and (2) reminds the jury of the other evidence already heard about this particular transaction or meeting (such as recorded telephone calls or surveillance testimony from other officers). In addition, jurors may end up taking notes in the same way the prosecutor creates the demonstrative timelines, which effectively means that the jurors will have the demonstrative with them in deliberations.

Alternatively, the prosecutor may be able to call a witness at the end of the trial to testify about summary demonstratives and display them to the jury, with the judge's permission. Exhibit numbers should be included in such demonstrative aids, as they will assist jurors, opposing counsel, and the court in finding the underlying evidence that is summarized. Before the demonstrative is displayed, the prosecutor should also endeavor to have the jury instructed that the jurors will not be able to see it during deliberations, which will cue them to take notes about the evidence the demonstrative aid summarizes.

Conclusion

Prosecutors may use summaries and demonstratives to present and summarize complex evidence to juries in public corruption cases. Whether a prosecutor uses a summary exhibit or a demonstrative aid will largely turn on the type of evidence the prosecutor is presenting and whether the prosecutor wants the jury to be able to consider the summary or demonstrative aid as evidence or simply use the summary or aid to assist the jury in understanding the presentation of the evidence.

CHAPTER 4.3

Defenses in Public Corruption Prosecutions

Peter J. Henning

Peter J. Henning was Professor of Law at Wayne State University Law School and the author and coauthor of numerous books and articles in the area of public corruption, including The Prosecution and Defense of Public Corruption: The Law and Legal Strategies, *published by LexisNexis.*

INTRODUCTION

State prosecutors play an important role in combatting public corruption.[1] Some state attorneys general have units devoted to investigating and prosecuting government officials for misconduct, and local prosecutors in larger jurisdictions often devote resources to pursuing such cases. Prosecutors and investigators have developed innovative investigative techniques and refined legal theories for obtaining convictions. At the same time, a sophisticated white collar corporate defense bar has grown primarily to defend executives and companies accused of private fraud. Former prosecutors often seek lucrative employment with the private defense bar, bringing with them the "tricks of the trade" to defend private clients with a zeal (and a budget) not often

1 Kelly v. United States, 140 S. Ct. 1565, 1571 (2020) (reversing conviction and observing that "federal fraud law leaves much public corruption to the States (or their electorates) to rectify").

seen in other areas of the law. When called on to defend public officials from corruption charges, the defense bar often employs the same tactics developed in white collar, bet-the-company cases. Perhaps even more than in private fraud cases, the stakes are high in a corruption case against a public official who has built a career on reputation and trust. Because of the high stakes, a defendant's response to such an accusation—from investigation through trial—is predictably ferocious.

The purpose of this chapter is to describe some of the various defenses that can be offered in a public corruption case and suggest means by which they can be countered. As much as any area of the law, each corruption case has its unique aspects, ranging from the form of the benefit, the conduct by the official, and the background and involvement of any cooperating witnesses. No two cases are alike, so the goal is not to try to catalogue every possible variation of the defenses. Nor is it likely that only one defense will be offered; there may be different combinations of defenses employed that are among those highlighted here, and there may be defenses that are not included in this chapter. Instead, the hope is that the prosecutor can *anticipate* what kinds of defenses may arise and take steps as early as during the investigation to develop evidence to respond to likely defenses. By considering the types of defenses commonly offered, a prosecutor can better predict what defenses might be used in a specific case and then focus on gathering and presenting evidence that both addresses the elements of the public corruption offense and minimizes, if not negates, a potential defense.

Before looking at the defenses, it is worth considering what types of defense claims will (almost) never arise in a public corruption case. There will rarely be an alibi claim, that the defendant was watching television at home when the bribe was paid or the benefit conferred. Nor will there likely be an issue of eyewitness identification or, except in rare cases, the collection and analysis of forensic evidence. In most corruption cases, there is no dispute about who was involved and what payment or benefit was provided. Like most other white collar crime prosecutions, the key issue is the intent of the defendant: Did he or she know a payment was in exchange for an exercise of government authority; was there a general (or specific) awareness of the nature of the transaction; and did the person act in a good faith belief the conduct was legal? Issues of intent mean that circumstantial evidence will be crucial, whether to prove what was in the defendant's mind as expressed in an email or text message or to corroborate the testimony of a cooperating witness[2] who is also tainted by the stain of corruption.

I. "It Wasn't a Bribe/Kickback/Unlawful Gratuity," Cooperating Witnesses/Informants, and Character Witnesses

A common defense in public corruption cases is to claim that "it wasn't a bribe" (or kickback or unlawful gratuity), so there was no crime. This defense is particularly common in prosecutions that feature the testimony of a cooperating witness who claims to have paid a bribe—that is, given something of value in exchange for the performance of an official act—or witnessed such a quid pro quo arrangement. Using this approach, the public official denies that any type of nefarious payoff occurred and along the way accuses the government's cooperating witness of lying, or at least misinterpreting an apparently innocent interaction between an official and a member of the public. The defense may also call character witnesses in an effort to strengthen the defendant's assertion that any payment received was lawful.

A. *The "No Nefarious Payment" Defense*

For the "it wasn't a bribe" defense to be effective, the defense attorney must develop a motive for the witness to lie or at least to have not comprehended what was really taking place. Potential or pending criminal charges against a cooperating witness often furnish a motive to curry favor with the prosecution, making the cooperator vulnerable to defense attacks on credibility. The defense may additionally, or alternatively, claim the witness is simply

2 This chapter uses "cooperating witness" or "cooperator" to mean a charged defendant who has agreed to provide useful information and testify and "confidential informant" to mean an individual who provides useful and credible information to law enforcement regarding criminal activities and from whom law enforcement expects to obtain additional useful and credible information in the future. *Accord* Guidelines Regarding the Use of Confidential Informants §§ I(B)(6), I(B)(7) (U.S. Dep't of Justice 2001), https://www.justice.gov/archives/ag/attorney-general-renos-confidential-informant-guidelines-january-8-2001 (providing similar definitions for confidential informant and cooperating witness). For a more detailed examination of cooperators and informants, see Chapter 2.5. For examples of ways witnesses can be corroborated, see Chapter 1.2, Part II(C).

mistaken about whether the public official's acts were corrupt and may seek to admit evidence that the public official had an otherwise unblemished record of public service in rebuttal. If a case rests largely on the uncorroborated testimony of a bribe payer, this defense strategy can be fatal to the prosecution. Because payoffs are made in secret, usually with only the cooperating witness and the public official present, meaningful evidence to confirm that the payment was illicit may be difficult to obtain.

On the other side, it is even more important to trace the bribe after it has been delivered to the public official. In some instances, large deposits will appear in a defendant's bank account shortly after the payoff. In other instances, illicit payments may go directly toward paying off an existing personal debt. In the federal bribery prosecution of the former mayor of Detroit, Kwame Kilpatrick, the government introduced evidence from Kilpatrick's bank accounts that showed, during a six-year period, over \$500,000 in cash deposits and another \$282,000 in cash payments for credit card bills.[3] This evidence was the linchpin of the prosecution's effort to show how he was being bribed, and it corroborated the testimony of cooperating witnesses who provided cash to Kilpatrick or his conspirators.[4] Even without a one-to-one correspondence between the bribe and the deposit, a pattern of cash deposits and withdrawals goes a long way toward establishing corruption, particularly where there is no credible alternative explanation for cash to be flowing to the defendant. Any potential source of corroboration of the payoff or benefit should be explored prior to filing charges to confirm that the payment truly was a quid pro quo.

B. *Cooperating Witnesses/Informants*

To reduce the later effectiveness of the "it wasn't a bribe" defense, during the investigation the prosecutor should aggressively seek to corroborate the

---

3 Robert Snell, *Kwame Kilpatrick on Trial: Feds Grilled Kilpatrick Kin Over Gifts, Loans*, Det. News (Nov. 27, 2012), http://blogs.detroitnews.com/kwamekilpatrick/2012/11/27/day-29-feds-call-key-detroit-official-wrap-up-extortion-victim/#liveblog-entry-3736; Allan Lengel, *Updated: For Kwame, It Was Good to Be the King*, Deadline Det. (Sept. 24, 2012), https://www.deadlinedetroit.com/articles/2000/updated_for_kwame_it_was_good_to_be_the_king.

4 United States v. Kilpatrick, No. 10-20403, 2013 U.S. Dist. LEXIS 111723, at *44-46 (E.D. Mich. Aug. 8, 2013). Kilpatrick's 28-year sentence was commuted to time served in early 2021. Christine Ferretti, Sarah Rahal, Melissa Nann Burke, *Kwame Kilpatrick's Commutation Met with Praise, Scorn*, Det. News (Jan. 20, 2021), https://www.detroitnews.com/story/news/local/wayne-county/2021/01/20/kwame-kilpatricks-commutation-met-with-praise-scorn/4229754001/.

statements of a confidential informant or cooperating witness—or even a potential cooperating witness—if it appears likely that a coconspirator might choose to cooperate.[5] A good starting point for developing effective corroboration is to establish *how* the bribe payer obtained the payoff money. The source and amount of the funds can often be established through bank records, loan documents, or corporate financial reports. If the benefit is less tangible, such as hiring a relative or awarding a contract to a favored bidder, then documents showing how ordinary transactions work will be crucial to show how this one was outside the norm. Telephone records, visitor logs, email and text messages, appointment books, and electronic calendars can provide valuable proof of communications between the cooperating witness and the defendant, even if none are particularly incriminating themselves. A course of regular communications also may be established through interviews of administrative assistants, co-workers, and other business associates. Even without going back in time to record the words that were exchanged between the defendant and the cooperating witness, corroborating the cooperator with objective proof on even undisputed facts can help establish to a jury that he or she is a credible witness. Introducing exhibits during the cooperator's testimony that enable the prosecutor to recreate for the jury what happened when, for example, the defendant was bribed, can make that testimony more persuasive and memorable. A claim that a cooperating witness is untrustworthy may be also undermined by showing that the defendant trusted the person at the time the crime was committed.

In some cases, there may be proof that the cooperating witness spoke about the illicit payment with one or more third parties, and perhaps even showed them the money, before he or she was aware of any criminal investigation. Prosecutors may be able to call the third party to testify about the cooperator's statements if the defense argues that the cooperating witness fabricated testimony to gain favorable treatment by the government.[6]

5 For more about confidential informants and cooperating witnesses, see Chapter 2.5. Part IV(B) of that Chapter lists some defenses prosecutors should anticipate.

6 Federal Rule of Evidence 801(d)(1)(B) permits the introduction of a witness's prior consistent statement as an exception to the rule against hearsay "to rebut an express or implied charge that the declarant recently fabricated it or acted from a recent improper influence or motive in so testifying." FED. R. EVID. 801(d)(1)(B). State rules of evidence often contain similar provisions, but may be more limited. *See, e.g.*, GA. CODE ANN. § 24-6-613(c) (2020) ("A prior consistent statement shall be admissible to rehabilitate a witness if the prior consistent statement logically rebuts an attack made on the witness's credibility."); ILL. R. EVID. 613(c)(i), (ii) (2021) (prior consistent statement admissible "for rehabilitation purposes only and not substantively as a hearsay exception" to rebut claim of improper influence, motive to testify falsely, or recent

If a confidential informant or cooperator who is working proactively with the investigation will be a featured witness at trial, the prosecutor should make every effort to corroborate all contacts between that person and the public official. If meetings can be safely and legally recorded, that is optimal—and it is even better if law enforcement officers can also monitor each meeting in real-time. If it is not possible to record or monitor the meetings, the witness should be debriefed by law enforcement soon after each meeting and the witness's description of what happened should be carefully documented. It is possible that the defendant will claim that the cooperator said certain things if the meetings are not adequately memorialized, and recording every meeting can help respond to allegations of entrapment.

A common defense is to assail the cooperating witness as a "con man." An essential component of many undercover investigations is an informant or cooperating witness who provides information, makes introductions, and sometimes sets up meetings between public officials and agents posing as bribe payers. Individuals who agree to perform these "intermediary" functions for an investigation are often motivated by money, hope for lenient treatment for crimes they have committed, or other benefits—motivations that, as discussed in the next paragraphs, can be exploited on cross-examination by the attorney for the officials they ensnare. The "con man" defense is frequently used in cases in which the defendant's conversations have been recorded. It is a standard tactic to contend that the cooperator had unrecorded meetings with the defendant outside the presence of government agents. The defense will contend that during those unrecorded meetings, the cooperator tricked the defendant into making statements or acting in a way that appears consistent with the defendant's guilt. Once the "con man" had the defendant properly programmed, the argument goes, that unwitting defendant appeared at a recorded meeting to make incriminating statements.

The motive for the cooperator's conduct can be attacked by pointing to the receipt of benefits or by the person's own exposure to punishment.[7] These

---

fabrication); Wyo. R. Evid. 801(d)(1)(B) (2020) (statement admissible as an exception to the rule against hearsay if it is "consistent with [the witness's] testimony and is offered to rebut an express or implied charge against him of recent fabrication or improper influence or motive").

7 Prosecutors are obliged to provide information to defense counsel about any benefit provided to, or hoped for by, a testifying informant or cooperating witness. *See, e.g.*, Giglio v. United States, 405 U.S. 150, 154 (1972); Justice Manual §§ 9-5.001, 9-5.002 (U.S. Dep't of Justice 2020), https://www.justice.gov/jm/justice-manual; Model Rules of Prof'l Conduct

arguments can be difficult to rebut if the investigation has not been structured with these potential defenses in mind. The first step to rebutting claims of misconduct by an informant or cooperating witness is to carefully control such a witness during the investigation and ensure that material information about the case flows only one way: from the witness to law enforcement. Whether it is necessary to provide information to help an informant to effectively work proactively for law enforcement should be carefully considered; generally, an informant should never be "fed" any facts about the case that could taint his testimony.[8] Substantial efforts should be made to monitor and record all contact between the informant or anyone acting on his or her behalf (spouse, assistant, etc.) and the target.[9] If those recordings are monitored, they may be admissible through an agent who monitored and maintained custody of the recording. If practicable, the role of the informant should be reduced and an undercover agent should be introduced to be the primary contact for the target at an early stage of the investigation. Prosecutors can also avoid problems at trial if they do not call the informant to testify. Instead, if possible, introduce the recordings through the agents. If it is essential that the informant be called as a witness, prosecutors should corroborate with independent evidence as much of the expected testimony as possible and consider structuring the testimony so that the informant testifies only about matters that have been corroborated.

Regardless of who will testify, if possible, all conversations with the target about the payoff should be recorded, and, when practicable, it should be stated in straightforward, clear terms that the payment is for a specific act.[10] It is much more difficult for a defendant to advance a credible "con man" claim to discredit the government's investigation if the recorded conversations discuss the payoff in clear, understandable language. Moreover, to the extent possible, the statements should come from the target and not the cooperator so there is no claim that words were put into the official's mouth. Of course, an official may be suspicious of stilted attempts to explicitly outline the quid pro quo, so this may not be possible in all cases.

Another way for the prosecution to deal with claims of improper conduct by the cooperator, especially one who made bribe payments or served as

---

r. 3.8(d) (Am. Bar Ass'n 2020). *See also* Chapter 5.1, Part III.

8 *See also* Chapter 2.5, Part III(C).

9 *See also* Chapter 2.5, Part III(F).

10 *See also* Chapter 2.5, Part IV(A).

a conduit, is through appropriate treatment of the person during the investigation. The cooperating witness should not be perceived by the jury as having escaped punishment for a crime simply because he or she agreed to inculpate the defendant.[11] If the jury has that perception, it might reject the witness's testimony, which may result in the acquittal of the defendant. Generally, a criminally culpable cooperating witness should be required to plead guilty to some crime.[12] A cooperating witness will be more credible if he has pled guilty to and admitted responsibility for the crime(s) about which he is testifying—particularly as he will not be perceived to be "getting away with" committing the crime for which the defendant is on trial.[13]

The relationship between the cooperator and government agents can be fertile ground for the defense to raise questions about whether prosecutors are allowing the "real bad guy" to escape punishment and suggest that the investigation was tainted by the cooperator's bias. Interactions between an agent and a cooperator that are not fully documented or contain communications that are in questionable taste can support defense arguments that the government gave favorable treatment to a criminal in an effort to impugn an otherwise upstanding public servant. Text messages, emails, and recorded communications that include what might be seen as too familiar or informal banter can have a disastrous effect, undermining the testimony of both the cooperator and any agents called as witnesses.

---

11 For a discussion of various means to use to secure a witness's testimony—including cooperation agreements, non-prosecution agreements, and immunity orders—and potential benefits and disadvantages to each, see Chapter 1.8, Part II(A).

12 *See id.* In at least one federal district, the Southern District of New York, prospective cooperating witnesses are thoroughly debriefed by prosecutors and law enforcement agents prior to being "signed up" as cooperators. Prospective cooperating witnesses are also required to plead guilty to both the original charges, if any, and any additional federal crimes to which they admit during their debriefings. It is common for judges in that district to, when they are sentencing cooperators, consider both the guidelines range that includes all of the conduct to which the cooperators plead guilty and the guidelines range that would have likely applied had the cooperator not agreed to cooperate with the government. The judges will generally, but not always, impose a sentence that is lower—sometimes substantially so—than what the cooperator would have likely received with a straight guilty plea.

13 Prosecutors must be careful not to imply that the guilt of the defendant is proven by the cooperator's plea. *See, e.g.*, United States v. Baez, 703 F.2d 453, 455 (10th Cir. 1983) ("A codefendant's guilty plea may not be used as substantive evidence of a defendant's guilt."). In particular, the government cannot argue "to the jury that the coconspirators' convictions established the evidence of a conspiracy, an element of the crime with which defendants were charged." United States v. Austin, 786 F.2d 986, 991 (10th Cir. 1986).

Especially in the period leading up to trial, prosecutors and investigators must be very careful in all interactions with cooperating witnesses. The conviction of Senator Ted Stevens in 2008 on corruption charges was reversed because the prosecutor failed to turn over notes of meetings with the key cooperator showing that he told different stories during the investigation.[14] Witness preparation is crucial in a corruption case, but it must be approached carefully to avoid claims that the witness's story was somehow shaped by the prosecutor, or that exculpatory evidence was generated and then withheld.[15]

C. *Character Witnesses*

To bolster the claim that a transaction or payment was not corrupt, the defense may offer testimony from "pillars of the community" that the defendant has a reputation for good character. Especially for elected officials, there are any number of community leaders who have received benefits through the intercession of the defendant and will testify to the person's good character. Prosecutors can address duplicative character evidence by asking the judge to place limits on the number of such witnesses the defense may call.[16] Next, if permitted by the relevant rules of evidence, the prosecutor can object if a character witness attempts to testify about specific good acts performed by the defendant.[17] On cross-examination of a character witness, specific instances of the defendant's misconduct can be raised.[18] The Advisory Committee Notes state that

---

14 *See, e.g.*, U.S. Dep't of Just., Off. of Prof'l Resp., Investigation of Allegations of Professional Misconduct in United States v. Theodore F. Stevens, Crim. No. 08-231 (D.D.C. 2009) (EGS) 11-12, 19, 666 (Aug. 15, 2011), https://www.leahy.senate.gov/imo/media/doc/052412-081511Report.pdf. *See also* Brady v. Maryland, 373 U.S. 83, 87 (1963); Giglio v. United States, 405 U.S. 150, 154 (1972). After years of litigation, an appellate board lifted sanctions that the U.S. Department of Justice proposed imposing against two of the line prosecutors in the case, concluding that USDOJ did not follow its own internal procedures. Goeke v. Dep't of Justice, 122 M.S.P.R. 69, 80-81 (M.S.P.B. 2015). In the end, the USDOJ was ordered to pay over $640,000 in legal fees to prosecutors' attorneys. *See* Kat Greene, *O'Melveny, Others Win Fees from DOJ in Ted Stevens Fallout*, Law360 (Aug. 16, 2016), https://www.law360.com/articles/829385/o-melveny-others-win-fees-from-doj-in-ted-stevens-fallout.

15 For more on ethical witness preparation, see Chapter 5.1, Part II(A).

16 *Accord* Fed. R. Evid. 403 (court may exclude relevant evidence if its probative value is substantially outweighed by the "needless[]" presentation of "cumulative evidence").

17 *Accord* Fed. R. Evid. 405 (permitting, when evidence of a person's character is admissible, testimony about the person's reputation, Fed. R. Evid. 405(a); only when character is "an essential element of a charge, claim, or defense," may specific instances of the person's conduct be proven, Fed. R. Evid. 405(b)).

18 Fed. R. Evid. 405(a).

> [t]he express allowance of inquiry into specific instances of conduct on cross-examination in subdivision (a) and the express allowance of it as part of a case in chief when character is actually in issue in subdivision (b) contemplate that testimony of specific instances is not generally permissible on the direct examination of an ordinary opinion witness to character.[19]

In rare instances, after a defendant has placed his or her character in evidence, the prosecution may choose to rebut with negative character witnesses.[20] But this can be risky because on cross-examination the defense could raise specific instances of conduct to show the defendant's good character, the very thing the prosecution wants to keep out.

Another defense tactic that is a way of showing good character without necessarily doing so through specific character witnesses is to call people who dealt successfully with the public official without being extorted or otherwise subjected to misconduct. They may testify that they did not feel any pressure to provide a benefit, or if the case involves outside business with the official, that they did so without regard to the person's position. For example, in the prosecution of Mike Hubbard, the former Speaker of the Alabama House of Representatives, for ethics violations, the prosecution alleged that he channeled contracts to his printing and media businesses by using the power of his office, but Hubbard asserted that he obtained the business legitimately and ethically through long-standing friendships and business contacts.[21] A rebuttal to this defense tactic is to request the court to rule that evidence of noncriminal conduct to negate the inference of criminal conduct is generally irrelevant.[22] In

---

19 Fed. R. Evid. 405 advisory committee's note.

20 Fed. R. Evid. 404(a)(1)(A) ("a defendant may offer evidence of the defendant's pertinent trait, and if the evidence is admitted, the prosecutor may offer evidence to rebut it").

21 Mike Cason, *Alabama House Speaker Mike Hubbard Convicted on 12 Counts*, AL.com (last updated Jan. 13, 2019), https://www.al.com/news/index.ssf/2016/06/house_speaker_mike_hubbard_con.html. This case is described in Chapter 1.3, Part III(C). *See also* Ex parte Hubbard, No. 1180047, 2020 Ala. LEXIS 54 (Ala. Apr. 10, 2020) (describing case and affirming in part and reversing in part defendant's convictions).

22 *See* State v. Brooks, 873 N.W.2d 460, 475 (Neb. Ct. App. 2016) ("Courts applying character evidence rules similar to those in Nebraska have also stated that evidence of prior *good* acts is inadmissible to prove that a defendant acted in conformity therewith on a given occasion."); United States v. Grimm, 568 F.2d 1136, 1138, (5th Cir. 1978) ("Evidence of noncriminal conduct to negate the inference of criminal conduct is generally irrelevant."); United States v. Russell, 703 F.2d 1243, 1249 (11th Cir. 1983) (same).

analogous contexts, this type of defense is obviously absurd: If a man is on trial for robbing a bank, evidence that he visited three other banks without robbing them is not relevant to the determination of whether he is guilty of the bank robbery in question.

II. The "Official Act" Defense

A variation of the "it wasn't a bribe" defense is one based on *McDonnell v. United States*, 136 S. Ct. 2355 (2016), in which the conviction of the former governor of Virginia on extortion and honest services fraud charges was overturned. The issue in the case was whether the governor's actions on behalf of a campaign donor who gave him expensive gifts worth over $175,000 were "official acts." To construe honest services fraud and Hobbs Act extortion, the statutes McDonnell was charged with violating,[23] the parties agreed to use "official act" in the federal bribery statute, 18 U.S.C. § 201(a)(3), which was defined as "any decision or action on any question, matter, cause, suit, proceeding or controversy, which may at any time be pending, or which may by law be brought before any public official, in such official's official capacity, or in such official's place of trust or profit."[24] While the parties disputed whether § 201(a)(3) encompassed the steps that McDonnell was accused of taking to assist the donor, they agreed that the government would be required to show that McDonnell took an "official act" to assist the donor to prove that he was guilty of honest services fraud or extortion.

The Court held that "[s]etting up a meeting, talking to another official, or organizing an event (or agreeing to do so)—without more—does not fit that definition of 'official act.'"[25] The Court did not explain what the "without more" meant, but it is clear that conduct by a senior official that involves just a meeting, communication with another official, or organization of a public function do not rise to the level of an "official act" when those are everyday acts that do not entail any exercise of authority. The "more" must be linked to some type of

---

23 McDonnell was charged with honest services fraud, in violation of 18 U.S.C. §§ 1343, 1346, and 1349, and Hobbs Act extortion, in violation of 18 U.S.C. § 1951(a), as well as violating 18 U.S.C. § 1014 by making a false statement. McDonnell v. United States, 136 S. Ct. 2355, 2365 (2016). For more on this case, see Chapter 1.3, Part I(B).

24 18 U.S.C. § 201(a)(3) (2018).

25 *McDonnell*, 136 S. Ct. at 2372.

decision that implicates the official's power, such that there is something that the benefit is given in exchange for apart from acts the Court seemed to find almost trivial.

This type of case would not appear at first glance to have much significance for state and local corruption prosecutions because it involves the application of a provision of federal law—§ 201(a)(3)—to a prosecution for violating federal statutes. Yet, the language the Court used may be implicated in cases brought under state law because the Court was discussing generally the requirements for proving the quid pro quo necessary for bribery. It described how public officials at all levels act in explaining why a more limited approach to establishing the object of a corrupt agreement was necessary:

> The basic compact underlying representative government *assumes* that public officials will hear from their constituents and act appropriately on their concerns—whether it is the union official worried about a plant closing or the homeowners who wonder why it took five days to restore power to their neighborhood after a storm. The Government's position could cast a pall of potential prosecution over these relationships if the union had given a campaign contribution in the past or the homeowners invited the official to join them on their annual outing to the ballgame.[26]

The official prosecuted was a state governor, and the statutes used in the case—the Hobbs Act and the right of honest services statute—incorporate a generic form of bribery that may apply in any type of prosecution. Thus, defendants may use *McDonnell* to argue that the same reading of what constitutes an "official act" should apply to narrow the concept of corruption, regardless of the particular language of a state or local bribery statute. As discussed below, the actual language of state statutes varies in how broadly or narrowly corruption is construed.[27] One example of a narrow state court interpretation of corruption was in *Commonwealth* v. *Veon*,[28] where the Pennsylvania Supreme Court cited to the analysis of an official act in overturning a conviction for a too-broad reading of what acts violate a conflict-of-interest statute for receipt of a "private

26 *Id.*
27 See Chapter 3.1, Part III for an overview of state bribery statutes.
28 150 A.3d 435, 447 (Pa. 2016).

pecuniary benefit."[29] The Pennsylvania court followed the tenor of *McDonnell* in rejecting a conviction for conduct that, in the court's view, was part of the ordinary political process:

> The trial court's jury instruction here made of the statute a meat axe, finding (or creating) a conflict of interest on every dais, at each parade, and at every ribbon-cutting, given that the very nature of seeking to satisfy one's constituents and secure re-election all but requires the taking of official action to secure intangible political gains. This criminalization of politics is a bridge too far.[30]

The impact of the *McDonnell* decision will be to encourage officials to claim that corruption statutes were not intended to criminalize politics as usual and that the acts they are accused of undertaking in exchange for a payment or benefit are more akin to the meeting/talking/organizing description of what is *not* an "official act." The farther away the conduct is from a typical exercise of authority, the more this defense can be effective, so that the public official admits receipt of a financial benefit, but denies any connection between that benefit and any *improper* use of office. Instead, it is portrayed as customary constituent service or providing some other government entitlement that does not involve any use of authority, just facilitating action for a citizen. The object of all of these arguments is to disassociate the payment from the public official's authority.

A. *Scrutinize Statutory Language*

In light of this narrowing view of corruption, prosecutors may scrutinize their state's statute to determine if state law contemplates a broad or narrow view of what constitutes bribery and should investigate and charge accordingly.[31] If the statute has terms like "official act," "official authority," or "use of office" to denote the benefit sought by the payment, and does not use terms broader that those in § 201(a)(3), then *McDonnell*'s analysis may well apply to limit the scope of that element of the offense. However, some statutes do not require a quid pro quo in order for a criminal violation to occur, or define "official act" (or its analogue) broadly. When charging violations under

---

29 *Id.*

30 *Id.* at 447-48.

31 *See* Chapter 3.1.

those statutes, linking the benefit to a specific exercise of authority may not be necessary. For example, Alabama makes it a crime for a public official to "use or cause to be used his or her official position or office to obtain personal gain for himself or herself, or family member of the public employee or family member of the public official . . . ."[32] Unlike a bribe, this provision reaches conduct in which the prestige of office and meeting with the official, when done for personal enrichment, can be enough for a conviction.[33] This type of law means that that buying access to an official through gifts and other benefits may be a state crime even if it was just to set up a meeting or arrange an introduction with another official, the types of conduct that might not be sufficient "without more" to establish a violation of § 201(a)(3) (or other statutes that depend on its "official act" definition) after *McDonnell*.

B. *Abnormalities May Negate a Defense of Politics as Usual*

A strong factual rebuttal to an "official act" defense is evidence that the defendant received the money in return for a *specific* act. Absent direct evidence, circumstantial proof may suggest that the purpose of the payment must have been to bribe the public official to undertake a specific action not for a benign purpose. For example, evidence that establishes the temporal relationship between the payment of the money and an identifiable act can be effective in asking the jury to draw an inference of a quid pro quo. In states where officials are permitted to also have non-government sources of income, evidence that a public official performed no legitimate service or that the payment is disproportionate to the services rendered can also be useful. If the public official changed a position without reason or undertook extraordinary efforts on behalf of the bribe payer, that unusual behavior may constitute the "something

---

32 Ala. Code § 36-25-5(a) (2020). For further information about criminal conflicts of interest, see Chapter 3.4.

33 *See, e.g.*, Ex parte Hubbard, No. 1180047, 2020 Ala. LEXIS 54, at *7 (Ala. Apr. 10, 2020) (concluding "the State was required to prove (1) that Hubbard was a public employee or public official (2) who solicited or received a 'thing of value' (3) from a lobbyist, a lobbyist's subordinate, or a 'principal,' and (4) that he did so intentionally").

In a bribery case, the Indiana Court of Appeals similarly found *McDonnell* inapposite. Tanoos v. State, 137 N.E.3d 1008, 1018 (Ind. Ct. App. 2019) ("While *McDonnell* may be relevant to the discussion, it does not govern our decision, as it concerned interpretation of the federal bribery statute's definition of 'official act' in the context of jury instructions. Its context is wholly distinct from that before us.").

more" described in the *McDonnell* opinion that moves the case from innocuous political conduct to criminal.[34]

The defense may also contend that a payment was a campaign contribution, and therefore any official act is not a bribe but the way in which political campaigns are financed. The defense is likely to cite to the following passage from the Supreme Court:

> Serving constituents and supporting legislation that will benefit the district and individuals and groups therein is the everyday business of a legislator. It is also true that campaigns must be run and financed. Money is constantly being solicited on behalf of candidates, who run on platforms and who claim support on the basis of their views and what they intend to do or have done. Whatever ethical considerations and appearances may indicate, to hold that legislators commit the federal crime of extortion when they act for the benefit of constituents or support legislation furthering the interests of some of their constituents, shortly before or after campaign contributions are solicited and received from those beneficiaries, is an unrealistic assessment of what Congress could have meant by making it a crime to obtain property from another, with his consent, "under color of official right." To hold otherwise would open to prosecution not only conduct that has long been thought to be well within the law but also conduct that in a very real sense is unavoidable so long as election campaigns are financed by private contributions or expenditures, as they have been from the beginning of the Nation.[35]

An effective rebuttal can be made by proof that the payment was never reported as a campaign contribution to the appropriate election authority, that the payment exceeded campaign contribution limits, or that the payment

---

34 *See* United States v. Percoco, No. 16-CR-776 (VEC), 2019 U.S. Dist. LEXIS 20629, at *7 (S.D.N.Y. Feb. 8, 2019) ("Percoco accepted approximately $285,000 in payments from [a national energy company], funneled through a 'low-show' job for his wife . . . In exchange, Percoco pressured state officials to approve two agreements in order to benefit [that energy company] . . . .").

35 McCormick v. United States, 500 U.S. 257, 272 (1991).

otherwise violated state election law limiting how contributions can be made or properly reported.[36]

III. The Diminished Capacity Defense

A defense sometimes raised in public corruption cases is diminished capacity.[37] This defense may be employed when the public official is charged with a crime that requires proof of specific intent, which most corruption crimes do. Typically, the defense will argue that because of the public official's use of alcohol or drugs, heart disease, stroke, or other medical condition, the official did not have the mental capacity to form the specific intent required to commit the offense.[38]

Rebutting this defense can follow three lines. First, the prosecutor may challenge the defendant's evidence of any addiction or medical condition. The defendant's treating physician, nurses, associates, and employees can be interviewed to obtain relevant information, and the defendant's medical records can be examined to the extent they may be available under various privacy laws. If there is an expectation that the defendant may claim diminished capacity, the investigatory stage is better for developing this type of evidence because the

---

36 *See* Evans v. United States, 504 U.S. 255, 278 (1992) (Kennedy, J., concurring) ("Readers of today's opinion should have little difficulty in understanding that the rationale underlying the Court's holding applies not only in campaign contribution cases, but in all § 1951 prosecutions. That is as it should be, for, given a corrupt motive, the *quid pro quo*, as I have said, is the essence of the offense.").

37 Diminished capacity has different definitions in different jurisdictions, but is generally "a type of evidence . . . admitted to rebut the specific intent required to convict the defendant of the crime charged." Henry F. Fradella, *From Insanity to Beyond Diminished Capacity: Mental Illness and Criminal Excuse in the Post-*Clark *Era*, 18 U. Fla. J.L. & Pub. Pol'y 7, 48 (2007) (quoting Chesney E. Falk, *Comment, Criminal Law—*State v. Phipps: *The Tennessee Court of Criminal Appeals Accepts "Diminished Capacity" Evidence to Negate Mens Rea*, 26 U. Mem. L. Rev. 373, 383 (1995)).

38 *See, e.g.*, United States v. Mister, 553 F. Supp. 2d 377, 389 (D.N.J. 2008) (permitting evidence of defendant's limited intellectual functioning because knowledge that the money he received was a bribe or corrupt payment was an element of the charged offense); Max Johnston, *Attorneys Grapple with "Diminished Capacity" Defense for Inman Trial*, Interlochen Pub. Radio (July 15, 2019), https://www.interlochenpublicradio.org/post/attorneys-grapple-diminished-capacity-defense-inman-trial (describing expected diminished capacity defense of state representative charged with extortion, soliciting a bribe, and lying to the FBI).

grand jury may be able to obtain evidence that a court might be reluctant to order. The prosecutor may also gather any video or audio evidence showing the defendant interacting normally with others, such as during a radio or television appearance, at a campaign rally, or appearing at a hearing or other public function. Facts developed in this inquiry may establish that the defendant was functioning at a level sufficient to hold him criminally responsible. Second, the prosecutor may hire an expert to assist in preparing for cross-examination of the defense expert and the treating physician. The prosecutor may prepare for cross-examination by interviewing the defense expert and reviewing the defense expert's writings on the subject in question. Third, the prosecution may call its own expert in rebuttal to establish that the defendant's acuity was sufficient to form the requisite intent.[39]

IV. Entrapment and "Outrageous Government Conduct"[40]

Entrapment is a frequently threatened, but less often offered, defense in public corruption cases when there is an undercover sting operation or a cooperator who sought out potential recipients of bribes.[41]

In its first decision recognizing the defense, the Supreme Court described entrapment as "the conception and planning of an offense" by a law enforcement officer and the "procurement of its commission by one who would not have perpetrated it except for the trickery, persuasion, or fraud of the officer."[42] Jurisdictions typically apply either an objective or subjective approach to entrapment. The objective theory looks at the conduct of law enforcement to determine whether the defendant was improperly enticed to commit the offense

---

39 *Accord* United States v. Shenghur, 734 F. Supp. 2d 552 (S.D.N.Y. 2010) (detailing, after competency hearing, judge's consideration of defense and government experts, taped conversations of the defendant, results of psychological tests, and immigration records, along with judge's own observation of defendant's in-court demeanor).

40 This section is based in part on Peter J. Henning, The Prosecution and Defense of Public Corruption: The Law and Legal Strategies § 15.03(4) (Matthew Bender, 2020 ed.).

41 For more on undercover operations, see Chapter 2.5.

42 Sorrells v. United States, 287 U.S. 435, 454 (1932). For additional discussion of entrapment, see Chapter 2.5, Part V(A).

because of government misconduct.[43] The subjective theory also considers whether the offense was induced by the government, but focuses on whether the defendant was predisposed to commit the offense.[44] Federal courts and the majority of states fall into this second category.[45]

Some states have codified the entrapment defense. For example, Connecticut provides that "it shall be a defense that the defendant engaged in the proscribed conduct because he was induced to do so by a public servant, or by a person acting in cooperation with a public servant, for the purpose of institution of criminal prosecution against the defendant, and that the defendant did not contemplate and would not otherwise have engaged in such conduct."[46] Washington state's statute provides:

> (1) In any prosecution for a crime, it is a defense that:
>
> > (a) The criminal design originated in the mind of law enforcement officials, or any person acting under their direction, and
> >
> > (b) The actor was lured or induced to commit a crime which the actor had not otherwise intended to commit.
>
> (2) The defense of entrapment is not established by a showing only that law enforcement officials merely afforded the actor an opportunity to commit a crime.[47]

---

43 Sosa v. Jones, 389 F.3d 644, 647 (6th Cir. 2004) ("The 'objective' theory of entrapment focuses on the conduct of the government, rather than individual predisposition, and has been consistently raised as an alternative formulation of the entrapment defense in concurring or dissenting opinions by Supreme Court justices. Under this theory, entrapment occurs when the government induces or instigates the commission of a crime by one not ready and willing to commit it, rather than merely providing the opportunity to commit a crime." (citations omitted)).

44 *Id.* ("The 'subjective' theory of entrapment focuses on the predisposition of the defendant and is the formulation of the defense adopted by the federal courts."). *See also* PAUL MARCUS, THE ENTRAPMENT DEFENSE §§ 1.05, 2.01 (Matthew Bender, 2020 ed.).

45 MARCUS, *supra* note 44, at § 2.01 n.10.

46 CONN. GEN. STAT. ANN. § 53a-15 (2020).

47 WASH. REV. CODE § 9A.16.070 (2020).

In other jurisdictions and the federal courts, entrapment is a common law defense with its parameters defined by reference to case law or the Model Penal Code.[48]

A. *Defendant Predisposition*

The subjective approach requires the factfinder—typically the jury—to determine both if there was government inducement *and* if the defendant was predisposed to commit the offense. A predisposed defendant is ready and willing to commit the crimes such as are charged in the indictment, whenever opportunity was afforded.[49] Predisposition "focuses upon whether the defendant was an 'unwary innocent' or instead, an 'unwary criminal' who readily availed himself of the opportunity to perpetrate the crime."[50] The emphasis is on the defendant's propensity to commit the offense rather than whether there was government misconduct, but the government must have induced the offense.[51] In a subjective theory jurisdiction, if the factfinder concludes that a defendant is predisposed, the defense of entrapment will not prevail. Testimony about the public official's readiness to accept the bribe, reputation, prior convictions, and other bad acts all can help establish a predisposition. Thus, one risk to defendants in using an entrapment defense is that the government will be able to introduce evidence of other prior conduct that might not be admissible otherwise.[52]

Federal courts of appeal have implied that the amount of an inducement might be relevant in determining if the will of the target was overcome, but have yet to find that a bribe or other monetary inducement was so high that

---

48 Model Penal Code § 2.13, LexisNexis (Am. Law Inst. 2020); Marcus, *supra* note 44, at § 1.05A. For a lengthy discussion of the history of Supreme Court entrapment jurisprudence and a discussion of federal circuit courts' approaches to the two-prong subjective analysis, see United States v. Mayfield, 771 F.3d 417, 424-38 (7th Cir. 2014) (en banc).

49 Sorrells v. United States, 287 U.S. 435, 451 (1932).

50 Mathews v. United States, 485 U.S. 58, 63 (1988).

51 *See, e.g.*, State v. Lively, 921 P.2d 1035, 1042 (Wash. 1996) (subjective entrapment state noting that defendants are "responsible for demonstrating that they were improperly induced to commit a criminal act which they otherwise would not have committed").

52 *See, e.g.*, United States v. Bumagin, 136 F. Supp. 3d 361, 371 (E.D.N.Y. 2015) (granting government's motion in limine to introduce "a wide variety of evidence," including that the defendant was a "high-ranking member of Russian organized crime," his disposal of firearms, his prior fraud convictions, and the fact he discussed other crimes during recordings of the charged crime, a robbery conspiracy, if defendant argued he was entrapped).

it, alone, overcame the need to consider predisposition. In the Abscam case, a district judge overturned the jury verdicts convicting two defendants by finding that they were entrapped when "in their zeal to make sure that the defendants would accept the tendered payments, the government agents offered such attractive inducements as to preclude any reliance upon the defendants' acceptance of the money as proof of predisposition."[53] The Third Circuit Court of Appeals reversed, finding that "[e]ven if the dollar amount offered were relevant to disprove predisposition, a question which we do not decide, we find nothing in the record to support the district court's conclusion that in today's inflationary times, city councilmen would view sums of $30,000 or $10,000 as so large or generous as to overcome an official's natural reluctance to accept a bribe."[54]

B. *Government Conduct*

Investigators can, in some cases, go too far in trying to entice a private citizen to pay a bribe that crosses the line into entrapment. In *United States v. Barta*,[55] the Seventh Circuit Court of Appeals overturned the conviction of a defendant by finding entrapment as a matter of law because of "plus" factors in the government's conduct. As part of an undercover sting, a cooperating witness and FBI agent sought to induce a pharmacy benefits company owner named James Barta to funnel a payment through the agent to an official at a Los Angeles county hospital. In describing how the government's efforts amounted to entrapment, the circuit court found:

> The FBI frequently emailed and called Barta, with no response from Barta. These were "repeated attempts at persuasion." The FBI invented false deadlines for Barta to commit to the deal and invented false problems for the Los Angeles County hospital system. These were "fraudulent representations." The FBI significantly sweetened what would have already been an attractive deal to Barta and his co-defendants. Here we have "promises of

---

53 United States v. Jannotti, 501 F. Supp. 1182, 1200 (E.D. Pa. 1980).

54 United States v. Jannotti, 673 F.2d 578, 599 (3d Cir. 1982); *accord* United States v. Cromitie, 727 F.3d 194, 221 (2d Cir. 2013) ("Even if we were to accept the premise that an offer of money might, in some unlikely circumstances, be so large as to constitute outrageous government conduct, we do not believe a line should be drawn at a fixed dollar amount. . . . [O]nly an offer significantly higher [than $250,000 to bomb synagogues and launch missiles at an air force base] would require us to consider whether due process limits had been exceeded.").

55 776 F.3d 931 (7th Cir. 2015).

> reward beyond that inherent in the customary execution of the crime." And the FBI pressed Barta—both directly and through [a codefendant]—to make a deal that it had reason to believe Barta would be making mainly to benefit his less fortunate friend, [the codefendant]. Here we have "pleas based on need, sympathy, or friendship." The presence of all these plus factors shows that the government induced Barta to commit a crime, one that the government concedes he had no predisposition to commit. That is enough to establish entrapment as a matter of law.[56]

This case shows the danger when investigators push too hard to lure in a defendant who has an otherwise spotless background, making it more difficult to establish that the person was an unwitting criminal. As the Seventh Circuit noted, "[t]he government's conduct here, including its persistence, posed an impermissible risk that Barta's criminality was created rather than caught."[57]

1. Outrageous Government Conduct and Due Process

The Supreme Court recognized "outrageous government conduct" as a defense in the early 1970s, but soon concluded that it usually "should result in prosecution of government officials rather than exculpation of criminal defendants."[58] Outrageous government conduct—which is sometimes termed "outrageous government misconduct"—resembles entrapment but does not require a defendant to show he or she lacked predisposition.[59] Rather, an outrageous government conduct defense is a claim of a violation of due process.[60] An accused public official may pose this defense—or a somewhat conceptually

56 *Id.* at 937 (citations omitted).

57 *Id.* at 939.

58 Ian Deitz, *Public Corruption*, 57 Am. Crim. L. Rev. 1143, 1153 (2020) (citing United States v. Hampton, 425 U.S. 484, 490 (1976); United States v. Russell, 411 U.S. 423, 431-32 (1973)).

59 United States v. Black, 733 F.3d 294, 306 n.9 (9th Cir. 2013) (citation omitted).

60 United States v. Napier, 787 F.3d 333, 341 (6th Cir. 2015).

related claim of vindictive[61] or selective[62] prosecution—by claiming that the government targeted him because he is a political enemy of the incumbent administration or a member of some group or organization deemed to be undesirable. Targeting a political rival for investigation or prosecution or bringing a case purely to advance the political career of the prosecutor, to be clear, constitute abuses of prosecutorial discretion.[63] But claims of this nature have been rarely if ever successful in federal court, typically because there is little evidence that a defendant was inappropriately targeted for prosecution.[64]

---

61 To demonstrate an actual vindictive motive, the defendant must show that "(1) the prosecutor harbored genuine animus toward the defendant or was prevailed upon to bring the charges by another with animus such that the prosecutor could be considered a 'stalking horse,' and (2) [the defendant] would not have been prosecuted except for the animus." United States v. Koh, 199 F.3d 632, 640 (2d Cir. 1999) (internal quotation marks omitted). A federal district judge granted a request for a hearing to explore whether a tax prosecution of a public official was vindictive after the defendant made a showing that only he and his codefendant—out of many clients served by the same tax preparer, who allegedly treated the tax returns of his clients similarly—had been targeted for prosecution. United States v. Williams, No. 20-55, 2020 U.S. Dist. LEXIS 186902, at *28-29 (E.D. La. Oct. 8, 2020) (granting a "limited evidentiary hearing" when defendant claimed vindictive prosecution for the defendants to "probe the similarities between them and other [tax preparer] clients proffered as comparators," along with whether the one defendant's refusal to meet with an agent and that defendant's status as a public official resulted in his prosecution); *but see* United States v. Hastings, 126 F.3d 310, 314-15 (4th Cir. 1997) ("a person's public renown may be properly considered among other factors when deciding whether to pursue criminal sanctions for a violation of the law" because of the increased media coverage and resulting general deterrence).

62 "A prosecution . . . cannot be motivated by a suspect's exercise of constitutional rights through participation in political activity." *Hastings*, 126 F.3d at 313, 315 (reversing dismissal of indictment ordered by district court that concluded a defendant was subjected to selective prosecution because of his political party because defendant did not meet his burden of proof).

63 *See, e.g.*, Chapter 5.1, Part I(A); Sandra Caron George, *Current Development 2004-2005: Prosecutorial Discretion: What's Politics Got To Do with It?*, 18 Geo. J. Legal Ethics 739, 740 (2005) (describing former U.S. Attorney Thomas DiBiagio's directive to his staff to charge "front page" public corruption cases in early November 2004); Letter from James B. Comey, Dep. Att'y Gen., U.S. Dep't of Justice, to Thomas DiBiagio, U.S. Att'y, Dist. of Md. (July 16, 2004), http://www.baltimoresun.com/news/local/bal-comeyletter071604,1,4439273.htmlstory (criticizing then-U.S. Attorney Thomas DiBiagio's direction to his staff to bring political corruption cases timed to assist the incumbent president's election).

64 United States v. Cyprian, 23 F.3d 1189, 1196-97 (7th Cir. 1994) (rejecting argument that it was inappropriate for government to use information supplied by a political opponent to indict defendant); *Williams*, No. 20-55, 2020 U.S. Dist. LEXIS 142030, at *3 (defendant's "claim[] that the federal government initiated an investigation into him based on a referral from a political rival" insufficient to show selective or vindictive prosecution); United States v. Rahman, S5 93 Cr. 181 (MBM), 1995 U.S. Dist. LEXIS 18512, at *2 (S.D.N.Y. Dec. 13, 1995) (defendant unsuccessfully argued "decision to prosecute was driven by the motive of assisting his political and religious opponent, President Hosni Mubarak of Egypt, and was brought about by pressure

The outrageous government conduct defense is available only in cases in which law enforcement conduct violated "that 'fundamental fairness, shocking to the universal sense of justice,' mandated by the Due Process Clause of the Fifth Amendment."[65] Unlike entrapment, this claim is not a jury issue; therefore, the judge has discretion in determining when to hear evidence on this issue.[66] If the judge hears a motion to dismiss on this ground prior to trial, the discovery allowed by the hearing can damage the prosecution's case. Moreover, the hearing itself can be a painful, protracted affair from the prosecution's point of view.[67]

Typically, the defense will subpoena documents from law enforcement agencies and seek the testimony of agents—and sometimes even the prosecutors—in an effort to show outrageous conduct that "shocks the conscience." Another avenue for obtaining evidence that puts the government in a bad light is scouring public posts on social media. Entries on Facebook, Twitter, Snapchat, and the like can be fertile ground for showing potential misconduct.[68] Prosecutors should be especially aware that defense counsel and the media will scrutinize any government comments for evidence of bias.[69] Prosecutors and

---

from Senator Alfonse D'Amato of New York on Attorney General Janet Reno"); United States v. La Rouche Campaign, Crim. No. 86-323-K, 1987 U.S. Dist. LEXIS 9233, at *13-14 (D. Mass. Aug. 29, 1987, revised Mar. 31, 1988) ("Although defendant alleges that these private entities were influenced by persons in the government who were opposed to his political influence, he has failed to provide any competent evidence that would support an inference that these entities or persons were acting at the government's direction.").

65 United States v. Russell, 411 U.S. 423, 432 (1973) (citation omitted).

66 United States v. Fuentes-Verdugo, No. 19-00010-05-CR-W-BP, 2019 U.S. Dist. LEXIS 119856, at *18 (W.D. Mo. May 10, 2019) (noting that "claims of outrageous government conduct are questions of law to be resolved by the court and not a jury").

67 Whether to grant such a hearing is typically in the discretion of the trial court. *Compare* United States v. Voigt, 89 F.3d 1050, 1068 (3d Cir. 1996) (concluding district court likely committed harmless error by not conducting an evidentiary hearing in case where defendant alleged government misconduct, given the record that was developed at the defendant's trial) *with* United States v. Al Kassar, 660 F.3d 108, 122 (2d Cir. 2011) (concluding district court did not err in denying a hearing where there were "no material facts in dispute related to the alleged government misconduct").

68 *Accord* Brendan Brosh, Alison Gendar, & Adam Nichols, *Staten Island Cop Bragged of Being a Gangsta on MySpace*, N.Y. Daily News (Nov. 4, 2007), https://www.nydailynews.com/news/crime/staten-island-bragged-gangsta-myspace-article-1.255077 (detailing social media posts by a New York City Police Department officer that cast him in a negative light).

69 Corruption cases brought in New Orleans were reversed after it was revealed that several high-ranking federal prosecutors were opining about those cases through online, anonymous comments. United States v. Bowen, 799 F.3d 336, 339, 358 (5th Cir. 2015).

law enforcement should control and limit public statements and social communications to avoid saying something that might jeopardize a case or their ability to continue to practice law.[70]

The prosecution may attempt to limit the scope of any hearing on a claim of government misconduct. One way to limit the scope would be to ask the court to require the defendant to sign an affidavit, under penalty of perjury, to support every allegation of outrageous government conduct made. Another way to limit the hearing would be to ask the court to require a proffer before the defense is permitted to call a government employee as a witness. Based on the proffer, the prosecutor may be able to object on the grounds of relevance, privilege, or another basis to prevent witnesses from being called.

2. Putting the Government on Trial

An informal version of the same defense is the strategy of "putting the government on trial." Evidence developed to support the outrageousness argument could be used to cross-examine an agent or cooperating witness to show bias, to impeach the direct testimony, or to raise questions about the reliability of the person's recollections. In jurisdictions in which there is a deep vein of mistrust of the government, the insinuation that the government "crossed the line" can have a visceral jury appeal even though it is not technically a defense to a criminal charge—and indeed may well contain an admission that the defendant engaged in the charged conduct but wants to avoid being held responsible for it.

3. Preventing a Defense of Outrageous Government Conduct

The best protection from the outrageous government conduct claim is to follow the relevant guidelines, including on undercover investigations,[71] concurrent proceedings,[72] making public statements about an investigation

---

70 One of the Louisiana prosecutors who posted the anonymous comments referenced in note 69 was disbarred. *In re* Perricone, 263 So. 3d 309, 319 (La. 2018). For additional guidance on public statements, see Chapter 5.3.

71 *See* Chapter 2.5.

72 *See* Chapter 2.8.

or case,[73] the timing of bringing criminal charges,[74] and the like. Staying as far away from the line between permissible and impermissible tactics as possible will defuse most claims of a due process violation in the conduct of the investigation.

A final note about undercover or other proactive investigative techniques as it relates to this type of defense involves the nature of investigative targets and their conversations. Public officials, and those who seek to corrupt them, are usually a wary lot. As such, they often act and speak in an indirect manner, frequently declaring that the payments are not bribes, are not illegal, are not in return for anything, are campaign contributions, or even not a payment at all. Very often, cooperating witnesses, and sometimes undercover agents, perhaps in an effort to allay a target's suspicion, allow such remarks to go unchallenged. This can undermine an otherwise productive undercover operation for the government and may support an entrapment or outrageous government conduct defense.

V. "I Was Conducting My Own Investigation"

Another defense public officials, particularly law enforcement, sometimes advance is to contend that the official knew he was being bribed and that he was playing along with it in order to investigate and eventually prosecute the offeror of the bribe. For example, then-sheriff Jim Traficant was caught on tape admitting that he accepted bribes from organized crime. He claimed that he was conducting his own secret sting operation seeking to catch criminals in the act of corrupting law enforcement. He was acquitted of those bribery charges, but was later subject to a federal judgment for unpaid back taxes on the bribe money.[75]

---

73 *See* Chapter 5.3.

74 *See* Chapter 5.2.

75 Traficant v. Comm'r of Internal Revenue Serv., 884 F.2d 258, 260, 267 (6th Cir. 1989), *aff'g* 89 T.C. 501, 534 (1987). Traficant was later elected to serve Ohio in the U.S. Congress, and convicted of, among other things, felony racketeering, bribery, and fraud for using his congressional office to solicit bribes and kickbacks. United States v. Traficant, 368 F.3d 646, 648-49 (6th Cir. 2004), *aff'g* 209 F. Supp. 2d 764, 786 (N.D. Ohio 2002); Matt Schudel, *James A. Traficant Jr., Colorful Ohio Congressman Expelled by House, Dies at 73*, Wash. Post (Sept. 27, 2014), https://www.washingtonpost.com/politics/james-a-traficant-jr-colorful-ohio-congressman-expelled-by-house-dies-at-73/2014/09/27/fa98868a-4431-11e4-9a15-137aa0153527_story.html.

If the defense is offered, the government can rebut it by showing that the person was acting out of greed rather than altruism. A rebuttal may establish the following: (1) the public official's job did not include investigating this type of crime; (2) no steps were taken by the official to notify a law enforcement agency with power to investigate of this type of crime of the official's "investigation"; and (3) no investigative steps were in fact taken by the official beyond the receipt of money or other benefits.

The government may also show the lack of a good-faith investigation by seeking the return of the bribe paid to the public official. This may take the form of a demand letter to defense counsel or, if that fails, through a court order or subpoena. If the public official cannot return all of the original currency, especially if the official claims payment was part of an undercover investigation in which the serial numbers were recorded, the prosecution has a strong argument that the defense is a sham.

VI. Employees Accused of Work-Related Fraud and Abuse

Although public corruption connotes misconduct by high-level officials, false statements, embezzlement, and kickbacks received by lower government officials may also constitute public corruption.[76] These cases against lower-level public employees may involve the submission of falsified expense vouchers, inflated overtime, or acceptance of gifts and cash for steering contracts to favored vendors. Other types of fraud can involve reimbursement for travel or other expenses incurred by government employees. The defenses to charges in this area are usually not legal defenses, but rather equitable arguments that urge jury nullification.[77] Typical equitable defenses tend to be based on the concepts that the employee somehow deserved the illicit funds (e.g., if the person submitted a voucher to be compensated for unreimbursed work-related expenses or for expenses he could have incurred but chose not to, or is generally overworked

---

76 See Chapter 1.5 for a discussion of these types of prosecutions.

77 Commentators have argued defendants should be prevented from informing juries of their power to nullify, Steven M. Warshawsky, *Opposing Jury Nullification: Law, Policy, and Prosecutorial Strategy*, 85 Geo. L.J. 191, 192 (1996), and that defense attorneys should be subject to ethical sanctions for doing so, Kimberly Del Frate, *Comment, The Elephant in the Room: Attorney Accountability for Jury Nullification Arguments in Criminal Trials*, 52 Cal. W.L. Rev. 163, 187-89 (2016).

and underpaid) or that the misconduct was somehow authorized (e.g., that a boss knew about it and permitted it or that everyone else was doing something similar).

The prosecution can rebut these equitable defenses by showing that the regulations are clear and that the employee knew or should have known of the obligation to comply. Investigation of the defendant's work history, including examining leave records and interviewing co-workers and supervisors, can lead to valuable evidence that the defendant did not work extra hours or otherwise deserve a self-help bonus. As for authorization, in many cases, the conduct may be so egregious (e.g., forged receipts) that the defendant cannot reasonably claim the conduct was allowed. In appropriate cases, the prosecution can call the defendant's supervisor or other appropriate officials to establish that the defendant was not given permission to engage in the unlawful conduct. In cases where the defendant asserts that other employees engaged in the same type of misconduct without prosecution, it may become an issue of intent, but a defense of "selective prosecution" is unavailable unless the defense can establish an invidious basis for the selection (e.g., race).

In kickback cases, defendants sometimes claim that the secret additional payments were actually funneled to government programs, such as schools or day care programs. The prosecutor can effectively challenge such a defense by showing that the defendant's personal spending increased once the money started flowing.

VII. The "Attorney Advice" Defense

A public corruption defendant may assert that the conduct was done in reliance on the advice given by an attorney. This defense may arise in cases involving improper campaign contributions made or received with guidance from an attorney or involving conflicts of interest that were vetted and approved by an attorney, but only when intent is an element of the crime charged.[78]

78 *See* United States v. Roti, 484 F.3d 934, 935 (7th Cir. 2007) ("Advice of counsel is not a free-standing defense, though a lawyer's fully informed opinion that certain conduct is lawful (followed by conduct strictly in compliance with that opinion) can negate the mental state required for some crimes, including fraud."); United States v. Lord, 710 F. Supp. 615, 617 (E.D. Va. 1989) (explaining that the federal conflict of interest charge does not require proof of specific

To offer a full-scale "advice of counsel" defense requires the defendant to have provided all relevant facts to the attorney, to have sought the advice in order to comply with and not avoid the law, and to have acted in the manner instructed by the attorney.[79] The assertion of this defense waives the attorney-client privilege for communications about the conduct at issue in the prosecution.[80] Therefore, once the prosecutor knows that the defendant intends to assert the advice of counsel defense, the prosecutor may seek to interview the attorney. This interview often reveals either that the attorney did not render legal advice as claimed by the defendant, or that the legal advice was based on the defendant's misrepresentation of the operative facts. The attorney may be willing to cooperate with the prosecution to show that there was nothing untoward in the attorney's representation.

In those rare instances in which the attorney supports the defendant's claim of reliance on professional advice, the prosecutor may employ a legal expert to testify that the advice provided was inaccurate, absurd, or unpersuasive to an intelligent public official. Alternatively, the prosecutor may consider whether the attorney who provided the advice participated in a criminal conspiracy.

Short of a complete advice-of-counsel defense, a defendant may attempt to show good faith and lack of criminal intent by arguing that he or she consulted with an attorney, without fulfilling all of the elements for a complete advice-of-counsel defense. Importantly, a defendant seeking to offer an imperfect advice-of-counsel defense might argue that there is no waiver of attorney-client privilege because the legal advice is not offered as a justification for the conduct, but only as evidence to show lack of a corrupt intent and good faith. The prosecutor may challenge this type of evidence as irrelevant. The government can also argue that the defendant is trying to get in an advice-of-counsel defense through the back door without fulfilling the requirements for that claim or waiving attorney-client privilege, and is thus inappropriately trying to use the privilege as both a sword and a shield.[81]

---

intent, so advice of counsel is not a defense).

79 *See* Markowski v. SEC, 34 F.3d 99, 105 (2d Cir. 1994).

80 *See* United States v. Ortland, 109 F.3d 539, 543 (9th Cir. 1997) ("The privilege which protects attorney-client communications may not be used both as a sword and a shield.").

81 "The attorney-client privilege cannot be used as both a shield and a sword, and [a defendant] cannot claim in his defense that he relied on [the attorney's] advice without permitting the prosecution to explore the substance of that advice." United States v. Workman, 138 F.3d 1261,

VIII. The Speech or Debate Protection

"The constitutions of forty-three states contain a privilege for state legislators analogous to the privilege that the federal Constitution provides members of Congress, and the common law has frequently recognized a similar protection as well."[82] The privilege generally protects legislators from inquiry into legislative acts or the motivation for actual performance of legislative acts, but it does not completely immunize legislators from prosecution under corruption laws as long as prosecutors can prove the case without inquiring into legislative acts.[83] Note that some states view their protection as identical to that provided by the federal Constitution, so case law in the federal courts may be applicable.[84]

In the context of defenses, it is important to note that a legislator does not offer this protection as a defense so much as a means to exclude certain evidence from being introduced at trial. The state and federal courts generally provide that "legislative acts" cannot be used to obtain an indictment or to prosecute a member of the legislature or other representative body.[85] The reason is that the immunity provided in the constitutions protects them from being questioned about their conduct as a legislator, and so this evidence is not admissible to prove a charge. Thus, the fact that a representative introduced

---

1264 (8th Cir. 1998) (citations omitted). *Accord* United States v. Scully, 877 F.3d 464, 476 (2d Cir. 2017) ("[D]efendants are entitled to an advice-of-counsel instruction only if there are sufficient facts in the record to support the defense.").

82 Steven F. Huefner, *The Neglected Value of the Legislative Privilege in State Legislatures*, 45 Wm. & Mary L. Rev. 221, 224, 236-37, 237 n.54 (2003) (categorizing states into categories and listing seven states without constitutional legislative privilege: California, Florida, Iowa, Mississippi, Nevada, North Carolina, and South Carolina).

83 *See* United States v. Brewster, 408 U.S. 501, 525-27 (1972). The protection afforded to legislators, including local elected representatives, is discussed more fully in Chapter 1.3, Part I(A).

84 *See, e.g.*, Marsh v. Pettway, 109 So. 3d 1118, 1122 (Ala. 2013) (Moore, C.J., concurring) ("Because the Speech or Debate Clause in the Alabama Constitution is identical in substance, and virtually identical in wording, to the federal Speech or Debate Clause, federal decisions construing the federal clause should be 'highly persuasive' in understanding the meaning of [the section in the Alabama constitution titled "immunity of legislators"]."); Edwards v. Vesilind, 790 S.E.2d 469, 476, 477-83 (Va. 2016) (noting that the Speech or Debate Clause in the Virginia constitution was "'derived from' the similar provision in the federal Speech or Debate Clause found in Article I, Section 6 of the United States Constitution" and citing cases analyzing the federal clause in construing Virginia's clause (citations omitted)).

85 *See* United States v. Menendez, 831 F.3d 155, 165 (3d Cir. 2016).

a bill after receiving a questionable payment could not be offered as further proof that the quid pro quo was fulfilled. Of course, in those jurisdictions that only require a corrupt agreement and not its fulfillment, this evidence may be unnecessary.[86]

Prosecutors investigating legislative corruption must be aware of what potential evidence will be excluded because of legislative immunity. A corrupt agreement may be proven without relying on conduct or statements that are "legislative acts," but only if the alternate proof is collected prior to trial. Furthermore, this issue arises in pre-trial proceedings and may divert time and attention away from preparing for the presentation of the case. Many states and the federal system allow an immediate appeal on this issue rather than having to wait until after a conviction, which may slow the prosecution.[87]

Conclusion

Given the career-ending high stakes of public corruption cases, prosecutors can reasonably anticipate that defendants will assert every possible defense. It is critical to a successful prosecution to anticipate those defenses and build the investigation in a way that can prevent or withstand those defenses at trial. Furthermore, anticipating defenses can speed the prosecution and prevent momentum-destroying delay resulting from pretrial motions and hearings.

86 *See Brewster*, 408 U.S. at 526 (holding that a violation of 18 U.S.C. § 201(c) requires only "taking or agreeing to take money for a promise to act in a certain way. There is no need for the Government to show that appellee fulfilled the alleged illegal bargain; acceptance of the bribe is the violation of the statute, not performance of the illegal promise").

87 *See, e.g.*, *Menendez*, 831 F.3d at 164 (explaining that the appeals court had jurisdiction over Speech or Debate Clause issues under the collateral order doctrine).

Section Five

Ethical & Strategic Considerations in Corruption Cases

This section addresses some ethical and strategic issues that may arise in corruption cases.

In addition to providing a roadmap to discussions elsewhere in the Manual that address potential ethical issues, Chapter 5.1 surveys ethical issues that might be more likely to arise in a corruption case than other types of criminal cases, including the need to ensure that political considerations do not infect the exercise of discretion, and suggests that prosecutors' offices consider recusals and conflict walls when appropriate.

Chapter 5.2, by New Jersey Attorney General Office prosecutors Anthony Picione and Peter Lee, discusses the timing of charges in corruption cases. This chapter also discusses factors to consider when determining whether to charge an entity.

Finally, in Chapter 5.3, the former Reporter for the American Bar Association's Standards for Criminal Justice: Fair Trial & Public Discourse, Cardozo Law Professor Jessica Roth, addresses public statements in corruption cases. In this chapter, Professor Roth shares her insights about how prosecutors can ethically discharge their sometimes-competing duties to protect a defendant's rights, including the right to a fair trial, and to keep the public informed.

Chapter 5.1

Ethical Issues for Corruption Prosecutors: An Overview

Victor Olds, Beverly M. Ma, Amie N. Ely

Victor Olds serves as New York Governor Andrew Cuomo's Special Counsel for Public Integrity and a Lecturer-in-Law at Columbia Law School. His previous positions include First Deputy District Attorney at the Westchester County District Attorney's Office, Chief of the Professional Responsibility Bureau at the Bronx County District Attorney's Office, Assistant Attorney General in Charge at the New York State Attorney General's Office, and Assistant United States Attorney for the Southern District of New York, where he was a prosecutor in the Public Corruption Unit and a member of the Securities and Commodities Fraud Task Force.

Beverly M. Ma is Chief of the Civil Litigation Bureau, and the Deputy Chief of Staff, in the Bronx County District Attorney's Office. Her previous experience has focused on complex civil litigation, including litigation in the areas of ethics and professional responsibility.

Amie N. Ely is the Director of the Center for Ethics & Public Integrity, National Attorneys General Training & Research Institute, National Association of Attorneys General.

Introduction

Potential ethical issues that can arise for corruption prosecutors are discussed throughout this Manual, including in later chapters in this section. This chapter collects these issues in one place, provides a map to locate discussions elsewhere in this book, and addresses additional topics that are not discussed at length in other chapters. The ethics issues referenced in this chapter may lead to motions by a defendant, bar complaints, or the appearance of impropriety to the public. The focus is primarily on the ethical duties of prosecutors—rather than civil enforcers—although some of the same concepts apply in civil cases. Ethics rules addressing conflicts among clients or designed to protect clients' autonomy and decision-making authority rarely apply to prosecutors, as they are generally understood to have "the state" or "the people" as their client.[1] However, as noted below, when prosecutors are found to abuse the substantial discretion and trust embodied by their offices, they can face harsh disciplinary consequences, including disbarment.

I. Political Issues

Corruption prosecutions may call into question a prosecutor's political motivation—whether fairly or not.[2] As a result, corruption prosecutors should be aware of standards addressing political motivations by prosecutors, and be familiar with when and how recusal and walls can be used to cure what might be loosely described as potential political conflicts.[3]

---

1 Fred C. Zacharias, *The Professional Discipline of Prosecutors*, 79 N.C. L. Rev. 721, 726 (2001) (citations omitted).

2 *See, e.g.*, Anthony S. Barkow & Beth George, *Prosecuting Political Defendants*, 44 Ga. L. Rev. 953, 955-56 (2010). *See also* Chapter 1.3, Part I(C)

3 Bruce A. Green & Rebecca Roiphe, *Rethinking Prosecutors' Conflicts of Interest*, 58 B.C. L. Rev. 463, 469-76 (2017) (describing potential conflicts of interest for prosecutors, and noting arguments that "to varying degrees, virtually all prosecutors' political preferences may influence their decision-making in cases involving public officials. Indeed, it is not unusual for critics to charge in such cases that prosecutors are biased, either because they are members of the same political party or because they are members of a different one.").

A. *Prosecutors Should Not Make Decisions Based on Political Considerations*

The American Bar Association's Criminal Justice Standards for the Prosecution Function, which are aspirational and not binding,[4] counsel against prosecutors using "partisan or other improper political or personal considerations" when they exercise their discretion, including in pursuing or discontinuing criminal charges.[5] The Standards treat political "interests or relationships" as potential conflicts of interest that prosecutors should not permit to affect their "professional judgment or obligations," and direct that prosecutors "should not allow interests in personal advancement or aggrandizement to affect judgments regarding what is in the best interests of justice in any case."[6]

The same standards also counsel that if a prosecutor has a significant political relationship with another lawyer, that prosecutor

> should not participate in the prosecution of a person who is represented by the other lawyer, unless the relationship is disclosed to the prosecutor's supervisor and supervisory approval is given, or unless there is no other prosecutor who can be authorized to act in the prosecutor's stead. In the latter rare case, full disclosure should be made to the defense and to the court.[7]

While those standards cannot provide grounds for bar discipline, gross abuse of authority—including using prosecutorial powers to punish political rivals—may be conduct prejudicial to the administration of justice under a state's rules of professional conduct.[8] Bar discipline authorities in Arizona cited Rule 8.4(d) of Arizona's Rules of Professional Conduct when they concluded prosecutors abused their authority to "exact political revenge."[9] Two Maricopa

---

4 ABA Standards for Criminal Justice: Prosecution Function s. 3-1.1(b) (Am. Bar Ass'n 2017), https://www.americanbar.org/groups/criminal_justice/standards/ProsecutionFunctionFourthEdition/.

5 *Id.* ss. 3-1.6(a) (generally), 3-4.4(b)(i) (pursuing or dropping charges).

6 *Id.* s. 3-1.7(f).

7 *Id.* s. 3-1.7(h).

8 *See* Model Rules of Prof'l Conduct r. 8.4(d) (Am. Bar Ass'n 2020) ("It is professional misconduct for a lawyer to: . . . engage in conduct that is prejudicial to the administration of justice."). *See also id.* r. 3.8, cmt. 1 ("a systematic abuse of prosecutorial discretion could constitute a violation of Rule 8.4").

9 Bruce A. Green & Samuel J. Levine, *Disciplinary Regulation of Prosecutors as a Remedy*

County, Arizona prosecutors were disbarred and another was suspended after they criminally charged and civilly sued several local politicians and judges with whom they had disputes.[10]

The state's supreme court later concluded that by filing and maintaining a civil racketeering suit against judges for judicial acts they took in criminal cases—despite the fact that the judges were absolutely immune from civil damages for the complained-of acts—two of the prosecutors violated Rule of Professional Conduct 8.4(d).[11] The court also concluded that a criminal complaint the prosecutors filed against a judge lacked probable cause and was designed to compel him to recuse himself from grand jury matters, which violated both Rule 8.4(d) and Rule 3.8(a), which requires prosecutors to bring only charges that are supported by probable cause.[12]

B. *Recusal and Conflict Walls*

Prosecutors at any level may face conflicts of interest in corruption cases involving political friends or foes. United States Attorneys General have recused themselves, including for these reasons, at least fifteen times over the last thirty years.[13] For example, former United States Attorney General John Ashcroft recused himself on three occasions. The first two recusals related to investigations of people or entities that had made campaign contributions for or against Ashcroft in the past.[14] The third recusal was notable because Ashcroft cited no reason for it other than an abundance of caution due to his close ties to senior White House aides. The investigation focused on whether senior White House personnel, including Lewis "Scooter" Libby, had illegally disclosed the

---

for Abuses of Prosecutorial Discretion: A Descriptive and Normative Analysis, 14 OHIO ST. J. CRIM. L. 143, 159-60 & nn.101-06 (2016) (quoting *In re* Thomas, PDJ-2011-9002, at 68 (Ariz. Apr. 10, 2012), http://archive.azcentral.com/ic/news/0410Thomas-Aubuchon.PDF (internal quotation omitted)).

10 *Thomas*, PDJ-2011-9002, at 232; *In re* Alexander, 300 P.3d 536, 551 (Ariz. 2013).

11 ARIZ. RULES OF PROF'L CONDUCT r. 8.4(d) (2020); *Alexander*, 300 P.3d at 546-47; *In re* Aubuchon, 309 P.3d 886, 894 (Ariz. 2013). The elected county attorney, Andrew Thomas, did not contest his disbarment, so the state supreme court did not review the allegations regarding his actions in the 247-page disciplinary judge opinion and order. *Aubuchon*, 309 P.3d at 888 n.2; *Thomas*, PDJ-2011-9002, at 232.

12 ARIZ. RULES OF PROF'L CONDUCT r. 3.8(a); *Aubuchon*, 309 P.3d at 896.

13 CONG. RES. SERV., LEGAL SIDEBAR: A BRIEF HISTORY OF ATTORNEY GENERAL RECUSAL 1 (Mar. 8, 2017), https://fas.org/sgp/crs/misc/recusal.pdf.

14 *Id.*

identity of an undercover Central Intelligence Agency officer. After Ashcroft recused himself, the deputy attorney general appointed a special prosecutor to handle the investigation.[15]

State attorneys general have recused themselves from overseeing public corruption cases. During his campaign, former Alabama Attorney General Luther Strange had used a printing business owned by the Alabama Speaker of the House, Mike Hubbard.[16] After Strange was elected, Hubbard was investigated by his office for using that same business to misappropriate political party funds, so Strange recused himself from that investigation.[17] More recently, Alabama Attorney General Steve Marshall recused himself from prosecuting a district attorney because they served together in the Alabama District Attorneys Association.[18]

In some states, if a local elected prosecutor has a conflict, the entire office must be recused.[19] This is also the practice recommended by the National District Attorneys Association.[20] In others, recusal of a prosecutor and the

---

15 *Id.*; Barkow & George, *supra* note 2, at 957-58.

16 *AG Luther Strange Explains Recusal in Hubbard Case*, WVTM 13 (June 11, 2015), https://www.wvtm13.com/article/ag-luther-strange-explains-recusal-in-hubbard-case/3831022.

17 *Id.* This case is described in Chapter 1.3, Part III(C).

18 Elizabeth White, *Attorney General's Office Releases Details in Lee County DA Indictment*, WBRL (Nov. 9, 2020), https://www.wrbl.com/alabama-news-2/attorney-generals-office-releases-details-in-lee-county-da-indictments/.

19 In Georgia, statutes provide that assistant district attorneys' authority derives from the elected district attorney, Ga. Code Ann. § 15-18-19(b) (2020), and that if a "district attorney's office is disqualified from interest or relationship to engage in a prosecution," the district attorney is required to notify the attorney general, who is then required to appoint or designate a new prosecutor. *Id.* § 15-18-5(a). If no appointment or designation is made, it is reversible error for an assistant district attorney in the conflicted district attorney's office to proceed with the case. McLaughlin v. Payne, 761 S.E.2d 289, 294 (Ga. 2014) ("When the elected district attorney is wholly disqualified from a case, the assistant district attorneys—whose only power to prosecute a case is derived from the constitutional authority of the district attorney who appointed them—have no authority to proceed."). Georgia is not alone, at least for recusals of district attorneys, in requiring that the entire local prosecutor's office be recused if the elected prosecutor has a conflict. *See, e.g.*, 55 Ill. Comp. Stat. 5/3-9008(a-15) (2020); *accord* Better Gov't Ass'n v. Office of the Special Prosecutor (*In re* Appointment of Special Prosecutor), 129 N.E.3d 1181, 1184-85 (Ill. 2019) (describing appointment of special prosecutor upon petition of victim's family, who alleged, pursuant to 55 Ill. Comp. Stat. 5/3-9008(a-10) (West 2010), that state attorney's office did not properly investigate nephew of Chicago's mayor for homicide because of political considerations).

20 Press Release, Nat'l Dist. Att'ys Ass'n, National District Attorneys Association Statement on Prosecutorial Best Practices in High Profile Cases (Mar. 27, 2019), https://ndaa.org/

implementation of solid conflict walls may be sufficient, provided that the conflict wall is legally adequate and factually well-documented.[21] In a territory where recusal of the elected attorney general and implementation of conflict walls could have been sufficient, a conviction was still reversed when the defendant credibly alleged that the attorney general had ignored the wall and his office was unable to disprove the defendant's claim.[22] In Virginia, the court of appeals held that while screening a conflicted line prosecutor—who had previously represented the defendant—would have been sufficient to cure the conflict, the office had failed to meet its burden to prove it had implemented effective screening procedures.[23]

More recently, national and state prosecutors' organizations raised concerns about the actions of the elected prosecutor in Cook County, Illinois.[24] The Cook County State's Attorney's Office initially investigated an actor for staging a phony hate crime on himself and charged him with sixteen felonies.[25] Prosecutors later dropped all charges against the actor.[26] The elected State's Attorney made conflicting statements about why her office dropped the charges and whether she had recused herself from the case due to personal connections with potential witnesses.[27] The Illinois Prosecutors Bar Association publicly characterized the dismissal as "abnormal," noted that the recusal was legally inadequate, and stated that "the State's Attorney has failed in her most

---

wp-content/uploads/NDAA-Press-Release-on-Prosecutorial-Best-Practices-in-High-Profile-Cases.pdf [hereinafter NDAA Press Release] ("[W]hen a chief prosecutor recuses him or herself, the recusal must apply to the entire office, not just the elected or appointed prosecutor.").

21 *See, e.g.*, Lux v. Commonwealth, 484 S.E.2d 145, 150-53 (Va. Ct. App. 1997) (noting split of authority regarding whether screening is sufficient to address conflict posed by presence of a former counsel for a defendant in a prosecutor's office, or whether entire office must be disqualified); *see also* People v. Tennessen, 2009 Guam 3, ¶ 50 (Guam 2009), *overruled in part by* Barrett-Anderson v. Camacho, 2018 Guam 20, ¶ 19 (Guam 2018).

22 *Tennessen*, 2009 Guam at ¶ 50.

23 *Lux*, 484 S.E.2d at 152.

24 NDAA Press Release, *supra* note 20; Press Release, Ill. Prosecutors Bar Ass'n, IPBA Statement on Jussie Smollett Case Dismissal (Mar. 28, 2019), http://www.ilpba.org/announcements/7249825 [hereinafter IPBA Press Release].

25 Megan Crepeau & Jason Meisner, *Report Finds "Abuses of Discretion" but No Criminal Wrongdoing in Kim Foxx Handling of Jussie Smollett Case*, Chi. Trib. (Aug. 17, 2020), https://www.chicagotribune.com/news/criminal-justice/ct-jussie-smollett-kim-foxx-dan-webb-report-20200817-avbaer4kezasnp4ih3fms7a3sq-story.html.

26 *Id.*

27 *Id.*

fundamental ethical obligations to the public."[28] Later, a court concluded that because her recusal was invalid, a special prosecutor should be appointed to investigate the actor and determine if charges should be brought, and to examine the conduct of the state's attorney and her staff.[29] After bringing new charges against the actor, the special prosecutor concluded that the State's Attorney and several members of her office should be referred to the Illinois Attorney Registration and Disciplinary Commission for, among other things, issues related to her partial recusal.[30]

II. The Investigation and Charges

A. *Witnesses*

A prosecutor must prepare witnesses to fulfill the duties of competence and diligence, but must do so within the bounds of other ethical obligations.[31] As the Fourth Circuit Court of Appeals, sitting en banc, concluded:

> Thorough preparation demands that an attorney interview and prepare witnesses before they testify. No competent lawyer would call a witness without appropriate and thorough pre-trial interviews and discussion. In fact, more than one lawyer has been punished, found ineffective, or even disbarred for incompetent representation that included failure to prepare or interview witnesses.[32]

28 IPBA Press Release, *supra* note 24.

29 Crepeau & Meisner, *supra* note 25.

30 *Id.*; Press Release, Special Prosecutor Dan K. Webb of Winston & Strawn Concludes Investigation into the Cook County State's Attorney's Office and Chicago Police Department's Handling of the Jussie Smollett Case (Aug. 17, 2020), https://www.prnewswire.com/news-releases/special-prosecutor-dan-k-webb-of-winston--strawn-concludes-investigation-into-the-cook-county-states-attorneys-office-and-chicago-police-departments-handling-of-the-jussie-smollett-case-301113238.html.

31 *See, e.g.*, Peter J. Henning, *The Pitfalls of Dealing with Witnesses in Public Corruption Prosecutions*, 23 Geo. J. Legal Ethics 351, 353 (2010).

32 United States v. Rhynes, 218 F.3d 310, 319 (4th Cir. 2000) (en banc).

Preparing witnesses thus flows from an attorney's fundamental duties of competence and diligence.[33]

While witness preparation is appropriate and necessary, witnesses cannot be "coached" to provide false testimony.[34] More specifically, lawyers cannot "counsel or assist a witness to testify falsely, or offer an inducement to a witness that is prohibited by law."[35] The ethical duty of candor to the court forbids knowingly offering false evidence, including testimony, and permits refusing to offer evidence reasonably believed to be false.[36] If a witness offers material testimony that a lawyer later learns is false, the lawyer is required to take reasonable remedial measures, including, if necessary, disclosure to the tribunal.[37]

Prosecutors should also take care to comply with Rules 4.2 and 4.3—which cover communicating with represented and unrepresented persons—when interacting with witnesses.[38] Other chapters in this Manual provide some guidance about ethically using confidential informants and cooperating witnesses.[39]

B. *Bringing Complex Charges*

Competence in the context of complex investigations and charges requires prosecutors to obtain training, skills, and experience appropriate to the prosecutor's level of responsibility. Just as filing a complaint or obtaining an indictment without probable cause can lead to bar discipline,[40] bringing a case that the prosecutor lacks sufficient training and experience to handle

---

33 Model Rules of Prof'l Conduct rr. 1.1, 1.3 (Am. Bar Ass'n 2020). *Accord In re* Wolfram, 847 P.2d 94, 96, 100, 104 (Ariz. 1993) (suspending criminal defense attorney from the practice of law for eighteen months because he failed to interview witnesses and failed in other aspects of representation).

34 *See, e.g.*, Henning, *supra* note 31, at 353; Model Rules rr. 3.3(a)(3), 3.4(b).

35 Model Rules r. 3.4(b).

36 *Id.* r. 3.3(a)(3). The rule contains an exception: a criminal defense attorney who reasonably believes his client's testimony is false may not refuse to offer it. *Id.*

37 *Id.*

38 *Id.* rr. 4.2, 4.3.

39 *See* Chapter 2.5, Part V(B); Chapter 1.8, Part II(A).

40 *In re* Aubuchon, 309 P.3d 886, 894-95 (Ariz. 2013) (prosecutor suspended after she, among other things, "violated her responsibility as a prosecutor in violation of [Arizona Rule of Professional Conduct] 3.8(a) and prejudiced the administration of justice in violation of [Rule] 8.4(d)" when she knowingly filed a criminal complaint against a judge without probable cause in an effort to avoid a hearing and compel the judge's recusal from another case).

competently can also lead to censure. In the same disciplinary matter involving the three Maricopa County, Arizona prosecutors, the state supreme court concluded that the most junior prosecutor's "responsibilities in a complex RICO lawsuit relative to her limited legal experience and insufficient preparation"[41] constituted a violation of Rule 1.1, which requires lawyers to provide "competent representation to a client," which, in turn, "requires the legal knowledge, skill, thoroughness and preparation reasonably necessary for the representation."[42]

C. *Use of the Grand Jury*

In the grand jury context, prosecutors must provide accurate legal instructions, fulfill the role required by any relevant grand jury statutes, and present sufficient evidence to establish probable cause to charge a defendant.[43] Failure to do so may constitute attorney misconduct under a state's rules against dishonesty and against any conduct prejudicial to the administration of justice.[44]

A former attorney general and district attorney in Kansas was suspended from the practice of law for, among other things, failing to properly advise a citizen's grand jury of the applicable law.[45] Then-district attorney Phil Kline misled the grand jury as to both the applicability of a relevant statute as well as the proper interpretation of that statute.[46] When the grand jury learned of the proper interpretation of the law, it concluded that it did not have proper

---

41 *In re* Alexander, 300 P.3d 536, 543-44 (Ariz. 2013).

42 Ariz. Rules of Prof'l Conduct r. 1.1 (2020). *Accord* Model Rules r. 1.1 (same).

43 *In re* Kline, 311 P.3d 321, 372-84 (Kan. 2013) (finding that prosecutor's actions with the grand jury violated rule 8.4(c), (d), and (g)); Bruce A. Green, *Prosecutors and Professional Regulation*, 25 Geo. J. Legal Ethics 873, 876-77 (2012). *Accord* Lacey v. Maricopa Cty., 693 F.3d 896, 913-14, 918 (9th Cir. 2012) (prosecutor who authorized arrest without probable cause not entitled to qualified immunity in civil suit brought under 42 U.S.C. § 1983 alleging prosecutor violated the Fourth Amendment).

44 *See Kline*, 311 P.3d at 381-84; Model Rules r. 8.4(c), (d).

45 *Kline*, 311 P.3d at 375-77. *See also In re* Complaint of Leonhardt, 930 P.2d 844, 949 (Or. 1997) (disbarring local prosecutor in Oregon who "pursued criminal charges without evidence or probable cause" and also "falsified public records and then lied about those alterations to lawyers, the court, the public, and her own staff").

46 *Kline*, 311 P.3d at 375-84. Given that Kline had been directly involved in the federal litigation, it was clear that he knew that a federal judge disagreed with his interpretation. *Id.* at 373-74.

grounds to issue the subpoena it had already served.[47] The state supreme court suspended Kline from the practice of law for misleading the grand jury and for failing to treat the grand jury as the "independent and objective body" that, by statute, it was.[48]

Prosecutors thus should endeavor to inform the grand jury of the law that applies to any conduct it is considering, including any material statutory amendments or court decisions interpreting the relevant law that materially undercut the prosecution's theory of the case.

Finally, prosecutors must abide by any applicable grand jury secrecy requirements. Chapter 1.2 details the prosecution of former Pennsylvania Attorney General Kathleen Kane for, among other things, violating her state's grand jury secrecy laws.[49]

D. *Timing of Charges*

A major decision for a public corruption prosecutor is the question of when to file charges.[50] In general, an important goal of these cases is to bring perpetrators to justice as quickly as possible to halt an ongoing injury to the public. Yet other concerns may require delaying filing charges. For example, the prosecutor may have sufficient evidence to prosecute one individual, but may still be investigating a broader criminal scheme.[51]

Prosecutors may enlist lower-level offenders' assistance in pursuing higher-level, more culpable targets.[52] This practice, while perhaps aimed at ensuring justice for the most culpable, has a potential downside. It allows the crime, and the resulting frequently undisclosed public injury, to continue. On the other

---

47 *Id.* at 375-84.

48 *Id.* at 377-78, 381, 398.

49 *See* Chapter 1.2. For additional discussion of grand jury secrecy requirements, see Chapter 2.8, Parts III(B)(1), and III(C), and Chapter 5.3, Part I.

50 For a fuller discussion of timing of charges, see Chapter 5.2.

51 *Accord* Justice Manual § 9-27.230 (U.S. Dep't of Justice 2020), https://www.justice.gov/jm/jm-9-27000-principles-federal-prosecution (discussing factors to consider in bringing or declining to bring federal criminal charges).

52 *Id.* (noting that relative culpability is an appropriate consideration in deciding to bring charges); *see also* Chapters 1.8, Part II(A) (discussing securing testimony through cooperation agreements, immunity orders, and non-prosecution agreements); 2.5 (discussing use of cooperating witnesses).

hand, moving prematurely to expose an ongoing crime may allow the highest-level criminals to escape justice.

E. *Potential Impact on Public Services*

Public corruption prosecutions have a unique potential to impact public access to services. Public corruption crimes may involve violations without any direct or obviously negative impact on the public.[53] In fact, from the vantage point of the people being served, the services provided by the perpetrators could not only appear acceptable, but vital to their concerns and interests. Would it matter, for example, if an immediate arrest and prosecution of a public official would shut down the only available daycare center providing much-needed services to a struggling community before a replacement is available? And is a public corruption prosecutor even allowed to consider such concerns in determining when and what charges to file?[54]

F. *Disclosure of the Investigation*

Another unique consideration in prosecuting public corruption is whether and when to notify the government body that is employing the corrupt official of the ongoing investigation and underlying crime.[55] While general guidelines permit disclosure of confidential information under some circumstances,[56] deciding how and when to disclose a particular criminal investigation

---

53 *Accord* Justice Manual § 9-27.230, cmt. 2 ("While public interest, or lack thereof, deserves the prosecutor's careful attention, it should not be used to justify a decision to prosecute, or to take other action, that is not supported on other grounds. Public and professional responsibility sometimes will require the choosing of a particularly unpopular course.").

54 *Id.* at § 9-27.260 (listing impermissible considerations in determining whether to prosecute, including "[t]he possible effect of the decision on the attorney's own professional or personal circumstances"); *see also supra* Part I(A) & Chapter 5.2, Part III.

55 For further discussion of the timing of covert and overt aspects of a corruption prosecution, see Chapter 2.2. For discussion of similar challenges when investigating judges, see Chapter 1.1, Part V(A).

56 Model Rule 3.6 states that a lawyer may give warnings of danger regarding certain behavior where there is a likelihood of "substantial harm" to the public interest. Model Rules of Prof'l Conduct r. 3.6(b)(6) (Am. Bar Ass'n 2020). Subdivision (b)(7) of the Rule makes clear that the general provision is applicable to criminal cases as well. Moreover, where a criminal prosecution has commenced, the disclosures are accorded even greater specificity, including, for example, information going to the identity, residence, and occupation of a defendant. *Id.* at r. 3.6(b)(7)(i). Prosecutors, specifically, may not make extrajudicial statements that have a substantial likelihood of heightening public condemnation of the accused "except for statements

can be challenging. Timing of any notice prior to filing charges and arresting a target is a critical strategic consideration. If the fact of the investigation is disclosed to the target's employer too early, or perhaps at all, the investigation could be compromised in any number of ways. The employer could alter personnel assignments in an effort to minimize damage of the ongoing criminal activity, but in a manner that also could inadvertently alert the target to the investigation. Revealing an investigation too soon carries a risk of destroyed evidence and of the target's flight.[57] In certain instances, disclosure of an investigation is governed by law rather than prosecutorial discretion, such as where a grand jury proceeding has been commenced,[58] or after a federal wiretap interception has ended.[59] In the earlier, pre-indictment stages of an investigation, no such statutory secrecy obligations typically apply, and the corruption prosecutor may balance the competing interests of secrecy and disclosure.

As a practical matter, prosecutors may have professional or personal relationships with the members of agencies whose employees may be under investigation.[60] Maintaining a good relationship for possible future investigations could depend on whether the agency heads believe they were treated fairly in having been timely and properly informed of persons and activities under scrutiny within their offices.

---

that are necessary to inform the public of the nature and extent of the prosecutor's action and that serve a legitimate law enforcement purpose." *Id.* at r. 3.8(f).

57 *See* Chapter 2.2, Part II.

58 *See* Fed. R. Crim. P. 6(e) (imposing an obligation of secrecy on a government attorney concerning matters occurring before a federal grand jury).

59 *See* 18 U.S.C. § 2518(d) (2018) (requiring disclosure of certain information from a wiretap, absent a court order permitting nondisclosure, within ninety days of the termination of interception).

60 In New York City, for example, the Department of Investigation, which is responsible for investigating corruption within the city's agencies, not only works closely with local, state, and federal prosecutors on public corruption investigations, but also engages in non-investigatory activities with city agencies such as helping them to establish practices and procedures designed to ensure compliance with the City's rules and regulations. *DOI's Mission & History*, N.Y.C. Dep't of Investigations, https://www1.nyc.gov/site/doi/about/mission.page (last visited Apr. 21, 2021). A late-breaking revelation that DOI investigators were working with city commissioners to improve their agencies' operations while simultaneously secretly investigating those agencies' personnel could strain professional relationships and make future investigations difficult.

G. *Interactions with the Media*

Public corruption cases require prosecutors to balance the public's legitimate interest in knowing about allegations against corrupt officials with other interests, such as the integrity of ongoing investigations, the privacy and reputational interests of those identified as subjects or targets during an investigation, and a defendant's right to a fair trial. Chapter 5.3 of this section addresses the ethical and constitutional issues that may arise when prosecutors make public comments relating to corruption cases.

III. Discovery and Disclosure

Discovery and disclosure issues are touched on throughout this Manual, including in Part V(D) of Chapter 2.5 (addressing confidential informants and cooperating witnesses) and Part II(B)(3) of Chapter 2.8 (addressing concurrent proceedings). In addition to the guidance provided by those authors, we make a few additional observations here.

A. *Understand the Scope of Your Obligations*

In addition to complying with their state's discovery statute, prosecutors should ensure they understand due process requirements and the scope of their state's rules of professional conduct.[61] Prosecutors should be aware that exculpa-

---

61 *See* Model Rules r. 3.8(d). *See also* Giglio v. United States, 405 U.S. 150, 154-55 (1972); Brady v. Maryland, 373 U.S. 83, 87 (1963). Both federal and state lawmakers have addressed failures to comply with *Brady* requirements. In 2020, Congress passed the Due Process Protections Act, which requires federal judges to "issue an order at the outset of all criminal proceedings that 'confirms' the government's *Brady* disclosure obligations and the 'possible consequences' of *Brady* violations." Reed Brodsky, et al., *Due Process Protections Act Sends a Message to the Government*, N.Y.L.J. (Dec. 2, 2020), https://www.law.com/newyorklawjournal/2020/12/01/due-process-protections-act-sends-a-message-to-the-government/. These orders will subject federal prosecutors who fail to comply with their constitutional discovery obligations to being found in contempt of court, among other consequences. *Id. See also* Cal. Pen. Code § 1424.5 (2020) (requiring courts to inform the State Bar of California of intentional *Brady* violations); Press Release, State of N.Y. Unified Court Sys., Chief Judge DiFiore Announces Implementation of New Measure Aimed at Enhancing the Delivery of Justice in Criminal Cases (Nov. 8, 2017), http://ww2.nycourts.gov/sites/default/files/document/files/2018-05/PR17_17.pdf (requiring all judges in New York to order prosecutors to timely disclose *Brady* and *Giglio* material).

tory or impeachment information known by any agency who assisted with the case will be imputed to the prosecutor if the agency is deemed to be a member of the "prosecution team."[62] Even if a discovery or disclosure violation does not require the reversal of a conviction, it can result in attorney discipline.[63] Moreover, some states have concluded that ethical disclosure requirements are broader than what is required by due process, and cover even non-material exculpatory evidence.[64] Other states have concluded that the obligations are coterminous.[65]

B. *Keep Records of What You Provided*

In complying with due process, statutory, and ethical discovery obligations, prosecutors should keep careful records of exactly what is provided. Although a general "open file" policy may be common practice, such a policy provides little guidance about what documents should actually be included in that file.[66] It may also be insufficient to defend against later allegations that exculpatory evidence was withheld.[67] A prosecutor in North Dakota argued that a memo containing exculpatory information was provided to her legal

---

62 *See* Chapter 2.8, Part II(B)(3).

63 State v. Valdez, 770 P.2d 313, 318 (Ariz. 1989) (holding that "in cases where there has been misconduct of either the prosecutor or defense counsel, but reversal is not required, the proper remedy will be affirmance, followed by institution of bar disciplinary proceedings against the offending lawyer, if such proceedings are warranted"), *rev'd on other grounds*, Krone v. Hotham, 890 P.2d 1149, 1151 (Ariz. 1995).

64 Those states include California, the District of Columbia, New York, North Dakota, Texas, and Virginia; this is also the view of the ABA. *In re* Petition to Stay the Effectiveness of Ethics Op. 2017-F-163, 582 S.W.3d 200, 205-09 (Tenn. 2019) (collecting cases and concluding that Tennessee "decline[s] to interpret Rule 3.8(d) as providing any greater ethical obligation upon prosecutors than the constitutional obligations under *Brady* and its progeny," *id.* at 209); *see also* Green & Levine, *supra* note 9, at 162 (noting split in materiality requirement); ABA Comm. on Ethics & Prof'l Responsibility, Formal Op. 09-454 (2009).

65 Those states include Colorado, Louisiana, North Carolina, Ohio, Oklahoma, Tennessee, and Wisconsin. *Petition to Stay*, 582 S.W.3d at 208-09.

66 The USDOJ counsels its prosecutors not to use the term "open file," as material may "be inadvertently omitted from production and the prosecutor will then have unintentionally misrepresented the scope of materials provided." Justice Manual § 9-5.002, Step 3(A) (U.S. Dep't of Justice 2020), https://www.justice.gov/jm/jm-9-5000-issues-related-trials-and-other-court-proceedings. The Justice Manual also notes that "because the concept of the 'file' is imprecise, such a representation exposes the prosecutor to broader disclosure requirements than intended or to sanction for failure to disclose documents . . . that the court may deem to have been part of the 'file.'" *Id.*

67 *See* Disciplinary Bd. v. Feland, 820 N.W.2d 672, 676 (N.D. 2012).

assistant to copy and send.[68] The legal assistant, in turn, said that she thought that the memo was included, but did not "know for certain," and the memo was not on any discovery checklists in the prosecutors' file.[69] The disciplinary hearing panel concluded that the prosecutor violated North Dakota Rule of Professional Conduct 3.8(d) by failing to disclose the memo, suspended her from the practice of law for sixty days, and ordered her to pay the costs of the disciplinary proceeding—over $11,000.[70]

C. *Be Prepared to Have a Speedy Trial*

The collapse of the prosecution of Ted Stevens, a former United States Senator from Alaska, is a cautionary tale for corruption prosecutors.[71] Even in complex, high-profile prosecutions, the defendant has a right to a speedy trial.[72] Senator Stevens, indicted just months before he faced re-election, asked for a speedy trial rather than seeking a delay as prosecutors expected.[73] Although Stevens was convicted at trial, the trial court reversed the conviction due to disclosure issues, and the U.S. Department of Justice declined to seek a new trial.[74] Disciplinary proceedings were launched against the prosecutors, and one of the prosecutors committed suicide.[75] The USDOJ Professional Misconduct Review Attorney assigned to review recommendations by the Office of Professional Responsibility described the case as one including "supervisory failures[,] . . . a frantically short [fifty-seven]-day period between indictment and trial and . . . the high octane pressure and 'scorched earth' defense tactics that accompanied the prosecution of one of the most senior members of the United States Senate . . . ."[76] An article co-authored by a former federal prose-

---

68 *Id.*

69 *Id.*

70 *Id.* at 677.

71 Barkow & George, *supra* note 2, at 975-83.

72 *See* U.S. CONST. amend. VI, § 1.

73 Barkow & George, *supra* note 2, at 976, 983.

74 *Id.* at 978-79.

75 Charlie Savage, *Stevens Case Prosecutor Kills Himself*, N.Y. TIMES (Sept. 27, 2010), https://www.nytimes.com/2010/09/28/us/politics/28stevens.html. For a longer discussion of the Stevens case, see Carrie Johnson, *Report: Prosecutors Hid Evidence In Ted Stevens Case*, NPR (Mar. 15, 2012), https://www.npr.org/2012/03/15/148687717/report-prosecutors-hid-evidence-in-ted-stevens-case.

76 *See* Memorandum from Terrence Berg, Prof'l Misconduct Review Unit Att'y, to Joseph A. Bottini, Assistant U.S. Att'y 4 (undated), attached as Exhibit B to Response to the U.S. Dep't of Justice Office of Prof'l Responsibility Final Report (Jan. 25, 2012), https://www.leahy.senate.gov/imo/media/doc/052412-BottiniResponse.pdf. *See also* U.S. DEP'T OF JUST., OFF. OF PROF'L

cutor concluded that "it is unclear whether the Stevens case's collapse resulted from deliberate misconduct by the prosecutors or mere (albeit enormously consequential) incompetence and lack of resources."[77]

One lesson from the Stevens prosecution is that the prudent prosecutor will be prepared to provide discovery, try the case, and comply with pretrial or trial-related disclosure obligations when, or soon after, a case is formally charged.

IV. Trial

A. *Witnesses*

In addition to the points made above in Part II(A), prosecutors may have additional obligations when they suspect, but are not sure, that a trial witness has lied. The Ninth Circuit Court of Appeals has held that prosecutors have a duty, at a minimum, to investigate the testimony of their witness if they have a "strong suspicion" that the witness has committed perjury.[78] Potential credibility issues may be most likely to arise when introducing the testimony of cooperating witnesses and confidential informants; for guidance about such witnesses, see Chapter 2.5.

B. *Evidence*

Corruption cases may include voluminous exhibits. For guidance about how to effectively introduce this kind of evidence, see Chapter 4.2.

Resp., Investigation of Allegations of Professional Misconduct in United States v. Theodore F. Stevens, Crim. No. 08-231 (D.D.C. 2009) (EGS) 11-12, 19, 666 (Aug. 15, 2011), https://www.leahy.senate.gov/imo/media/doc/052412-081511Report.pdf.

77 Barkow & George, *supra* note 2, at 983. In the end, a merit review board reversed the suspension of two federal prosecutors, concluding that the USDOJ violated its own procedures, resulting in the prosecutors likely receiving harsher discipline. Goeke v. Dep't of Justice, 122 M.S.P.R. 69, 73, 80-81 (M.S.P.B. 2015).

78 *See* Morris v. Ylst, 447 F.3d 735, 744 (9th Cir. 2006).

C. *Jury Addresses*

Jury addresses provide the corruption prosecutor with the opportunity to set the stage for the trial to come, and, later, to sum up sometimes-complex evidence and testimony and argue that the jury should convict the defendant. They are thus extremely important, but are one of the areas where prosecutors can—unwittingly or intentionally—cross an ethical line. Chapter 4.1 of this Manual discusses some potential ethical issues that can arise during jury addresses. Notably, at least one lawyer has been reprimanded for repeatedly violating defendants' rights in jury addresses across multiple trials, even though none of those jury addresses resulted in a reversal of any defendants' convictions.[79]

V. When Disciplined, Prosecutors Can Face Harsh Punishment

The comments to the Model Rules of Professional Conduct opine that "[a] lawyer's abuse of public office can suggest an inability to fulfill the professional role of lawyers."[80] State bars have considered prosecutors' abuse of a position of trust as an aggravating factor in imposing discipline.[81] The ABA's Standards for Imposing Lawyer Sanctions recommend disbarment "when a lawyer in an official or governmental position knowingly misuses the position with the intent to obtain a significant benefit or advantage for himself or another, or with the intent to cause serious or potentially serious injury to a party or to the integrity of the legal process."[82]

---

79 *In re* Martinez, 462 P.3d 36, 41-43, 46 (Ariz. 2020).

80 Model Rules of Prof'l Conduct r. 8.4 cmt. 7 (Am. Bar Ass'n 2020).

81 *See, e.g.*, Off. of Disciplinary Counsel v. Cappuccio, 48 A.3d 1231, 1240 (Penn. 2012) (holding that misconduct of attorneys serving in public positions "speaks directly to the integrity of the legal system by placing the reputation of those tasked with serving and protecting the public at issue"); *In re* Marinoff, 819 So. 2d 305, 312-13 (La. 2002) (holding that "an attorney occupying a position of public trust is held to a higher standard of conduct than an ordinary attorney" and suspending from the practice of law an assistant city attorney who left the scene of an accident he caused and lied about what happened); People v. Larsen, 808 P.2d 1265, 1265, 1267 (Colo. 1991) (reversing grievance committee recommendation that former district attorney be suspended for a year and a day and requiring three year suspension in light of his position as district attorney).

82 ABA Standards for Imposing Lawyer Sanctions s. 5.21 (Am. Bar Ass'n 2019).

In one extreme case, the Oregon Supreme Court concluded that the "integrity of the legal process" was damaged by a prosecutor in Oregon who pursued charges without evidence or probable cause, falsified documents, and then lied about the documents she falsified to other lawyers, the public, judges, and her own staff—and then, in a separate criminal case against her fiancé, tried to use her influence to alter the course of the prosecution.[83] Citing both her conduct and the fact that the conduct resulted in her being convicted of multiple felonies, the court disbarred her.[84]

The same standards suggest suspension if such a lawyer "knowingly fails to follow proper procedures or rules, and causes injury or potential injury to a party or to the integrity of the legal process."[85] Prosecutors have been suspended for inappropriately threatening to bring criminal charges and for criminal or ethical violations that cast their office in a negative light. A county attorney in Kansas who also had a civil practice was suspended from the practice of law under this standard when he threatened opposing counsel in a civil case that he would file criminal charges against his client in an effort to force the civil case to settle.[86]

The Ohio Supreme Court suspended the former attorney general, Marc Dann, for six months after he pled guilty to soliciting improper compensation and filing false financial disclosure forms, both misdemeanors, in connection with actions he took while he was the attorney general.[87] In rejecting his request for a lesser sanction, the court concluded that "Dann's criminal and ethical violations reflect poorly on his fitness to practice law and the legal profession as a whole, but also cause incalculable harm to the public perception of the attorney

---

83 *In re* Complaint of Leonhardt, 930 P.2d 844, 847-49 (Or. 1997).

84 *Id.* at 850.

85 ABA Lawyer Sanctions s. 5.22. *See also id.* s. 5.23 ("Reprimand is generally appropriate when a lawyer in an official or governmental position negligently fails to follow proper procedures or rules, and causes injury or potential injury to a party or to the integrity of the legal process."); *id.* s. 5.24 ("Admonition is generally appropriate when a lawyer in an official or governmental position engages in an isolated instance of negligence in not following proper procedures or rules, and causes little or no actual or potential injury to a party or to the integrity of the legal process.").

86 *In re* Holste, 358 P.3d 850, 858-59 (Kan. 2015) (suspending lawyer for two years, with leave for him to file for early reinstatement after six months).

87 Disciplinary Counsel v. Dann, 979 N.E.2d 1263, 1265, 1271 (Ohio 2012).

general's office and those government agencies, departments, and institutions that the attorney general advises and represents."[88]

Courts often consider the motive of a lawyer who committed misconduct in determining what kind of sanction to impose. When the Kansas Supreme Court concluded that a former attorney general and former district attorney violated the rules of professional conduct, it found that his "efforts at casting a favorable public image toward himself... was clearly an improper motive" when his statutory duty was elsewhere.[89]

Conclusion

Competence, diligence, honesty, lack of personal or political bias, and fairness in the administration of justice are qualities any prosecutor must cultivate. Particularly in the complex and vigorously-defended realm of public corruption prosecutions, prosecutors should be prepared to face increased scrutiny as to whether they are meeting their ethical obligations. Supervisors should ensure that corruption prosecutors have adequate training and resources. Decisions should be made without regard for political or personal concerns. Offices should also consider developing policies that help guide the discretion of prosecutors charged with holding corrupt officials accountable—including guidance for when recusals are warranted and how to ensure and document the effective imposition of conflict walls.

By both being viewed as—and truly being—apolitical, corruption prosecutors can discharge their requirements to seek justice and respond to potential defense motions claiming improper use of their prosecutorial powers.

---

88 *Id.* at 1269.

89 *In re* Kline, 311 P.3d 321, 395 (Kan. 2013).

Chapter 5.2

The Timing of Charges in Corruption Cases

Anthony A. Picione, Peter Lee

Anthony A. Picione serves as Assistant Attorney General and the Deputy Director of the Office of Public Integrity and Accountability, New Jersey Division of Criminal Justice.

Peter Lee serves as Deputy Attorney General and the Chief of the Corruption Bureau within the Office of Public Integrity and Accountability, New Jersey Division of Criminal Justice.

Introduction

This chapter examines issues commonly faced by prosecutors in determining when to file criminal charges in corruption cases. The public filing of criminal charges always carries significant consequences, but targets charged with corruption may experience collateral consequences beyond those faced by the typical defendant. These amplified consequences pose unique challenges for prosecutors during the investigation and charging of a criminal case. In determining whether and when to file charges in a corruption case, prosecutors must carefully consider whether the case is strong enough to result in a conviction, which public interests will be served by filing the charges at a given time, the strategy for achieving a resolution of the case, and any ethical issues that might be raised by the timing of the charges. Prosecutors are often presented with the added difficulty of making these determinations in an environment of heightened public attention and political sensitivities. Nevertheless, the decision to file charges must always be made at a time and in a manner to best promote the interests of justice.

I. Legal Considerations: Is the Case Ready to be Charged?

A. *What, if Any, Charges Should Be Filed?*

At the most basic level, corruption cases are the same as all other criminal cases: A prosecutor should file charges only when an investigation has revealed sufficient evidence to meet the legal requirements for proving the target has committed a crime. A prosecutor must answer several questions before concluding a case is ready to be charged: What, if any, crimes have been committed? Who committed those crimes? Does sufficient admissible evidence prove the legal elements of each of those crimes? Only after these questions have been answered should the prosecutor consider *when* to file corruption charges.[1]

Identifying a crime to be charged should not be taken lightly—especially in corruption cases. As a first step, the prosecutor must determine if the evidence indicates that some type of criminal activity has taken place. If it has, the prosecutor must then identify the specific statutes that have been violated and determine whether sufficient evidence exists to prove each element of those statutes.

Corruption investigations often begin with referrals from a variety of sources, including anonymous tips, concerned citizens, victims, other public agencies, and even political or personal enemies of the accused. Such referrals may contain vague allegations, opinions, speculative conclusions, or descriptions of conduct that is not criminal. Prosecutors should not rely only on statements made in referrals to bring criminal charges and should always

---

1 *See* ABA Standards for Criminal Justice: Prosecution Function s. 3-4.3(a) (Am. Bar Ass'n 2017), https://www.americanbar.org/groups/criminal_justice/standards/ProsecutionFunctionFourthEdition/.

scrutinize allegations for bias before commencing an investigation.[2] If they do not, and the source is later revealed to have impure motives, that bias may jeopardize an otherwise strong case.

Unless and until the investigation reveals sufficient evidence to prove the defendant violated the law, the prosecutor cannot file charges.[3] Conduct that appears upon first impression to be criminal may not actually violate a specific statute. Unless admissible evidence proves each element of a crime, charges cannot be filed. If a prosecutor believes that additional investigation may uncover evidence necessary to prove a crime, he or she should delay filing charges to allow that investigation to proceed.

Another important consideration is whether to file multiple criminal charges. If the evidence supports charging multiple counts, that may impact the timing of the charges. For example, in some jurisdictions corruption statutes contain mandatory or elevated sentencing provisions.[4] Severe criminal penalties may augur protracted litigation by defendants, which in turn may necessitate more pre-emptive investigation and preparation by the prosecution. Inter-office policies or procedures may also dictate what charges to file. For example, there may be a policy that requires a prosecutor to charge the most serious, readily provable charge.[5] When prosecutors do have discretion to

---

2 While prosecutors should carefully scrutinize claims by, for example, political rivals, federal courts have rejected claims that reliance on information provided by a defendant's enemy is inappropriate. United States v. Cyprian, 23 F.3d 1189, 1196-97 (7th Cir. 1994) (rejecting argument that government should not have used information supplied by a political opponent to indict defendant). *See also* United States v. Williams, No. 20-55, 2020 U.S. Dist. LEXIS 142030, at *3 (E.D. La. Aug. 10, 2020) (defendant's "claim[] that the federal government initiated an investigation into him based on a referral from a political rival" insufficient to show selective or vindictive prosecution). ABA Standards for the Prosecution Function s. 3-4.4(a)(vii), (b) (advising that in the exercise of discretion, a prosecutor should consider the views and motives of the victim or complainant and, in filing and maintaining charges, should not consider partisan, political, or personal considerations or improper biases).

3 Model Rules of Prof'l Conduct r. 3.8(a) (Am. Bar Ass'n 2020) (ethical violation for prosecutor to file charge without probable cause); *In re* Complaint of Leonhardt, 930 P.2d 844, 949 (Or. 1997) (disbarring local prosecutor in Oregon who "pursued criminal charges without evidence or probable cause" and also "falsified public records and then lied about those alterations to lawyers, the court, the public, and her own staff").

4 *See, e.g.*, N.J. Stat. Ann. § 2C:43-6.5 (2020) (imposing mandatory minimum periods of imprisonment for the conviction of certain corruption-related crimes).

5 *See, e.g.*, Memorandum from U.S. Att'y Gen. John Ashcroft to All Fed. Prosecutors §§ I.A., II.C. (Sept. 22, 2003), http://www.usdoj.gov/opa/pr/2003/September/03_ag_516.htm.

decide what charges to bring, it must be exercised even-handedly and consistently, particularly in corruption cases.

B. *Who Should be Charged?*

1. Individuals

Once sufficient evidence proves that a crime has occurred, the prosecutor must determine who to charge. The prosecutor must evaluate whether the evidence is sufficient to prove that a particular person violated a specific criminal statute. Evaluating the evidence can be a time-consuming and complex task. With cases involving multiple targets, the prosecutor must consider whether sufficient admissible evidence supports charges against each target, and may have to decide whether to delay charging some targets until the investigation yields sufficient evidence to support charging others. In addition to considering the evidence against each target, the prosecutor also must consider whether the order and manner of charging the defendants will help to achieve the prosecution's objectives in the case. One such objective may be securing cooperation from some defendants, which might warrant charging those defendants earlier in the case—perhaps under seal—with the hope that they will provide additional evidence against the remaining targets.

Assessing the evidence against each target for each element of each crime to be charged is challenging in any complex multi-defendant case. With corruption cases in particular, prosecutors must carefully consider whether admissible evidence will prove each count beyond a reasonable doubt as to every target they are considering charging. Targets often have differing levels of culpability—for example, accomplice targets who are not public servants may not know the full scope of a corrupt government actor's duties and responsibilities.

2. Corporations and Organizations

The presence of corporations or organizations that have potential criminal liability may further complicate charging decisions. The "Principles of Federal Prosecution of Business Organizations" section of the Justice Manual guides how federal prosecutors investigate and charge such organizations, and may also be useful for state prosecutors to consult when considering whether to charge a corporation or organization.[6] Because corporations and organizations "act" through their owners, directors, officers, and high managerial employees, prosecutors in states where such entities can face criminal liability must consider whether to charge the entity itself or just the individual(s) involved. Prosecutors faced with that decision should assess whether charging the entity would be in the public interest. Factors to consider may include:

1. The seriousness of the offense and whether criminal charges against the entity are necessary to protect the public;

2. The ownership and command structure of the entity, including whether top decision-makers directly participated in the crime;

3. Whether charging the entity is necessary to ensure the appropriate disgorgement of criminally-derived assets as restitution or forfeiture,[7] or to revoke the organization's charter;[8]

4. The purpose being served by the entity (a nonprofit organization serving handicapped children might warrant different treatment than a for-profit corporation, for example); and

5. The extent to which criminal charges would harm blameless employees or investors. [9]

The key here is consistency and fairness—attempting to treat like situations in the same manner, but being flexible enough to adjust for the individual circumstances of each case.

After assessing the seriousness of the crime and the risk the entity poses to the public, prosecutors should consider the relationship of the perpetrators to the entity—if a corporation is little more than the alter ego of those who used it to commit criminal acts, that weighs heavily in favor of charging that

---

6 Justice Manual §§ 9-28.010 to 9-28.1600 (U.S. Dep't of Justice 2020), https://www.justice.gov/jm/justice-manual.

7 For more on asset forfeiture and restitution, see Chapter 6.4.

8 For more on this and similar remedies, see Chapter 6.3, Part II.

9 *See* Justice Manual § 9-28.300 (outlining ten factors for federal prosecutors to consider in determining whether to criminally charge a corporation).

organization. To assess the relationship between the individual perpetrators and the entity, prosecutors may consider:

1. The positions of the perpetrators in the entity (e.g., high-level executives versus low-ranking employees);[10]

2. Whether the entity has separate legal counsel that operates independently from the perpetrators;[11]

3. Whether the entity has cooperated with prosecutors investigating the perpetrators;[12] and

4. Whether the entity has made remedial efforts (including by disciplining or terminating wrongdoers, or maintaining or initiating a corporate compliance program).[13]

It is also useful to consider whether charges are necessary to return misappropriated funds to the victims of the crime—whether they are individuals or the public treasury. Sometimes it may be necessary to charge the entity criminally; other times, a non-prosecution or deferred prosecution agreement can ensure the same result. Moreover, in some states, criminal charges against a corporation provide grounds to revoke its charter—an appropriate penalty for an organization that appears likely to continue victimizing others.[14]

In assessing whether to charge an entity, it may also be appropriate to consider whether criminal charges are necessary for specific or general deterrence. Factors to consider here include:

1. Whether the entity is a repeat violator;[15]

---

10 *See id.* § 9-28.500.

11 *Accord id.* § 9-28.800 (discussing role of compliance department, including whether it is empowered to "prevent and detect misconduct and to ensure that corporate activities are conducted in accordance with applicable criminal and civil laws, regulations, and rules").

12 *See id.* § 9-28.900.

13 *See id.* § 9-28.1000.

14 *See, e.g.*, N.J. Stat. Ann. § 2C:43-4 (2020); Md. Code Ann., Corps. & Ass'ns § 1-405 (2020) (revoking charter in context of organized crime). States take various approaches to corporate charter revocation. *See* Kyle Noonan, *The Case for a Federal Corporate Charter Revocation Penalty*, 80 Geo. Wash. L. Rev. 602, 614-16 (2012). *See also* Chapter 6.3, Part II.

15 Justice Manual §§ 9-28.300, 9-28.600.

2. Whether misconduct is pervasive in the entity's industry;[16]

3. Whether charging one organization would encourage other similarly-situated entities to comply with the relevant laws;[17] and

4. Whether non-prosecution agreements that require financial or compliance monitoring, or civil or administrative enforcement would better deter future criminal behavior by this entity or others.[18]

C. *When Should Charges be Filed?*

As in all criminal cases, a prosecutor should generally charge only when the case is ready to be tried, unless countervailing concerns—such as if the defendant is expected to flee or poses a serious ongoing risk to the community—require acting more quickly. Once formal charges have been filed, the prosecutor has the obligation to provide discovery to the defendant.[19] The state's ability to secure additional evidence is hampered by the end of the grand jury investigation and the resulting loss of the power to subpoena witnesses and documents prior to trial.[20] Prosecutors must be prepared to respond to pretrial motions. Judges may weigh in on both their impression of the quality of the evidence and the jury appeal of a case, and, in some states, may pressure the parties to resolve the case. Because corruption cases are often closely watched by the public and the press, the "court of public opinion" may also comment on the strength of the case or the wisdom of the charges.[21] Defendant(s), the court, and the public may identify apparent weaknesses in the state's case, including in the investigation. Finally, the speedy trial clock is ticking, and prosecutors must be prepared to face the crucible of trial, where the state's evidence will be judged by the trier of fact.[22]

---

16 *See id.* § 9-28.200 (observing that "corporations are likely to take immediate remedial steps when one is indicted for criminal misconduct that is pervasive throughout a particular industry, and thus an indictment can provide a unique opportunity for deterrence on a broad scale").

17 *Id.*

18 *Id.* §§ 9-28.200, 9-28.1100, 9-28.1200.

19 *See* Chapter 5.1, Part III (summarizing discovery and disclosure requirements).

20 *See* Chapter 4.3 (discussing potential defenses in corruption cases and recommending prosecutors seek to counter them during the investigation).

21 *See* Chapter 5.3.

22 *See* Chapter 5.1, Part III(C) (recommending prosecutors be prepared to have a speedy trial).

Against this backdrop, a prosecutor who has taken sufficient time to secure clear, concrete, convincing evidence is well rewarded. That evidence can assure the court of the seriousness of the charges—and (in jurisdictions where judges weigh in on the advisability of a guilty plea) perhaps cause the judge to persuade the defendant to make the compromises necessary to achieve a just resolution of the case. The evidence can be used to defeat defense motions to dismiss the case or to limit the scope of the case, or to respond to defenses.[23] A prosecutor should never seek to try a criminal case in the court of public opinion.[24] However, because corruption cases are often closely watched and well publicized, strong evidence may discourage meritless motions and unnecessary hearings, as the resulting publicity about the overwhelming evidence against the defendant will benefit neither the defendant nor the defense attorneys. Perhaps most important, that evidence means that a reasonable defendant, upon reviewing the discovery materials, may well choose to accept responsibility for his crimes and plead guilty. Put simply: no argument that a defendant should plead is more powerful than the presentation of overwhelming evidence that he will be convicted and face harsher penalties after trial than those being offered in the proposed plea resolution. If a defendant in a well-investigated case nonetheless chooses to proceed to trial, the prosecutor will be positioned to prove the charges—and the public may well benefit from a full airing of the defendant's crimes.

D. *Charging Corruption in New Jersey State Court: Issues and Opportunities*

How the factors discussed above are applied to the timing of charges may be best illustrated by considering them in the context of a particular state. New Jersey, for example, has significant enhanced penalties for prosecutions of certain crimes involving public officials. If a public official is engaged in official misconduct,[25] bribery,[26] tampering with public records,[27] false representations in connection with government contracts,[28] theft by deception of over $10,000,[29]

---

23 *See* Chapter 4.3.

24 *See* Model Rules of Prof'l Conduct rr. 3.6, 3.8(f) (Am. Bar Ass'n 2020). *See also* Chapter 5.3.

25 N.J. Stat. Ann. § 2C:30-2 (2020).

26 *Id.* § 2C:27-2.

27 *Id.* § 2C:28-7.

28 *Id.* § 2C:21-34.

29 *Id.* § 2C:20-4.

or any other enumerated offenses as part of his public employment, the public official faces mandatory incarceration in state prison, without parole, for ten years for a first degree crime, five years for a second degree crime, two years for a third degree crime, and one year for even a fourth degree crime.[30] This stands in stark contrast to the penalties faced by non-public officials or by defendants in non-corruption cases, where there is a presumption against incarceration for first offenders convicted of third and fourth degree crimes, and where first offenders convicted of first and second degree white collar crimes face a presumption of imprisonment but with no term of parole ineligibility.[31] Corruption defendants also face mandatory forfeiture of their public pensions, mandatory forfeiture of their office (for public officials), and permanent disqualification from future office.[32] Finally, defendants can face large monetary penalties, including corruption profiteering penalties of $500,000 for first degree crimes, $250,000 for second degree crimes, and $75,000 for third degree crimes.[33]

The New Jersey Division of Criminal Justice (DCJ) also has a policy of requiring that the most serious criminal offense provable by the evidence be pled to by a defendant in corruption matters, after due regard is given to defendant's willingness to cooperate with law enforcement authorities.[34] This requirement is, of course, tempered by the prosecutor's duty to seek justice in every case, which ensures that DCJ prosecutors consider the individual circumstances of each case. This flexibility may result in prosecutors initially charging and accepting a guilty plea to less serious charges, in the interests of rewarding a quick acceptance of responsibility or cooperation against others, and conserving prosecutorial and investigative resources. If the defendant is unwilling to quickly accept responsibility for his crimes, however, the charges and any corresponding plea offer may well include more serious offenses, particularly when an ongoing investigation uncovers additional evidence. Some of the considerations that can guide DCJ prosecutors' decisions in this regard include:

---

30 *Id.* § 2C:43-6.5.

31 *Id.* § 2C:44-1(d), (e).

32 *See* N.J. Stat. Ann. § 43:1-3.1 (2020) (pension forfeiture); N.J. Stat. Ann. § 2C:51-2(a), (d) (forfeiture of and disqualification from public office). *See also* Chapter 6.3, Part I.

33 N.J. Stat. Ann. § 2C:30-8(d).

34 *See* Memorandum from N.J. Att'y Gen. Stuart Rabner to Dir. of Criminal Justice & Cty. Prosecutors § 3(a), (d) (May 31, 2007), http://www.nj.gov/oag/dcj/pdfs/guidelines-pros-pub-officials.pdf.

1. The defendant's position and the seriousness of the crime (for example a low-level data entry clerk may warrant a more generous plea offer than a constitutional officer like a county sheriff, even if they might be charged with the same degree of crime);

2. The willingness of the defendant to plead guilty and take responsibility for his conduct early, thereby obviating the need for further investigation;

3. The defendant's willingness and ability to cooperate in the investigation and prosecution of this or other corruption schemes;

4. The quality and persuasiveness of the evidence against the defendant;

5. The state's disposition of like charges or similar criminal conduct in the past; and

6. Other relevant individual characteristics of the defendant, such as the motive for the crime, the defendant's place in the criminal scheme relative to others, the ability of others to influence defendant's conduct, or the defendant's willingness to make restitution for his crimes.

Ultimately, the overarching question in all corruption cases is the same as that in all criminal cases: What is the right result? In trying to reach this result, a prosecutor should consider what charging decisions and plea offers suggest about the seriousness and strength of the case. The initial charges will also form an impression in both counsel and in the defendant about the likelihood of an acceptable plea offer. Prosecutors should also consider how to best handle minor targets who may be important witnesses against those with greater culpability. In larger corruption cases, it is common to have low-level participants who may not be able to afford to hire private counsel; oftentimes, these defendants only obtain representation after they are charged. As such, the state's ability to negotiate a pre-charge resolution with them is extremely limited. The best strategy for the case as a whole may be to "flip" these lower-level participants, securing their cooperation early so that they can be witnesses against more culpable actors in the scheme.[35] The initial charges against such a

35 *See* Chapter 1.8, Part II(A) (summarizing cooperation agreements, non-prosecution

participant may impact his or her willingness to plead guilty to a cooperation agreement.

If charges are filed publicly against a defendant—and sometimes even if they are not—a prosecutor should assume that uncharged participants in the scheme will quickly learn about those charges. This initial charging decision by the state may thus impact those targets' deliberations about whether to cooperate in the investigation and prosecution. For example, if charges against a lower-level cooperating defendant seem too harsh, they may cause similarly-situated uncharged targets to conclude that the cooperating defendant made a mistake by cooperating and that their best course of action is to refuse, leaving the state to its own investigation and proofs.[36] In contrast, initial charges that seem too lenient may make the state appear unable or unwilling to hold members of the scheme responsible for their actions, and higher-level participants who are charged later in the investigation may cite those charges to argue for more lenient treatment.

Indeed, a prosecutor should be ready for defendants to argue that their charges—and sentences—should be commensurate with those of other defendants in the same case, as well as defendants charged in arguably similar cases elsewhere in the state. The defense bar is always watching and comparing. In New Jersey, DCJ press releases in other cases have been cited during plea negotiations and sometimes even submitted to the court in support of arguments that the defendant faces disproportionately harsh charges compared to those in other, purportedly similar cases. And courts—perhaps seeking to dispose of corruption cases that may lead to long, complex, multi-defendant trials—are often willing to use these comparisons to undercut the state when expressing what they believe are reasonable plea dispositions and also later when sentencing defendants. Thus, it behooves a prosecutor to weigh charging decisions carefully to ensure that they are fundamentally fair and support a coherent

---

agreements, and immunity orders); Chapter 2.5 (addressing the use of confidential informants and cooperating witnesses).

36 Note, however, that some prosecutors' offices have a policy of requiring cooperating witnesses to plead guilty to every crime they committed, with the expectation that the judge will impose a substantially shorter sentence than the cooperating witness would otherwise receive if he or she fulfills the requirements in the cooperation agreement. *See* Chapter 4.3, n.12 (detailing procedure used in the Southern District of New York); *see also* Chapter 1.8, Part II(A) (summarizing methods of securing testimony, including cooperation agreements, non-prosecution agreements, and immunity orders).

strategy for the case as a whole, and to consider the precedent that might be cited even in unrelated cases.

II. Timing and Methods of Charging

A. *Charging Vehicles: Complaints, Indictments, and Informations/ Accusations*

Often, a prosecutor must decide not just what crimes to charge, but also *how* to charge them—for example, what pleading vehicle to use. In New Jersey, a prosecutor may begin the criminal legal process by complaint—either complaint-summons if the defendant is to surrender, or complaint-warrant, if the defendant is to be arrested. Alternatively, a prosecutor may choose to initiate the case by indicting the defendant and then obtain a summons or warrant only after the indictment is returned by the grand jury. Indictments may also be sealed, allowing defendants to be located or ongoing aspects of the investigation to be completed, including cooperation by the charged defendant.

As mentioned above, corruption schemes may involve participants who differ in culpability levels, public service positions, and personal wealth. Some targets may obtain private counsel very early in the investigation, allowing the prosecutor and defense counsel to discuss a pre-indictment resolution and cooperation. Other targets may be unwilling to retain counsel until they are charged, or be unable to afford an attorney and not receive court-appointed counsel until after they are charged. A pre-indictment resolution may pose ethical issues[37] and is difficult—if not impossible—with an unrepresented target, and the lack of a defense attorney may hamper attempts to secure a target's cooperation against other, more culpable participants in the scheme. In New Jersey, prosecutors can charge an unrepresented target by complaint; if the target qualifies financially, the court will appoint counsel.[38] If the target is not indigent, he or she will be advised by the court to retain counsel. Either way, once representation has been secured, discussions can begin with the attorney about whether his or her client wishes to cooperate or pursue some other

37 *See, e.g.*, Ben Kempinen, *The Ethics of Prosecutor Contact with the Unrepresented Defendant*, 19 Geo. J. Legal Ethics 1147, 1154-55 (2006).

38 *See* N.J. Stat. Ann. §§ 2A:158A-2, 2A:158A-5.2 (2020).

pre-indictment resolution.[39] This practice can obviate the need for a grand jury presentation and avoid questions from grand jurors about why other targets are not being charged or why the prosecutor has made certain charging decisions.

A target who is a flight risk presents special challenges to consider when deciding when to file charges, particularly if the investigation is still incomplete and ongoing. If there is sufficient evidence of the underlying crime, charging by complaint-warrant may be an ideal option. That will allow the state to obtain an arrest warrant for the target, seek pretrial detention (or some condition of release that will decrease the probability of flight), continue the investigation of other participants in the scheme, and obtain additional evidence against the target—both on the charges in the complaint and other charges that might be included in an indictment. Further, in New Jersey, the state is only required to provide pre-indictment discovery if it chooses to make a plea offer,[40] which allows the investigation to proceed more covertly than if the same defendant were indicted.

Conversely, indictments provide a vehicle to charge multiple defendants together while also lending an added legitimacy to the prosecution by showing that the grand jury—comprised of citizens from the same pool from which a trial jury would be drawn—has found probable cause that one or more crimes were committed. As such, a defendant may take an indictment more seriously and be more inclined to either cooperate or resolve the case in some other fashion before the trial. If the investigation is complete, there may be no need to take the interim step of charging via complaint. Where a large portion of the investigation has already occurred before—or been presented to—an investigatory grand jury, a prosecutor can simply present a proposed indictment to that grand jury—along with any necessary supplemental evidence to establish probable cause for each element of each proposed charge against each proposed defendant—to initiate a criminal case against the defendant(s).

Filing an indictment under seal may be useful to avoid publicity that might adversely impact an ongoing investigation, or to ensure that all of the defendants are located and arrested at the same time.[41] Sealing can be a useful

---

39 *See* Chapter 1.8, Part II(A); Chapter 2.5.

40 *See* N.J. Ct. Rules 3:13-3(a), (b)(1) (requiring discovery prior to indictment only where the state has made a plea offer).

41 *See id.* 3:6-8(a) (discussing the return of an indictment and providing that the "judge may direct that the indictment shall be kept secret until the defendant is in custody or has been

tool when the primary investigation is complete but a collateral matter, such as attempts by one or more defendants to tamper with witnesses or evidence, is still being investigated. In such a case, an indictment charging the underlying criminal scheme may be sealed while the tampering investigation continues, and all of the charges can be unsealed at the same time.

Finally, in some jurisdictions, a defendant can agree to waive the right to be indicted by a grand jury and consent to the filing of a criminal information or accusation. This charging vehicle may be appropriate when, for example, a defendant has agreed to cooperate or to enter a guilty plea during the early stages of an investigation. When appropriate, the information can also be filed under seal to preserve a cooperating witness's ability to work proactively with investigators.[42]

B. *Statutes of Limitations*

Statutes of limitations can impact the timing of charging decisions. If prosecutors choose to forego charging certain crimes in an initial indictment, they may consider whether they want to charge those crimes in the future and must be sure to file any additional charges within the applicable limitations period. Further, different criminal offenses may have different limitations periods, which could require that less serious but more readily provable crimes be charged earlier in an investigation, and more serious crimes be added once evidence has been uncovered. Additionally, different jurisdictions may require different types of charging documents to satisfy the statutes of limitations. For example, in New Jersey, only crimes alleged in an indictment are considered "charged" for the purpose of satisfying the applicable statute of limitations.[43]

Prosecutors may also consider entering into an agreement with defense counsel to toll the statute of limitations in some cases. Such a tolling agreement may allow for pre-indictment plea negotiations, for example. Prosecutors should take special care to ensure that a tolling agreement is enforceable in

---

released pending trial and in that event it shall be sealed by the clerk . . . ."); *see also In re* Essex Cty. Grand Jury Investigation into Fire at Seton Hall Univ., 845 A.2d 739, 756 (N.J. Super. Ct. Law Div. 2003) (discussing stay of discovery while indictment under seal).

42 *See* Chapter 1.8, Part II(A); Chapter 2.5.

43 *See* N.J. Stat. Ann. § 2C:1-6(d) (2020) ("A prosecution is commenced for a[n indictable] crime when an indictment is found and for a nonindictable offense when a warrant or other process is issued . . . .").

their jurisdiction, however, and thoughtfully draft the agreement to encompass all of the potential charges they may want to bring should plea negotiations break down or the investigation reveal information unknown to the government at the time the tolling agreement was signed.

III. Additional Considerations Regarding Timing of Charges

A. *Public Interest and Public Safety*

Public safety is obviously of paramount concern to a prosecutor. Filing charges can stop an ongoing criminal scheme and prevent additional crimes from occurring—important goals that may warrant filing charges soon after sufficient evidence has been gathered. In corruption cases, citizens may be deprived of honest representation in government each day that an investigation continues without criminal charges. Actions taken by public servants who are ultimately adjudged to be corrupt may be voided—either legally or in the public perception—and then be reconsidered by others at a later date, delaying the public's business, wasting taxpayer money, and potentially undercutting public trust in the government.[44] The need to preserve citizens' trust in government and conserve government resources may mean that it is in the interest of justice to file corruption charges at the first available opportunity after sufficient evidence is obtained.

B. *Case Strategy*

In cases involving multiple targets, prosecutors may consider how filing charges publicly is likely to impact the overall strategy for the case. As discussed above, both the crimes charged and the charging instruments themselves may affect a defendant's decision about whether to cooperate. So, too, does the timing of charges. Charging can also lead to scrutiny of the case by the press and the public, potentially drawing premature—and perhaps unwanted—attention and ending the possibility of proactive investigation.[45] It may also cause any uncharged defendants to cease or hide ongoing criminal activity and to

44 See Chapter 6.3, Part I for a discussion of removing corrupt officials from office.
45 See Chapter 2.5 for a discussion of such investigations.

be unwilling to discuss past criminal activity. Even unsubstantiated rumors about police investigation can cause targets to refuse to answer telephone calls, change cellular telephones, stop meeting with past associates, and change their patterns of movement. Charging just one defendant can have an even more drastic effect and can effectively end an investigation. Such concerns sometimes weigh toward a decision to delay charging, or to charge a defendant under seal.

Conversely, and particularly in historical investigations, charging may make a point that the investigation is serious and may encourage reluctant witnesses to cooperate. Charging lower level conspirators one by one may put pressure on the remaining, uncharged conspirators to volunteer to cooperate.

There is no "one-size-fits-all" approach to determine the "right" time to file charges in every case. Public safety concerns that encourage charging quickly sometimes conflict with case strategy factors that suggest a more measured approach, for example. Prosecutors should consider these sometimes competing interests in determining who to charge, when to charge them, what charges to file, and even whether to file a complaint or an indictment in the first instance.

C. *Media Issues*

Public corruption investigations and allegations often draw a great deal of public attention, garnering media interest.[46] Unfortunately, headlines like "Corruption Investigation Continues Methodically and Professionally" do not attract readers, so reporters may be quick to share their opinions about an investigation they believe to have proceeded slowly. For example, in New Jersey, the investigation of a state assemblyman who was alleged to have viewed images of child pornography on his state-issued computer generated public speculation about how long it would take for the assemblyman to be charged. One news outlet even posted a clock counting down the days, hours, minutes, and seconds between the initial allegations and when the assemblyman was charged.[47] While popular with the public, the clock put tremendous pressure on the investigation, and risked encouraging haste that was not beneficial to investigating

---

46 *See* Chapter 5.3.

47 *Neil Cohen Finally Charged*, The Cranford Pundit (Dec. 18, 2008, 9:36 AM), https://cranfordpundit.wordpress.com/2008/12/18/neil-cohen-finally-charged/; Bob Ingle, *Where is Cohen Case?*, Politics Patrol (Oct. 3, 2008), http://blogs.app.com/politicspatrol/2008/10/03/where-is-cohen-case/.

the sensitive and serious allegations. With that said, the public outcry and the need to keep public confidence did warrant a prompt investigation. The case was ultimately successful, as the agencies investigating the allegations added additional staff to the case who worked long hours to ensure that the investigation was completed both as carefully and as quickly as possible.

D. *Other Pressures*

Victims—whether individuals or agencies that have been defrauded—concerned citizens, and civic organizations can also create pressures that may influence a prosecutor's decision with respect to the timing of charges in corruption cases. While all criminal charges should be prosecuted in a timely manner, accelerating the filing of charges in response to these types of external pressures raises the risk that charges are brought before full consideration is given to the merits of a case. Under such circumstances, legal deficiencies, evidentiary omissions, and failures to predict and address potential defenses in the case are more likely to occur. Although the concerns of outside groups cannot and should not be ignored, a prosecutor who hastily brings charges to meet an arbitrary deadline expected by others is more likely to be unsuccessful. When the evidence and law dictate, a prosecutor must be prepared to delay or decline filing criminal charges, regardless of any outside pressures.[48]

IV. Ethics and Politics in the Timing of Corruption Charges

A. *Remaining Impartial and Avoiding Conflicts of Interest*

Ethical considerations factor significantly into deciding when to file charges in corruption cases. Prosecutors should avoid making decisions based on bias, economic or professional self-interest, political partisanship, and other improper influences—and be sensitive to even the appearance of such improprieties.[49] The ethical standards that govern the conduct of prosecutors in

---

48 *See* ABA Standards for Criminal Justice: Prosecution Function ss. 3-4.4(a), (b) (Am. Bar Ass'n 2017), https://www.americanbar.org/groups/criminal_justice/standards/ProsecutionFunctionFourthEdition/.

49 *Id.* s. 3-1.7; Chapter 5.1, Part I(A).

other situations also apply when making decisions about the timing of charges in corruption cases.[50] If an individual line prosecutor, the attorney general or other elected prosecutor, or the office itself has a conflict of interest, it may be necessary to, as appropriate, seek a waiver of the conflict, establish walls to segregate any conflicted prosecutor(s), or agree to recusal.[51] Identifying and addressing any such conflicts early in an investigation may prevent or mitigate later allegations that politics or other sinister motives infected the case.

B. *Avoiding Allegations of Partisanship*

Whether the chief prosecutor is elected or appointed, the intrusion of politics sometimes is an unavoidable aspect of a line prosecutor's job. One of the most difficult burdens faced by corruption prosecutors is making decisions, including when to bring charges, in a politically charged environment. Whatever the ultimate charging decision—or whenever it is made—a prosecutor or the office itself may be accused of partisanship. When confronted with such a situation, the best recourse for a prosecutor is to make decisions independently from any political pressures or one's own political beliefs and affiliations.[52]

Election season is a particularly fraught time for corruption prosecutors—especially if the target of an investigation is on the ballot. Action will invariably lead to allegations that a prosecutor has attempted to affect the outcome of an election; inaction may lead to other complaints and perhaps even require an expensive and time-consuming special election if an elected target is later indicted. To address these concerns, a practice common in prosecutors' offices during an election cycle is to remind staff that their investigative and prosecution activities must not be influenced by politics—a reminder that is frequently accompanied by an admonition to notify supervisors of any matters with political implications. One such memorandum from the United States Department of Justice states simply that "[l]aw enforcement officers and prosecutors may never select the timing of investigative steps or criminal charges for

---

50 *See* Model Rules of Prof'l Conduct rr. 1.7-1.9, 3.8 (Am. Bar Ass'n 2020) (discussing conflicts of interest for attorneys generally, and detailing special responsibilities for prosecutors).

51 *See* Chapter 5.1, Part I(B); ABA Standards for the Prosecution Function s. 3-1.7(a).

52 *See* ABA Standards for Criminal Justice: Prosecutorial Investigations s. 3.6 (Am. Bar Ass'n 2014), https://www.americanbar.org/content/dam/aba/publications/criminal_justice_standards/Pros_Investigations.pdf.

the purpose of affecting any election, or for the purpose of giving an advantage or disadvantage to any candidate or political party."[53]

Faced with the possible repercussions of bringing corruption-related charges during a politically sensitive time, such as an election cycle, a prosecutor may choose to delay bringing charges until the relevant event has passed. In some states, investigations may be required to cease during the certain periods.[54] Some prosecutors' offices may have set "quiet" or "dark" periods in advance of an election, during which time the office refrains from filing charges, serving subpoenas, or taking other overt action on sensitive matters that might bring into question the motives of the office.

Even such quiet periods, however, may require reasonable exceptions. For example, if the statute of limitations deadline is approaching, a prosecutor may need to decide whether to charge a case, notwithstanding an election. Regardless, barring any statute of limitations concerns, the quiet period ends after the election is over, and the investigation or prosecution may then continue in the normal fashion. Of course, other offices operate entirely differently, and may require their prosecutors to bring charges—even in corruption cases—whenever the evidence is sufficient to support them. Regardless of which approach an office decides to use in its corruption cases, protecting those cases from accusations of partisanship requires the prosecutors in a given office to use a consistent approach in deciding when to file charges in corruption cases.

---

53 Memorandum from the U.S. Att'y Gen. to All Dep't Emps., Re: Election Year Sensitivities 1 (Mar. 9, 2012), http://www.justice.gov/sites/default/files/oip/legacy/2014/07/23/ag-memo-election-year-sensitivities.pdf; *see also* Letter from Sen. Sheldon Whitehouse to Attorney General William Barr (Sept. 14, 2020), https://www.whitehouse.senate.gov/imo/media/doc/200914_Letter%20to%20Barr%20RE%20Intervening%20in%20E%20Jean%20Carroll%20Suit.pdf 2 n.5 (citing 2008 and 2016 attorney general memoranda with identical language). For more on investigation of crimes around the time of an election, see Chapter 1.7 (addressing election crimes).

54 *See, e.g.*, Ga. Code Ann. § 45-15-17(d) (2020) ("Nothing contained in this Code section shall authorize the Attorney General to commence or carry on any investigation or to issue any subpoenas to anyone for the purpose of investigating any member of the General Assembly while the General Assembly is in any regular or called session.").

Conclusion

Corruption prosecutors, like all prosecutors, must:

1. Apply consistent procedures in all cases, regardless of any target's political affiliation;

2. File charges that properly reflect the seriousness of the offense;

3. Choose the proper charging vehicle;

4. Consider the timing of any charges; and

5. Do their best to ensure that defendants receive fair trials in the face of increased press interest.

If political considerations infect the process, every decision and the case itself is subject to attack. The often high-profile nature of corruption cases means that media, victims, citizens, and others may well weigh in on the timing and necessity of charges. Prosecutors cannot bend to external pressure to file a case quickly, as a decision to file charges prematurely may lead to years of litigation and an unjust outcome. Prosecuting public corruption cases will never be easy, but it is important work that, when approached fairly and consistently, does more than perhaps any other area of prosecution to uphold the rule of law.

Chapter 5.3

Media Relations in Criminal Corruption Cases

Jessica A. Roth

Jessica A. Roth is a Professor of Law at Benjamin N. Cardozo School of Law and Co-Director of Jacob Burns Center for Ethics in the Practice of Law. She was an Assistant United States Attorney in the Southern District of New York from 2002-2009 and served as the Reporter for the American Bar Association's Standards for Criminal Justice: Fair Trial & Public Discourse.

Introduction

Public corruption cases frequently attract significant media attention. Often, they involve high-profile individuals and allegations that cut to the core of the public trust. Thus, prosecutors handling such cases may find themselves in a difficult position, having to balance the public's legitimate interest in being kept informed on matters of heightened public concern with other equally important interests, including the integrity of ongoing investigations, the privacy and reputational interests of those identified as subjects or targets during an investigation, and a defendant's right to a fair trial. This chapter provides practical guidance for prosecutors in handling such matters, consistent with their legal and ethical responsibilities and best practices.

I. The Model Rules of Professional Conduct

Several rules in the American Bar Association Model Rules of Professional Conduct apply to prosecutors bringing high-profile criminal cases. The first is Rule 1.6 (Confidentiality of Information), which imposes a duty on lawyers to maintain confidentiality of information related to the representation of a client.[1] Since the prosecutor's client is the public,[2] this means the prosecutor is required to maintain the confidentiality of all information gained during the investigation he or she conducts on behalf of the public, barring a permitted reason for disclosure. While an investigation is ongoing, there rarely is a good reason for public disclosure. The strategic reasons against disclosure are clear. For example, it could jeopardize the investigation by tipping off potential targets and witnesses. Moreover, many state and federal rules governing grand jury secrecy make it illegal for prosecutors and agents to disclose material occurring before the grand jury.[3] Thus, during the investigatory stage of a matter, it rarely will be appropriate for a prosecutor to comment on the existence of an investigation, its scope, targets, or subjects, or to publicly discuss evidence gathered during the investigation.

The presumption against public comment is justified not only by the necessity of maintaining the integrity of the investigation, but also because prosecutors have a duty to avoid unnecessarily causing reputational harm to potential targets and witnesses. These concerns are part of the rationale for the grand jury secrecy rules.[4] The ethics rules also reflect these concerns. For example, Rule 3.8 (Special Responsibilities of a Prosecutor) provides that prosecutors

---

1 Model Rules of Prof'l Conduct r. 1.6 (Am. Bar Ass'n 2020).

2 *See* ABA Standards for Criminal Justice: Prosecutorial Investigations s. 1.2 (Am. Bar Ass'n 2014), https://www.americanbar.org/content/dam/aba/publications/criminal_justice_standards/Pros_Investigations.pdf ("The prosecutor's client is the public, not particular government agencies or victims.").

3 *See* Trump v. Vance, 140 S. Ct. 2412, 2427 (2020) (citing Sara S. Beale & William C. Bryson, Grand Jury Law & Practice § 5:1 at 5-3 (2d ed. 2018) ("[T]he federal system and most states have adopted statutes or court rules" that "impose sharp restrictions on the extent to which matters occurring before a grand jury may be divulged" to outside persons.); Wayne R. LaFave et al., 3 Criminal Procedure § 8.5(b) (4th ed. Dec. 2020 update), Westlaw. The federal grand jury secrecy provisions are set forth in Federal Rule of Criminal Procedure 6(e). Fed. R. Crim. P. 6(e).

4 *See, e.g.*, Douglas Oil Co., v. Petrol Stops Northwest, 441 U.S. 211, 219 (1979) ("by preserving the secrecy of the [grand jury] proceedings, we assure that persons who are accused but exonerated by the grand jury will not be held up to public ridicule").

shall "refrain from making extrajudicial comments that have a substantial likelihood of heightening public condemnation of the accused . . . ."[5] When an individual has a high public profile, such as holding a public office, merely being associated with a criminal investigation may cause grave reputational harm—and may even cause the person to lose an election—even if no charges ultimately are filed or the person is acquitted at trial.[6] For that reason, prosecutors should be particularly careful to avoid publicly identifying office holders as subjects or targets of investigations when an election is near. Moreover, in rare cases where the existence of a particular investigation into a public figure has been widely reported—and the investigation has been concluded with a decision not to bring charges—it may be appropriate for a prosecutor to so state publicly.[7] However, if the prosecutor decides against filing charges or the grand jury does not indict, the prosecutor should not comment on the evidence that was gathered or characterize the behavior of the target of the investigation.[8]

---

5 Model Rules r. 3.8(f).

6 *See, e.g.*, Stern v. State *ex rel.* Ansel, 869 S.W.2d 614, 622 (Tex. Ct. App. 1994) ("an elected official's reputation may be irreparably harmed by public disclosure [that he or she is a subject of grand jury investigation] even though investigation of the allegations reveals no basis for prosecution").

7 *See, e.g.*, Press Release, U.S. Dep't of Justice, U.S. Att'y's Off., S. Dist. of N.Y., Acting U.S. Attorney Joon H. Kim Statement on the Investigation Into City Hall Fundraising (Mar. 16, 2017), https://www.justice.gov/usao-sdny/pr/acting-us-attorney-joon-h-kim-statement-investigation-city-hall-fundraising (announcing declination of charges against New York City Mayor Bill DiBlasio, citing concern about "unduly influenc[ing] the upcoming campaign and Mayoral election" as reason for issuing rare public statement about the status of an investigation); Press Release, U.S. Dep't of Justice, U.S. Attorney's Office, S. Dist. of N.Y., Statement of U.S. Attorney Preet Bharara Relating to Moreland Comm'n Investigation (Jan. 11, 2016), https://www.justice.gov/usao-sdny/pr/statement-us-attorney-preet-bharara-relating-moreland-commission-investigation (announcing no charges related to interference with the operation, and closing, of the Moreland Commission Established by New York Governor Andrew Cuomo, citing insufficient evidence).

8 The widespread criticism of former FBI Director James Comey's public remarks regarding Hillary Clinton's use of a private email server while she was Secretary of State, made in conjunction with his decision not to recommend prosecution, reflects this principle. *See, e.g.*, Memorandum from Dep. Att'y Gen. Rod J. Rosenstein to the Att'y Gen. 1 (May 9, 2017), https://www.justice.gov/oip/foia-library/moss/download (noting the "longstanding principle" that "we do not hold press conferences to release derogatory information about the subject of a declined criminal investigation"); Open Letter from Former Fed. Prosecutors and High-Ranking Officials of The U.S. Dep't of Justice 1 (Oct. 30, 2016), http://nafusa.org/wp-content/uploads/2016/10/20161030_DOJ-Letter-with-signatories.pdf (noting that "evidence uncovered during the course of an investigative inquiry" may be "incomplete, misleading or even incorrect, and releasing such information before all of the facts are known and tested in a court of law can unfairly prejudice individuals and undermine the public's faith in the integrity of our legal

Rule 3.8(f) provides an exception to the general "no comment" rule for statements that "are necessary to inform the public of the nature and extent of the prosecutor's actions and that serve a legitimate law enforcement purpose."[9] This exception should not be read too broadly, and the first phrase must be understood in conjunction with the second. Thus, in a rare situation where there is widespread public panic or fear—such as when an active shooter has been at large—prosecutors may disclose developments in an investigation necessary to quell that panic. Prosecutors also may release information necessary to protect potential victims, encourage the public to come forward with evidence, or to solicit help in apprehending a fugitive.[10] In public corruption cases, this exception rarely will be applicable during the investigation stage.

Finally, Rule 3.6 (Trial Publicity) provides additional reason for a prosecutor to refrain from making public statements about a matter during an investigation: the potential impact on the defendant's ability to obtain a fair trial.[11] The closer to an anticipated trial date prosecutorial statements are made, the more likely they are to materially prejudice the proceeding, including by making it harder to seat an unbiased jury.[12] However, statements made during the investigative stage also have that potential.[13]

Three additional points bear noting. First, the trial publicity rule applies not only to the prosecutors directly involved in a matter, but also any other lawyers in the same agency.[14] Second, any comments to the media or to the public are subject to this rule—even if they are not "on the record." Third, Rule 3.8 requires prosecutors to "exercise reasonable care" to prevent employees, law

---

process.").

9 Model Rules r. 3.8(f).

10 *See, e.g.*, *In re* Brizzi, 962 N.E.2d 1240, 1248 (Ind. 2012) (criticizing prosecutor's statements at press conference that did not serve any law enforcement purpose such as "protecting potential victims or apprehending suspected perpetrators still at large").

11 Model Rules r. 3.6.

12 *See* Gentile v. State Bar of Nev., 501 U.S. 1030, 1044 (1991) (statement made on eve of voir dire more likely to cause difficulties in seating an unbiased jury than statement made six months before trial).

13 *Accord* United States v. Bowen, 799 F.3d 336, 355 (5th Cir. 2015) (granting new trial where anonymous pretrial postings online by members of prosecutor's office "gave the prosecution a tool for public castigation of the defendants that it could not have used against them otherwise, and in so doing deprived them of a fair trial").

14 *See* Model Rules r. 3.6(d) ("No lawyer associated in a firm or government agency with a lawyer subject to paragraph (a) shall make a statement prohibited by paragraph (a).").

enforcement personnel, investigators, and other persons assisting the prosecutor or associated with the case from making statements that the prosecutor would not be permitted to make.[15] Thus, prosecutors must educate their own staff and other members of law enforcement about the risks associated with disclosing information about pending investigations to the public and make reasonable efforts to prevent them from doing so.[16]

Once charges have been filed, or an individual has been arrested, all the foregoing rules still apply, but the concerns identified in Rule 3.6 (Trial Publicity) become particularly important. Rule 3.6(a) provides that a lawyer who is participating in a matter "shall not make an extrajudicial statement that the lawyer knows or reasonably should know will be disseminated by means of public communication and will have a substantial likelihood of materially prejudicing an adjudicative proceeding in the matter."[17] In the criminal context, this rule reflects the prosecutor's professional duty to help protect a defendant's constitutional right to a fair trial, before a jury that is not tainted by pretrial publicity.[18]

The rule identifies, in part (b), certain matters that a lawyer may state, notwithstanding part (a). These include:

> (1) the claim, offense or defense involved and, except when prohibited by law, the identity of the persons involved;
>
> (2) information contained in a public record;
>
> (3) that an investigation of a matter is in progress;

---

15 *Id.* r. 3.8(f).

16 The National District Attorneys Association Guidelines similarly call for prosecutors to take affirmative steps to train law enforcement personnel on these issues, urging prosecutors to "assist law enforcement and other investigative agencies in understanding their statutory responsibilities with respect to the release of criminal justice information" and assist in the training of agencies within their jurisdiction "on subject matters to avoid when discussing pending criminal investigations or prosecutions with the media." NAT'L DIST. ATT'YS ASS'N, NATIONAL PROSECUTION STANDARDS s. 2-14.6 (3d ed. 2009).

17 MODEL RULES r. 3.6(a).

18 *See* U.S. CONST. amend. VI ("In all criminal prosecutions, the accused shall enjoy the right to a speedy and public trial, by an impartial jury of the State and district wherein the crime shall have been committed"); Sheppard v. Maxwell, 384 U.S. 333, 362 (1966) ("Due process requires that the accused receive a trial by an impartial jury free from outside influences.").

(4) the scheduling or result of any step in litigation;

(5) a request for assistance in obtaining evidence and information necessary thereto;

(6) a warning of danger concerning the behavior of a person involved, when there is reason to believe that there exists the likelihood of substantial harm to an individual or to the public interest; and

(7) in a criminal case, in addition to subparagraphs (1) through (6):

(i) the identity, residence, occupation and family status of the accused;

(ii) if the accused has not been apprehended, information necessary to aid in apprehension of that person;

(iii) the fact, time and place of arrest; and

(iv) the identity of investigating and arresting officers or agencies and the length of the investigation.[19]

Thus, in public corruption cases, once criminal charges have been publicly filed, prosecutors ordinarily may disclose the charges, including the criminal complaint or information, and certain limited information about the arrest and each stage of the proceedings in court. They also may disclose that the investigation is ongoing (if it is). When charges are disclosed, for example in a press release, prosecutors should include a "statement explaining that the charge is merely an accusation and that the defendant is presumed innocent until and unless proven guilty."[20] Editorializing or commenting on the charges should be avoided—even though the temptation to do so, in part for general deterrence purposes, may be great.[21]

---

19 Model Rules r. 3.6(b).

20 Model Rules r. 3.6 cmt. 5(6). *See, e.g.*, *In re* Brizzi, 962 N.E.2d 1240, 1245-46 (Ind. 2012).

21 In recent memory, two prominent federal prosecutors were criticized for making comments that went beyond the matters contained in the charging documents in public corruption cases. *See, e.g.*, United States v. Silver, 103 F. Supp. 3d 370, 378-79 (S.D.N.Y. 2015) (chastising Southern District of New York United States Attorney Preet Bharara for remarks at

The exception that threatens to swallow the rule and authorize prosecutors' release of considerable other information is that set forth in part (b)(2), for "information contained in a public record."[22] There has been some litigation about what exactly this means.[23] The safer course, which is most consistent with the interest in preserving a defendant's right to a fair trial, is to construe "public record" as those documents contained in the publicly-available court file, or documents in the possession of the prosecutor's office or an investigative agency that are deemed a "public record" under applicable state open records laws. Under this standard, information that has appeared in the media does not automatically become "information contained in a public record."

Rule 3.6(c) also provides a limited exception for a lawyer, including a prosecutor, to respond to the "substantial undue prejudicial effect of recent publicity not initiated by the lawyer or the lawyer's client."[24] The rule states that such response "shall be limited to such information as is necessary to mitigate the recent adverse publicity."[25] Pursuant to this exception, a prosecutor, for example, may make limited comment to counter claims by the defense or a third party of prosecutorial misconduct or irregularities in the investigation.[26]

---

press conference following New York State Assembly Speaker's arrest, and speech at local law school given the next day, "that appeared to bundle together unproven allegations regarding the [d]efendant with broader commentary on corruption and a lack of transparency in certain aspects of New York State politics" which could lead some members of the public and media to interpret the United States Attorneys' remarks as his personal commentary on the defendant's character or guilt); Kelly Selesnick, *Innocent Until Proven Guilty: Will Patrick Fitzgerald's Public Statements Prejudice Rod Blagojevich's Trial?*, 23 Geo. J. Legal Ethics 827, 828-30, 835 (2010) (discussing criticisms of Chicago United States Attorney Patrick Fitzgerald for comments at a press conference announcing charges against Illinois Governor Rod Blagojevich, including that the governor's conduct "would make Lincoln roll over in his grave").

22 Model Rules r. 3.6(b)(2).

23 *See, e.g.*, Att'y Grievance Comm'n v. Gansler, 835 A.2d 548, 567, 569 (Md. 2003) (prospectively holding that "public record" within meaning of Rule 3.6 means "public government records—the records and papers on file with a government entity to which an ordinary citizen would have lawful access" not, as respondent argued, "anything in the public domain . . . [including] media reports" prior to or separate from the investigation); *Brizzi*, 962 N.E.2d at 1247 (endorsing *Gansler*'s prospective definition of "public record," with caveat that "on file" does not require "such formalities as file stamping or entry on a case docket.").

24 Model Rules r. 3.6(c).

25 *Id.*

26 The rare public statement by the Office of Special Counsel Robert Mueller in the course of his probe into Russian interference in the 2016 presidential election and related conduct that certain media accounts of witness statements to the Special Counsel were not accurate, provides an example of an extrajudicial statement falling within r. 3.6(c). *See* Mark Mazzetti & Sharon

The official comment to Rule 3.6 enumerates certain subjects that are particularly likely to materially prejudice a proceeding, particularly a criminal jury trial.[27] These include:

> (1) the character, credibility, reputation or criminal record of a party, suspect in a criminal investigation or witness, or the identity of a witness, or the expected testimony of a party or witness;
>
> (2) in a criminal case or proceeding that could result in incarceration, the possibility of a plea of guilty to the offense or the existence or contents of any confession, admission, or statement given by a defendant or suspect or that person's refusal or failure to make a statement;
>
> (3) the performance or results of any examination or test or the refusal or failure of a person to submit to an examination or test, or the identity or nature of physical evidence expected to be presented;
>
> (4) any opinion as to the guilt or innocence of a defendant or suspect in a criminal case or proceeding that could result in incarceration;
>
> (5) information that the lawyer knows or reasonably should know is likely to be inadmissible as evidence in a trial and that would, if disclosed, create a substantial risk of prejudicing an impartial trial; or
>
> (6) the fact that a defendant has been charged with a crime, unless there is included therein a statement explaining that the charge is merely an accusation and that the defendant is presumed innocent until and unless proven guilty.[28]

LaFraniere, *Mueller Statement Disputes Report That Trump Directed Cohen to Lie*, N.Y. Times (Jan. 18, 2019), https://www.nytimes.com/2019/01/18/us/politics/buzzfeed-cohen-russia-tower.html.

27 Model Rules r. 3.6 cmt. 5.

28 *Id.*

This list is extensive, in effect counseling prosecutors to try their cases in a court of law, not in the court of public opinion. In evaluating the propriety of public statements, courts generally consider not only the statement's content, but also its proximity to trial.[29] The closer to trial it is made, the more likely it will be deemed to pose a "substantial likelihood of materially prejudicing" the proceeding.[30] Extrajudicial statements made during trial also are subject to this rule, given the risk that jurors may be exposed to media accounts of prosecutors' out-of-court statements. Sequestration is rare, especially in public corruption cases. Although judges typically instruct jurors to avoid any media accounts about the case in which they are sitting, it is always possible—particularly in today's digital media environment—that jurors will be exposed to some extrajudicial information about the case. It is incumbent upon prosecutors not to heighten that risk, particularly by discussing evidence that may not be admitted at the trial.

Notwithstanding the foregoing, prosecutors have a duty to provide the public with information about matters of public concern, which includes criminal prosecutions brought in its name. Thus, to the extent doing so is consistent with their other professional obligations, as discussed above, prosecutors may facilitate the public's access to such information.[31] Practical suggestions for doing so, in a manner that minimizes the risk of violating the prosecutors' professional responsibilities or the defendant's constitutional rights, are set forth in Part III.

II. Other Sources of Guidance

In addition to the Model Rules of Professional Conduct, several other sources offer professional guidance for prosecutors. For example, the ABA's Criminal Justice Section publishes detailed Standards that address many of these issues at an even more granular level.[32] These Standards are aspirational

---

29 *See* Gentile v. State Bar of Nev., 501 U.S. 1030, 1044 (1991); United States v. Bowen, 799 F.3d 336, 355, 358 (5th Cir. 2015).

30 *See* Model Rules r. 3.6(a).

31 For an example of a case where prosecutors facilitated access to information by creating a website containing public documents, see Chapter 1.1, Part III(B).

32 *See Criminal Justice Standards*, Am. Bar Ass'n, https://www.americanbar.org/groups/criminal_justice/standards/ (last visited Apr. 17, 2021).

and, unlike the Model Rules of Professional Conduct, are not intended to serve as the basis for professional discipline.[33] One set of Standards, Fair Trial and Public Discourse, goes beyond the Model Rules of Professional Conduct, suggesting that prosecutors should be even more circumspect in making public statements about ongoing cases. For example, these Standards provide that prosecutors should not deliberately insert information into a public record, such as a complaint, solely to circumvent the prohibition on extrajudicial statements that tend to unnecessarily heighten condemnation of the accused.[34] They also counsel prosecutors to consult with their supervisors before making any public statement.[35] They add to the list of topics that prosecutors ordinarily should not discuss the "race, ethnicity, creed, religion, or sexual orientation"[36] of an accused or witness, in light of research demonstrating that statements about race in particular can be prejudicial to potential jurors.[37] They also draw particular attention to "perp walks"—which have on occasion been used in public corruption cases[38]—and make clear that law enforcement personnel "should not exercise their authority over an individual in a manner deliberately designed to increase the likelihood that images of the individual in custody will be disseminated . . . by means of public communication."[39]

The ABA Criminal Justice Section's Standards for the Prosecution Function also contains more detailed guidance about many of these issues. For example, they explicitly note that in light of the prosecutor's "duties of confidentiality and loyalty," the prosecutor "should not secretly or anonymously provide non-public information to the media, on or off the record, without appropriate authorization."[40] They also state that, when a prosecutor declines

---

33 ABA Standards for Criminal Justice: Fair Trial & Public Discourse s. 8-1.1(c) (Am. Bar Ass'n 2013), https://www.americanbar.org/content/dam/aba/publications/criminal_justice_standards/fair_trial_commentaries.pdf.

34 *Id.* s. 8-2.1(c).

35 *Id.* s. 8-2.1(a).

36 *Id.* s. 8-2.2(a)(ii).

37 *See* Laurie L. Levenson, *Prosecutorial Soundbites: When Do They Cross the Line?*, 44 Ga. L. Rev. 1021, 1038-42 (2010) (summarizing how prosecutorial comments on a defendant's race can be particularly prejudicial).

38 *See, e.g.*, Zimmerman v. Corbett, 195 F. Supp. 3d 695, 699 (M.D. Pa. 2016), *rev'd on other grounds*, 873 F.3d 414 (3d Cir. 2017).

39 ABA Fair Trial & Public Discourse § 8-3.2(a).

40 ABA Standards for Criminal Justice: Prosecution Function s. 3-1.10(g) (Am. Bar Ass'n 2017), https://www.americanbar.org/groups/criminal_justice/standards/ProsecutionFunctionFourthEdition/.

charges, she may make a public statement explaining that decision "but must take care not to imply guilt or otherwise prejudice the interests of victims, witnesses or subjects of an investigation."[41]

Both sets of standards address lawyers, including prosecutors, serving as commentators for the media. Both provide that no lawyer should do so in any case in which that lawyer is involved; and instruct lawyers to provide commentary only to the extent that they are informed about the relevant facts and the law, and that the commentary serves to educate the public and does not risk prejudicing a proceeding—by, for example, opining on the likely outcome or sensationalizing the matter.[42]

In addition to the ABA Criminal Justice Standards, the National District Attorneys Association publishes "best practices" standards for prosecutors. NDAA's provisions regarding statements to the media are consistent with those set forth in Model Rule of Professional Conduct 3.6.[43] As noted above, NDAA's National Prosecution Standards also urge prosecutors to educate members of law enforcement about these limits on the disclosure of information to and communications with the media.[44]

The U.S. Department of Justice has also issued guidance to its prosecutors about communications with the media in federal cases that is largely consistent with the Model Rules of Professional Conduct.[45] In some respects, like the ABA Standards, these internal directives go further, providing more detailed guidance. For example, they discourage "perp walks"[46] and state that, if a prosecutor makes a press statement in conjunction with an arrest, that statement "should include only incontrovertible, factual matters, and should not include subjective

---

41 *Id.* s. 3-1.10(c). For further discussion of public declination statements, see note 7 *supra* and accompanying text.

42 ABA Standards for the Prosecution Function s. 3-1.10(i); ABA Fair Trial & Public Discourse s. 8-2.4.

43 *See* Nat'l Dist. Att'ys Ass'n, National Prosecution Standards s. 2-14.1 to 2-14.5 (3d ed. 2009).

44 *Id.* s. 2-14.6.

45 *See* 28 C.F.R. § 50.2 (2020) (providing guidance about the "[r]elease of information by personnel of the [USDOJ] relating to criminal and civil proceedings").

46 28 C.F.R. § 50.2(b)(7) (2020) (directing that USDOJ staff "should take no action to encourage or assist news media in photographing or televising a defendant or accused person being held or transported in Federal custody. Departmental representatives should not make available photographs of a defendant unless a law enforcement function is served thereby").

observations."[47] In addition, the USDOJ's Justice Manual (previously the United States Attorney's Manual) has an entire section on contacts with the media that provides useful guidance.[48]

III. Practical Guidance

Establishing office policies on relations with the media, well in advance of any particular high-profile case, may prevent difficulties that could arise in such a case. Such policies may designate what information may be disclosed, when, and by whom on behalf of the office. Training on such policies should be repeated with sufficient regularity that line prosecutors and other relevant staff, including any media relations or public information officers, are familiar with the policies before they ever receive a call from the media. Developing and implementing standard policies will help prosecutors and staff plan for intense media interest in cases of heightened public concern, respond promptly to media inquiries when they arise, and forestall allegations that the office's dissemination of approved information in a high-profile corruption case was politically motivated. Such policies also may counsel prosecutors and law enforcement agents regarding the various consequences that may flow from the unjustified release of information or public statements, which can include

---

47 *Id.* at § 50.2(b)(3)(iv).

48 Justice Manual §§ 1-7.001 to 1-7.900 (U.S. Dep't of Justice 2020), https://www.justice.gov/jm/jm-1-7000-media-relations (last visited Apr. 17, 2021).

dismissal of an indictment,[49] reversal of a conviction,[50] professional discipline,[51] civil liability,[52] and even criminal sanction.[53]

---

49 *See, e.g.*, Bank of Nova Scotia v. United States, 487 U.S. 250, 255-60 (1988) (holding that violations of grand jury secrecy rules could lead to dismissal of an indictment where it "substantially influenced the grand jury's decision to indict" or where "the structural protections of the grand jury have been so compromised as to render the proceedings fundamentally unfair, allowing the presumption of prejudice"); United States v. Walters, No. 16 Cr. 338 (PKC), 2017 U.S. Dist. LEXIS 85478, at *25-31 (S.D.N.Y. Mar. 1, 2017) (entertaining motion to dismiss indictment in light of FBI agent's unauthorized release of grand jury material to the press, but denying it upon finding that the leak did not undermine the "fundamental fairness of the process that resulted in this indictment").

50 *See, e.g.*, Sheppard v. Maxwell, 384 U.S. 333, 340, 362-63 (1966) (setting aside conviction in light of defendant's deprivation of a fair trial due in part to prejudicial extrajudicial statements by members of law enforcement); United States v. Bowen, 799 F.3d 336, 355 (5th Cir. 2015) (granting new trial because of prosecutors' anonymous online postings about defendants).

51 *See, e.g.*, *In re* Brizzi, 962 N.E.2d 1240, 1241 (Ind. 2012) (prosecutor disciplined for public statements that had substantial likelihood of materially prejudicing a proceeding and heightening public condemnation of the accused); Amended Findings of Fact, Conclusions of Law and Order of Discipline at 23, 24, N.C. State Bar v. Nifong, No. 06 DHC 35 (Disciplinary Hearing Comm'n, N.C. State Bar July 24, 2007), http://www.ncbar.gov/Orders/06DHC35.pdf (disbarring former North Carolina District Attorney Michael Nifong for, *inter alia*, his public comments about the evidence and the guilt of the accused in the Duke lacrosse case); Aversa v. United States, 99 F.3d 1200, 1216 (1st Cir. 1996) (referring Assistant United States Attorney to federal and state disciplinary bodies to consider action based on prosecutor's "false, misleading, self-serving, unjust and unprofessional" statements to the press about the defendant).

52 *See, e.g.*, Fattah v. United States, Civ. No. 14-1092, 2017 U.S. Dist. LEXIS 74886, at *1-2 (E.D. Pa. May 17, 2017) (denying government's motion for summary judgment in civil action where government conceded that it had improperly released defendant's tax information); Lauro v. Charles, 219 F.3d 202, 203 (2d Cir. 2000) (holding that intentional staging of a "perp walk" for media consumption, which served no law enforcement purpose, violated the Fourth Amendment and could provide the basis for civil liability but for qualified immunity based on the state of Fourth Amendment law at the time). *But see* Ganek v. Leibowitz, 874 F.3d 73, 77, 80 (2d Cir. 2017) (dismissing claims against federal prosecutors and their supervisors because of qualified immunity despite false information contained in search warrant application that was circulated in the press).

53 *See, e.g.*, *Walters*, 2017 U.S. Dist. LEXIS 85478, at *2 (noting that FBI agent was "currently the subject of a criminal investigation by the [USDOJ's] Public Integrity Section" for leaking grand jury material); Jon Hurdle & Richard Pérez-Peña , *Kathleen Kane, Former Pennsylvania Attorney General, Is Sentenced to Prison*, N.Y. Times (Oct. 24, 2016), https://www.nytimes.com/2016/10/25/us/kathleen-kane-former-pennsylvania-attorney-general-is-sentenced-to-prison.html (recounting conviction of former Pennsylvania Attorney General for illegally disclosing grand jury material to the press and then lying about that disclosure to another grand jury). For further details of the prosecution of Kathleen Kane, see Chapter 1.2.

Office policies may emphasize the need for prosecutors to keep information about ongoing investigations confidential. They also may emphasize the need for prosecutors, once charges have been publicly filed, to avoid characterizing the facts or engaging in rhetoric that suggests a personal opinion of the accused's guilt, tends to unnecessarily heighten public condemnation of the accused, or otherwise would make it difficult for the accused to obtain a fair trial. In general, public statements should not stray from the facts as alleged in the charging document, other publicly filed court documents, and the facts related to the arrest. Pre-conviction press conferences are particularly fraught with danger, and should be approached with caution because they "allow the type of unconstrained and extemporaneous discussion that potentially exacerbates prejudice to defendants . . . ."[54]

In most social media formats, it is difficult to announce charges without characterizing them—and is almost impossible to include the requisite statement that the charges are merely allegations and the accused is presumed innocent until proven guilty. As a result, prosecutors should be careful about using social media in publicizing arrests or charges. Making a brief announcement that a significant action was taken by the prosecutor's office, with a link to a full press release, may be an acceptable approach.

Conclusion

None of the foregoing is meant to suggest that prosecutors should discourage the media from reporting on criminal cases or make it difficult for the public and the media to obtain public information about the prosecutors' activities or priorities. To the contrary, office policies on media relations should facilitate the media's access to public information. Moreover, there is no reason why prosecutors cannot participate in general public dialogue about important matters of public concern, including public corruption. A problem arises only when prosecutors do so in the context of ongoing cases. By consulting ethical rules and professional standards that guide prosecutors' ability to provide information to the media, ensuring that members of their team also understand those limitations, and developing and applying thoughtful media policies for

54 Anthony S. Barkow & Beth George, *Prosecuting Political Defendants*, 44 Ga. L. Rev. 953, 1009 (2010).

their offices, prosecutors can properly balance their ethical duties, a defendant's right to a fair trial, and the public's interest in being kept informed about the administration of criminal justice in matters involving public corruption.

Section Six

Civil & Administrative Enforcement, Asset Forfeiture, & Collateral Consequences of Corruption

Criminal prosecution is only one of several enforcement mechanisms to address corruption. This section describes other avenues for government attorneys to fight corruption.

This section starts with a chapter by the first-ever director of government ethics for the District of Columbia's Board of Ethics and Government Accountability (BEGA), Darrin Sobin. He explains how BEGA and other bodies with similar powers investigate, adjudicate, and penalize corrupt acts.

The second chapter describes some ways to address corruption by bringing civil cases under federal law, focusing on the Racketeer Influenced and Corrupt Organizations (RICO) Act and 42 U.S.C. § 1983. That chapter addresses standing issues that may arise—even for attorney general offices—and profiles several corruption-related cases that used those statutes.

The third chapter summarizes some of the state court remedies that can provide important adjuncts to criminal cases or cases seeking civil fines, including forfeiture of office, forfeiture of pensions, bans on future public employment, cancellation of certificates of formation, and suspension or debarment of a contractor.

The section ends with a chapter by the Chief of the Program Management and Training Unit within the Money Laundering and Asset Recovery Section at the United States Department of Justice, Alice Dery. She discusses why and how to use asset forfeiture in public corruption cases, including how it can be used to provide direct assistance to victims.

Chapter 6.1

Administrative Remedies: How Ethics Boards Deter & Punish Corrupt Behavior

Darrin P. Sobin

Darrin P. Sobin is the chief programs officer for the District of Columbia Bar. Mr. Sobin previously served as D.C.'s first director of government ethics and served in the D.C. Attorney General's Office as a counselor of government ethics and legal ethics. Any opinions or conclusions set forth in this chapter are solely those of the author, Mr. Sobin, and are not attributable to the D.C. Bar or to the D.C. Board of Ethics and Government Accountability.

Introduction

In recent years, efforts by states and local jurisdictions to combat public corruption have expanded beyond traditional criminal investigation and prosecution to include watchdog boards and commissions with authority to impose civil sanctions. These administrative bodies generally are made up of three to seven part-time board members who serve as adjudicators, and a full-time agency director who also investigates and prosecutes the enforcement proceedings. These independent governmental entities typically have three features: (1) the board members serve terms and cannot be removed except for cause; (2) the director has expansive investigatory powers, including subpoena authority; and (3) the board can impose sanctions on wrongdoers, such as public censure or a fine.[1]

In the District of Columbia, the D.C. Board of Ethics and Government Accountability (BEGA) has all three of these features.[2] Prior to BEGA's creation in 2012, redress of a government employee's ethical misconduct in the District was limited. Typically, the local inspector general would investigate to determine if alleged misconduct appeared to be criminal and would decide whether to refer it to a prosecutor's office. If the matter was not accepted for prosecution, the IG's office would prepare a report and forward it to the agency where the malfeasant employee worked for personnel action, such as informal discipline, suspension, or termination. Numerous problems arose with this approach, including inconsistent—and sometimes no—employee discipline across different agencies for the same type of misconduct; no public accountability or transparency, as personnel records are private; and no ability to sanction high-level elected officials. Worse, an employee could avoid discipline by simply resigning or transferring to a different District agency. As a result, ethical misconduct that was not sanctioned criminally or disciplined by an agency where the malfeasant employee continued to work went unaddressed. BEGA was created to fill this gap.[3]

---

1 *See infra* note 2; *see also, e.g.*, *Mission/History*, L.A. City Ethics Comm'n, https://ethics.lacity.org/mission/ (last visited Apr. 22, 2021); *Enforcement*, N.Y.C. Conflicts of Interest Bd., https://www1.nyc.gov/site/coib/the-law/enforcement.page (last visited Apr. 22, 2021); *About the Ohio Ethics Commission*, State of Ohio Ethics Comm'n, http://www.ethics.ohio.gov/about/index.html (last visited Apr. 22, 2021).

2 BEGA was established by the Board of Ethics and Government Accountability Establishment and Comprehensive Ethics Reform Amendment Act of 2011, D.C. Law 19-124 (2012), which is codified at D.C. Code §§ 1-1161.01 to 1-1164.01. Regarding the three features noted in the text, see D.C. Code § 1-1162.02 (establishing BEGA); *id.* § 1-1162.03(j) (setting forth qualifications for board members, including that they can be removed only for good cause); *id.* § 1-1162.11(3) (setting forth powers of the Director of Government Ethics, including subpoena power); *id.* § 1-1162.21 (setting forth potential penalties for violation of the Code of Conduct). Unless otherwise indicated, all citations to statutes and regulations in this chapter refer to the version current at the time of publishing.

3 Robert J. Spagnoletti & Darrin P. Sobin, *The Dawn of Ethics Reform in the District of Columbia Government?*, Washington Lawyer 28, 29 (Apr. 2015), https://www.dcbar.org/getmedia/f28dc6bd-7ae2-42da-984f-0acda8a53a00/WashingtonLawyerApril2015.pdf.

I. Advice

An important component of administrative ethics bodies is the ability to offer training and binding advice. Certainly, effectively preventing ethics violations is more efficient than investigating and punishing violations. Mark Davies, the former Director of the New York Conflicts of Interest Board, would often remark that for any ethics enforcement system to be effective, there needs to be a set of clearly understood and straightforward rules.[4] While ignorance of the law may generally be no excuse, it is easier for an employee to comply with standards that have been explained than it is for them to guess at what the rules might be. As a result, training and advice are an important part of any ethics scheme. This can include providing information about the ethics standards that govern agency employees and the consequences of violating those standards. As part of its mandate to provide ethics advice, BEGA released a plain-language Ethics Manual, which is available online.[5] While general advice (like that contained in an ethics manual) is useful, employees facing ethics questions require more specific guidance. Ethics officials should be cautious and as informed as possible about material facts when offering advice about a specific issue or incident, lest such guidance later be used as a defense to an enforcement action. In the District, a "safe harbor" provision immunizes an employee who is following guidance given by an ethics officer, but the exception applies only if that employee fully and accurately discloses all material facts.[6] Moreover, the safe harbor applies only prospectively.[7] An employee who asks whether past conduct was ethical risks having that query viewed as a confession.

II. Transparency

Public transparency, along with training and advice, is important. The old adage about sunlight being the best disinfectant is true on multiple levels. In

---

4 *Accord* Mark Davies, *Governmental Ethics Laws: Myths and Mythos*, 40 N.Y.L. Sch. L. Rev. 177, 179 (1995).

5 Darrin P. Sobin, Gov't of D.C. Bd. of Ethics and Gov't Accountability, Ethics Manual: The Plain Language Guide to District Government Ethics (Nov. 1, 2014), https://bega.dc.gov/sites/bega/files/publication/attachments/Ethics_Manual_-_11.1.14.pdf [hereinafter D.C. Ethics Manual].

6 *See* D.C. Code § 1-1162.19(d).

7 *Id.* § 1-1162.19(a).

the context of civil ethics enforcement, privacy concerns of employees must be weighed against the public's right to be informed, keeping in mind that ethics complaints might be initiated for political or other ill-intentioned motives. In the District, public disclosure of an investigation occurs through a series of stages. For a preliminary investigation to be initiated, the director must receive an allegation that, if true, would result in an ethics violation.[8] The preliminary investigation, conducted confidentially,[9] involves reviewing records and documents, interviewing witnesses, and seeking an explanation from the alleged offender. Thereafter, the matter becomes public and the identity of the alleged offender is disclosed only if: (1) there is reason to believe an ethics violation has occurred, and (2) public disclosure would not harm any additional investigation by the director.[10] If the investigation results in the filing of ethics charges, the matter becomes public and an open and adversarial hearing ensues.[11] Like most court proceedings, the hearing is open to the public, and there is document production and witness testimony.[12] If the hearing results in a formal adjudication of misconduct and a sanction is imposed, the sanction itself is also likely to be public.[13]

Another area in which transparency is important is the operation of the ethics board itself. In the District, the ethics board must publish ethics opinions and enforcement decisions.[14] BEGA's Director is also required to post online a quarterly report that includes the status of each complaint it received, including if an investigation is ongoing or completed, information about fines and penalties imposed by the board, as well as any allegations that were dismissed, and all political contributions.[15] Not only does this keep the public informed of how tax dollars are being used (i.e., the number of investigations), but there is a public record of each matter that informs citizens of potential ethics problems in the agencies that provide public services. Ultimately, this type of transparency increases the credibility of the ethics body as an entity committed to

---

8 *Id.* § 1-1162.12(a).

9 *Id.* § 1-1162.12(d).

10 *Id.*

11 *Id.* § 1-1162.14(a)(1).

12 *Id.* § 1-1162.14(b) (providing that hearings "shall be of record" and held in accordance with the District's administrative procedures).

13 *Id.* § 1-1162.21.

14 *See id.* § 1-1162.19(b).

15 *Id.* § 1-1162.20.

acting above-board—something that is particularly important given its role in discovering and addressing unethical behavior.

III. Investigations

In this section, we address the important role that investigatory authority plays in enforcement. It begins with the tools available to the ethics body. In the District, BEGA's director has discretion to commence a preliminary investigation and to compel employees and public officials to cooperate with investigations without first consulting the Board.[16] Other tools, like the issuance of subpoenas, require Board approval.[17] Each of these investigative tools, as explained below, helps to ensure that BEGA is able to uncover ethics violations.

A. *Subpoena Authority*

Subpoena authority is critical to obtaining the cooperation of private or other non-governmental entities such as banks, email vendors, or government contractors. Subpoenas can be used both to obtain documents (subpoenas *duces tecum*) and testimony (subpoenas *ad testificandum*), and the BEGA board may petition a court for an order requiring compliance in the event of non-compliance.[18] Subpoenas should generally not be used to obtain records from other governmental entities, however, as overuse within the government could result in lawmakers deauthorizing this powerful tool (mandatory cooperation by officials and government employees is addressed below).

B. *Jurisdiction*

To be most effective, administrative ethics bodies should have jurisdiction over all government employees (subordinate and independent agencies alike), elected officials, members of boards and commissions (paid or unpaid), and, if possible, government contractors. Unfortunately, BEGA does not have

16 *See id.* §§ 1-1162.11(1), (6), 1-1162.12.

17 *See id.* §§ 1-1162.11(3).

18 *See id.* §§ 1-1162.11(3), 1-1162.18.

authority over government contractors,[19] and, as a result, it has been unable to investigate even what may appear to be clear ethical violations by them. With respect to employees, it is important that an ethics body operate outside of the regular employee grievance process often required by union-sponsored collective bargaining agreements. In most instances, a grievance process is triggered by a personnel action (i.e., suspension or termination), so if an ethics body lacks authority to impose personnel-related sanctions, it avoids triggering that grievance process. Instead, sanctions should be limited to civil penalties such as fines or censures.[20]

C. *Mandatory Reporting*

It should be an affirmative obligation for government employees to report credible information about an ethics violation.[21] This is not intended to catch every instance of using a government computer for personal reasons or time and leave abuse, such as late work arrivals or early departures. Rather, it is intended to address the temptation for an agency to withhold allegations of serious misconduct by its employees and to handle the matter internally because of the risk that public disclosure might result in negative publicity.

D. *Mandatory Cooperation*

Cooperation by those with information or evidence is key to a successful investigation. The temptation to resist investigatory efforts because of personal relationships with colleagues or fear of supervisors is very real. As a result, cooperation with an investigation should be mandatory to encourage complete and truthful witness disclosures.[22]

---

19 *See id.* § 1-1162.01a.

20 Rosenblum v. New York City Conflicts Bd., 964 N.E.2d 1010, 1010-11, 1014-15 (N.Y. 2012) (explaining that the New York Conflicts of Interest Board may impose a fine on a tenured teacher for an ethics violation even though the Department of Education is authorized to penalize the employee under separate personnel law for the same act).

21 D.C. Ethics Manual, *supra* note 5, at 8-9 (citing D.C. Mun. Regs. tit. 6B, § 1801.1); *see also* D.C. Mun. Regs. tit. 6B, § 1801.3(k).

22 *See* D.C. Code § 1-1162.11(1); D.C. Mun. Regs. tit. 6B, §§ 1801.2, 1801.3.

E. *No Retaliation*

The other side of compelling employees to report and cooperate is the guarantee that they will not be retaliated against for doing so. While whistleblower laws can be an effective deterrent against retaliation, actions brought by employees under such statutes can be burdensome, expensive, and lengthy. Moreover, the government—not the retaliator—must pay for any judgment or settlement a whistleblower receives. If retaliation is also forbidden in the ethics code, however, it can be efficiently investigated and sanctioned by the same ethics board handling the underlying ethics complaint.[23]

F. *Anonymous Hotline*

Just like compulsory reporting, anonymity encourages the reporting of misconduct.[24] It is important to note, however, that anonymity cannot be guaranteed to those who identify themselves to ethics authorities in the first instance, particularly if they are determined to be necessary witnesses. This is because of the open and adversarial nature of an enforcement hearing, should an investigation proceed to that stage. An accused employee has a limited right to discovery prior to any evidentiary hearing, which includes the names of witnesses who will be called in the proceeding. Although the discovery rules differ across jurisdictions, an ethics prosecutor should carefully consider whether it is necessary to require a complainant who has requested confidentiality to testify, particularly if only hearing witnesses' names must be disclosed. In many instances, ethics violations can be proven either through documentary evidence alone or by witnesses who have not requested confidentiality. If a complainant has exculpatory information, however, disclosure of that information—and perhaps also the complainant's name—is provided by BEGA. While *Brady* v. *Maryland*[25] has been held not to apply in civil cases (and thus is unlikely to apply to administrative ethics proceedings),[26] under the rules that

---

23 *See* D.C. Code § 1-1162.13(d).

24 *See id.* § 1-1162.02(a)(9) (requiring BEGA to establish a telephone hotline to receive anonymous complaints about ethics violations).

25 373 U.S. 83, 87 (1963) (holding that "suppression by the prosecution of evidence favorable to an accused upon request violates due process where the evidence is material either to guilt or to punishment, irrespective of the good faith or bad faith of the prosecution").

26 SEC v. Neil, No. C 14-122 WHA, 2014 U.S. Dist. LEXIS 88223, at *14-15 (N.D. Cal. Jun. 27, 2014); Miles v. City of Pittsburgh, No. 10-1135, 2011 U.S. Dist. LEXIS 99782, at *5 (W.D. Pa. Sept. 6, 2011); SEC v. Pentagon Cap. Mgmt., 08 Civ. 3324, 2010 U.S. Dist. LEXIS 120247, at *3

govern BEGA enforcement proceedings, the director has an obligation to disclose evidence that is "material to the preparation of the respondent's defense."[27] Whether or not this requirement applies elsewhere, it is a better practice to provide exculpatory evidence to those facing ethics charges, in my view, as it ensures they receive a full measure of due process.

G. *Staff*

Finally, any effective ethics entity must have sufficient staff to carry out its functions. In addition to administrative support, attorneys, investigators, and auditors are, in my view, essential.

Because an ethics board often interprets and implements ethics laws and regulations, attorneys should comprise a large portion of the staff. In fact, it is possible that, in some states, prosecuting an ethics matter or providing legal advice concerning ethics rules to government officials and employees would constitute the practice of law.

Investigators, too, are important to have on staff. Investigators are trained to locate and ferret out information from witnesses and to track down necessary documentary evidence. On the criminal side, of course, police and other law enforcement officers serve this role and work with prosecutors. On the administrative enforcement side, law enforcement officers are not available and so investigators are necessary. The temptation to have an attorney act alone as both investigator and prosecutor should be avoided at all costs. This is because attorneys who are the sole witnesses to facts put themselves at risk of being called as necessary witnesses by opposing counsel and, as a result, disqualified from prosecuting the case.[28] In the District of Columbia's ethics board, not only do attorneys and investigators work in tandem, but all witness interviews are electronically recorded.

If resources permit, auditors are also greatly beneficial to an ethics enforcement body. Some ethics entities have no choice but to have auditors on

---

(S.D.N.Y. Nov. 12, 2010).

27 D.C. Mun. Regs. tit. 3, § 5511.3(b).

28 Rule 3.7(a) of the Model Rules of Professional Conduct states that lawyers are, with few exceptions, not permitted to act as advocates at a trial in which they are likely to be "necessary witness[es]." Model Rules of Prof'l Conduct r. 3.7(a) (Am. Bar Ass'n 2020).

staff, especially if statutory duties include auditing.[29] In the District of Columbia, the ethics board is charged not only with enforcement of the ethics laws, but also with oversight of lobbyist activities[30] and yearly financial disclosure statement reporting by government officials.[31] These filings must be reviewed, preferably by auditors who have the skill and experience to review voluminous documentation for irregularities.

H. *Internal Deadlines*

Many ethics entities have deadlines for completing investigations that are either internal and self-imposed for performance measurement purposes or statutorily mandated.[32] In either case, it just makes good sense to have these deadlines. Aside from serving as an effective motivator for staff, deadlines help assure the public that ethics investigations are being handled promptly and professionally. Deadlines also help to keep an investigation focused, give some certainty to complainants and respondents, and thereby prevent the appearance of being politicized or wasteful of taxpayer funds. Indeed, Congress mandated that its own Office of Congressional Ethics complete and close any investigation within forty-five days after a thirty-day preliminary review.[33] In the District, BEGA has a self-imposed, informal deadline of 120 days to complete an investigation and either dismiss it or ask the Board members to issue a charging document. Sometimes, of course, through no fault of the ethics office, an investigation is delayed. The delay may occur because the target of the ethics investigation is also subject to a related civil, criminal, or administrative investigation.[34] When that happens, the ethics case is informally stayed pending resolution in the parallel case. Additionally, when necessary, a closed

---

29 BEGA is charged, for example, with providing the annual auditing of all public financial disclosure reports that are filed. *See* D.C. Code § 1-1162.24(g).

30 *See id.* §§ 1-1162.27 to 1-1162.32.

31 *See id.* §§ 1-1162.24, 1-1162.25.

32 In the District, for example, the Director of Government Ethics generally must present evidence to the Ethics Board concerning a complaint within thirty business days of the initiation of a formal investigation. *See id.* § 1-1162.13(e).

33 U.S. Office of Cong. Ethics, Rules for the Conduct of Investigations r. 7(D), 8(C) (2015) (preliminary review to be completed within thirty calendar days and "second-phase review" to be completed within forty-five calendar days, with a potential fourteen-day extension), https://oce.house.gov/sites/congressionalethics.house.gov/files/OCE_Rules_Conduct_Investigations.pdf.

34 For more on concurrent or parallel proceedings, see Chapter 2.8.

investigation can be re-opened if new facts are discovered as long as the statute of limitations does not bar re-opening.[35]

I. *Coordination with Law Enforcement Authorities*

As most ethics bodies can only impose civil fines, they are not generally considered to be law enforcement entities. While coordination and cooperation between ethics bodies and law enforcement authorities is important, it should be approached with care to avoid jeopardizing either investigation. Turf battles should be avoided at all cost, and ethics bodies should keep in mind that the best penalty for a serious ethics violation or corrupt act is a criminal conviction, regardless of who takes credit. Moreover, because a criminal conviction requires proof beyond a reasonable doubt and criminal cases are often subject to much greater scrutiny than are ethics cases, a criminal prosecution team may be concerned about an ethics investigation unintentionally endangering a related criminal investigation. Certainly, no ethics body or director wants to be accused of tampering with a criminal investigation. As a result, law enforcement authorities, inspectors general, and the like will generally only refer cases to an ethics body when a criminal case is not viable.

When there are parallel investigations,[36] compelled statements in an administrative proceeding or internal investigation can potentially impact criminal prosecutions, although warnings given to the targets may help protect both administrative and criminal investigations. To reduce the risk to a criminal case, ethics prosecutors and investigators may wish to consider giving one of three types of warnings if a parallel criminal case exists or is anticipated.

A *Kalkines* warning is an advisement of rights administered to government employees that compels them to respond to questions or face disciplinary action that could include termination.[37] At the same time, however, the warning waives the government's right to use those statements in a criminal investigation or prosecution.[38] Because a *Kalkines* warning provides for "use immunity" for the statements, a criminal prosecution team even inadvertently exposed to such compelled statements could not use those statements in any way and

---

35 In the District, complaints of ethical misconduct must be made within five years after the discovery of the alleged violation. *See* D.C. Code § 1-1162.13(c).

36 *See* Chapter 2.8 (addressing concurrent or parallel proceedings).

37 Kalkines v. United States, 473 F.2d 1391, 1393-94 (Ct. Cl. 1973).

38 *Id.*

would also have the burden to show that it did not rely on the compelled statement to build its criminal case.[39]

A *Garrity* warning is also an advisement of rights to government employees, but it strikes a slightly different balance between an employee's Fifth Amendment right to remain silent and the employer's right to require answers during an internal investigation.[40] A *Garrity* warning waives the government's right to discipline an employee who chooses not to respond to questions, but permits the use of voluntary statements in a later criminal proceeding against the employee. As a result, information an ethics body obtains after providing a *Garrity* warning to a target could, unless there are state laws to the contrary, generally be later provided to a criminal team conducting a parallel investigation without fear of tainting that investigation.

A *Miranda* warning is the well-known constitutionally required advisement of rights against self-incrimination in criminal matters, and is only required when the target has been arrested.[41] While *Miranda* warnings are not required in ethics investigations, as investigators do not have the power to arrest a target, statements obtained after such warnings could be used in both an ethics case and any subsequent criminal investigation and trial.

In the District of Columbia, BEGA investigators do not give *Kalkines*, *Garrity*, or *Miranda* warnings. This is because BEGA has neither criminal jurisdiction nor personnel authority over government employees and, if possible criminal liability were to be at issue, the matter would be referred to law enforcement. Moreover, in the District, an affirmative ethical obligation requires employees to cooperate with an ethics investigation, whether or not the employee is the subject of the investigation.[42] To be sure, employees who are the subject of an investigation may refuse to answer questions on Fifth Amendment grounds against self-incrimination either during the investigatory or contested hearing stages of a matter.[43] In my experience, the D.C. Ethics Board interprets

---

39 Kastigar v. United States, 406 U.S. 441, 444-45 (1972). *See also* Chapter 2.8, Part III(B)(3).

40 Garrity v. New Jersey, 385 U.S. 493, 500 (1967). For examples of both *Kalkines* and *Garrity* warnings, see Nat'l Ass'n of Letter Carriers, Garrity *and* Kalkines *Warnings*, Postal Record 37, 37 (July 2005), http://www.branch343.org/Contract-Talk/Garrity-Kalkines-Warnings_contlk07_05.pdf.

41 Miranda v. Arizona, 384 U.S. 436, 498-99 (1966).

42 *See* D.C. Code § 1-1162.11(1); D.C. Mun. Regs. tit. 6B, §§ 1801.2, 1801.3.

43 *See* D.C. Code § 1-1162.14(c).

this provision expansively to include not just possible criminal liability but civil liability (i.e., ethics board-imposed fines) as well.

IV. Enforcement Proceedings

In the District of Columbia, a contested ethics proceeding begins at the conclusion of an investigation conducted by the Director of Government Ethics. The Director then drafts a Notice of Violation, which is a detailed charging document, similar to an indictment, that describes the alleged misconduct and includes any ethics provisions that were allegedly violated.[44] The Notice of Violation is provided to the ethics board, which must vote on whether there is reason to believe that a violation has occurred.[45] If the case is approved by the board, the Notice of Violation is then served on the respondent, who must provide a written response.[46] A contested hearing is then scheduled.

Several aspects of BEGA hearings ensure that the respondent receives necessary due process, that hearings are handled efficiently, and that government resources are conserved. One aspect is that the hearings are open and adversarial proceedings.[47] To ensure respondents receive adequate due process, prior to the hearing they receive discovery (including documents that might be used as exhibits) and are provided with the names of witnesses, and both parties have the opportunity to file motions in limine.[48] The hearing itself is either recorded electronically or transcribed by a court reporter, and witnesses testify under oath.[49] The board chairperson presides over the proceeding and rules on admissibility of testimony and exhibits.[50] Like a regular civil or criminal trial, the Director of Government Ethics, as the prosecutor, has the burden of proof: the director must prove by substantial evidence that the respondent violated the District's Code of Conduct.[51] There is direct examination, cross-examination,

---

44 D.C. Mun. Regs. tit. 3, § 5509.1.

45 *See* D.C. Code § 1-1162.14(a)(1).

46 D.C. Mun. Regs. tit. 3, §§ 5508.1, 5509.2.

47 *Accord id.* § 5505.1 (requiring the recording of all meetings).

48 *Id.* §§ 5511.3 (discovery); 5511.8 (pretrial motions).

49 *Id.* §§ 5505.1 (recording); 5517.4 (witnesses under oath).

50 *See, e.g., id.* § 5517.3 (Board Chairperson's authority over cross-examination).

51 *Id.* § 5518.1. The Code of Conduct that BEGA has jurisdiction to enforce is defined by the D.C. Official Code. *See* D.C. Code § 1-1161.01(7). Substantial evidence is "such relevant evidence

and re-direct examination.[52] Opening statements are permitted and a respondent need not testify if doing so would be incriminating.[53] Respondents may be represented by counsel (although they are not entitled to court-appointed counsel if they cannot afford an attorney), or may proceed pro se.[54] Board members also are allowed to ask questions of a witness. The proceeding is open to the public.[55]

As in other administrative proceedings, a certain amount of hearsay is permissible during BEGA hearings.[56] While perhaps not technically a hearsay issue, counsel for respondents will sometimes argue that even documents they agree are authentic and admissible should only be admitted by a sponsoring witness so that the witness can be cross-examined about the contents of those documents. For instance, if a bank statement is offered into evidence to show a deposit on a certain day, the respondent's counsel might agree the bank statement is authentic and admissible, but nonetheless demand a bank employee be called as a witness to be cross examined about it. There is a good argument that the respondent could simply request to publish to the board the relevant portions of the bank statement and make an argument about what conclusions should be drawn from that data. In my opinion, however, the better course is to, when possible, use a sponsoring witness to introduce the document, even if it is the BEGA investigator who reviewed and relied upon the document when making his or her investigatory findings. The respondent would still be free to obtain the testimony of a bank employee if he or she wished to challenge the contents of the bank statement.

A. *Judicious Use of Subpoenas and Witnesses*

Care should be taken to avoid even appearing to abuse subpoena power. Ethics prosecutors and boards that are fortunate enough to have the ability to

---

as a reasonable mind might accept as adequate to support a conclusion." Wash. Canoe Club v. D.C. Zoning Comm'n, 889 A.2d 995, 998 (D.C. 2005) (citation omitted). *See also* § 1-1162.14(b) (applying administrative procedures set forth in D.C. Code §§ 2-501-2-510 to BEGA hearings).

52 D.C. Mun. Regs. tit. 3, § 5517.2.

53 *Id.* § 5517.5(b), (c) (permitting opening statements); D.C. Code § 1-1162.14(c).

54 D.C. Mun. Regs. tit. 3, § 5502.2(d).

55 *See* D.C. Code § 1-1162.15(a) (referring to the proceeding as "adversary . . . and open").

56 D.C. Mun. Regs. tit. 3, § 5507.11 ("The [Ethics] Board may admit hearsay evidence during an adversarial hearing if it determines it will be relevant and material to the resolution of any factual issue in dispute in the matter before the Board.").

issue subpoenas should serve them only when necessary. In many jurisdictions, government employees are required to cooperate with investigations, which includes appearing as a witness in a hearing,[57] so they need not be subpoenaed. Subpoenas should be issued as a matter of course for private citizens, however, to ensure their appearance at a proceeding. Special care should be taken with a respondent's request for witness subpoenas, however. While the respondent should be permitted to use subpoenas to secure the testimony of necessary witnesses, subpoena power should not be used to waste time or needlessly present cumulative evidence.[58] If a respondent wishes to subpoena a multitude of witnesses and the evidentiary purpose of such witnesses is not clear, the ethics board may consider denying the request if the respondent cannot make a proffer as to the witnesses' anticipated testimony or why it would be material to his case.

B. *Incentives to Settle/Negotiated Dispositions*

In the District of Columbia, the ethics board has the authority to dispose of a case in three ways: dismissal;[59] a finding of misconduct (after a contested proceeding);[60] or, where facts are not in dispute, through a settlement agreement known as a "negotiated disposition."[61] Typically, a negotiated disposition will either occur at the outset of an investigation, if the matter is simple and facts are undisputed, or after an investigation concludes but before the matter is charged through a Notice of Violation.[62] The negotiated disposition sets forth in writing the undisputed facts and the ethics provision that was violated.[63] It also includes an agreed-upon sanction.[64] It is signed by the director/prosecutor and the respondent before being presented to the ethics board for approval.

---

57 *See* D.C. Mun. Regs. tit. 6B, § 1801.3 ("An employee shall fully cooperate with any investigation, enforcement action, or other official function of the Office of Government Ethics."). This regulation, which is a provision in the District Personnel Manual, is an enforceable part of the Code of Conduct. *See* D.C. Code § 1-1161.01(7)(E).

58 *Accord* Fed. R. Evid. 403 (permitting courts to exclude relevant evidence if its probative value is substantially outweighed by, for example, the danger of undue delay, wasting time, or the needless presentation of cumulative evidence).

59 D.C. Code §§ 1-1162.15(a)(4), 1-1162.16(a).

60 *Id.* § 1-1162.15(a)(1).

61 *Id.* § 11162.21(a)(4)(A)(v); D.C. Mun. Regs. tit. 3, § 5902.

62 *Accord* D.C. Mun. Regs. tit. 3, § 5902.2 ("The Director of Government Ethics or respondent can initiate a negotiated disposition at any point after an investigation has been opened by the Director and prior to the issuance of a final Order of the Ethics Board.").

63 *Id.* § 5902.11(a).

64 *Id.* § 5902.11(b).

Several compelling reasons may incentivize a respondent to enter into a negotiated disposition. First, the respondent has the opportunity to help frame the narrative in the negotiated disposition through consultation and negotiation with the director. Although the negotiated disposition is public, it avoids the issuance of a notice of violation, which does not include the respondent's version of the events. Second, a negotiated disposition avoids a potentially embarrassing and costly public proceeding for the respondent. Third, there is some certainty with respect to a possible sanction because the director and the respondent agree to a specific penalty and then together recommend its approval by the board. In its first five years of operations in the District, the ethics board did not once reject a proposed negotiated disposition.

V. Imposition of Sanctions

If it finds that the respondent committed an ethics violation, the ethics body must then determine what, if any, sanction to impose. As described below, the penalties that the board can impose include fines and restitution and non-financial penalties like community service.[65] Alternatively, the board can decide to impose no penalty at all, particularly if criminal sanctions are sufficient.[66] Finally, the board has discretion to permit a remorseful ethics violator to expunge the record of a low-level violation.[67] Most important though, and as further set out below, is that the board has authority to compel compliance with its sanctions including wage garnishment, property attachment, or contempt proceedings in court.

A. *Fines*

In the District of Columbia, the ethics board may impose fines of up to $5,000 per violation or, in the case of an unlawful gift or contribution, to triple the amount of the unlawful funds.[68] The multiplier is important because it takes

---

65 D.C. Code § 1-1162.21(a)(1), (3).

66 *Accord id.* § 1-1162.15(a)(2), (3) (ethics board has power to refer matter to the D.C. U.S. Attorney or D.C. Attorney General for enforcement or prosecution).

67 *See, e.g., id.* § 1-1162.21(a)(4)(A)(iv) (noting respondent may seek expungement after successful completion of probation); D.C. Mun. Regs. tit. 3, § 5902.16 (providing procedure for subject of a negotiated disposition to apply for expungement).

68 *See* D.C. Code § 1-1162.21(a)(1).

away any incentive for a wrongdoer to view the $5,000 maximum fine as simply the cost of doing business when an improper gift might far exceed that amount. As an example, in one recent ethics board case, a public official was convicted of taking a $50,000 bribe.[69] Theoretically, the ethics board could have imposed a fine of $150,000, which is substantial by any measure. That upper limit allowed the board to negotiate a settlement with the official that was much more than $5,000.[70] Once the board imposes a fine (or approves a negotiated disposition with a fine attached), it is expected that the respondent will immediately satisfy that amount. Of course, that does not always happen, so it is important that any order imposing fines be converted into a court judgment. In the District, the ethics board may file a petition for enforcement in Superior Court.[71]

B. *Restitution*

Normally, if a matter is serious enough to warrant restitution, then a fine will also be levied. In the District, there is only one ethics provision that makes restitution mandatory.[72] That occurs in cases of nepotism. When nepotism is discovered, the improperly hired relative is immediately fired and the hiring government employee/relative is required to refund every penny of salary paid to the improperly hired relative.[73] In one case handled in the District, this amounted to six months of wages, or roughly $26,000. As with fines, restitution orders can be converted to court judgments.

C. *Collecting on Judgments*

The old adage that only suckers pay judgments is as relevant today as it was when the debtors prisons closed more than 100 years ago. Fortunately, BEGA has several options to collect on judgments:

---

69 *See* Negotiated Disposition, *In re* M. Brown, No. 1057-001, 1 (D.C. Bd. of Ethics & Gov't Accountability July 8, 2015), https://bega.dc.gov/sites/bega/files/publication/attachments/1057-001_-_M.Brown-Negotiated_Disposition_Redacted.pdf.

70 *Id.* at 2 ($12,000 fine).

71 *See* D.C. Code § 1-1162.21(a)(5)(A).

72 *See* D.C. Mun. Regs. tit. 6B, § 1806.5.

73 *Id.* § 1806.4 ("Any hiring decision secured or effectuated in violation of this section shall be rescinded immediately."); *id.* § 1806.5 ("[A] public official who violates" the regulation forbidding nepotism "shall pay restitution to the District of Columbia for any gains received by the relative.").

1. Garnishment

For respondents who remain employed by the District following an ethics violation, it is relatively easy to work with the payroll office to garnish their wages until the fine or restitution amount is satisfied. If the respondent is no longer employed by the District, the two options are: (1) withhold part or all of the employee's last paycheck and apply it to the fine amount; and/or (2) withhold any unused vacation leave rather than permitting the employee to "cash it in." In the District, and perhaps in other jurisdictions, withholding an employee's retirement pay to satisfy a judgment is not permitted.[74]

2. Attachment of Property

Most jurisdictions have special laws and regulations governing the ability to attach real or personal property to satisfy a judgment.[75] Again, it is recommended that ethics bodies work with their attorney general's office or other appropriate government entity to determine if attachment is a viable option for collecting on an outstanding judgment.

3. Contempt

In the District, the ethics board's establishment legislation permits it to request that a respondent with an unpaid judgment be held in contempt of court and incarcerated.[76] This is based on similar legislation to allow parents who owe child support to be incarcerated until they bring their payments up to date.[77] This is a remedy of last resort and to date has not been utilized. It remains, however, a powerful incentive for a respondent to satisfy any unpaid fines.

---

74 *See* D.C. Code § 1-629.04(d).

75 *See, e.g.*, D.C. Code §§ 16-501 to 16-533 (DC attachment and garnishment statutes).

76 *See* D.C. Code § 1-1162.21(a)(5)(c) (nonpayment punishable by contempt of court); D.C. Code § 11-944 (describing power of Superior Court judges to punish contempt of court, including with imprisonment).

77 Notably, the Supreme Court has required, in the child support context, "procedures that assure a fundamentally fair determination of the critical incarceration-related question, whether the [alleged contemnor] is able to comply with the [court] order." Turner v. Rogers, 564 U.S. 431, 435 (2011). Presumably, a similar analysis would be required before incarcerating a respondent for not complying with a judgment requiring him to pay an ethics fine.

D. *Non-Monetary Sanctions*

Fines are not the only way to punish ethics violations. Many factors go into deciding a proper sanction. Claims of ignorance of the law are very common, and it can be difficult to prove that the respondent intended to commit an ethics violation. In those cases and others with mitigating factors, alternatives to fines like the following should be considered:

1. Community Service

In the District, a respondent can be required to provide a certain number of hours of community service. This can be imposed by itself or in combination with other sanctions.[78]

2. Public Censure or Admonition

The board can make a finding that the respondent violated an ethics rule without imposing a fine or other financial penalty. This censure or admonition is published on the ethics board's website.[79]

3. Non-Public Informal Admonition

This is more akin to a warning letter, in that it advises respondents that they committed an ethics violation but that no other sanction will be imposed.[80] It is confidential and is not published on the website nor is it otherwise publicly available. It is available only for the lowest-level violations, such as a one-time minor misuse of government property.[81]

E. *No Penalty: Criminal Sanctions Are Sufficient*

As stated earlier, a criminal conviction is the best outcome for any serious ethics violation. That being said, criminal penalties do not have to be the

---

78 *See* D.C. Code § 1-1162.21(e) (explaining that "all equitable remedies at law shall be available for violations of the Code of Conduct, which may be in addition to any civil penalty prescribed in this chapter"); D.C. Mun. Regs. tit. 3, § 5902.12(g) (community service as a sanction for a negotiated disposition).

79 *See* D.C. Code § 1-1162.21(a)(4)(A)(ii).

80 *Id.* § 1-1162.21(a)(4)(A)(iii).

81 *Id.* § 1-1162.21(a)(4)(A)(iii)(I).

only sanction. While an ethics body should be sensitive to perceptions it has "piled on" by bringing ethics allegations against, for example, a defendant who received a lengthy sentence of incarceration and substantial financial penalties, there are some good reasons for imposing administrative sanctions as well. First, if the criminal penalty is simply inadequate to account for the misconduct, an administrative sanction may ensure that the ethics violator is properly held accountable. Second, in cases in which the government has lost property or resources and no restitution was ordered in the criminal case, restitution can be sought before the ethics board. However, in many cases that come before the ethics board in the District that resulted in criminal prosecution, the board tends to close the matter without further inquiry or sanction.[82]

F. *Expungement*

On the other end of the spectrum is the board's ability to expunge someone's record of an ethics violation.[83] In my experience, this is generally considered long after a matter has ended, and is usually granted only for low-level violations in which an individual has paid any fines and restitution, is genuinely remorseful, and has not committed any additional ethics violations.

Conclusion

The foregoing is intended to offer guidance with respect to administrative options to combating government corruption. The ethics board approach is not intended to replace criminal enforcement, but it, importantly, fills a gap created when a criminal prosecutor declines prosecution and a government personnel authority declines to impose discipline on an employee. To that end, an independent ethics body can ensure that employees across agencies of state and local governments are held to the same high ethical standards, which helps to establish and maintain a culture of ethical conduct and to increase citizens' trust in their government.

---

82 *Accord id.* § 1-1162.15(a).

83 *See id.* § 1-1162.21(a)(4)(A)(iv).

Chapter 6.2

Civil Corruption Enforcement in Federal Court: Using § 1983 & RICO to Fight Corruption

Amie N. Ely

Amie N. Ely is the Director of the Center for Ethics & Public Integrity, National Attorneys General Training & Research Institute, National Association of Attorneys General.

Introduction

Some attorney general offices have successfully used federal civil actions to hold corrupt officials accountable. In this chapter, we analyze federal court standing requirements for AGOs and examine several enforcement actions under two statutes: 42 U.S.C. § 1983 and the Racketeer Influenced and Corruption Organizations Act, or RICO (18 U.S.C. §§ 1961-1968). Each of these statutes has been successfully used by AGOs to address corruption.

I. Federal Court Standing

An AGO must have standing to bring any case in federal court.[1] While states are "not normal litigants for the purposes of invoking federal jurisdiction" and are entitled to "special solicitude" in the standing analysis,[2] they still must show an injury-in-fact. That requirement can be met by harm to any of the following kinds of interests: (1) proprietary or financial interests, (2) *parens patriae*, and (3) sovereign interests.[3]

First, an AGO has standing to seek redress for harms to the state's own proprietary or financial interests. For this form of lawsuit, a state need only meet the "ordinary demands of Article III" by establishing "injury-in-fact, causation and redressability."[4] If, for example, a politician's misdeeds both violated a federal statute and resulted in direct harm to the public fisc, an AGO should typically have standing to bring a civil case against that politician seeking repayment to the state for the financial harm directly caused by the misdeeds.[5]

Second, AGOs may have *parens patriae* standing to bring suit. "States can bring actions *in parens patriae* where there they have (1) a quasi-sovereign interest, (2) an interest apart from the interests of private parties, and (3) injury to a sufficiently substantial segment of their population."[6] As the Supreme Court explained in greater depth, to bring a *parens patriae* suit on behalf of its citizens, "the State must articulate an interest apart from the interests of particular private parties, *i.e.*, the State must be more than a nominal party. The State must express a quasi-sovereign interest."[7] That interest can be "in the health

---

1 Chapman v. Tristar Prods., Inc., 940 F.3d 299, 307 (6th Cir. 2019); Rosenblum v. John Does 1-10, No. 3:20-cv-01161-MO, 2020 U.S. Dist. LEXIS 132517, *3 (D. Ore. July 25, 2020).

2 Massachusetts v. EPA, 549 U.S. 497, 518, 520 (2007).

3 Maryland v. United States, 360 F. Supp. 3d 288, 308-09 (D. Md. 2019) (citing Texas v. United States, 809 F.3d 134, 152-55 (5th Cir. 2015), *aff'd by an equally divided court*, 136 S. Ct. 2271 (2016)).

4 Gov't of Manitoba v. Bernhardt, 923 F.3d 173, 178 (D.C. Cir. 2019) (citing West v. Lynch, 845 F.3d 1228, 1230 (D.C. Cir. 2017)).

5 *Accord* Alfred L. Snapp & Son, Inc. v. Puerto Rico, 458 U.S. 592, 601-02 (1982).

6 Washington v. Geo Grp., Inc., 283 F. Supp. 3d 967, 978 (W.D. Wash. 2017) (citing *Snapp*, 458 U.S. at 607). At least one court has treated *parens patriae* as separate from the quasi-sovereign interest. *See* Dist. of Columbia v. Trump, 291 F. Supp. 3d 725, 735-36 (D. Md. 2018).

7 *Snapp*, 458 U.S. at 607.

and well-being—both physical and economic—of its residents in general."[8] More specifically, the injury to its citizens must be of the type "that the State, if it could, would likely attempt to address through its sovereign lawmaking powers."[9] While the Court has not specified precisely what proportion of the state's citizens must be impacted by such an injury, it must be "a sufficiently substantial segment of its population."[10] Courts have also suggested that *parens patriae* is a doctrine that must be invoked explicitly.[11]

Courts have thus concluded that a complaint alleging injury to just a handful of specific citizens will be insufficient to provide an AGO with standing to sue,[12] as will a complaint seeking payment of damages directly to citizens who were allegedly injured by a defendant.[13] Moreover, while a state has a generalized interest in combatting fraud, it must show injury or threatened injury to citizens inside its own borders to have standing to seek redress.[14]

Third, the state has standing to protect its sovereign interest in "the power to create and enforce a legal code, both civil and criminal,"[15] which includes defending the constitutionality of state statutes and attacking federal regulatory action that would preempt state law.[16] Notably, states do not have a sovereign interest in enforcing federal law; that right belongs to the United States alone.[17]

---

8 *Id.*

9 *Id.*

10 *Id.*

11 Lynch v. Nat'l Prescription Adm'rs, Inc., 787 F.3d 868, 873 (8th Cir. 2015) (collecting cases).

12 Illinois v. Life of Mid-America Ins. Co., 805 F.2d 763, 766-67 (7th Cir. 1986) (dismissing RICO case brought by Illinois AGO for lack of standing).

13 New York v. Seneci, 817 F.2d 1015, 1017-18 (2d Cir. 1987) (dismissing RICO case brought by New York AGO for lack of standing).

14 Utah Div. of Consumer Prot. v. Stevens, 398 F. Supp. 3d 1139, 1145-46 (D. Utah 2019). Notably, this case involved a federal telemarketing statute that explicitly provided AGOs with the power to bring a civil action against telemarketers in federal court; the court determined that such a statute did not, itself, fulfill the standing requirement under the facts of the case. *Id.* at 1145, 1147-48.

15 *Snapp*, 458 U.S. at 601.

16 Va. House of Delegates v. Bethune Hill, 139 S. Ct. 1945, 1951 (2019) (state attorney general has standing to defend constitutionality of state statute, under that state's law); Wyo. *ex rel.* Crank v. United States, 539 F.3d 1236, 1242 (10th Cir. 2008) ("Federal regulatory action that preempts state law creates a sufficient injury-in-fact . . . ." (collecting cases)).

17 *Utah Div. of Consumer Prot.*, 398 F. Supp. 3d at 1144 (holding that "although the State's sovereign interest in enforcing its own laws may give it standing to assert its state law claims, the

Some federal statutes, however, expressly grant AGOs authority to seek restitution for their citizens, including those grounded in consumer protection.[18] For example, 15 U.S.C. § 15c explicitly grants attorneys general the right to bring a civil action, as *parens patriae*, to secure monetary relief for antitrust violations.[19] Courts have also generally permitted AGOs to prove *parens patriae* standing under a variety of federal statutes that lack a provision authorizing states to sue.[20]

II. Section 1983

Section 1983 provides a cause of action for "the deprivation of any rights, privileges, or immunities secured by the Constitution and laws" of the United States.[21] When a case "is grounded on a protection of the Fourteenth Amendment or on one of the protections of the Bill of Rights, the appropriateness of § 1983 for redress is unlikely to be questioned."[22]

Several AGOs have used § 1983 against individual police officers, their offices, and/or the towns that oversee them, typically under a *parens patriae* theory of standing, for ongoing violations of citizens' constitutional rights.[23]

---

sovereign interest in enforcing the Telemarketing Act belongs to the United States, not Utah").

18 Federal statutes include 15 U.S.C. § 15c (2020) (authorizing AGO suit for violations of federal antitrust law); *id.* § 1679h(c)(1) (authorizing suit by a state's "chief law enforcement officer" for violations of federal law governing credit repair organizations); *id.* § 1681s(c) (authorizing suit by a state's "chief law enforcement officer" against credit reporting agencies); *id.* § 5712(a) (authorizing AGO suit against pay-per-call services); *id.* § 6103(a) (authorizing AGO suit against telemarketers); *id.* § 6309(c) (authorizing suit by a state's "chief law enforcement officer" to enforce professional boxing safety requirements); *id.* § 7804(a)(1) (authorizing AGO suit against sports agents for violating certain federal laws); *id.* § 6504(a)(1) (authorizing AGO suit to enforce laws protecting children's online privacy); *id.* § 7706(f)(1) (authorizing AGO suit against violators of federal laws addressing "spam" emails). Margaret Lemos, *Aggregate Litigation Goes Public: Representative Suits by State Attorneys General*, 126 Harv. L. Rev. 486, 496 n.39 (2012).

19 15 U.S.C. § 15c(a)(1) (2020).

20 Jason Mazzone & Stephen Rushin, *State Attorneys General as Agents of Police Reform*, 69 Duke L.J. 999, 1042-43 (2020). *But see* Illinois v. Life of Mid-America Ins. Co., 805 F.2d 763, 766 (7th Cir. 1986) (suggesting in dicta "it is not clear to us that Congress, in enacting the RICO statute, intended to permit . . . a *parens patriae* proceeding").

21 42 U.S.C. § 1983 (2020).

22 Joseph G. Cook & John L. Sobieski, Jr., Civil Rights Actions ¶ 7.06 (2019).

23 *See, e.g.*, Mazzone & Rushin, *supra* note 20, at 1030-31. *See also* Chapter 1.8, Part IV(B)

The Third Circuit Court of Appeals is the only federal appellate court to have considered whether *parens patriae* standing is available to AGOs seeking to use § 1983 to enjoin corrupt police departments;[24] as discussed below, that court concluded that the AGO did have standing.[25]

A. *Pennsylvania AGO Case Against Borough of Millvale Police Officers*

In *Pennsylvania* v. *Porter*, the Pennsylvania AGO brought a federal civil case under § 1983 against several officials in the Borough of Millvale—including a police officer named Frank Baranyai, the chief of police, the borough council, and the mayor—alleging that Baranyai was violating the rights of citizens in that town to be "free from physical violence, mistreatment, threats, harassment, illegal detention, illegal arrests, and illegal searches and seizures."[26] After a bench trial, the court enjoined Baranyai and his codefendants from continuing the complained-of abuse of authority.[27]

In concluding that the AGO had *parens patriae* standing, the Third Circuit Court of Appeals noted its substantial sovereign interest in, *inter alia*: (1) preventing the "lawless exercises of the powers its laws confer upon police officers hired by its subdivisions;" (2) addressing the risk that public confidence in these subdivisions would be undermined if local officials did not property discharge their duties; and (3) averting physical abuse of its citizens by a corrupt policeman, which it concluded were "no different in kind from the Commonwealth's interest in preventing poisoning by toxic waste or maiming by unsafe automobiles."[28]

The court also noted that the AGO argued persuasively that it was a particularly apt plaintiff because: (1) individual victims would likely be able to seek only damages, not an injunction; (2) the costs to an individual victim to investigate and litigate a lawsuit was likely substantial and would deter bringing such a

---

(describing consent decree entered into by Illinois AGO and Chicago Police Department).

24 *See* Mazzone & Rushin, *supra* note 20, at 1044.

25 Pennsylvania v. Porter, 659 F.2d 306, 316 (3d Cir. 1981) (en banc). *But see id.* at 333-34 (Garth, J., concurring in part and dissenting in part).

26 *Id.* at 309.

27 Pennsylvania v. Porter, 480 F. Supp. 686, 705 (W.D. Pa. 1979), *aff'd in part and rev'd in part*, 659 F.2d at 325.

28 *Porter*, 659 F.2d at 315; *see also Porter*, 480 F. Supp. at 694-95.

case; and (3) the risk of intimidation and retribution in police misconduct cases was high and would also act as a deterrent to individual victims.[29]

B. *New York AGO Case Against the Town of Wallkill*

In a case the federal district court judge described as "strikingly similar" to *Pennsylvania* v. *Porter*, the New York AGO sought injunctive relief against, and the imposition of a federal monitor over, police in the Town of Wallkill.[30] The New York AGO alleged the Wallkill police engaged in systemic misconduct, including by "routinely and openly us[ing] their powers to target women, critics, and perceived enemies of the Department, by making traffic stops without having reasonable suspicion to do so and by committing various acts of harassment, all in violation of the federal and state law."[31]

The court found, among other things, that the injunctive relief sought by the AGO would protect both current and future potential victims; and that private plaintiffs would face substantial legal, financial, and practical burdens to bringing suit.[32] As a result, the court easily concluded that the state had *parens patriae* standing and that the court had the power to enter the consent decree.[33]

C. *Illinois AGO Case Against the City of Chicago*

More recently, the Illinois AGO brought a § 1983 action against the City of Chicago alleging its police engaged in a repeated pattern of using excessive force in a way that disproportionately harmed the city's minority residents.[34] Like Pennsylvania and New York before it, the Illinois AGO sought to enjoin the police from future unconstitutional law enforcement practices. The AGO relied upon evidence that included a U.S. Department of Justice report finding that there was a pattern or practice of the unconstitutional use of force and that the accountability mechanisms by the city were inadequate and significantly

---

29 *Porter*, 659 F.2d at 315-16.

30 New York v. Town of Wallkill, 01-Civ-0364 (CM), 2001 U.S. Dist. LEXIS 13364, at *1, *9 (S.D.N.Y. Mar. 16, 2001).

31 *Id.* at *2.

32 *Id.* at *17-21.

33 *Id.* at *21-22.

34 Illinois v. City of Chicago, 912 F.3d 979, 981-82 (7th Cir. 2019); Illinois v. City of Chicago, No. 17-cv-6260, 2019 U.S. Dist. LEXIS 15360, at *3 (N.D. Ill. Jan. 31, 2019). For more information about this case, see Chapter 1.8, Part IV(B).

contributed to the repeated constitutional violations.[35] And like its counterpart in New York, the Illinois AGO entered into a consent decree that provided forward-looking, injunctive relief.[36]

III. Civil RICO

Local and state governments have filed suits against corrupt officials under the federal RICO Act.[37] Congress passed RICO to provide new weapons to address organized crime—and, in particular, its infiltration of legitimate businesses.[38] Congress directed courts to construe RICO liberally to achieve its remedial purpose,[39] and while organized crime was the impetus for the Act, the statute is "not limited in application to organized crime."[40]

RICO is notoriously complex and the caselaw in one circuit may require dismissal of a case that in another circuit would survive. Accordingly, any AGO considering using this powerful tool should research and wield it carefully and expect vigorous pretrial motion practice.[41] One AGO enforcement action against a corrupt mayor and his cronies, discussed below, illustrates a generally successful use of this statute to fight corruption. An enforcement action against

---

35 *City of Chicago*, 2019 U.S. Dist. LEXIS 15360, at *3-4.

36 *Id.* at *27. Earlier in the case, the district court suggested that the AGO likely had *parens patriae* standing to advance its § 1983 claim, which it confirmed in its decision entering the consent decree. *Id.* at *24; Illinois v. City of Chicago, No. 17-cv-6260, 2018 U.S. Dist. LEXIS 139061, *35-37 (N.D. Ill. Aug. 16, 2018) ("The Court need not definitively resolve at this time any issues regarding [the Illinois AGO's] standing, as those issues remain underdeveloped on the current record.").

37 *See, e.g.*, Alan Vinegrad, Note, *Government Corruption and Civil RICO: Providing Compensation for Intangible Losses*, 58 N.Y.U. L. Rev. 1530, 1533 & nn.17-18 (1983) (collecting cases); Twp. of Marlboro v. Scannapieco, 545 F. Supp. 2d 452, 455 (D.N.J. 2008).

38 *See, e.g.*, G. Robert Blakey, *Time-Bars: RICO—Criminal and Civil—Federal and State*, 88 Notre Dame L. Rev. 1581, 1595 (2013).

39 *Id.* at 1598 & n.29 (citation omitted).

40 Nat'l Org. for Women, Inc. v. Scheidler, 510 U.S. 249, 260 (1994) (quoting H.J. Inc. v. Nw. Bell Tel. Co., 492 U.S. 229, 248 (1989) (internal quotation marks omitted)).

41 Perhaps because of its complexity and power, federal prosecutors can only charge criminal RICO with the approval of the Organized Crime and Gang Section of the USDOJ. Justice Manual § 9-110. 210 (U.S. Dep't of Justice 2020), https://www.justice.gov/jm/jm-9-110000-organized-crime-and-racketeering#9-110.210.

a former governor exemplifies some of the challenges an AGO might face in bringing a federal RICO case against a corrupt official.

A. *RICO Requirements*

The USDOJ has published a lengthy manual that provides a comprehensive overview of civil RICO requirements for federal government attorneys.[42] While some aspects of that guidance are inapplicable to state AGOs—such as the requirement that USDOJ's Organized Crime and Gang Section review charging documents before they are filed[43] or the use of civil investigative demands under 18 U.S.C. § 1968[44]—the manual provides a comprehensive overview of how to investigate and litigate a RICO case, as well as examples of successful cases prosecuted by the USDOJ.

1. Statutory Elements

To succeed on a civil RICO claim, a plaintiff "must show that the defendants were responsible for the '(1) conduct (2) of an enterprise (3) through a pattern (4) of racketeering activity.'"[45] A *pattern* of racketeering activity means at least two "predicate acts" within a particular time period.[46] Predicate acts are, in turn, defined by statute, and include violations of state law, including—of particular interest to the anticorruption enforcer—bribery and extortion;[47] a number of acts indictable under federal law, including various fraud and obstruction offenses, violations of the Hobbs Act,[48] money laundering, and

---

42 Civil RICO: A Manual for Federal Attorneys (U.S. Dep't of Justice 2007) (referring to the Organization Crimes and Racketeering Section, which is now the Organized Crime and Gang Section), https://www.justice.gov/sites/default/files/usam/legacy/2014/10/17/civrico.pdf.

43 *Id.* at 6-8.

44 *Id.* at 114-29.

45 Cullen v. Margiotta, 811 F.2d 698, 712-13 (2d Cir. 1987) (quoting Sedima, S.P.R.L. v. Imrex Co., 473 U.S. 479, 496 (1985) (footnote omitted)).

46 18 U.S.C. § 1961(5) (2018); *see also Cullen*, 811 F.2d at 713.

47 18 U.S.C. § 1961(1)(A).

48 *Id.* at § 1951(a) (criminalizing interference with interstate commerce, robbery, and extortion).

illegal money transmission;[49] illegal acts related to labor organizations and unions;[50] and securities fraud.[51]

2. Standing

Unlike some federal statutes,[52] RICO does not provide explicit authority for AGOs to sue, but instead appears to treat them similarly to other private plaintiffs. As a result, an AGO must show (1) that the state has suffered an injury; and (2) "that this injury was caused by the predicate acts of racketeering activity that make up the violation of § 1962."[53] If there is no link between the injury the state suffered and a predicate racketeering act, an AGO will not have standing to pursue a racketeering case.[54]

The general standing analysis discussed above applies in RICO cases. Courts have been amenable to two standing arguments from state or local government plaintiffs in civil RICO corruption cases: (1) a defendant's misappropriation of funds from a state-administered or state-funded account directly injured the state;[55] or (2) under *parens patriae*, a "state's interest in protecting the right of its citizens to honest and impartial government officials is substantial: although the losses to individual citizens are perhaps de minimis, the collective loss suffered when government entities are operated through illegality and corruption is significant."[56] This more expansive definition of injury does not, however, relieve the state from its burden to show that the injury for which it seeks recompense was caused by a predicate act, and to allege both that predicate act and the injury that flowed from it.[57]

---

49 *Id.* at § 1961(1)(B).

50 *Id.* at § 1961(1)(C). For more on union-related corruption, see Chapter 1.6.

51 *Id.* at § 1961(1)(D).

52 *See supra* note 18 (collecting statutes).

53 Brandenburg v. Seidel, 859 F.2d 1179, 1187 (4th Cir. 1988).

54 *See id.* ("a civil RICO complaint is vulnerable to a motion to dismiss if it fails to allege either an adequate injury . . . or an adequate causal nexus between that injury and the predicate acts of racketeering activity alleged" (citations omitted)); *see also* discussion *infra* Part III(C)(2) regarding West Virginia v. Moore, 895 F. Supp. 864, 866 (S.D.W. Va. 1995).

55 *See, e.g.*, Missouri v. W.E.R., 55 F.3d 350, 356-57 (8th Cir. 1995).

56 Vinegrad, *supra* note 37, at 1547. While some courts have found this to be an "injury," others have not. *See, e.g.*, *West Virginia*, 895 F. Supp. at 870-71.

57 *See, e.g.*, City of New York v. Jam Consultants, 889 F. Supp. 103, 105 (S.D.N.Y. 1995); *Moore*, 895 F. Supp. at 868-70.

Knotty standing issues can arise in RICO cases. AGOs should carefully research standing requirements in their circuits and their federal district courts early in an investigation to ensure that they can build, charge, and litigate a successful case. As an example, one court concluded that a municipal government's interest in its "general economy" or "ability to carry out its functions" is not a sufficient injury for RICO purposes, but that a direct injury to its business or property—including its right to recover salary payments to an employee who fails to perform his duties or performs corruptly—does provide standing.[58] Had the plaintiff alleged only the injury to the general economy, for example, rather than investigating and being prepared to prove the salary paid to the defendant, this aspect of the case would likely have been dismissed. Similarly, in *Illinois v. Life of Mid-America Insurance Co.*, the Seventh Circuit Court of Appeals dismissed a RICO case brought by the Illinois AGO for lack of standing, concluding that the complaint did not allege an injury to the interest of the state, but only to eight specific consumers.[59] Had that AGO instead also alleged that a wider range of consumers faced an ongoing risk of injury from the defendant, the result may have been different.

3. Interstate Nexus

Finally, an AGO must also show that the enterprise or its activities has some nexus with interstate commerce.[60] This is typically a rather low bar. In one case, a private plaintiff alleged that the RICO defendants participated in a scheme to require workers to contribute to a corrupt political machine to be considered for promotions.[61] The Second Circuit Court of Appeals concluded that the plaintiff showed a sufficient effect on interstate commerce:

---

58 *City of New York*, 889 F. Supp. at 105 (quoting Town of West Hartford v. Operation Rescue, 915 F.2d 92, 104 (2d Cir. 1990)). *But see infra* Part III(C)(2)(b).

59 Illinois v. Life of Mid-America Ins. Co., 805 F.2d 763, 766-67 (7th Cir. 1986). The court also suggested in dicta that it was not clear if Congress intended for states to enforce RICO as *parens patriae*. *Id. But see* New York v. Mid Hudson Med. Grp., P.C., 877 F. Supp. 143, 146 (S.D.N.Y. 1995) (collecting cases where "the statute the attorneys general sued under did not specifically give them standing" but standing was found). One commentator has suggested that Congress amend RICO to explicitly provide standing to state AGOs. Beth S. Schipper, Note, *Civil RICO and* Parens Patriae: *Lowering Litigation Barriers Through State Intervention,* 24 Wm. & Mary L. Rev. 429, 449 (1983).

60 18 U.S.C. § 1962.

61 Jund v. Hempstead, 941 F.2d 1271, 1285 (2d Cir. 1991).

the non-contributing victims who were denied promotions had less money to spend on items obtained through interstate commerce.[62]

B. *RICO Remedies*

RICO provides both injunctive and monetary relief. Successful private and AGO plaintiffs are also entitled to treble damages and attorneys' fees,[63] but only if they establish that the defendant's violation of the RICO statute was the proximate cause of injury to their business or property.[64] The monetary relief sought by the plaintiffs must be designed to compensate them for the damage caused by the RICO violation; as a result, for example, an AGO that alleges that a defendant's actions caused damages to *parens patriae* interest in the right of its citizens to an honest government cannot then seek damages for individual citizens whose businesses and property were harmed by the defendants.[65]

Federal courts have not ruled consistently on whether any plaintiff other than the U.S. government may obtain injunctive relief. The Second and Seventh Circuit Courts of Appeals have concluded that injunctive relief is available to any successful plaintiff,[66] while the Ninth Circuit Court of Appeals allows only the U.S. government to obtain an injunction against a defendant found liable for civil RICO.[67] The USDOJ takes the position that only it has the power to

---

62 *Id.*

63 18 U.S.C. § 1964(c). The USDOJ has concluded that it is not entitled to seek such damages. *See* Civil RICO, *supra* note 42, at 27-28.

64 *See, e.g.*, Anza v. Ideal Steel Supply Corp., 547 U.S. 451, 458 (2006).

65 *Accord* New York v. Seneci, 817 F.2d 1015, 1017-18 (2d Cir. 1987) (dismissing RICO case brought by NY AGO).

66 Chevron Corp. v. Donziger, 833 F.3d 74, 137 (2d Cir. 2016) (granting equitable relief to a private plaintiff); Nat'l Org. for Women, Inc. v. Scheidler, 267 F.3d 687, 695 (7th Cir. 2001), *rev'd on other grounds*, 537 U.S. 393 (2003) (same, and collecting cases where courts suggested in dicta that injunctive relief was available for private plaintiffs (in the Eighth Circuit), acknowledged that it was an open question (in the First and Third Circuits), or expressed doubt about its availability (in the Fourth and Fifth Circuits) (citations omitted)); *see also* Absolute Activist Value Master Fund Ltd. v. Devine, No. 2:15-cv-328-FtM-29MRM, 2016 U.S. Dist. LEXIS 52263, at *13-14 (M.D. Fla. Apr. 19, 2016) (collecting cases and concluding injunctive relief was available to private civil RICO plaintiff).

67 Religious Tech. Ctr. v. Wollersheim, 796 F.2d 1076, 1088 (9th Cir. 1986). A handful of cases in the Third Circuit have also rejected a private right of equitable relief. *See* Minnesota v. Sanofi-Aventis U.S. LLC, 18-cv-14999 (BRM) (LHG), 2020 U.S. Dist. LEXIS 82957, *33-34 (D.N.J. Mar. 31, 2020) (collecting cases).

seek injunctive relief.[68] Forms of injunctive relief expressly permitted by statute include:

> ordering any person to divest himself of any interest, direct or indirect, in any enterprise; imposing reasonable restrictions on the future activities or investments of any person, including, but not limited to, prohibiting any person from engaging in the same type of endeavor as the enterprise engaged in, the activities of which affect interstate or foreign commerce; or ordering dissolution or reorganization of any enterprise, making due provision for the rights of innocent persons.[69]

Courts have concluded that injunctive relief under § 1964(a) also includes "injunctions, disgorgement of wrongdoers' ill-gotten gains, restitution of illegally obtained profits, divestiture or dissolution, appointment of a receiver and others to assist the court in executing its duties, and constructive trusts."[70]

Courts have been split on whether non-USDOJ plaintiffs can obtain disgorgement of a corrupt official's salary. District courts in Illinois,[71] Indiana,[72] New Jersey[73] and West Virginia[74] have concluded that because the damages are pegged to the plaintiff's loss—and not the defendant's gain—a defendant cannot be required to refund his salary to his government employer, but district courts in New York have allowed the recovery of the salaries of corrupt public officials as damages.[75]

---

68 Civil RICO, *supra* note 42, at 28-33 & 33 n.29 (collecting cases and acknowledging it took this position before the Supreme Court in Scheidler v. Nat'l Org. for Women, Inc., 547 U.S. 9, 16 (2006) and Scheidler v. Nat'l Org. for Women, Inc., 537 U.S. 393, 411 (2003)).

69 18 U.S.C. § 1964(a).

70 Civil RICO, *supra* note 42, at 11-12 (citations omitted); *see also id.* at 21-26 (providing additional examples of these species of relief).

71 Claire's Stores, Inc. v. Abrams, No. 86 C 9851, 1989 U.S. Dist. LEXIS 12224, at *14-15 (N.D. Ill. Oct. 13, 1989).

72 Indiana *ex rel.* Zoeller v. Pastrick, 696 F. Supp. 2d 970, 974, 984-86 (N.D. Ind. 2010).

73 Twp. of Marlboro v. Scannapieco, 545 F. Supp. 2d 452, 460-61 (D.N.J. 2008).

74 West Virginia v. Moore, 895 F. Supp. 864, 870-71 (S.D. W. Va. 1995).

75 City of New York v. Jam Consultants, 889 F. Supp. 103, 105-06 (S.D.N.Y. 1995).

C. *RICO Cases Against Corrupt Officials*

The Indiana AGO used civil RICO to hold accountable politicians in East Chicago who, for years, ran the city like a fiefdom. The West Virginia AGO's RICO case against a corrupt former governor, however, was dismissed by a federal district judge who acknowledged that other courts would have permitted it to proceed. These two cases are discussed below.

Other states have also brought civil RICO cases in other contexts,[76] and some citizens have filed RICO suits against corrupt officials.[77] In at least one case, discussed below, plaintiffs have also alleged violations of state racketeering laws.[78]

1. Illinois AGO Case Against the Former Mayor of the City of East Chicago

a. The Scheme and the Charges

In 2004, the Indiana AGO and the City of East Chicago filed a civil RICO complaint alleging that East Chicago's mayor, Robert A. Pastrick, and his associates were essentially running the city as if it belonged to them, drawing "little distinction between government affairs, political affairs, and personal affairs."[79] The complaint named over two dozen individuals and corporate entities as defendants.[80] It alleged that Pastrick led them in managing and operating the city as a RICO enterprise in violation of federal and state law, and included allegations that the defendants violated Indiana state law by committing theft

---

76 For example, the Florida AGO filed suit alleging RICO and other violations against a health care corporation it alleged unlawfully inflated charges to receive excessive Medicare payments. Florida v. Tenet Healthcare Corp., 420 F. Supp. 2d 1288, 1292-93 (S.D. Fla. 2005). The corporation settled with the AGO for $7 million in 2006. *Fla. AG, Tenet Reach Agreement on All State Issues*, Ins. J. (Feb. 22, 2006), https://www.insurancejournal.com/news/southeast/2006/02/22/65745.htm.

77 Cullen v. Margiotta, 811 F.2d 698, 704 (2d Cir. 1987); Jund v. Hempstead, 941 F.2d 1271, 1273-75 (2d Cir. 1991).

78 *See* Indiana *ex rel.* Zoeller v. Pastrick, 696 F. Supp. 2d 970, 974, 975 (N.D. Ind. 2010). More than thirty states have racketeering statutes. For an overview, see John E. Floyd, RICO State by State: A Guide to Litigation Under the State Racketeering Statutes (2d ed. 2011).

79 *Pastrick*, 696 F. Supp. 2d at 974, 975.

80 *Id.* at 974 n.1.

and official misconduct.[81] Individual defendants included Frank Kollintzas, a long-serving city councilman,[82] who had been charged and convicted of related federal criminal charges in 2003.[83]

The AGO showed[84] that Pastrick, who had been elected as mayor in 1971 and reelected every term through 2003, and his associates used the city to further Pastrick's political interests, and their own financial interests, in a variety of ways:

- Job applications included a signature for the applicant's political sponsor;
- New hires were given the "opportunity" to "contribute" a percentage of their salary to a "slush" or "flower" fund that was used to finance campaigns, and appears to have resulted in tens of thousands of dollars in cash that were spent to assist Pastrick and his cronies during election periods;[85]
- During the periods before elections, as many as fifty to ninety new employees were hired and were encouraged to vote for Pastrick;
- Many city department heads and contractors who were awarded city contracts were somehow affiliated with the Pastrick political machine; and
- In the 2003 election, Pastrick and others worked to literally buy the votes of absentee voters.[86]

---

81 *Id.* at 974.

82 *Id.* at 974-76.

83 United States v. Kollintzas, 501 F.3d 796, 798 (7th Cir. 2007). Kollintzas fled to Greece prior to being sentenced. Bill Dolan, *Corruption in the Region: Former East Chicago City Councilman Frank Kollintzas, Infamous for Sidewalks-for-Votes Scandal, Remains at Large After Fleeing to Greece in 2005*, Nwi.com (Jan. 25, 2018), https://www.nwitimes.com/news/local/crime-and-courts/corruption-in-the-region-former-east-chicago-city-councilman-frank/article_f09c8559-45ed-5aba-b96d-6e5f825989a1.html.

84 The defendants eventually elected not to defend against the allegations; as a result, the federal district court found as true the allegations in the complaint and held a hearing to determine the damages due to the city and to the state by Pastrick and others. *Pastrick*, 696 F. Supp. 2d at 974-75. The facts here are primarily are derived from that court's findings of fact.

85 These contributions were, perhaps unsurprisingly, not entirely voluntary. *Id.* at 975.

86 *Id.* at 975-76. For more on election-related crimes, see Chapter 1.7.

Pastrick and his associates also engaged in specific schemes linked to particular elections. One was described as the "sidewalks for votes" scheme. Despite the fact that East Chicago's Board of Public Works did not approve any bids that had been submitted, the defendants caused contractors to perform millions of dollars of work on sidewalks and parking lots on public and private property, and on trimming trees, in an effort to improve Pastrick's, Kollintzas's and others' chances of reelection in 1999.[87] To cover up their crimes, the defendants falsely represented that the city had authorized the program, caused contractors to submit invoices and bids under $75,000 to circumvent Indiana state bidding laws, and backdated contracts.[88] In the end, nearly $24 million was paid to contractors as part of this scheme—an amount of money that entirely depleted the city's general fund by the May 1999 primary and caused its account to be overdrawn by several million dollars.[89]

In an effort to finance the sidewalks for votes scheme, the defendants developed other schemes, first tapping into casino revenue being held in a trust fund, then arranging for corrupt bond authorizations of nearly $15 million.[90]

In addition to the financial investigation that proved how the defendants misused the city's money, the AGO obtained evidence from similarly-sized cities to show that East Chicago was being mismanaged. For example, it showed that East Chicago's employment of over 1,000 people was far in excess of the number of employees in a nearby city,[91] and that fees from riverboat casinos by another similar city went through its city council to be appropriated and disbursed—not to a trust fund that was spent entirely at the discretion of the mayor, as was the practice under Pastrick.[92]

b. RICO Standing Analysis

The AGO successfully defeated a motion to dismiss on standing grounds.[93] The district court applied federal standing requirements but looked to state law to determine if the AGO alleged an injury that was cognizable

87 *Id.* at 976; *see also* United States v. De La Cruz, 469 F.3d 1064, 1065-66 (7th Cir. 2006).
88 *Pastrick*, 696 F. Supp. 2d at 976-77; *De La Cruz*, 469 F.3d at 1065-66.
89 *Pastrick*, 696 F. Supp. 2d at 977.
90 *Id.* at 977-78.
91 *Id.* at 978.
92 *Id.*
93 Indiana *ex rel.* Carter v. Pastrick, 384 F. Supp. 2d 1261, 1266-67 (N.D. Ind. 2005).

under RICO.[94] The court concluded that state statutes granting the AGO the right to recover misappropriated municipal funds meant that the AGO acquired the right to pursue collection on behalf of the city from which Pastrick and his cronies stole, "mak[ing] the Attorney General the owner of the property that has allegedly been injured because the Attorney General has the exclusive right to pursue recovery for that property."[95] The court also found that, in the alternative, the AGO had standing under Seventh Circuit caselaw holding that if an injured party was under the "'continuing control or influence of the defendant or his henchman,' even parties only *indirectly* injured could recover under RICO."[96]

c. The Judgment

In the end, the AGO successfully obtained a judgment against Pastrick and several of his codefendants of more than $108 million.[97] The district court found it had not proven that some of the requested damages were sufficiently tied to the racketeering scheme alleged in the complaint, however.[98] The decision thus illustrates the need for AGO attorneys to be prepared to carefully follow the money and to demonstrate a "causal connection" between a corrupt defendant's scheme and the damages the AGO requests. The office also sought as injunctive relief an order prohibiting the defendants from ever again holding positions of public office, as well as a forensic accounting of two non-party entities it believed had been misused by the racketeers, which the court denied.[99]

---

94 *Id.* at 1267. The court framed this analysis as looking to state law to determine if there was a "property interest." *Id.* at 1266.

95 *Id.* at 1267-68.

96 *Id.* at 1268 (quoting Carter v. Berger, 777 F.2d 1173, 1178 (7th Cir. 1985)).

97 *Pastrick*, 696 F. Supp. 2d at 990.

98 *Id.* at 986-88.

99 *Id.* at 991-98. The court opined, in dicta, that it was likely that only USDOJ could obtain injunctive relief, but ruled that, in any event, the AGO had not "attempted to even articulate, much less prove, their entitlement to this injunction." *Id.* at 991. Note that in at least some states, a separate action could have been brought in state court to seek to bar the defendants from holding state office in the future. *See* Chapter 6.3, Part I(B).

2. West Virginia AGO Case Against the Former Governor

a. The Scheme and the Charges

After former West Virginia Governor Arch Moore pled guilty to federal mail fraud, filing false tax returns, extortion, and obstruction charges and was sentenced to thirty-three months in federal prison,[100] the West Virginia AGO filed a complaint in federal court alleging that he violated civil RICO, as well as breaches of contract and of fiduciary duty, fraud, malfeasance, and unjust enrichment.[101] It also sought punitive damages.[102]

As he admitted when he pled guilty to federal charges,[103] during his 1984 campaign for governor, Moore accepted several cash contributions in violation of state election law and for his personal use.[104] He did not report this cash on his campaign finance disclosure statements or on his tax returns.[105] Moore also accepted a kickback from a coal company that received a refund of premiums it paid into a fund to provide benefits to coal miners who were disabled by pneumoconiosis (perhaps better known as "black lung disease").[106] Moore also helped the same company with an enforcement issue by directing state officials to give the company six months to cure certain environmental problems.[107]

b. RICO Standing Analysis

The court granted summary judgment to the former governor on the RICO counts, finding that the state had not alleged an adequate injury or the linkage of that injury to a predicate act.

First, it found that the state had not alleged or shown that Moore intervened to cause the return of the premiums to the coal company and thus the

100 Lawyer Disciplinary Bd. v. Moore, 591 S.E.2d 338, 341 (W. Va. 2003).

101 West Virginia v. Moore, 895 F. Supp. 864, 866 (S.D. W. Va. 1995).

102 *Id.*

103 *Lawyer Disciplinary Bd.*, 591 S.E.2d at 342-43.

104 *Moore*, 895 F. Supp. at 867; *Lawyer Disciplinary Bd.*, 591 S.E.2d at 343.

105 *Moore*, 895 F. Supp. at 867.

106 *Id.* at 867, 871; *Lawyer Disciplinary Bd.*, 591 S.E.2d at 345.

107 *Moore*, 895 F. Supp. at 868.

refund of those premiums was not an injury for which the state could seek redress under RICO.[108]

Second, it found that the provision of a salary and benefits to the governor did not constitute an injury for RICO purposes, as the state would have paid a salary and benefits to *someone*, even as it recognized that other courts found that payments to corrupt officials were recoverable under RICO and thus a cognizable injury.[109]

Third, it found that the AGO was not entitled to recover the kickback paid to Moore by the coal company, as that was not a cognizable injury to the state, although it again recognized that other courts had concluded that receipt of a bribe by an official established an injury to the government that employed him.[110]

Finally, it concluded that the state had not adequately proven that Moore's failure to declare as income the money with which he was bribed resulted in an increase to his tax liability.[111] It also opined that civil RICO was not the appropriate mechanism for a state to pursue a defendant for tax fraud, and suggested that the state instead seek relief under West Virginia state law.[112] Once again, it noted that at least one court, the Seventh Circuit Court of Appeals,[113] disagreed with its analysis, although the Sixth Circuit Court of Appeals had also concluded that an AGO could not bring a civil RICO case in federal court to obtain treble damages on a tax case.[114]

---

108 *Id.* at 868-70.

109 *Id.* at 870-71.

110 *Id.* at 871.

111 *Id.* at 871-72.

112 *Id.* at 872.

113 Ill. Dep't of Revenue v. Phillips, 771 F.2d 312, 312 (7th Cir. 1985).

114 *Moore*, 895 F. Supp. at 872 (citing Mich. Dep't of Treasury, Revenue Div. v. Fawaz, 848 F.2d 194, No. 86-1809, 1988 U.S. App. LEXIS 6206, *6 (6th Cir. May 9, 1988) (characterizing the Michigan AGO as seeking to "designate the district courts as collection agencies for unpaid state taxes, presumably because he can there pursue treble damages" in a case that followed the conviction of the defendant in state criminal court for failing the pay the same taxes, which included an order of restitution)).

c. The Judgment

Even though it dismissed the RICO and several other counts, the district court denied Moore's motion for summary judgment on state law counts that alleged he was unjustly enriched by his corrupt conduct and his unlawful campaign contributions.[115] Moore eventually settled with the West Virginia AGO by agreeing to pay $750,000, and was later disbarred.[116]

Conclusion

In some cases, civil corruption enforcers can hold corrupt officials accountable by alleging § 1983 or civil RICO violations in federal court. The injunctive relief available under a § 1983 action—and potentially available under RICO—can provide both individual and general deterrence and prevent ongoing acts of corruption. Treble damages under RICO can be a powerful tool to make the state whole and deter wrongdoing. When embarking on an investigation that might warrant bringing a federal civil corruption case—particularly under RICO—an AGO attorney should thoroughly research the applicable caselaw in the relevant circuit and district to avoid dismissal and increase the likelihood of recovering meaningful relief.

---

115 *Id.* at 872, 874-75.

116 Lawyer Disciplinary Bd. v. Moore, 591 S.E.2d 338, 341 (W. Va. 2003).

Chapter 6.3

Collateral Consequences of Corruption: Forfeiture of Office, Loss of Pension, Ban on Future Public Employment, & Other Tools

Amie N. Ely

Amie N. Ely is the Director of the Center for Ethics & Public Integrity, National Attorneys General Training & Research Institute, National Association of Attorneys General.

Introduction

State attorney general offices can use a variety of civil and administrative mechanisms to address corrupt behavior by government officials and by those in the private sector. In addition to pursuing civil damages,[1] AGOs can also seek remedies that divest defendants of the status they abused to commit the offense, or prevent them from having access future government employment or contracts. These remedies include:

- Forfeiture of public office;
- Forfeiture of pension;

1 *See, e.g.*, Chapter 6.2.

- A ban on future public employment;
- Cancellation of certificates of formation of a company; and
- Suspension or debarment of a contractor.

This chapter examines how these tools can be used to address the abuse of office or commission of crimes by government officials, and to ensure that those in the private sector who benefited from or facilitated such malfeasance are less likely to have opportunities to do so in the future.[2]

I. Tools to Address Corruption by Officials

In at least some states, statutes provide for the forfeiture of the office or pension of government employees who commit misconduct.[3] Some states provide for prospective relief, banning people from future public office if they are convicted of certain crimes or have abused their position.

A. *Immediate Penalties: Forfeitures of Public Office and Pension*

Particularly in cases where a high-ranking official has been convicted of a crime, removal from office "is not to punish the officer, but to improve the public service. The public interest demands that public affairs be administered by officers upon whom rests no stigma . . . of any offense involving a violation of their official duties."[4]

---

2 This chapter does not provide an exhaustive overview of the laws across the United States; instead, it provides some examples in an effort to encourage prosecutors and enforcers to consider these administrative remedies when they may be appropriate. The National Conference of State Legislatures has, however, gathered at least some of the relevant laws. Mark Quiner, *Ethics & Public Corruption Laws: Penalties*, Nat'l Conf. of State Legislatures (Mar. 3, 2021), https://www.ncsl.org/research/ethics/50-state-chart-criminal-penalties-for-public-corr.aspx. Readers may also be interested in the Union Corruption chapter, which discusses the use of court-appointed monitors, another tool that might be appropriate to consider in some corruption cases. *See* Chapter 1.6, Part III.

3 For an overview of state official misconduct laws, *see* Chapter 3.2, Part I.

4 State *ex rel.* De Concini v. Sullivan, 188 P.2d 592, 599 (Ariz. 1948) (removing attorney general from office).

More practically, these provisions can also reduce legal, political, financial, and personal costs to taxpayers when a powerful elected official is convicted.[5] In the 1990s, governors from Arizona and Arkansas were found guilty by federal juries; while the Arizona governor stepped down within hours of the verdict, the Arkansas governor remained in office for several weeks.[6] During that time, he made hundreds of appointments to state boards and commissions and spent millions of dollars in state funds—likely to prevent the incoming, opposite-party governor from filling those positions and funding projects of his choosing.[7] Lawsuits were filed attacking the decisions the Arkansas governor made during the period between his conviction and his resignation.[8] For about an hour—after the convicted governor announced he would step down but changed his mind—Arkansas had two people claiming to be the rightful governor.[9]

Statutes providing for removal from office upon conviction can reduce uncertainty about who is the appropriate officeholder and prevent costly litigation—in dollars, time, and trust in government—over whether an officeholder had the power to make decisions after his conviction.

1. Forfeiture of Public Office

Most states have constitutional or statutory provisions that permit or require the removal from office of officials convicted of certain crimes.[10] Those statutes often, but not always, require a "conviction"[11] and may also require that

---

5 Tim Delaney, *Keeping the Taint of Guilt Out of Office: Proposals to Clarify Arizona's Public Office Vacancy Statute*, 31 Ariz. St. L.J. 95, 100-01 (1999).

6 *Id.*

7 *Id.*

8 Elana Cunningham Wills, *Constitutional Crisis: Can the Governor (or Other State Officeholder) Be Removed From Office in a Court Action After Being Convicted of a Felony?*, 50 Ark. L. Rev. 221, 222 n.3 (1997).

9 *Id.* at 224-25.

10 Susan L. Thomas, Annotation, *What Constitutes Conviction Within Statutory or Constitutional Provision Making Conviction of Crime Ground of Disqualification For, Removal From, or Vacancy in, Public Office*, 10 A.L.R. 5th 139, *2a (2020).

11 Courts have "taken widely divergent positions regarding when a conviction occurs for the purpose of removing a public officer." Delaney, *supra* note 5, at 98. Some conclude that a defendant has been convicted for this purpose when guilt has been determined—whether by plea or verdict—but others find convictions upon the entry of a judgment or when appeals are final. *Id.* at 99 (collecting cases). At least one state statute provides for forfeiture of office "upon the entry of the [guilty] plea." 51 Okla. Stat. § 24.1(E). Unless otherwise indicated, all citations

the offense be connected to the defendant's official position to warrant removal from office.

For example, in New Jersey, forfeiture of a government official's office requires a conviction that is "involving or touching" the defendant's public office, a crime involving dishonesty, or a crime requiring a sentence of over three years in prison.[12] For the first category, the offense must be "related directly to the person's performance in, or circumstances flowing from, the specific public office, position or employment held by the person."[13] Thus, a New Jersey police officer who sexually assaulted an acquaintance while he was neither on duty nor in his uniform was not subjected to statutory forfeiture, as there was no proof that the crime "involve[d] or touch[ed] upon" his position as an officer or involved dishonesty and he was permitted to plead guilty to a crime that did not require a sentence of at least three years in prison.[14]

Some states provide for forfeiture only for certain crimes. For example, Idaho has a number of statutes that require an official to forfeit an office when convicted of a particular type or category of crime.[15] Oklahoma is an example of a state with broader forfeiture requirements, however, as it provides that an official will forfeit his office upon any plea of "guilty or nolo contendere to a felony or any offense involving a violation of his or her official oath."[16]

In some states, no conviction is required. If a court determines that the conditions for disqualification are met, the officeholder can be removed from office. For example, in Arizona, officials who are not permitted to acquire certain interests are "forever disqualified from holding any office" if a court

---

to statutes in this chapter refer to the version current at the time of publishing.

12 N.J. Stat. Ann. 2C:51-2(a)(1), (2) (requiring forfeiture of office if defendant is convicted of a "crime of the third degree or above," which is a crime requiring a sentence of at least three years in prison, N.J. Stat. Ann. § 2C:43-6(a)(3)).

13 State v. Hupka, 1 A.3d 640, 647 (N.J. 2010) (quoting N.J. Stat. Ann. § 2C:51-2(a)(3)).

14 *Id.* at 651, 653.

15 *See, e.g.*, Idaho Code § 18-1307 (providing for forfeiture of office for any officer convicted of bribery or corruption-related crimes); *id.* § 63-3076(4) (forfeiture of office for unlawfully divulging income tax information); *id.* § 18-2702 (forfeiture of office for being convicted of requesting or accepting bribes). Pennsylvania takes a similar approach. 65 Pa. Cons. Stat. § 121 ("Any person . . . who pleads nolo contendere or guilty, or is convicted . . . of extortion, embezzlement, bribery, malfeasance or misfeasance in office, or fraudulent conversion of public moneys or property, or for any misdemeanor in office, shall forfeit his office.").

16 51 Okla. Stat. § 24.1(E).

determines that they, in fact, acquired those interests.[17] As a result, a court will remove such an official from office even if he is never convicted of a separate crime related to acquiring those prohibited interests. Other states do not allow removal from office by a judicial proceeding absent a conviction, but instead require the official to be impeached.[18]

Finally, in at least some states that provide for removal upon conviction, reversal of that conviction allows a defendant to return to his office.[19]

2. Forfeiture of Pension/Retirement Benefits

Some state statutes allow for the forfeiture of a state pension or other retirement benefits if a government employee commits misconduct. For example, in Illinois, a member of the General Assembly who is convicted of a felony relating to, arising out of, or in connection with his service as a member can be required to forfeit his pension.[20]

At least some states require prosecutors to initiate a separate proceeding to seek forfeiture of an official's pension. In New York, after an official is convicted of "any crime related to public office," a district attorney or the attorney general (depending on which office has jurisdiction) must initiate an action in the court in the county where the defendant was convicted, and must prove, among other things, that the crime related to public office.[21]

The forfeiture of pensions can provide an additional deterrent to corrupt activity, even in instances where defendants were convicted by another prosecutor. State AGOs have sought forfeiture of pensions of officials who were

---

17 Ariz. Rev. Stat. § 38-447; State *ex rel.* Smith v. Bohannan, 421 P.2d 877, 881-82 (Ariz. 1966) (removing officeholder who admitted his misconduct but had not been convicted of a crime).

18 Wills, *supra* note 8, at 235 ("Indeed, no one could seriously argue that under our state constitution a sitting governor or other state officer could be legally removed from office for criminal conduct through judicial proceedings absent any adjudication of guilt by a court.").

19 *See, e.g.*, Summerour v. Cartrett, 136 S.E.2d 724, 725 (Ga. 1964); State v. Blazer, 619 S.W.2d 370, 372-74 (Tenn. 1981).

20 *See* 40 Ill. Comp. Stat. 5/2-156. *See also* Ariz. Rev. Stat. § 13-713(A); Fla. Stat. § 112.3173(3); Mo. Rev. Stat. § 105.669(1).

21 N.Y. Retire. & Soc. Sec. Law § 157(2), (7). Note that the statute will be amended to permit forfeiture only after the official's sentencing on the underlying criminal case if voters ratify amendments to Section 7 of Article V of the New York Constitution. *Id.*

convicted of federal crimes. For example, the Michigan AGO secured the forfeiture of the state-paid portion of the pensions held for thirteen Detroit Public School employees who were convicted in federal court for participating in a $2.7 million kickback scheme.[22]

B. *Prospective Penalties: Ban on Future Public Employment*

Statutes that ban people who have been convicted of certain crimes from being again employed by state government are typically designed to "preclude those who have once violated the public trust from having a second opportunity."[23]

Some states restrict all felons from seeking or holding public office. Tennessee disqualifies a person convicted of any felony from "qualifying for, seeking election to or holding a public office in this state" unless his citizenship rights have been restored.[24] If that person was an elected public official and committed the offense of conviction in his official capacity or the offense involved the duties of his office, even the restoration of citizenship rights will not restore eligibility to seek or hold a public office.[25]

Some states disqualify an official who was convicted while in office from future public employment. Nevada, for example, provides that a public officer's conviction for "any felony or malfeasance in office" will disqualify him "from ever afterward holding any public office in this State."[26]

---

22 Lori Higgins, *Convicted Former Detroit Principal Loses Portion of Pension*, DET. FREE PRESS (July 28, 2017), https://www.freep.com/story/news/2017/07/28/detroit-principal-pension-scandal/520790001/; *Schuette Initiates Pension Forfeiture Action Against Ex-Detroit Principals, Superintendent Convicted of Accepting Bribes*, MICHIGAN.GOV (undated), https://www.michigan.gov/ag/0,4534,7-359--396306--,00.html; *Schuette Secures Forfeiture of State-Funded Pensions from Eight Detroit Principals Convicted of Bribery*, MICHIGAN.GOV (May 1, 2017), https://www.michigan.gov/ag/0,4534,7-359-92297_47203-410510--,00.html.

23 Cicchetti v. Morris County Sheriff's Office, 947 A.2d 626, 638 (N.J. 2008) (alteration and citation omitted).

24 TENN. CODE ANN. § 40-20-114(a). While the statute provides for disqualification only for "infamous crime[s]," the definition of infamous crimes was expanded in 1981 to include all felonies. May v. Carlton, 245 S.W.3d 340, 345 (Tenn. 2008) (citing Gaskin v. Collins, 661 S.W.2d 865, 866 (Tenn. 1983)).

25 TENN. CODE ANN. § 40-20-114(b).

26 NEV. REV. STAT. ANN. § 197.230.

Other states ban future public employment only if an official abused his office or was convicted of certain crimes. In New Jersey, if the requirements for forfeiture of current office are met, the official "shall be forever disqualified from holding any office or position of honor, trust or profit under this State or any of its administrative or political subdivisions."[27] In Idaho, a legislator who is convicted of certain crimes that involve abusing his legislative power—such as altering a bill, or offering or accepting a bribe—is "forever disqualified from holding any office in this state."[28]

Some states have provisions that require candidates to be rejected from civil service positions if they were previously convicted. In Illinois, candidates for public employment "who have been guilty of infamous or disgraceful conduct" are to be rejected.[29]

II. Tools to Address Corruption by the Private Sector

While corruption's blackletter definition is the abuse of public power for private gain, private sector individuals and entities may conspire with, abet, or assist[30] a corrupt government official. AGOs and other enforcers often have tools that allow them to address private sector malfeasance that may be particularly appropriate to deploy when private actors assist corrupt government actors. While some of the examples below may not fall within the strictest definition of "corruption," the cancellation of certificates of formation and the suspension or debarment of contractors are measures that enforcers should be aware of and consider using when private sector actors improperly assist corrupt government officials.

---

27 N.J. Stat. Ann. § 2C:51-2(d).

28 Idaho Code § 18-4706.

29 20 Ill. Comp. Stat. Ann. 415/8b.4; *see also* John F. Decker, *Collateral Consequences of a Felony Conviction in Illinois*, 56 Chi.-Kent L. Rev. 731, 747 (1980).

30 While conspiracy and aiding and abetting have distinct definitions—at least in the federal system—the generic term "assist" will be used here to encompass both, as well as assistance that may not rise to the level of violating a criminal statute. 18 U.S.C. § 2(a) (aiding and abetting); *id.* at § 371 (conspiracy).

A. *Cancelling Certificates of Formation or Dissolving Trusts*

In at least some states, the state attorney general has the power to dissolve companies, corporations, and nonprofits that have been misused.[31] As the 2016 revision of the Model Business Corporation Act contains a provision permitting a state's attorney general to petition a court for dissolution if "the corporation has continued to exceed or abuse the authority conferred upon it by law,"[32] states that do not currently grant this power to the attorney general may do so in the future.

This tool could be used to dissolve a company that has been used to, as an example, provide cover for bribes to a politician. Two recent examples of AGOs dissolving companies illustrate the potential use of this power.

1. Delaware AGO Cancelling Certificates of Formation

In Delaware, the attorney general may initiate proceedings to cancel the certificate of formation of any domestic limited liability company if the company abuses or misuses its limited liability company powers, privileges, or existence.[33] To do this, the attorney general files a request for cancellation in the Delaware Court of Chancery,[34] which then has the power to cancel the certificate of formation and appoint third parties to administer and wind up the affairs of the now-defunct company.[35]

This power emanates from recent statutory amendments. National press coverage suggests it is having its intended effect of discouraging the misuse of corporations, as a commentator warned that "corporate counsel, tax counsel

---

31 *See, e.g.*, Del. Code Ann. tit. 6, § 18-112; Kan. Stat. § 17-6812; Mo. Rev. Stat. § 347.143; N.Y. Not-for-Profit Corp. Law § 1101; Or. Rev. Stat. § 63.661. As noted in Chapter 1.4, convictions under state antitrust laws may also require the dissolution of a corporate charter. *See* Chapter 1.4, n.10 and accompanying text.

32 Denis Demblowski, *Analysis: Can Delaware Cancel My Company?*, Bloomberg Law, Jan. 17, 2020, https://news.bloomberglaw.com/bloomberg-law-analysis/analysis-can-delaware-cancel-my-company (explaining that the Model Business Corporation Act § 14.30(a)(1) (Am. Bar Ass'n 2016) permits an attorney general to petition a court for dissolution if "the corporation has continued to exceed or abuse the authority conferred upon it by law").

33 Del. Code Ann. tit. 6, § 18-112(a).

34 *Id.*

35 *Id.* at § 18-112(b).

and compliance professionals may need to take a second look at the potential implications of the statute."[36]

Since the statute's enactment in 2018, the Delaware AGO successfully used it to dissolve companies that were used to commit crimes. In the first use of the new statute, Backpage.com entered into a consent judgment agreeing to the eventual cancellation of its certificates of formation.[37]

In late September 2019, the Delaware AGO filed six Court of Chancery actions to dissolve fifteen limited liability companies.[38] In most of these cases, the companies or the individuals running them had been convicted of crimes, and the companies were used in some way to carry out those crimes.[39] In two, the companies themselves had been placed on the federal Office of Foreign Assets Control Specially Designated Nationals List for laundering drug money, and had failed to comply with Delaware's requirements for maintaining a business entity.[40]

Several of those fifteen companies were dissolved in October 2020. The Delaware Court of Chancery approved a stipulation of consent judgment dissolving two limited liability companies that had been formed and used to facilitate unlawful payments to suppress negative publicity about a candidate for office in advance of an election.[41] Later that month, the same court dissolved

---

36 Demblowski, *supra* note 32.

37 Jennings v. Backpage, C.A. No. 2018-0838-SG, 2019 Del. Ch. LEXIS 446, at *3-4 (Del. Ch. June 11, 2019).

38 Jeff Montgomery, *Del. AG Sues to Dissolve 15 Crime-Tied Biz Entities*, LAW360 (Sept. 20, 2019), https://www.law360.com/articles/1201317/del-ag-sues-to-dissolve-15-crime-tied-biz-entities.

39 Del. News Desk, *AG Wants to Wrap Up Criminal LLCs*, THE BEACON (Sept. 20, 2019), https://www.milfordbeacon.com/news/20190920/ag-wants-to-wrap-up-criminal-llcs.

40 Verified Compl. at 1, Jennings v. Oyster Invs. LLC, C.A. No. 2019-0758 (Del. Ch. Sept. 19, 2019), https://attorneygeneral.delaware.gov/wp-content/uploads/sites/50/2019/09/Smile-Group-Complaint-1.pdf.

41 Jennings v. Essential Consultants LLC, C.A. No. 2019-0755-AGB (Del. Ch. Oct. 1, 2020), https://attorneygeneral.delaware.gov/wp-content/uploads/sites/50/2020/10/JudgeReviewed_73775894_Proposed-Order-of-Consent-Judgment-2019-0755-AGB-10-1-2020.docx-.pdf; *see also* Karl Baker, *Delaware Dissolves Shell Companies Created to Pay Off Women by Trump-Fixer Michael Cohen*, DEL. NEWS J. (Oct. 5, 2020), https://www.delawareonline.com/story/news/2020/10/05/delaware-dissolves-llcs-created-pay-off-women-trump-fixer-michael-cohen/3623443001/ (describing the circumstances of the case and quoting Delaware Attorney General Kathleen Jennings as stating, "We expect every Delaware business to

six Delaware entities that had been used to launder millions of dollars from a foreign government to assist in the commission of tax fraud and other crimes.[42]

2. New York AGO Dissolution of Charitable Trust

Under New York law, the AGO has the power to bring an action for dissolution of a not-for-profit corporation if the corporation "procured its formation through fraudulent misrepresentation or concealment of a material fact."[43] The AGO can also dissolve a not-for-profit corporation that:

- Exceeded the authority conferred upon it by law;
- Violated any provision of law whereby it has forfeited its charter;
- Carried on, conducted, or transacted its business in a persistently fraudulent or illegal manner; or
- By the abuse of its powers contrary to public policy of the state, has become liable to be dissolved.[44]

The New York AGO sought to use these powers to dissolve a charitable trust controlled by a politician, alleging it was improperly used to, among other things, assist his campaign. After the judge denied the defendants' motions to dismiss,[45] the parties settled. In a subsequent order, the state court judge noted that the parties agreed to dissolve the foundation under judicial supervision, annul its certificate of incorporation, and end its corporate existence.[46] It also agreed to provide nearly $2 million it had raised through the charity to legitimate charitable organizations.[47]

---

follow the law, full stop, and my office will not hesitate to use our full authority to stop criminal abuse of a Delaware LLC or corporation.").

42 Press Release, Del. Dep't of Justice, DOJ Secures Manafort and Gates-Connected Entity Dissolutions (Oct. 26, 2020), https://news.delaware.gov/2020/10/26/doj-secures-manafort-and-gates-connected-entity-dissolutions/.

43 N.Y. Not-for-Profit Corp. Law § 1101(a)(1).

44 *Id.* at § 1101(a)(2) (quotation marks omitted, phrases bulleted, and punctuation and capitalization modified to increase readability).

45 People v. Trump, 62 Misc. 3d 500, 521 (N.Y. Sup. Ct. 2018).

46 People v. Trump, 66 Misc. 3d 200, 201-02 (N.Y. Sup. Ct. 2019).

47 *Id.* at 202; David A. Farenthold & Joshua Partlow, *Trump Ordered to Pay $2 Million to Charities Over Misuse of Foundation, Court Documents Say*, Wash. Post (Nov. 7, 2019), https://www.

B. *Suspension or Debarment of Contractors*

Criminal and civil violations provide a basis for suspension or debarment under federal law and in at least some states.[48] In the Federal Acquisition Regulations (FAR), contractors may be debarred for:

- Committing civil fraud or a criminal offense in connection with obtaining, attempting to obtain, or performing a public contract;[49]

- Violating federal or state antitrust laws;[50]

- Committing crimes of "embezzlement, theft, forgery, bribery, falsification or destruction of records, making false statements, tax evasion, violating Federal criminal tax laws, or receiving stolen property;"[51]

- Affixing a "Made in America" inscription to a product that was not so made;[52] or

- Committing "any other offense indicating a lack of business integrity or business honesty that seriously and directly affects the present responsibility of a Government contractor or subcontractor."[53]

Under the FAR, suspension is a temporary exclusion of a contractor from eligibility to contract with the federal government for up to a year, typically while an investigation into the alleged misconduct is ongoing.[54] Debarment

washingtonpost.com/politics/trump-ordered-to-pay-2-million-to-charities-over-misuse-of-foundation-court-documents-say/2019/11/07/b8f804e2-018e-11ea-9518-1e76abc088b6_story.html.

48 *See, e.g.*, 48 C.F.R. § 9.406-2(a) (listing causes for debarment in the Federal Acquisition Regulations System).

49 *Id.* at § 9.406-2(a)(1).

50 *Id.* at § 9.406-2(a)(2). As noted in Chapter 1.4, convictions under state antitrust laws can lead to debarment, which often forbid a contractor from bidding on state or local contracts for a term of years. *See* Chapter 1.4, n.8 and accompanying text.

51 48 C.F.R. § 9.406-2(a)(3).

52 *Id.* at § 9.406-2(a)(4).

53 *Id.* at § 9.406-2(a)(5).

54 *Frequently Asked Questions: Suspension & Debarment*, U.S. Gen. Servs. Admin. (Dec. 8, 2020), https://www.gsa.gov/policy-regulations/policy/acquisition-policy/office-of-acquisition-policy/gsa-acq-policy-integrity-workforce/suspension-debarment-division/suspension-debarment/frequently-asked-questions-suspension-debarment; Pascale Helene

is a similar restriction on eligibility to contract with the government, but is typically for three years and requires the government to prove by a preponderance of the evidence that debarment is appropriate.[55] If the government meets that burden, the contractor then has the opportunity to "demonstrate present responsibility"—that is, show that notwithstanding the earlier misconduct, it has ethical integrity and should be trusted to "perform without violation in the future, given the context of past conduct and performance."[56]

The United States General Services Administration Office of Inspector General maintains a list of state and federal websites that list contractors who have been debarred or are otherwise ineligible to contract with the United States.[57]

Like the federal government, at least some states have provisions permitting or requiring the debarment of contractors for corruption-related offenses. For example, in New York, being convicted of bribery, defrauding the government, or other corruption-related offenses subjects contractors, vendors, and grantees to debarment.[58]

Similarly, in Maryland, a conviction in its state courts for bribery, attempted bribery, or conspiracy to bribe requires the debarment of a contractor if the crime was "committed in furtherance of obtaining a contract with a public body."[59] Debarment is permitted but not required if those crimes were committed by a contractor but were not in an effort to obtain a contract with a public body, committed in another state, or the subject of a federal conviction.[60] Other grounds for discretionary debarment in Maryland include being

---

Dubois, *Domestic and International Administrative Tools to Combat Fraud & Corruption: A Comparison of U.S. Suspension and Debarment with the World Bank's Sanctions System*, 2012 Univ. of Chi. Legal Forum 195, 214 (2012), https://chicagounbound.uchicago.edu/cgi/viewcontent.cgi?article=1497&context=uclf.

55 Dubois, *supra* note 54, at 209, 214.

56 *Id.* at 207.

57 *Suspension & Debarment Sites by State*, U.S. Gen. Servs. Admin., Office of Inspector Gen. (Feb. 1, 2016), https://www.gsaig.gov/content/suspension-and-debarment-sites-state.

58 *No. 192: Executive Order Imposing Continuing Vendor Integrity Requirements in State Contracts*, N.Y. State (Feb. 15, 2019), https://www.governor.ny.gov/news/no-192-executive-order-imposing-continuing-vendor-integrity-requirements-state-contracts.

59 Md. Code Ann., State Fin. & Proc. § 16-202(a).

60 *Id.* at § 16-202(b)(1)-(2). Debarment is also permitted if a person admitted "during the course of an official investigation or other proceeding . . . , in writing or under oath, acts or

convicted in any state or federal court of (1) any crime "incident to obtaining, attempting to obtain, or performing a public or private contract";[61] or (2) "fraud, embezzlement, theft, forgery, falsification or destruction of records, or receiving stolen property."[62] Maryland also allows reciprocal debarment of those debarred under the FAR.[63]

New Jersey provides for debarment of a person convicted of bribery;[64] making unlawful threats to influence official or political matters;[65] offering, accepting, or receiving an unlawful benefit for the official behavior of a public servant;[66] official misconduct;[67] or several other offenses.[68] A person convicted of one of the enumerated offenses is, with limited exceptions, automatically restricted from bidding, contracting, or conducting any business with the state for either five or ten years, depending on the seriousness of the offense.[69]

In cases where suspension or debarment is available, attorneys for the government may wish to ensure that corporations that have been used in the service of corrupt acts are no longer permitted to obtain government contracts.

Conclusion

Divesting corrupt officials of the status they abused, preventing them from future government employment, or taking away their pensions can protect taxpayers from paying for untrustworthy services. When the private sector is involved in government corruption, the vehicles used to carry out or conceal that corruption can be cancelled, dissolved, or debarred. In states where these remedies are available, prosecutors should consider using them to deter and penalize corruption, and to reduce opportunities for bad actors to continue to prey upon the public.

---

omissions that would constitute bribery, attempted bribery, or conspiracy to bribe, under the laws of the State, another state or the United States." *Id.* at § 16-202(b)(3).

61 *Id.* at § 16-203(a)(1)(i).

62 *Id.* at § 16-203(a)(1)(ii).

63 *Id.* at § 16-203(c).

64 N.J. Stat. Ann. § 2C:27-2.

65 *Id.* at § 2C:27-3.

66 *Id.* at §§ 2C:27-11 (offering) & 2C:27-10 (accepting or receiving).

67 *Id.* at § 2C:30-2.

68 *Id.* at § 2C:51-2(f) (listing offenses that require forfeiture of office).

69 *Id.*

CHAPTER 6.4

Asset Forfeiture in Public Corruption Cases

Alice W. Dery

Alice W. Dery is the Chief of the Program Management and Training Unit within the Money Laundering and Asset Recovery Section at the United States Department of Justice.

INTRODUCTION

Beginning in 1990 and continuing over a period of more than twenty years, Rita Crundwell, the comptroller for the city of Dixon, Illinois, stole more than fifty-three million dollars from the city.[1] While she used that money to establish herself as a leading breeder of quarter horses, the city of Dixon struggled to pay its bills. The United States Attorney for the Northern District of Illinois prosecuted Crundwell for wire fraud and money laundering and she was sentenced to nearly twenty years in prison in 2013.[2] Similarly, former Cuyahoga County, Ohio, commissioner Jimmy Dimora was convicted of thirty-three federal counts by the U.S. Attorney for the Northern District of Ohio

1 Press Release, U.S. Dep't of Justice, U.S. Attorney's Office, N. Dist. of Ill., Former Dixon Comptroller Rita Crundwell Sentenced to Nearly 20 Years in Federal Prison For $53.7 Million Theft from City (Feb. 14, 2013), https://www.justice.gov/usao-ndil/pr/former-dixon-comptroller-rita-crundwell-sentenced-nearly-20-years-federal-prison-537. For examples of forfeiture and restitution orders in state cases, see Chapter 1.5, Part IV.

2 *Id.*; United States v. Crundwell, 735 F.3d 743, 744 (7th Cir. 2013).

and sentenced to twenty-eight years in prison for taking more than $166,000 worth of bribes in the form of cash, home improvements, lavish meals at high-end restaurants, and gambling trips to Las Vegas and Canada.[3]

In addition to the jail sentences of Crundwell and Dimora, complete justice for the city of Dixon and Cuyahoga County required recovering the stolen funds and returning them to their residents. In many cases of this kind, the primary means of recovering and returning funds to victims of crime is asset forfeiture.

This chapter discusses asset forfeiture and its role in holding those guilty of public corruption accountable for their crimes.[4]

I. What is Asset Forfeiture?

Asset forfeiture is the recovery by the government of money or property that constitutes the proceeds of a crime, facilitated a crime, or is otherwise connected to a crime. Asset forfeiture has its roots in federal common law, dating back centuries and used originally in connection with *in rem* proceedings in admiralty, piracy, and customs violations. Congress expanded forfeiture in the 1970s and 1980s as a weapon against organized crime syndicates and drug trafficking organizations. In addition, Congress codified the English common law practice of using forfeiture as a means of criminal punishment, first with regard to racketeering and drug offenses,[5] and later for additional crimes and related

---

3 *See* Press Release, Fed. Bureau of Investigation, Former Cuyahoga County Commissioner Jimmy Dimora Convicted of Racketeering (Mar. 9, 2012), https://archives.fbi.gov/archives/cleveland/press-releases/2012/former-cuyahoa-county-commissioner-jimmy-dimora-convicted-of-racketeering.

4 Given the different forfeiture practices across states, this article focuses on federal forfeiture law. Many state laws import concepts or language from the federal forfeiture laws. For example, Nevada has incorporated the concept of substitute assets into its criminal forfeiture law, Nev. Rev. Stat. Ann. § 207.420(3), and Maine has incorporated the language of 21 U.S.C. § 853(n) related to ancillary hearings on third party interests into its forfeiture law, Me. Rev. Stat. Ann. tit. 15, § 5826(5). Unless otherwise indicated, all citations to statutes in this chapter refer to the version current at the time of publishing.

5 *See* United States v. Bajakajian, 524 U.S. 321, 332 n.7 (1998) ("It was only in 1970 that Congress resurrected the English common law of punitive forfeiture to combat organized crime and major drug trafficking [as] . . . [']an innovative attempt to call on our common law heritage to

conduct for which property could be forfeited civilly.[6] With this expansion came an increase in the use of forfeited funds to compensate victims of financial crimes, including embezzlement and bribery. Over the past decade, the U.S. Department of Justice has returned more than $8.5 billion to such victims of financial crimes.

II. Why Use Asset Forfeiture?

Forfeiture is a particularly effective tool against public corruption because it takes away the principal incentive for the crime—financial gain—while punishing corrupt officials by denying them the fruits of their crimes. In many cases, the publicity generated by the forfeiture and liquidation of criminal proceeds can highlight the efforts of law enforcement and magnify the deterrent effect. For example, the sale of Crundwell's horses, memorabilia, and other property generated international press coverage, and her case would eventually become the subject of an award-winning documentary film.[7] Similarly, following Jimmy Dimora's conviction at trial, he forfeited his share of his residence and retirement fund, among other assets, that were proceeds of the crime.[8] The investigation and prosecution of Dimora and his coconspirators received widespread media attention and caused Cuyahoga County to reorganize its governance structure,[9] in addition to receiving approximately $3.5 million in forfeited funds through remission from the USDOJ.[10]

---

meet an essentially modern problem.'" (citations omitted)), *superseded by statute*, USA PATRIOT Act, Pub. L. No. 107-56, 115 Stat. 272, *as recognized in* United States v. Jose, 499 F.3d 105, 109 (1st Cir. 2007).

6 *See, e.g.*, 28 U.S.C. § 2461(c) (stating that "[i]f a person is charged in a criminal case with a violation of an Act of Congress for which the civil or criminal forfeiture of property is authorized, the Government may include notice of the forfeiture in the indictment or information" and "[i]f the defendant is convicted of the offense giving rise to the forfeiture, the court shall order the forfeiture of the property as part of the sentence in the criminal case").

7 *See* All the Queen's Horses (Gravitas Ventures 2017).

8 James F. McCarty, *Jimmy Dimora Cuts a Deal with Prosecutors; Forfeits Pension and Half of House*, Cleveland.com (Mar. 14, 2012), https://www.cleveland.com/countyincrisis/2012/03/jimmy_dimora_cuts_a_deal_with.html.

9 *See* Andy Kim, *Cuyahoga County's Road to Recovery from Corruption*, Governing (Nov. 2010), https://www.governing.com/topics/politics/Cuyahoga-Countys-road-recovery-from-corruption.html.

10 *See* Pat Galbincea, *Cuyahoga County Gets $3.5 Million Restitution Check from the Federal Government*, Cleveland.com (May 20, 2011), https://www.cleveland.com/metro/2011/05/

In addition to recovering stolen funds, asset forfeiture is an effective way to remove the tools of the trade from the criminal. When bribery and corruption rise to the level of racketeering, it is possible to forfeit the business or enterprise of the corrupt person. Forfeiture can protect and benefit the community harmed by the criminal activity. For example, the government has forfeited drug houses and turned them over to non-profit organizations to help redevelop neighborhoods blighted by drugs and crime. In one case, the government forfeited approximately one thousand acres of land in Tennessee that was used to illicitly grow marijuana and donated the land to the state for use as a wildlife refuge.[11] In sum, asset forfeiture effectively removes the tools of crime from the criminals and their organizations, deprives them of the proceeds of crime, and recovers property that may be used to compensate, and otherwise benefit, victims.

III. What Can Be Forfeited?

Depending on the crime, the government can forfeit a wide variety of property and interests in property, including:

- The proceeds of the crime, including anything of value obtained as a result of the crime and property traceable to those assets;[12]
- Property used to facilitate the crime, i.e., property used to make the crime easier to commit or harder to detect;[13] and

---

cuyahoga_county_gets_35_millio.html (noting that the bulk of the restitution came from the widow of a lawyer who masterminded a scheme to steer no-bid commercial appraisal contracts to a particular firm in return for kickbacks). *See also* McCarty, *supra* note 8 (explaining that Dimora, after conviction, agreed to forfeit half his share of his family's $438,000 home, his commissioner's pension valued at $122,383, and a $3,600 Ohio State football jersey received from a contractor).

11 Press Release, U.S. Dep't of Justice, Justice Department Transfers 1,000 Acres of Land in Cannon County, Tenn., to State of Tennessee (Jun. 13, 2012), https://www.justice.gov/opa/pr/justice-department-transfers-1000-acres-land-cannon-county-tenn-state-tennessee. For more information about real property transfers, *see* Asset Forfeiture Policy Manual Ch. 4, § V (Money Laundering and Asset Recovery Section, U.S. Dep't of Justice 2019), https://www.justice.gov/criminal-afmls/file/839521/download.

12 *See, e.g.*, 18 U.S.C. § 981(a)(1)(C).

13 *See, e.g.*, *id.* § 981(a)(1)(B).

- Property involved in money laundering, including the money being laundered and the money and other property that is commingled with it.[14]

To be forfeitable, property must be connected to a crime for which forfeiture is statutorily authorized.[15] There is no federal common law for forfeiture, and there is no general forfeiture statute that covers all crimes. However, forfeiture is available for more than two hundred different federal and state crimes.[16] Perhaps the best known forfeiture statutes allow the forfeiture of drug proceeds and any type of property used to commit a drug offense.[17] In addition, forfeiture is authorized for all money and property involved in money laundering offenses.[18] Criminal proceeds are forfeitable in mail and wire fraud cases,[19] bribery cases,[20] and honest services fraud cases,[21] among others. In Racketeer Influenced and Corrupt Organizations cases, property acquired or maintained through the racketeering activity is forfeitable.[22]

Under federal forfeiture law, property is considered anything of value, both tangible and intangible, including everything from cash, cybercurrency, real property, and cars to website domain names, liquor licenses, bar licenses, and medical licenses.[23] In *Crundwell*, the government forfeited 400 quarter

14 *See, e.g.*, *id.* §§ 981(a)(1)(A), 982(a)(1).

15 Alice W. Dery, *Overview of Asset Forfeiture*, ABA Bus. L. Today, June 2012, at 2, https://www.americanbar.org/content/dam/aba/publications/blt/2012/06/full-issue-201206.pdf.

16 *Id.*

17 *See* 21 U.S.C. §§ 853(a), 881(a).

18 18 U.S.C. §§ 981(a)(1)(A), 982(a)(1).

19 *Id.* § 981(a)(1)(D)(v)-(vi).

20 While 18 U.S.C. § 981(a)(1)(C)-(D) does not included references to all federal bribery statutes, it does provide for forfeiture of property "which constitutes or is derived from proceeds traceable to a violation of" any offense "constituting a specified unlawful activity" under 18 U.S.C. § 1056(c)(7). Section 1056(c)(7), in turn, defines specified unlawful activity as including, e.g., "bribery of a public official, or the misappropriation, theft, or embezzlement of public funds by or for the benefit of a public official." 18 U.S.C. § 1056(c)(7)(B)(iv).

21 While "specified unlawful activity" under 18 U.S.C. § 1056(c)(7) does not explicitly include violations of the honest services fraud statute, 18 U.S.C. § 1346, that section operates to define the "scheme or artifice to defraud" in mail and wire fraud statutes to include "a scheme or artifice to deprive another of the intangible right of honest services" rather than creating a separate crime. United States v. Boscarino, 437 F.3d 634, 636 (7th Cir. 2006). Because mail fraud (18 U.S.C. § 1341) and wire fraud (*id.* §1343) statutes are defined as specified unlawful activities, criminal proceeds obtained through an honest services fraud scheme are forfeitable. *Id.* § 981(a)(1)(D)(v)-(vi).

22 *Id.* § 1963(a)(1).

23 *See* 21 U.S.C. § 853(b).

horses, vehicles, trailers, tack, a luxury motor home, jewelry and personal belongings, real property in Illinois and Florida, along with her interest in royalties earned from breeding the horses.[24]

The pretrial preservation tools of asset forfeiture are the single most important technique for ensuring that a perpetrator does not dissipate assets.[25] These tools fill the legislative gap in the restitution statutes, which provide no mechanism for preserving assets until after sentencing.[26] Criminal and civil forfeiture statutes allow pretrial restraint of the proceeds of most fraud offenses.[27] After the defendant's assets are seized and forfeited, the government has the power to return the proceeds from the liquidation of those assets, minus government costs and expenses, to the victim, using the restoration or remission processes discussed below.[28]

IV. Types of Forfeiture

A. *Criminal Forfeiture*

Criminal forfeiture is an *in personam* action, because it is pursued as part of a criminal case against a defendant, and the forfeiture of assets is part of the criminal sentence.[29] Criminal forfeiture requires a criminal conviction, and only the defendant's interest in the property can be forfeited.[30] In cases where the forfeiture involves property other than proceeds of crime or property that is commingled with legitimate property, only the criminally-involved property is forfeitable.[31] In addition, because a criminal forfeiture order is an *in personam* judgment against the defendant, the court can order the defendant to pay a money judgment or to forfeit substitute assets not implicated in the crime if

24 *See* Press Release, U.S. Dep't of Justice, U.S. Attorney's Office, N. Dist. of Ill., *supra* note 1.

25 Alice W. Dery et al., *Restraining and Forfeiting Assets for Crime Victims*, U.S. Att'ys' Bull., Sept. 2013, at 45, 47, https://www.justice.gov/sites/default/files/usao/legacy/2013/09/16/usab6105.pdf.

26 *Id.*

27 *Id.*

28 *Id.*

29 *Types of Federal Forfeiture*, U.S. Dep't of Justice, http://www.justice.gov/afp/types-federal-forfeiture (last updated Dec. 16, 2020).

30 Dery, *supra* note 15, at 2.

31 *Id.*

the directly forfeitable assets have been dissipated and are otherwise no longer available.[32] In *Crundwell*, the Court ordered certain specific property that was traceable to the crime forfeited, but it also ordered her to pay a money judgment for the entire amount she stole, not just the monies the government could locate.[33] Any proceeds earned from the sale of the traceable property were offset against the amount she owed on her money judgment.[34] After sentencing, the government continued to locate assets and forfeit them as substitute assets to collect on the money judgment.[35]

If a defendant pleads guilty, at least one of the offenses to which she pleads must support the forfeiture.[36] If the defendant is convicted by trial, a second, forfeiture phase of the trial takes place, in which the government bears the burden of proving the connection between the property and the criminal conduct.[37] This is sometimes referred to as a bifurcated trial. Whereas in the main trial the government must prove a defendant's guilt beyond a reasonable doubt, in the forfeiture phase it must only prove by a preponderance of evidence a nexus between the property and the crime.[38] If the government meets its burden, the court grants a preliminary order of forfeiture as to the defendant's interest in the property.[39] The forfeiture becomes final after the court conducts an ancillary hearing to address the interests of any third parties in the specific property forfeited.[40] The ancillary hearing is essentially a quiet title action as to any third party claims against the property.[41] Once the third-party claims to the seized property are resolved, the court enters a final order of forfeiture, which transfers title of the property to the government, minus any interests of third parties.[42]

---

32 *Id.*

33 *See* Press Release, U.S. Dep't of Justice, U.S. Attorney's Office, N. Dist. of Ill., *supra* note 1.

34 *Id.*

35 *See, e.g.*, United States v. Crundwell, 12 CR 50027-1, 2015 U.S. Dist. LEXIS 8808, at *2-3 (N.D. Ill. Jan. 27, 2015) (entering judgment against third-party citation respondents who had borrowed money from Crundwell, which required them to repay that loan to the United States government).

36 Dery, *supra* note 15, at 2.

37 *Id.* at 2-3.

38 *Id.*

39 *Id.* at 3.

40 *Id.*

41 *Id.*

42 *Id.*

B. *Civil Forfeiture*

Like criminal forfeiture, civil forfeiture is a judicial process, but it does not require a criminal charge or conviction.[43] Civil forfeiture is an *in rem* action because it is brought against the property itself, rather than a person.[44] Thus, if the government were pursuing a civil forfeiture action against a home, the case would be captioned *United States* v. *1234 Main Street, Anywhere, USA*. Like the forfeiture phase of a criminal trial, the purpose of the civil forfeiture action is to establish title to the property.[45]

Since civil forfeiture is a proceeding against the property and not the defendant, it is limited to property that is traceable to the offense, that facilitated the offense, or that was involved in a money laundering offense.[46] Substitute assets are not forfeitable in civil cases, nor can the government obtain a money judgment against the perpetrator.[47] An advantage of civil forfeiture is that property can be obtained even if the perpetrator dies, flees the jurisdiction, or otherwise evades prosecution.[48] As in any other civil case, the civil forfeiture case moves through discovery, motions practice, and ultimately trial by a judge or jury.[49] During the proceedings, claims may be submitted by third parties and must be resolved before the court may enter final judgment for the government.[50]

In civil forfeiture, the government can obtain civil restraining orders for bank accounts and real property instead of taking physical custody of the assets.[51] However, for those assets that can be easily moved or liquidated, physical seizure may be necessary.[52] The government may generally seize bank accounts, cars, boats, aircraft, jewelry, cryptocurrencies,[53] and other items of

---

43 *Id.*

44 *Id.*

45 *Id.*

46 *Id.*

47 *See* Craig Gaumer, *A Prosecutor's Secret Weapon: Federal Civil Forfeiture Law*, U.S. Att'ys' Bull., Nov. 2007, at 59, 66, https://www.justice.gov/sites/default/files/usao/legacy/2007/12/21/usab5506.pdf.

48 *See id.* at 68.

49 *Id.* at 64-66; Dery, *supra* note 15, at 3.

50 Dery, *supra* note 15, at 3.

51 Dery et al., *supra* note 25, at 47.

52 *Id.* (citation omitted).

53 *See, e.g.*, Press Release, U.S. Dep't of Justice, U.S. Attorney's Office, S. Dist. of N.Y.,

value pursuant to a seizure warrant issued by the court after demonstrating that legal restraint of the property would not be effective in preserving the asset.[54] Some investigative agencies, including the Drug Enforcement Administration, Federal Bureau of Investigation, and Internal Revenue Service Criminal Investigation Division, have the authority to seize certain items and institute administrative forfeiture proceedings, which do not require judicial action unless a third party claim is filed with the agency.[55] A civil forfeiture action may be stayed pending the conclusion of the criminal case.[56]

V. Returning Forfeited Assets to Victims

Two principal avenues are available to return forfeited assets to victims: remission and restoration. In remission, the U.S. Attorney General, acting through the Money Laundering and Asset Recovery Section (MLARS) or the seizing agency, directly compensates persons or entities that incurred a pecuniary loss from the offense underlying the forfeiture or a related offense.[57] In public corruption cases, the victim is generally a governmental unit or agency. The victim submits a petition to MLARS or the seizing agency requesting remission of the forfeited funds, up to the amount lost.[58] The petitioner must

---

Manhattan U.S. Attorney Announces Forfeiture of $28 Million Worth of Bitcoin Belonging to Silk Road (Jan. 16, 2014), https://www.justice.gov/usao-sdny/pr/manhattan-us-attorney-announces-forfeiture-28-million-worth-bitcoins-belonging-silk (noting previous seizure of Bitcoins before entry of order of forfeiture).

54 Dery et al., *supra* note 25, at 47.

55 *Id. See also generally* 19 U.S.C. § 1607; 18 U.S.C. § 983. Subject to certain limitations and strict noticing requirements, an administrative forfeiture is completed by the law enforcement agency that seized the assets. If no claimant steps forward to contest the agency's seizure, the courts are not involved in the process. If anyone files a timely claim to the property at issue, a civil or criminal judicial forfeiture case is automatically commenced, in which the court determines the forfeitability of the property. *See also* Dery, *supra* note 15, at 2.

56 Dery et al., *supra* note 25, at 47 (citing United States v. Contents of Nationwide Life Ins. Annuity, No. 1:05-CV-00196, 2008 U.S. Dist. LEXIS 29485, at *4-6 (S.D. Ohio Apr. 10, 2008); United States v. $247,052.54, No. C-05-4798 SC, 2007 U.S. Dist. LEXIS 52037, at *2 (N.D. Cal. July 6, 2007); United States v. All Funds on Deposit in Suntrust Account Number XXXXXXXXX8359, 456 F. Supp. 2d 64, 64-65 (D.D.C. 2006)). For a discussion about stays in other types of concurrent proceedings, see Chapter 2.8, Part IV.

57 Dery et al., *supra* note 25, at 48.

58 *Id.* at 48-49.

establish the loss amount through documented evidence such as internal audits or other evidence developed in the criminal case.[59]

In restoration, the U.S. Attorney formally requests that MLARS authorize the transfer of forfeited assets to the court to be applied toward satisfaction of the defendant's criminal restitution order.[60] The court, based on evidence submitted by the U.S. Attorney, determines the amount of the victim's loss.[61] Although the restoration decision is discretionary, MLARS will generally approve restoration as long as the victim otherwise meets the eligibility criteria for remission.[62]

MLARS has granted restoration in numerous domestic public corruption cases, including the following:

- Devin McCraney and Sharika Allison were employed by the Beaumont, Texas, Independent School District as Chief Financial Officer/Director of Finance and Comptroller, respectively.[63] Between 2010 and 2013, McCraney and Allison embezzled $4,041,705.27 from the school district.[64] McCraney pleaded guilty to fraud upon programs receiving federal funds[65] and Allison pleaded guilty to conspiracy to commit fraud upon programs receiving federal funds.[66] Both were ordered to pay restitution, jointly and severally, to the school district.[67] MLARS restored approximately $889,615.33 in partial satisfaction of the $4,041,705.27 restitution order.[68]

---

59 *Id.* at 49.

60 *Id.* at 50.

61 *See id.* at 50; 18 U.S.C. § 981(e)(6) (permitting forfeited funds to be provided as restoration to any victim of the offense giving rise to the forfeiture); *id.* § 3664(e) (court resolves dispute as to the proper amount of restitution by a preponderance of the evidence).

62 *See* Dery et al., *supra* note 25, at 50.

63 Indictment at 1-2, United States v. McCraney, 99 F. Supp. 3d 651 (E.D. Tex. 2015) (No. 1:14-CR-1), ECF No. 1.

64 *Id.* at 3-4.

65 Factual Basis and Stipulation as to McCraney at 1, *McCraney*, 99 F. Supp. 3d 651 (No. 1:14-CR-1), ECF No. 28.

66 Factual Basis and Stipulation as to Allison at 1, *McCraney*, 99 F. Supp. 3d 651 (No. 1:14-CR-1), ECF No. 32.

67 Judgment as to Allison at 7, *McCraney*, 99 F. Supp. 3d 651 (No. 1:14-CR-1), ECF No. 56; Judgment as to McCraney at 8, *McCraney*, 99 F. Supp. 3d 651 (No. 1:14-CR-1), ECF No. 54.

68 *See* Judgment as to McCraney at 9, *McCraney*, 99 F. Supp. 3d 651 (No. 1:14-CR-1), ECF No. 54.

- David J. Bertnagel used his position in the Finance Department of the Town of Plymouth, Connecticut, to unlawfully deposit the town's checks into his personal checking account, causing a loss to the town of more than $800,000.[69] On February 22, 2015, Bertnagel was convicted of theft from a local government in violation of 18 U.S.C. § 666(a)(1)(A) and ordered to forfeit funds from several bank accounts, as well as jewelry and numerous precious gemstones, stamps, and coins.[70] MLARS applied the forfeiture toward his restitution obligation to the town of Plymouth.

- Lorena Loren used her position as executive director of the St. Clair, Michigan, Housing Commission to steal $336,240.62 in U.S. Department of Housing and Urban Section 8 Housing Choice Voucher Program funds to pay her personal and family expenses.[71] On August 29, 2017, Loren was convicted of conspiracy to commit federal program fraud in violation of 18 U.S.C. §§ 371 and 666(a)(1)(A) and ordered to forfeit $336,240.62, which would be satisfied in part by her full pension benefits and the sale of a rental property used to commit fraud.[72] MLARS applied the forfeited funds towards her restitution judgment.

- Joe L. Russell, II was the Chief Deputy of Administration for the Rutherford County, Tennessee, Sheriff's Office, where he and two coconspirators defrauded the county by creating an enterprise to sell e-cigarettes to the county's inmates, while illegally pocketing fees and commissions owing to the county. [73] On January 20, 2017, Russell pled guilty to wire fraud in violation of 18 U.S.C. § 1343, honest services fraud in violation of 18

---

69 Affidavit of Special Agent Ron W. Offutt at 3-5, United States v. Bertnagel, No. 3:15-CR-24-JAM (D. Conn. Jan. 20, 2015), ECF No. 2.

70 Plea Agreement at 1, 4-5, Attachment A, *Bertnagel*, No. 3:15-CR-24-JAM (D. Conn. Feb. 20, 2015), ECF No. 16. Bertnagel also pled guilty to making and subscribing a false tax return, in violation of 26 U.S.C. § 7206(1). *Id.* at 1.

71 Press Release, U.S. Dep't of Justice, U.S. Attorney's Office, E. Dist. of Mich., Former Executive Director of St. Clair Housing Commission Sentenced on Fraud Charges (Mar. 21, 2018), https://www.justice.gov/usao-edmi/pr/former-executive-director-st-clair-housing-commission-sentenced-fraud-charges.

72 *See* Amendment to Stipulated Preliminary Order of Forfeiture at 1-3, United States v. Loren, No. 2:17-cr-20527 (E.D. Mich. Dec. 21, 2017), ECF No. 14.

73 *See Joe Russell Sentenced in JailCigs Scheme*, News Channel 5 (Nov. 16, 2017), https://www.newschannel5.com/news/joe-russell-sentenced-in-jailcigs-scheme; Press Release, U.S. Dep't of Justice, U.S. Attorney's Office, M. Dist. of Tenn., Rutherford County Tennessee Sheriff Indicted by Federal Grand Jury (May 27, 2016), https://www.justice.gov/usao-mdtn/pr/rutherford-county-tennessee-sheriff-indicted-federal-grand-jury.

U.S.C. §§ 1343 and 1346, and Hobbs Act extortion under color of official right in violation of 18 U.S.C. § 1951.[74] He was ordered to pay $52,500 in restitution and to forfeit $52,234.41, an amount which equaled all proceeds he received from the enterprise.[75]

- Rhonda Williams and Gary Williams used their positions as executive director and maintenance supervisor of the Cotton Plant, Arkansas, Housing Authority, respectively, to defraud the U.S. Department of Housing and Urban Development of approximately $732,177.80 by soliciting and accepting bribes and kickbacks from housing authority contractors and using housing authority equipment and materials for construction of their personal residence.[76] On September 2, 2016, the Williamses pleaded guilty to conspiring to commit wire fraud and money laundering and were subsequently sentenced and jointly ordered to pay restitution of $732,177.80 and to forfeit $145,000 in cash seized from their home, the money in four bank accounts, one sport utility vehicle, a boat, and a trailer.[77]

- Sheila Silas Cochran, Clerk of the Marion County, Alabama, Circuit Court, defrauded the Court of $62,028.49 by writing checks to herself and removing cash from the criminal restitution account safe for personal use.[78] On March 31, 2016, Cochran pled guilty to theft of government funds, in violation of 18 U.S.C. § 666(a)(1)(A), and agreed to the forfeiture of $42,074.54 from her retirement funds, which MLARS

---

74 *See* Petition to Enter a Plea of Guilty at 4-5, United States v. Russell, No. 3:16-CR-117-002 (M.D. Tenn. Jan. 20, 2017), ECF No. 168; Judgment at 1-2, United States v. Russell, No. 3:16-CR-117-002 (M.D. Tenn. Nov. 16, 2017), ECF No. 252.

75 *See* Judgment at 7-8, United States v. Russell, No. 3:16-CR-117-002 (M.D. Tenn. Nov. 16, 2017), ECF No. 252; Press Release, U.S. Dep't of Justice, U.S. Attorney's Office, M. Dist. of Tenn., Former Rutherford County Tennessee Sheriff's Administrative Chief Deputy Sentenced on Federal Corruption Charges (Nov. 16, 2017), https://www.justice.gov/usao-mdtn/pr/former-rutherford-county-tennessee-sheriffs-administrative-chief-deputy-sentenced.

76 *See* Press Release, U.S. Dep't of Justice, U.S. Attorney's Office, E. Dist. of Ark., Couple Sent to Prison for Scheme to Steal HUD Funds Intended for the Cotton Plant Housing Authority (July 28, 2017), https://www.justice.gov/usao-edar/pr/couple-sent-prison-scheme-steal-hud-funds-intended-cotton-plant-housing-authority.

77 *Id.*; Final Order of Forfeiture at 1, United States v. Williams, No. 4:16-CR-166 (E.D. Ark. Nov. 1, 2017), ECF No. 49.

78 *See* Plea Agreement at 3-4, United States v. Cochran, No. 6:16-CR-101 (N.D. Ala. Mar. 31, 2016), ECF No. 2.

applied towards the $62,028.49 she owed in restitution to the Marion County Clerk's Office.[79]

Conclusion

Pursuant to USDOJ policy, victims of financial crimes have first priority to funds that are forfeited over any law enforcement uses or other equitable sharing of the funds.[80] In other words, every dollar of forfeited funds, less government expenses, is returned to victims who demonstrate a pecuniary loss and otherwise meet the regulatory requirements for remission. Recovery of stolen funds can add to the overall sense of justice to the victim community. In the *Crundwell* case, the federal government recovered more than ten million dollars of the stolen funds, while the city recovered an additional forty million dollars from civil settlements with its bank and auditors.[81] Dixon then used those funds for projects to improve the city whose trust Crundwell abused, with its administrator observing that the city was "very fortunate to recover the amount of money that it did and is putting it to good use."[82]

---

79 *Id.* at 1, 13.

80 *See* Asset Forfeiture Policy Manual, *supra* note 11, at Ch. 14, § II(A)(3).

81 Rachel Rodgers, *Crundwell Recovery: Five Years Later*, Shaw Media (Apr. 14, 2017), https://www.shawlocal.com/2017/04/14/crundwell-recovery-5-years-later/a7nasm0/.

82 Angie Sharp, *Dixon, Illinois Begins to Use Money from Crundwell Case*, WQAD8 (May 23, 2014), https://www.wqad.com/article/news/local/drone/8-in-the-air/dixon-illinois-begins-to-use-money-from-crundwell-case/526-1179c1ef-b091-40ca-845f-16d2489055f0.

Index A

Select Sources

Title 19

Title 21

Title 26

Title 28

Title 29

INDEX B

States and Other Jurisdictions

A

C

D

O

P

R

S

T

U

V

W

Index C

Topics

A

B

C

D

E

F

G

H

I

J

K

L

M

N

V

W

Y